Law, S

ESSAYS IN MODERN LEGAL HISTORY

Law, Society, and the State represents the first collected work on the inter-action of law and society within communities, societies, and states in common law jurisdictions of the former British empire. While the collection focuses on Canada, the areas covered range from southeast Asia to the United States, encompassing the themes of comparative colonial legal experiences; disorder, unrest, and state intervention; gender and the law; and the archival sources of the central state, local police forces, and the legal profession.

The essays reveal the rich diversity of the evolution of colonies into states; the conflicts between the laws of England and the laws and customs of indigenous peoples and European settlers; the problems of governance in mixed colonial societies; the social control functions of state, community, and family; and the roles of religion, race, gender, class, and poverty in law-making and law-giving. The original essays use diverse sources skilfully to explore the history and historiography of different jurisdictions, pointing in this way to further fields of scholarship. An analytical introduction by the editors identifies and assesses the themes of the volume and places the essays and their findings into the larger historical and legal context of the common law world and its societies both east and west.

LOUIS A. KNAFLA is a professor in the Department of History, University of Calgary.

SUSAN W.S. BINNIE is the research coordinator for the Law Society of Upper Canada Archives, Osgoode Hall, Toronto.

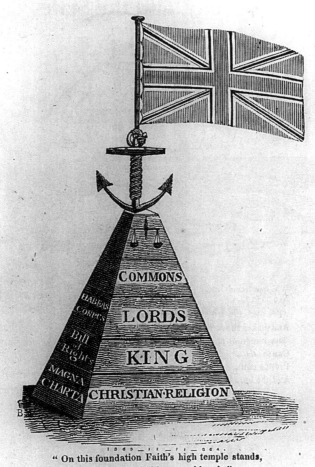

COMMONS

HABEAS CORPUS

LORDS

Bill of Rights

KING

MAGNA CHARTA

CHRISTIAN RELIGION

"On this foundation Faith's high temple stands,
As Atlas fix'd, not rais'd by mortal hands."

THESE ARE

THE LAWS OF ENGLAND.

A print satirizing English legal and political institutions c. 1820 as epitomized
by Magna Carta, habeas corpus, and the liberties of the free-born English
(Copyright British Museum)

LAW, SOCIETY, AND THE STATE:

Essays in Modern Legal History

Edited by
Louis A. Knafla and Susan W.S. Binnie

UNIVERSITY OF TORONTO PRESS

Toronto Buffalo London

© University of Toronto Press Incorporated 1995
Toronto Buffalo London
Printed in Canada

ISBN 0-8020-0535-7 (cloth)
ISBN 0-8020-6971-1 (paper)

Printed on acid-free paper

Canadian Cataloguing in Publication Data

Main entry under title:

Law, society, and the state : essays in modern legal history

Based on papers prepared for a conference held in
1992 at Osgoode Hall and sponsored by the Law
Society of Upper Canada.
ISBN 0-8020-0535-7 (bound) ISBN 0-8020-6971-1 (pbk.)

1. Law – Canada – History. 2. Law – History.
3. Sociological jurisprudence. I. Knafla, Louis A.,
1935–   . II. Binnie, Susan W.S. (Susan Wendy
Strickland), 1941–   .

KE394.L38 1994   340'.115'0971   C94-932769-7
KF345.L38 1994

University of Toronto Press acknowledges
the financial assistance to its publishing program
of the Canada Council and the
Ontario Arts Council.

Contents

Foreword
DAVID SUGARMAN
ix

Acknowledgments
xi

1 *Introduction*
Beyond the State: Law and Legal Pluralism
in the Making of Modern Societies
LOUIS A. KNAFLA and SUSAN W.S. BINNIE
3

Part One: Colonial Legal Experience

2 The Anderson Case and Rights in Canada and England
PAUL FINKELMAN
37

3 From Fishing Schooner to Colony:
The Legal Development of Newfoundland, 1791–1832
CHRISTOPHER ENGLISH
73

4 William Osgoode, John Graves Simcoe, and the Exclusion
of the English Poor Law from Upper Canada
RUSSELL C. SMANDYCH
99

5 Law-Making and Social Change in Colonial Trinidad, 1900–1950
KUSHA HARAKSINGH
130

6 Asian Customary Laws through Western Eyes:
A Comparison of Sri Lankan and Hong Kong Colonial Experiences
ANTON COORAY
145

Part Two: Disorder, Dissent, and the State

7 Imperial Authority and Colonial Officialdom
of Upper Canada in the 1830s:
The State, Crime, Lunacy, and Everyday Social Order
RAINER BAEHRE
181

8 The Blake Act of 1878: A Legislative Solution to
Urban Violence in Post-Confederation Canada
SUSAN W.S. BINNIE
215

9 Civil Liberties and the Law:
California during the First World War
DIANE M.T. NORTH
243

10 Wagging Tongues and Empty Heads:
Seditious Utterances and the Patriotism of Wartime
in Central Alberta, 1914–1918
JONATHAN SWAINGER
263

11 Treaties, Trains, and Troubled National Dreams:
Reflections on the Indian Summer in Northern Ontario, 1990
ANTHONY HALL
290

Part Three: Gender and the Law

12 'If a Man's Wife Does Not Obey Him, What Can He Do?':
Marital Breakdown and Wife Abuse in Late Nineteenth-Century and
Early Twentieth-Century Ontario
ANNALEE E. GÖLZ
323

13 Locking Them Up:
Incarcerating Women in Ontario, 1857–1931
WENDY RUEMPER
351

14 'Just Plain Everyday Housekeeping on a Grand Scale':
Feminists, Family Courts, and the Welfare State
in British Columbia, 1928–1945
DOROTHY E. CHUNN
379

15 The 'Incorrigible,' the 'Bad,' and the 'Immoral':
Toronto's 'Factory Girls' and the Work of
the Toronto Psychiatric Clinic
JENNIFER STEPHEN
405

Part Four: Archival Sources in Legal History

16 'Law-ways,' 'Law-jobs,' and
the Documentary Heritage of the State
LOUIS A. KNAFLA
443

17 The Archives of the
English and Welsh Police Forces: A Survey
CLIVE EMSLEY
465

18 Towards a Canadian Police Historiography
GREG MARQUIS
477

19 Private Sector Legal Archives in Canada:
A Source of Concern
RICHARD KLUMPENHOUWER
497

20 Waiving History Goodbye?
Lawyers' Records and the Scholar
PETER MOORE
514

Contributors
525

Table of Cases
529

*Table of Statutes, Charters,
and Proclamations*
531

Index
535

Foreword

It is a real pleasure to write the foreword for *Law, Society, and the State: Essays in Modern Legal History*. The distinguished contributions that fill this book had their origin in papers prepared for the 1992 conference sponsored by the Law Society of Upper Canada and held at Osgoode Hall, Toronto. The conference was supported as well by the Social Sciences and Humanities Research Council of Canada and by The Osgoode Society for Canadian Legal History, a body that has played a seminal role in encouraging research and writing in the history of Canadian law. International conferences devoted to the theme of law, society, and the state in history have been relatively rare, but the recent dramatic growth of interest in the history of law and society undoubtedly justifies this welcome attempt to stimulate a challenging, broad-ranging, and interdisciplinary treatment of this fascinating theme. The editors have compiled a volume which, I believe, will become a milestone in the writing of Canadian legal history, as well as an important contribution to the history of law in other common law jurisdictions. As this collection amply testifies, modern legal history has not only come of age, but is increasingly concerned to describe, analyse, and philosophize upon the political, economic, and cultural significance of law, legal ideas and ideologies, and legal institutions.

The co-editors and their associates have produced a group of excellent essays. The first three parts of the book address the experience of law in a colonial context, public order, disorder and sedition, and gender and the law. In the concluding part of the book some of the relevant archives in Canada and elsewhere are considered, particularly in the light of the problems that they may give rise to and the increasing demands that will be made on them by 'law and society' histories in the future. The book is prefaced by an interesting introduction, which explores the utility of a pluralistic perspective to ordering and organization, an approach that helps to integrate modern legal history within contemporary debates in history and social and legal theory concerning the role of law and legal institutions as brute force and the producers of meaning, value, and power.

In sum, the authors of this collection make an important contribution to the understanding of the past and present, as well as to the future growth of this exciting new area of studies. When set alongside the pioneering efforts of, for example, The Osgoode Society's *Essays in the History of Canadian Law*, Constance Backhouse's *Petticoats and Prejudice*, and the recent collections *Canadian Perspectives on Law and Society: Issues in Legal History* (edited by Wesley Pue and Barry Wright) and *Glimpses of Canadian Legal History* (edited by Dale Gibson and Wesley Pue), it becomes abundantly clear that interdisciplinary legal history flourishes in Canada.

David Sugarman
Department of Law,
Lancaster University

Acknowledgments

The preparation of this volume has involved many people, either directly or indirectly. The fact that the proposal for the book sprang from a large and international conference of common law legal historians, held at the Law Society of Upper Canada in May 1992, has broadened the numbers of persons involved beyond normal expectations, even for a volume of multi-authored, edited essays. The editors recognize that this project benefited at the outset from a positive sense of involvement and direction contributed by those scholars, including legal historians from around the world, who helped to organize and participated in the original conference. It has also profited from the dedication of the particular authors whose work is included in this volume.

Nineteen authors are represented in the collection. Their work was selected from more than fifty papers presented at the conference as well as from a number of subsequent submissions, after thorough peer evaluation. The resulting chapters focus on four major conference themes: colonial law, law and gender, disorder and the state, and legal archives. Although the focus is primarily Canadian, the studies reach out to other common law settings, representing altogether eight common law jurisdictions.

The editors gratefully acknowledge the financial support of the Law Society of Upper Canada and the Social Sciences and Humanities Research Council of Canada, which made publication of the volume possible. While naming some individuals necessarily omits many of those concerned, we are especially grateful to the staff of the University of Toronto Press: to former editor Laura Macleod, who encouraged the project from the outset; to editor Gerry Hallowell, who took over the volume and saw it to conclusion; and to assistant editor Rob Ferguson and managing editor Anne Forte in Toronto. We are also greatly indebted to John McLaren and to two anonymous readers for the Press for their helpful remarks; to Peter Oliver and Marilyn MacFarlane of the Osgoode Society for their continued interest and advice; to Kathy Johnson for expert copyediting; and to others, including Mariana Valverde, Karen Dubinsky, and Andrew Rodomar, for assistance in many different ways.

The Law Society of Upper Canada provided the setting for much of the editorial work, and we extend our appreciation to the treasurer, benchers, and staff of the Law Society for their support. We also thank the reference librarians of the Great Library for assisting with historical-legal queries. All the members of the Archives Department of the Law Society contributed their time most generously, and we are especially grateful to Ann-Marie Langlois and Elise Brunet for their interest and encouragement, and to former staff members Roy Schaeffer and Carolyn Strange for initiating the idea of an international conference. Expert typing assistance for the manuscript was provided by three capable and willing students, Beth Gerwin, Asha Gosein, and Anita MacCallum.

Louis A. Knafla
Susan W.S. Binnie

Law, Society, and the State

1 *Introduction*
Beyond the State: Law and Legal Pluralism in the Making of Modern Societies

LOUIS A. KNAFLA AND SUSAN W.S. BINNIE

Prolegomena

In the rapid expansion of legal historiography over the past two decades, legal-historical writers have increasingly turned their attention to socio-legal writing. Where once the traditional areas of legal history were the nation-state and the history of the law, courts, and professions, these have now been supplemented first with the rise of the history of crime and the criminal law, and more recently with the expansion of the study of civil and regulatory disputes in the history of law and society.[1] The major studies of Rubin and Sugarman, and Cornish and Clark, represent a leading edge in these fields in British history.[2] In the United States, 'law and society' studies have brought a rich texture to legal-historical writing, which is now being reflected in work in Australia, New Zealand, and Canada. In none of these countries, however, is the literature sufficiently developed to allow a synthetic survey beyond, for example, the institutional and overarching analyses of Lawrence Friedman.[3]

In Canada as well as in other Commonwealth countries there has also been a growth of legal historiography. These post-colonial societies, however, have lacked both the fundamental institutional histories of the Western European countries and the broader normative studies of law and society.[4] Some pioneering efforts have demonstrated the richness of the heritage, the wealth of the sources, and the breadth and depth of some of the questions to be posed and examined.[5] Given the fact that historical thought, like history itself, waits for no person, the essays in this volume have been brought together to serve as mirrors, or reflections, of current research and writing on law and society both within and outside the more traditional framework of the state.[6]

The nineteen essays published here stem in large part from a conference on 'Law, State and Society in History' planned by the Law Society of Upper Canada and held at Osgoode Hall, Toronto, in May 1992. In the editors' view, the essays selected comprise a useful window into the growing historiography on the interface of law, history, and the state in modern times. More specifically, they contribute to the development of Commonwealth and Canadian legal-historical studies with respect both to the history of law and to the history of law and society.

The emergence of recent scholarship on the history of state formation dates in part from a series of international conferences organized by Charles and Louise Tilly in the 1960s and 1970s, which inspired a generation of essays and books primarily concerned with Europe and North America.[7] The new approach drew too on the earlier work of the *Annales* school in France,[8] and its focus later diversified to other continents particularly Africa and the subcontinent of India, in the 1970s and 1980s.

Interest in state formation was also furthered by developments in a number of related disciplines, including political and social theory, as the late 1960s and 1970s witnessed the rise of alternative modes of scholarship in both Europe and North America. Neo-Marxist thinkers in France, Germany, and England revisited marxist thought, and their re-examinations of the writings of earlier authors, including Karl Marx and Evgeny Pashukanis, inspired a spate of writing in which law and the state became central issues.

The fruitfulness of new historical schools influenced by such developments, including that founded by E.P. Thompson at the University of Warwick in the mid-1970s, led to further empirical work exploring the parameters of crime, class, and alternative cultures from a critical perspective.[9] Developments emphasizing the role of the state gave a new direction and impetus to studies of law in societal context in the 1980s.[10] Soon the central focus was no longer the state, but communities and societies. What now marks this general area of research, thought, and writing is the way in which earlier issues – for example, law and the state and law and social class – are being informed by the rise of original scholarship on race, gender, work, and culture in the late 1980s and early 1990s. It is within this framework and from these perspectives that the conference was created and this volume planned.

The four parts of the volume parallel, with some changes, the themes and organization of the conference, and include a broad selection from the approximately fifty papers presented there.[11] While the parts have been shaped to reflect four major themes as set out below, the essays frequently transcend their individual subjects as a number of them bear on several themes. In practice, the parts and their titles should be regarded as signposts, serving the interests of topical groupings as well as thematic or interpretive ones. A brief overview of the rationale, role, and purpose of the sections follows.

Part One of the volume focuses on colonial law. It is now evident from the historiography of colonial common law jurisdictions and colonial relations with the imperial British state that the evolution of colonies into states was not simply a series of separate and unique events. Instead, these transitions and the meanings of particular series of events can be illuminated by considerations of context, conjuncture, and interaction in comparison with other settings. Thus any understanding of the interface of law, society, and the state in colonial and post-colonial common law settings must stem from and begin with the colonial circumstances. These experiences form the first part of the volume. The rich diversity of this literature is represented by studies ranging from the subcontinent of India to Southeast Asia, the Caribbean, the United States, and Canada.

The transition from colony to republic, commonwealth, or nation-state was often accompanied by considerable travail and, at times, bloodshed. In the colonial period the laws of the conqueror, or settlers, had to face the customs of indigenous peoples as well as the attitudes and customs of later immigrants. Government during colonial and post-colonial periods was frequently problematic. Political relations between indigenous and settler societies were often contentious in situations of colonially imposed economic structures and contested ideological stances. Resulting conflicts tended to occasion disorders and dissent, which at times were interpreted by states as politically threatening or seditious. Intervention by the colonial or national state was seen as mandatory for the protection of the 'social order.' While much has been written on state intervention in European history, much less has been written on the subject for North America, and Part Two contains some recent research on disorder, dissent, and state intervention in Canada and the United States.

The internal divisions of peoples and societies that occurred in worlds 'discovered' by Europeans were not limited, however, by the boundaries of geography or necessarily restricted to political, legal, and economic spheres. The containment of potentially divisive conflict deriving from religion, race, gender, or other sources was frequently a state-assumed responsibility with restraints operating both through the visible institutions of the state (the so-called social control agencies) and through less visible institutions such as the family.

Part Three is dedicated to conflicts relating to gender and sexuality. Building upon the new historiographies of feminism and criminality, the studies selected here reflect how gender and sexuality were spoken of in legal discourse, and how women's lives were affected by the rise of the prison and the welfare state – primarily in Canada (where these subjects are still in their formative periods of research). The chapters also demonstrate how new approaches to court records can provide flesh and bone to the statute law and case files, thereby joining the disciplines of history and law.

Finally, both history and law as social sciences depend upon evidence derived from written sources. As scholars push forward into new fields in these disciplines, the multivarious records that have come down to them must be made available through practical aids that assist the researcher in probing vast series of legal records with new questions.

Part Four contains several chapters that provide guidelines and insights for researchers in common law settings. These essays discuss and assess the archives of the state, local police forces, and law societies and professions. In addition, the authors raise needed questions concerning a number of *problematiques* that have come to attract and occupy both the scholarly community and the reading public.

The Law of the State:
Law from the Perspective of State Formation

The rise of the nation-state can be attributed to certain developments in Western Europe in the sixteenth and seventeenth centuries. These include the growth of royal power in France, England, and Spain; the supremacy of the Crown over the feudal nobility; the transformation of religious institutions to serve the interests of the dynastic central state; the development of secular bureaucracies; the rise of modern diplomacy with its assumptions about the sovereignty of nation-states; and the advent of modern, non-feudal warfare by national citizen armies under the aegis of the state. More important, however, for the purposes of this essay is the fact that the rise of the nation-state was accompanied by the growth of 'state law': that is, central courts that operated independently under the Crown, administered secular law, and, over the following centuries, exercised an ever-increasing supervision over regional and local courts.

In addition, in countries such as England and the Low Countries sovereignty was enjoined between the monarch and an elected assembly, resulting in the institution and supremacy of statute law. In this sense England could be considered a nation-state from the thirteenth century, but the 'parliamentary sovereignty' that came to define the law of England as such is a phenomenon that was completed only in the twentieth century, after a tortuous history.[12] In the meantime, in much of modern Europe the rise of republican governments or constitutional monarchies by the close of the French Revolution was accompanied by a secular sovereignty rooted in centralized national institutions, which claimed the ultimate authority to make law.

State formation theory relates to the institutions and laws created by the secular authority of the central state and the powers that were assumed in their making. With respect to the law, these institutions included central legislatures, courts, police, criminal law, prisons, and asylums. According to many writers of the 1970s and 1980s, the study of these institutions revolved inherently around the nation-state, which was regarded not only as their maker but also as their administrator. And according to many European legal historians, the rise of institutions of 'law and order' such as the modern police, galleys, hulks, and prisons was due primarily to the desire of the central state to gain control over those people who represented the sources of disorder, dissent, and revolt.[13]

For Marxist and some neo-Marxist analysts of the law, these forms of state control were predicated on certain requirements of capitalism. For example, analyses of the 'disciplining' of labour forces allowed law to be seen as directly 'instrumental' in relation to the purposes of the capitalist state.[14] For other writers the state was less directly implicated in questions of social control. For instance, as Morton Horowitz revealed in his study of the transformation of American law in the early national period, judges could see the common good expressed by entrepreneurs and industrialists who trampled the rights of individual and group interests in order to provide the benefits of a capitalist economy.[15] More recently, other versions of neo-Marxist approaches have emphasized ideological elements relating to law, and have developed explanations for the consent of the many to rule by the few.[16] These perspectives express a need to theorize the continuing legitimacy accorded by members of the working class to rule by societal élites, a situation captured in the term 'hegemony' rather than in the simplified view of a necessarily repressive state acting against members of subordinate classes. In this respect, the notion of the state as 'a major instrument of centralization and normalization' relying on the use of state law is also called into question when we recognize that law exists in the customs of local communities, and that these communities, 'whether culturally, socially or economically organized – [reflect] felt and lived systems of values which may require rehearsing and rededication, but not enforcement in a formal sense.'[7]

Regardless of the view of state formation adopted, the records generated by the institutions of the centralized secular state continue to comprise the major database for legal historians of the modern era, which is defined in Europe and North America as the period from the eighteenth century to the present. These include, for the common law world, documents in record groups housed in state archives (national or provincial) under the authority of the legislature and the Crown (attorneys and solicitors general and ministers of justice). They range from statutes, proclamations, and central and regional court records to police, prison, and asylum records. They also include the various reports, correspondences, and statistics gathered and prepared under the auspices of these institutions and their agencies.

Much of the legal-historical research undertaken in the common law world has been based on the records of the 'state' as defined above, and thus many research topics have been those capable of illumination in terms of the historical stories emanating from the institutions that spawned the records. The range of such studies is clearly vast. It comprises on the one hand subject-specific research and its accompanying methodologies from the imposition and administration of central laws and codes to the controlling functions of professional police forces, the surveillance functions of secret services, and the social control mechanisms of jails, prisons, and asylums. It also includes on the other hand studies of social, economic, religious, and political history that have used the legal records of the state to document, illuminate, or expand the context of their subjects. Thus law from the perspective of the state has a central symmetry and meaning that has attracted amateur and professional research and readership since at least the mid-nineteenth century. It has also formed both the core and essence of legal-historical writing.

Legal Pluralism:
Law from the Perspective of the Community

A practising lawyer's conception of law stems from the cases in which she or he is involved, and the experiences of legal education and legal culture in the jurisdiction where these cases take place. A practising historian's conception stems purely from the record group or groups that form the base of his or her research projects. In the instance of either lawyers or historians, law is defined as the medium in and with which they work. The conceptions with which lawyers, historians, sociologists, or criminologists work determine the kind of history they will produce. Thus traditionally legal history has focused on the history of the law and legal institutions of the state, whereas sociolegal (law and society) history focuses on the normative rules and ordering of social institutions. While the former includes the law declared by rulers, legislators, and judges, the latter includes the rules, norms, and customs of corporations, unions, churches, communities, and families.

Both legal and sociolegal history draw upon the ambiguities of the past in spite of their differing conceptions of law. But the sociolegal historian is more inclined to gather up all the debris a society leaves behind in order to create a larger, more diverse, and, in the end, less focused environment that aspires to the sum of its collective subjectivities.[18]

Historians by tradition have left legal pluralism in the hands of anthropologists, lawyers, and sociologists. But a historian's perspective can be equally useful. Let us begin with what legal pluralism is not: namely, state law. In Canada, for example, state law could encompass all purely 'legal' records: those of law courts at the national or provincial level and of legal departments of governments at the three respective levels. Other legal records concerning the state are not, however, in its custody. These include the papers of bodies created by statute, such as law societies, and the papers of bar associations and legal professionals, such as judges, lawyers, court officials, and arbitrators. Some of these, especially the records of 'legal professionals,' have received much less attention than the legal records of the state, which have traditionally embodied the working definition of 'legal records.' Legal pluralism, however, includes less tidy categories: persons or organizations that dispense or participate in normative rule-making functions. This covers a wide range, from legal departments or personnel of business corporations, public utilities, municipalities, schools, hospitals, and unions to the legal business of private and public charities, community organizations, churches, and other bodies.

Currently there is a major debate in the legal literature over the boundaries of legal pluralism. For some writers it is the opposite of state law: the normative rules and orders of non-statal institutions. For others it is the equivalent of both state legal and non-statal normative ordering. The view adopted here is that legal pluralism is based on non-statal rules and customs, and that its value is in providing (1) a perspective on state law that is both different and useful, (2) a comparative device for the study of rules within and outside the state, and (3) a tool for examining the customs and rules of non-statal institutions, including local communities and social organizations.[19]

There is, however, another dimension to legal pluralism that has not necessarily been part of its currently established borders. Law is not just positive law; it is also certain ways of thinking about the external world, and ways of thinking that have infused other institutions so that we cannot consider them without the law. Nicos Poulantzas, for instance, wrote at length about the 'juridical subject,' the individual as conceived in law and liberal philosophy and the ways in which law reinforces certain concepts of the individual.[20] For instance, in the example of Anatole France's ironic comment that the law forbids us all, rich or poor, to sleep under the bridges of Paris, such equality is self-evidently mythical.[21] But ideas such as 'equality' and 'rights' and other maxims, precepts, and modes of legal thought about individuals, law, and society carry powerful messages that become part of societal thinking.[22] The messages have often been at the heart of much social theory and anthropological research and writing that has yet to become fully appreciated by historians of law and society.[23]

Moreover, anthropologists, in examining the customs of ancient civilizations and communities, have also done considerable work in defining the legal environment. They have employed the terms 'law-ways' and 'law-jobs' to represent the ways in which disputes are heard and resolved, and the people who hear and resolve them.[24] Thus 'law-ways' serves as a term to denote all the different ways in a society in which disputes are resolved, whether by state, quasi-state, or non-statal institutions. And 'law-jobs' denotes all those individuals who take part in a particular dispute-resolution system, from legislators to councillors, judges, and local magistrates to arbitrators and referees, and from professionals to amateurs. In addition, anthropologists are examining what the law means to people: how it works in society at the conscious and unconscious levels, a subject that will be discussed below under legal culture and ideology.

While the terms 'state formation' and 'legal pluralism' are not used by the authors of the essays in this volume, the terms can assist us in gaining a better understanding of the major issues discussed in the essays, and can provide a medium for the analysis of comparative studies in these and other contexts. It is important in terms of colonial state formation, for instance, to recognize that English law did not survive intact in the colonies. As McLaren has pointed out, 'For too long the assumption among legal historians of the common law about legal culture has been that of "metropolitanism" – the flowing of law, legal institutions and legal ideology from the colonizing power or mother country to the colonial outposts where it was supposedly greeted with unalloyed enthusiasm and applied without question. The truth is that English law in its substance or procedures only partially survived in the colonies.'[25]

It is also useful to have in mind, for example, the fact that there are multiple levels of government in the Canadian system, two of which are represented in legal process as 'the Crown in right of Canada' and 'the Crown in right of the province.'[26] In some instances the legal conflicts are 'within' the state, making it apparent that, even in law, states are not unitary or monolithic. It is equally useful to have in mind that 'case law' is not necessarily made by supreme or superior courts. Every decision of a 'state' judge may be a precedent, whether it is made in federal or provincial court.

This idea of legal pluralism takes on most significance at the point at which the law at issue goes beyond the institutions of the state, and involves quasi- or non-statal organizations. Originally this occurred at the level of the family and the community, and it is at this level that many sociolegal historians have begun to discuss and write about 'law and society.' These terms are seen as interdependent: 'law' as an institution regulating normative (customary) behaviour, and 'society' as the structures and institutions of the community. The point at which they become engaged is called 'living law': the active work and thought of the life process, the theatre where disputes between people and between people and institutions take place.[27]

The concept of legal pluralism also assists us in coming to terms with the subject of 'legal culture,' and with the idea of legal ideology. Both notions derive partly from the French concept of *mentalité* (mental structures of cultural history), while approaches to law as ideology have been further developed and applied by French structuralist and English cultural theorists. Cultural history,[28] represented in the work of the fourth generation of the *Annales* school, is the study of society in its temporal, spatial, and human dimensions, comprising structure (the long-term milieu), conjuncture (the vernacular, medium term), and event (the current action or point).[29] The premise is that all activities or determinations (human or institutional) stem from mental structures (*mentalités*), and that the task of the historian is to 'read' the community's mind, from its 'texts,' for the purposes of perceiving what it is, what it means, and how it works.[30]

In the 1970s French structuralists raised the role of ideology to a central position, developing the concept of the ideological institutions of the capitalist state, or 'ideological state apparatuses.'[31] These included schools, churches, universities, and other major institutions that might assist in disseminating ideological viewpoints, including those relating to the law. Concepts of legal ideology, in the more subtle (that is, non-instrumental and non-economistic) neo-Marxist versions of the 1980s, were strongly influenced by the earlier work of the Italian theorist Antonio Gramsci and his view of ideology as a vital aspect of social structure or as sets of beliefs that assisted in holding a society together.[32]

Legal culture, then, is a broad historical term that comprises a community's legal mind, and includes legal ideology as one aspect of legal relations: culture implies those assumptions, beliefs, and customs that lie behind and inform its normative law. It provides the theoretical framework and historical context from which the law of the community can be interpreted. It sees law not only as positive law, but also as legal ways of thinking, which may be as important as formal written law. For instance, as American social theorists such as Macaulay have demonstrated[33] (following in the footsteps of sociologists, including Weber and Durkheim),[34] the practised mores and customs surrounding commercial relations mean that the resort to law is relatively unused in society. Again, from Marx on the theft of wood[35] to E.P. Thompson on gleaning,[36] the evidence of unwritten rights' becoming assumed as unwritten law is considerable. It is in these ways that concepts of legal culture and ideology can assist in shaping the research agendas of historians concerned with the interface and interaction of law in society.

In effect, the task of the 'law and society' historian is not only to discern the normative law of the community in which the research is taking place, but also to see the law in its multidimensional context – its local and borrowed origins; its written and unwritten customs; its formal and informal practices; its main and subsidiary streams; its rules and customs, whether established, receding, or developing; its vernacular practices (the laws that are used fully, partially, or not at all); and its meaning (how law is perceived) for the various socioeconomic groups of the community (business, labour, immigrants, Native peoples, women, etc).

Legal pluralism is a useful concept for the study of law, society, and the state because it forces both the lawyer and the historian to go beyond the traditional confines of their disciplines, to view the law from where it began (from the ground up) and where it has been generally practised (in the local community). Adding the perspectives of the anthropologist and the social theorist to that of the lawyer and the historian, the 'law' becomes a much more dynamic institution, one whose rules and societal processes are in daily practice, constantly in flux, continually challenged, and always in the process of being refined and created. The law has traditionally been interpreted in the common law world as providing stability to an otherwise ever-changing environment. But the law must also be recognized, and especially in colonial societies, as a factor of adaptation and change. We must remember that the common law began as common custom, and developed as such throughout the early modern era and into the nineteenth century. Thus the common law tradition represents an evolutionary rather than a static or radical legal system. Perceiving law as legal pluralism assists us in achieving that understanding.

Colonial Legal Experiences

The development of state law in colonial settings offers a rich field for comparative research. The five chapters in Part One of this book provide effective case studies of pluralism in practice. The cases cover a wide gamut of contexts and situations, including relations and conflicts between formal law and customary practice as well as interactions between state law and religion-based or indigenous laws. They range too from processes of replacing earlier colonial systems with English common law to the development of law, legal institutions, or law-jobs in newly settled colonial territories. The settings thus furnish insights into the nature of legal processes reflective of legal cultures lying outside as well as inside state systems of law. The authors take advantage of pluralist conceptions of law to emphasize the interaction between law, legal cultures, and the socioeconomic and political contexts of legal development.

Aspects of the processes of the reception of English law, the initial and formal step in the development of state law in colonial settings, provide focuses for several papers, and the approaches allow potential comparisons with other common law colonial cultures. In the North American context, Christopher English's paper considers the shaping of English law on the island of Newfoundland, the result of a political decision made in England to recognize and legitimize illegal settlement undertaken there for the purpose of the North Atlantic fishery. Legal developments are analysed in his paper as the outcome of interactions between the imperial government's applications of colonial law and the particular setting, with limitations on the form of law effectively set by the characteristics of

Newfoundland settlement. Thus legal procedures and the structure of the courts remained far simpler than on the mainland, reflecting the basic nature of settlement life. In contrast, Russell Smandych explores the formal reception of law, in this instance in the colony of Upper Canada under conditions of early loyalist settlement. His discussion of reasons for the simultaneous adoption of English common law and the rejection of the specific legislative area of the English poor law serves as a useful case study of legal reception. In effect both studies throw light on the growth of common law legal culture in situations of colonial settlement as opposed to colonial conquest.

Turning to an alternative form of common law reception process, Anton Cooray analyses legal contexts in Sri Lanka and Hong Kong, where systems of colonial and local law were established well before the introduction of English common law. In these instances, the reception of English law occurred after the territories were ceded to Britain by the Netherlands and China, respectively. In Sri Lanka a combination of mixed races and legal cultures in the indigenous population, together with a history of earlier colonization, created a setting where the indigenous laws and the Romano-Dutch colonial law interacted with the English colonial law to form a new legal system. In Hong Kong the reception of common law took place in the context of an established system of Chinese customary law, which failed to survive under new conditions of English colonization. This situation bears some similarities to the English model in Quebec, where French civil law was first jettisoned in the aftermath of the conquest in 1760 but, in contrast to Hong Kong, eventually survived.

In Trinidad the reception of common law, as analyzed by Kusha Haraksingh, took place in a different form of colonial society. Here English law was developed partly to further the interests of an élite white settler minority drawn to the island by the lure of profits from sugar cultivation. Haraksingh describes the development and applications of certain laws in relation to the imported labour force of black and Indian workers, and considers the results for both Moslem and Hindu segments of the population. Thus one can see in Trinidad clear parallels with other colonial settings as, for instance, the early history of English law in British Columbia and its discriminatory treatment of Asian immigrants. In both cases a dominant élite was able to shape certain laws and use them to serve its own ends.

However, as suggested, the examination of the interaction and interrelations of legal cultures in these papers is not limited to simple narratives.

The accounts illustrate complex areas of interaction, including the gap between law 'in the books' and 'law in action' in the colonial environment. Equality before the law in principle versus practice emerges as a major theme in several chapters. If common law systems are widely seen as unable to provide equal treatment of unequal legal subjects, this disparity has manifest implications for settings where the subjects of law are divided not only by race, class, and gender, but also by culture and religion. Several problematic situations of this kind are examined in Haraksingh's study of Trinidad. The author establishes the failure of landowning white settlers to recognize the rights of labourers, especially the right to organize as granted in law, and he identifies the use made of master and servant legislation by employers against indentured labour.[37] As we know, similar practices predominated in other colonies – for instance, in Australia's colonial society in regions such as Queensland.

Turning to mid-nineteenth-century Upper Canada, Paul Finkelman is concerned with the working out of legal relations within a common law political 'triangle' formed by the imperial government, the post-colonial United States, and the Province of Canada. Relations between states are examined in the context of a legal dispute over the fate of the escaped slave John Anderson. Here the courts reached an impasse over conflicting legal and political traditions. In explaining distinctions in legal theory and legal practice in three common law jurisdictions in response to the issue of race, Finkelman's paper goes further towards illuminating the role of legal ideology through exploring motives and belief systems in relation to legal culture. Both Haraksingh's and Finkelman's analyses add considerable empirical detail to the view that the law in practice must be distinguished from the law in books.

Several of the chapters in the first two parts are revealing of the attitudes and approaches of those trained in one system of law towards other legal cultures. Some contributions serve to identify areas of conflict between colonial law and established religious or secular customs. Still others demonstrate the degree to which 'English law' was capable of undergoing modification, by undertaking an examination of the nature of such adjustments in relation to particular features of new colonial settings. For example, marriage customs and laws of property ownership and inheritance frequently reflected the effects of changing legal cultures in colonial settings. Customary or religious patterns of marriage in precolonial societies tended to present administrative difficulties for colonial regimes. Under English law a major use of marriage records was to establish legitimacy or lines of descent and inheritance for succession to private property. With marriage customs holding an important place in most religious systems, conflict between legal cultures was likely and occurred in several settings. This is illustrated in the failure of the administration in Trinidad to recognize either Muslim or Hindu marriages, and in Newfoundland's hasty legislation of formal marriage laws to replace the customary marriages of the pre-colonial era.

Other issues of legal succession appear in the problems surrounding Chinese customary practices of joint family inheritance and exclusion of female descendants in Hong Kong, as described by Cooray. State law did not necessarily always prevail in such conflicts of law and custom. Indeed, the strategic resistance of local communities under powerful colonial regimes is striking. As Haraksingh points out, the recognition of religious marriages in Trinidad was eventually included in formal state law only after strong and persistent public demands. In fact, even 'British' administrators did not necessarily have a clear view of the state of the law of marriage pertaining to British and native unions, as the parallel Canadian experience of Prince Rupert's Land in the nineteenth century illustrates.

Similarly, in the Newfoundland cases of *Lundrigan* and *Butler* discussed by Christopher English, major law reforms were prompted by a conflict between custom and state law. Here local courts staffed by a non-professional judiciary forced repayment of debts incurred in the fishery and imposed harsh physical punishments on offenders. The resulting local outcry was sufficiently strong for long-delayed legislative changes and judicial reforms to be brought forward, approved at Westminster, and implemented. The source of conflict lay in the demands of merchants for repayment of overdue credit from local fishermen. But the attempt to use civil legal remedies to control customary means of financing the fishery backfired. Legislative change and judicial reform were a direct consequence. Once again state law appears to have been modified to fit local customary practice. One notes that a similar pattern could be seen in early nineteenth-century Lower Canada, when 'English' common law courts of common pleas were established for litigating local commercial law where Quebec litigants and judges held sway.

Even in so-called settler societies, where the population brought English law with them, not all law or legislation was perceived as relevant. Blackstone's *Commentaries* stated: 'Such colonists carry with them only so much of the English law as is applicable to their own situation and the condition of an infant colony,'[38] and went on to explain that in conquered territories indigenous laws remained in force until altered.[39] The modification of English law and legal institutions in local colonial settings is demonstrated in the role of laymen in the legal system in Newfoundland, outlined in English's chapter. In Upper Canada, as Russell Smandych describes, the decision not to adopt all forms of English legislation was made by ruling elements, and it succeeded in modifying the received body of law. However, the first legislature of Upper Canada was made up, in Simcoe's words, of 'Men of a lower Order' who refused to increase taxes to pay for government measures despite their agreement with the principles of such measures. A poor law would have been an additional expense. Indeed, if Governor Simcoe had considered English poor law legislation appropriate in the Upper Canadian setting, any proposal could have floundered on the issue of taxation. In the Canadian context too, financial considerations were instrumental in precluding the early construction of goals in the Maritimes as well as in Western Canadian colonies. This suggests that exclusionary decisions in the field of law may have been motivated as much by economic considerations as by social or political factors.

What can be said about the relationships between distinct and different systems of law in different colonies, as described by several authors? Pluralist systems that contained divergent legal cultures rarely seem to have remained stable in the examples considered, even when formal state recognition was granted to alternative systems of legal culture. Chinese succession law, in Anton Cooray's view, was eventually eclipsed in Hong Kong because the English common law did not recognize customary forms of succession, and resort to the common law was always possible in cases of dispute. In Trinidad the introduction of village councils (*panchayats*, or traditional conciliatory dispute settlement mechanisms) failed in the face of the availability of common law adversarial opportunities.

At the same time Haraksingh suggests that the indigenous leadership in pre-independent Trinidad came to rely on formal state law as a means of achieving political goals. Thus, in addition to customary political methods such as protest and riot, Haraksingh identifies legal culture as a means to economic and political ends. This perspective on law as an *in situ* site of political struggle has a resonance with many colonial experiences in the nineteenth and twentieth centuries. It also informs Tony Hall's chapter on native rights in the following section.

The initial paper on Upper Canada moves beyond periods of early settlement or conquest to analyse some of the legal and political relations among Britain, the United States, and Canada West at the time of the outbreak of the Civil War in the United States. Finkelman's detailed study of the John Anderson case allows an investigation of the complex interactions between three closely related jurisdictions. In spite of the common legal heritage and Canada's position under the imperial colonial thumb, the three countries failed to reach agreement over the case. The impasse was not only the result of different ideological stands between Britain and Canada over the issue of slavery; it also involved different approaches to the use of legal decisions to effect political goals. The story of the Anderson case shows how the predominantly conservative ideology of the Upper Canadian judiciary clashed with the anti-slavery perspective of the Court of King's Bench at Westminster. However, the fact that the United States did not respond more vigorously to the refusal to extradite Anderson can be attributed to other factors, including the domestic crisis of secession and a change of administration, and not to any coincidence of views between US interests and the law courts at Westminster. In effect, Finkelman speaks to the political implications of legal judgments in common law jurisdictions with diverging political ideologies and goals. These kinds of issues are also intrinsic to the cases of sedition and dissent that are considered in part Two. They demonstrate some of the cross-relationships between the studies in this book.

Disorder, Dissent, and State Intervention

Disorder has traditionally been studied from the perspective of the 'great' historical events: strikes, revolts, rebellions, and revolutions. But disorder also has a more pervasive role in the historical process, particularly when it is examined either as the more subtle forms of violence within the private confines of the family, or as public violence in the local community and the state. While violence in the family, and especially against women, is a theme in some of the studies on gender and the law in this volume, violence in the sense of public disorder and dissent against the state is also the focus of Part Two in settings ranging from Ontario and Alberta to California.

The question of 'state' intervention in resolving disorder requires definition. The criminal law has historically been the preserve of the monarch or the central state. And the ultimate use of the sanction over life and death has been in the defence of the state against treason and sedition in times of war or rebellion. The enforcement of measures against disorder, however, has often fallen first upon the shoulders of the local community, and second upon those of the regional or central state. What has been important in measuring success (from the perspective of the nation-state) is the extent to which the various levels of government have been able to work together, either to enlist the support of the local population or to find alternative ways to prevent or suppress disorder.

A useful example of the effective functioning of the state in a time of crisis is that of California in suppressing dissent during the First World War. As Diane North reveals, the state not only took the initiative in arresting and imprisoning 'dissidents,' but it also implemented the surveillance of people designated as such by private organizations who were concerned with the 'ethnic cleansing' of non-white, non-Christian society. In this regard the state was successful, because it gave overt support to the politically and economically powerful members of Californian society. This was accomplished by enacting legislation to empower county and city governments to arrest and imprison for various acts of civil disobedience, as well as by assisting corporations and institutions of the federal government to do the same where they had jurisdiction.

The role of the state in Canada was somewhat different. In Upper Canada and later in Alberta the provinces took the initiative in dealing with disorder and dissent. As Rainer Baehre demonstrates in his study of the origins of prisons and asylums in Upper Canada, the province, after failing to obtain the approval of the imperial authority to reform its institutions of social control, sent officials to other jurisdictions (particularly Massachusetts and New York) to examine their experiments. It then borrowed what had looked to be most appropriate for Upper Canada. Later, after Confederation, the provincial governments were equally conspicuous. As Jonathan Swainger reveals in his study of dissent in central Alberta during the First World War, the Alberta courts took the unusual position of gradually restricting the interpretation of political dissent, to the extent that by 1918 few individuals could be convicted. Using a strict application of proving 'intent,' the Alberta courts set a new standard for civil liberties in Canada and upheld the ideology of the rule of law. In so doing they restricted the state's field of legitimate action in favour of abstract notions of fairness and justice. They also provided a clear alternative to the legal reasoning adopted by the United States Supreme Court in 1919 – one that permitted a wide definition of the terms under which a person could be convicted (*Schenck v. U.S.*). What made the Alberta Supreme Court rule significant is that it resulted very clearly from judicial support for the perspective of the local community: the view that working-class European immigrants who had settled the farms of central Alberta had pro-German and anti-British, pro-peace, and anti-war cultural mindsets, which entitled them to opinions that were not actionable unless there was evidence that the expression of those opinions in public places could be tied directly to hindering the prosecution of the war in Europe.

The exercise of legal-political power by the central state also lay at the doorstep of the aboriginals of Long Lake Reserve 58 in northern Ontario in 1990, when they took the step of blocking the Canadian National Railway in frustration at federal government inaction over their land claims. In the end the province and municipal officials assisted in making a breakthrough with Ottawa that enabled the Indians to make their point (that the federal government may have been trespassing) while allowing the normal commerce of the country to return to its movement. In each situation, however, although separated by several thousand miles and seventy years, the role of the local community and its legal culture was decisive in bringing about a resolution of the problem.

The use of state violence often presents difficulties for governments, especially democratic ones. If violence is the legal preserve of the state, then the question of violence, whether legitimate or illegitimate, and its forms, whether armed or unarmed, as well as the limits to state uses of violence, are usually controversial. At one level Rainer Baehre argues that the institution of prisons and asylums is a form of state-legitimatized violence against its 'dangerous classes': criminals, lunatics, First Peoples, and the destitute. In terms of the state's response to riot, seen as an illegitimate form of violence, Susan Binnie argues that the assembly of several thousand militia in Montreal to prevent Catholic-Protestant conflict was a panicked reaction to an outcome fostered by the state's previous hesitancy to intervene to control sectarianism. Perhaps at a more controversial level, Tony Hall suggests that the Indians of Long Lake 58, by using violence as a means to gain national attention for the plight of Indian society in the face of the failure of federal and provincial politicians to come to terms with their longstanding claims, were engaging in a form of violence made legitimate by the illegitimate acts of governments who granted public and private corporations unlawful access to and use of aboriginal lands.

In all of these studies comparative contexts lend themselves to analysis. The first comparative question concerns the sources of law. Baehre, in his study of the origins of prisons and asylums in Upper Canada, has been able to document the way in which local dignitaries and concerned reformers travelled to the United States to search out proven institutions that would serve the 'bourgeois egalitarian' needs of the colony. Finding those needs expressed by the Boston Prison Discipline Society and at the Albany state prison, they went on not only to establish permanent lines of communication in North America, but also to extend those links to France, Germany, and Great Britain. This is in clear contrast with Swainger's study of the evolution of judicial reasoning in Alberta, where the judges essentially created their own legal doctrine from a strand of British custom to meet the needs of local communities.

A second comparative question concerns the extent of interaction between the different levels of government in different nation-states. North's study of civil liberties in California demonstrates that the three levels in the United States could work very efficiently, given a common ground and purpose of action. She shows with great care how federal, state, and local governments interacted with professional aplomb, and were supported at each critical juncture by the courts. The studies of Binnie, Swainger, and Hall, however, suggest that the levels of government were not, and still may not be, nearly as enmeshed in Canada. Their cooperation at critical moments was stumbling at best. Moreover, the governments in these studies did not have the ears of the judiciary, which suggests that the latter may have been much less 'political,' regardless of the level, than it was in the United States.

The political context expressed in all five studies is somewhat similar. In each 'event' there was a political consensus of the ruling élite, whether it was the Whigs and Tories in Upper Canada, the Reform party in Quebec and Ontario, or the Progressive party in California. Disorder or dissent was handled by a political élite that had a non-partisan edge, co-opting its political adversaries into the process. As Hall concludes prophetically, even today governments will create a consensus to resolve a dispute because they cannot afford not to. In addition, the resolution of such disputes has often taken the form of creating new institutions, both bureaucratic and impersonal, which over time have come to form the institutional foundations of the bureaucratic central state. Thus one sees, for example, from the early nineteenth to the late twentieth century a shift from a paternalistic to an impersonal state.

Finally, some interesting questions arise from the sociolegal context. The question of what is the 'law' – that of the sovereign state, the colony, province or state, or the local community, is always a vexing one. What we find in these chapters is that the law is often in flux, seldom certain. For Upper Canada, in both the Baehre and Smandych essays, the law of England was not necessarily good for the colony if it conferred too much authority or marked too large a break from its past. As Baehre's chapter suggests, the conservative judges were able to make decisions relevant to changing social and economic conditions, at least in some fields. For the

Confederation of Canada later in the nineteenth century, Susan Binnie concludes that the Blake Act was used to threaten sparring sectarians either to end their conflagrations or to suffer the exercise of the majesty of the law. The law enacted, however, was rather tame and limited; it was rarely used again, left to expire on the dust heap of *fragmenta antiqua*. In Alberta, the law of the nation-state concerning sedition was an open field, lacking in specificity, and the judges devised a multicultural and ideological solution to give flesh to its bones. And in the area of aboriginal rights and the land law, the law remains nothing less than a quagmire, taking us in the 1990s back to the proclamations of 1670, 1763, and all that.

The law is also, as we recall, a larger environment than simply law *qua* law. It is often treacherous to look at one aspect of the law from its own internalist perspective. This is brought home to us in several of the chapters. In Upper Canada the laws created for prisons and asylums were part of a larger law, one that was concerned with establishing a more general law of social welfare. It inspired the vision of a new and more humanitarian society. In California the law relating to sedition was not concerned primarily with sedition, but with legislating a new social order based on a white, middle-class, Christian society. And in contemporary Canada the law concerning First Nations is not English law but in the end the *jus gentium*, the law of nations; one that can only be informed by, and understood at, the intersection of history, law, anthropology, and comparative civilizations.

Gender and the Law

The major expansions of research initiatives in legal history over the past two decades have included a growth of innovative work in the general area of women and the law. New historiographies have been developed and new fields of women's history established, and these developments have included work on the criminality of women, the history of women's offences, and analyses of penological practice in relation to female offenders.

At the same time, influential new emphases were under development in studies of ideological perspectives and cultural practices, especially in the work of European social theorists. The theorizations were taken up by feminist historians and applied to relations between ideological perspectives, gender, and sexuality. These newer approaches have assisted in enlarging perspectives on the role of law in women's history and the relation of women to the law. One result has been new views of state legal systems from feminist perspectives that encompass and highlight the patriarchal features of law and legal relations.

The chapters in Part Three address a range of issues in Canadian settings while at the same time contributing to these broader histories of women and the law. For instance, major focuses common to two of the studies are the nature and effect of shifting social ideologies and attitudes regarding women's roles, and the use of state institutions to control women's behaviour. As Wendy Ruemper describes, under the aegis of the nineteenth-century ideology of maternal feminism, middle-class North American women became identified as appropriate mentors of female conduct; members of the working class were exhorted to identify with and, where necessary, learn suitable patterns. The ideology of women's 'separate sphere' together with the perceived benefits of maternal feminism formed one foundation for the development of separate prisons for women, run by women, in late nineteenth-century Canada. Meanwhile, the staffing of reformatories by educated, white, middle-class women as exemplars of idealized female conduct, and the adoption of strict prison regimes designed to discipline working-class inmates, demonstrated the state's involvement in practical applications of social control measures relating to the labour force. Jennifer Stephen's study of the Toronto Psychiatric Clinic demonstrates these focuses, first in the efforts made by middle-class, male psychiatrists to control the lives and sexuality of young working-class women according to this model of female behaviour and, second, in the state's involvement in the these processes. Drawing on the medical diagnosis of 'feeble-mindedness' upheld by those in the eugenics movement, clinic staff were able to categorize female referrals and play an advisory role in the processes of the state, such as imprisonment and deportation, used to control them.

By the turn of the century, roles for middle-class women sanctioned by ideological justifications were undergoing a major expansion, especially in relation to the caring and nurturing professions most akin to women's roles in the domestic workplace. In addition, female participation was seen as an acceptable part of the professionalization of social welfare, as described in David Rothman's well-known work on the correctional reforms of the Progressive era in the United States.[40] In Canada the activities of so-called first-wave feminists of the post-suffragist period were marked by involvement in organizations concerned with moral purity issues and welfare reform ranging from temperance unions to children's aid societies. Thus, Dorothy Chunn shows how middle-class women in British Columbia active in social welfare and politics furthered the intro-

duction of family courts in the 1940s. In Chunn's view, the similarity of
the women's ideological positions eclipsed their political divisions. In
effect, shared class positions and ideologies as well as gender linked the
feminists who served as prime movers behind the British Columbia Family
Court. The court was part of a significant and broader move constituting
one element in a shift of emphasis found in a number of capitalist countries from social control measures to a social welfare state. Social control,
however, stands as a principal theme of the chapter in which Stephen, for
the post-First World War period, examines the approach of the Toronto
Psychiatric Clinic with its recommendations for the moral regulation of
working-class girls. Under the direction of Dr Clarence Hincks and Dr
Charles Clarke, the clinic operated within a dominant paradigm resting
on biological determinism as favoured by members of the eugenics movement, and it promoted interventions in the lives of the referred women.

In contrast to the shift away from state social control measures to social
welfare approaches, marital relations as reflected in state law and legislation remained private and highly patriarchal in nature throughout much
of the nineteenth century and into the twentieth. Dependency is another
face of patriarchy. One of the prevailing assumptions was the husband's
duty of care of his wife. At the same time, contemporary states were
highly reluctant to intervene in domestic relationships, except in cases of
visible abuse and/or where wives demanded intervention, and civil remedies such as divorce were available only to women who could afford
expert legal advice. Annalee Gölz's paper demonstrates that women who
experienced severe marital abuse or neglect could, by mid-century, obtain
recourse in the Ontario courts, but that their remedies were both limited
in application and not necessarily effective. The selectivity of the judiciary
in applying relevant legal devices was exercised principally in cases where
lengthy patterns of abusive behaviour were established with no evidence
of fault on the part of the wife. Court interventions did not, however,
necessarily prevent recurrent abusive conduct, which suggests that state
interventions in cases of marital abuse did not mean state control of such
behaviour.

Gölz's analysis also offers insights into the alternative informal enforcement of appropriate marital and domestic roles, in addition to the limits
set on community interventions into marital relationships, and adds to
our knowledge of the informal mechanisms for marital dispute resolution
in this period. Stephen's chapter, by contrast, explores the activities of a
recognized medical institution which for a time achieved a quasi-statal
role. Its female patients stood accused of such common behaviours as

frequent job changes, sexual relations outside marriage, and unmarried motherhood. In proposing interventions in the lives of these young women, the clinic staff influenced state agencies in the field of criminal justice and immigration. Established punitive legislation provided the basis for the proposals made to criminalize some women and deport others, but the clinic's support for measures of regulation and control against these women supplied professional legitimacy to interventionist policies that fundamentally affected many lives.

One of the major problems for legal-historical research in the field of women's history is that records may be sparse or unavailable. Wendy Ruemper's use of official institutional records resolves the problem of availability while raising other interesting questions. For instance, what are the effects of changes in policing practices on the incidence of 'victimless' crimes such as vagrancy and prostitution, and thus on offence categories that form part of criminal justice records for prison populations? Gölz, Stephen, and Chunn in turn respond in different ways to problems of developing adequate databases from limited sources. Gölz's examination of marital desertion and violence builds on a wide range of legal records from the central state down to the local community. She includes civil suits for criminal conversation, police and county court records for non-support cases, and alimony cases under provincial legislation. Stephen draws on the records of the psychiatric clinic and the doctors who staffed it to establish the relationships between the clinic and state agencies. Chunn employs political, institutional, and non-judicial manuscript sources in her analysis of feminist participation in the development of the family court in British Columbia. All of these studies have elements of a legal pluralistic perspective.

The work of these authors, as well as that of others in the volume, underscores the significance of the nature, content, limitations, and availability of legal, quasi-legal, and non-legal records for legal-historical research. Some current concerns in these areas are addressed in Part Four, which explores not only the extent to which the records of the central state are still being catalogued and relatively unused, but also how legal records from local areas, as well as quasi-legal and non-statal records, can be used to illuminate the facts and theories of the history of law in society.

Archival Sources in Legal History

The archives of the central state in the common law world date from the early Middle Ages, and for England's courts of record from the advent of legal memory in 1189. English common law, however, was always much more than the law adjudicated in the central common law courts. The common law was nothing less than the forms, procedures, and customs that various people brought to it. These included the folk, feudal, manorial, and ecclesiastical courts in the Middle Ages, the borough, franchise, and liberty courts of early modern times, and the commercial, statutory, and administrative tribunals of the industrial age. The more restrictive, and generally known, view of the common law is that it is composed of statutory prescriptions and judicial precedents that articulate the declared law. The broader view, which stretches the legal imagination, perceives it as common custom, a large umbrella that has seconded those legal developments deemed worthy of retention, and cloaked those 'laws' in its language, formularies, and substantive rules.[41] The latter view is instructive more for its insights into how common law was formed and works than for its technical accuracy.

The term 'law-ways,' which has been described above, originated from legal-anthropological studies of Native peoples, especially in Africa, Southeast Asia, and North America. An understanding of how law evolves through the customs, folkways, and law-ways of a society to its established systems of dispute resolution can be seen instructively in studies drawn from colonial Africa. Louis Knafla, exploring the documentary heritage of the state, uses the comparative laboratory of African experiences to illustrate the potential breadth of law-related sources that can provide us with a meaningful understanding of what is law and how it works in society. Breaking these sources down into statal, quasi-statal, and non-statal legal records, he relates the study of law in society to the common law world of England and of its Canadian colonies, concluding with recent examples of documentary strategies that point in the direction of records retention in these categories.

By and large, the records of the central common law courts in Britain and a few of its colonies, and their successor states and provinces, have been admirably retained at least until the mid-twentieth century. As Knafla narrates, the retention has at times been uneven, and the problems of finding relevant materials are major, although not on a par with questions of their future retention and access.[42] The records extant remain, none the less, diamonds in a rough and sometimes uncharted terrain. They are major untapped resources symbolizing the role of the Crown and the nation-state as the fountain of all justice, and providing both a juridical framework and a foundation for legal studies in the common law world.

The archival problem emerges more significantly with the regional or local courts, whether in Britain or in its former colonies and successor provinces and states.[43] As is well known, the great bulk of litigation occurred, and still occurs, in regional or local courts. Because they lack stature in their lower 'state' hierarchy as well as the ability to make unchallengeable decisions, there has been less effort to keep their records. The nation-state has also been less willing to finance their preservation, let alone legislate their survival at the enforced expense of local authorities. That many such records have survived is due to the local pride and interest of the custodians and archivists. The difficulties of using such records are much less than with those of the central courts, because they are less voluminous and forbidding. But the information they contain is also perhaps more important to sociolegal historical research. It is there, in the local courts, that life on the streets, in the shops, and in the homes of the country becomes vividly revealed.

The legal records of the state, however, are in themselves simply one part of legal memory in the larger scheme of life that is encompassed in the notions of legal pluralism and legal culture. Prominent examples of such records that are not generally within the direct jurisdiction of the central state provide the focus of two sets of essays in Part Four: by Clive Emsley and Greg Marquis on the archives of the police, and by Peter Moore and Rick Klumpenhouwer on the records of the legal profession. These two kinds of legal records are characterized here as quasi- and non-statal legal records, respectively. While each chapter has a particularly relevant story and message for the future of state law and law and society studies, each essay and set of essays has independently reached some remarkably similar conclusions.

The 'police,' whether in Britain or other common law countries, arose in the nineteenth century as professional forces created by statute to serve primarily local interests. As Emsley and Marquis reveal for Britain and Canada, there is no specific legislation for the preservation of their records, and the problem of who 'owns' them and therefore sets access and use policies is clouded. As a result, many police records pertaining to the work of their forces in the communities are no longer extant, and those that are lack both retention and access policies. With these problems, it is no wonder that their history has been written largely by amateurs in the form of hagiography, creating myths that have been preserved in both scholarly and popular literature from one generation to another. Given the importance of, for example, the records of local constables both as 'evidential' (in their own history) and as 'informational' (in their contents) sources, their preservation is essential if such quasi-statal legal records are to be available for the future exploration of how the law works in society.

Similar problems beset the profession of law. The official and private papers of judges and lawyers, and of law societies and bar associations, are equally important for the legal record of the community. First, these are prominent professions and organizations in their own right. Their records reflect not only the roles played by leading members of society, but also the history of major organizations that traditionally have been self-regulating. Second, their records contain more 'case' materials than those of the central and local courts combined. Client files, depositions, and examinations for discovery are created for many more disputes than those that go beyond the initial statement of claim and into the halls of justice. Thus, for some subjects, the history of law and of society can be written in more depth if and when such legal records exist and can be consulted.

But as private organizations, jealously mindful of the privilege of solicitor-client relations, the legal profession has been reluctant to schedule formally the preservation of records by its professional bar and law societies, let alone those of its members. Moore and Klumpenhouwer reveal the extent of this reluctance in their essays on the records of lawyers and the profession in Australia and Canada. Their findings are similar, and the themes in some ways parallel those of the records of police forces. The problems of jurisdiction, privacy, preservation, and access loom prominently in these essays. But it must be remembered that the essentially legal records of these quasi- and non-statal bodies are not in isolation. What is written here could easily be duplicated for the legal records of similar organizations, from public utilities, schools, hospitals, and community organizations to private corporations, trade unions, and all the professions.

Epilogue

'Many are called but few are chosen.' The phrase has been used by the prominent Canadian archivist Terry Cook to characterize archival situations in which, typically, many historical files are wanted but few are found or made available.[44] However, in describing the difficulties in and problems of legal archives, the future should not be seen with despair. As Rick Klumpenhouwer explains, archivists are becoming more active in framing the questions that lead to retention, preservation, and access schedules. Models for state and local regions have been devised recently with the interests of researchers and the broader demands of sociohistorical studies in mind.[45] The effects of professional specializations, which have drawn the custodians and the users of the records apart, may have run their course. The age of decreasing public resources may spur users to become more demanding of retention, and archivists to become more involved in drawing quasi- and non-statal organizations into the mindset of archival culture so that those organizations can see and understand the relevance of their records as part of society's 'documentary heritage.'[46] Developments such as these can only enhance the future of law and society studies.

In the end the trilogy of law, society, and the state relates to the double role of law: law as a mechanism of the nation-state harbouring its idealized perspectives, as well as an expression of the customs, rules, and regulations of its communities. The importance of the trilogy is to maintain two crucial perspectives: that the history of the law as ideology 'upstairs' is best informed by how it works in practice 'downstairs'; and that one cannot write the history of law in society without the archival records and the resulting knowledge of the legal and customary institutions and traditions. That much is evident. If the essays in this volume and the ideas that inform them have any significance that is larger than their data, it is the connection between historical reality and the present. As one reviewer wrote in relation to this volume and feminist legal historical scholarship, 'Life as it is lived ... can only be understood fully in terms of the close association between the law and its institutions and patriarchy but ... at the same time, the present experience of women is an extension of that history.' So too for other aspects and faces of the law, current experience remains an outgrowth and a development of that past which the present authors attempt to explore in this volume.

NOTES

1 The paradigm and a corresponding critique have been formulated by David Sugarman, 'Legal Theory, the Common Law Mind and the Making of the Textbook Tradition,' in *Legal Theory and Common Law*, ed. William Twining (Oxford: Basil Blackwell 1986), 26–61.

2 *Law, Economy and Society. Essays in the History of English Law 1750–1914*, ed. G.R. Rubin and David Sugarman (Abingdon: Professional Books 1984), and David Sugarman, 'Simple Images and Complex Realities: English Lawyers and their Relationships to Business and Politics, 1750–1950' (1993), 11 *Law*

and History Review, 257–301; and W.R. Cornish and G.deN. Clark, *Law and Society in England 1750–1950* (London: Sweet and Maxwell 1989).

3 Lawrence M. Friedman, *A History of American Law*, 2d ed. (New York: Simon and Schuster 1985). For a more profound examination of the interaction of social and legal change in the nineteenth and twentieth centuries, see Friedman, *Total Justice* (New York: Russell Sage Foundation 1985).

4 For definitions, see, for example, *Law and Society: a Critical Perspective*, ed. Tullio Caputo, Mark Kennedy, Charles E. Reasons, and Augustine Brannigan (Toronto, New York, and London: Harcourt Brace Jovanovich 1989).

5 For Canada, see the volumes of the Osgoode Society for Canadian Legal History, including *Essays in the History of Canadian Law*, vols 1–4, edited by David Flaherty (1981, 1983), Philip Girard and Jim Phillips (1990), and Jim Phillips, Tina Loo, and Susan Lewthwaite (1994); also Constance Backhouse, *Petticoats and Prejudice: Women and Law in Nineteenth-Century Canada* (Toronto: Osgoode Society 1991), and Louis Knafla, *Law and Justice in a New Land: Essays in Western Canadian Legal History* (Toronto: Carswell 1986). For Africa, see, for example, B.O. Nwabueze, *A Constitutional History of Nigeria* (London: C. Hurst and Co. 1981), and Martin Channock, 'Writing South African Legal History' (1989), 30 *Journal of African History*, 265–88. For Asia, see M.B. Hooker, *A Concise Legal History of South-East Asia* (Oxford: Clarendon Press 1978), and his studies of Indonesia, Java, and Malaysia; and the controversial work of Masaji Chiba, *Legal Pluralism: Toward a General Theory Through Japanese Legal Culture* (Tokyo: Tokai University Press 1989).

6 For wide-ranging commentary on these 'mirrors' in the United States see Aviam Soffer, 'Beyond Mirrors: Lawrence Friedman's Moving Pictures' (1988), 22 *Law and Society Review*, 995–1016.

7 See Charles Tilly, 'Reflections on the History of European State-Making,' in his *The Formation of National States in Western Europe* (Princeton: University Press 1975), 3–83.

8 Traian Stoianovich, *French Historical Method: The Annales Paradigm* (Ithaca: Cornell University Press, 1976); Guy Bourdé, *Les Ecoles historiques* (Paris 1983); and Lynn Hunt, 'French History in the Last Twenty Years: The Rise and Fall of the Annales Paradigm' (1986), 21 *Journal of Contemporary History*, 209–24.

9 For interesting interviews of Thompson and other scholars of his generation see *Visions of History* by MARHO, the Radical Historians Organization, ed. Henry Abelove et al. (Manchester: Manchester University Press 1983).

10 David Sugarman's collected studies on law, economy, and the state in modern Britain and William Cornish and G.deN. Clark's treatise on law and society in modern England are prominent examples (supra note 2). See also Sugarman's critique, 'Writing "Law and Society" Histories' (1992), 55:2 *The Modern Law Review*, 292–308.

11 Six papers were in a separate 'Canadian State Trials' section for future publication by the Osgoode Society for Canadian Legal History.

12 See David Lieberman, *The Province of Legislation Determined* (Cambridge: Cambridge University Press 1989), for the history and its debate.

13 See, for example, *The Emergence of Carceral Institutions: Prisons, Galleys and Lunatic Asylums 1550–1900*, ed. Pieter Spierenberg (Rotterdam 1984).

14 *Marxism and Law*, ed. Piers Beirne and Richard Quinney (New York: John Wiley 1982).

15 Morton Horowitz, *The Transformation of American Law, 1780–1860* (Cambridge: Harvard University Press 1977).

16 For instance, Bob Jessop, *The Capitalist State* (Oxford: Martin Anderson 1982).

17 From comments made by John McLaren in reviewing this volume. The editors wish to acknowledge his very helpful review.

18 As another author has put it: 'historical debris which have been allowed to deteriorate into disorder': R.C. Alston, 'Preserving the Record' (October 1992), 20:88 *Archives*, 181–9, at 182.

19 Some of the landmarks in the history of legal pluralism within the context of this volume are as follows: M.B. Hooker, *Legal Pluralism: An Introduction to Colonial and Neo-Colonial Laws* (Oxford: Clarendon Press 1975); *People's Law and State Law: The Bellagio Papers*, ed. Antony Allott and Gordon R. Woodman (Dordrecht: Foris Publications 1985); John Griffiths, 'What Is Legal Pluralism?' (1986), 24 *Journal of Legal Pluralism*, 1–55; Sally Engle Merry, 'Legal Pluralism' (1988), 22 *Law and Society Review*, 869–96; and Brian Z. Tamahana, 'The Folly of Legal Pluralism' (1993), 20 *Journal of Law and Society*, 192–217.

20 For discussion of the 'juridical subject' and the 'isolation effect,' see *Political Power and Social Classes*, trans. Timothy O'Hagan (London: New Left Books 1968) and *State, Power and Socialism* trans. P. Camiller (London: New Left Books 1978).

21 'La majesteuse égalité des lois, qui interdit au riche comme au pauvre de coucher sous les ponts, de mendier dans les rues et de voler du pain': Anatole France, *Le Lys rouge* (Paris: Calmann-Levy 1906), chapter 7.

22 For some of the problems regarding women before the law, see T. Brettel Dawson, 'Sexual Assault Law and Past Sexual Conduct of the Primary Wit-

ness: The Construction of Relevance' (1987–8), 2 *Canadian Journal of Women and the Law*, 310–34.

23 Especially Marshall Sahlins, *Islands of History* (Chicago: University Press 1985).

24 For example, K.N. Llewellyn and E. Adamson Hoebel, *The Cheyenne Way*, 2d ed. (Norman: University of Oaklahoma Press 1978). See also William Twining, 'Llewellyn and Hoebel: A Case Study in Interdisciplinary Collaboration,' in *Law and Social Inquiry: Case Studies of Research*, ed. Robin Luckham (Uppsala and New York 1981), 17–33.

25 From comments by reviewer John McLaren.

26 The third level, municipal government, is the creature of the province but acts under its own name.

27 Eugene Ehrlich, *Fundamental Principles of the Sociology of Law* [1936] trans. W. Moll (New York: Arno Press 1975).

28 Lynn Hunt, in *The New Cultural History*, ed. Lynn Hunt (Berkeley and Los Angeles: University of California Press 1989), 7; Roger Chartier, 'Intellectual History or Sociocultural History? The French Trajectories,' in *Modern European History: Reappraisals and New Perspectives*, ed. Dominick LaCapra and Steven L. Kaplan (Ithaca: Cornell University Press 1982).

29 Two useful critiques are those of Robert Darnton, 'Intellectual and Cultural History,' in *The Past Before Us: Contemporary Historical Writing in the United States*, ed. Michael Kammen (Ithaca: Cornell University Press 1980), and François Furet, 'Beyond the Annales' (1983), 55 *Journal of Modern History*, 389–410.

30 Pierre Bourdieu, *Distinction: A Social Critique of the Judgment of Taste*, trans. Richard Nice (Cambridge: Harvard University Press 1984), for his concept of 'habitus,' which has defined the field of legal culture. Equally important here is Michel Foucault; see, for example, his essays in *The Foucault Reader*, ed. Paul Rabinow (New York: Viking Press 1984).

31 Louis Althusser, *Essays on Ideology* (London: Verso 1984), and Poulantzas, *Political Power and Social Classes*, supra note 20.

32 Among English theorists influenced by the work of Antonio Gramsci, the author of *Selections from the Prison Notebooks*, ed. Quintin Hoare and Geoffrey Nowell Smith (London: Lawrence and Wishart 1971), are Raymond Williams, E.P. Thompson, and Stuart Hall.

33 Robert Macaulay, 'Non-contractual Relations in Business: A Preliminary Study' 28 *American Sociological Review* 55–67.

34 Emile Durkheim, *The Division of Labour in Society* (London: Free Press of Glencoe 1964), 374–411; Max Weber, *Economy and Society*, ed. G. Roth and C. Wittich (New York: Bedminster Press 1968), 333–7.

35 Karl Marx, 'Debates on the Law on Thefts of Wood' in Karl Marx and
    Friedrich Engels, *Collected Works* (New York: International Publishers 1975),
    vol. 1, 224–63.
36 E.P. Thompson, *Customs in Common* (London: Merlin Press 1991).
37 As studied by Douglas Hay and Paul Craven. See their research report
    'Master and Servant in England and the Empire: A Comparative Study' 31
    Labour La Travail, 175–84.
38 *Commentaries I*, 4th ed. (Oxford: Clarendon Press 1770), 107–8.
39 Citing the *ratio decidendi* in *Calvin's Case* (1608), 77 E.R., 377 [7.1a] (Exch.
    Ch.). The only complete reports of this case are in manuscripts: British
    Library, Hale MS 47, fols 150–71, and Sloane MS 2716, fols 1–37. For the
    case, see Louis A. Knafla, *Law and Politics in Jacobean England* (Cambridge:
    Cambridge University Press 1977), 66–80, 202–53.
40 David Rothman, *Conscience and Convenience: The Asylum and Its Alternatives in
    Progressive America* (Boston: Little, Brown 1980).
41 See, for example, L.A. Knafla, 'Common Law and Custom in Tudor Eng-
    land: Or, "The Best State of a Commonwealth" ' in *Law, Literature, and the
    Settlement of Regimes*, ed. Gordon J. Schocket (Washington: Folger
    Shakespeare Institute 1990), 171–86; and, more generally, J.G.A. Pocock,
    'The Ancient Constitution Revisited: A Retrospect' in his *The Ancient Consti-
    tution and Feudal Law*, rev. ed. (Cambridge: Cambridge University Press
    1987), 253–87.
42 Note that some Canadian state archives have begun to exercise restrictive
    rules for certain categories of material following the passage of privacy
    legislation and freedom of information acts.
43 Douglas Hay, 'Archival Research in the History of the Law: A User's
    Perspective' (Summer 1987), 24 *Archivaria*, 36–46.
44 Terry Cook, ' "Many Are Called but Few Are Chosen": Appraisal
    Guidelines for Sampling and Selecting Case Files' (Summer 1991), 32
    Archivaria, 25–50.
45 For example, the *Report of the Interministerial Committee on Court Records*,
    abridged, English-language edition by Jessica Pottier (Montreal: Ministry of
    Cultural Affairs 1991), and Richard J. Cox, 'A Documentation Strategy Case
    Study: Western New York' (Spring 1989), 52 *American Archivist* 192–200.
46 Hans Booms, 'Society and the Formation of a Documentary Heritage:
    Issues in the Appraisal of Archival Sources' (Summer 1987), 24 *Archivaria*,
    69–105.

Part One

COLONIAL
LEGAL EXPERIENCE

2 The Anderson Case and Rights in Canada and England

PAUL FINKELMAN

In 1860 Canadian authorities arrested a fugitive slave named John Anderson, on a charge that he had killed a white man while fleeing from bondage in Missouri. This set the stage for the last attempt to remove a fugitive slave from Canada.[1]

In 1860–1 Canadian abolitionists litigated Anderson's incarceration in three different courts; British abolitionists brought the case to the Court of Queen's Bench at Westminster; politicians discussed the case in Parliament; and diplomats in Washington and London sparred over Anderson's status. Ultimately, a Canadian court released Anderson on a technicality. The Americans never officially requested Anderson's extradition, and the case just faded away.

Despite its anticlimactic ending, the Anderson case briefly threatened to lead to a confrontation between Great Britain and the United States. Coming at the end of the antebellum period, however, it was quickly overshadowed by the secession crisis. In Canada and Great Britain its significance lasted longer, causing, according to one scholar, 'a rethinking of the rights of Canadians within the British empire.'[2]

Anderson's case reveals how slavery shaped nineteenth-century diplomacy. The failure of the United States government to secure Anderson suggests that southern critics of the Webster-Ashburton treaty correctly complained that it would do little to help them recover fugitive slaves in Canada. Finally, the case illustrates the uncertain protection that Canada offered fugitive slaves, and the extent to which racism and Negrophobia affected Canadian law and politics.

John Anderson's Flight to Freedom

In September 1853 a slave named Jack absconded from his master, determined to find freedom. Three days into his flight, a white named Seneca P. Digges challenged Jack on his absence from his master's residence. Jack ran from Digges, who sent his slaves to catch him. Jack eluded the slaves, only to encounter Digges. In the ensuing scuffle Jack stabbed Digges two or three times, and escaped. Digges subsequently died from his wounds.[3]

Jack travelled by foot to Chicago, where abolitionists helped him get to Detroit and then to Canada. In 1854 Missouri's governor sought Jack's extradition, but he 'was nowhere to be found.'[4] Changing his name to John Anderson, he remained in safe obscurity, studying briefly at the William Bibb Institute, becoming a mason and plasterer, and eventually buying a house in Caledonia, a small town about twelve miles south of Hamilton, Canada West.

In March 1860 his fortunes changed when a black former friend told a magistrate that Anderson was wanted for stabbing a man in Missouri. William Mathews, a justice of the peace in nearby Brantford, then issued a warrant for his arrest. Mathews also brought Samuel Port, a Windsor policeman, to identify Anderson. Officer Port told Mathews that Anderson was wanted for murder in Missouri. Hoping to share in a thousand-dollar reward offered by Missouri, Port informed James H. Gunning, a Detroit slave-catcher, about Anderson. Gunning notified the family of Seneca Digges, who slowly took steps to have Anderson returned for trial.[5]

While in custody Anderson admitted he had stabbed a white man while escaping from Missouri. Anderson did not know the man's name, nor, until Mathews told him, that he had died. For a month Mathews waited for someone from the United States to proceed against Anderson. Meanwhile, Samuel B. Freeman, a lawyer and a founding member of the Anti-Slavery Society of Canada, intervened on Anderson's behalf.[6] By 28 April 1860, the last day of the court session, no one had formally asked for Anderson's extradition. On the advice of Justice Archibald McLean of the Court of Queen's Bench for Upper Canada, Mathews released Anderson, who went to Simcoe, about ten miles south of Brantford. Two days after Anderson's release, Gunning returned to Canada with evidence from Missouri and secured a warrant for Anderson's arrest. By August Anderson was again in the Brantford jail.[7]

This time Gunning was prepared. A witness from Missouri identified Anderson as one 'Jack Burton,' belonging to a Missouri slaveowner named Moses Burton.[8] Gunning also submitted the deposition of a Missouri slave, who stated that he had seen a slave named Jack stab Digges. This was the only witness who could place the slave Jack at the scene of the stabbing.[9] On 28 September, after a one-day hearing, Mathews concluded that the evidence sustained the charge that Anderson was the same 'Jack' who did 'wilfully, maliciously and feloniously stab and kill one Seneca T.P. Diggs.' Mathews ordered Anderson jailed 'until he shall be delivered by due course of law.'[10] This delivery could commence only when a formal warrant for his extradition arrived from the United States. The entire matter would then be forwarded to the governor general, who would have the final say on the extradition request.

A few days after this decision Anderson petitioned the governor general of Canada, asking not to be returned to Missouri. Anderson conceded he had stabbed Digges, but argued that it was necessary to 'obtain his liberty.' Anderson noted that when he encountered Digges, 'his pursuers being at his heels with clubs,' he acted on his 'first impulse,' and 'dashed against said Digges with an open knife.' Trapped between the pursuing slaves and their master, Anderson had acted to gain his freedom. He urged the governor general not to return him to Missouri because in the encounter with Digges he had 'only used such force as was necessary to maintain that freedom' to which he was entitled as a human being.[11]

Although Anderson sought help from the governor general, in the short term his liberty would be in the hands of various Upper Canadian judges, who would rule on the legitimacy of his arrest and incarceration. In the long term his fate was in the hands of the government of Lord Palmerston in London. Palmerston would be guided by internal English politics, his own anti-slavery and anti-American views, and the requirements of the Webster-Ashburton treaty of 1842.

Fugitive Slaves and the Webster-Ashburton Treaty

The Webster-Ashburton treaty 'reduce[d] the threat of a third Anglo-American war' by resolving longstanding disputes over boundaries, waterways, and the suppression of the African slave trade.[12] Under Article X, the treaty's last substantive provision, extradition was available for persons 'charged with the crime of murder, or assault with intent to commit murder, or piracy, or arson, or robbery, or forgery...' The treaty provided for extradition only if 'upon such evidence of criminality as, according to the laws of the place where the fugitive or person so charged shall be found, would justify his apprehension and commitment for trial, if the crime or offence had there been committed.'[13] Anderson's case turned on whether Anderson, as a slave seeking his freedom, had committed a crime recognized by Upper Canadian law, or whether the stabbing of Digges was simply an incident in his assertion of his natural right to freedom.

The fact that thousands of American slaves had escaped to Canada complicated the negotiations over the extradition provision. Most slave states could easily charge these slaves with theft, since the clothes they wore belonged to their masters, they sometimes took horses to facilitate their escape, and, in a sense, they had stolen themselves from their masters. Some slaves also committed more serious crimes, including battery and homicide, while escaping.

Throughout the treaty negotiations British officials opposed the return of fugitive slaves. Henry Stephen Fox, the British ambassador to the United States, 'warned against making any provision for giving up runaway slaves.'[14] Lord Palmerston, the foreign secretary, endorsed this position. His successor, Lord Aberdeen, opposed slavery on both religious and political grounds.[15] In 1840 the British drafted an extradition treaty but delayed proposing it, because the British refused to accept one of the key 'demands of the United States ... the extradition of runaway slaves and of "all persons" regardless of their nationality or citizenship.'[16] The British saw no point in negotiating with the Van Buren administration and its slaveholding secretary of state, John Forsyth. An extradition treaty became possible after 1841, when the New Englander Daniel Webster became secretary of state.[17]

Lord Ashburton, the special British envoy appointed to negotiate the treaty, opposed the return of fugitive slaves.[18] He refused to include theft and burglary in the list of extraditable offences because he believed they would be used as excuses to demand the return of runaway slaves.[19] The governor general of Canada had wanted the right to extradite military deserters, and Ashburton had been 'very desirous to secure the delivery of mutineers; but did not press it, lest it should involve, on the part of his Government, the delivery of slaves.'[20]

Although Ashburton had kept theft and burglary out of the treaty, abolitionists feared that fugitive slaves charged with robbery, murder, attempted murder, or arson would be extradited under the treaty. Shortly before the treaty was signed, the governor general of Canada extradited Nelson Hackett, a slave who had stolen a horse, saddle, gold watch, and beaver coat while escaping from Arkansas. Canadian authorities determined that the stolen watch and coat were unnecessary for his escape, and this reduced Hackett, in the eyes of Canadian officials, from a fugitive slave to a common thief. When an Arkansas grand jury indicted Hackett for larceny, the governor general approved his extradition to Arkansas. However, when he arrived in Arkansas Hackett was not tried for larceny, but instead was returned to slavery.[21]

The Hackett case made British abolitionists fearful that local officials might act unilaterally under the proposed treaty, and send fugitive slaves back to the United States. British abolitionists believed that 'local Canadian authorities had conspired with Hackett's American pursuers to mislead the new governor [Sir Charles] Bagot, and secure the slave's return to Arkansas.'[22] Thus the British abolitionists wanted the final authority to return fugitives to rest with Whitehall. Only then could they 'hope to have any influence.'[23]

Shortly after the United States Senate ratified the treaty, a group of American abolitionists met with Ashburton to express their fears about Article X. Ashburton assured them that Britain would not allow the extradition of fugitive slaves on false charges of murder or larceny. The Americans 'left, wholly satisfied.' Lewis Tappan, a founder of the American and Foreign Anti-Slavery Society, told an English ally, 'Our fears respecting any action in Canada adverse to the safety of fugitive slaves subsided.' If Ashburton 'was sincere – which we could not doubt – it seems to us impossible that your Government will allow any practice contrary to the intentions of the framers of the Treaty in Canada.'[24]

Nevertheless, British abolitionists remained concerned. The abolitionist Charles Stuart said the treaty was 'a horrible pledge from us, to make ourselves runaway slave-catchers for the United States.'[25] In November Ashburton assured a group of British abolitionists of his determination to protect fugitive slaves. He told Thomas Clarkson that 'real criminals' would be surrendered without 'respect to colour & condition & therefore the Slave committing [a] crime will be treated like any other person,' but 'that acts necessarily connected with the fact of emancipation cannot be dealt with as crimes.' Dr Stephen Lushington, an anti-slavery member of Parliament, assured his fellow abolitionists 'that by nothing short of the most forced and "treasonable construction," could the clause be made to bear on fugitive slaves finding refuge in Upper Canada.'[26] Lord Aberdeen promised that if 'an evil use be made' of Article X he would urge its abandonment.[27]

Clearly, the British did not believe that the treaty allowed for the extradition of fugitive slaves. But that understanding did not guarantee that a slave who had committed a crime in the United States might not be extradited under the treaty. British abolitionists certainly took no comfort when the House of Commons, by a vote of fifty-nine to twenty-five, refused to exempt all runaway slaves from the operation of Article X.[28]

In response to abolitionist pressure, the British government ordered all colonial governors to send extradition records to England before acting on them. London then sent all colonial governors 'detailed instructions about extradition procedures,' which 'indicated that Britain would follow the narrowest view of her obligations under Article 10 and that slave-holders would face difficulty in recovering their chattels from the British colonies.'[29] As late as June 1843 Charles Stuart still complained about the treaty. But by the year's end abolitionists became more optimistic, when the governor of the Bahamas refused to extradite fugitive slaves who had escaped by boat, even though they were charged with murder in Florida.[30] The combined work of American and British abolitionists had successfully shaped the British interpretation of Article X, which reluctant American officials apparently accepted.[31]

Southerners evidently understood British intentions towards the extradition of fugitive slaves, for they were immediately fearful. John C. Calhoun fumed over British 'treachery' in the negotiations.[32] Senator Thomas Hart Benton of Missouri opposed the treaty 'on many grounds,' including its failure to spell out 'how far' the extradition clause 'applies to the largest class of fugitive offenders from the United States – the slaves who escape with their masters' property, or after taking his life – into Canada and the British West Indies.' Benton considered the extradition provision 'the merest hoax' because extradition was possible only if 'the offense is ... one for which the fugitive could be arrested and tried, if committed at the place of apprehension.' But Benton asked, 'Who supposes that in the abolition dominions of Great Britain, the murder or robbery of a master by his slave will be admitted to be a crime for which the perpetrator should be delivered up to justice? ... Who expects a warrant, a decision, or a certificate against a slave, under such circumstances?'[33] Echoing Benton, Louisiana Senator Charles M. Conrad argued that if a slave killed his master while escaping, 'would not an English judge ... decide that *according to the laws of England,* there is no criminality?'[34]

President John Tyler was also unhappy with the extradition provision. He complained to Webster, 'If a slave kills his master and flees, a Nassau jury or court would declare the act to have been committed in self defence and without malice.' He thought the 'main point' of an extradition treaty was 'unprovided for.' Despite some southern opposition and Tyler's reservations, most of the Senate, including a majority of southerners, voted for the treaty.[35] Their desire to avoid a war with England outweighed their reservations about the extradition clause. As Senator Conrad noted, many who did 'not entirely approve this treaty' were 'willing to vote for it as the price of peace.'[36]

Before the Court of Queen's Bench in Upper Canada

Given the British interpretation of the Webster-Ashburton treaty, it seems that Anderson stood little chance of being returned to the United States. However, the treaty had been signed in 1842. By 1860 British policy might have changed. Even without a policy change, Anderson's actions might not be interpreted as self-defence, and could conceivably lead to his extradition. Anderson's best hope for avoiding extradition was to leave Canada. To accomplish this he had to find a court that would release him from the Brantford jail. John A. Macdonald, the attorney general of Canada West, believed that Anderson should be held for possible extradition. So too did Justice of the Peace Mathews. This suggests a huge gap between Canadian politicians and British leaders. That gap was partially caused by the ambiguities of mid-nineteenth-century theories of international law and the commitment to legal formalism on the part of Canadian jurists. It was also exacerbated by a growing hostility towards blacks on the part of some Canadians.

In November Anderson asked the Court of Queen's Bench in Toronto for a writ of habeas corpus. The court heard arguments in late November, but delayed judgment until 15 December, when the court ruled that Anderson had committed a crime recognized by Upper Canadian law, and so could be extradited under the Webster-Ashburton treaty. The court, by a vote of two to one, remanded Anderson to the Brantford jail 'until a warrant shall issue upon the requisition of the proper authorities of the United States of America, or of the state of Missouri.'[37]

The Court of Queen's Bench faced three questions: (1) Was Anderson charged with a crime that allowed for his extradition under the Webster-Ashburton treaty? (2) Was Anderson's alleged crime cognizable by law in Upper Canada? (3) Did there appear to be sufficient evidence under Canadian law to convict him? If the court answered yes to these questions, it would hold Anderson for extradition to the United States. If the court concluded that any of these questions could not be answered in the affirmative, the court had to release Anderson. Reflecting nineteenth-century legal positivism,[38] Chief Justice John Beverley Robinson noted that courts had to 'conform to what the law required, and are not at liberty to act upon considerations of policy, or even of compassion, when a duty is prescribed.'[39]

But of course what the 'law required' in a case involving treaty obligations was a question of policy as well as law. The meaning of the 'prescribed' duty turned on how the court approached what was a conflict-of-laws question. Put simply, the Upper Canadian court had to decide whether it would enforce Anglo-Canadian concepts of law and justice, or those of the United States. Justice Archibald McLean noted in dissent that 'the law of England, or rather of the British Empire' did 'not recognise slavery within the dominions of the Crown.' Starting with this proposition, McLean wrote:

> Could it be expected from any man indulging in the desire to be free, which nature has implanted in his breast, that he should quietly submit to be returned to bondage and to stripes, if by any effort of his strength, or any means within his reach, he could emancipate himself? Such an expectation, it appears to me, would be most unreasonable, and I must say that, in my judgment, the prisoner was justified in using any necessary degree of force to prevent what to him must inevitably have proved a most fearful evil.

This analysis led McLean to the critical question: 'Can, then, or must, the law of slavery in Missouri be recognized by us to such an extent as to make it murder in Missouri, while it is justifiable in this province to do precisely the same act?'[40] McLean thought not.

Unlike northern judges in the United States, McLean was not constrained by a proslavery Constitution.[41] He was not obligated to enforce the law of bondage to preserve a federal union. Paraphrasing the American Declaration of Independence, McLean noted that 'all men are born equal and possessed of certain inalienable rights, amongst which are life, liberty, and the pursuit of happiness.' In the United States only 'the first of these' was 'accorded to the unfortunate slaves,' but in Upper Canada McLean would protect all these rights, and 'in administering the laws of a British province,' he would 'never ... recognize as law any enactment which can convert into chattels a very large number of the human race.'[42]

The other two justices rejected McLean's position. Chief Justice Robinson thought the evidence presented to Mathews provided enough probable cause to hold Anderson in jail under Upper Canadian law.

But assuming that Anderson had done what the evidence purported to prove, had he committed a murder? After a careful review of the case, the court concluded that when he stopped Anderson, Digges 'was acting under legal authority as much as if he had been armed with process.'[43] This was because Missouri law authorized all whites to stop any slave who was away from his master's residence without a pass. The court thus construed Anderson's act to be the same as if a Canadian in legal custody had killed a policeman. Such a killing would be murder in Canada and thus an extraditable offence under the 1842 treaty. The court remanded Anderson to jail 'until a warrant shall issue upon the requisition of the proper authorities of the United States of America, or of the state of Missouri.'[44]

For Chief Justice Robinson, Anderson's status as a slave had nothing to do with the case. The case was not about a slave gaining his freedom at all costs, but about someone using deadly force to resist lawful authority. Where McLean saw a slave fighting for his freedom, Robinson saw a criminal resisting the police.

Did the Court of Queen's Bench reach the correct decision in this case? On both choice-of-law theory and public policy grounds, Robinson's decision was arguably wrong.

The English *Law Magazine and Law Review* asserted that Anderson could not be given up, because whatever he had done, it was in self-defence. The author of this article argued that the whole question turned on whether Anderson could be 'charged upon such evidence of criminality as, according to the law of Canada, would justify his apprehension and commitment' on a murder charge. Since Digges could not have legally seized Anderson in Canada, Anderson had a right to defend himself, even if it meant killing Digges. In other words, had Robinson analysed Anderson's actions in the light of Canadian law rather than in the context of Missouri law, he would have released Anderson.[45] 'Junius Junior,' an anonymous Canadian, argued much the same point in a pamphlet subtitled *Seven Ways of Proving that Anderson Should Not Be Remanded.*[46]

British public policy also suggested that Anderson should be released. Great Britain generally opposed the extradition of fugitive slaves. None had been returned since the signing of the 1842 treaty. Because a treaty was at issue, Chief Justice Robinson was clearly wrong in thinking that he should approach this case as if it were an ordinary murder trial. In Parliament Lord Palmerston took this position, arguing that it was 'clear as day' that the Webster-Ashburton treaty required that 'the American Government must establish that Anderson committed an offence which by the law of England is murder, and that they must give proof which would be sufficient to satisfy an English justice of the peace that he ought to be committed to be tried on that accusation.' Palmerston thought 'no English lawyer would place the act [of Anderson] under the heading of murder.' Under the treaty, if Anderson could not be tried for murder in Canada on the facts presented by Missouri authorities, then he could not be returned to Missouri for trial.[47]

The Anderson Case in England

After the Court of Queen's Bench in Upper Canada refused to release Anderson, Canadian and British Abolitionists turned to other courts to obtain relief. Meanwhile, abolitionists looked to the Palmerston government to prevent his extradition. Had the case gone this far it is likely that Palmerston would have protected Anderson. But, as it happened, the British government was not tested.

On the same night that the Court of Queen's Bench issued its opinion, William H. Harris, a black leader in Toronto, chaired a pro-Anderson mass meeting.[48] In early January 1861 news of the Canadian decision reached London. The case electrified English abolitionists, rejuvenating their movement just as it had brought the moribund Anti-Slavery Society of Canada back to life. Abolitionists who had more or less dropped out of the antislavery struggle reemerged to raise funds for Anderson, apparently appalled that a British court, even one in Canada, might consider sending a slave back to America. Similarly, the English Ladies Association in Aid of the Coloured Refugees, which had previously aided fugitives in Canada, raised money for Anderson and other blacks in Canada.[49]

News of the case also led to a flurry of official activity. In conformity with existing policies, on 9 January 1860 the colonial secretary, the Duke of Newcastle, ordered Canada's acting governor general, Sir William Fenwick Williams, not to issue a warrant for extradition without authorization from London. The government considered this a case 'of the gravest possible importance, and Her Majesty's Government are not satisfied that the decision of the Court at Toronto is in conformity with the view of the Treaty which has hitherto guided the authorities in this country.'[50] In February Lord Palmerston told Parliament that Newcastle had ordered Fenwick Williams 'not to surrender Anderson to the American Government until he had received positive instructions from Her Majesty's Government to do so.' Palmerston assured Parliament that there was 'no chance of Anderson being surrendered until the question shall have been fully and completely considered.'[51]

Meanwhile, on 15 January the British and Foreign Anti-Slavery Society (BFASS) applied for a writ of habeas corpus from the Court of Queen's Bench at Westminster. The BFASS hoped this writ would compel authorities in Toronto to send Anderson to London, where his case would be heard. After deliberating for less than half an hour, the court issued the writ, despite Chief Justice Sir Alexander Cockburn's recognition that this action might be 'inconsistent with that higher degree of colonial independence, both legislative and judicial, which has happily been carried into effect in modern times.'[52]

This writ had the potential to cause great damage in the empire. It was the first time an English court had ever issued such a writ to Canadian authorities. Edwin John James, arguing for the BFASS, told the English judges that 'the Crown has power to issue the writ of habeas corpus to any part of her possessions, that Canada is a possession of the British Crown, and that the Queen ... has the right to have an account of the imprisonment of her subjects in her own dominions.' While no English court had ever directed a writ of habeas corpus at Canada, English courts had issued such writs to the Isle of Man, Jersey, Guernsey, and Ireland, and other parts of the empire. James argued that Canada 'as a possession of the British Crown' was no different from those places.[53]

Whether this was a fair characterization of Canada is unclear. By 1860 Canada 'had wrested from Britain the grant of a wide autonomy' and was moving 'toward full independence in domestic matters.'[54] Canada was far more independent than the Isle of Man, Jersey, or Guernsey had been when English writs had been served in those places. After 1849 the Province of Canada had virtual self-government on local questions under 'responsible government.'[55] Upper Canada had a fully developed court system, and the courts had ruled that some English laws were not enforceable in Upper Canada. Since the Constitutional Act of 1791[56] the legislature of Upper Canada, not the monarch, had established the courts. Similarly, Canadians in their own legislatures had enacted their own law.[57]

The 1791 act and the subsequent history of Canada implied that Canadian courts were parallel, not subordinate, to English courts. But the issue was complicated. Despite 'responsible government,' the governor general could still reject bills, the home government could disallow Canadian laws, and Parliament could pass legislation that was binding in the Province of Canada. Moreover, 'foreign affairs were still wholly under

British control.'[58] Thus the final interpretation of the Webster-Ashburton treaty lay with the governor general or with Whitehall. Certainly most Canadians understood this. But whether an English court could issue a writ that was enforceable in Upper Canada was another matter. Lord Justice Crompton asked Edwin James if 'the courts in Westminster have now a concurrent jurisdiction with the local [Canadian] courts in granting this writ.' James answered, 'The fact that Canada has both a separate legislature and judicature makes no difference. The Superior Courts in England have a concurrent jurisdiction with the courts in Canada as to issuing writs of *habeas corpus*.'[59]

The chief justice worried that Canadians would disobey the English writ and treat it 'with disobedience and contempt,' but James responded: 'Your lordship will not assume that.' But the court was not so sanguine. The chief justice feared people would consider this 'an interference with the independence of the colonial judicature,' and the court would embarrass itself with 'the attempt to exercise a jurisdiction which we have no means of enforcing.' James argued that 'the sheriff of Toronto is a British subject,' implying that he would obey a writ from an British court. James reiterated his point: 'If it is a British possession, and he is a British subject, there cannot be a question on earth.'[60]

Although uncertain about its jurisdiction, the English court nevertheless issued the writ. The English judges accepted the argument that a writ of habeas corpus was the right of all people within the jurisdiction of the British Crown, and they could direct the writ to anywhere the Union Jack flew, unless expressly prohibited by Parliament.[61] While most of the English press applauded the decision, many British legal scholars agreed with their Canadian counterparts that the court at Westminster had no jurisdiction over the matter.[62]

Although angry over the English writ, Canadians had few options if the writ was served. To reject the writ out of hand might force a crisis that no one in Canada or Great Britain wanted. However much the writ led to 'Canadian restiveness – the congenital tic of outraged colonials,' as one English historian has characterized the Canadian response,[63] Canadians were not about to follow South Carolina's recent example of secession. As the *Upper Canada Law Journal* explained, Canadians were 'united in the opinion that the English Court, in sending a writ of *habeas corpus ad subjiciendum* to Canada, has done wrong.' This led to a 'feeling of resistance' among Canadians who were annoyed by the action of the English court. But when they spoke 'of a feeling of resistance,' Canadians did 'not desire to depict overt acts of treason.' The *Law Journal* declared, 'We do not intend to indorse the absurd stories circulated in the neighbouring States, about "the ring of 1775." Such stories were a libel on our loyalty. While determined to resist encroachments on our rights as an independent colony, by all constitutional means, there never was nor is there, the slightest intention to kindle the flame of rebellion.'[64]

Although indignant that a British court had the audacity to overrule a Canadian court, Canadians had no interest in challenging British sovereignty. As the *Upper Canada Law Journal* noted, Anderson could appeal to 'Her Majesty in Privy Council,' a right with which 'Canada is at present satisfied.'[65]

Curiously, neither Court of Queen's Bench – the one at Toronto or the one at Westminster – acknowledged that in the end Anderson's fate would not rest with a court. International extradition was a political question. Ultimately the Palmerston ministry, not a court of law, would decide whether what Anderson did constituted murder under the Webster-Ashburton treaty. As Palmerston told the House of Commons, 'There is a general impression that the decision of the Court of Queen's Bench in Canada would have the effect of rendering it necessary that Anderson should be given up. But it has no bearing on that point.' The Canadian decision determined only whether Anderson was 'to be taken out of the custody' of the Brantford jailer. The final decision rested with the governor general of Canada, who took orders from the ministry. The undersecretary for the colonies, Chichester-Fortescue, made the same point two weeks later, noting that no court had 'the competency' to 'deliver him up to any foreign Power.' The Undersecretary reminded Parliament that Anderson 'can only be delivered up under the hand and seal of the Governor General.'[66]

Had activists on both sides of the issue acknowledged the fact that the final decision in this case rested with the governor general or with Palmerston, the tensions caused by the English writ might have been averted. Instead, pressure would have been focused on Palmerston. Although Palmerston had never been much of a reformer, he had always been associated with antislavery. In 1853 he had been 'one of the most prominent of the social figures to meet Mrs. Harriet Beecher Stowe.' Moreover, 'his deepseated hostility to the United States' made him less than anxious to return a fugitive slave.[67] Palmerston's foreign secretary, Lord John Russell, was even more committed to antislavery.

The antislavery sentiments of the administration, however, might have been counterbalanced by other considerations. Throughout his career Palmerston feared an American invasion of Canada.[68] Had the United

States pressed the issue, it is at least remotely possible that Palmerston would have sacrificed John Anderson for peace on the St Lawrence frontier. Equally important, both Palmerston and Lord Russell 'were averse to interference in the judicial and legislative procedures of the colonies.'[69] They were reluctant to overrule local decision-makers on local matters.

For reasons of both foreign policy and internal imperial policy, a court decision freeing Anderson would have solved some delicate problems for Palmerston. If pressed by the United States, Palmerston might have found it easier to blame the release of Anderson on the courts than on his own actions. Similarly, if the case led to a conflict between the metropolis and the colony, Palmerston might have preferred the justices of the Queen's Bench to be the point men.

Given these considerations, the strategy of the BFASS may have been shrewdly correct. Despite the antislavery sentiments of the British leaders, foreign policy is not always guided by the principles of the leading dramatis personae. And sentiments might be balanced against other sentiments. Palmerston's foreign policy 'was intimately entwined with, and to a very large degree formed by domestic politics.'[70] Thus the persistence of the abolitionists in litigating for Anderson's freedom had four values. First, it could and ultimately did lead to Anderson's release from jail. Second, it kept the case in the public mind, preventing a quiet or secret extradition. Third, it gave the abolitionists a focus for their cause and a new visibility. Finally, it helped put pressure on Palmerston to do the right thing.

The application for a English writ of habeas corpus was ideal for these tactics. The English press carried news of the case at Westminster, generally applauding the result.[71] The writ placed the Anderson case in the forefront of the Anglo-Canadian legal world and threatened to cause a major crisis in imperial legal and political relations. From the abolitionist perspective, the English writ was a perfect way of forcing Palmerston and Russell to intervene on behalf of freedom.

Round Two in the Canadian Courts

The potential crisis between the English and Canadian courts over the English writ ultimately never materialized. While Canadians fumed about this symbolic loss of judicial autonomy, friends of Anderson found a way to further his cause while avoiding an Anglo-Canadian confrontation: they appealed to another Upper Canadian court, which did issue a writ of habeas corpus.

On 1 February 1861 Anderson's lawyers applied to the Court of Common Pleas in Toronto for a writ of habeas corpus. Anderson could gain another hearing at another court because of the jurisdictional anomalies of the early Upper Canadian courts. As an Ontario Supreme Court Justice explained six decades later: 'In those days the decision of any court or any judge in *habeas corpus* proceedings was not final. An applicant might go from judge to judge from court to court and the last applied to might grant the relief refused by all those previously applied to.'[72]

Beyond these anomalies of the Canadian court system, there was a strong legal reason for the Court of Common Pleas to hear Anderson's case after the Court of Queen's Bench had rejected his plea for freedom. In Common Pleas Anderson's lawyers raised arguments that had not been brought before Queen's Bench. In other words, the case before Common Pleas was not res judicata because the points of law were new.

Samuel B. Freeman had argued before Upper Canada's Court of Queen's Bench that Anderson should be set free because the evidence presented to Justice of the Peace Mathews was insufficient to authorize his extradition. Freeman argued that 'according' to Canadian law 'the homicide was justifiable' and 'would not amount to murder' because Digges was attempting to reduce Anderson to slavery.[73] Freeman's argument was excellent abolitionist theory. It was also a theory that the English Court of Queen's Bench later accepted. Moreover, it seemed to be the theory to which the Palmerston government subscribed, as had all English governments since the adoption of the Webster-Ashburton treaty. But this theory did not persuade a majority of the justices of Toronto's Court of Queen's Bench, who ruled that Anderson's act did constitute murder, and that he could be extradited under the treaty.

Before the Court of Common Pleas, Anderson's counsel offered an argument that was narrower and far less political. Anderson's lawyers argued their client was in jail on a technically insufficient warrant of commitment. The technicality was a simple one. The warrant charged that Anderson did 'wilfully, maliciously and feloniously stab and kill' Digges. However, the Webster-Ashburton treaty specified that extradition was possible only for murder. Since to 'feloniously stab and kill' might include a lesser offence than murder, Anderson's counsel argued that he could not be extradited for the crime for which he was committed. The lawyer for the Canadian government did little to resist this argument; he presented a weak case and admitted that he had 'no desire unduly to press the case against the prisoner.'[74] While lawyers and judges had alluded to this question when the case was before the Canadian Queen's Bench, this claim had not been formally raised or answered.

The Court of Common Pleas happily accepted this argument. Chief Justice William H. Draper noted that the charge that Anderson did 'feloniously stab and kill' Digges 'would be an insufficient statement in an indictment for murder in any of our Courts.'[75] The court determined that Anderson must be released on the insufficiency of the warrant. Upon his release, Anderson commented 'that he never thought there was so much law in Canada.'[76] Although out of jail, Anderson could still have been rearrested under a better warrant, but that was unlikely.

As soon as the weather permitted, Anderson left Canada for England, where he was lionized, fêted, educated, and eventually shipped off to Liberia.[77] Among those speaking out for Anderson when he arrived in England was the eighty-year-old Charles Stuart, who had warned of the dangers of the Webster-Ashburton treaty nearly two decades earlier.[78] It is not implausible to argue that the strong abolitionist opposition to the extradition clause in 1842–3, which Stuart spearheaded, was critical for establishing the British policy that led to Anderson's freedom.

John Anderson, Canadian Racism, and the Law

For Canadians Anderson's case was a major event, which a turn-of-the-century Ontario lawyer claimed 'caused more excitement ... than any other one had ever made before or since' and was 'watched over with the greatest interest by the legal profession and by governments and politicians of the British provinces.'[79] Subsequent scholars have endorsed this view. Patrick Brode, concentrating on the case as an aspect of Canadian history, notes that when the British court issued the writ of habeas corpus it 'caused a rethinking of the rights of Canadians within the British empire.' Brode argues that the 'nationalistic resentment aroused by this imperial interference ... was a measure of the sense of nationhood Canada had achieved by 1860.'[80] In Britain the case was also a major event. English 'law journals were full of the case,' and it 'provided more interest to law journals than any other case of the period.'[81]

Anderson's case also illuminates the history of Canadian race relations. While justly proud of their heritage as a beacon of real liberty just north of the 'land of the free,' Canadians were not immune to the virus of racism.[82] In the 1840s Charles Stuart had found 'horrible prejudice,' particularly in western Canada, while a black Canadian 'cited numerous examples of color prejudice' in arguing that 'fugitive blacks would be better off emigrating to Jamaica.'[83] Robin Winks notes that in the '1840s and 1850s the Negro found himself distinctly unwelcome in many areas of the provinces,' where 'prejudice rose as the number of Negroes rose.'[84] Jason Silverman offers the most extreme analysis, arguing that after the adoption of the 1850 fugitive slave law many Canadians were 'frustrated and angry at the sudden influx of black refugees.' Canadian newspapers often reflected popular 'ambivalence' towards fugitive slaves, and some papers published 'vicious racist propaganda.'[85] During the Civil War one fugitive told an American investigator that there was 'as much prejudice against the black man in Canada as there is in the States,' while another complained Canadians were more prejudiced than southern slaveholders.[86] American blacks, Silverman concludes, 'did not find in Canada what they had been promised. On the contrary, they often found antagonism and resentment.'[87]

Silverman and Winks may have overargued their position. Statements made during the Civil War may indicate that these fugitives were already laying the psychological groundwork for a return to the United States in anticipation of a total end of slavery. Canadian race relations, like those in the northern United States, were complex.

In the north, for example, it was possible to find communities that offered blacks full equality and integrated facilities, while another city in the same state barely tolerated blacks.[88] Canada may have been equally diverse. The black utopias of Canada provided a safe haven for numerous fugitive slaves and native-born Canadian blacks. Racism in some parts of Canada must be balanced with the success of blacks in other parts of the country.[89]

Anderson's case illustrates this complexity. Before his arrest Anderson had worked his way from a penniless fugitive to a homeowner with a viable trade. Anderson's troubles with a Brantford politician who was hostile to blacks must be contrasted with his ability to hide in Simcoe for an entire summer. The legal and political aspects of this case also illustrate the complexity of Canadian race relations.

The Canadian judiciary certainly was almost too anxious to rush Anderson to judgment. Anderson's case was heard in three different courts, and with the exception of Justice McLean's dissent on the Court of Queen's Bench, no Upper Canadian judge showed any sympathy for Anderson and his plight. Even the court that released Anderson did so on a technicality, while rejecting the main thrust of his lawyer's argument. Some Canadian politicians, including Attorney General John A. Macdonald, were equally unsympathetic to Anderson and other fugitive slaves.[90]

At the same time, many Canadians were truly outraged at the possibility of Anderson's extradition. The leading white advocate of Anderson's release was George Brown, the 'unrivaled' leader of the reformers in Upper Canada.[91] Thomas Henning, the secretary of the Anti-Slavery Society of Canada, told his English counterpart that 'the cry here is throughout the land, Anderson is not a *murderer* but a *Hero* and he *must* not be given up.'[92] Henning seems to have accurately understood the sentiments of his countrymen. A mob threatened the Court of Queen's Bench when that forum denied Anderson relief. Only the intervention of Anderson's lawyer prevented a riot. More than 2,500 Montreal residents signed a pro-Anderson petition. White and black residents throughout British North America objected to returning Anderson.[93] 'The Canadian press reported daily on the clamor, comparing Anderson to Garibaldi, to a ravished Negro maid seeking to escape from her abductor, and to the manly symbol of all Africa.' Black Canadians and white abolitionists in the country organized rallies in support of Anderson.[94] When Anderson was finally released, The Toronto Globe, a mainstream paper edited by the antislavery activist George Brown, heartily congratulated 'the people of Canada on the narrow escape we have thus made from what would have been a deep and indelible stain on the fair fame of our country.'[95]

Relying on a technicality, the Canadian judges of Upper Canada's Court of Common Pleas may have ultimately saved Canada's 'fair fame,' but they and other Canadian judges also put that 'fair fame' into jeopardy. Had the Canadian judges been more sensitive to the problem of slavery itself, Anderson might have been released for substantive reasons at any of his three hearings.

Brode, defending Canadian nationalism, argues that 'in view of the accusations against Anderson, William Mathews would have been delinquent in his duty if he had not had him arrested.'[96] Yet racial bias played an important part in Mathews's decision to hold Anderson for extradition. Arrogant, authoritarian, and quick to judge blacks, Mathews was also a politician in a notably racist town. In 1846, fourteen years before Anderson's arrest, 'white residents of Brantford asked that the Negroes there – fifteen families – be sent away' to a more remote and unsettled area of Canada West.[97] By 1860 race relations had worsened. Mathews, a politician with no legal training, embodied this hostility towards blacks and American fugitive slaves. He was, in Brode's language, 'a bumbling racist.'[98] His approach to the case reflected his prejudices.

It is also not clear that under the law and the rules of extradition Mathews should have jailed Anderson. The initial incarceration followed an accusation by an angry acquaintance. While technically not hearsay,[99] this was certainly flimsy evidence on which to arrest and hold someone for a month.[100] Officer Port, who identified Anderson at this time, had never actually seen him, so his identification was hardly reliable. The second incarceration was based on Gunning's affidavit, which recounted that 'Jack' had committed a murder in Missouri in 1853, and ended with the phrase 'this deponent doth verily believe.'[101] But Gunning had never been to Missouri and had never seen either 'Jack' or Anderson. In his dissent Justice McLean suggested that Gunning's 'doth verily believe' was not precise enough to justify an arrest. McLean noted that Missouri had not issued any warrant. He decried 'the absence of any more positive information than mere belief' of a crime, and stated that Mathews should 'have hesitated before issuing a warrant to apprehend the prisoner.' McLean said that Mathews could not have been charged with 'any dereliction of duty' if he had 'called for some proof of a murder having been committed, and of the identity of the party accused as the murderer.'[102]

The evidence presented to Mathews was also suspect. No testimony placed Anderson at the scene where Digges died. The only evidence of his having been there was an affidavit sworn by a slave in Missouri about another slave named 'Jack.'[103] Although Anderson's own lawyer inexplicably failed to challenge this affidavit, a trained judge might have found it unacceptable. The judge might have demanded that the slave himself be brought to Canada West to testify at the hearing. Since whites from Missouri were able to make the trip, there was obviously no technical reason for the slave not to come. Had the slave come, however, then he would have been immediately free.[104]

It is not clear if an affidavit of a slave could have been legally presented in a Missouri court. Slaves in Missouri could testify in criminal cases against other slaves, but the Missouri law was silent on their giving affidavits.[105] Certainly if a slave's affidavit was inadmissible in Missouri, a Canadian court should not have accepted the same affidavit. Anderson's lawyer should have challenged the affidavit on these grounds; but even when he failed to do so, there was no reason for Mathews to accept it at face value. An Upper Canadian court could reasonably have refused to accept the affidavit because of the enormous potential for coercion: a master could compel a slave to agree to the contents of an affidavit. Where slave testimony was involved, the only certain way of securing honest and fair testimony would have been to bring the slave to the court.

Anderson had of course admitted that he did stab a white man while escaping from Missouri. Anderson did not recant this admission, but neither did he view it as a confession of guilt. Anderson did not confess to stabbing Digges. He did not know who he had stabbed. Nor did he confess to killing anyone. He had no personal knowledge that he had killed anyone. Furthermore, even Anderson's admission that he had stabbed someone, assuming that it was Digges, did not necessarily provide probable cause for holding Anderson, owing to the strict grounds for extradition under the Webster-Ashburton treaty.

As already noted, Article X of the treaty provided for the extradition of persons 'charged with the crime of murder, or assault with intent to commit murder ... upon such evidence of criminality as, according to the laws of the place where the fugitive or person so charged shall be found, would justify his apprehension and commitment for trial, if the crime or offence had there been committed.'[106] Anderson was clearly charged with murder in Missouri, and murder was a crime that Canada recognized. But did what Anderson had done in Missouri constitute murder in Canada?

Digges initiated the violent contact by stopping Anderson, ordering his slaves to chase Anderson, and by assaulting Anderson with a stick. In these circumstances it would not have been unreasonable for a Canadian court to conclude that Anderson had committed the lesser offence of manslaughter or even justifiable homicide on the ground of self-defence. In the Court of Queen's Bench Justice McLean, in dissent, had argued this position.[107]

Making Sense of the Canadian Result

Beyond complicated issues of international law, the Canadian courts that heard Anderson's habeas corpus petitions faced three identical questions: (1) Was there sufficient evidence to hold Anderson for subsequent extradition as a murderer? (2) Could a fugitive slave accused of murder be extradited under the 1842 treaty? (3) Was the warrant of commitment technically correct?

The Court of Queen's Bench in Upper Canada ruled against Anderson on all three grounds. Chief Justice Robinson believed that the evidence in support of the allegations against Anderson was sufficient to return him for trial in Missouri. Robinson rejected any notion that Anderson's slave status might affect his offence. The court acknowledged problems with the warrant for commitment, especially because it did not allege that Anderson had committed a murder. But Robinson believed such 'defects' were 'not fatal, for there is not the same necessity for an adherence to technical terms in a warrant as in an indictment.' Robinson felt that 'when a legal cause for the imprisonment appears upon the evidence, the ends of justice are not allowed to be defeated by a want of proper form in the warrant.'[108]

The Court of Common Pleas showed some sympathy for Robinson's position on the first two issues. Chief Justice Draper refused to rule out an extradition of a fugitive slave merely because as a slave he might be denied a fair trial or enslaved even if acquitted of the crime. He also offered one example of a situation where a fugitive slave might be returned for a murder trial: if the slave had killed a police officer in a free state in order to prevent his return to a slave state. But at the same time Draper indicated slaves ought to have a right to fight for their freedom, and that the Queen's dominions had become the land of the free for American slaves. Thus Draper faced a dilemma: 'I am reluctant, on the one hand ... to declare that ... 4,000,000 slaves in the Southern States may commit assassination in aid of escape on any part of his route to this province and find impunity and shelter on his arrival here. I am reluctant, on the other hand, to admit that Great Britain has entered into Treaty obligations to surrender a fugitive slave who, as his sole means of obtaining liberty, has shed the blood of the merciless task-master who held him in bondage'.[109]

Fortunately for Draper, he did not have to face these questions. Unlike Chief Justice Robinson, Draper believed that the warrant was defective and that the court had no choice but to discharge Anderson. An English – or Canadian – court could not remand a prisoner to jail on a defective warrant.

There are four possible reasons for the different results in these two cases. Taken together, they explain why Anderson was set free by one court after another had refused to do so.

First, the arguments of counsel on behalf of Anderson seem to have improved in the second case. Samuel Freeman did a better job in the second case, where he was also joined by two new counsel, one of whom 'was a noted conservative.'[110] This political bipartisanship may have helped Anderson, while the new barristers may have helped shape the arguments on his side. In particular, before the Court of Common Pleas Anderson's lawyers stressed the defects of the warrant of commitment, while before the Court of Queen's Bench they noted that it was defective, but foolishly conceded that this was not the key issue of the case. In other words, in the second case the lawyers chose to argue law and were content to win on a technicality, while in the first case they were far more concerned with asserting antislavery theory. Had they vigorously argued the insufficiency of the warrant in November, the Court of Queen's Bench might have released Anderson.

Second, the two courts differed in their analyses of the case. Queen's Bench focused on the fact that Anderson had killed Digges. That was enough for Chief Justice Robinson to believe that he should stand trial in Missouri. Common Pleas, however, focused on the requirements of the Webster-Ashburton treaty. In a concurring opinion, Common Pleas Judge William B. Richards noted that 'if it were not for the Treaty, and the Act of Parliament carrying it out, we should be obliged to discharge the prisoner from custody, though it was clearly shown that he had committed murder in the State of Missouri. If it does not appear that he has committed some offence against the Queen's peace, we have no right to detain him in custody, except under the authority of the Act of Parliament.'[11] Such an analysis led the Common Pleas judges to demand strict adherence to the treaty, in ways the Queen's Bench justices did not do.

Personalities and personal prejudices also may have affected the way the two courts approached the case and the judgments they reached. Chief Justice Robinson, a descendant of slaveowning Virginia loyalists, had a 'low opinion of blacks' and little tolerance for their presence in Canada. Extremely conservative, Robinson seemed more concerned with order than justice. Lord John Russell, the English foreign secretary who had worked with Robinson in Canada, wrote of the Anderson case: 'I believe the law is against Chief Justice Robinson but he cannot bear liberty in any form.'[12] Draper, although a Tory, was far less conservative than Robinson. Moreover, the other Common Pleas judges, John H. Hagarty and William B. Richards, were 'pronounced liberals.'[13] The different outcomes of the two cases underscore how personalities and personnel can affect the scales of justice.

Finally, the outcome was doubtless affected by the political problems the case had caused. For Canada West's attorney general, John A. Macdonald, the Anderson case was an embarrassment. Macdonald felt some obligation to support his political allies Justice of the Peace Mathews and Chief Justice Robinson. But Macdonald realized that as attorney general he would be held responsible if somehow Anderson was actually returned to the United States. Macdonald tried to straddle the issue. As attorney general, he might have been instrumental in getting Anderson out of jail. An opinion by the attorney general that Anderson's actions were not such that he could be extradited under the Webster-Ashburton treaty probably would have ended the case before it reached the Court of Queen's Bench in Upper Canada. Indeed, when he first got wind of the case, while it was in the hands of Justice of the Peace Mathews, he might have intervened on behalf of freedom. That Macdonald did not do so suggests that he was unsympathetic to Anderson's plight.

Macdonald ignored the case when it was before Mathews.[114] Once the case was headed for Queen's Bench, Macdonald apparently worked behind the scenes to secure a result favourable for Anderson. He clearly hoped the courts would solve his dilemma; thus he privately agreed to provide public funds for Anderson's defence, and interposed no objections to any of the procedural motions of Anderson's lawyer.[115]

Since the 'reactions in Canada to the court [of Queen's Bench] decision were almost entirely critical,'[116] Macdonald had to distance himself from the decision to avoid a political backlash. Macdonald personally tried to stay clear of the case, while in the end defending Canadian nationalism against both the court at Westminster and the government at Whitehall. Appealing to popular emotions, Macdonald claimed that 'Anderson was better off being tried "by the *Magna Carta*, by the law of the land" than by any Cabinet whatever.'[117] This was nonsense, of course, since in the end Anderson's greatest chance for freedom lay with the governor general or the English cabinet.

Probably more important to Macdonald than the reaction of the Canadian electorate was the impact of the case on Macdonald's aspirations for greater Canadian autonomy. Macdonald hoped to lead Canada to a new level of independence in the British empire. He could hardly accomplish this if Canada followed a policy towards slaves that was diametrically opposed to Great Britain's, in conflict with the spirit and possibly the letter of the Webster-Ashburton treaty, and at odds with nearly eight decades of antislavery British jurisprudence.

Macdonald, an ambitious politician, was still recovering from the embarrassing 'Orange Affair,' which had forced him to abandon the Crown Prince and the Duke of Newcastle when they visited his hometown of Kingston.[118] The confederation that Macdonald looked forward to 'would have been impossible ... unless the Imperial Government had given its blessing.' Despite the Orange fiasco, the trip to the Province of Canada helped convince Newcastle that confederation was a good idea.[119] But Macdonald could not know this in the winter of 1860–1. He only knew that the Anderson case was potentially a greater embarrassment than the Orangemen.

If Canadians tried to force the extradition of Anderson, the British would intervene and be more reluctant than ever to give Canada political autonomy. No one could predict the result if the Canadians ignored a writ from the Court of Queen's bench in England. Macdonald, anxious to avoid another embarrassment, doubtless wanted the Anderson case to go away. This explains why the Crown counsel only halfheartedly resisted the suggestion that the warrant was defective. Here was an easy way out of the problem with the least political damage.

The Court of Common Pleas must have wanted to limit the political damage too, even though a majority of the justices were Macdonald's political opponents. Canada's jurists had their own reasons for wanting the case to end and Anderson to go free. Looming in the background was the writ of habeas corpus issued by the English court. If an Upper Canadian court did not release Anderson, then an English court would demand he be brought to Westminster. If the writ was served it would create a huge constitutional crisis in Canada. By discharging Anderson, the court avoided this crisis.

In addition to the English writ, the Court of Common Pleas explicitly recognized that no matter what the Canadian courts did, the governor general, at the direction of the Palmerston ministry in London, would refuse to sign a warrant of extradition. As Chief Justice Draper noted in his opinion, in an extradition case the judge's 'decision is not binding on the Government to whom he must certify the same, and the evidence, and on whom rests the ultimate responsibility of surrendering or refusing to surrender the prisoner.'[120]

In releasing Anderson, the Court of Common Pleas made life easier for the Macdonald-Cartier ministry in Canada, prevented a crisis with the mother country, and avoided forcing the governor general to overrule the recommendation of a Canadian court. In addition, the politically reformist common pleas justices had the satisfaction of knowing that they helped strike a blow against slavery while simultaneously pleasing the majority of the Canadian public. The only parties to the case whom they might have offended were Justice of the Peace Mathews and the United States government. Mathews, a small-minded man in a small office in a small town, was of no consequence to them. Canadians were rarely concerned with what might offend the United States; and in late February 1861 everyone in Canada knew that the United States had far greater things on its collective mind than the decisions of a court in Toronto.

Making Sense of the American Response

While all this was happening, neither the Buchanan administration nor the Missouri government did much to regain Anderson. On 2 October

1860 Secretary of State Lewis Cass wrote to R. Douglas Irvine, the British chargé d'affaires in Washington, asking that 'Her Britannic Majesty's Government ... issue the necessary warrant to deliver up' Anderson. Irvine immediately forwarded this letter to Foreign Secretary Russell. On 27 October this message was transmitted to Sir Edmund Head, the acting governor general of Canada, as well as to the prime minister's office.[121]

Given the pace of intragovernmental communication and transatlantic mail, the English authorities acted relatively expeditiously. But it was not fast enough for the Americans. On 2 November Secretary of State Cass wrote the British ambassador, Lord Lyons, asking why 'the requisition' had 'never been forwarded to Canada.' Cass feared that Anderson would be released from custody. A day later Lyons told Cass that he had forwarded the material to London rather than directly to Canada. Lyons immediately telegraphed officials in Canada, requesting that Anderson be held in custody. The officials responded that Anderson was in jail 'waiting requisition.'[122]

Curiously, no formal 'requisition' had actually been sent. Cass's vague and general communication of 2 October 1860 was little more than a note – hardly a document that would allow for an international extradition. In mid-December Lord Lyons explained to Acting Governor General Williams, 'I do not know anything of the facts of the case, except what I have read in the newspapers.'[123] The American government had failed to supply even the most basic information on the case. As late as 12 February 1861 Foreign Secretary Russell told Parliament that 'no communication has taken place between Her Majesty's Government and that of the United States' on the Anderson case 'beyond the original demand,' which had been insufficient to justify an extradition. Russell later explained to Parliament: 'Now what the American Government did was of the very simplest character. They stated that a man of colour had been guilty of murder, without saying what his name was or anything else.'[124]

In 1860 'something of a *rapprochement* between Great Britain and the United States took place.'[125] This may explain the federal government's lackadaisical pace in sending the proper requisition for the extradition. The Buchanan administration fully understood that this *rapprochement* did not apply to slavery. In January 1861 the American ambassador in London, George M. Dallas, reported to Secretary of State Jeremiah S. Black that Anderson's case had 'awakened ... much interest' and 'invoked ... much professional astuteness to defeat the operation of the Xth Article of the Treaty of 1842.' Dallas reminded Black of 'the pungent and uncompromising hostility to social bondage' in England. Dallas thought it would be 'expedient' for the United States to take part in the legal proceedings in London, if Anderson was sent there under the writ of habeas corpus issued by the court at Westminster.[126] But this was more a showing of the flag than anything else: the British were not going to give up Anderson and American officials in London understood this. Short of a military confrontation, the United States could not expect any movement on the British side.

Even in the unlikely event that some American administration would have been willing to confront Great Britain over the fate of a fugitive slave, in 1861 the nation was certainly in no position to do so. When the case began, Buchanan's administration was about to become a lame duck. By the time Dallas wrote Black, Lincoln had been elected and the union had started to fall apart.

At another time Anderson's case might have been a major issue for American domestic politics and Anglo-American relations. American abolitionists would have been outraged when it seemed that Canadian authorities might actually extradite the fugitive. Similarly, southerners would have expressed deep concern when the Toronto court released Anderson and allowed him to go to England, where his freedom would be secure.

But the timing of the case explains the silence of Americans. When Anderson was first tried, the United States was in the throes of the most important presidential election in the nation's history. Most of the antislavery movement was focused on Lincoln's campaign and where it might lead. In the early stage of this case only the abolitionist Gerrit Smith, who lived in central New York State, seemed concerned with Anderson's fate. It is also likely that the American antislavery movement was relatively unconcerned about Mathews's decision. After all, the action of an unknown justice of the peace in a small village did not, in the long run, matter very much. Abolitionists knew that the important decisions were made at much higher levels. They doubtless expected the higher Canadian courts, and certainly the governor general, to be on the side of freedom.

The Court of Queen's Bench for Upper Canada must have severely disappointed American abolitionists. Newspapers in Detroit, Buffalo, and other northern cities commented on the dangers the case posed to fugitive slaves. Gerrit Smith went to Toronto to speak on Anderson's behalf. But in general most American abolitionists ignored the decision of the Queen's Bench. The ruling came down on 15 December 1860, and news of it reached the United States slowly. The *Liberator*, the nation's most important antislavery paper, did not cover the Anderson case until

31 December, when it carried a story – written before the Queen's Bench decision – that discussed the potential dangers of the case. The *Liberator* subsequently ignored the case.[127]

By the time Americans knew about the Queen's Bench decision, Lincoln's election, South Carolina's secession, and the impending dissolution of the Union diminished the importance of Anderson's case. American abolitionists may have anticipated that the English antislavery movement would fight for Anderson's freedom. The case was not as much an American issue as an Anglo-Canadian one. Moreover, only five days after the Upper Canada Court of Queen's Bench had ruled against Anderson, South Carolina had left the union.

The timing of the case was awkward for southerners. If the Canadian or British courts had immediately freed Anderson, and Buchanan had been unwilling or unable to gain custody of Anderson, then the case could have become one more immediate cause of secession. Southerners, who were looking for excuses to leave the union, could have pointed to the Webster-Ashburton treaty as another example of how the federal government did not protect southern interests.

In fact, the initial hearings in Canada West more than satisfied southerners. They had no reason to complain. Not until 11 February 1861 – after Americans found out about the writ of habeas corpus – did anyone in Congress raise the question of the Anderson case. On 25 February the Senate finally sent Buchanan a resolution, written by Senator James S. Green of Missouri, asking the president for information and diplomatic correspondence 'relative to the extradition of one Anderson.'[128] By this time the court in Toronto had released Anderson, and although he could not leave for England until the St Lawrence thawed, the chances of rearresting him were slim.

In less than a fortnight Buchanan would leave office. Seven deep-south states had already left the union. By March the new administration of Abraham Lincoln and Secretary of State William F. Seward was far more concerned with the Civil War and maintaining good relations with England than it was with the fate of a former slave whose freedom was won at the expense of a meddling slaveholder in Missouri nearly a decade before.

NOTES

I thank Dr Kenneth Winn of the Missouri Historical Society for helping me obtain some sources for this article, and Susan Binnie, Seymour Drescher,

Louis Knafla, and Jon Swainger for their superb comments on an earlier draft.

1 Canada consisted, between 1841 and 1867, of Canada East, formerly called Lower Canada (and, after 1867, Quebec) and Canada West, formerly called Upper Canada (and, after 1867, Ontario). In this article the term Canada refers to the Province of Canada, the combination of Canada East and Canada West.

2 Patrick Brode, *The Odyssey of John Anderson* (Toronto: The Osgoode Society 1989), xi.

3 Harper Twelvetrees, ed., *The Story of the Life of John Anderson, Fugitive Slave* (1863, reprint ed.; Freeport, NY: Books for Libraries Press 1971), 13–17; Brode, supra note 2, at 8–11; William Teatero, *John Anderson: Fugitive Slave* (Kingston, Ont.: Treasure Island Books 1986), 11–14.

4 Twelvetrees, supra note 3, at 19–23; Brode, supra note 2, at 14.

5 Twelvetrees, supra note 3, at 23, 24–5; Brode, supra note 2, at 20–3. Brode says that the Digges family contacted officials in Washington to help with the extradition, but there is no indication that the state department became involved in the case until the fall of 1860.

6 Teatero, supra note 3, at 24.

7 Brode, supra note 2, at 25.

8 'An Act to pay the expenses incurred in the prosecution of the slave "Jack," alias Anderson, for murder, committed in Howard county,' Act of 27 March 1861, 21 *Missouri Laws, 1860–1861* 534 (1861).

9 Digges's son Benjamin had seen the killing, but could not positively identify Anderson as his father's killer because he was only eight at the time and had not been close enough to the stabbing to actually see what happened. Benjamin Digges could only say that Anderson was 'about the colour and size of the man, but I would not swear he is the man.' In *Re John Anderson* (1860), 20 UCQBR 124, at 132.

10 Ibid., at 133.

11 John Anderson to 'His Excellency the Governor-General of Canada' [Edmund Walker Head], 1 October 1860, in Peter Ripley, ed., *The Black Abolitionist Papers: Canada, 1830–1865*, vol. 2 (Chapel Hill and London: University of North Carolina Press 1986), 431–3 (hereinafter cited as Ripley, *Canada*).

12 Howard Jones, *To the Webster-Ashburton Treaty: A Study in Anglo-American Relations, 1783–1843* (Chapel Hill: University of North Carolina Press 1977), xi.

13 'A Treaty to Settle and Define the Boundaries Between the Territories of the United States and the Possessions of Her Britannic Majesty in North America ... And for the Giving up of Criminals, Fugitives From Justice, in

Certain Cases,' ratifications exchanged and entered into force, 13 October, 1842, Article X, in *Treaties and Other International Agreements for the United States of America, 1776–1990*, ed. Charles I. Bevans, 12:88 (herein after cited as Webster-Ashburton treaty).

14 Albert B. Corey, *The Crisis of 1830–1842 in Canadian American-Relations* (New Haven: Yale University Press 1941), 174.

15 Bertram Wyatt-Brown, *Lewis Tappan and the Evangelical War Against Slavery* (Cleveland: Case Western Reserve University Press 1969), 253.

16 Corey, supra note 14, at 174–5.

17 Ibid.

18 Alexander Baring, the first Baron Ashburton, was a retired banker by this time. Married to the eldest daughter of Senator William Bingham of Pennsylvania, Ashburton had a keen understanding of American politics, and some sympathy for the United States, while at the same time being totally opposed to slavery.

19 Corey, supra note 14, at 177.

20 'Speech of Mr. Benton, August 18, 1842,' *Congressional Globe*, 27th Cong., 3rd Sess., Appendix, 12n, quoting the American and Foreign Anti-Slavery Society.

21 64 *Hansard's Parliamentary Debates* (3d Ser.) 640–1, debate of 27 June 1842 ('Fugitives from the United States') (hereinafter cited as *Hansard*; all cites are to the 3d series of *Hansard*); Roman J. Zorn, 'Criminal Extradition Menaces the Canadian Haven for Fugitive Slaves, 1841–1861' (1957) 38 *Canadian Historical Review*, 284–87. Hackett was the last fugitive slave extradited from Canada to the United States.

22 David M. Turley, ' "Free Air" and Fugitive Slaves: British Abolitionists Versus Government Over American Fugitives, 1834–61,' in *Anti-Slavery, Religion, and Reform: Essays in Memory of Roger Anstey*, ed. Christine Bolt and Seymour Drescher (Folkestone, England: Wm. Dawson and Sons 1980), 173.

23 Ibid., at 177.

24 Jones, supra note 12, at 150. Tappan to John Beaumont, 17 November 1842, reprinted in *A Side-Light on Anglo-American Relations, 1839–1858*, ed. Annie Heloise Abel and Frank J. Klingberg (Washington: The Association for the Study of Negro Life and History 1927), 105; 'Speech of Mr. Benton, August 18, 1842,' *Congressional Globe*, supra note 20; and 'Speech of Mr. Conrad,' Ibid., 59.

25 Zorn, supra note 21, at 288–90. Stuart, quoted in Anthony J. Barker, *Captain Charles Stuart: Anglo-American Abolitionist* (Baton Rouge and London: Louisiana State University Press 1986), 245.

26 Ashburton to Thomas Clarkson, 17 March 1843, and 'Minute Books of the British and Foreign Anti-Slavery Society, November 28, 1842,' both reprinted in Abel and Klingberg, supra note 24, 33n and 105–7n. Barker, supra note 25, at 246; Ripley, *Canada*, supra note 11, at 162n.

27 Aberdeen, quoted in Betty Fladeland, *Men and Brothers: Anglo-American Antislavery Cooperation* (Urbana: University of Illinois Press 1972), 317.

28 Zorn, supra note 21, at 288–90. 72 *Hansard* 564–79 (Debate of 1 August 1843). See also *British and Foreign Anti-Slavery Reporter*, 23 August 1843.

29 Zorn, supra note 21, at 290–1.

30 Joshua Leavitt to Joseph Soule, 12 January 1844; Lewis Tappan to John Beaumont, 30 January 1844; Joshua Leavitt to 'My dear Friend,' [John Scoble?], 2 February 1844, all in Abel and Klingberg, supra note 24, at 167–9; 169–75; 175–6; and Zorn, supra note 21, at 291. Barker, supra note 25, at 254–5.

31 Fladeland, supra note 27, at 319.

32 Ibid., at 318. The term is Fladeland's, not Calhoun's.

33 'Speech of Mr. Benton, August 18, 1842,' *Congressional Globe* supra note 20, quoted at 1, 12, 22.

34 'Speech of Mr. Conrad,' 18 August 1842, Ibid., quoted at 58 (emphasis in orginal). To support his position, Conrad included as a note to his speech an 'account, given by the notorious Tappan, of a conference which took place between Lord Ashburton and a committee of the American and *Foreign* Anti-Slavery Society,' which was published in the New York *Courier and Enquirer*. Ibid., at 59.

35 Jones, supra note 12, at 149, 161–5; John Tyler to Daniel Webster, 7 August 1842, in *The Papers of Daniel Webster: Diplomatic Papers, Series 3, 1841–1843*, vol. 1, ed. Kenneth E. Shewmaker, et al. (Hanover, NH, and London: University Press of New England 1983), 671–2.

36 'Speech of Mr. Conrad,' 18 August 1842, *Congressional Globe*, supra note 20, quoted at 59.

37 *Anderson*, supra note 9, at 192–3.

38 On this problem in the United States, see Robert M. Cover, *Justice Accused: Antislavery and the Judicial Process* (New Haven: Yale University Press 1975).

39 *Anderson*, supra note 9, at 174.

40 Ibid., at 186, 187–8.

41 On the moral dilemma of slavery and jurisprudence, see Cover, supra note 38; for examples of judges who found a way out of their dilemma, see Paul Finkelman, '*Prigg* v. *Pennsylvania* and Northern State Courts: Antislavery Use of a Proslavery Decision' (1979), 25 *Civil War History*, 5–35. On the proslavery constitution, see William M. Wiecek, *The Sources of Antislavery*

Constitutionalism, 1760–1848 (Ithaca: Cornell University Press 1977) and Paul
Finkelman, 'Slavery and the Constitutional Convention: Making a Covenant
with Death,' in *Beyond Confederation: Origins of the Constitution and American
National Identity*, ed. Richard Beeman (Chapel Hill: University of North
Carolina Press 1987), 188–225.

42 *Anderson*, supra note 9, at 188.

43 Ibid., at 172.

44 Ibid., at 192–3.

45 'The Case of Anderson, The Fugitive Slave' (1861), 10 *The Law Magazine
and Law Review* 368, quoted at 370.

46 Junius Junior [pseud.] *A Review of the Judgments of the Bench in the Anderson
Extradition Case: Or, Seven Ways of Proving that Anderson Should Not Be
Remanded* (Toronto: Printed for the Publisher 1861); reprinted in *Slavery,
Race, and the American Legal System: Fugitive Slaves and American Courts*, vol. 4,
ed. Paul Finkelman (New York: Garland, 1988), 445–92.

47 161 *Hansard* 222–4 debate of 8 February 1861.

48 Ripley, *Canada*, supra note 11, at 160n.

49 Allen P. Stouffer, *The Light of Nature and the Law of God: Antislavery in
Ontario, 1833–1877* (Baton Rouge: Louisiana State University Press 1992),
134–6. Peter Ripley, ed., *The Black Abolitionist Papers: The British Isles,
1830–1865*, vol. 1 (Chapel Hill and London: University of North Carolina
Press 1985), 365n, 360n.

50 Sir Frederick Rogers to Edmund Hammond, 16 January 1861, containing
Newcastle's instructions of 9 January 1861 to the governor-general of
Canada, printed in *Correspondence Respecting the Case of the Fugitive Slave,
Anderson* (London: Harrison and Son, 1861), 2–3, quoted at 3, reprinted in
*British Parliamentary Papers: United States of America: Correspondence and other
Papers Relating to Fugitive Criminals and the Slave Trade, 1842–90*, vol. 46
(Shannon: Irish University Press 1971), quoted at 118–19 (hereinafter cited
as *Anderson Correspondence*, with pagination from the original document,
followed by reprint pagination in brackets).

51 161 *Hansard* 222, debate of 8 February 1861.

52 'Transcript of the Arguments in Westminster Hall, January 15, 1861, in the
Queen's Bench, In Re Anderson, From the short-hand Notes of Messrs.
Reed, Robeson & Woodward' (hereinafter cited as 'Westminster Transcript')
printed in 'Message from the President of the United States, Communicating,
In compliance with a resolution of the Senate, information relative to the
extradition of one Anderson, a man of color,' 26 February 1861, Senate, Ex.
Doc. No 11, 36th Cong., 2d Sess. at 44 (hereinafter cited as Sen. Doc. No 11).

53 Ibid., at 19.

54 Edgar McInnis, *Canada: A Political and Social History*, 4th ed. (Toronto: Holt, Rinehart and Winston 1982), 299.

55 Ibid., 275–9.

56 36 Geo. III, c. 31 (1791).

57 Brode, supra note 2, at 72, 74. Brode cites, at 72, a Canadian decision in *Leith v. Willis* (1836), 5 UCQB (OS) 101, declaring that the English Gin Acts were of no effect in Upper Canada.

58 McInnis, supra note 54, at 299.

59 Quoted in Brode, supra note 2, at 73.

60 'Westminster Transcript,' supra note 52, at 41.

61 Ibid., at 43–4.

62 Brode, supra note 2, at 75. Robert C. Reinders, 'Anglo-Canadian Abolitionism: The John Anderson Case' (1975), 19 *Renaissance and Modern Studies*, 72. For an English critic of the English court's action, see Thomas Tapping, 'The Case of Anderson, the Fugitive Slave' (1861), 11 *The Law Magazine and Law Reporter*, 42. See also *The Law Times*, 19 and 26 January and 2 and 9 February 1861.

63 Robert C. Reinders, 'The John Anderson Case, 1860–61: A Study in Anglo-Canadian Imperial Relations' (1975), 66 *Canadian Historical Review* 393, at 410.

64 'The English Writ of *Habeas Corpus*' (March 1861) *The Upper Canada Law Journal*, 53. On reactions in Canada and Great Britain, see Reinders, 'Anglo-Canadian Abolitionism,' supra note 62, at 72–98.

65 'English Writ,' supra note 64, quoted at 72.

66 161 *Hansard* 222–23, debate of 8 February 1861.

67 Jasper Ridley, *Lord Palmerston* (London: Constable 1970), 276–7, quoted at 549, 548.

68 Ibid., at 540.

69 Reinders, 'Anglo-Canadian Abolitionism,' supra note 62, at 83.

70 David F. Krein, *The Last Palmerston Government: Foreign Policy, Domestic Politics and the Genesis of 'Splendid Isolation'* (Ames: Iowa State University Press 1978), 9.

71 Reinders, 'Anderson Case,' supra note 63, at 406.

72 Justice William Renwick Riddle, 'The Slave in Upper Canada' (1919), 4 *Journal of Negro History* 372, quoted at 394.

73 *Anderson*, supra note 9, at 135.

74 *In re Anderson*, 11 Upper Canada Reports: Common Pleas 41–51 (1861), quoted in Reinders, 'Anderson Case,' supra note 63, at 411.

75 'Judgment of Chief Justice Draper,' printed in *Anderson Correspondence*, supra note 50, at 36–40 [152–6], quoted at 37 [153].

76 Quoted in (March 1861) *The Upper Canada Law Journal* 53.

77 For example, see *Report of a Great Meeting Held in Exeter Hall, London, On Tuesday Evening, July 2nd, 1861, for the Purpose of Welcoming John Anderson, The Fugitive Slave, to England* [1861].

78 Barker, supra note 25, at 298.

79 J.E. Farwell, speaking in 1912 to the Ontario Bar Association, quoted in Reinders, 'Anderson Case,' supra note 63, at 393.

80 Brode, supra note 2, at xi, xii.

81 Reinders, 'Anderson Case,' supra note 63, at 400.

82 Robin Winks, *The Blacks in Canada: A History* (New Haven and Montreal: Yale University Press and McGill-Queen's University Press 1971), 142.

83 Barker, supra note 25, at 244–5.

84 Winks, supra note 82, at 142, 143.

85 Jason Silverman, ' "We Shall be Heard!": The Development of the Fugitive Slave Press in Canada' (1984), 65 *Canadian Historical Review*, 54, reprinted in *Articles on American Slavery: Fugitive Slaves*, vol. 6, ed. Paul Finkelman (New York and London: Garland 1989), 386–401.

86 Jason Silverman, 'The American Fugitive Slave in Canada: Myths and Realities' (1980), 19 *Southern Studies* 218.

87 Jason Silverman, *Unwelcome Guests: Canada West's Response to American Fugitive Slaves, 1800–1865* (Millwood, NY: Associated Faculty Press 1985), viii. Daniel G. Hull, *The Freedom-Seekers: Blacks in Early Canada* (Agincourt: The Book Society of Canada 1981), 96–106, describes the discrimination in education that blacks in Canada faced.

88 See Paul Finkelman, "Prelude to the Fourteenth Amendment: Black Legal Rights in the Antebellum North" (1986), 17 *Rutgers Law Journal*, 415–82.

89 William H. Pease and Jane H. Pease, *Black Utopia: Negro Communal Experiments in America* (Madison: State Historical Society of Wisconsin 1963); Winks, supra note 82, at 142–271.

90 Macdonald's hostility to blacks is revealed in a letter to Chief Justice J.W. Ritchie of New Brunswick. In 1868 Ritchie asked Macdonald why Canada still retained a death penalty for the crime of rape. Macdonald replied: 'We found it necessary, or rather judged it expedient to return the life penalty principally on account of the influx of blackguards of all kinds from the United States, who can cross and recross our border at will and occasionally commit all kinds of outrages. We have thought it well also to continue it on account of the frequency of rapes committed by negroes, of whom we have too many in Upper Canada. They are very prone to felonious assaults on white women: If the sentences and punishment were not very severe there would be a great dread of the people taking the law into their own hands.'

Letter from John A. Macdonald to Chief Justice J.R. Ritchie (8 June 1868) in National Archives of Canada, Manuscript Group 26A, 854–5 (8 June 1868). I am indebted to Professor Jon Swainger for sharing this information with me.

91 McInnis, supra note 54, at 343.

92 Reinders, 'Anderson Case,' supra note 63, at 398. Thomas Henning is quoted Ibid., at 399.

93 Fred Landon, 'The Anderson Fugitive Case' (1922), 7 *Journal of Negro History*, 242.

94 Winks, supra note 82, at 175–6; Twelvetrees, supra note 3, at 43–52; Ripley, *Canada*, supra note 11, at 430.

95 Toronto Globe (following 16 February 1861), quoted in Twelvetrees, supra note 3, at 81.

96 Brode, supra note 2, at 23.

97 Winks, supra note 82, at 146.

98 Brode, supra note 2, at 97.

99 Normally the statement of a third party concerning something someone else has said had happened is hearsay. However, one of the exceptions to the hearsay rule is an admission made against the interests of the speaker – in this case, Anderson's admission that he stabbed someone.

100 Landon, supra note 93, at 237, argued that Mathews admitted that he was holding Anderson 'pending the receipt of necessary evidence' and that Mathews mistreated Anderson, 'keeping him ironed, permitting no Negro friends to see him, not even admitting Rev. Walter Hawkins, the Negro preacher.'

101 *Anderson*, supra note 9, at 125.

102 Ibid., at 175 (McLean J. dissenting).

103 Ibid., at 130.

104 Slaves were free, or at least had a claim to freedom, the moment they entered a free jurisdiction under *Somerset v. Stewart*, Lofft 1 (1772). See Wiecek, '*Somerset*: Lord Mansfield and the Legitimacy of Slavery in the Anglo-American World' (1975), 42 *University of Chicago Law Review*, 86, at 129, and Paul Finkelman, *An Imperfect Union: Slavery, Federalism, and Comity* (Chapel Hill: University of North Carolina 1981), 162.

105 *The Revised Statutes of the State of Missouri* (St Louis: J.W. Dougherty 1845), 1090.

106 Webster-Ashburton treaty, supra note 13, at Article X.

107 *Anderson*, supra note 9, at 174–88.

108 Ibid., at 162.

109 'Judgment of Chief Justice Draper,' printed in *Anderson Correspondence*, supra note 50, at 40 [156].

110 Brode, supra note 2, at 91.
111 'Judgment of Mr. Justice Richards,' printed in *Anderson Correspondence*, supra note 50, at 41 [157].
112 Brode, supra note 2, at 16–17, and Russell to Newcastle, 9 January 1861, quoted in *Anderson Correspondence*, supra note 50, at 70.
113 Brode, supra note 2, at 91.
114 Reinders, 'Anglo-Canadian Abolitionism,' supra note 62, at 74, argues that Macdonald 'had early shown an interest in the case,' but this interest was after Mathews ordered Anderson held for extradition.
115 Ibid., 74–5.
116 Reinders, 'Anderson Case,' supra note 63, at 396–8, quoted at 398. See also Fred Landon, 'Canadian Opinion of Southern Secession, 1860–61' (1920), 1 *Canadian Historical Review*, 255.
117 Brode, supra note 2, at 107–8.
118 In September 1860 the anti-Catholic Orange Order demonstrated in Kingston in front of a boat carrying the Prince of Wales, the Duke of Newcastle, and Macdonald. Although legal in Canada, the Orange Order was banned in Great Britain. Macdonald was forced to leave the boat and abandon the English emissaries in order to placate his own constituents. Donald Creighton, *John A. Macdonald: The Young Politician* (Toronto: Macmillan of Canada 1952), 299–303. The Anderson case and the 'Orange Affair' were merged in a brief but bitter debate in Parliament between Nova Scotia-born Thomas C. Haliburton and Samuel Chichester-Fortescue, the undersecretary for foreign affairs. 161 *Hansard* 225–6, debate of 22 February 1861.
119 Arthur R. M. Lower, *Colony to Nation: A History of Canada* (Toronto: Longmans 1961), 318.
120 'Judgment of Chief Justice Draper,' printed in *Anderson Correspondence*, supra note 50, at 40 [156].
121 Ibid., at 1–2 [117–18].
122 Mr Cass to Mr Irvine, 2 October 1860; Mr Cass to Lord Lyons, 2 November 1860; Lord Lyons to Mr Cass, 3 November 1860; Lord Lyons to Mr Cass, 6 November 1860; N.F. Williams (by telegram) to Lord Lyons, 6 November 1860, all in Sen. Doc. No. 11, supra note 52, at 43–4.
123 Lord Lyons to Sir W. Williams, 14 December 1860, in *Anderson Correspondence*, supra note 50, at 50–1 [166–7].
124 161 *Hansard* 342, debate of 12 February 1861, and 162 *Hansard* 258–9, debate of 22 March 1861.
125 Robin Winks, *Canada and the United States: The Civil War Years* (Baltimore: Johns Hopkins Press 1960), 5.

126 Mr Dallas to Mr Black, 16 January 1861, printed in Sen. Doc. No. 11, supra note 52, at 4.

127 'A Fugitive Slave Claimed at Toronto,' *The Liberator*, 31 December 1860. Brode suggests that this was because William Lloyd Garrison, the editor of the *Liberator*, and Gerrit Smith were feuding, and as long as Smith was involved in the case, Garrison's paper would ignore it. Brode, supra note 2, at 52–3.

128 *Congressional Globe*, 36th Cong., 2d Sess., Senate Debate of 11 February 1861, 841; Sen. Doc. No. 11, supra note 52.

3 From Fishing Schooner to Colony: The Legal Development of Newfoundland, 1791–1832

CHRISTOPHER ENGLISH

> With reference to her jurisprudence and judicial establishments, Newfoundland is still in a state of the most helpless infancy.
>
> *William Dawe* v. *John Broom et al.* (1822), per Tucker CJ[1]

In 1832 Newfoundlanders could look back upon a rapid, heady, and sometimes bewildering transformation in the political and economic life of the island, achieved within their lifetimes. The institutions and practice of the law had not only caught up to reflect the reality of island life, but had also begun to delineate the very context in which society would function. In 1790 the legal regime still reflected the requirements of a century-old statute that reserved Newfoundland as an adjunct of the migratory fishery.[2] In 1793 William Knox, formerly an undersecretary of state in the Home Office, which was responsible for the colonies between 1782 and 1801, told a parliamentary committee examining the state of trade with the island that 'Newfoundland had been considered, in all former times as a great English ship moored near the Banks during her fishing season, for the convenience of the English Fishermen. The Governor was considered as the Ship's Captain, and all those who were concerned in the Fishery business, as his crew, and subject to naval discipline while there, and expected to return to England when the season was over.'

The island was to be employed simply as a summer land base upon which the staple product of an inshore fishery and that of the Grand Banks could be landed and cured. The policy marked a happy conjunction between the interests of west-of-England merchants, who dominated the trade in the seventeenth century, and English imperial policies, which sought to deny Spanish, French, and American claims to territory or access to a closed fishery. Both a national economic asset and a 'nursery for seamen,' the Newfoundland fishery contributed significantly to England's global strategic power.[3]

Westminster discouraged settlement. Fishermen were to return to their home ports in England and Ireland in the autumn. Those who 'over-wintered,' or who succumbed to the lure of squatting on land, especially on the 'French Shore' north from Cape Bonavista,[4] did so contrary to statute. In response, hesitantly and often grudgingly, the legal bases for the orderly settlement of local disputes were offered in a series of ad hoc arrangements effected under the royal prerogative. Resident magistrates were nominated and left in place to deal with minor crimes in the absence of the seasonal governor (1729). Customs officers were appointed to suppress smuggling (1739), and a court of vice-admiralty (1744) was established to save the expense and time of transporting captured prizes, for example, back to England. 'King William's Act' (1699) had required that criminal cases be pursued in England. A court of oyer and terminer (1750) in St John's permitted their local resolution while the governor was resident. These initiatives signalled, albeit reluctantly, that settlement was a growing and finally ineluctable reality.

Given the entire dependence of the economy on the cod fishery, these jurisdictions inevitably infringed the statute of 1699, which had reserved all disputes in the fishery for adjudication in English courts. Accordingly, much of the eighteenth-century system of prerogative arrangements was called into question when an aggrieved litigant, Richard Hutchings, appealed successfully to the Devonshire quarter sessions at Exeter in 1787. The result was widespread uncertainty about the legality of magistrates' judgments on matters dealing with the fisheries, and commercial chaos; by 1791, twelve hundred writs concerning debts in the fishery were outstanding. The magistrates themselves had been noticeably unenthusiastic about the propriety of hearing such cases for at least a decade. They continued to sit as a convenience to the trade and to satisfy the governor, but 'did it negligently, rather consulting the inclinations of the parties, and proceeding as arbitrators, not as judges, in such causes as they undertook to try.' The law officers of the Crown in London ruled that neither the governor nor his surrogates could hear fisheries matters. The court of vice-admiralty was popularly held to retain jurisdiction, but it too was unenthusiastic and could not accommodate the flood of petitions. A pariiiamentary committee was told that, more often than not, petitions were bounced back and forth between vice-admiralty and governor. Aaron Graham, secretary to each seasonally resident governor in Newfoundland between 1779 and 1791, advised Governor Mark Milbanke in 1789 to appoint a court of common pleas with a criminal as well as a civil jurisdiction. All cases would go before a jury. London's failure to issue instructions for the 1790 fishing season, according to Graham, prompted Milbanke to leave the question of a jury to the choice of the parties. However, London then ruled the option of common pleas (always limited to a civil jurisdiction) ultra vires. By way of providing a short-term solution it appointed John Reeves, legal adviser to the board of trade, as the island's first chief judge to preside over a court of civil jurisdiction during the fishing season of 1791. As a result of his report the court was renewed for 1792, with its jurisdiction expanded to criminal matters. Parliamentary hearings in 1793 affirmed these initiatives.[5]

The pressure of immigration, which accompanied the unprecedented prosperity of the war years between 1793 and 1815, led to the permanent establishment of the court in 1809.[6] Two years later the provision in the statute of 1699, which had reserved the island to uses consequent upon the fishery on an annual basis, was effectively amended to permit private title to property, though in practice it was to be granted only upon thirty-year leases.[7] No attention was paid to the extensive lands along the coast; these were out of reach of the governor in St John's and had for many years been effectively alienated from Crown use by squatters. A system of courts and legal title to property gave substance to official recognition that there was a permanently settled population that required these structures for orderly and peaceful development. The reach of the law was applied to social relations, embracing new marriage acts (noted below) and the emergence of public institutions: two schools in 1804; a postal service in 1805; a newspaper, the *Royal Gazette*, in 1807, to be joined by three more by 1820; philanthropic societies; and a hospital, which opened in 1814. In a society in which the Church of England was to be pre-eminent in fact if not in law, there was room for religious toleration. The loyalty to the British Crown of Roman Catholic James O Donel, Prefect apostolic from 1784, was a consideration in his elevation to a bishopric in 1796. He and his few priests ministered to the waves of Irish immigrants who arrived during the Napoleonic Wars. They were permitted their own chapels and, by 1811, their own cemetery.[8]

If much had been accomplished to distinguish the era after 1815 from that of twenty-five years earlier, Newfoundlanders, as they were beginning to see themselves, were far from *maîtres chez eux*. As always in their history, they remained vulnerable to imperial priorities and to their dependence on a staple product open to the vagaries of international demand and markets. London ignored local pleas to continue to reserve the fishery to Newfoundlanders, a monopoly achieved during the wars with France from 1793 and with the Americans from 1812. Local outrage greeted the peace settlements of the treaties of Paris of 1814 and 1815, because they reaffirmed French treaty rights to land and dry fish all the way along the coast from Cape St John in the north to Cape Ray on the Cabot Strait. Three years later an Anglo-American convention permitted American fishing from Ramea on the south coast, west and north to the tip of the Northern Peninsula, along the coast of Labrador (returned to Newfoundland's jurisdiction in 1809), and through the Gulf of St Lawrence to the Magdalen Islands. By 1822 French and American ships were said to account for fully two-thirds of the fishery. Equally serious was the post-war depression, which set in during late 1814 and led to bankruptcies, unemployment, and domestic unrest. Rival gangs of immigrant Irish fought out their ancient feuds in the streets of St John's. A general air of malaise and helplessness followed from a popular realization that a choice of fishing-berths and the unprecedented wages of the war years were a thing of the past. Exports of 1,200,000 quintals of fish at war's end had declined to half that quantity two years later. Local hardship was increased by a series of bitterly cold winters and disastrous fires that swept through St John's and the leading outports of Harbour Grace and Carbonear in Conception Bay. According to a contemporary observer, 'the starving population became a lawless banditti: they broke open the merchants' stores, carried off their property by wholesale, seized the vessels which arrived with provisions, and set the police altogether at defiance.'[9]

While times were difficult, it was popularly perceived that some inhabitants fared worse than others. Even in the relatively prosperous days of the war the need for relief of the destitute had been apparent. Governor William Waldegrave (1797–1800) was instrumental in forming a Committee for the Relief of the Poor, which cared for three hundred people during the winter of 1797–8. The Roman Catholic Bishop Scallan fed ten at his table in the bitterly cold winter of 1816–17. Governor Sir Charles Hamilton in 1822 encouraged relief by matching private donations of £370. At the same time, however, almost £100 more than that sum was allocated from official sources to deport paupers.[10]

Despite these setbacks and dangers to law and order, it was clear in the post-war era that there could be no return to the past. The population had increased to 40,000 (12,000 in St John's).[11] The migratory seasonal fishery was dead. Ships constructed locally pursued the inshore and Grand Banks fishery. Sealing in the spring of the year offered an alternative source of income, which complemented a summer fishery now extended to the French Shore north from Cape Bonavista. This in turn opened up regular voyages to the coast off Labrador. In short, by 1815 the statutory regime of 1699 and 1775 lay in tatters. A settled population, public institutions, property rights, and a system of judicature embracing sessional, vice-admiralty, and supreme courts made the island a colony in all but name. The final pressure point, in part a product of the reforms since 1791, was the demand for recognition and political institutions. Forcefully advocated locally, and granted because they accorded with imperial policy, these took the form of colonial status in 1825 and representative government in 1832.[12]

The law played a key role in guiding and articulating the changes of this important and transitional era. The legal system legislated in 1791–2, uniting law and equity and complemented by magistrates and governor's surrogates, seems to have worked satisfactorily and smoothly.[13] However, the changes and new demands of the war years required flexibility and further reforms in the law. Colonial Secretary Lord Bathurst wrote Governor Sir John Duckworth in 1812: 'There can be no question that the present situation of [the] fishery from the long continuation of the War, and the great change which the recent introduction of the Seal Fishery must necessarily have occasioned, even if the War were now to terminate, will require a revision of the Laws and Instructions at present in existence.'[14]

All these developments – economic, social, constitutional, and political – involved the use of the law, and the law set limits on what could be accomplished in terms of reform and a greater degree of home rule. Its institutions, personnel, and sanctions mediated the process of reform. A new Judicature Act in 1824 preceded the important change in Newfoundland's status within the empire the following year and the achievement of representative political institutions in 1832.[15] For two reasons that will be briefly canvassed, commentators have largely ignored these changes. The remainder of these remarks will discuss the reasons for this disregard, outline the changes, and illustrate the central role that law played during the period.

The first factor in this neglect centres on a historiography, which, with only minor variations, emerged in 1793 and rapidly became an unquestioned orthodoxy. From what has been argued so far, it is apparent that

Newfoundland fitted no model of colonial development. Commentators, from John Reeves in 1793 through D.W. Prowse a century later and A.H. McLintock in 1941, have found the island's failure to follow the more typical path from settlement or conquest, to colony, to nation, by turns curious and exasperating. In this respect McLintock's subtitle says it all: *A Study in Retarded Colonization.* Optimistic, progressive, and Whiggish in their assumptions, these writers attributed Newfoundland's failure to follow the North American norm for colonial development to a conspiracy between generations of West Country merchants and entrepreneurs in league with their branch managers in Newfoundland and their parliamentary allies at Westminster. The enforcement and perpetuation of a migratory fishery had perverted the course of history. Finally, however, this static and selfish barrier to settlement and self-actualization was surmounted, and the natural evolution of a people towards the local rule of law, representative institutions, and self-government could take place. In this light, the period from 1790 to 1832 is an entr'acte, less important for what it was than for what it portended. 'The late Georgian era,' Prowse noted in 1895, 'is the transition period in our history between the bad old days of tyranny, corruption and violence, and the dawning of the brighter day of civilization and progress.' In 1832 Newfoundland shucked off her aberrant past. Emerging from the limbo of a fishing-station denied settlement, she assumed her rightful place in the mainstream of British North American colonial development.[16]

McLintock's is the sole monograph to pay close attention to the period before 1832. In the fifty years since its publication no one has fleshed out or challenged its assumptions. McLintock broke new ground, mining the governors' reports to the Colonial Office but accepting them uncritically. Amid sweeping and sometimes paternalistic generalizations, he was committed to expose, less often to explain, Newfoundland's anomalous existence. Recently a new generation has been concerned to explain what happened without necessarily making reference to external models. Matthews, O'Flaherty, and Cadigan have tried to reconstitute a local perspective using their own visions and methodologies.[17] Up to this point, however, no serious attempt has been made to situate Newfoundland in a wider North American and imperial context.

Difficulties in tracking down legal sources and, perhaps, a reluctance by the non-legally trained to tackle them may also be a factor in the lack of attention paid to the period. The Judicature Act of 1824 is more often referred to than summarized, and is seldom analysed. The Royal Charter (1825), which proclaimed the act into force effective 2 January 1826, is often confused with the statute itself. The Charter is placed in 1832 by one respected commentator.[18] The fact that we are dealing with imperial statutes before 1832 may present some problems in terms of local access. A private source has reprinted the Charter, but it is not widely available; although a worthy and important first step in collecting the documents bearing on the evolution of judicature, it is in itself incomplete, and overlooks, for example, the act that extended the civil jurisdiction of the Supreme Court to Labrador in 1811.[19]

Other essential building-blocks in this process are not readily accessible. The Rules of the Supreme Court and the Rules of the Supreme Court on Circuit, issued under the auspices of the Charter in 1825 to take effect with the court's first session in 1826, are essential to an understanding of how the revised judicial system was to function. The first predecessors to the current Rules of the Supreme Court, 1986, for some years they contained rules of criminal procedure as well. Published in 1847 in a monograph that has become a collector's item, they, like the Charter, are not readily available. The rules offer a fitting adaptation of English judicial practice to local realities. The forms of action and pleadings were simplified and streamlined, especially when the court went on circuit to the northern and southern districts of the Avalon Peninsula. Agents for litigants, including special pleaders – professionally unqualified but experienced laymen, some of whom had argued cases since the 1790s – were recognized and, upon request, entered upon the Barristers' Roll from 1826. In contrast to the situation in Britain and Europe, the local bar was not divided between barristers and solicitors. In this a North American norm was preferred. The magistrates continued to serve in sessional courts much as they had done since 1729, although their fellow laymen within the judicial system, the much-criticized surrogates, disappeared in 1824. While the Supreme Court chief justices after the arrival of Caesar Colclough from Prince Edward Island in 1813, through Francis Forbes (1816) and Richard Tucker (1822) were graduates of English inns of court, there was still room for laymen to serve as lawyers and assistant judges (assessors). The rules provided for the eventuality of attorneys' being licensed and regulated within their own statutorily regulated profession, but time and experience would be the gauge of when that was to be accomplished. In short, the rules offer an example, consistent with the preceding two centuries of judicial development on the island, of pragmatism adapted to local circumstance and experience.[20] 'Finally, the constitutional instruments that led to the establishment of representative government in 1832 are rarely cited. They were reproduced only in the first two editions of the Consolidated Statutes of Newfoundland (1877 and 1916).

These two factors – a simplistic historiography that prevailed for almost two centuries, and difficulties associated with tracking down and interpreting law-related documents – may help to explain our lack of knowledge of a judicial regime that was centrally important to life in Newfoundland between 1791 and 1832. The Judicature Act (1824), for example, signalled changes to the system of courts and their personnel, and to the rules of practice. It was the benchmark against which later amendments were introduced, and remains the basis for today's Judicature Act.

The account that follows is preliminary, and concerned with some basic building-blocks centring on the act of 1824, the Royal Charter of 1825, and the achievement of representative government in 1832. The latter embraced a popularly elected house of assembly, an appointed legislative council, and a governor. The central theme emphasizes the place assumed by the Supreme Court as the highest judicial power on the island. By tracing the evolution and powers of the court we may discern a continuity that linked the statutory definition and practical application of the judicial regime of the early nineteenth century with the preceding statutory history of the island. Operating for half a dozen years before the attainment of representative government, the judicial regime remained untouched by the events of 1832.

While significant local agitation for a political voice continued to be inchoate and unfocused for some years after 1815, life for many was more profoundly touched by the collapse of fish prices, markets, and wages. The propertied class had cause, especially in the face of immigrant violence and natural disasters, to fear for its positions and possessions. The governors, by no means uncaring men, sought means – land grants, private charity, emigration, or deportation – to contain and relieve the pressure of vulnerability and despair.[21] Their dispatches to London are full of such news and pleas for assistance. But London had ignored similar requests in the past. It was not the level of local despair that turned Westminster in the direction of reform, but a timely contiguity between local needs and a change in the basic direction of imperial policy. As so often in Newfoundland's past, the imperial factor would be determinative.

In the aftermath of a peace settlement in 1815 that contained France within the European balance of power, Britain retreated behind the Channel and the Royal Navy to put her house in order. Before seizing the opportunities offered by industrialization and empire, she sought to contain domestic agitation for fundamental social and economic change by relying on a mixture of repression and internal reform. Repression was employed at Peterloo in 1819, and brought the formation of a London police force a decade later. Reform assumed various guises: political, in the Reform Bill of 1832; religious, with Catholic emancipation in 1829; economic, with industrialization; and commercial, with liberalized trade and the repeal of the Corn Laws in 1846. Of a piece was a retreat from the financial, administrative, and military obligations of empire under the altruistic mantle of extending representative institutions to the white outposts of empire in the 1820s and responsible government in the late 1840s. While they recognized that Newfoundland was a late candidate for colonial status, it was easier and cleaner for British policy-makers to treat her as if she had shared the common experience of several generations of settled government and political institutions enjoyed by the mainland colonies of British North America.

In both London and St John's this proved a convenient fiction. A colony required uninterrupted governance. In 1818 the governor became a year-round resident, a few years after the chief justice of the Supreme Court. Chief Justice Caesar Colclough, the first lawyer to preside over the court since John Reeves's seasonal sittings in 1791 and 1792, was transferred from a similar post in Prince Edward Island to St John's in 1813. His stay of two years was an unhappy one. He departed, his nerves shattered, to be succeeded by Francis Forbes (1816–22). While he and Governor Hamilton (1818–24) differed in their attitudes to what the law was and what it might accomplish in Newfoundland, they were each eminently qualified to shape the process whereby the common law, as mandated by the Judicature Act of 1792 and reaffirmed by the act of 1809, would be adopted 'as far as the same can be applied to suits and complaints arising in the islands.'[22]

Two more statutory developments in Newfoundland marked a shift in imperial policy that complemented and recognized the changed nature of local circumstances. Precisely why colonial governments were so assiduous in seeking to regularize personal relations within officially sanctioned marriage ties is unclear. Whether it was a genuine problem or one they invented, they made it an early and pressing priority. Perhaps it was simply seen as a consequence flowing naturally and rightly from the recognition of year-round settlement. In any case, by imperial statute all marriages contracted before 5 January 1818 were legitimized. Thereafter all marriages were to be celebrated by persons in Holy Orders. But due to the 'peculiar and extreme difficulty' in procuring a priest, the parties might exceptionally swear an oath before a magistrate or person duly authorized by the governor. An exemption was offered to Quakers and Jews.[23] The need to take into account local circumstances was underlined by the need for a successor statute within seven years. In stipulating that the rites must be those of the Church of England, the act of 1824 was probably clarifying rather than narrowing the intent of the predecessor act of 1817. Extending the period for automatic legitimization to 25 March 1825, it reiterated much of the former act but permitted new agents to perform marriages. 'By reason of the great extent of the ... island, and the want of internal communication between the different parts,' it was not possible for all candidates to reach a Church of England church or chapel. Now the governor might empower a full-time teacher or a preacher of religion to perform the ceremony. However, there must be no cutting of corners: loss of licence and a fine of between £10 and £50 would be imposed on those marrying candidates who might have availed themselves of Church of England rites. In the absence of teacher or preacher, a marriage witnessed by two credible observers was valid. In all cases a certificate must be delivered to the governor or nearest Church of England priest within a year. This would be recorded in a Book of Marriages from which copies would be available. Since further changes might be required in response to new circumstances (the act bears the same date as the Judicature Act, 17 June 1824), its duration was limited to five years.[24] Once legally married, people needed the security of title to property. A policy that encouraged the regularization of domestic relations raised once again the tangled question of rights to land. Palliser's Act in 1775 had opened the door in permitting the seasonal use by private persons of lands not employed in the fishery.[25] However, there was no provision for the recognition of adverse possession or possession via fee simple or lease, as the act had reiterated traditional prohibitions against overwintering and the succeeding judicature Acts of 1792 and 1809 did not refer to property rights.

The prosperity of the fishery, the exigencies of war in cutting off supplies from Britain, and a growing population probably contributed to the decision to offer leases on crown lands for private cultivation in order to feed the poor. Governor Gambier offered eighty acres in 1803, and urged Whitehall to rethink its policies. Dr William Carson, a vocal and persistent advocate of political reform after his arrival in 1808, had a large property on Portugal Cove Road by 1812 and was pamphleteering against the 'anti-settlement laws' the following year. At the same time

Governor Sir Richard Keats (1813–15) offered to 250 'industrious individuals' four-acre lots where hay, potatoes, and vegetables could be grown. Finally, in 1811 a statute marked a clear break with the policy of opposition to settlement and the use of land for anything but the fishery. Recognizing that some 'ships rooms' (prime waterfront land in the heart of St John's harbour) were not being employed for the fishery, the act envisioned establishing new rooms at the western extremity of the harbour. Accordingly, 'it shall be lawful for the same [ships rooms] to be granted, let and possessed as private property, in like manner as any other portions of land in Newfoundland ... anything in [King William's Act of 1699] ... or ancient custom ... not withstanding.' As noted above, thirty-year leases rather than possession in fee simple became the order of the day.[26]

Revisions and additions to the law on marriage and property implemented the requirement for year-round residence by colonial officials. In a period of change, the findings of a parliamentary committee in 1817 added to the pressure for legislative revision. The committee was appalled at the news of economic crisis, poverty, famine, and rioting during the hard winter of 1816–17. Merchants' agents in Newfoundland cautioned against sending out supplies that few local fishermen could afford and that might be targeted for pillage the following winter. Forty-five pages of testimony from eight merchants, only one of whom resided in Newfoundland, were attached to the committee's one-page report. It stressed the 'pressing urgency' of recognizing 'the Sufferings experienced by the great majority of a very exhausted Population, amounting, unless speedily provided against, to the certainty of absolute Famine; and which has already involved in its consequences the violation of private property and the destruction of civilized order. Unless ... immediate relief ... be granted ... the horrors of the ensuing winter will, if possible, be still further aggravated and increased.'[27] All these factors contributed to the framing of a new Judicature Act in 1824.

The act, initially effective for five years, continued the process of legal reform begun in 1791 and confirmed in 1809. The most voluminous of the Judicature Acts to date, it contained thirty-six clauses and articulated five major themes. These concerned jurisdiction, personnel, procedures, property, and new policy initiatives. The jurisdiction of 'the Supreme Court of Newfoundland' embraced civil and criminal matters, as had its predecessors since 1792, but with a wider ambit.[28] It was a court of record with 'all the powers of the Courts of King's Bench, Common Pleas and Exchequer and of the High Court of Chancery' (section 1). As well, it encompassed oyer and terminer, not mentioned by the acts since 1791 and presumably outside them, reaching all crimes and misdemeanours on the Grand Banks, seas, and islands visited by ships engaged in the fishery. By this power the Supreme Court shared jurisdiction over, if it did not annex, suits on trade and commerce in the Americas previously exercised by the Court of Vice-Admiralty. Was a shared jurisdiction intended in respect of all matters touching admiralty? While an admiralty jurisdiction was not enumerated under section 1 of the act, it may have been implied. Section 4 provided for appeals from the Supreme Court to the High Court of Admiralty in England. From the vantage-point of the 1840s, one who had been in daily contact with matters judicial since 1832 referred to the court's proceedings on 'the crown side, plea [civil] side, equity side and admiralty side.'[29] Nevertheless, the Court of Vice-Admiralty continued to sit, presided over by a sole judge who was paid the comfortable sum of £500 per annum, below the £1,000 paid the chief justice but within reach of the £700 paid the puisne judges of the Supreme Court. Perhaps this was simply the latest in a series of moves by which the jurisdiction of admiralty was limited in favour of the magistrates and the Supreme Court. We remain uninformed as to the functioning of admiralty in Newfoundland.

The court's equitable power was noteworthy. The predecessor acts had not adverted to it specifically, though they had assigned exclusive powers in probate to the chief justice. This was confirmed in 1824, when a power of administration of the estates of intestates was added and a parens patriae power over infants and lunatics was confirmed. Insolvency matters were assigned to the court because it supervised the activities of trustees. In uniting law and equity in the Supreme Court, the act is said to have been in the forefront in British North America. Having prescribed equitable powers by statute, Newfoundland was spared debates about the capacity and practice of colonial governors, under the authority of the great seal, acting as chancellor or establishing courts to do so. In contrast to other Maritime jurisdictions,[30] however, the Supreme Court did not excercise jurisdiction over matrimonial causes until 1947 and over divorce until 1967. Judicial conservatism, political caution, the absence of immigrants from New England, and the influence of the Roman Catholic hierarchy may have been determinative in this regard, but this remains a hypothesis.

The court's criminal and civil jurisdiction was exercised, consistent with the predecessor acts, 'according to the rules and course of the law of England, as far as the situation and circumstances of the said colony will permit' (section 10). In criminal and the appropriate civil cases, issues of fact were to be tried before a jury in St John's during at least one term every year, as decided by the governor. Criminal cases outside the capital in which a jury could not be raised would be decided by a circuit judge and three assessors who, beyond being laymen as in 1792, must now be justices of the peace. The fitness of the assessors in any given case could be challenged in open court 'upon the special ground of direct interest or affection.' A guilty verdict would require the concurrence of the judge and two of the assessors, delivered in open court. In the event, there was no need to resort to the use of assessors, at least to 1847.[31] This speaks to the willingness of jurors to serve, for they were regularly summoned in anticipation of the annual tour of the circuit courts. The act did not stipulate a property qualification for jurors.

Evidently a greater informality was to attend the sittings of the Supreme Court on circuit. Less prescriptive and rigorous rules governed its procedures. Perhaps in the light of the provision for lay assessors, its jurisdiction was not as wide as that of the Supreme Court sitting in St John's, or of the Supreme Court when it sat on the central circuit when in the capital city. Circuit courts outside St John's had no jurisdiction over treason or misprisions of treason, felonies not within benefit of clergy, or suits pursuant to statutes on the trade or revenue of the British colonies in America (section 9).

In civil cases where a jury was requested but could not be found, the act provided for the judge to act alone. But in actions over £50 all evidence was to be recorded in writing against the possibility of an appeal. In trials under £50 the judge exercised his discretion according to the importance of the matter and the likelihood of appeal. The use of summonses in actions over £10 and the discretionary sanctions of arrest and the attachment of personal chattels were retained from the acts of 1792 and 1809.

Appeals, excepting admiralty as noted above, lay to the Supreme Court en banc for actions, as provided for in the Royal Charter the following year, over £50 (up from £40 in 1809), with the traditional provisions for notice and security. An innovation was to grant the court exclusive jurisdiction in disputes over land. The final avenue of appeal lay to the Privy Council in judgments over £500 (up from £100 in 1809).[32] In sum, these procedures offered an expeditious route for appeals. In their simplicity they mark a departure from the norm of having to invoke the rule nisi, still typical of other British North American common law jurisdictions.[33] This last example offers evidence, perhaps, of the modernizing potential of statutory reform.

Some of the personnel changes brought by the act have been referred to. The single chief justice of 1792 and 1809 was joined by two assistant judges, barristers of England or Ireland 'or in some of His Majesty's Colonies or Plantations' of three years' standing. The surrogate judges were abolished in favour of the Supreme Court justices' going on circuit through northern, southern, and central districts at least once a year.[34] Suits might be transferred among circuit courts and the Supreme Court on the test of convenience. The abolition of the surrogate courts extended to the Labrador coast, where a court had been permitted in 1809 and established in 1811. The governor might set up a summary court of civil jurisdiction there. Presumably the difficulty in gathering a jury in Labrador accounted for the bar to a criminal jurisdiction.

Three broad procedures for hearings by magistrates were retained from previous acts. First, actions for debt to a value of 40s and for wages for seamen under £5 would be heard summarily by two justices of the peace sitting in courts of general session. Second, the act continued well-established procedures for priorities of claim: (1) wages of fishermen, seamen, and now domestics; (2) creditors for supplies issued in the current season; (3) creditors for debts incurred within two years; and (4) all other creditors. Third, existing procedures for dealing with insolvents were perpetuated. It appeared that these courts had worked well enough in the past to be continued into the future.

For the first time the act of 1824 regulated rights to private property. The Supreme Court had exclusive jurisdiction to resolve disputes over 'title to any lands, tenements, right of fishery, annual rent or other matter where ... rights in future may be bound.' Registration was compulsory for 'all deeds, wills, and other assurances whereby any lands or tenements ... may be granted, conveyed, devised, mortgaged, charged or otherwise affected.' The chief clerk of the Supreme Court and each of the clerks of the circuit courts would act as registrars.

Finally, two new areas of public policy were announced. Via the royal prerogative, charters would be issued to incorporate towns with powers to make bylaws on policing, fire protection, 'prevention or abatement of nuisances,' and the imposition of 'such reasonable and moderate rates and assessments upon the inhabitants and householders ... as may be necessary.' In the furtherance of efficient and responsible local government, a new system for supervising and licensing retail outlets for the sale of ale and spirits was provided for.

Second, the act for the first time noticed the legal profession. Requests for the attachment of a defendant's goods for debt, for example, might be sworn by the plaintiff 'or his ... lawful attorney.' As with municipal government, the royal prerogative would provide rules and procedures for 'the admission of barristers, attorneys and solicitors' and for 'the fees, poundage or perquisites to be lawfully demanded by any officer, attorney or solicitor in the ... courts.'

To take account of the future evolution of the colony, the term of the act was set at five years from the date it was proclaimed in the Charter (19 June 1825). While the Charter reiterated many of the purposes and provisions of the act, it added further details concerning such issues as the financial thresholds for appeals, noted above, and the bases upon which counsel might be regulated. Its most immediate effects lay in proclaiming the act in force as of 2 January 1826, the opening of the first session of the reconstituted Supreme Court, and the appointments of the assistant judges. Joining Chief Justice Richard Alexander Tucker were John William Molloy, recently chief clerk of the Supreme Court (himself soon to be removed, allegedly for incompetence, and replaced by Edward Brenton), and Augustus Wallet Des Barres. Captain Patterson was appointed as assistant judge on the Labrador coast.[35]

Whether intended to do so or not, colonial status and a functioning judicial regime soon raised the question of political institutions and representative government. The latter, of course, is not the sole means by which people may be governed and still bring their voice home to those in authority,[36] but in post-Napoleonic British North America it had become the accepted way.

Whatever the merits of the pre-1832 system, it was unacceptable to local reformers and no longer endorsed in Whitehall, where there was even an air of *mea culpa*. Lord Goderich, the colonial secretary, admitted in 1832 that ancient British policy

> was to prevent the colonization of the island, and to render this kingdom the domicile of all persons engaged in the Newfoundland fisheries. The common interest or convenience of those persons virtually defeated ... various statutes respecting them, long before Parliament admitted the necessity of repealing those laws ... Notwithstanding the growing population and wealth of Newfoundland, no plan has hitherto been adopted for regulat[ing] such of the internal affairs of the colonists as demanded the enactment of laws specially adapted to their peculiar situation.

The result was judicial overreaching and an evident requirement for local changes and improvements. Since the government was unwilling to encumber British statute-books with colonial legislation, there was no other source of relief, Goderich noted, than a degree of self-government. This practical concern meshed nicely with Whiggish ideology, which assumed that there was no need even to provide a rationale for colonial government: 'the difficulty would consist rather in finding valid arguments for withholding it.' Finally, there was the example of mainland British North America: 'Representative assemblies are not only recommended by abstract considerations drawn from the genius and principles of our Government, but by a long course of experiments ... leading to the same general result.'[37] All would not be smooth sailing, but the colonial secretary was confident that a cooperative venture, modelled on the British experience and taking into account local variations, would succeed.

Beyond history, practice, and ideology lay the imperial interest. Among the acts extended by Parliament to remain in force during the transition to representative government – Marriage, Judicature, and Fisheries – the last was of key concern.[38] The first two would be open to the house of assembly and legislative council to revise; the fisheries, to the extent that they affected imperial interests, were reserved for Parliament. After two years 'so much of that statute as relates to the navigation and commerce of this kingdom may then be revised by Parliament, with the benefit of the assistance to be anticipated from the labours of the Council and Assembly.' In addition, certain revenues would remain reserved. All those raised by parliamentary authority would be consigned to Newfoundland, subject to the sums stipulated for the support of the governor, judges, colonial secretary (Newfoundland), and attorney general. But the Crown's prerogative remained unaffected. Rents and the proceeds of the sale of Crown lands, escheats, fines and forfeitures, would adhere to the Crown, though all would be applied to civil or military government, 'or towards objects strictly and exclusively local.'[39]

Of the three remaining constitutional documents that formed the basis for representative government in 1832, the commission to Governor Sir Thomas Cochrane (1825–33), and his instructions broadly sketched the changes in his powers consequent on his governing with the advice and consent of council and assembly. The third proclaimed the nine districts of fifteen members, and the electoral rules to be employed in the election of the island's first legislature in 1832. According to his commission, the governor would continue to play an important role in the life of the island. He commanded the armed forces and presented benefices to the

Bishop of Nova Scotia, who exercised religious jurisdiction in Newfoundland. The judicial system was little touched by these changes in political life. In the light of the act of 1824, which assigned jurisdiction over oyer and terminer to the Supreme Court, the power of the governor to appoint commissioners of oyer and terminer is curious. In addition, he appointed justices of the peace, sheriffs, and other officers; and he had the power of pardon and reprieve, except for treason and wilful murder.

Cochrane's instructions stipulated that legal powers not exercised by either courts or governor could fall to the legislature. Further, the legislature should address the question of jurors' qualifications. At the same time a long list of subjects was reserved for reference to England before local legislation could be proclaimed: the re-enactment of previously vetoed bills; reductions in governmental revenues; lotteries; the property of non-residents; the naturalization of aliens and divorce; suspension of the operation of religion; the remission of fines over fifty pounds or forfeitures; and, unsurprisingly, constitutional changes touching on the council or assembly and declarations of war.

The continuing importance of the judicial structure for the new constitutional regime was reflected in the fact that twenty-four of the governor's sixty-five instructions concerned the law. And after 1832 the law continued to be closely interwoven with governance. The question of jurors' qualifications and the membership of Chief Justice Henry John Boulton on the legislative council were to lie at the heart of the political confrontation of governor, council, and assembly, often a three-cornered rivalry, during the first decade of representative government.[40]

The statutes and constitutional documents to 1832 described a judicial regime. But what was their significance for the development of the law in Newfoundland? In effect they brought Newfoundland more closely in line with the mainland colonies. Certainly the achievement of representative government is an obvious parallel. The same is true of the legal system, though it differed in important ways from the mainland pattern: for example, in the unity of law and equity; the directness and ease of appeal; the narrower jurisdictions and simpler rules employed by the Supreme Court on circuit outside St John's; the absence of a divorce jurisdiction; and, in debt, the continuing priority ascribed to actions for seamen's, fishermen's, and domestics' wages and for current suppliers to the fishery. Whether the overall direction of imperial policy for Newfoundland reflected the wider one of devolution to the colonies via representative institutions can, at present, only be inferred. To this point we remain relatively uninformed about the possible influence of local opinion, lay and legal, on the content of the imperial statutes framed for Newfoundland, and on the instructions issued under the royal prerogative to the governor between 1824 and 1832. One example, however, has become notorious.

Lay opinion was galvanized against the surrogate courts in the cases of *Lundrigan* and *Butler* in 1819 and 1820. James Lundrigan sustained a default judgment in surrogate court, presided over by Rev. Frederick Hamilton Carrington in Harbour Grace in 1819, for a debt of thirteen pounds to a fisheries supply firm in Conception Bay. His house and goods in Cupids were ordered attached but were not possessed, owing to the resistance of his wife, who threatened to blow out the brains of the constable executing the order. Subpoenaed the same day to attend court in Port de Grave on 5 July 1820, he refused and instead went fishing. Arrested that night, he was confined aboard a navy ship and charged before the court on 6 July with 'divers contempt of Court and resisting constables in the execution of their duty, and particularly for refusing and neglecting to attend' when summoned the previous day. He was sentenced to thirty-six lashes by the presiding surrogates, the recently appointed Rev. John Leigh and Naval Commander David Buchan. Lundrigan, an epileptic, sustained fourteen lashes before collapsing. He was cut down upon his undertaking to deliver the house and goods to his creditor. The severity of the sentence and the eviction of Mrs Lundrigan and her children made it a cause célèbre. A day later the court meted out the same punishment to Butler on much the same facts.

The public outrage, which may have been aggravated by the fact that one of the accused was Roman Catholic and both were native-born, was marked and sustained. It is credited with translating the theoretical calls for reform by such persons as Dr William Carson and Patrick Morris into a practical cause, combining ethnic consciousness, an attack on mercantile greed, sensitivity to the local rights of private property, and opposition to the harsh summary justice rendered in the two cases. Actions by both Butler and Lundrigan for trespass and assault were heard against Leigh and Buchan in the Supreme Court on 9 November. Despite strong criticisms of their actions by the jury and by Chief Justice Forbes in *Lundrigan,* the right of the surrogate court to punish for contempt was sustained. Forbes immediately acceded to a defence motion for permission to appeal to the privy council, although in the end the appeal did not proceed. Three days after the verdict, a meeting in St John's mobilized popular support for the twin causes of abolishing the surrogate courts and winning representative government. A petition was forwarded through the governor to Whitehall. Sympathizers in the House of Commons and the House of Lords brought Lundrigan's case forward for debate. Lord Bathurst, the colonial secretary, instructed Governor Hamilton that legal reforms were contemplated and that the surrogates should avoid infliction of corporal punishment in like cases. In short, the cases are credited with giving a crucial impetus to the reforms that led to the Judicature Act of 1824, the appointment of an executive council to advise the governor in 1825, and, despite the opposition of official opinion in 1825, to the new constitutional regime of 1832.[41]

As benchmarks for further research we may pose some larger questions about the significance of law, legal practice, and legal culture in early nineteenth-century Newfoundland. Clearly the colony comprised a legal community in the process of change and adaptation. In a generation it had moved from a statutory regime frozen in its historical origins as 'a great English ship moored near the Banks during the fishing season' to one distinguished by permanent settlement, an established judicature, colonial status, and representative government. The law was the agent for framing, facilitating, and mediating this transition. This should not surprise us. For the law – as statute, prerogative writ, charter, substance, and community practice – had historically been the mechanism by which imperial strategic and economic interests, the fishery, and settlement had coexisted, however uneasily, and evolved. The law – as precedent and practice, institutions and personnel – was familiar. It appears to have been popularly accepted and widely deferred to. However, two caveats must be offered. First, there were still considerable gaps in the law. By 1832 policing had barely been addressed. As noted above, title to land was restricted to thirty-year leases granted by the governor. What he granted he presumably could refuse to renew. Leases were probably confined largely to St John's; but for generations land around the coast had been occupied and exploited by individual and idiosyncratic forms of adverse possession unsanctioned by the law. In 1834 the Real Chattels Act provided that all real property was to be treated as chattels real. The act gave rise to much litigation and conflicting judical opinion. Was the English law of real property applicable to Newfoundland? Had it been so before 1832? Or was the unstated purpose of the statute to apply strictly to inheritances? Three years later English criminal law was received into Newfoundland.[42] A second consideration is that statutes and governor's instructions were not the sole source of legal authority. At the local level, and without reference to the courts, disputes continued to be mediated by informal means: compromise, reimbursement, arbitration, and violence. In the last case, especially when liquor was involved, the parties might slug it out and afterwards repair to the local tavern, where the losing party bought the rounds. We are at the very earliest stages of exploring the nature and functioning of informal and popular sources of dispute resolution.

As the vehicle for easing Newfoundland from fishing-station to settled colony, the law was instrumentalist. It offered a means and a context by which the pretensions of the settlers to legal status and a voice in government might be squared with changes in imperial policy. The latter, after 1815, counselled a retreat from colonial obligations in favour of a global imperial strategy. Like imperial policy-makers before 1832, later Newfoundland legislators would use the law to realize policy goals, whether in education, health, road-building, public works, or regulating the legal profession.

Did the judges view their adjudicative functions not merely as discovering and applying legal rules but as mandating them to frame social and economic doctrine? The claim has been advanced on behalf of Francis Forbes by two commentators.[43]

There was scope for judicial intervention on several fronts. In politics, the chief justice chaired the legislative council. In religion, the Church of England was not formally 'established,' but it was clearly preeminent. The meaning and implications of the two terms would be at issue in the sectarian debate and violence that distinguished the first decades of representative government. And in the economy the continued predominance of the fishery, the perpetuation in statute of the priorities assigned to fishery-related claimants in debt, and the laws on current supply offered scope for judicial interpretation and policy-making.

In addition to the bench, the lawyers themselves, translated via statute from their informal role as special pleaders to the professional status of barrister and solicitor, would influence the evolution of the law and its values. What collective role they assumed in setting standards for admission and in training future practitioners remains to be explored. Other professions, clerical and medical, seem to have been unable or unprepared to exhibit that 'collective autonomy, cohesion and public image' which, Wilfrid Prest suggests, 'may well provide the most effective conceptual framework for the historical study of men of the law.'[44] And in the profession there appear to have been subsets of cohesion. David Bell has noticed the dynastic propensities of the profession in New Brunswick, a phenomenon already apparent in Newfoundland.[45] The Carters and the Emersons in St John's were on the way to establishing legal dynasties. Each would provide luminaries of bar, bench, and politics by mid-century.

What wider role might lawyers play as mediators between the people and the new constitutional and legal regime? They were organized, accredited, self-regulating, and socially prominent in the community. They seemed well placed to assume important roles in the resolution of conflicts and to mediate the process of modernization and the emergence of new institutions.

These questions are highly speculative, and court the danger of adopting external models. Mid-century Upper Canadian judges differed markedly from their American counterparts. How much more so might Newfoundlanders? Denied the eighteenth-century colonial experience and dependent upon a sea-based rather than a land-based economy, they were ignored by the immigrants from New England who profoundly influenced legal cultures from the Strait of Cabot to the Great Lakes. Newfoundland looked east rather than west; its population was drawn from West Country and Irish sources, which, after the early nineteenth century, remained unrenewed. Isolated and distant, would she recognize or emulate North American models? And in a local bar in which there were few trained lawyers? The experience of lawyers and of the law in other jurisdictions must, at this stage, be limited to a comparative framework.

We have noted that while much of the law was adopted from England it was also adapted to local circumstances. Judge Des Barres's retort to counsel William Hayward's citation of *Chitty* is possibly apocryphal, but it retains its force: 'Chitty, Mr Hayward! Goodness me, what does Mr Chitty know about this Country? He was never in Newfoundland.'[46] Tucker CJ's comment in *Dawe v. Broom*, cited at the outset of this paper, was not simply a cry of despair. It also recognized that Newfoundland, and the law in Newfoundland, were different. What it lacked in English rules and procedures also saved it from becoming snarled in the twelve pettifogging technical objections offered by Dawe in that case.[47] Dawe, counsel to either or both Lundrigan and Butler before the Supreme Court in 1820, was identified by Governor Hamilton as the only trained lawyer on the island. Dawe argued that the English rules of pleading had been abrogated. The answer from the bench was that the renowned Blackstone had held that reception of law was a selective process, necessarily tailored to local needs. Bench and bar in the first third of the nineteenth century faced the challenge of teasing out from English precedent and practice what best suited Newfoundland. As historians we face a comparable challenge. We still need to know much about these men, what they did, and how they saw themselves within the legal culture of their era.

NOTES

1 E.P. Morris, ed., *The Reports, 1817–1828. Decisions of the Supreme Court of Newfoundland* [1829] (St John's 1901), 401.
2 (1699) 10 and 11 William III, c. 25; (1775) 15 Geo. III, c. 31.
3 Great Britain, House of Commons, *Reports from the Committee on the State of the Trade to Newfoundland. Severally reported in March, April and June 1793* (London 1793), vol. 10, 413. Keith Matthews, 'A History of the West of England-Newfoundland Fishery,' D.Phil. thesis, Oxford University (1968).
4 Frederic F. Thompson, *The French Shore Problem in Newfoundland* (Toronto: University of Toronto Press 1961).
5 Keith Matthews, 'Richard Hutchings,' *Dictionary of Canadian Biography* (Toronto: University of Toronto Press 1983), vol. 5, 443–4 (hereinafter cited as DCB); *State of the Trade to Newfoundland, Second Report*, April 1793, testimony of Aaron Graham, vol. 10, 433–9; Christopher English, 'The Development of the Newfoundland Legal System to 1815' (1990), 20 *Acadiensis*, 89–119; Peter Neary, 'John Reeves,' *DCB*, vol. 6, 636–7; Frederic F. Thompson, 'Mark Milbanke,' ibid., vol. 5, 595–6; (1791) 31 Geo. III, c. 29; (1792) 32 Geo. III, c. 46. Reeves heard 138 cases between 10 September and 31 October 1791, and 120 the following year between 3 September and 30 October. He delivered an exhaustive and uncompromising exposé to the Parliamentary Committee in 1793, *State of the Trade to Newfoundland, Third Report* (1793) vol. 10, 463–78.
6 (1809) 49 Geo. III, c. 27.
7 (1811) 51 Geo. III, c. 45. For a discussion of the practice that predated the recognition of reality by the statute, see Patrick O'Flaherty, 'The Seeds of Reform: Newfoundland, 1800–1818' (1988), 23 *Journal of Canadian Studies*, 39–59. The act did not stipulate thirty-year leases, but D.W. Prowse, *History of Newfoundland from the English Colonial and Foreign Office Records* (London: Macmillan 1895), notes them. They anticipated the provision of one of the earliest acts of the Newfoundland Parliament, which stipulated that (for the purposes of inheritance) all property in Newfoundland was to be treated as chattels real: (1834) 4 William IV, c. 18 (Nfld).
8 Melvin Baker, 'The Government of St. John's, Newfoundland, 1800–1921,' Ph.D. thesis, University of Western Ontario (1980); Raymond J. Lahey, *James Louis O Donel in Newfoundland, 1784–1807* (St John's: Newfoundland Historical Society 1984); C.J. Byrne, ed., *Gentlemen-Bishops and Faction Fighters: The Letters of Bishops O Donel, Lambert, Scallan and other Irish Missionaries* (St John's: Jesperson 1984).

9 John Mannion, 'Patrick Morris,' *DCB*, vol. 8, 626–34; Lahey, *O Donel*, supra note 8; Byrne, *Gentlemen-Bishops*, supra note 8; Lewis Amadeus Anspach, *A History of Newfoundland* (London: Sherwood, Gilbert and Piper 1827), 263–73; Frederic F. Thompson, 'Francis Pickmore,' *DCB*, vol. 5, 672. According to Paul O'Neill, *A Seaport Legacy: The Story of St John's, Newfoundland* (Erin: Press Porcepic 1976), vol. 2, at 574, there were eight uniformed policemen in St John's in 1825. A quintal is 112 pounds of dried fish.

10 O'Flaherty, 'Seeds of Reform,' supra note 7, 43–4; Raymond J. Lahey, 'Thomas Scallan,' *DCB*, vol. 6, 691; Phillip Buckner, 'Sir Charles Hamilton,' ibid., vol. 7, 377.

11 Great Britain, Colonial Office, CO 194, 'Abstract Census and Return for the Several Electoral Districts of Newfoundland, 1793–1830,' Maritime History Archives, Memorial University of Newfoundland. The returns of the period are said not to be reliable, and other commentators put the island's post-war population as high as 70,000.

12 For a summary of the impact of the war on the fishery, see Shannon Ryan, 'Fishery to Colony: A Newfoundland Watershed, 1793–1815', in *Atlantic Canada Before Confederation*, ed. P.A. Buckner and David Frank (Fredericton: Acadiensis 1990), 138–56. For the Royal Charter, 1825, see Newfoundland Law Reform Commission, *A History of the Newfoundland Judicature Act, 1791–1984, Complete with a Table of Disposal* (St John's: Law Reform Commission 1989), vol. 1, 13, and Edward M. Archibald, ed., *Digest of the Laws of Newfoundland* (St John's: Henry Winton 1847), 21. Representative government did not come by statute but by a series of instructions issued to Governor Sir John Cochrane under the royal prerogative. See Newfoundland, Consolidated Statutes, 1916, 3d series (St John's: Robinson 1919), vol. 1, Appendix, 3–46. For official policy during the period, see Phillip Buckner, 'The Colonial Office and British North America, 1801–50,' *DCB*, vol. 8, xxiii–xxxvii.

13 A very preliminary survey of materials for a reconstruction of the criminal law is in English, 'Law to 1815,' supra note 5, at 110–13.

14 Ryan, 'Fishery to Colony.' supra note 12, at 156.

15 (1824) 5 Geo. IV, c. 67.

16 John Reeves, *History of the Government of the Island of Newfoundland* (London: J. Sewell 1793); Prowse, supra note 7, at 304; A.H. McLintock, *The Establishment of Constitutional Government in Newfoundland, 1783–1832: A Study of Retarded Colonization* (London: Longmans, Green 1941).

17 Keith Matthews, 'West of England-Newfoundland Fishery,' supra note 3; 'Historical Fence Building: A Critique of Newfoundland Historiography'

(1978), 74 *Newfoundland Quarterly*, 21–30; 'The Class of '32: St John's Reformers on the Eve of Representative Government' (1977), vol. 6 *Acadiensis*, 80–94; Patrick O'Flaherty, 'Government in Newfoundland before 1832: The Context of Reform' (1988), 84 *Newfoundland Quarterly*, 25–30; 'Seeds of Reform,' supra note 7. O'Flaherty provides an inclusive historiographical survey of contemporary nineteenth-century historians and commentators in *The Rock Observed* (Toronto: University of Toronto Press 1979), 49–81. Among eight relevant *DCB* entries by O'Flaherty several are noted below. Sean Cadigan, 'Seamen, Fishermen and the Law: The Role of the Wages and Lien System in the Decline of Wage Labour in the Newfoundland Fishery,' in *Jack Tar in History: Essays in the History of Maritime Life and Labour*, ed. Colin Howell and Richard J. Twomey (Fredericton: Acadiensis Press 1991), 105–31; Sean Cadigan, 'The Role of the Fishing Ships' Rooms Controversy in the Rise of a Local Bourgeoisie: St John's, Newfoundland, 1775–1812', (unpublished 1992); Sean Cadigan, 'Merchant Capital, the State and Labour in a British Colony: Servant-Master Relations and Capital Accumulation in Newfoundland's Northeast Coast Fishery, 1775–1799' (1991) *Journal of the Canadian Historical Association*, n.s. II, 17–42.

18 Prowse, supra note 7, at 422; Frederic F. Thompson, 'John Holloway,' *DCB*, vol. 6, 323; W.S MacNutt, *The Atlantic Provinces: The Emergence of a Colonial Society, 1712–1857* (Toronto: McClelland and Stewart 1965), 177.

19 (1811) 51 Geo. III, c. 45, is missing from Newfoundland Law Reform Commission, *History of the Newfoundland Judicature Act*, supra note 12.

20 Newfoundland, General Rules and Orders of the Supreme Court of Newfoundland and General Rules and Orders of the Circuit Courts of Newfoundland, in *History of the Newfoundland Judicature Act*, supra note 12, 21–35; Archibald, *Digest*, supra note 12; J.M. Bumsted, 'Caesar Colclough,' *DCB*, vol. 6, 160–4; Patrick O'Flaherty, 'Sir Francis Forbes,' ibid., vol. 7, 301–4; C.H. Currey, *Sir Francis Forbes* (Sydney: Angus and Robertson 1968); (1833) 3 William IV, c. 6 (Nfld), An Act to declare the qualifications and character of Persons admitted to practice as Barristers and Attornies of the Supreme Court of this Island; (1834) 4 William IV, c. 23 (Nfld), An Act to Incorporate a Law Society in Newfoundland.

21 O'Flaherty, 'Seeds of Reform,' supra note 7, passim; Frederick Jones and George Story, 'Lewis Amadeus Anspach' *DCB*, vol. 7, 114; Buckner, 'Hamilton,' supra note 10; W.H. Whiteley, 'Sir John Duckworth,' *DCB*, vol. 5, 273–6.

22 (1792) 32 Geo. III, c. 46, s 1; (1809) 49 Geo. III, c. 27, s 1.

23 (1817) 57 Geo. III, c. 51.

24 (1824) 5 Geo. IV, c. 68.

25 (1775) 15 Geo III, c. 31, s 2; W.H. Whiteley, 'Sir Hugh Palliser,' *DCB*, vol. 4, 597–601.

26 O'Flaherty, 'Seeds of Reform', supra note 7, at 44–6; MacNutt, *Atlantic Provinces*, supra note 18, at 140, 142; (1811) 51 Geo. III, c. 45; Prowse, *History*, supra note 7, at 386.

27 Great Britain, House of Commons, *Select Committee on Newfoundland Trade with Minutes of Evidence Taken before the Committee and an Appendix*, 22 June 1817; MacNutt, *Atlantic Provinces*, supra note 18, at 177. All quotations in the section that follows are from (1824) 5 Geo. IV, c. 68.

28 A change from 'the Supreme Court of Judicature of the Island of Newfoundland' in the act of 1809.

29 Archibald, *Digest*, supra note 12, at 45.

30 J.A. Clarence-Smith and Jean Kerby, *Private Law in Canada* (Ottawa: University of Ottawa Press 1975), 219. Nova Scotia had divorce courts from 1758, New Brunswick from 1785, and Prince Edward Island from 1833–5.

31 Archibald, *Digest*, supra note 12, at 58.

32 (1809) 49 Geo. III, c. 27, s. 5.

33 Clarence-Smith, *Private Law*, supra note 30, at 217.

34 For the boundaries of the districts, see Archibald, *Digest*, supra note 12, at 52. In fact there were four courts, as the Supreme Court also sat as the circuit court for St John's in the Central District.

35 J.B. Cahill, 'Edward Brabazon Brenton,' *DCB*, vol. 7, 104–5.

36 O'Flaherty, 'Context of Reform,' supra note 17.

37 'Royal Instructions' (27 July 1832), Goderich to Governor Sir Thomas Cochrane, Consolidated Statutes, 1916, 33, 35.

38 (1832) 2 & 3 William IV, c. 78, continued (1829) 10 Geo. IV, c. 17, which itself had continued the Judicature and Marriage Acts to 31 December 1832 or until the new constitutional regime in Newfoundland chose to repeal them. (1832) 2 & 3 William IV, c. 79 did the same for (1824) 5 Geo. IV, c. 51, on the fishery.

39 'Royal Instructions,' supra note 37, at 40.

40 Hereward and Elinor Senior, 'Henry John Boulton,' *DCB*, vol. 9, 69–72; Gertrude E. Gunn, *The Political History of Newfoundland* (Toronto: University of Toronto Press 1966).

41 Patrick O'Flaherty, 'James Lundrigan,' *DCB*, vol. 6, 409–11; John Hewson, 'John Leigh,' ibid., 392–3; William Kirwin, 'David Buchan,' ibid., vol. 7, 114–16; John Mannion, 'Morris', supra note 9; O'Flaherty, 'Forbes', supra note 20, and 'William Carson,' *DCB*, vol. 7, 151–6; Provincial Archives of Newfoundland and Labrador (hereinafter cited as PANL), GN 5/1/B/1,

Minutes of the Surrogate Court, *Graham McNichol and Co. v. James Lanregan [sic] and James Hollochan*, Harbour Grace, 6 May 1819 (Surrogate Ct); *R. v. James Lundrigan*, Port de Grave, 5 July 1820 (Surrogate Ct); *R. v. James Lundrigan*, Port de Grave, 6 July 1820; PANL, GN 5/2/A/1, Minutes of the Supreme Court, *Lundrigan v. Buchan and Leigh*, St John's, 9 November 1820 (S.C.); *A Report of Certain Proceedings of the Inhabitants of the Town of St John [sic] in the Island of Newfoundland* (St John's: S. Ryan 1821).

42 (1834) 4 William IV, c. 18 (Nfld); (1837) 1 Victoria, c. 4 (Nfld).
43 Currey, *Forbes*, supra note 20, at 14–19, and O'Flaherty, 'Forbes,' ibid., provide analyses of some leading cases.
44 Wilfrid Prest, ed., *Lawyers in Early Modern Europe and America* (London: Croom Helm 1981).
45 D.G. Bell, 'The Transformation of the New Brunswick Bar, 1785–1830' (unpublished 1987).
46 Prowse, *History*, supra note 7, at 423.
47 Buckner, 'Hamilton,' supra note 10, at 377.

4 William Osgoode, John Graves Simcoe, and the Exclusion of the English Poor Law from Upper Canada

RUSSELL C. SMANDYCH

Introduction

The first legislature of Upper Canada, meeting in September 1792, enacted that in all matters relating to property and civil rights the civil law of England was to be adopted, with the exception of 'the laws of England respecting the maintenance of the poor and bankruptcy.'[1] The particular direction taken by the development of Upper Canadian poor relief institutions and practices was profoundly affected by this decision. The action also made the subsequent history of poor relief in the colony radically different from that of other British North American colonies in the period after the American Revolution.[2] However, the decision made in Upper Canada in 1792 was not unprecedented; both the English poor law and English bankruptcy law had been excluded from the pre-1791 province of Quebec.

Social and legal historians of the colony, having noted the failure to adopt the English poor law, have only speculated about the reasons for this rejection. This study attempts to uncover the specific historical circumstances that led to the exclusion of the law,[3] and in doing so to contribute to Canadian legal-historical scholarship on the reception of English law.[4] An additional goal is to determine the political and legal culture of Upper Canada in the 1790s.[5]

This essay reviews the historiography to show why previous investigators have been unable to explain the absence of the poor law from Upper Canada, and then examines the broader macrohistorical context within which poor relief developments occurred. In addition, information is introduced concerning the specific steps taken by colonial officials, both in England and in Upper Canada, to fashion the new province in British North America into a particular kind of 'well-ordered' society. Comparative evidence is also presented on the exclusion of the English poor law and English bankruptcy law from pre-1791 Quebec. In the final part of the study, documents from the initial session of the colony's first legislature are examined. This provides additional, albeit still not definitive, evidence of why the legislature of Upper Canada decided not to follow the example of other British North American colonies. In addition to bringing us much closer to solving the puzzle of the missing Upper Canadian poor law, this study offers critical insights into the character of the political and legal culture of the colony in the 1790s.

The Historiography of the Missing Upper Canada Poor Law

The question of why early Upper Canadian legislators did not adopt the English poor law has been considered by a number of historians.[6] In *Social Welfare in Ontario*, Richard Splane offered what was to become the most influential account. According to Splane, the decision was a practical choice made by Lieutenant-Governor John Graves Simcoe. Splane argued that Simcoe was probably 'conscious of the practical difficulties of transplanting the English poor law administration' into a society which, 'at least at the onset, manifestly lacked the ability to undertake the responsibilities associated with the English-type poor law.' In Splane's view, one of the major obstacles to the adoption of the English poor law was the lack of a tax base to provide 'sufficient funds to maintain any persons who became destitute and who applied for public assistance.' Consequently, he concluded that 'even if the English poor law had been nominally brought into the province by the act of 1792, it would have remained, for lack of local tax support, a dead letter for an indefinite period.'[7]

Splane also argued that the decision was influenced by the prevailing Upper Canadian belief that 'any necessary assistance, not merely for the survival of the population but also for the economic development of the province, should come from the British government.' Rather than being opposed in principle to the idea of the government providing assistance to those in need, Upper Canadians believed that such assistance should come directly from the British government. In Splane's view, the idea that the rejection of the English poor law represented a rejection of the principle of public support for the poor is 'hardly ... conceivable in a colony whose birth and early survival, until well after 1792, were dependent upon extensive measures of public assistance granted by a public body – the only one capable of providing it, the British government.'[8]

Contemporary Canadian social historians have tended to draw liberally on Splane's interpretation.[9] For instance, Brereton Greenhous concludes that Simcoe probably rejected the English poor law because he realized that it 'was not suited to the condition of the province.' Given that New Brunswick had adopted 'a system of poor relief copied almost exactly from that of the mother country' five years earlier, Greenhous speculates that Upper Canada may have learned from New Brunswick's difficulties, which were

> an excellent example of the complications which arose when a highly mobile, thinly settled and financially insecure community, very similar to itself, tried to adapt to its use a Poor Law designed for a comparatively static, socially immobile, wealthy and well settled environment. There were good and obvious reasons, on the basis of New Brunswick's five years' experience, for leaving poor relief in private hands as much as possible, so that it might be offered in kind rather than demanded in cash, and then supplying any needed balance upon a provincial rather than a parish level.[10]

To date, only one historian has challenged Splane's interpretation. J.C. Levy, in exploring possible reasons for Upper Canada's failure to enact a law modelled on that of England, suggests that the decision reflected the acceptance of a 'principled social vision,' as opposed to pragmatic considerations.[11] Key elements of this 'principled social vision' included the belief that charity should be private and voluntary, and that the colony offered ample opportunities to individuals who were self-reliant and industrious. In part, the decision may have stemmed from the belief that Upper Canada was 'a vigorously self-reliant society founded upon individual initiative exploiting almost unlimited resources. The fittest would survive; the temporarily distressed would be looked after by family or by locally organized private charity; those who could not "make a go of it" would perish or move on; and government would play a minimal role.'

Levy examines a number of other factors which suggest that 'the Upper Canadian rejection of the poor law was indeed the rejection of a principle rather than merely of a set of inconvenient administrative specifics.' He argues that if the colonists had simply reasoned that they

would not be able to administer an English-style poor law, they would not
have had to enact exclusionary legislation. 'Even if the legislature had
done nothing,' the poor law of England would not have been brought
into force. Given this likely course of events, Levy maintains that 'the
action actually taken by the legislature can ... be interpreted at the very
least as a peculiarly emphatic rejection of the Poor Law.'

Levy also notes that the rejection of the English poor law in 1792 was
coupled with the explicit rejection of English bankruptcy law. He argues
that although this latter decision by Simcoe and his advisers may appear
unrelated to their rejection of the English poor law, both actions were
likely taken for similar reasons. Like the existing English poor law, which
sought to mitigate the plight of the poor by providing them with a
guaranteed level of public support, the English bankruptcy law of the
1790s was aimed at alleviating the lot of insolvent debtors. This was done
by enabling debtors to pay their creditors a part of the debt they owed
instead of being sentenced to a debtors' prison until they were able to
pay the entire amount. What these laws had in common was their effective denial of individual responsibility. According to Levy, the importance
early Upper Canadians attached to 'self-reliance' and 'individual responsibility' could well account for the rejection of the poor law.

Finally, Levy speculates that any decision by Simcoe to reject the English poor law in favour of a more 'voluntaristic' approach to dealing with
the poor was based on an informed assessment of the contemporary
English debate over the adequacy of the existing law. At the very time
that Simcoe and his advisers were deciding on the kind of poor relief
system that was to be adopted in the province, the English tradition of
public support for the poor (by way of compulsory taxation) was being
subjected to increasing 'attack from the proponents of voluntarism.' In
Levy's view, Simcoe 'could scarcely have lived the life he did' without
acquiring a knowledge of the conflicting currents of English opinion on
the subject of voluntary versus compulsory poor relief.

Rainer Baehre, in 'Paupers and Poor Relief in Upper Canada,' remarks
that when the Upper Canadian legislators 'rejected the English Poor Law
system in the 1790s ... they were likely responding to the almost universal
criticism of poor relief practices in England in that period.'[12] The most
stinging criticism levelled at the late eighteenth-century English poor law
was that, contrary to its intended purpose of providing relief to the
deserving poor, the law worked instead to foster 'growing pauperism,
indigence and vice.' One of the pernicious features of the law most
denounced by contemporary critics was the practice of subsidizing the

wages paid to labourers by means of the poor rates. This practice, which later came to be referred to as the 'Speenhamland system,' was widely condemned by critics for the effect it had on discouraging 'the able-bodied from working, finding a job, or providing for themselves and their families.'[13]

Other Upper Canadian historians offer similar speculative accounts. In his recent investigation of the reasons for the absence of an English-style court of chancery in Upper Canada, John Weaver comments that the 'explicit elimination of the poor laws [from Upper Canada in 1792] suggests a desire to be rid of old country obligations.' Weaver notes that the statute passed in 1792, which explicitly rejected the English poor laws and bankruptcy legislation, did not clearly rule out the establishment of an English-style court of chancery or equity. In considering why Upper Canadians accepted some but not all elements of contemporary English law, Weaver concludes that 'if the [English] poor laws were omitted specifically, then failure to omit equity implies an introduction of it into Upper Canada.'[14] In another recent study concerned with how Upper Canada's Tory magistrates went about providing relief to the poor in the absence of an English-style law, David Murray, summarizing the current state of speculation about the reasons for the missing poor law, comments as follows:

> We do not know precisely why Governor Simcoe excluded the Poor Law from the English laws adopted by the newly formed Upper Canadian legislature. It may have been due to administrative concerns; the absence of clearly defined parishes, the difficulties inherent in levying a poor rate, or the fear of creating a pauper class. Criticism of the Poor Law and poor rates was endemic in England at the end of the eighteenth century, although not all critics went as far as Edmund Burke's precepts for the poor: 'Patience, labour, sobriety, frugality, and religion should be recommended to them; and all the rest is down-right fraud.'[15]

There are several reasons for the speculative nature of previous accounts. One is the absence of primary historical documentation that provides direct evidence of the rationale underlying the decision to exclude the English poor law from Upper Canada. A second is that historians have not defined the question of exclusion as pertinent to explaining later developments and changes. At a more theoretical level, it can be argued that the inability of historians to account for the decision of 1792 resides in their collective failure to investigate the economic, political, and ideological context in which the decision to exclude the English poor law was made. In what follows, an attempt is made to develop an explanation that is based on direct archival evidence from the 1790s, and that situates the events that occurred in Upper Canada in 1792 in a broader macrohistorical context.

The Search for a 'Well-Ordered' Society:
The Loyalist Foundations of the Province

Let the Canadians have a Constitution formed on the principles of Canadians and the English upon principles of Englishmen but let there be no wild theories.

Edmund Burke, 1791[16]

To begin to understand why the English poor law was excluded, and the parts played by Lieutenant-Governor Simcoe and Chief Justice Osgoode in this decision, we are obliged to consider two historical events: the creation of the province in 1791, and the framework of government and law-making effected by the enactment of the Constitutional Act of 1791 in Britain. The history of the province of Upper Canada was tied to the outcome of the American Revolution and directly related to the failure of counterrevolutionary forces to end the American hostilities that broke out in 1776. Among the resulting exodus of British Loyalists from the American colonies – an estimated 50,000 persons who had 'hoped and worked and fought for the defeat of the rebellion'[17] – just under 7,000 individuals, consisting 'largely of farmers and artisans, with only a sprinkling of intellectuals and office holders,' travelled to the old province of Quebec.'[18] Most of these Loyalists took up grants of land in the southwestern part of the province, which was soon to become the province of Upper Canada.

In the decades following the British victory of 1760, the French-speaking population of Quebec was allowed to continue to use pre-existing French 'Canadian' laws for the purpose of settling 'all controversies relating to property and civil rights.'[19] But the steady stream of Loyalists to the province after 1776 led to increasing opposition to the 'non-representative' system of government and to the legal system, favoured by French-Canadians, that was provided for under the Quebec Act of 1774.[20] In 1785 Loyalist military officers, led by Sir John Johnson, began petitioning the King 'on behalf of the Loyalists they had led into the province.'[21] This early petition, along with the many others that followed, stressed that Loyalist emigrés to the province, like their 'fellow sufferers' in Nova Scotia and New Brunswick, desired 'the enjoyment of British laws and customs, for which they had fought and courted exile.'[22] Although the Loyalists who settled in the upper part of the province were not alone in their desire to be governed according to the British model, their concerns were given more attention by prominent English statesmen of the day.[23] The arrival of the Loyalists was thus instrumental in the division of the old province of Quebec into Upper and Lower Canada.

From 1789 to 1791 'the key to Canadian politics' was in London.[24] During this period a plan to divide the province of Quebec into Upper and Lower Canada was formalized, debated, and finally agreed upon by English parliamentarians. The major objective of the plan, which came to be embodied in the Constitutional Act of 1791, was to satisfy the Loyalists' desire to be governed by a system based on 'British laws and customs.' In explaining the rationale underlying the act, Lord Grenville, its original author, informed his fellow peers that the Quebec Act had to be replaced because (Upper) Canada now had a population that not only was well acquainted with 'British privileges,' but that 'had retired to that country for the express purpose of enjoying them in greater perfection than they could elsewhere.' In his view, the people deserved 'the blessings of the English constitution,' which was by far 'the best in the world.'[25] Similarly, William Pitt, who introduced the Canada Bill in the House of Commons, stated that the intention of the proposed act was to provide Upper Canada with 'the very image and transcript of the British constitution,' or at least as close an approximation as was practically possible in the fledgling province.[26]

The Constitutional Act of 1791 represented the written cornerstone of Upper Canada's political constitution,[27] and it provided the legislative framework for provincial government that was to prevail in the colony for some fifty years. In addition, the act gave concrete expression to the kind of 'well-ordered' society that leading provincial and British officials hoped Upper Canada would become. It provided the basis for a system of representative but not responsible government, and stipulated that the colony was to have a bicameral legislature comprising a legislative council with at least seven residents appointed by the lieutenant-governor for life, and a lower house of assembly consisting initially of sixteen members elected by voters in the various counties of the province at least every four years. A third body was the executive council, made up of members appointed by the lieutenant-governor to advise him on his decisions and implement government policy.[28]

Although it created a representative form of government, the act vested a great deal of political power in the hands of the lieutenant-governor and the government in London. Even after a bill had passed through both houses of the legislature, the lieutenant-governor had the power to withhold royal assent and reserve the bill for consideration by the home (British) government. In turn, the lieutenant-governor's power to decide on legislation was also controlled. Specifically, any approved bill could still be disallowed by the government in London within two years of its passage.[29] Thus the act created a much less democratic and autonomous system of local government than that which had existed in the Thirteen Colonies prior to 1776. These features were clearly the outcome of a conscious effort made by its drafters 'to avoid the evils occasioned by the American Revolution.'[30]

One unifying concern shared by British government officials, including Lord Grenville and Pitt, and the original entourage of provincial officeholders led by Simcoe and Osgoode, was the desire to fashion Upper Canada into a particular kind of 'well-ordered' society – an opposing model to the powerful and undisciplined country that emerged out of the American Revolution, and a positive exemplar of the kind of prosperous and orderly society premised upon British political institutions and practices. Although it is clear that leading British government officials and members of the Upper Canadian 'Tory-Loyalist' governing élite shared this view, there is considerable disagreement among historians about whether and for how long the colonists as a whole held to such a conservative vision. Closer attention to this debate is necessary because it bears directly on the subsequent analysis of the outcome of the initial session of the first provincial legislature, in which electors voted against introducing a poor law based on the English version.

The extent to which the Loyalist origins of the province had an enduring political effect was first described in the writings of S.F. Wise, who argued that one of the most salient features of early Upper Canada was a pervasive conservatism.[31] In Wise's view, the sources of conservative thought were twofold. The first was the 'emotional compound of loyalty to King and Empire' and 'antagonism to the United States' brought to the colony by its Loyalist founders. The second consisted of the 'Toryism of late-eighteenth century England' brought by Simcoe and his entourage, and crystallized in the Constitutional Act of 1791. Wise concludes that 'the joining of these two counter-revolutionary outlooks' in early Upper Canada had major consequences for the province's development. Most significantly, he maintains that these forms of conservative thought gave rise to nearly 'fifty years of oligarchic rule' by an 'authoritarian and paternalist elite.'[32] In his various studies, Wise analyses the assumptions and beliefs shared by members of the governing élite, its character and makeup, and the manner in which its conservative 'world view' was conveyed to citizens. Wise's findings support the argument that the governing élite was indeed concerned with developing a 'well-ordered' society, and that it also succeeded for some time in convincing its citizens that they should share this desire. However, more recent investigations by Jane Errington and George Rawlyk,[33] Donald Akenson,[34] and Paul Romney[35] have begun to raise questions about the prevalence of such a conservative frame of mind.

Errington and Rawlyk's critique focuses on the putative attitudes of Loyalist founders towards the United States. Specifically, they deny the claim that post-1784 Loyalists displayed a consistently negative attitude. Against the claim that they shared a bitter hatred for the United States that led them to 'reject all things American,' Errington and Rawlyk argue that throughout the period from 1784 to 1812 Upper Canadians coexisted with and were greatly influenced by the new republic to the south. Rather than attempting to 'erect unbreachable psychological barriers to all American influences,' Errington and Rawlyk maintain that 'even the most pro-British Loyalist, as he looked back from his early nineteenth-century vantage point, would not have denied the very important positive role that the new republic south of the border had actually played in colonial development.' Although 'Upper Canada was a British colony and many of its residents were firmly committed to their King and the British constitution, it was, during its formative stage, also very much an American community.'[36]

In his study of the Irish immigrant experience in the colony, Akenson questions the notion that most Upper Canadians were staunchly politically conservative. He provides a detailed account of the development of Leeds and Lansdowne Township during the 'Loyalist era' from 1789 to 1816. Contrary to historians who have explored the dominant ideology that prevailed in the pre-1815 period, Akenson argues that one can best obtain a sense of what it was like to have lived there – and what Irish immigrants experienced after their arrival – by investigating the day-to-day social and economic activities of people. Akenson portrays pioneer life in the township before 1815 as a 'competitive individualistic game' in which individuals concerned with making a living entered into economic agreements and alliances with each other. The emphasis given to practical concerns, and in general the 'atomistic' way of life of early settlers, had a profound effect in shaping not only the economic relationships of settlers but also their attitudes towards civic arrangements. He maintains that this pragmatic approach to life helps to explain the absence of a strong 'collective culture' and shared 'ideology' among the settlers.[37] Thus Akenson brings into question the extent to which Upper Canada's governing class may be seen to have shared a conservative political ideology and sense of 'providential mission' that led them to give up their own vested economic interests for the greater good of the province.

The argument hinted at by Akenson concerning the importance of self-interest in understanding the actions of Upper Canada's governing class is explicitly taken up in more recent work by Romney. In one of his related essays,[38] he criticizes authors who have argued that leading members of the governing élite were motivated by a consuming sense of 'providential mission.'[39] According to Romney's views of these authors, whom he labelled 'Nostalgic Tory zealots,'[40] the sense of providential mission shared by members of the Tory governing élite led them to place their own (economic, political, and class) interests behind what they considered to be the best interests of Upper Canada. In Romney's view, the tendency on the part of 'Nostalgic Tories' to accept such assumptions as the starting-point for analyses of the governing élite's role in shaping the political and legal culture has led them to offer interpretations that place undue emphasis on a shared conservative ideology at the expense of their vested self-interests. In addition, he criticizes these authors for fostering the 'romantic' image that the colony was settled by a politically docile population that submitted to the rule of an authoritarian-paternalist élite.

Although the arguments made by Romney and others point to added complexities involved in attempting to gain a sense of the dominant ideology that pervaded Upper Canada, they in no way undermine the thrust of the interpretation advanced by Wise and like-minded historians. Like the province itself, the complexion of the governing élite that came to rule over the colony took on a very 'Loyalist' and 'Tory' tinge. Whether motivated by its sense of 'providential mission' or by vested self-interest, the province's Tory governing élite was undeniably concerned with fashioning it into a particular kind of 'well-ordered' society.

Planning for the Government of Upper Canada, 1789–91: The Roles of Simcoe and Osgoode

The idea of creating a 'colonial nobility' along the lines envisaged by English supporters of the Constitutional Act was never implemented in

Upper Canada,[41] but something similar emerged in the province in the ruling Tory élite. The important appointed positions in the first legislative and executive councils were occupied by leading Loyalist emigrés and the officials who accompanied Lieutenant-Governor John Graves Simcoe in the summer of 1792. The views held by Simcoe and the men who became his advisers are relevant to our inquiry into the poor law.

By the time he arrived in Upper Canada on 24 June 1792, Simcoe had spent eighteen months preparing to establish his government.[42] One of the first steps was to arrange for the appointment of executive and legislative councillors. In consultation with Pitt, Lord Grenville, and Henry Dundas,[43] some appointments were made before Simcoe's departure from London in September 1791, although they were not completed until the following spring.[44] A key figure in Simcoe's government was William Osgoode, who, in addition to having been appointed lord chief justice of Upper Canada,[45] was Simcoe's choice for speaker of the legislative council and chairman of the executive council.[46] Other individuals appointed to serve as executive councillors included Jacques Baby, Richard Cartwright, Robert Hamilton, and Peter Russell,[47] all of whom were, or who went on to become, prominent merchants, landowners, and government administrators.[48]

There seems little doubt that Simcoe felt closest to Osgoode, and there is evidence that he reciprocated Simcoe's regard.[49] In his correspondence to Dundas in the months prior to his departure for Upper Canada, Simcoe confirmed his good opinion of Osgoode's appointment on several occasions. For example, on 2 June 1791, in one of many letters to Dundas, Simcoe alluded to Osgoode's appointment as chief justice when he said, 'The Administration of public justice has been nobly provided for in the selection of a Gentleman to fill its Principal Office of such respectable personal & professional Character as may ensure the equal & just execution of its responsible Duties.'[50] On 12 August 1791 Simcoe wrote to Dundas again, detailing his views on the civil and military appointments being made for Upper Canada, and commenting that 'in regard to legal Appointments, the placing of so respectable a Man as Mr. Osgoode at the Head of the law Department leaves me nothing to desire on that Subject, and I shall be well content without the slightest wish for Recommendation in any of the legal situations or vacancies that may happen, provided that secondarily to Integrity & Ability they be filled by such persons as appear to have the most Influence, and exert it in support of His Majesty's Government.'[51] Although both Simcoe and Osgoode communicated by letter with Dundas and others about Upper Canadian matters, it is clear that meetings were held in London between Simcoe, Osgoode, and their political superiors at which many questions were settled.[52]

In addition to travelling to Upper Canada to take up his post as lieutenant-governor, Simcoe was given the responsibility of delivering the formal government instructions to Lord Dorchester for his job as governor in chief of (Upper and Lower) Canada, which made him Simcoe's political superior.[53] On several occasions both in England and after arriving in Quebec, Simcoe broached the question of the extent to which he would be answerable to Lord Dorchester. In the month before his departure Simcoe wrote to Grenville and Dundas about a number of concerns, including his uncertainty over the extent of his civil and military authority. It is significant that Grenville appears to have shared Simcoe's belief that the government instructions for colonial officials in Canada needed to be made clearer. In an internal Colonial Office memo dated 22 June 1791, Grenville is quoted as follows:

In drawing the Instructions for the Governor & Lieut. Governor two points will require particular attention.
    First Wether [sic] and what particular directions be given him for the exercise of his discretion as to dividing the province into Counties & and together with all the other points preliminary to the Elections ... [and]
    Secondly. The Directions to be given him as to cases wherein he is to negative reverse or affirm acts presented to him – Something of this appears in the old Colonial Instructions, but it is imperfect & inadequate to the present case.[54]

The instructions turned out to contain detailed and explicit statements about Dorchester's various powers and responsibilities.[55] For our purposes, the most pertinent instruction to Dorchester was one outlining the official steps to be followed in enacting legislation in the colony. On this matter, Dorchester was told

that all Laws assented to by You in Our Name, or reserved for the signification of Our Pleasure thereon, shall when transmitted by You, be fairly abstracted in the Margins and accompanied with very full and particular Observations upon each of them, that is to say, whether the same is introductory to a new Law, declaratory of a former Law, or does repeal a Law then before in being; And You

are also to transmit in the fullest manner, the Reasons and Occasion
for proposing such Laws, together with fair Copies of the Journals
and Minutes of the Proceedings of the said Legislative Council and
Assembly, which you are to require from the Clerks, or other proper
Officers in that behalf, of the said Legislative Council and Assembly.

Given this wording, it would seem a simple matter to uncover evidence
for the rationale underlying the exclusion of legislation from Upper
Canada. However, although Simcoe and Osgoode were required to report
back to London through Dorchester in the 'fullest manner' about their
reasons for proposing laws, no evidence has been found of any formal or
informal discussion about the exclusion of the English poor law.

One possible reason for this omission is that the officials concerned
did not consider the poor law to be important in comparison with other
significant matters, such as emigration and military defence.[56] A second
possibility may lie in dissatisfaction with the system in operation in England. Given the prominence of the late eighteenth-century English poor
law debate and the fact that Simcoe and Osgoode were both in England
at the height of this debate, it is unlikely that they remained unaware of
concerns expressed by critics over the adequacy of England's 'public'
poor relief system. During the year before his appointment, Simcoe was
elected to the English House of Commons.[57] It is very likely that he sat
in sessions of Parliament in which the poor law came up for debate.[58]
Osgoode, prior to his appointment as the first chief justice and chief
legislative draftsman for Upper Canada, spent several years practising law
in London, building a career as a 'moderately distinguished' lawyer.[59]
Like Simcoe, Osgoode 'was a man of profoundly Tory principles,'[60] and
undoubtedly shared his views on the important issues of the day.

Although Simcoe and Osgoode travelled separately to take up their
positions in Upper Canada, they had ample opportunity upon arrival to
share their views on whether the English poor law was suited to the
colony. Indeed, Osgoode lived with Simcoe and his family from the time
of his arrival until the middle of December 1792. An unsigned daily
journal entry by Lady Elizabeth Simcoe for 29 December 1792[61] reads:
' "The Gov" walked to the landing at Ft. Scholper – the weather so mild
we breakfasted with the door open into the Garden – Mr. Chief Justice
Osgoode is now in his own house which is so near he always comes to us
in [the] Even[ing]. Till within this fortnight he resided with us not
having been able to meet with any Home that suited him – Lt S[imcoe]
finds him a very agreeable companion.'[62] This document helps to explain

the absence of any written correspondence between Osgoode and Simcoe with regard to the poor law.

Whatever their personal views on the poor law Simcoe and Osgoode's power to enact legislation was still limited in several ways. It was important that their position did not conflict with that of the government in London, which, because of the Constitutional Act of 1791, held veto power over any legislation passed in the province. Moreover, any legislation introduced by Osgoode and Simcoe required the votes of a majority of elected members in the province's House of Assembly. One of the assumptions of previous investigators is that Simcoe and Osgoode had the power to enact legislation. However, it may have been the elected members of the assembly who pushed for its exclusion. This hypothetical possibility will be explored in more detail after an examination of the important earlier experience of legislation in Quebec.

The Exclusion of English Social Legislation from Quebec

One of the elements missing from previous attempts to explain the 'missing' Upper Canadian poor law is a consideration of the broader economic, legal, and constitutional relationships that linked Upper Canada, and, before 1791, the old Province of Quebec to Britain. Although we know that the English merchants and Loyalists who settled in Quebec before 1791 were required to follow the existing law of Quebec in all matters relating to property and civil rights, this practice had implications for enacting a poor law that are not immediately apparent. Moreover, Quebec's earlier legal and constitutional circumstances help to explain why the rejection of the English poor law in Upper Canada was coupled with the rejection of English bankruptcy legislation. A crucial finding that emerges from this comparative research is that the decision made in 1792 was not unprecedented. Significantly, it points to another unexplored possibility – that Simcoe and Osgoode may never have made a formal decision to omit English poor law and bankruptcy law, and that the decision was perhaps made long before.

When the defeat of the French at Quebec in 1759 paved the way for the English takeover of the province, English merchants were among the first to arrive. As early as 1764 they had increased the level of trade between Britain and Canada to 296,000 pounds sterling annually.[63] Although minuscule in number compared with the 60,000 French 'Canadians' who remained in the province after 1760, these merchants constituted a significant element in the population. Government officials like

General James Murray, the first governor of Quebec from 1763 to 1766, and Colonel Guy Carleton, his successor from 1768 to 1778, recognized that they were a powerful economic group whose interests had to be taken into account.[64]

When Murray was appointed Governor of Quebec in 1763, he received essentially the same instructions as those given to the governor of New York in 1754.[65] These included the power to call an assembly, establish courts of justice, and make laws 'for the public peace, Welfare, & good Government of [the] province' that were not 'repugnant, but as near as may be agreeable, to the laws & Statutes of this our Kingdom of Great Britain.'[66] He was further authorized to consider what had taken place in other colonies, and in particular in the most recently formed colony of Nova Scotia, when establishing courts of justice.[67] During his short tenure as governor, Murray, with the advice of legal officials who came from Nova Scotia, set up the province's legal system in such a way that it would conform as closely as possible to the English model.[68]

Guy Carleton (later Lord Dorchester), appointed governor in 1768, was given similar instructions from London on how to govern the province.[69] However, it is clear that Carleton used his powers differently from Murray. Whereas the latter appeared to try to make laws for Quebec that were 'agreeable, to the laws & Statutes' of Britain, Carleton seems to have done everything in his power to keep English civil law from being introduced into Quebec. He spent four years as governor of Quebec in England (from 1770 to 1774) lobbying for the enactment of the Quebec Act.[70] When he returned to Quebec in 1775 he brought with him the law he wanted in order to retain the support of the French-Canadian *seigniors* (or wealthy landowners),[71] and the instructions he was supposed to share with residents about how the act was to be implemented.[72] Most importantly, the Quebec Act allowed for the introduction of 'the Laws of England' to serve 'at least in part [as] the Rule for ... decision in all Cases of personal Actions grounded on Debts, Promises, Contracts, and Agreements, whether of a Mercantile or other Nature.'[73]

Theoretically and legally, the act allowed for the introduction of English poor law and bankruptcy law into Quebec. But actions taken by Carleton before and after the enactment of the Quebec Act, effectively ruled out that possibility. As several historians have pointed out, Carleton intentionally ignored instructions calling for him to clarify its intent, refusing even to make them public until near the end of his tenure.[74] This suggests that even if there were a number of English residents of the province who wanted laws concerning the maintenance of the poor and bankruptcy that conformed to the English model, they probably would not have known that they had the right to try and have those laws introduced.

Another step taken by Carleton explicitly excluded existing English bankruptcy law from being introduced in the province. In 1768 he received a reply from the Earl of Hillsborough, who had recently been appointed first secretary of the new Department of State for the Colonies, to several letters sent to the government of London the previous fall. In concluding his generally positive response, Hillsborough commented:

> I have, in the mean Time, His Majesty's Commands, to express His Satisfaction in your prudent conduct relative to the Applications mentioned in your Letter No. 17. to have been made to you for a Commission of Bankruptcy, as it is impossible to conceive, that it could ever be His Majesty's Intention signified, either by the Proclamation, or by the Ordinance for the Establishment of Courts of Judicature, to extend Laws of that particular and municipal Nature to the Colony, even if the Intention had been to have overturned the Customs of Canada, and it would be full as reasonable to make a poor Rate under the 43rd of Elizabeth, or to execute any other Act of Parliament of England, in Quebec, however intended for any local or particular purpose in this Kingdom.[75]

While the meaning of Hillsborough's comment is not entirely clear, his references to the English bankruptcy and poor laws are unmistakable. The 'Letter No. 17' mentioned by Hillsborough had been sent to England by Carleton. Dated 21 November 1767, it enclosed 'a petition from British merchants in Canada, stating their objections to the complete enforcement in Canada of the English bankruptcy laws.' In the same letter Carleton informed government officials that he agreed with the petitioner's argument, and that he had already refrained from introducing English bankruptcy laws in the province.[76]

Besides providing a precedent for the rejection of English bankruptcy law in a British North American colony, Hillsborough's letter to Carleton coupled mention of English bankruptcy law with a reference to the Elizabethan poor law. This linkage suggests two possibilities: first, that the English merchants of Quebec may not have been great supporters of the English poor law, and either Carleton or the petitioners may have made specific recommendations about it in other correspondence sent to Hillsborough; second, and as is more explicitly suggested in the letter, that these laws were perceived to be of a very 'particular and municipal Nature,' and they were never intended to be introduced to replace customs already existing in Quebec.

Legislation resembling the English poor law was never enacted. As far as can be determined, the English law relating to bankruptcy was also never introduced in Quebec, despite the fact that the Montreal merchants later changed their views on the usefulness of English bankruptcy legislation.[77] It is therefore possible that the action taken in Upper Canada by Simcoe and Osgoode followed a Quebec precedent. Evidence concerning the proceedings of the initial session of the first legislature of Upper Canada provides additional support for the view that Simcoe and Osgoode may have had little choice in the matter of the poor law.

Who Pushed for Excluding the Poor Law?
Evidence from the First Session of the Legislature at Newark,
17 September to 15 October 1792

Historians have pointed out that Osgoode, following Simcoe's orders, drafted many of the eight statutes that were passed in the first provincial legislature that met at Newark from 17 September to 15 October 1792.[78] Moreover, although other pieces of legislation introduced in this session were debated on the floor, there is no evidence of any debate on the poor law or bankruptcy law in either the Legislative Council or the House of Assembly. In commenting on Osgoode's role in drafting the legislation, Colgate remarks that 'Osgoode, at the instigation of Simcoe, assisted by the attorney general and supported by the executive council, prepared for submission to the legislative council a bill making English law the law of Upper Canada. The Legislative Council approved the measure and it passed the assembly without dissent.'[79] In his discussion of the enactment of the statute in *The Life of John Graves Simcoe*, Riddell writes:

> Simcoe and the legal officers, the Chief Justice and Attorney-General, were English to the core, and the Executive Council also were almost a unit; the Province at large was populated almost wholly by English-speaking people, and there could be no doubt that English Law was sincerely desired by practically all. A Bill prepared at Simcoe's request by Chief Justice Osgoode was introduced in the Legislative Council; it rapidly passed its various stages and was sent down to the House, which speedily concurred.[80]

Although these descriptions of what happened in the first legislature may be accurate, there is a need to know why the various bills were dealt with in certain ways. In particular, why was there no recorded discussion or debate surrounding the exclusion of the poor law? Apart from Riddell's account, the only secondary source that sheds light on this matter is that offered by S.R. Mealing. According to Mealing, Simcoe

> was disappointed in the social status and education of the members of the legislative assembly when he first met them, but in five sessions their objects seldom conflicted with his. Most of the legislation put before them, especially in their first session, was altogether uncontroversial: the adoption of English civil law and of jury trials, of standard English weights and measures and of tavern licensing, and the provision of jails and courthouses in each of the four administrative districts. During his whole term of office, the assembly rejected only two measures that he was anxious for – a land tax and an education bill.[81]

As required by his official instructions, Simcoe sent copies of the journals and proceedings of the Legislative Council and the House of Assembly back to London.[82] In a covering letter addressed to Dundas, Simcoe described how various bills had been handled in the legislature, and offered his views of the appointed and elected members. These two primary data sources, along with other relevant secondary sources, give a good idea of why Simcoe was disappointed in the members of the assembly. One of the main reasons, and one not insignificant to the 'missing' poor law, was that the members of the assembly opposed his determined effort to introduce a land tax, which he felt was needed to raise revenue for the province. Simcoe's letter to Dundas is worth quoting at length for the vivid picture it draws of Simcoe's assessment of how well the first session went:

> In my passage from Montreal to Kingston, I understood that the general Spirit of the Country was against the Election of half pay Officers into the Assembly: and that the prejudice ran in favour of Men of a Lower Order, who kept but one Table, that is who dined in Common with their Servants ...
> ... The House of Assembly consisted chiefly in the most active Characters in the several Counties ... At their first meeting, they were active and Zealous for particular measures, according to the

promises they had made, or the Instructions they had received, many projects were accordingly framed, which only required a little time to evince their impropriety or Futility. Having Officers to create and Salaries to bestow, they were rather too Liberal of their Patronage, and pledged their Credit to the payment of 174 [pounds], annually to different Officers; the Legislative Council made no Engagements, but of course their Expences must be equal. – The Sum of 348 [pounds] was therefore the first Item – A Bill was in its progress for the building of Gaols and Court Houses in the four Districts – And many of the Members were not averse to Parliamentary Wages. – All these Charges were to be defrayed by a Duty of Six pence per Gallon on all spirit and wine passing thro' the Country, which it was presumed would produce a Revenue of 1500 [pounds], and a Bill for that purpose actually passed. It had been suggested to them in conversation that a County rate was the natural supply for the Discharge of all expenses contracted by the County, but the Answer was that the smallest Tax on real property would prevent Emigration. It was replied, that the Quit Rent Originally imposed at four shillings and two pence per hundred Acres and which far exceeds any projected Rate, did not prevent the Coming in of settlers, but all arguments were useless to persons actuated by their fears. The House of Assembly consisted entirely of Land holders, the Duty on Rum was therefore their only expedient to answer the demands of the Province, and all opposition in the House of Assembly was useless.[83]

As J.K. Johnson documents in his recent study, *Becoming Prominent*, 'the first two parliaments of Upper Canada (from 1792 to 1800) were both very small and quite similar in composition.'[84] Despite what Simcoe had heard about 'the general Spirit ... against the Election of half pay Officers,' Johnson found that nine of the seventeen members in the first parliament (from 1792 to 1796) 'were on half pay from Loyalist regiments.' The rest of the seats were filled 'by men whose loyalty during the revolution had been manifested in non-military ways.' Johnson notes that a certain 'levelling' process went on in the assembly between 1792 and 1812. This resulted from an increased predilection by electors to reject members of the Loyalist civil and military establishment as their representatives. Instead, they began to elect those whom Simcoe termed 'Men of a Lower Order' to Parliament.[85] Despite these tendencies, it is clear that the first legislature was still dominated by Loyalist 'Land holders' who had little sympathy for a property tax, regardless of the good causes on which it might be spent. In concluding his covering letter to Dundas, Simcoe commented that while 'upon the whole I have no reason to be dissatisfied with the Disposition of the Assembly ... I confess myself much at a loss for a proper Subject for taxation.'[86]

One could provide more detail about how the bills worked their way through the Legislative Council and the House of Assembly, but it is sufficient to note that the statute enacted to adopt the civil law of England passed through both chambers of the legislature without comment or discussion.[87] One of the assumptions in the accounts offered by previous investigators is that Simcoe and Osgoode had the power to enact the legislation that excluded the English poor law. However, the evidence presented here suggests that, regardless of how they felt personally, Simcoe and Osgoode saw that such legislation would be opposed by the elected members of the assembly. The removal of any contentious items could also explain why there was no debate on the bill as it passed through both chambers of the legislature.

Conclusions

The story of the 'missing' Upper Canadian poor law provides added insight into the political culture of Upper Canada in the 1790s as well as the economic interests of those who first gained control of the province's legal system. More specifically, the findings are consistent with Errington and Rawlyk's analysis of the colony's early political culture,[88] as well as with Romney's critique of the 'Nostalgic Tory' school.[89]

First, the manner in which the newly elected Loyalist members of the legislature rejected the English poor law and bankruptcy law shows that they did not share any consuming sense of 'providential mission.' In other words, nothing led them to set aside their personal economic interests in order to further the general good of the province. Second, it is clear that the colony was not peopled by politically docile settlers deferring to an authoritarian-paternalist élite. Indeed, in contrast to the kind of 'well-ordered' society which Simcoe and British government officials envisioned, members of the assembly favoured a government that would reduce the cost for the élite of supporting less fortunate Upper Canadians to a minimum. At the same time, as shown in Simcoe's letter to Dundas, the élite enjoyed the economic rewards that flowed from political patronage and 'Salaries to bestow.' Even the first putative 'Tory-Loyalist' legislators did not hesitate to rely on the assembly to enact laws that coincided with their own economic and personal interests.

Although we may never be able to obtain conclusive evidence of the rationale underlying the decision to exclude the English poor law, it is telling that Upper Canadians living in the province more than two decades later thought they knew why the decision was made.[90] In January 1819 the Kingston *Chronicle* published a lengthy editorial on the causes and prevention of pauperism, in which an anonymous writer informed readers about the history of efforts that had been undertaken to deal with the problem in England.[91] The English system, the writer argued, was seriously flawed because it was geared towards responding to pauperism rather than preventing it from developing in the first place.[92] A similar view was expressed in the *Chronicle* in June 1819, in the published minutes of a meeting of 'the Magistrates and Inhabitants of the Town & Township of Kingston' held for the purpose of agreeing on a plan for providing relief to the local poor. In a declaration intended to spell out the general views held by Kingston-area residents on the subject of poor relief, Thomas Markland, the leading Tory magistrate who chaired the meeting stated: 'A reasonable support of the Poor is the duty of every Christian community. In most civilized countries provision is made for it by law. But, the English system of laws on the subject having been found to be attended with serious evils, our Provincial Legislature in their general adoption of the laws of England, excepted the Pauper Laws, and have not yet provided any substitute.'[93]

What is revealing about these items is that they indicate serious efforts were made later to inform Upper Canadians about the 'evil' consequences attendant on adopting an English-style poor law. Moreover, individuals such as Markland claimed that they were aware of the rationale that underlay the decision to exclude the law from being introduced into the province. Contrary to the view that 'pragmatic considerations' weighed heavily on the minds of the legislators of 1792,[94] Upper Canadians writing thirty years later believed that the English poor law was rejected because it was inherently flawed.[95]

Despite the efforts made here to draw reasonable inferences from known sources of data, the question of why the English poor law was not adopted in Upper Canada cannot be considered closed. It is possible that Simcoe and Osgoode made their decision alone, but there is no hint of this in their voluminous correspondence.[96] It remains, however, for future studies to ask why Upper Canadians seem to have resented the idea of adopting a formal poor law as late as the 1830s. One line of inquiry that merits further investigation is the possibility that Upper Canadian 'Tory-Loyalists' brought their resentment of the poor law with them from the

United States, since we know that many of the pre-revolutionary colonies modelled their poor relief systems on the English model.[97] It is also possible that some direct discussions of the reasons for exclusion might yet be found in the records and correspondence of other leading early Loyalists who became Simcoe's advisers, such as Peter Russell, Richard Cartwright, and Robert Hamilton.[98] In any case, a more complete picture of the reasons underlying the rejection of the law must include the question of why Upper Canadians later felt that they had the answer to the puzzle.

NOTES

The author would like to thank The Osgoode Society for the research award it granted to facilitate the research for this study. He would also like to thank his colleague, Nicholas Tavuchis, for his editorial assistance, and the volume editors for their additional editorial advice.

1 Statutes of Upper Canada (1792), 32 George III, c. 1., 'An Act Introducing the English Civil Law into Upper Canada,' in *Documents Relating to the Constitutional History of Canada, 1791–1818*, ed. A. Doughty and D. McArthur (Ottawa: Historical Documents Publication Board 1914), 83–4 (hereinafter cited as *Constitutional Documents, 1791–1818*).

2 Unlike the colonies of New Brunswick and Nova Scotia, where arriving Loyalists had decided to create poor relief systems based largely on the poor law that existed in England. Brereton Greenhous, 'Paupers and Poorhouses: The Development of Poor Relief in Early New Brunswick' (1968), 1 *Histoire sociale / Social History*, 103–26; Charles Thomas, 'The Administration of the Poor Law in Nova Scotia, 1749–1937,' MA thesis, Dalhousie University (1938); James Whalen, 'New Brunswick Poor Law Policy in the Nineteenth Century,' MA thesis, University of New Brunswick (1968), and 'The Nineteenth Century Almshouse System in Saint John County' (1971), 7 *Histoire sociale / Social History*, 5–27; R. Williams, 'Poor Relief and Medicine in Nova Scotia, 1749–1783,' in *Medicine in Canadian Society: Historical Perspectives*, ed. S. Shortt (Montreal and Kingston: McGill-Queen's University Press 1981).

3 This is part of a larger work that uses the history of Upper Canada to address a number of theoretical questions about the development of law, social welfare, and social control. This work includes Russell Smandych, 'The Upper Canadian Experience with Pre-Segregative Control,' Ph.D. thesis, University of Toronto (1989); 'Tory Paternalism and the Politics of Penal Reform in Upper Canada, 1830–1834: A "Neo-Revisionist" Account

of the Kingston Penitentiary,' in (1991), 12 *Criminal Justice History: An International Annual*; 'Rethinking "the Master Principle of Administering Relief" in Upper Canada: A Response to Allan Irving' (1991), 27 *Canadian Review of Social Policy*, 81–6; 'Review of D. Garland, *Punishment and Modern Society: A Study in Social Theory*' (1991), 16 *Canadian Journal of Sociology*, 205–7; and Russell Smandych, Catherine J. Matthews, and Sandra Cox, *Canadian Criminal Justice History: An Annotated Bibliography* (Toronto: University of Toronto Press 1987).

4 Canadian legal historians have displayed interest in addressing questions surrounding the reception of English law. One of the most frequently asked questions is why the English law pertaining to particular subjects was received differently in the different British North American colonies or Canadian provinces (after 1867). For examples, see Simon N. Verdun-Jones, 'The Evolution of the Defenses of Insanity and Automatism in Canada from 1843 to 1979: A Saga of Judicial Reluctance to Sever the Umbilical Cord to the Mother Country?' (1979), 14 *University of British Columbia Law Review*, 1–73; David G. Bell, 'A Note on the Reception of English Statutes in New Brunswick' (1979), 28 *University of New Brunswick Law Journal*, 195–201, and 'The Reception Question and the Constitutional Crisis of the 1790s in New Brunswick' (1980), 29 *University of New Brunswick Law Journal*, 157–72; John C. Bouck, 'Introducing English Statute Law into the Provinces: Time for a Change?' (1979), 57 *Canadian Bar Review*, 74–87; and J.E. Coté, 'The Introduction of English Law into Alberta' (1964), 3 *Alberta Law Review*, 262–92. Several dozen other studies of this type are listed in Smandych, Matthews, and Cox, *Canadian Criminal Justice History*, supra note 3.

5 Some of the most important recent students of the Upper Canadian 'Tory-mind' and its legacy on Upper Canada's political and legal culture include Blaine Baker, 'The Juvenile Advocate Society, 1821–1826: Self-Proclaimed Schoolroom for Canada's Governing Elite' (1985) *Canadian Historical Association, Historical Papers*, 74–101, and ' "So Elegant a Web": Providential Order and the Rule of Secular Law in Early Nineteenth-Century Upper Canada' (1988), 38 *University of Toronto Law Journal*, 184–205; Jane Errington and George Rawlyk, 'The Loyalist-Federalist Alliance of Upper Canada" (1984), 14 *American Review of Canadian Studies*, 157–76; Jane Errington, *The Lion, the Eagle and Upper Canada: A Developing Colonial Ideology* (Kingston and Montreal: McGill-Queen's University Press 1987); David Howes, 'Property, God and Nature in the Thought of Sir John Beverley Robinson' (1985), 30 *McGill Law Journal*, 365–414; David Mills, *The Idea of Loyalty in Upper Canada, 1784–1850* (Kingston and Montreal: McGill-Queen's University Press 1988); and Paul Romney, 'From the Types Riot to the Rebellion: Elite Ideology,

Anti-Legal Sentiment, Political Violence, and the Rule of Law in Upper Canada' (1987), 79 *Ontario History*, 113–44, 'Very Late Loyalist Fantasies: Nostalgic Tory History and the Rule of Law in Upper Canada,' in *Canadian Perspectives on Law and Society: Issues in Legal History*, ed. W. Pue and B. Wright (Ottawa: Carleton University Press 1988), 'Re-Inventing Upper Canada: American Immigrants, Upper Canadian History, English Law, and the Alien Question,' in *Patterns of the Past: Interpreting Ontario's Past*, ed. R. Hall, W. Westfall, and L. MacDowell (Toronto: Ontario Historical Society 1988), and 'From Constitutionalism to Legalism: Trial by Jury, Responsible Government, and the Rule of Law in Canadian Political Culture' (1989), 7 *Law and History Review*, 121–74.

6 Rainer Baehre, 'Paupers and Poor Relief in Upper Canada' (1981), *Canadian Historical Association: Historical Papers*, 57–80; Jack A. Blyth, *The Canadian Social Inheritance* (Toronto: Copp Clark 1972); G.P. de.T. Glazebrook, *Life in Ontario: A Social History* (Toronto: University of Toronto Press 1971); Greenhous, supra note 2; Richard B. Splane, *Social Welfare in Ontario, 1791–1893: A Study of Public Welfare Administration* (Toronto: University of Toronto Press 1965); Susan Houston, 'The Impetus to Reform: Urban Crime, Poverty and Ignorance in Ontario, 1850–1875,' Ph.D. thesis, University of Toronto (1974); J.C. Levy, 'The Poor Laws of Upper Canada,' in *Law and Society in Canada in Historical Perspective*, ed. D. Bercuson and L.A. Knafla (Calgary: University of Calgary Studies in History No 2 1979); David Murray, 'The Cold Hand of Charity: The Court of Quarter Sessions and Poor Relief in the Niagara District, 1828–1841,' in *Canadian Perspectives on Law and Society*, supra note 5; John Weaver, 'While Equity Slumbered: Creditor Advantage, A Capitalist Land Market, and Upper Canada's Missing Court' (1990), 28 *Osgoode Hall Law Journal*, 871–914.

7 Splane, supra note 6, at 66–7.

8 Ibid., at 68.

9 For instance, see Blyth, supra note 6, at 17; Glazebrook, supra note 6, at 100; Greenhous, supra note 2, at 103.

10 Greenhous, supra note 2, at 103–4.

11 Levy, here and below, supra note 6, at 24–33.

12 Baehre, supra note 6, at 58.

13 More detailed studies of the nature of late eighteenth-century English ideas on poverty and the debate over the adequacy of the 'old' English poor law are provided in Crowther, *The Workhouse System 1834–1929: The History of an English Social Institution* (Athens: University of Georgia Press 1982); Gertrude Himmelfarb, *The Idea of Poverty: England in the Early Industrial Age* (New York: Vintage Books 1985); Norman Longmate, *The Workhouse*

(London: Temple Smith 1974); and J.R. Poynter, *Society and Pauperism: English Ideas on Poor Relief, 1795–1834* (London: Routledge and Kegan Paul 1969).

14 Weaver, supra note 6, at 875.

15 Murray, ibid., at 179.

16 Cited in F.H. Soward, 'The Struggle Over the Laws of Canada, 1783–1791' (1924), 5 *Canadian Historical Review*, 334.

17 Gerald M. Craig, *Upper Canada: The Formative Years, 1784–1841* (Toronto: McClelland and Stewart 1963), 3.

18 David Bell, 'The Loyalist Tradition in Canada,' in *Canadian History Before Confederation: Essays and Interpretations* ed. J. Bumstead (Georgetown, Ont.: Irwin-Dorsey 1972), 210.

19 William Smith, 'The Struggle Over the Laws of Canada, 1736–1783' (1920), 1 *Canadian Historical Review*, 166–86.

20 Arthur R.M. Lower, *Colony to Nation: A History of Canada* (Toronto: McClelland and Stewart 1977), 66–77.

21 John Johnson (1741–1830) was a leading Loyalist emigré and military officer who fled to the province of Quebec in the spring of 1776 after losing the Mohawk valley to the Americans. In 1790 Lord Dorchester, the governor of Quebec, recommended that Sir John Johnson be appointed the first lieutenant-governor of Upper Canada. This had significant consequences later for Simcoe's relationship with Dorchester: see E. Thomas, 'Sir John Johnson.' *Dictionary of Canadian Biography*, vol. 6, 352–4.

22 'Petition of Sir John Johnson ... and others in Behalf of the Loyalists settled in Canada.' Dated London, 11 April 1785, and signed by Colonel Guy Johnson and others, in *Documents Relating to the Constitutional History of Canada, 1759–1791*, 2d ed., vol. 1, part 2, ed. A. Shortt and A. Doughty (Ottawa: Historical Documents Publication Board 1907) (hereinafter cited as *Constitutional Documents, 1759–1791*); Craig, supra note 17, at 9.

23 Soward, supra note 16; Craig, supra note 17, at 9; Lower, supra note 20, at 126–7.

24 Soward, supra note 16, at 325.

25 Cited in Craig, supra note 17, at 17.

26 Cited in Lower, supra note 20, at 127.

27 Aileen Dunham, *Political Unrest in Upper Canada, 1815–1836* (Toronto: McClelland and Stewart 1963), 29.

28 Ibid., at 45–6; Splane, supra note 6, at 21.

29 (1791) 31 George III, c. 31, 'The Constitutional Act of 1791,' in *Constitutional Documents, 1759–1791*, 1031–51.

30 Lower, supra note 20, at 127–8.

31 S.F. Wise, 'Tory Factionalism: Kingston Elections and Upper Canadian Politics, 1820–1836' (1965), 47 *Ontario History*, 205–25; 'Upper Canada and the Conservative Tradition,' in *Profiles of a Province*, ed. E. Firth (Toronto: Ontario Historical Society 1967); 'Colonial Attitudes from the Era of the War of 1812 to the Rebellions of 1837,' in *Canada Views the United States: Nineteenth Century Political Attitudes*, ed. S.F. Wise and R.C. Brown (Toronto: Macmillan 1967); 'Sermon Literature and Canadian Intellectual History,' in *Canadian History Before Confederation*, supra note 18; 'God's Peculiar Peoples,' in *Studies in Canadian Social History*, ed. M. Horn and R. Sabourin (Toronto: McClelland and Stewart 1974); 'Liberal Consensus or Ideological Battleground: Some Reflections on the Hartz Thesis' (1974) *Canadian Historical Association, Historical Papers*, 1–14; 'John Macaulay: Tory for All Seasons,' in *To Preserve and Defend: Essays on Kingston in the Nineteenth Century*, ed. G. Tulchinsky (Kingston and Montreal: McGill-Queen's University Press 1976).

32 Wise, 'Upper Canada and the Conservative Tradition,' supra note 31, at 21.

33 Errington and Rawlyk, supra note 5.

34 Donald H. Akenson, *The Irish in Ontario: A Study in Rural History* (Kingston and Montreal: McGill-Queen's University Press 1984).

35 Romney, 'Very Late Loyalist Fantasies' and 'From the Types Riot to the Rebellion,' supra note 5.

36 Errington and Rawlyk, ibid., at 159.

37 Akenson, supra note 34, at 79, 97–8.

38 Romney, 'Very Late Loyalist Fantasies,' supra note 5.

39 The two authors criticized in particular by Romney are Baker ('The Juvenile Advocate Society' and ' "So elegant a Web" ') and Howes ('Property, God and Nature'), supra note 5.

40 Romney, 'Very Late Loyalist Fantasies,' ibid., at 141.

41 Dunham, supra note 27, at 32.

42 S.R. Mealing, "John Graves Simcoe," *Dictionary of Canadian Biography*, vol. 5, 755.

43 Henry Dundas (1742–1811), elected to the British House of Commons in 1774, held many high government appointments, including treasurer of the navy (1784–1800) and secretary of state for home affairs (June 1791) and for war (1794–1801). *The Correspondence of Lieut. Governor John Graves Simcoe*, ed. E.A. Cruikshank, vol. 1 (Toronto: Ontario Historical Society 1923), 34 (hereinafter cited as *Simcoe Correspondence*).

44 Simcoe was concerned that appropriate appointments be made to the government of Upper Canada. In a letter to Dundas, he remarked that 'it may be for the King's Service not to appoint without a more particular Enquiry,

more Persons to the Executive or Legislative Council, than shall be necessary to give Birth to the Functions of the New Government': *Simcoe Correspondence*, Simcoe to Dundas, 12 August 1791.

45 Arthur R.M. Lower, 'Three Letters of William Osgoode First Chief Justice of Upper Canada' (1965), 57 *Ontario History*, 183.

46 William Colgate, 'William Osgoode, Chief Justice' (1953), 31 *Canadian Bar Review*, 272.

47 Fredrick H. Armstrong, *Handbook of Upper Canadian Chronology and Territorial Legislation* (London: University of Western Ontario, Lawson Memorial Library, Centennial Publication 1967), 13, 33.

48 Edith Firth, 'The Administration of Peter Russell, 1796–1799' (1956), 48 *Ontario History*, 163–81; Douglas McCalla, 'The "Loyalist" Economy of Upper Canada, 1784–1806' (1983), 16 *Histoire Sociale/Social History*, 279–304; George Rawlyk, 'The Honourable Richard Cartwright, 1759–1815' (1985), 33 *Historic Kingston*, 15–41; Bruce Wilson, *The Enterprises of Robert Hamilton: A Study of Wealth and Influence in Early Upper Canada, 1776–1812* (Ottawa: Carleton University Press 1983).

49 Although both Simcoe and Osgoode wrote to many contemporaries, there is little correspondence between them.

50 *Simcoe Correspondence*, 'Memorandum from J.G. Simcoe to Hon. Henry Dundas,' 2 June 1791.

51 National Archives (NAC), MG 11, CO 42, vol. 21, reel C–13, 606, 'Quebec, Despatches and Miscellaneous, 1789–1792,' 252–3, Wm Osgoode to the Right Honourable Henry Dundas, Secretary of State, 12 August 1791.

52 Indicatively, in the same letter he wrote to Dundas on 12 August 1791, Simcoe mentioned 'the Conversation which [he] had the Honour to hold' with Dundas about 'the detail[s] of the Upper Canadian Government' when he had recently 'waited upon' him at the Treasury. Moreover, Simcoe concluded his letter by stating that if Dundas was 'desirous of any further Elucidation on the Subject' he would be pleased to arrange to meet him for a 'personal interview.'

53 NAC, *Simcoe Papers*, MG 23, HI1, series 3, book I, Evan Nepean to J.G. Simcoe, 10 September 1791.

54 NAC, MG 11, CO 42, vol. 21, reel C–13,606, 'Quebec, Despatches and Miscellaneous, 1789–1792,' 243–4, 'Remarks of Ld. Grenville relative to Commissions & Instructions under the Canada Bill,' memo dated 22 June 1791.

55 'Instructions to Lord Dorchester as Governor of Upper Canada,' dated 16 September 1791, in *Constitutional Documents, 1791–1818*, 33–48.

56 Much of the correspondence Simcoe wrote before arriving in Upper Canada is concerned with emigration and military defence. See Malcolm

MacLeod, 'Fortress Ontario or Forlorn Hope? Simcoe and the Defence of Upper Canada' (1972), 53 *Canadian Historical Review*, 149–78. For a more detailed discussion of Simcoe's emigration policy, see Smandych, 'The Upper Canadian Experience with Pre-Segregative Control,' supra note 3, at 136–44; Craig, supra note 17, at 20–41; Lillian Gates, *Land Policies of Upper Canada* (Toronto: University of Toronto Press 1968), 24–38.

57 Simcoe was elected to the English House of Commons in the same election as Edmund Burke, who we know made comments about the state of the English poor law and about the 'Canada Bill.' William R. Riddell, *The Life John Graves Simcoe: First Lieutenant-Governor of the Province of Upper Canada, 1792–96* (Toronto: McClelland and Stewart 1926), 79–80, 90.

58 During his brief parliamentary career, Simcoe is reported to have made only two speeches in the House of Commons, one of which was on the new constitution for Quebec (Mealing, supra note 42, at 754).

59 William Colgate, 'Letters from The Honourable Chief Justice William Osgoode: A Selection from his Canadian Correspondence, 1791–1801' (1954), 46 *Ontario History*, 78–9; *Friends of the Chief Justice: The Osgoode Correspondence in the Archives of the Law Society of Upper Canada*, ed. D. Hay and R. Paley (Toronto: The Law Society of Upper Canada 1990).

60 Hay and Paley, 'Introduction,' supra note 59, at vi.

61 Colgate, supra note 46, at 273; Mary Beacock Fryer, "A Note: Mrs. Simcoe from Neglected Sources" (1990), 82 *Ontario History*, 306–9.

62 NAC, *Simcoe Papers*, MG 23, HI5, reel A606, unsigned journal diary with cover title '1792–1793–1794.'

63 Smith, supra note 19, at 167–8.

64 Lower, supra note 20, at 64–73. It is significant to note that many of these 'English' merchants were actually traders from New England or demobilized British soldiers.

65 Smith, supra note 19, at 168.

66 'Commission of Captain-General & Governor in Chief of the Province of Quebec,' dated 28 November 1763, in *Constitutional Documents, 1759–1791*, supra note 22, at 175–6.

67 'Instructions to Governor Murray,' ibid., at 187.

68 Smith, supra note 19, at 168–72.

69 'Instructions to Our Trusty and Well beloved Guy Carleton Esquire, Our Captain General and Governor in Chief in and over Our Province of Quebec in America and of all Our Territories Dependent thereupon Given,' in *Constitutional Documents, 1759–1791*, supra note 22, at 301–24.

70 Lower, supra note 20, at 67.

71 Smith, supra note 19, at 169.

72 'Instructions to Our Trusty and Well beloved Guy Carleton,' supra note 22, 594–614.
73 Supra note 22, Instruction 12, 599. The specific provision of the Quebec Act referred to in this instruction states that 'Resort shall be had to the Laws of *Canada*, as the Rule for the Decision (of all matters relating to property and civil rights) ... until they shall be varied or altered by any Ordinances ...' supra note 22, at 573.
74 He was finally forced to do so because of a protest raised by the province's chief justice. Smith, supra note 19; Soward, supra note 16; A.L. Burt, 'The Tragedy of Chief Justice Livius' (1924), 5 *Canadian Historical Review*, 196–212.
75 'Hillsborough to Carleton, Whitchall, March the 6th, 1768,' supra note 22, at 298. Carleton's letters were sent while he was still lieutenant-governor of the province.
76 Ibid., editor's note, 297.
77 Additional research is required in order to understand the controversy over the application of English bankruptcy legislation in pre-1791 Quebec. Sources of information on the history and outcome of this controversy include 'Plan of a Code of Laws for the Province of Quebec; Reported by the Advocate-General, James Marriott, London, MDCCLXXIV (1774),' *Constitutional Documents, 1759–1791*, 453; Baron Maseres, *Considerations on the Expediency of procuring An Act of Parliament For the Settlement of the Province of Quebec [with supplement]* (London 1766); *The Maseres Letters, 1766–1786*, ed. W. Wallace (Toronto: Oxford University Press 1919); and E. Arthur, 'Francis Maseres,' *Dictionary of Canadian Biography*, vol. 6, 491–6.
78 Colgate, 'Letters from the Honourable Chief Justice William Osgoode,' supra note 59, 77–8, and 'William Osgoode, Chief Justice,' supra note 46, 274–5; Riddell, supra note 57, at 176–7; Duncan Campbell, *John Graves Simcoe* (Toronto: Morang 1906), 85.
79 Colgate, 'William Osgoode, Chief Justice,' supra note 46, 275.
80 Riddell, supra note 57, at 176–7, 173–88.
81 Mealing, supra note 42, at 756.
82 *Simcoe Correspondence*, J.G. Simcoe to Henry Dundas, Navy Hall, Niagara, 4 November 1792, 6 November 1792; NAC, MG 11, CO 42, no. 317, reel B–281, 'Original Correspondence – Secretary of State – Upper Canada, 1792–92,' 60–99, 'Journal and Proceedings of the House of Assembly of the Province of Upper Canada' and 'Journal of the Legislative Council of Upper Canada,' 17 September to 15 October 1792.
83 *Simcoe Correspondence*, Simcoe to Dundas, Niagara, 4 November 1792.

84 J.K. Johnson, *Becoming Prominent: Regional Leadership in Upper Canada, 1791–1841* (Montreal and Kingston: McGill-Queen's University 1989), 124.
85 Johnson, Ibid., at 124, 127–8.
86 Ibid., at 127–8.
87 It should also be noted that the 'Rum Tax Bill' passed by the assembly was subsequently defeated on its second reading in the Legislative Council. This led Simcoe to tell Dundas, in a letter of 4 November 1792, that 'The Legislative Council were more cautious and moderate, and I have good reason to believe, will be found to constitute a seasonable [sic] check upon any precipitate Measure, without throwing the Burthen of a Negative upon Government.' Simcoe wanted the tax bill defeated because he felt it would antagonize the Montreal merchants who produced most of the alcohol sold in Upper Canada.
88 Errington and Rawlyk, supra note 5.
89 Romney, 'Very Late Loyalist Fantasies,' ibid.
90 This argument is documented in more detail in Smandych, 'Pre-Segregative Control,' supra note 3.
91 Kingston *Chronicle*, 22 January 1819.
92 Given that residents of the Midland District were going to be meeting soon to consider changing the manner in which they dispensed relief to the poor, this anonymous author felt it was important to point out that 'every Christian country has necessarily attempted some plan for remedying this evil, and in every case, to a greater or less degree, such attempt has failed. – England, in the present day, exhibits the most astonishing instance of a complete failure ... The mischief it appears, is not at its height [in Upper Canada]; and a new system is loudly called for. Warned thus by example, it would be little short of madness, for a new community, to have recourse to any similar expedients, for the support of its indigent members': Kingston *Chronicle*, 22 January 1819.
93 Ibid., 18 June 1819. At an earlier meeting held in the Midland District for the purpose of improving methods of preventing pauperism, residents of the district were similarly told that 'it will be well for you to keep in remembrance, that mischiefs of every kind, have been produced in England, by the operation of Poor Laws, and therefore you cannot be too careful in avoiding the adoption of any system, which may have the least approximation to that which has been found so extremely pernicious': ibid., 19 February 1819.
94 Splane, supra note 6.
95 There is also a great deal of evidence that this negative sentiment towards

English 'Pauper Laws' lasted well into the 1830s. See Smandych, 'Pre-Segregative Control,' supra note 3.

96 Although not integrated in the text of the present study, my research also included examining William Osgoode's personal correspondence held in the National Archives of Canada: *Osgoode Correspondence*, MG23, HI10.

97 For examples of the English influence on pre-revolutionary American poor laws and poor relief practices, see James W. Ely Jr, ' "There are few subjects in political economy of greater difficulty": The Poor Laws of the Antebellum South' (1985) *American Bar Foundation Research Journal*, 849–79, and 'Poor Laws of the Post-Revolutionary South, 1776–1800' (1985), 21 *Tulsa Law Journal*, 1–22.

98 Supra note 48. The correspondence and records of these and many other leading early Upper Canadian 'Loyalists' are located in the Ontario Archives and the National Archives of Canada.

5 Law-Making and Social Change in Colonial Trinidad, 1900–1950

KUSHA HARAKSINGH

Introduction

A recurring characteristic of many colonial societies is a degree of ethnic
and cultural heterogeneity, often a result of the forces that scattered
people across the globe in an age of imperial expansion. The plural
composition of the society is often accompanied by a legal regime in
which a variety of legal systems coexist, as in colonial Ceylon or the East
African dependencies. In the case of the Caribbean island of Trinidad,
however, except for special marriage and divorce laws for the Hindu and
Muslim population, there was for all practical purposes a uniform legal
system.[1] Arguably, this uniformity could have facilitated a move towards
greater social cohesion among the island's disparate groupings, but that
process was to founder in the wake of the law's emphasis on order rather
than development.[2] The force of the general law was directed in the first
place at maintaining control: the strategy was to prevent the two major
groups at the bottom of the social and economic system – the descendants of black ex-slaves and of Indian indentured workers – from establishing any common front.[3] Thus, the requirements of order and stability in
a colonial polity served to neutralize the law's tendency to foster a sense
of common identity or to construct political and other bridges in a
segmented society. The island's cultural pluralism continued to be juxta-
posed with formal legal uniformity. The predictable consequence was that
many of the law's subjects embraced what can only be called an underground existence in which legal rules were deliberately avoided. People
came to hold a jaundiced view of the legal system, even as they conceded

a certain status to judges and practitioners.[4] At the same time, especially among the large population that traced its origins to indentured migrants from India, the centralist form of law effected a strengthening of ethnic identity.[5]

The Setting

In many respects colonial Trinidad stood in stark contrast to its Caribbean neighbours. It was what West Indian historians like to call a late-developing colony. It had been captured by the British from Spain only in 1797, when some of the older British islands had passed their golden age of sugar production. When slavery was abolished in 1838 Trinidad was underpopulated and largely unexplored; substantial areas of land were untouched, and some of the existing sugar plantations were relatively new by Caribbean standards. The second half of the nineteenth century witnessed major changes, including the advent of large central sugar factories and the incursion of modern technology into the production process. These innovations were facilitated by the system of indentured labour, which, over the period from 1845 to 1917, brought 145,000 immigrants from India to Trinidad.

The Indians entered a colony that was sharply divided between white society at the top and the black ex-slaves and their descendants at the bottom. Whether or not by design, Indians were placed between the two as a buffer group. White society was divided into two sections – British officials and white creoles (that is, locally born persons of French, Spanish, Irish, or English descent). French creoles dominated the white creole group. The French, who were largely engaged in cocoa production, experienced a major improvement in their fortunes at the beginning of the century, when prevailing prices for cocoa were high. Whatever the tensions among the whites, however, they were still united in their attitude towards the labouring population of blacks and Indians.

One thing they agreed on was the notion that only those with a real stake in the island could have its true interests at heart. 'Stake' usually meant land ownership. This attitude, combined with the received colonial office wisdom concerning the special circumstances of Trinidad – the mixture of races and nationalities, doubts about the allegiance of Spanish and French creoles, and the increasing number of Indian immigrants – precluded the introduction of representative political institutions. The result was the familiar system of colonial law-making, in which, real authority resided with official members of the Trinidad legislature under

the general direction of the governor. Only at the very end of the period
– in 1950 – was an effective measure of constitutional change introduced,
and then only after sustained agitation; this change gave elected members
a majority in the legislative and executive councils, and established a
quasi-ministerial system. Even so, informal networks and the rules of
social distance kept access to the corridors and to the substance of power
firmly in the hands of persons of rank and privilege. In this situation,
progressive law-making to accord greater rights to the working population
or to facilitate the process of constitutional development could more
easily be activated by outside stimuli, which in turn were often prompted
by local disturbance and riot. But the frequency of strikes and riots[6]
confirmed the members of the power élite in their determination to
emphasize the law's regulatory and proscribing functions, and to resist
even the faintest glimmer of a breach in their dominant position. Thus,
a recurring cycle was set in train: disquiet and agitation, often culminat-
ing in civil disturbance and riot; official inquiry, often conducted by
external commissioners; and new legal arrangements, which worked (if
at all) only for the briefest moment, and ended with another recurrence
of the cycle.

Law and Labour

The grudging progress of labour legislation in the first half of this century illustrates the character of colonial law-making in Trinidad.[7] For the
labouring poor, change came slowly. The employers believed that every
ground had to be defended, often in ways that rendered legal innovation
meaningless. For example, in 1933, when the restrictive common law
doctrine of restraint of trade was rendered inapplicable to trade unions,
activists in the sugar plantation sector still found it difficult to organize
workers who worked and lived on lands belonging to their employers.
The employers merely denied union organizers access to the estates, so
that while it was legitimate to combine for trade union purposes, it was
nevertheless nearly impossible to achieve that combination. The resort by
employers to such strategies ensured that what appeared to be new rights
and opportunities were often hollow. Peasants growing sugar and cocoa
on their own or rented lands had an experience similar to that of plantation workers, marked by the distinction between paper rights and real
rights. The disillusionment with the legal system that flowed from such
experiences deepened labour's sense of alienation and social distance.
  Both workers and peasants were heirs to legal traditions that operated

on assumptions somewhat different from those of western law. These non-western traditions were strongest among the Indian population, which had entered the island with a formidable religious and cultural baggage that in some ways would be strengthened by the encounter with western law.[8] Thus, while the lower orders of society as a whole would have one experience of the operation of the law, for the Indians there would be a different gloss to that experience, traceable to their particular frame of reference. These divergent trends would lead to complications when demands for constitutional change were articulated,[9] and would help to set the stage for a politics of racial competition in the 1950s.

Some of this was predictable even at the beginning of the century, when Trinidad was still a plantation society. If the memory of a past constructed on slave labour had dimmed at all, employers were reminded by the depression that hit the sugar industry in the mid-1890s that their economic salvation lay in compelling labour to perform. That compulsion was more easily achievable in the case of indentured as compared to free workers,[10] but the legal framework for its attainment was similar. Free workers were governed by the Masters and Servants Ordinance 1846, and indentured workers by various immigration ordinances that were consolidated in 1899. Both sets of legislation contained some clauses that recalled the so-called beneficent provisions of earlier slave codes, and that, in theory at least, provided some safeguard for workers' interests.[11] But the interpretation of these clauses and of the legislation in general was heavily influenced by developments in the common law relating to freedom of contract. The general trend favoured the employer, so that it hardly mattered that many workers had no real freedom to spurn the terms of employment that were offered to them. This absence of choice was related to individual circumstances, such as indebtedness or residence in accommodation belonging to their employers, or the inability to deal with employer strategies that successfully foreclosed alternative means of earning a livelihood. The tendency to favour the position of the employers, buttressed in part by the feeling that the claims of those who had a real stake in the society ought to be preferred above other competing interests, was strengthened by social contacts between the judiciary and the planters. Thus it was most unlikely that a worker would prevail over his employer in any matter involving the interpretation of either contractual or statutory terms that reached a court.

The presence of indentured labourers provided a mechanism to bring free labour to heel; if the occasion demanded, they could be used as a strike-breaking force. The indentureds were obliged either to work or to

face a penal sanction for breach of contract. It was not surprising, therefore, that when it became untenable largely in the face of nationalist
pressure in India, to maintain a system of indenture,[12] the employers
would look for a new means of compulsion. Nor was the device ultimately
resorted to entirely unpredictable. It took the form of vagrancy legislation
which reached the statute-book in 1920 as the Habitual Idlers Ordinance.
A habitual idler was defined as a person who had no visible means of
subsistence, who habitually abstained from work, and who had not
worked for at least four hours during each of three days of the week
before his arrest. It was not clear what constituted visible means or the
ability to work, or even what magic lay in the four-hour stipulation. And,
as was usually the case in this kind of legislation, the burden of proof
rested on the supposed idler to prove that he did have lawful means of
subsistence or that he had not habitually abstained from work.

Remarkably, the statute was passed without a dissenting vote. That fact
is enough to underscore the monopoly of legislative power enjoyed by
those who favoured the interests of the planters and employers. It is also
remarkable that the Colonial Office, though taking note of the far-reach-
ing nature of the legislation, did not object to it. In this situation it would
have been strange if judicial law-making had taken a different trend. But
this was not to be, as was demonstrated in the perennial conflict between
peasants and millers, which eventually in 1922 spawned litigation that
reached all the way to the Privy Council in London.[13]

The Ste Madeleine Sugar Company Limited, which owned the largest
mill in the island, had circulated in January 1919 a notice offering to buy
canes from growers on their list of suppliers at a certain price. In December 1921, two weeks before the start of reaping, the company issued a
new notice offering a lower price; the growers proceeded to supply the
company with canes and claimed the original price. The company insisted
on paying the reduced rate, and the growers went to court to claim the
difference. On its face, this case was about the validity of a contract, and
the Privy Council applied a contractual analysis. It held that an offer
could be withdrawn at anytime before it was accepted, and that no contract came into existence until the canes were actually delivered to the
company's mills; in those circumstances it followed that the 1919 offer
had been validly withdrawn.

In strict law the Privy Council was probably right, but that was cold
comfort to a peasant who had been induced to cultivate his plots by the
1919 notice. He might not have understood the mysteries of part performance, but he knew that he had relied on the company's word. Like

many appellate cases, this one turned partly on English usage – the literal meaning of 'cane' and 'canes', and of 'supply' and 'grow,' matters that undoubtedly would have appeared arcane to those whose usual language of communication was not standard English. Contract cases have a way of being dissolved into a simple maxim: 'keep your promise.' Many of the growers must have felt that the company was being allowed to renege on its obligations with impunity. The Privy Council judgment turned a blind eye to the realities of cane cultivation, with its long periods of growth and its inbuilt lack of manoeuvrability, factors that ensured that reasoning based on cases involving ordinary commercial contracts was bound to favour the millers. The council justified its finding that no contract was concluded until the canes were delivered by pointing out that the growers were not bound to sell to the company; this statement was true, but too simplistic: it ignored the monopoly conditions settled by arrangement among the various sugar-millers, which presented the grower with no alternatives except, as counsel argued, to grind the canes 'with his own molars.' There is little doubt that the Privy Council's decision confirmed the growers' beliefs that some people could get away with anything, that wealth and privilege obscured justice and fair play, and that the whole commercial and legal establishment was out to rob them of their just deserts.

These views undoubtedly would have been echoed by the working population as a whole, especially when the tortuous progress of labour legislation in the territory is considered. Sometimes what passed as a protective measure hid a sting in its tail. This had been the case with clauses in earlier immigration ordinances, which provided for the supply of rations to indentured workers; the inflated prices that were charged eventually led the workers themselves to seek the removal of the provision. The Truck Ordinance, which came into effect in 1920, prohibited the payment of wages to labourers otherwise than in money. Ostensibly, this was a safeguard for the worker, for when payment was made even partially in kind, serious abuse was likely to occur. Clearly, though, the measure was also intended to divert labour from small contractors and emerging middlemen with limited specie to the large planters and other established planters who could manage a money payroll. At other times, the proverbial coach-and-four were all too evident in the framing of the statute. This was the case with the Workmen's Compensation Ordinance of 1926. The stated aim of the ordinance was to provide compensation for a worker who became unemployed as a result of personal injuries arising out of and suffered in the course of employment; however, the test of who a workman was and what the course of employment was raised vexing issues. Moreover, no compensation was payable unless the injury had resulted in the disablement of the worker for a period of ten days; and agricultural workers, the largest group in the labour force, were effectively excluded from the legislation. At other times it seemed as if loopholes were hardly necessary. The Labour (Minimum Wage) Ordinance 1935, which empowered the governor to increase by proclamation the wages of any occupation if he was satisfied that they were unreasonably low, was simply not activated.[14]

Law and Indians

Owing to the circumstances of their arrival in Trinidad, Indians were relegated to a separate place in the legal landscape. The indenture contract defined their rights and obligations not only in the workplace, but also more generally. It was their 'constitution,' but the 'rights' it enshrined had little bearing on the reality of their situation. The predilections of the employer class served to blunt the edge of many provisions that were theoretically capable of safeguarding the interests of the Indians. In addition, recourse to the judicial system to uphold the rights of indentured labour usually proved ineffective in the face of the requirements of social distance in a small and heterogeneous colony, and one affected by entrenched biases relating to status and rank. The Indian view of the legal system was sharpened in cases involving breach of indenture terms, which, considering the ratio of hearings to population, achieved alarming proportions. Through the operation of the legal process the Indians discovered that not much store was set by oral promises, and their own notions of honour, based on being true to one's spoken word, were roughly assailed. In breach of contract cases, the Indians were almost invariably the ones charged with breach; that experience probably confirmed their impression that there was one law for the rich and another for the poor. The increased number of breach of contract suits and the higher incidence of incarceration in times of falling sugar prices suggest that the employers presumably used the legal process to shirk their economic obligations to their workers: an immigrant in jail did not have to be paid, and, on his release, the duration of his mandatory indentured servitude was simply lengthened by the time he had spent in confinement. This was an object lesson in the extralegal uses of the legal process. After a while the courts and the justice they were seen to dispense came to be held in such low esteem that the Indians would often not bother to complain, even about overtly illegal activities on the part of the planters. Thus when some employers unilaterally withheld wages or imposed petty fines for workplace offences, as if they were both complainant and judge, the Indians did not seek to mount a challenge in court.

Not surprisingly, the presence of Indians in the legal system as 'the accused' helped to fashion perceptions of them among other groups in society. Perhaps because their evidence was given under oaths taken on their own religious texts or holy books (other than the bible), it was thought that they had no real compulsion to tell the truth.[15] An imperfect understanding of the obligations imposed by caste membership and a studied awareness of the apparently strong ties to ancestral religion and customs led many judges to suppose that special care had to be taken with evidence given by Indians. In addition, there was a noticeable predisposition to extrapolate guilt from the faltering use of the English language, which until the middle of the twentieth century characterized the speech patterns of many Indians. In these circumstances, it is not surprising that the maxim 'innocent until proven guilty' was hardly applicable.

While doubt and suspicion about the quality of justice obtainable in the official courts were being sown among the Indians, they were making determined steps to resurrect their own traditional legal procedures. This was part of a general process of reconstituting, in the Caribbean setting, elements of Indian institutions and structures closely associated with their religious and social life, a development that was stimulated by the settlement in free villages of Indians who had completed their indentures. Further support for this process was provided by the ending of indenture in 1917. In many of the villages that sprang up on the margins of the sugar plantations, built on land that Indians acquired in exchange for surrendering their return passage and, more often, on outright purchase, village *panchayats* of the kind known in India took root.[16] In transplanting this institution the Indians were constructing a parallel legal process, which served to remind them that the forms of western procedure to which they were officially subject were not without serious blemish.

In particular, the *panchayat* comparison would have convinced them that the official Trinidad courts were not really concerned about finding the truth. The rules of evidence would have appeared mysterious to them, especially if the dispute involved past behaviour or matters of common knowledge, which villagers might have taken for granted. Nor would the adversary proceedings have led them to believe that fairness as they understood it was the goal. There was little place in the official courts for the consensus-seeking approach of the *panchayat*, or for the harmonious resolution of a situation of conflict.[17]

Inevitably, the traditional forum of the *panchayat* was bound to be undermined as state-sanctioned courts came to dominate the legal environment. This was partly a result of differential access to western education and the appearance of class alignments among the Indians. Some disputants, when dissatisfied with the outcome in the village tribunal, simply ignored the sanctions that had been levied. Others began fresh proceedings in the official courts. The likelihood that this course might be followed served to deter village leaders from sitting in *panchayat*; not only might they be called upon to give evidence about what had transpired before them in the informal hearing (which would have raised troubling questions about legal privilege), but they would certainly lose face should the law courts overturn their decision. In one case, which clearly revealed all of these pitfalls, a litigant was able successfully to sue another for defamatory words allegedly uttered while testimony was being given before a village *panchayat*; the defence of privilege was given short shrift, and another nail driven into the body of the unofficial forum.[18]

The *panchayat* was not the only casualty of the inescapable presence of western legal forms (though long after it had died as an arena in which legal disputes were entertained, it remained an instrument for resolving social tensions and as a vehicle for mobilizing collective efforts).[19] Other institutions that were similarly undermined but showed a remarkable longevity were the joint family and the reciprocal caste relations of the *jajmani*, or patron–client system. These were group-based structures, and naturally at odds with a legal system that set great store on the position of the individual. To survive in the new environment they had to acquire a character that was independent of legal support.

Some of the property acquisition in which Indians were involved after indenture was made possible only by the pooling of resources available to the joint family. However, the usual forms of landholding in Trinidad – tenancy in common and joint tenancy – were not adequate to cover the variety of arrangements that could subsist in a joint family situation. There was no way, for example, for the aged parent to ensure that his wish that the family holding remain a single entity free from partition would survive his death. Nor did the law give much attention to purely oral promises to convey a share of property for services such as looking after the welfare of parents or performing the required religious rites after their passing. Widows in particular were especially vulnerable, as were children who had lost both their parents. Those members of the family who were content to rely only on words and family sentiment to secure their interests were always likely to suffer disappointment, but attempts to fix their expectations in an appropriate legal form, where that was available, were costly and certain to generate family feuding.[20] Thus a major legal experience of Indians in Trinidad in the twentieth century was involvement in land cases, where it would come as a shock to many that title which they had regarded as inviolable and rights which they believed were assured were not immune from successful challenge.[21] Like the contract cases of indenture, these too would sully the image of the legal process; such a result was ensured by the law's insistence on evidence in writing, which is a feature of land cases, and by the mysteries of the doctrine of part performance, but even more by the fact that the procedure was not designed to promote compromise and harmony in the family. In western law there was bound to be a winner and a loser, and often what had been won on the floor of the court was poor exchange for what had been lost in the bosom of the family.

The devolution of family property was also rendered problematic by the non-recognition of Indian marriages.[22] The offspring of such marriages were in law illegitimate, and did not succeed on intestacy to the family property. Even in indenture some of the meagre savings of immigrant labourers had gone to the Crown on the ground that there were no heirs in the colony, and that it was virtually impossible, because of the transliteration of names, to trace relatives in India. Indeed, the naming system that western law seemed to demand – a forename (sometimes unfortunately described in official documents as a 'Christian' name) and a surname – created its own complications. This state of affairs could hardly have convinced sons and daughters of the justness of the legal system. The particular situation with respect to marriage spawned a vigorous campaign for the recognition of marriages performed according to Hindu and Islamic custom, which remedied the situation somewhat, though a process of registration was still mandatory. A further step was taken only in 1981, and was aimed at legitimating the so-called common law spouse and the offspring of common law unions.[23]

The caste-based workings of the *jajmani* system involved the exchange of goods and services, typically between a landed proprietor on the one hand and an artisan or landless labourer on the other. Some of the payment for services rendered was reckoned in ordinary commercial terms, but there was a large ritual element. Western law operated to enlarge the commercial nature of the transaction; in fact, the Truck Acts outlawed non-cash payments. In some respects this was a progressive situation, since some of the feudal tenor of the relations between the parties was reduced, but, as in India and as was the case with respect to joint property, the result was the creation of avenues for individual mobility that sharpened alignments between differently located members of the community.

The major difficulties in the encounter between Indians and western law in Trinidad arose from clashes of values. This was revealed in the preference for the claims of capital over those of labour, especially immigrant labour. Also, the law appeared to place greater value on individual than on joint endeavour. In the latter context the Christian bias of the content of western law was fairly obvious, promoting to some extent an 'underground' existence among Indians in which certain laws were deliberately broken.[24] For example, a shopkeeper in the Indian villages would not worry about selling liquor on Sundays, though that was against the trading laws; he fully understood that for his Hindu customers Sunday was far from a day of abstinence, and police efforts to lay a charge for Sunday trading were dismissed, somewhat accurately, as annoying attempts to elicit a bribe. Some Hindu religious men and village elders routinely smoked marijuana in conformity with the demands of polite behaviour and in defiance of the law. Some Indian Muslims and some Hindus married, in their customary rites, more than one 'wife.' Parents took back into their homes married daughters who had fallen out with their husbands, thus conspiring in the loss of consortium, a cause of action that was available until fairly recently.[25] Practitioners of traditional medicine hardly cared or understood that they were flouting some of the laws of the land, while certain practices, such as disposing of the remnants of religious celebrations in flowing watercourses, remained a matter of everyday occurrence.

Conclusion

The discussion of some aspects of the economic and social history of Trinidad in the first half of the twentieth century reveals a pool of disquiet about the operation of the law. Yet the irony was that the emerging leadership of the workers as a whole, as well as of the Indians, would turn to the law to allay this sense of unease. Workers at the bottom of the economic ladder and Indians who might have felt themselves to be on the fringes of the larger society both sought to come in from the cold on the basis of rights and privileges grounded in western law. In the former case this was noticeable in the demands for a legal regime that could foster the growth of trade unions, and in the latter case in the agitation for special marriage and divorce laws and for constitutional and electoral safeguards for social and cultural interests.

This strategy was bound to drive a wedge between the leaders and the flock. The leaders would consistently seek to redress an uncomfortable legal position by the application of yet more law, and the followers would be quick to see the futility of that approach. Nothing in their ordinary experiences was capable of convincing them that yet more law was the answer to their prayers. The law's incapacity to foster any meaningful changes in attitudes among the privileged was all too clear to them. This position was reached at a time when unofficial and informal forums of dispute resolution had been undermined, largely by the official courts themselves. Thus, while spokesmen pinned their hopes on legal intervention, the rank and file were disposed to look beyond that horizon. And at flashpoints in 1919–20, 1934–7, and 1946–7 they would leave the leadership behind and make the streets their arena of dispute settlement.

NOTES

1 Enacted in the 1930s only after a sustained public campaign. The history of law in Trinidad is a relatively underdeveloped subject, but many parallels are noticeable with places such as Guyana, Fiji, and Mauritius, all of which have significant overseas Indian populations.

2 This represented the continuation of a trend set in the nineteenth century. See D. Trotman, *Crime in Trinidad: Conflict and Control in a Plantation Society 1838–1900* (Knoxville: University of Tennessee Press 1986).

3 This is explored in the case of Guyana in W. Rodney, *A History of the Guyanese Working People* (Baltimore: John Hopkins University Press 1981), and in the case of Trinidad in K. Singh, *Race and class: Struggles in a Colonial State – Trinidad 1917–1945* (Calgary: University of Calgary Press 1994).

4 For a variety of reasons, over the last decade there has been a marked change in this attitude. A common sentiment regarding lawyers is expressed in the words of the principal of a leading secondary school in Trinidad, quoted in the *Trinidad Guardian*, 20 September 1991: 'Those who practise law seem to have no idea any longer of the purpose and function of law. Their whole purpose seems to be the preservation of law at all costs, regardless of the common good of the people for whom they were designed to serve ... In fact, it can be said of the practice of the law, that it

has sadly evolved to be one of the main tools in the disintegration and moral decay that is so dynamically evident in our present day society.' A case appealed to the Privy Council involving a dispute between the chief justice and a High Court judge over the non-rostering of the latter to preside in court has severely tarnished the image of the judiciary. See *Privy Council Appeal no 13 of 1993*, delivered 14 February 1994.

5 Other forces were also at work: See S. Ryan, *Race and Nationalism in Trinidad and Tobago* (Toronto: University of Toronto Press 1972), and Y. Malik, *East Indians in Trinidad: A Study in Minority Politics* (London: Oxford University Press 1971).

6 Details may be found in B.M. Brereton, *A History of Modern Trinidad, 1783–1962* (London: Heinemann 1981).

7 See C. Okpaluba, *The Evolution of Labour Relations Legislation in Trinidad and Tobago* (Trinidad: Institute of Social and Economic Research 1980), and R.D. Thomas, *The Development of Labour Law in Trinidad and Tobago* (Wellesley, Mass.: Calaloux Publications 1989).

8 M. Klass, *East Indians in Trinidad: A Study of Cultural Persistence* (New York: Columbia University Press 1961); A. and J. Niehoff, *East Indians in the West Indies* (Milwaukee: Milwaukee Public Museum 1960); and S. Vertovec, *Hindu Trinidad: Religion, Ethnicity and Socio-Economic Change* (London: Macmillan Caribbean 1992).

9 Indians lobbied for various types of constitutional safeguards, from communal electorates (familiar in other parts of the British empire) to schemes of proportional representation. In the end they would settle at Independence in 1962 for constitutional provisions that established various independent commissions, such as the Electoral Commission, the Judicial and Legal Service Commission, the Public Service Commission, and the Teaching Service Commission, and for the notion of 'consultation' with the leader of the opposition on certain matters. See Ryan, supra note 5, and Malik, ibid.

10 K. Haraksingh, 'Control and Resistance among Indian Workers: A Study of Labour on the Sugar Plantations of Trinidad 1875–1917,' in *India in the Caribbean*, ed. D. Dabydeen and B. Samaroo (London: Hansib Publishing 1987).

11 For example, the Masters and Servants Ordinance prevented employers from terminating certain contracts without adequate notice or 'good and sufficient cause,' and allowed the worker to resile from his contract 'in consequence of ill-usage by his employer'; and the Immigration Ordinance stipulated the rations payable to the workers and limited the hours of work.

12 Discussed in H. Tinker, *A New System of Slavery: The Export of Indian Labour Overseas, 1830–1920* (London: Institute of Race Relations 1974).
13 *Samuel Taylor v. Ste. Madeleine Sugar Company Ltd* (1921), Judgments of the Supreme Court of Trinidad and Tobago, vol. 5, 27–47.
14 Okpaluba, supra note 7, at 14–17.
15 A view reinforced by local officials who had any knowledge of nineteenth-century English writing on India, and by the opinions of Presbyterian missionaries from Canada, who from the 1860s strove to convert Trinidad's Hindus and Muslims to Christianity.
16 As defined by *Oxford English Dictionary* 2d ed., a *panchayat* is 'a council of five (or now usually more) persons, assembled as a jury or court of arbitrators, or as a committee to decide on matters affecting a village, community or body.' The term derives from the Hindi or Sanskrit for 'five.'
17 There is a large literature on this in the context of the Indian subcontinent. In a land case from Fiji, a son's promise in writing, made at the instance of a village panchayat, to provide his 'mother with food, clothes, all medical treatments, look after and carry out the funeral rites in full' was tendered in evidence not to concede any legal authority to the *panchayat*, but to establish a dealing in land. The son had made the promise in conjunction with the payment of a deposit and an agreement to pay the remainder: *Jai Kissun Singh v. Sumintra* (1970), 16 FLR 165 (CA).
18 *Sunamsing v. Ramkerising* (1897), Judgments of the Supreme Court of Trinidad and Tobago, vol. 1, 55–60.
19 Especially in relation to religious observances. See Klass, supra note 8.
20 Customary preferences sometimes created trouble. For example, an aged parent might be cared for by an unmarried daughter who discovered too late that all the property had been left to the sons of the family.
21 Litigation in these matters would raise (but not explicitly since the point was almost unnoticed) the issue of equity's role in a non-western tradition. In India, legal reformers had resolved any misgivings in this area by claiming that the application of just reasoning unified equity with the Dharmasastras. See A. Glucklich, 'Conservative Hindu Response to Social Legislation in Nineteenth Century India' (1986), 20(1) *Journal of Asian History*, 33–53.
22 Where problems were encountered, for whatever reason, the property was likely to suffer neglect and decay. A good example is V.S. Naipaul's childhood home, known locally as 'Hanuman House' and made famous in his novel *A House for Mr Biswas (1961)*.
23 *White Paper on Law Reform* (Trinidad and Tobago: Ministry of Legal Affairs 1978).

24 And, of course, among the black population, which this paper does not treat.
25 See S. Daly, *The Developing Legal Status of Women in Trinidad & Tobago* (Trinidad: National Commission on the Status of Women 1982).

6 Asian Customary Laws through Western Eyes: A Comparison of Sri Lankan and Hong Kong Colonial Experience

ANTON COORAY

Introduction

In their colonial legal histories Sri Lanka and Hong Kong provide contrasting examples of the inevitable conflicts between a dominant legal system and the customary usages and practices of indigenous peoples. In both countries indigenous laws and customs failed to resist the force of the organizational strength and claims to modernity of the received legal concepts and structures. In Sri Lanka three indigenous systems of law have survived four and a half centuries of western domination; but they have been subjected to considerable change, mainly to bring them in line with western-Christian views of morality and justice. In Hong Kong, in one and a half centuries of British rule, the customary laws of the Chinese, who make up almost 98 per cent of Hong Kong's population, never flourished and have been virtually annihilated by legislative intervention. In this paper I will explore the factors accounting for the different directions taken by the indigenous laws of Sri Lanka and Hong Kong. The introductory section provides an overview of the customary laws in the two countries as a prelude to a detailed examination of their development in the second and third parts. Finally, an attempt is made to compare and contrast the development of Colonial law in the two countries.

The state of the two countries at the time of British occupation was vastly different. Sri Lanka had a well-established social organization, and its social and cultural values had been subjected to three centuries of Portuguese and Dutch influence. Hong Kong was a hilly terrain with a small Chinese population, unexposed to any foreign presence and without a government establishment of its own. Since both Sri Lanka and Hong Kong were treated as conquered or ceded colonies, their governance had to be in accordance with the rule laid down in *Campbell v. Hall* [1] – that the laws of the colony continue in force until altered by the sovereign. In the case of Sri Lanka, existing laws meant a medley of laws: Roman-Dutch law administered by the Dutch in areas under their control; Kandyan law of the Kandyan kingdom; *Thesawalamai*, governing Tamils of the Northern Province; and Muslim law, obeyed by all Muslims. In Hong Kong the few thousand Chinese people living there at the time of the British occupation followed the customs and usages that prevailed in mainland China.

The indigenous laws of Sri Lanka continued to be recognized by the British government principally because they had been firmly established among the people and recognized by the country's previous western rulers. During the British period customary laws lost much of their vitality, mainly because of legislation and judicial decisions that abolished or modified parts of customary laws considered to be lagging behind the times. The judicial recognition of the right of those governed by a customary law to enter into legal transactions alien to it but recognized by common law also contributed to the declining importance of customary laws. Customary laws have a legitimate, though now much restricted, sphere of operation, and it is unlikely that in the context of a fully representative government structure they will be completely swept away by legislation.

Chinese law, by contrast, has received scant attention from law-makers, judges, and scholars. Hong Kong started life as a British trading-post, a gateway to lucrative trade relations with China, and the administration has taken the territory's continued success as a thriving trading centre as the primary, if not sole, consideration in policy formulation and implementation. In recent decades the government has shown a keen interest in improving standards of general welfare and in involving people in decision-making. But it has generally been non-interventionist, limiting its role to maintaining law and order and providing a healthy legal environment for trade and finance. As Margaret Thatcher is reported to have said, 'Democracy has not historically been the first concern of Hong Kong people. Their first concern has been sound administration and a rule of law with an independent judiciary under which they could concentrate on creating prosperity from their trade and industry.' [2]

In contrast to Sri Lanka, there has been hardly any legislative attempt to codify or reform Chinese customary law, the only legislative activity, starting in early 1970, was to abolish it. There is a paucity of judicial decisions dealing with substantive issues of Chinese law, and there has been no significant academic interest in the nature and extent of Chinese law's prevalence in Hong Kong.

The Indigenous Laws of Sri Lanka

As recorded in *Mahavamsa*, a chronicle believed to have been compiled in the sixth century, the history of Sri Lanka begins with the mythical advent, sometime in the fifth century BC, of Vijaya, who had been banished from India by his father Sinhabahu (begotten of a lion) the king of Sinhapura (the City of lions), in India. Vijaya founded the Sinhalese community (meaning descendants of the Lion) which, particularly because of the benevolent influence of Buddhism, was able to develop a distinct language, culture, and way of life. Apart from the Sinhalese, who today account for about 70 per cent of the population, the close proximity of the island to India attracted several waves of Indian settlers. The Tamil population, mainly resident in areas that are nearest to India, are mostly Hindu and speak the dominant language of South India, Tamil. Their culture and social practices have deviated little from the Indian model. Sri Lanka's infinite wealth of spices and precious stones attracted Muslim tradesmen, mainly from India, who brought with them legal and cultural values founded on the Islamic religion.

With the advent of the Portuguese in 1405 a new era began in the history of Sri Lanka, an era of western domination that ended in 1948, when Sri Lanka became an independent nation. The Portuguese captured parts of Sri Lanka's coastal areas and ceded them to the Dutch in 1656. The British occupation of Sri Lanka in 1796 established imperial control over the whole of Sri Lanka's coastal belt. The British overcame this territorial limitation in 1815 with the subjugation of the Kandyan kingdom in the interior of Sri Lanka, which had repelled previous attempts at invasion by the Portuguese and the Dutch.

Historical evidence of the Portuguese period is very limited.[3] The Portuguese had as their priorities trade and 'proselytising the pagan,' and appear to have introduced few changes to the native administrative structure, preferring to use it for their own purposes. However, it seems that under Portuguese rule the Sinhalese began to move away from their customary laws, while the Tamils and Muslims were relatively unaffected. The Sinhalese laws declined because the Portuguese took no positive steps to promote such laws, and the spread of Catholicism distanced the

Sinhalese from traditional practices that conflicted with Christian teaching. The customary laws of the Tamils of northern Sri Lanka were less influenced by the Portuguese, who held only a small area there and only for about forty years. The Mohammedans did not succumb to western religious and cultural influences, and continued to practise their religion and customs.

Like the Portuguese, the Dutch introduced no significant changes, but used the native administrative structure for their own purposes.[4] However, the Dutch contribution to the legal system was remarkable. They set up an elaborate system of courts: a *Raad van Justitie*, or a High Court of Justice, was established in each of three provincial centres. In each centre a civil court also was established, a *civiele Raad*, to ease the workload of the High Court. A number of country courts, or *Landradd*, exercised civil and some limited criminal jurisdiction, and were established in several towns primarily to relieve civil administrative officers of their judicial functions. Apart from these courts of record, which were structured on an original-appellate jurisdiction system, several Dutch and native officers exercised judicial functions in minor civil and criminal cases. Having established these courts, the Dutch used them to apply their laws as well as the established laws of the natives. Originally the Dutch had pursued a policy of applying their laws to both Europeans and Asians in their overseas possessions, but experience had shown the desirability of permitting the judges to take local customs into account.[5] As a senior administrative officer said in the early years, 'Justice is administered to the Dutch according to the laws in force in the fatherland and the statutes of Batavia. The natives are governed according to the customs of the country, if they are clear and reasonable, otherwise according to our laws.'[6] In pursuance of this policy the Dutch prepared three codes of native laws: *Thesawalamai*, a collection of laws and customs of the Jaffna Tamils; a collection of the customs of the Tamil-speaking people belonging to the Mukkuwan caste; and the Mohammedan Code, which regularized Muslim laws and customs.

The failure of the Dutch to codify the laws and customs of the Sinhalese who lived in the Dutch-controlled areas may be attributed to the movement of the Sinhalese, most of whom had become Christians during the period of Portuguese and Dutch rule, away from their traditional laws. In contrast, the Kandyan kings upheld the Sinhalese laws and customs in the interior of Sri Lanka, and resisted foreign invasion of their kingdom until 1815. While there has not been sufficient research into the application of Sinhalese laws by the Portuguese and the Dutch, Sir

Alexander Johnston, who served on the Supreme Court in the early years of British rule and who greatly contributed to the study of native laws, observed in 1807 that at a later stage of Dutch rule Sinhalese law in the coastal areas had been largely superseded by the Dutch law.[7]

British Attitudes to Indigenous Laws

In 1796, when the British East India Company occupied the coastal areas of Sri Lanka on behalf of the British government (commonly known as the maritime provinces, as distinguished from the interior Kandyan provinces), the administration of the country had to comply with the principle of British constitutional law and practice (recognized in cases such as *Campbell v. Hall*) that the laws of a conquered country continue in force until they are altered by the conqueror. The laws in force in the occupied territories were those administered by the Dutch government, namely, the Roman-Dutch law and native laws; the natives were subject to the Roman-Dutch law when native laws were silent. A proclamation made by Governor Frederick North on 23 September 1799 declared that justice should be administered in the maritime provinces according to the laws and institutions that subsisted under the Dutch government, subject to changes that might be made by lawful authority.

During the British period no attempt was made to abolish the Roman-Dutch law, in spite of views such as that of a senior puisne judge who wrote in 1886 that 'all remains of the Roman-Dutch law should be cut down and grubbed up, root and branch.'[8] The Roman-Dutch law extended its application beyond the maritime provinces and throughout Sri Lanka with the expansion of the British sovereignty; it continued as the common law of the land, governing persons subject to any indigenous law only as a residuary law. However, by legislative intervention and judicial interpretation its scope was substantially reduced. As was pointed out by the Privy Council in 1969, 'Although the Roman-Dutch law as applied in Ceylon under the [Dutch government] is the starting point of the common law of Ceylon, it is not the finishing point. Like the common law of England the common law of Ceylon has not remained static since 1799. In the course of time it has been the subject of progressive development by a cursus curiae ... as the courts of Ceylon have applied its basic principles to the solution of legal problems posed by changing conditions of society of Ceylon.'[9]

Adhering to the principle in *Campbell v. Hall*, the British authorities in Sri Lanka were committed from the very start 'to preserve inviolate to the natives of the Island their local habits, their ancient tenures, distinctions and religious observances.'[10] The Charter of Justice of 1801, which established the first Supreme Court of the island, directed the court to pay 'special attention to the religion, manners and usages of the native inhabitants living within its jurisdiction.'

In 1806 the government succeeded in promulgating two codes of customary law, one on *Thesawalamai* and the other on Muslim law. No code of the laws of the Sinhalese of the maritime provinces was ever compiled, because the Sinhalese were governed by the Dutch law rather than their ancient customs. With the subjugation of the Kandyan provinces in 1815, however, the colonial government became involved in the administration of the laws of the Kandyan Sinhalese. An agreement between the British authorities and the Kandyan native chiefs provided that the British would govern the Kandyan provinces in accordance with the native laws and institutions in force there. The British government, instead of extending the authority of the government of the maritime provinces to the newly annexed territory, appointed a board of commissioners, including a judicial commissioner, to supervise the administration of the Kandyan provinces by native officials.[11] In time this native-British mixture of administration proved ineffective, and the Charter of Justice of 1833 introduced a uniform system of civil and judicial administration throughout Sri Lanka.

The British administration in the maritime provinces made serious attempts to continue operating the system of courts established by the Dutch. However, the judges were uncooperative, and soon the Dutch courts were replaced with courts patterned on the British model. Thus, in the maritime provinces as well as in the Kandyan provinces, customary laws came to be administered by courts staffed with English civil servants and judicial officers. As the system took root, judicial predecent became the most reliable and authoritative source of native law.

Much of native law and the entirety of Kandyan law existed only in oral tradition at the time of the British occupation in 1796. The British judicial and administrative officers' compilation of native laws in digests and commentaries was continued by Sri Lankan scholars. These scholarly writings provided valuable evidence of customary laws and practices that might otherwise have been engulfed by the incoming tide of common law and English-based legislation. As happens in any legal system, the opinions of commentators often conflicted; litigation thus provided a practical forum for testing the strength of differing views on the meaning and effect of customary laws. In making their decisions judges listened to counsel's arguments, but could also draw on evidence from native chiefs and experts.

Even where legislative provisions affecting customary laws had been passed, it was left to the judiciary to interpret the legislator's intention. Since almost all legislation dealing with customary laws was enacted by the British colonial government, much of the authoritative interpretation had been accomplished by the time of independence, and was subsequently almost automatically followed. While judges gave effect to the clear intention of the legislature, they also felt bound to ensure that justice was done. As will be shown later, judicial interpretation of legislation affecting customary laws has frequently reflected the judges' concepts of justice and fairness.

At the same time, any parts of indigenous laws that existed in writing, either in digests and commentaries or in codes, were invariably too generalized,[12] because the information contained in them was collected by Dutch or English officers who had limited experience of Sri Lankan society and observed native laws from their own legal perspectives.[13] This enabled judges during the British period and thereafter not only to fill omissions in native laws with common law concepts, but also to use common law principles by analogy so as to interpret and develop customary legal principles.

The Sources and Application of Indigenous Laws

Indigenous laws continued to exist side by side with the two great imported legal systems, the Roman-Dutch law and the English law. Indigenous laws applied to certain sections of the Sri Lankan population and governed certain legal relationships. If a matter that fell within the scope of an indigenous law could not be resolved by reference to that law because it contained no applicable rule or had been abolished or had fallen into desuetude, the courts resorted to the common law.

Kandyan law applied to the Kandyan Sinhalese.[14] *Thesawalamai* applied to the Tamils of the northern and eastern provinces.[15] Muslim law applied to every believer in Islam irrespective of the believer's race or residence.[16] Thus a Christian Sinhalese could become a believer in Islam and be entitled to contract a Muslim marriage during the subsistence of his Christian marriage, without committing the offence of bigamy.[17]

The codification of the customary laws of the Muslims and Tamils was not accomplished in the same manner. The Mohammedan Code was enacted as an ordinance in 1806, and largely incorporated a translation of the code compiled by the Dutch. In the same year the government passed a regulation declaring that the *Thesawalamai* code, which had been put into force by the Dutch, would continue to be operative. An English translation of the code was later incorporated into the regulation.

In codifying indigenous laws and preparing commentaries and digests, lawyers were greatly influenced by the legal concepts with which they were familiar. For instance, the rule in the Dutch code of *Thesawalamai* that 'the wife being subject to the will of her husband may not give anything without the consent of her husband' is a verbatim reproduction of a sentence in Simon Van Leeuwen's *Commentaries on the Roman-Dutch Law*. This was because the concept of community of property, which restricted the wife's right to alienate matrimonial property, was common to both *Thesawalamai* and Roman-Dutch law.

The *Thesawalamai* and Mohammedan codes were far from comprehensive,[18] and their deficiencies were remedied principally by way of amending legislation. Sir Alexander Johnston, one of the first judges of the Sri Lankan Supreme Court, made representations to the Colonial Office in 1832 on 'Ceylon Native Laws and Customs' and suggested revisions to the Mohammedan Code.[19] In 1872 the government circulated among the chief Muslim inhabitants an expanded and revised version of the code compiled by natives conversant with Muslim law.[20] A revised version of the Mohammedan Code was published in the Ceylon Gazette of 24 April 1875 for general information, but no steps were taken to enact it fully. In 1886 parts of the draft Bill of 1875 dealing with Muslim marriages were enacted.[21] Some provisions of the code imposing restrictions on testamentary freedom had already been abrogated in 1844, with the enactment of the Wills Ordinance No 21 of that year, which enabled the making of a will free from any restrictions imposed by Roman-Dutch law or any customary law. The Mohammedan Code was finally repealed by the Muslim Marriage and Divorce Registration Ordinance No 27 of 1929 and the Muslim Intestate Succession and Wakfs Ordinance No 10 of 1931.[22] This account of the legislative history of the Mohammedan Code is illustrative of the active involvement of the colonial government in the development of native laws and of the part played by the governments in independent Sri Lanka. The *Thesawalamai* code was also modified and improved during and after the British period.[23]

When these codes were silent or imperfect, courts had to look for other sources, such as local customs, to fill the gaps or clarify defective provisions. If defects still remained after recourse to other available sources, judges decided the matter before them by reference to the common law.

Judicial Approaches to Indigenous Laws

At the outset it is important to note that the grant of independence under the 1947 Ceylon Independence Act did not affect judicial attitudes to indigenous laws in any significant way. Localization of the judiciary began early, with local judges sitting in the Supreme Court along with expatriate judges.[24] Local judges were and still are trained in the English legal tradition, and there is little difference between them and expatriate judges in their attitudes towards indigenous laws. English judges serving in Sri Lanka have, as a general rule, respected native customary practices. If in some cases English judges have found customary practices offensive, local judges have equally shown their disapproval of unjust customary laws before as well as after independence. The doctrine of binding precedent has ensured that legal positions established in cases decided during the early years of colonial rule continue to be followed by judges.

However, the fact that the indigenous laws had not been comprehensively codified gave a discretion to judges in choosing what source of law was relevant to a dispute before them. For example, judges had persistently rejected the argument that general principles of Muslim law governed Muslims resident in Sri Lanka *proprio vigore*. In one case it was observed that the whole of Muslim law was not received in Sri Lanka because the Prophet Mohammed had no right to impose his laws on the inhabitants of a British territory.[25] Reference to the general principles of Muslim law was considered appropriate only if they had been adopted by established local custom or if such reference was necessary to elucidate the meaning of a legislative provision.[26] General principles of Muslim law were held to be irrelevant if they were in conflict with legislation[27] or a local custom.[28] The preconditions judges imposed on the applicability of general principles of Muslim law meant that the Muslims of Sri Lanka tended to be governed only by those principles of Muslim law that they had voluntarily accepted as binding.

By refusing to accept a customary law – for example, because it had fallen into desuetude – judges were often able to reject any practices they thought unconscionable. In *Ratwatte v. Habana*,[29] the requirement that an owner of leased lands be carried in a palanquin by his tenants when on a journey was found to be obsolete. In *Siripina v. Korale*,[30] the court, rejecting a landlord's claim that he had a right to mine for gems in leased land without the tenant's consent, said, 'It certainly is extremely probable that in an eastern country like Ceylon, where the attitude of political inferiors towards their superiors is markedly servile, land owners could very frequently carry matters against the tenants with a high hand as regards gemming, as well as other things.' The court held that, whatever might have been done, there was no evidence that such a right was currently in force.

By demarcating the subject areas governed by indigenous law, the courts expanded the scope of the common law's applicability. Both Muslim law and Kandyan law, for example, considered gifts made inter vivos to be revocable, while under the common law they were irrevocable. In a number of cases courts held that where a person governed by Muslim law or Kandyan law made a gift and unequivocally declared his intention for the gift to be irrevocable, such gifts were governed by the common law and valid. In *Tikiri Kumarihamy v. de Silva*, the court observed that 'the tendency of the courts has been in the direction of restricting the power of revocation and thereby assimilating the Kandyan customary law to the common law of the land.'[31] A similarly accommodating judicial approach is seen in relation to the competence of a person governed by customary law to create a *fidei-commissum*, a civil law technique to control the inheritance of property.[32] The increasing use of the common law by persons governed by customary laws is also evident in the choice of Kandyans to enter into a marriage under the General Marriage Ordinance rather than under their customary law.[33]

Judges, however, cautioned against unrestricted extension of the general law to people governed by customary laws. In *Ummah v. Pathumma*, the Supreme Court held that the Roman-Dutch principle of collation, which ensured the equal distribution of a dead person's estate among his children, had no application to Muslims because their law of succession was founded on inequality of shares.[34]

In many cases judges gave effect to customary laws even when they seemed to be inconsistent with fundamental common law concepts, provided that the customary law was unambiguous and well established. In *Non Sooja*'s case,[35] for instance, the court recognized the Muslim legal principle that where a mother remarried the maternal grandmother was entitled to the child's custody, unless the new husband was a very close relative of the minor child. However, in *Lebbe Marikkar's Application for a Writ of Habeas Corpus*,[36] the Supreme Court refused to follow this general principle of Muslim law because it was 'wholly inconsistent with the universal practice in the civilized world.' In other words, considerable discretion lay with the court.

The Impact of British Rule on Indigenous Laws

The preceding discussion has shown the judges' limited scope in reforming indigenous laws, the major restraint being that judges had to apply customary laws if they were found to have legal force. In *Paththuma v. Seeni Mohammadu*,[37] for example, where a Muslim woman wanted to live separately when her husband married a second wife (as permitted by Muslim law), the court rejected her claim for maintenance: 'If an alteration of the law of maintenance is necessary with regard to Mohammadans under modern conditions the law must be altered by the legislature and not stretched by myself.' The legislature had no such restraint, as legislation as a source of law is superior to custom.

Legislative reform of customary law in Sri Lanka began with the abolition of slavery.[38] Dutch law recognized slavery, and Dutch burghers continued to keep slaves into the British period. In the northern and eastern Tamil areas, the status of people of certain lower castes was indistinguishable from slavery. The Sinhalese in the maritime provinces, however, had long given up slavery. One of the earliest steps taken by the British administration was the proclamation made by Governor North in 1801, which recognized as slaves only those who had been enslaved before 1796. Import and export of slaves were prohibited, and rules were made for the fair treatment of those already enslaved. North's successor, Thomas Maitland, attempted to control slavery, but it was left to his successor Robert Brownrigg to take more effective measures. Chief Justice Sir Alexander Johnston had also exercised his influence and persuaded many slaveowners to voluntarily free their slaves. In 1816 slaveowners submitted an address to the British government in which they contended that freeing the existing slaves might make them destitute and suggested a gradual abolition. Brownrigg took this opportunity to pass regulations declaring that any child born to a slave after 12 August 1816 would be a free person. Later in 1844 Ordinance No 20 was passed 'to provide for the total abolition of slavery in Ceylon.' It declared that 'slavery shall no longer exist in Ceylon, and all persons being slaves shall become free and entitled in every way to all the rights and privileges of free persons, and any other law or enactment to the contrary now in force notwithstanding.'

Some of the British reforms in Sri Lankan customary laws were the result of attempts to introduce uniformity in certain important areas rather than to abolish customary laws that offended western views of morality. The Age of Majority Ordinance introduced a common age of majority, thereby repealing customary rules. The Wills Ordinance of 1844 introduced freedom of testation, abolishing the Roman-Dutch and customary restrictions on testamentary freedom. The Adoption Ordinance of 1944 regulated the manner of lawful adoption without affecting any substantive rules of customary law.

Apart from legislation that sought to introduce rules of universal application and to that extent repealed or modified customary laws, legislation
was passed specifically to codify, modify, or repeal customary laws. Reference has already been made to the two early British codes and ordinances
that subsequently modified or replaced them. In relation to Kandyan law
the enactment of the Marriage and Divorce (Kandyan) Ordinance in 1859
and the Kandyan Succession Ordinance in 1917 should be mentioned as
the only attempts to enact any aspects of Kandyan law.

The part played by legislation in law reform may be further illustrated
by reference to the development of Kandyan marriage law and *Thesawalamai* rules relating to married women's rights to common matrimonial
property.

Marriage in Kandyan Law

During the time of the Sinhalese kings and well into the British period,
the Kandyan kingdom was an agricultural society.[39] Most Kandyans were
poor. Men went to work in the fields, and women attended to household
tasks. The rules relating to marriage and to matrimonial rights and duties
were fashioned to suit such a society.

The prevalence of caste distinctions imposed prohibitions on marriage
and sexual relations between persons belonging to different castes. During the time of the Kandyan kings, it was an offence for a woman to
marry a man of a lower caste. The British administration, by a proclamation made on 3 January 1821, declared illegal the 'inhuman practice' of
putting to death a woman who had violated caste rules by having sexual
relations with a person of a lower caste.[40] In *Mohamadu v. Dingiri Menike*,[41]
the court refused to recognize that a woman who committed adultery
with a man of low caste forfeited her rights to ancestral property. The
court observed that while there might very well have been sanctions
against women who indulged in such behaviour during the time of the
Sinhalese kings, there was no evidence that this was the current practice.
The Kandyan Marriage Ordinance No 13 of 1859 and its successors made
no reference to caste as an impediment with respect to Kandyan customary marriages.

The formalities required for a Kandyan marriage varied from region
to region, and depended greatly on the financial and social circumstances
of the parties. Among the poorer classes generally there were no formal
marriage ceremonies. The law relating to Kandyan marriages was modern-
ized by the 1859 ordinance, which was enacted in response to a large

number of petitions and deputations calling for reform. The ordinance abolished polygamy and polyandry in the Kandyan provinces, introduced a system of marriage registration, and provided that no unregistered customary marriage would thereafter be valid.

Kandyan law recognized polygamy and polyandry before their abolition in 1859, though even in the times of the Kandyan kings polygamy had been rare. Polygamy in its commonest form led to an association of two families by virtue of brothers marrying two or more sisters from another family. This arrangement ensured that the properties of the two families remained collectively in the same hands. The practice of polyandry was more firmly established. The brothers of a family cultivated their land in common, worked long hours, and stayed away from home guarding their crops from wild animals. A busy farmer could not give his wife the attention and companionship she demanded. If several brothers married one woman, they could take turns in attending to familial needs and help bring up the children of their common union while pooling whatever economic resources they possessed. As Kandyan society benefited from economic change and education under British rule, polygamy and polyandry lost their significance and social acceptance. In 1858 a deputation of Buddhist priests asked Governor Henry Ward to remove the 'stigma on their race and character' by abolishing associated marriages.[42]

While the prevalence of polyandry might have been on the decline at the time of its abolition in 1859, there is historical evidence that associated marriages did not disappear altogether. After the 1859 ordinance polyandrous marriages continued to be contracted informally with only one of the husbands registering the marriage. Over time, however, polyandry virtually disappeared, and research has shown that polyandry is rarely practised by the present generation of Kandyan Sinhalese.[43]

Kandyan marriage took two forms, *diga* and *binna*. In *diga* marriage, the wife left her family and went to live with her husband, forfeiting the right of inheritance to her father's estate in favour of her brothers and any sisters who were either unmarried or married under the *binna* form of marriage. By 1896, in *Kiriwante v. Ganetirale*,[44] where there was a conflict of views between institutional writers on Kandyan law regarding the right of a *diga* married daughter to share in her mother's estate, the court preferred the view that entitled the daughter to such a share. In *binna* marriage the husband moved into the wife's house, and occupied a subordinate position. The husband had to be prepared to leave if the wife's parents decided to dissolve the marriage, a move for which they did not require the daughter's consent.

By legislative intervention Kandyan marriage became a monogamous union, which had to be registered and which could be dissolved only on specified grounds. The distinction between *diga* and *binna* was retained, except that a *binna* marriage could not be dissolved by the wife's parents at their will. The effect of legislative reform has been to clarify the law while removing aspects incompatible with changing social values.

Women's Property Rights under Thesawalamai

Thesawalamai recognized community of matrimonial property. A husband brought his inherited property to the marriage and a wife brought her dowry property. They both cultivated their land. Any profits they made during the existence of their marriage were known as acquired property, and became common to them. It was not difficult for a judge to accept that the fruits of their labour must be held in common, particularly because community of property was known to Roman-Dutch law. However, the husband was the manager of the common property, and he could sell or mortgage the common property without his wife's consent. The wife was incompetent to give away anything without her husband's consent. The restriction on the wife's right to dispose of acquired property led the Supreme Court to equate the wife's right only to a mere interest in expectancy. In other words, the wife could enforce her right to a half of the acquired property only upon dissolution of the marriage.

The *Thesawalamai* rule that a husband could not give away by way of gift more than half the acquired property was interpreted by the majority in *Seelatchy v. Visuwanathan*[45] as giving the wife only limited rights. According to this decision, the wife could not prevent the husband from giving away their acquired property by way of gift. But if the marriage was dissolved, she could ask for a judicial decree setting aside the gift, provided that she could not be compensated for the loss of property in some other way. However, the dissenting view of Garvin, AJ was that a gift of more than half the acquired property by the husband was invalid, and that the wife could at once bring a vindicatory action. This minority view was followed in a long line of cases, which protected the rights of the wife in relation to the common matrimonial property.

The modification of the customary law of the Tamils relating to matrimonial property did not remove the incapacity of married women to dispose of the acquired property. A strong case can still be made for legislative reform on the lines of the Married Women's Property Ordinance of 1923 (which has no application to those governed by a customary law), thereby removing the disabilities that *Thesawalamai* imposes on married women.

Judges have been unable to liberate Tamil married women from the subordinate position they occupy under *Thesawalamai*. In the absence of research it is not known how frequently Tamil families of northern Sri Lanka place wives in this position, but case law presents instances in which wives have been so disadvantaged. What is perplexing is that the legislature has not passed legislation to make every Tamil woman a feme sole by extending the Married Women's Property Law Ordinance to cover those governed by *Thesawalamai*.

The preceding discussion suggests that the legislature and the judiciary have been active in the development of indigenous laws in Sri Lanka. While certain aspects of these native laws have been repealed or modified in the process, legislation and judicial decisions have at the same time fortified customary laws by formally recognizing and enforcing them. By contrast, the Hong Kong government and courts have been virtually passive observers, except perhaps for a recent spate of legislation that has virtually withdrawn all legal recognition of Chinese customary laws.

Chinese Customary Law in Hong Kong

Hong Kong, a barren island with a population of a few thousand Chinese and a few hundred Englishmen at the time of its formal occupation by the British in 1841, is today an international financial centre with a population of about six million. The history of the laws and customs of the Chinese, its native inhabitants who make up almost the whole of its population, has been one of subordination. Over the years Chinese customary law failed to withstand the challenges of socioeconomic change. Legislative reforms have repealed much of Chinese law, leaving it to apply only to certain land matters in the New Territories.

The formal occupation of Hong Kong in 1841 was facilitated by the Convention of Chuenpi, which ceded Hong Kong island to the British. Neither the British nor the Chinese were happy with the convention, which was never ratified. The chief superintendent of trade, Captain Charles Elliot, who was responsible for making the convention and who had already started the sale and development of land in the island, was recalled. Henry Pottinger, his replacement, succeeded in concluding the Treaty of Nanking in 1842. By this convention the Chinese government ceded Hong Kong island to the British 'to be possessed in perpetuity.'

An extension of the territory of Hong Kong was made possible by the conclusion of the Convention of Peking in 1860, by which Britain secured outright a part of the Kowloon peninsula and Stonecutters Island. In 1898 a further convention was signed, by which Britain secured a ninety-nine year lease of the New Territories, comprising the area north of Kowloon up to the Shenzhen River and 235 islands. The expiration of this lease in 1997 will occasion the transfer of sovereignty over Hong Kong to the Chinese authorities.[46]

At the time of British occupation, Hong Kong was part of the Chinese empire and, as evidenced by Elliot's two proclamations of 1841, Hong Kong's inhabitants were governed by Chinese law and custom. While these proclamations have been judicially recognized as solemn pledges to preserve Chinese law and custom,[47] Elliot's authority to issue them is in doubt; and in any event they were intended only as interim measures.[48] The Royal Charter dated 5 April 1843, which followed the formal cession of Hong Kong in 1842, made no reference to the state of the existing law. Therefore the legal basis for the continuation of Chinese law and custom can be said to be the rule in *Campbell v. Hall* that 'the laws of a conquered country continue in force, until they are altered by the conqueror.'[49]

Reception of English Law and Its Coexistence with Chinese Customary Law

The Hong Kong government took the first step towards modifying the protection afforded by *Campbell v. Hall* to the indigenous laws of Hong Kong soon after it established its Legislative Council.[50] The Supreme Court Ordinance No 15 of 1844, one of the first local ordinances, declared the law of England to be in force in Hong Kong, 'except where the same shall be inapplicable to the local circumstances of [Hong Kong] or of its inhabitants.' This formula, which permitted application in Hong Kong of the whole body of English law (in legislative, judicial, or common law form) received any time, past or future, was amended in 1846 to fix a reception date. A slightly amended section appeared in the Supreme Court Ordinance No 12 of 1873: 'Such laws of England as existed when the Colony obtained a local legislature, that is to say, on the 5th day of April, 1843, shall be in force within the Colony, subject to [some limitations relating to criminal law], and except so far as the said laws shall be inapplicable to the local circumstances of the Colony or of its inhabitants.' This meant that any parts of such English laws (common law or statute) that had been received in Hong Kong before 5 April 1843 could be excluded on the basis of their inapplicability to local circumstances.

This formula enabled judges to decide in appropriate circumstances that pre-existing English law was inapplicable on account of Hong Kong's peculiar local circumstances; in other words, they could declare that an English legal principle was inapplicable because it was opposed to Chinese law and custom. However, the Strickland Committee, which prepared a report in 1948 on Chinese law and custom,[51] expressed a strong view that English law could be excluded only when its application 'would lead to injustice or oppression or at all events to some result that is fundamentally inequitable,' a view that found judicial acceptance.[52]

The introduction of English Law Ordinance No 2 of 1966 establishes that English legislation received in Hong Kong before 5 April 1843 has no legal force in the colony if it conflicts with local circumstances; that English common law and equity must undergo modification to be suitable to Hong Kong's peculiar circumstances; and that English legislation received in Hong Kong after 5 April 1843 and local legislation are operative in spite of any inconsistency with local circumstances. However, since Chinese law and custom were repealed in the early 1970s, the 'inapplicability test' is virtually useless.

What is meant by Chinese law and custom? In *Ho Tsz Tsun v. Ho Au Shin* (1915), it was said that 'succession in the case of Chinese is governed by the aboriginal law, i.e., the laws and customs in force in that part of China of which Hong Kong formed an integral part before cession to Great Britain,' and that 'there is only one Chinese law, and there are no local customs varying it.'[53] But a contrary view was expressed in the 1969 case *In Re Wong Chio-ho and Another*: 'The correct law to apply is the Ch'ing law and custom as it existed in 1843 with such modifications in custom and in the interpretation of the law as have taken place in Hong Kong since that period.'[54] A similar stance was taken in *In Re Tse Lai-chiu*[55]; however, Hogan, CJ cautioned that in determining the applicability of English law several factors had to be taken into account: 'amongst the factors to be weighed would be the danger that a departure from what had long been accepted might itself cause hardship.'[56]

This liberal view, which seems to have paved the way for the development of Hong Kong's own brand of Chinese customary law, experienced a setback in 1990 in *In Re the Estate of Ng Shum (No 2)*.[57] In that case it was held that a Chinese customary marriage in 1944 was valid only if the form of marriage was recognised in Hong Kong on 5 April 1843. Section 7(2) of the Marriage Reform Ordinance No 68 of 1970 provides that a customary marriage celebrated before 7 October 1971 is valid only if it was contracted 'in accordance with the traditional Chinese customs accepted at the time of the marriage as appropriate for the celebration of marriage.' It was held that once the requirements of section 7(2) were satisfied, there arose a presumption of valid customary marriage. That presumption could be rebutted by proving that Chinese law and custom in existence in Hong Kong in 1843 did not recognize a marriage of the type in question.

The court recognized that Chinese law and custom could be modified by emerging local customary practices. However, it was not willing to accept that those practices could replace or radically alter Chinese law and custom as they existed in 1843. Hong Kong courts, by their hesitation to recognize the growth of Chinese customary law during the period of British rule, have tended to discourage the development of customary law. This may be contrasted with the attitude of the Sri Lankan judiciary, already described. In Sri Lanka the courts have not been slow to recognize customary laws as living systems. They have acknowledged the validity of new customary practices' superseding existing ones. Even the fact that a customary practice had been incorporated in a statute did not necessarily matter. For instance, on one occasion the Supreme Court held that a rule prescribed in the *Thesawalamai* code had fallen into desuetude. The court did this by regarding the code as a Dutch not an English statute, for the same reason that the colonial government, rather then enacting the *Thesawalamai* code as an ordinance, only made a proclamation to the effect that the code would remain in force. The court made use of the legal principle that Dutch statutes, unlike English statutes, could fall into desuetude.[58]

It can be argued that differences in the judicial attitudes to customary laws in Sri Lanka and Hong Kong can be attributed principally to the fact that the Sri Lankan government followed the rule in *Campbell v. Hall*, while the Hong Kong government passed legislation allowing Chinese customary law to operate only where English law could be proved inappropriate for Hong Kong. The judges in Hong Kong, as seen above, were reluctant to declare English law inappropriate to Hong Kong, and hesitated to expand the scope of Chinese law and thus make the application of English law more difficult.

Abolition of Chinese Law by Legislation

The Chinese law and customs that operated at the time of the British occupation of Hong Kong did not receive legislative or judicial encouragement to flourish as a living system. But while official backing was absent, the Chinese, especially those living in the rural areas, continued to follow their customary practices. Chinese law and custom governed marriage, concubinage, adoption, legitimacy, and succession to property. As Hong Kong underwent rapid economic change and people reaped the benefits of education, however, the relevance of age-old customary practices became less strongly felt.

Although legislation did refer to and recognize some revered Chinese customary practices, the role of legislation in the area of customary law became marginal. In fact, the most important function of legislation in relation to customary law was to abolish it in the 1970s. The way for legislative action had been prepared by the work of three committees appointed by the government to inquire into the state of customary laws in Hong Kong. The first committee, consisting of seven members under the chairmanship of Solicitor General George Strickland, was appointed in 1948. Two more, each manned by the attorney general and the secretary for Chinese affairs, were appointed in 1960 and 1965 to report on Chinese marriages. The committees made extensive inquiries and produced recommendations for improvement. In response to their recommendations several statutes, discussed below, were enacted in the 1970s to repeal much of the Chinese customary law. The Strickland Committee had been given wide terms of reference. Its mandate was to examine the extent of the application of Chinese customary law and to recommend whether Chinese law should be incorporated in an ordinance or be abolished. The committee was to recommend 'the best course, legislative or otherwise, to adopt in relation to Chinese law and custom in force in Hong Kong.' Its lengthy report explained the nature and scope of Chinese law and custom in Hong Kong as well as possible in view of the fact that there had been very little litigation and legislation on the subject. The committee found that while there was no accurate information on the prevalence of polygamous marriages, 'there could be little doubt that public opinion has come to regard monogamy as the rule' and recommended abolition, a position that had been strongly advanced by the Hong Kong Council of Women. The committee drew support from the Marriage Law of the People's Republic of China of 1950, which had emphasized the equality of rights between the sexes and had prohibited bigamy.

In referring to other areas of customary law the committee did not reject them out of hand. It recommended that customary law relating to matters such as adoption and intestate succession be modified in line with changing social circumstances. It suggested that its report be widely circulated to encourage public response. The committee had been disappointed by the lack of public interest in its deliberations; upon publication of the report, the government received only five replies. From 1957 to 1962 the Hong Kong Council of Women again vigorously campaigned for the abolition of polygamy and in 1958 the Governor directed the attorney general to conduct a fresh survey. Again, there was little public response. The attorney general published his report on Chinese marriages in Hong Kong in 1960; this report apparently received a more encouraging response from the public. The attorney general's committee recognized that Chinese customary marriages were on the decline, and concluded that the custom did not require repeal by legislation. The committee recommended that measures be taken to discourage concubinage, and suggested several ways in which a wife's matrimonial rights could be enhanced.

The third committee, which published its report in 1965, recommended the abolition of polygamous marriages. Having reviewed the work done by the earlier committees and evaluated the public reaction to changes, it concluded that reform of the law would be welcomed by the Chinese community. The government, acting on all these recommendations, published its White Paper on Chinese Marriages in Hong Kong in 1967, and in the 1970s enacted legislation that abolished the Chinese customary laws of marriage and related matters.[59] These amendments, however, left succession issues in the New Territories unaffected. As will be shown later, even that restricted area of Chinese customary law is likely to be swept aside soon.

Marriage

In 1915 it was said in *Ho Tsz Tsun v. Ho Au Shi and Others* to be 'a matter of common knowledge that polygamy is expressly recognised by Chinese law, that the children of the principal wife and those of the secondary wife or concubine are treated alike as the lawful children.'[60] In 1962 Macfee, J said in *Lui Yuk Ping v. Chow To*, 'It is, of course well known that in Hong Kong there is a large number of highly respectable Chinese ladies who are concubines, and I would certainly not be prepared to hold that their state of concubinage was other than perfectly proper, nor that their children, as a result of such union, were other than legitimate.'[61] But this did not mean that the majority of Chinese were adhering to the ancient traditions of customary law. In fact, barely eight years passed before the Marriage Reform Ordinance No 68 of 1970 was enacted to do away with customary marriages and concubinage. Section 5(1) of that ordinance stated that on or after 7 October 1971 no man might take a concubine and no woman might acquire the status of a concubine. Customary marriages contracted before that date were unaffected. Similarly, a woman who before that date became a concubine would continue to enjoy legal recognition. As a result, any children born of such a marriage or concubinage would be legitimate. The Marriage Reform Ordinance provided a mechanism for the preparation and maintenance of a register of customary marriages. A customary marriage so registered could be dissolved under the Matrimonial Causes Ordinance No 1 of 1967, like any monogamous marriage, or under the Marriage Reform Ordinance. The latter ordinance enabled a dissolution of marriage by public notice made by both parties to the marriage, as was permitted under Chinese customary law.

Adoption under Chinese Law

Adoption had a peculiar importance in Chinese law. Since only a son could succeed to family property, it was necessary, if there was no natural son, for the parents to adopt a male person related to the head of the family. The adopted son would perform other duties generally falling on a natural son, supporting the adoptive parents in their old age and performing sacrifices to the ancestral spirits. When a person died without leaving a natural or adopted son, a posthumous adoption had to be carried out to facilitate devolution of property.

In 1948 the Strickland Committee recommended the retention of customary adoption, subject to certain modifications. The committee thought it desirable to pass supplementary legislation on the English model, which permitted adoption by order of the court. The Adoption Ordinance of 1956 provided for a statutory form of adoption. The ordinance, modelled on the English Adoption of Children Act of 1926, ensured that the welfare of the child was taken into account in an adoption. The ordinance was in direct contrast with Chinese customary law and its view that the adopted child should serve the needs of the adopting family. The 1956 ordinance left adoption according to Chinese law and custom unaffected.

In 1971 and 1972 the original Adoption Ordinance was amended to provide that after 31 December 1972 an adoption in Hong Kong could be effected only in accordance with the ordinance. While from 1973 onwards no adoption effected according to Chinese customary law had any legal force, any customary adoption that took place before the end of 1972 remained valid. At present a child who has not been adopted under the Adoption Ordinance is not considered an adopted child for the purposes of the Intestates' Estates Ordinance. This means that a person who has been adopted only in the customary manner is not entitled to succeed to the property on the intestacy of the adopting parent or to maintenance on the adopting parent's death. The legislative reform of adoption makes it impossible for a family to adopt a male for the purpose of succeeding to family property, unless the stringent requirements set out in the Adoption Ordinance concerning the interests of the child are followed.

Intestate Succession

In the Chinese tradition property belonged to the family. When the head of the family died, the property devolved according to customary rules. According to Chinese customary law, the family property would upon intestacy automatically vest in the male members of the family. In 1920 the Supreme Court decided that taking out letters of administration was imperative under the Probates Ordinance of 1897.[62] This meant that Chinese customary rules relating to intestate succession, such as male inheritance to the exclusion of females[63] and an unmarried daughter's entitlement to maintenance but not to inheritance[64] were required to operate in conformity with procedural rules modelled on English law.

It has been said that Chinese customary law relating to intestate succession was in a very unsatisfactory condition. The rules were unclear, and it was common for parties to lead conflicting expert evidence. In most cases, after spending vast amounts of money on litigation, parties would come to a settlement regarding the distribution of the intestate's estate.[65]

The Intestates' Estate Ordinance No 1 of 1971 abolished the Chinese law of intestate succession. The ordinance declared that its provisions would apply in connection with any person (including Chinese) who died after the commencement of the ordinance on 7 October 1971. The ordinance, which was based on Part IV of the Administration of Estates (UK) Act of 1925, sought to abolish the inequality between men and women and to simplify the administration of an estate of an intestate by restricting the classes of relatives who could inherit.[66] Special provision was made to recognize customary marriages entered into before the Marriage Reform Ordinance in the distribution of an estate.

Survival of Customary Law in the New Territories

Lands governed by Part II of the New Territories Ordinance No 34 of 1910 escaped the legislative onslaught of the early 1970s.[67] Such lands are not governed by the new rules regulating distribution upon intestacy. The reason for this exemption is largely historical. When the New Territories were leased for a period of 99 years in 1898, there was a sizeable rural Chinese population in occupation. Upon the grant of the lease, Governor Blake issued a proclamation promising that the landed and commercial interests of New Territories' inhabitants would be safeguarded and that their usages and customs would not be interfered with.

The New Territories Ordinance of 1910 was enacted to ensure the continued observance of Chinese custom and usage in the newly acquired territory. In the early years of the British administration of the New Territories, Chinese leaders, British administrative officers, and the New Territories Land Court played important roles. But over the years the 1910 ordinance was revised a number of times, and the role of Chinese law in administration diminished. The special Land Court disappeared, and jurisdiction in respect of land governed by the ordinance is now vested in the District Court and the High Court. These courts are permitted to take into account any Chinese custom or customary right affecting such land.

The ordinance recognized two important Chinese customary practices: customary land trusts and intestate succession. A customary trust is set up by family institutions or other Chinese associations; its manager may be likened to a trustee. A customary land trust is not subject to the rule against perpetuity. Rules of devolution relating to these trusts are alien to common law.

Intestate succession to land situated in the New Territories is governed by Chinese customary law, which remains unaffected by the Intestates' Estates Ordinance. A recent review of land administration in the New Territories conducted by the government did not address the propriety of the continued recognition of the Chinese customary rules of intestate succession, which discriminate against women. This omission has been justified on the ground that, particularly in view of the statement in the Basic Law that 'the lawful traditional rights and interests of the indigenous inhabitants of the New Territories shall be protected by the Hong Kong Special Administrative Region' which will come into being in 1997, it would be inappropriate for the government to interfere with indigenous customary practices.

In June 1994, however, the government passed an ordinance to end discrimination against women in relation to intestate succession to rural lands. The New Territories Land (Exemption) Ordinance No 55 of 1994, which came into effect on 24 June 1994, exempts rural lands from the application of the discriminatory Chinese customary rules of intestate succession.

Last Wills and the Chinese

Last wills were not popular among the Chinese, because writing a last will was an act of contemplation of one's death, something the Chinese regard as inauspicious. In addition, last wills did not fit into the Chinese family tradition, in which property belonged not to an individual but to the family. If the head of the family was free to dispose of the family property as he willed, he would defeat the elaborate rules relating to intestate succession that vested rights to family property in family members. The ancient Chinese customary law therefore relied on intestate succession to ensure the perpetual devolution of property in the family. However, as Hong Kong society developed, many Chinese began to acquire personal property that could be easily transferred, and to use last wills for disposition of property. The making of a last will introduced an element of certainty, which Chinese customary rules of intestate succession failed to provide.

In the 1969 case of *In re Tse Lai-chiu, deceased*,[68] the Supreme Court had to decide whether English law, which recognized the freedom of testamentary disposition, was inconsistent with Chinese customary law. The court, having found that English law had application in Hong Kong unless its application would cause injustice or oppression, held that testamentary freedom could only be regarded as a sound, acceptable development in the circumstances then prevailing in Hong Kong. The court observed that the making of wills had gained general acceptance, and referred to the 1948 report of the Strickland Committee:

Although the point has never been expressly decided by the Courts of Hong Kong it has been long accepted as a matter of practice that, with the possible exception of a will relating to land in the New Territories, the English doctrine of freedom of alienation by will applies and that a Chinese testator is free to dispose of his property by will to his wife and daughters, as well as to his sons, notwithstanding that by Chinese law and custom a testator could not substantially alter the devolution of his property which would take place on his intestacy.[69]

The court held that although Chinese customary law governed succession on intestacy of Chinese persons, no such accepted practice prevented Chinese persons from making wills in accordance with English law.

The Chinese Wills Validation Ordinance of 1856 had provided that the will of a Chinese testator, made and authenticated according to Chinese law and usage, was valid as though it had been made in full compliance with English legal requirements. The court construed this provision to mean that the ordinance relaxed the rules relating to execution of wills by the Chinese, but did not lay down a rule that a Chinese could dispose of his property only in accordance with Chinese customary law, whatever it might have been.

After 1970 the Wills Ordinance clearly stated that a person could, by a will executed in accordance with the ordinance, dispose of all his property. Thus, even on the assumption that freedom of testamentary disposition is oppressive and unjust, an English-style will is effective because statutes passed after 1843 do not have to satisfy the condition that they are not unsuitable to Hong Kong. The ordinance recognizes the validity of a Chinese testator's will written in Chinese and signed by the testator, even if it is not executed in accordance with the rules set out in the ordinance.

Conclusion

In Sri Lanka the British inherited a well-developed set of customary laws, which continue to the present as living systems, notwithstanding inroads made by legislation and judicial decisions. Indigenous laws in Sri Lanka apply only to certain well-defined sections of the community and in respect of narrowly confined areas of law. Moreover, many people governed by an indigenous law either opt out of it altogether or enter into certain transactions that are governed by the general law of the land. Therefore, while indigenous laws have survived British colonial rule, their ambit of operation is relatively limited. In Hong Kong, Chinese law and custom withered away during the period of British colonial rule. The combined result of this trend and of legislation passed in the early 1970s has been to wipe out Chinese law and custom, except in relation to certain property matters in the New Territories.

In Sri Lanka two of the customary laws began as codes, while the other was carefully studied and documented by British judicial and administrative officers. These customary laws have changed with the times. In Hong Kong it was the Chinese law of Southern China as at 1843 that the British undertook to preserve. In mainland China that customary legal system underwent radical change, making it difficult to ascertain what the Chinese law and custom received in Hong Kong in 1843 had been.

In Sri Lanka the customary laws applied to particular communities in derogation of the common law. If a party to a dispute was able to prove that the matter before the court was governed by an indigenous law, common law had no application. Only when an indigenous law was silent did common law apply to the parties. In Hong Kong Chinese customary law was absorbed into the common law. This meant that English common law was applicable to the Chinese population, unless a party to litigation was able to prove that it was unsuitable to the Chinese. In Sri Lanka it was enough to prove the existence of a valid custom to override the common law, but in Hong Kong, in addition to proving the existence of a valid custom, one had to establish that to apply the English common law or a pre-1843 English statute in preference to the Chinese custom would cause injustice or oppression.

There is no dearth of judicial decisions in Sri Lanka on the nature and applicability of customary laws, but in Hong Kong judicial decisions on Chinese customary law are few, perhaps because of the Chinese tendency to rely on a system of internally operating norms to resolve disputes: 'There was a tendency among people to avoid litigation. They preferred to settle disputes outside the court. Many cases were settled within the family or *tsu*, the village or the guild. Elders and gentry members often acted as arbitrators. Only cases which failed to be settled by these means went to court.'[70] In fact, cases involving customary matters generally came before courts when the Chinese who wanted to do things according to their custom failed to observe procedural requirements prescribed by legislation – for instance, when letters of administration had not been obtained in the administration of the property of a Chinese intestate. This is in contrast to Sri Lanka, where litigation involving indigenous law has often come before the courts because parties disagreed on the nature and application of customary rules.

The British administration in Hong Kong failed to provide a system of amicable dispute resolution, and the courts never came to grips with Chinese culture.[71] In Sri Lanka local judges gained entry to the judiciary at a very early stage of colonial rule; by contrast, Hong Kong's courts have been almost entirely staffed by expatriate judges. Localization of the judiciary, though it has a high priority in view of the impending transfer of sovereignty to China, has been painfully slow. The chief justice remarked in 1911: 'It is an extraordinary fact that the Court of this Colony ... should be entirely in ignorance of Chinese law on any subject which concerns the family life and family law of those who form the bulk of its inhabitants.'[72]

In comparing the experiences of the two countries it is interesting to note that repealing parts of Asian laws on the ground that they were repugnant to the needs of modern times did not necessarily mean that the repealed customary practices ceased to exist. In relation to polyandry in the Kandyan kingdom it has already been noted that this traditional institution, which was useful in keeping family property undivided, took time to disappear. It was shown that when two brothers lived with a common wife, the marriage between one brother and the wife was registered, thereby giving it the appearance of a lawful monogamous marriage while in fact a polyandrous association was maintained. In Hong Kong, while only monogmous marriages are permitted by law, it is by no means certain that polygamous practices have completely disappeared. Recent newspaper reports indicate that Hong Kong Chinese businessmen who commute regularly between Hong Kong and China for business are known to maintain two wives, one in Hong Kong and the other in China.

An interesting illustration of customary traditions that continue to exist side by side with legislative innovations is provided by the importance of family relations in business activities in Hong Kong. It was shown that in the Chinese tradition the family as a unit was more important than its individual members in relation to property-holding. The development of Hong Kong's financial system on the English or the global pattern meant that in business individuals as well as legal entities mattered. Research into the role of families in Chinese business enterprises shows that while incorporation as a company is the most widely used form of business structure, strategic decisions are taken within the family circle. Yash Ghai, in a recent examination of the relevance of familial ties in business decision-making, concedes that

> it is possible that Hong Kong Chinese companies are at a stage of corporate development where the paterfamilias is dominant, but that as they expand (especially in overseas markets) more impersonal rules of organization will become important. It may also be that Chinese firms, although rooted in traditional social structures, find the formal legal system a useful auxiliary ... Hong Kong's role

as an entrepot and a financial centre may also find Hong Kong's developed and established legal system of great value. In short, it may be that I have overrated the role of law in Western capitalism and underrated it in Hong Kong.[73]

It must be pointed out, however, that familial business ties among the Chinese have generally operated within the law, and do not present a situation in which social custom and law are directly in conflict. The only area of concern for the law has been whether such family control of businesses may lead to an over-concentration of decision-making power, engendering malpractices such as awarding contracts to interested parties, in the absence of meaningful independent control. There has been no indication that Chinese customary law plays any significant part in the family control of business ventures.[74]

NOTES

1 (1774) Cowper 204.
2 Quoted in Yash Ghai, 'The Rule of Law and Capitalism: Reflections on the Basic Law,' in *Hong Kong China and 1997: Essays on Legal Theory*, ed. Raymond Wacks (Hong Kong: Hong Kong University Press 1993), 343–65, at 355.
3 For the Portuguese period, see P.E. Peiris, *Ceylon and the Portuguese 1505–1658* first published 1920 (Delhi: Sri Murugu Publications 1986).
4 For the Dutch period, see S. Arasaratnam, 'The Administrative Organisation of the Dutch East India Company in Ceylon' (1963), 8 *Ceylon Journal of Historical and Social Studies*, 1–13.
5 See T. Nadaraja, *The Legal System of Ceylon in Its Historical Setting* (Leiden: E.J. Brill 1972), at 12, where Dutch authorities are cited for this proposition.
6 A. Pavilioen, Commandeur of Jaffnapatnam (at present the Jaffna area) in a memoir left for his successor in 1665, now in the National Archives. Ceylon National Archives (hereinafter cited as CNA) 1/2671, 366.
7 See Johnston's 'statement of all such customary laws as are in use amongst respective classes of natives who inhabit the several parts of these settlements,' submitted to Governor Maitland, CNA 5/79, 44. He says that 'few or no customary laws peculiar to the Cyngalese [Sinhalese] can at present be discovered, because the policy observed by the Dutch has, in general, established amongst that class of people the law of Holland': at 45.

8 L.B. Clarence (senior puisne judge of the Supreme Court of Ceylon), 'The Administration of Justice in Ceylon' (1886), *The Law Quarterly Review*, 38–51, at 49 ff.

9 *Kodeeswaran v. The Attorney-General of Ceylon* (1969), 72 NLR (New Law Reports) 337, at 342 (PC).

10 See Instructions from H. Dundas, President of the Board of Control of the East India Company to Governor North, 13 March 1801. CNA 4/1.

11 See Vijaya Samaraweera, 'The Judicial Administration of the Kandyan Provinces of Ceylon, 1815–1833' (1971), 1 *The Ceylon Journal of Historical and Social Studies*, 123–50.

12 For instance, in 1811 the secretary of state wrote to Governor Wilson, drawing his attention to the need for a 'short and simple code of laws' prevailing among the natives. See *British Parliamentary Proceedings, House of Commons (RC)* 1831–2 (735–iv), xii, 165.

13 For instance, Sir John D'Oyly admitted, in a work left unfinished on his death in 1824, that for want of written authorities his outline of the Kandyan laws and customs might be 'imperfect and liable to many errors.' See C.J.R. Le Mesurier, T.B. Panabokke, and L.J.B. Turner, eds., *Sketch of the Constitution of the Kandyan Kingdom* (Colombo: Ceylon Government Press 1929).

14 Kandyan law was initially thought to be a territorial law. In *Kershaw v. Nicholl*, [1860–2] Ramanathan Rep. 157, a European woman permanently resident in the Kandyan provinces was held to be subject to Kandyan law. Twenty-five years later, in *William v. Robertson* (1886), 8 SCC (Supreme Court Circular) 36, a full bench of the Supreme Court, which did not take favourably to the position that Europeans brought up in the Christian tradition could be subjected to the Sinhalese customary laws, overruled *Kershaw v. Nicholl* and held that Europeans resident in the Kandyan provinces were governed by the Roman-Dutch law. The result of a series of decisions following the 1886 case is that Kandyan law governs Kandyan Sinhalese only.

15 See *Velupillai v. Sivakamipillai*, (1910) 13 NLR 74.

16 *Khan v. Maricar* (1913), 16 NLR 425.

17 *The Attorney General v. Read* (1964), 67 NLR 25 (PC).

18 *Chellappa v. Kanapathy* (1914), 17 NLR 294, at 295, and *Narayanan v. Saree Umma* (1919), 21 NLR 439, at 440.

19 See CO (Colonial Office) 54/123, 250.

20 See *Debates of the Legislative Council of Ceylon* 1873, 93.

21 As the Mohammedan Marriage Registration Ordinance No 8 of 1886, repealing sections of the original code to the extent of any inconsistency.

22 The first ordinance was later amended by Ordinance No 9 of 1934 and was replaced by the Muslim Marriage and Divorce Act No 13 of 1951 (subsequently amended in 1965 and 1969). The second ordinance was partly amended by the Muslim Mosques and Charitable Trusts or Wakfs Act No 51 of 1956.

23 See, for example, the Jaffna Matrimonial Rights and Inheritance Ordinance No 1 of 1911 and the Thesawalamai Preemption Ordinance No 59 of 1947.

24 As early as 1830 Sri Lankans, particularly Eurasians, were appointed as district judges and officers of what is now the Attorney-General's Department. Sir Harry Dias was the first Sinhalese judge of the Supreme Court appointed in 1878, though two Eurasians had by then already been elevated to the Supreme Court. With the expansion of the local bar, it became increasingly difficult for the colonial administration to resist the aspirations of the local community. See P.T.M. Fernando, 'The Legal Profession of Ceylon in the Early Twentieth Century: Official Attitudes to Ceylonese Aspirations' (1969–70), 19 *The Ceylon Historical Journal*, 1–15.

25 *Abdul Rahiman v. Ussan Umma* (1916), 19 NLR 175, at 184.

26 *Mangandi Umma v. Lebbe Marikkar* (1906), 10 NLR 1.

27 *Bandirale v. Mairuma Natchia* (1912), 16 NLR 235.

28 *Sule Amma v. Mohamadu Lebbe Padily* (1907), 10 NLR 109.

29 (1898), 3 NLR 110.

30 (1878), 5 NLR 326.

31 (1906), 9 NLR 202, at 209, aff'd on review in *Tikiri Kumarihamy v. de Silva* (1909), 12 NLR 74. For Muslim law see *Weerasekera v. Peiris* (1932), 34 NLR 287 (PC).

32 *Fidei-commissum* is a Roman-Dutch devise whereby a person could make a donation of his immovable property, specifying that it should devolve on successive donees and permitting only the ultimate donee to sell or otherwise dispose of the property. This devise, which had the effect of tying property in a family for generations, was abolished by legislation in 1973.

33 The legislature had intended the Kandyan marriage law and general law of marriage to exist side by side in the Kandyan provinces. *Sophia Hamine v. Appuhamy* (1922), 23 NLR 353.

34 (1913), 16 NLR 378, at 380.

35 (1930), 32 NLR 63.

36 (1890), 9 SCC 42.

37 (1921), 23 NLR 277.

38 For a good account of slavery and its abolition by the British see Colvin R. de Silva, *Ceylon under the British Occupation 1795–1833* (Colombo: The

Colombo Apothecaries' Co. Ltd 1953). This paragraph relies on the information collected in de Silva's book from archival material.

39 When the British annexed the Kandyan kingdom in 1815, they found a feudal system of land tenure. The kings had granted land to officials and private individuals for significant services rendered, had donated lands to Buddhist temples, or had retained lands to supply the needs of the king. Most people who were landless worked as tenants on lands granted to individuals, and were bound to render free services to the king and to temples. The British, who had agreed to respect the Kandyan laws and customs by the Convention of 1815 with Kandyan chiefs, taking the opportunity afforded by an unsuccessful Kandyan rebellion in 1817, passed a proclamation abolishing the right of the state to demand free services of the people, except in regard to road construction. After passing several ordinances regulating the system of land tenure, in 1892 an ordinance was passed to abolish service tenures altogether.

40 Cited in T. Nadaraja, *The Legal System of Ceylon* (Leiden: E.J. Brill 1972), 198.

41 (1933), 35 NLR 337.

42 See enclosures in No 163 of 9 December 1858, CO 54/338.

43 See Prince Peter of Greece and Denmark, *A Study of Polyandry* (The Hague: Mouton and Co. 1963), 130–57; Steven Kemper, 'Polygamy and Monogamy in Kandyan Sri Lanka' (1980), 9 *Journal of Comparative Family Law*, 299–323; S.J. Tambiah, 'Polyandry in Ceylon,' in *Caste and Kin in Nepal, India and Ceylon*, ed. Christoph von Furer-Haimendorf (Bombay: Asia Publishing House 1966), 264–358.

44 (1896), 2 NLR 92.

45 (1922), 23 NLR 97.

46 The annual government publication *Hong Kong* provides a useful introduction to the history and current affairs of the territory. *The Other Hong Kong Report*, published annually by the Chinese University of Hong Kong, is a critical review of current political and economic affairs. For Hong Kong's constitutional history, see Peter Wesley-Smith, *Constitutional and Administrative Law in Hong Kong*, 2 vols. (Hong Kong: China and Hong Kong Law Studies 1987).

47 *Ho Tsz Tsun v. Ho Au Shi* (1915), 10 HKLR 69. Rees-Davis, J said, at 80, that to apply the English Law to the Chinese family system would be to violate the assurance given in the proclamations.

48 See D.M.E. Evans, 'Common Law in a Chinese Setting: The Kernel or the Nut' (1971), 1 *Hong Kong Law Journal* 9–32, at 13.

49 As stated in *Campbell v. Hall*, supra note 1. Colonies acquired by

voluntary cession, or by cession after conquest, are in the same class as colonies acquired by conquest merely: *Summut v. Strickland*, [1938] AC 678 (PC).

50 On reception of English law generally, see Peter Wesley-Smith, 'The Reception of English Law in Hong Kong' (1988), 18 *Hong Kong Law Journal*, 183–217.

51 'Chinese Law and Custom in Hong Kong: Report of a Committee appointed by the Governor' (Hong Kong: Government Printer 1948).

52 See *Wong Yu-shi v. Wong Ying-kuen (No 1)*, [1957] HKLR 420, at 442–3, and *Re Tse Lai-chiu*, [1969] HKLR 159, at 177.

53 (1915), 10 HKLR 69, at 83 and 77.

54 [1969] HKLR 391, at 394.

55 [1969] HKLR 159.

56 Ibid., at 188.

57 [1990] 1 HKLR 67.

58 See, for instance, *Suppiah v. Thambiah* (1904), 7 NLR 151, where the Supreme Court held that a rule prescribed in the *Thesawalamai* code had fallen into desuetude.

59 See generally D.J. Lewis, 'A Requiem for Chinese Customary Law in Hong Kong' (1983), 32 *International and Comparative Law Quarterly*, 347–79.

60 (1915), 10 HKLR 69, at 80.

61 [1962] HKLR 515, at 523.

62 *Ho Cheng Shi v. Ho Sau Lam* (1920), 15 HKLR 35.

63 *Lau Leung Shi v. La Po Tsun* (1915), 10 HKLR 69.

64 *In Re Wong Chio-ho*, [1969] HKLR 391. An unmarried daughter has a right to receive a dowry. *Wong Pun Ying and Another v. Wong Ting Hong*, [1963] HKLR 37.

65 See, for example, *In Re Tse Lai-chiu, deceased*, [1969] HKLR 159, at 197.

66 The acting attorney-general, moving the second reading of the Intestates' Estates Bill. *Proceedings of the Hong Kong Legislative Council*, 16 December 1970, 264–5.

67 See Stephen Selby, 'Everything You Wanted to Know About Chinese Customary Law (But Were Afraid to Ask)' (1991), 21 *Hong Kong Law Journal*, 45–77.

68 [1969] HKLR 159.

69 The Strickland Committee, supra note 51, Appendix 1, at 115.

70 Ch'u T'ung-tsu, *Law and Society in Traditional China* (Paris: Mouton 1961), at 284, cited in Evans, supra note 48, at 12.

71 Recently a judge of the Supreme Court recommended the establishment of neighbourhood justice centres to help people settle their disputes amicably.

See 'Domestic Rows Need Local Hearing: Judge,' *South China Morning Post*, 28 April 1993.

72 *Li Chok-hung v. Li Pui-choi* (1911), 6 HKLR 12, at 53.

73 Yash Ghai, supra note 2.

74 On family and business, see Siu-lun Wong, 'The Chinese Family Firm: A Model' (1985), 36 *The British Journal of Sociology*, 58–72, and S.R. Clegg and S.G. Redding, *Capitalism in Contrasting Cultures* (Berlin: Walter de Gruyter 1990).

Part Two

DISSORDER, DISSENT,
AND THE STATE

7 Imperial Authority and Colonial Officialdom of Upper Canada in the 1830s: The State, Crime, Lunacy, and Everyday Social Order

RAINER BAEHRE

Introduction

In this paper my strategy is to examine crime and insanity as special-ized forms of popular resistance to legal, social, and moral order.[1] In so doing, I will try to link ideology and social change, culture and behav-iour, and political and social processes. More specifically, I will seek to re-evaluate the nature and degree of state intervention and its accompany-ing socially defined legitimacy in relation to crime and insanity as reflected in a complex of legal and proposed institutional reforms arising in the late 1820s and 1830s in Upper Canada. Two noted products of these developments were penal and lunacy reform: in particular, the Kingston penitentiary and its stillborn counterpart, initially a temporary asylum and then a model provincial lunatic asylum (completed only in 1849) at Toronto.

Such reforms were more than a 'panacea' for social disorder in the colony.[2] They represent what another observer on legal authority has described as important elements in the foundation of modern govern-ment.[3] While they did not solve problems of crime, insanity, or disrup-tions of the social order on a grand scale, these legal and institutional developments of social welfare precipitated between 1840 and 1867 the largest growth in any pre-Confederation government department, in terms of both personnel and capital expenditure.[4]

This reformation in the Upper Canadian state also contributed to a form of cultural revolution. The colonial response to crime and insanity in the era saw not only the introduction of 'rationalized' governance in the form of institutional structures, laws, and bureaucratic procedures, but also 'non-rationalized' governance – the introduction of a new moral code governing the public regulation of criminals and the insane.[5] In bringing into being this new moral–legal world, the colonial government of Upper Canada, acting with the willing compliance of the colonial office through the lieutenant governor, evinced what Paul Romney has described as the implementation of 'bourgeois egalitarianism.'[6] In other words, the state increasingly abandoned a system premised on providential design embodied in longstanding laws and institutions, and sought instead to fine-tune the rule of secular law. In specific situations, this meant implementing statutes and institutional rules and regulations more equitably and impartially.

Such reformulations of authority also came to guide all social welfare institutions almost immediately, and helped in the long term to redefine existing customs, traditions, and social relationships between 'normal' citizenry – the respectable and self-supporting members of society – and 'the dangerous classes' – the abnormal, the deviant, the dependent, and the outcast to whom criminals, lunatics, Amerindians, and the destitute were ascribed. Moreover, in reconfiguring state paternalism, in reconsidering obsolete, pre-industrial methods and views, and then in adopting what were by 1830s standards 'modern' methods, the Upper Canadian state began to operate more impersonally. In the words of the eminent English jurist Sir William Blackstone, it assumed the posture of 'a machine designed to contain the play of adversarial social forces.'[7] As recent commentators on the nature of the 'state' have effectively argued, however, the state must be understood less as a single cohesive political structure or apparatus and more as a process or as series of practices.[8] In this sense, the Upper Canadian state helped to manufacture over time a new 'common interest.'

I reject the view that the adoption of attitudes, laws, institutions, and customs that helped to legitimate and construct forms of social subjection and domination comprised hinterland vestiges of a developing, conformist frontier society. While American, British, and Upper Canadian links in establishing a general pattern of institutional and ideological change relating to the origins of the penitentiary and lunatic asylum in Upper Canada have been noted elsewhere,[9] the vectors of ideological change need to be reconsidered. By tracing and analysing their cultural transmission, I will attempt to place these reform ideas more firmly into the context of an ongoing and truly international discourse. The question naturally arises, therefore, as to which persons or class in Upper Canada was primarily responsible for initiating and promoting reform.

One view posits the colonial office and a ruling oligarchy as hostile towards reform and condoning arbitrary authority, even violence, in their attempt to maintain political hegemony. On this basis it has been argued (I think erroneously) that the divisions in Upper Canadian society along class, ethnic, and political lines somehow dictated or determined attitudes towards social reform. Sean Cadigan, for example, makes this point: 'The military-administrative elites of British and Loyalist gentry stock opposed attempts by merchants, mechanics, more prosperous farmers, and professionals to break into their preserves of political power.' They also struggled 'for limited political democracy, the separation of church and state, and reform in education, public health, and public morality.'[10] On the one hand, the view that political reformers of the day either initiated or stood on the side of social reform while the Tory-dominated oligarchy did not welcome it is untenable upon closer examination of the empirical evidence relating to penal and lunacy reform. On the other hand, several other recent studies pursue quite an opposite argument; namely, that the paternalistic Tories, not the reformers, were instrumental in introducing such changes.[11]

My intention is to help resolve this debate and apparent contradiction by demonstrating the relatively non-partisan nature and largely cooperative effort between these conflicting political factions at least on certain social reform matters. It will be suggested that colonial social reformers of differing political persuasions – Tory, Whig, reformer, and radical – demonstrated a remarkable consensus when it came to concerns relating to such issues of general social welfare. When they differed, it was on questions of detail such as cost, control of political appointments to civil service positions, and funding, and not on the overall thrust of social reform. In addition, the introduction into Upper Canada of a reformed prison system and a lunatic asylum was recognized and endorsed by imperial *and* colonial authorities, as well as by Tories, reformers, and radicals, as not just desirable but necessary. This attempt at social and moral reordering, while reflecting middle-class values and the introduction of strategies conducive to a liberal-bourgeois industrial order, were not the product of some abstract pre-industrial class conflict.[12]

Another related theme concerns timing, agency, and the actual 'growth of institutions' in Upper Canada. These developments are usually placed in the period following the Rebellions of 1837–8, the Durham Report (1839), and the subsequent arrival of Lord Sydenham and his administrative reforms.[13] Increasing state intervention, for example, is particularly evident during the 1840s in the field of education.[14] But interestingly, in the case of the reformed prisons and the penitentiary, the colony had already anticipated various reform measures in the 1830s. These ideals were never abandoned, despite the dramatic disruption and dislocation of the Rebellions and the near economic collapse of the colony. Moreover, it will be shown that the movement towards legal and institutional reform as reflected in penal and lunacy reform, while struggling along in an occasionally disjointed fashion, was overall a continuous development. In commenting on Sydenham's reforms, Charles Buller described the lieutenant-governor as having 'reaped the harvest after others prepared the soil and planted the seed.'[15] Furthermore, the necessity of such reforms as revamped prisons and the introduction of a model lunatic asylum, among others, in promoting social order was reaffirmed by Lord Durham in his investigation of the state of the colonies. Yet these significant aspects of The Durham Report have received scant attention.[16] Sections of the report reflected and helped to legitimate previous and ongoing colonial social reforms, and demonstrated how the state was part and parcel of the restoration and maintenance of moral and social order.

Criminal Law and Penal Reform

Studies of the incidence of crime and social disorder in Upper Canada, apart from those directly related to politics and ethnic conflict, have indicated clearly that there was no explosion of serious crime in the province, certainly not in the districts of London, Gore, and Niagara.[17] This is supported by examining the number and extent of serious non-political crimes in the province gleaned from the table of offences for which Kingston penitentiary convicts were sentenced in the years 1835–9.[18] Nevertheless, although serious crime was not a pressing problem in terms of its incidence, there existed pressures to initiate some major legal reforms of criminal and penal law and to modify attitudes towards criminal punishment. Foremost, by the end of the 1830s the number of capital crimes for which persons could be charged had been sharply reduced, a model penitentiary had been built at Kingston, and the architecture and rules and regulations of district jails were revamped.

John Blackwell has noted that a substantial list of capital offences remained on the books until the consolidation of English criminal law statutes in 1833. The passage of 'An Act to reduce the number of cases in which Capital Punishment may be inflicted' (1833) formally signalled the end of the legal framework of England's so-called bloody code. The code had been introduced into British North America with the Proclamation of 1763, reaffirmed with the Quebec Act of 1774, and finally formally adopted in the colony of Upper Canada in 1800,[19] with only a handful of amendments. This movement towards its reform was apparently initiated in the colony by Sir Peregrine Maitland, Upper Canada's lieutenant-governor in the 1820s. Maitland was the first person to attempt to reduce the incidence of public whipping and to end capital punishment for horse-stealing and sheep killing. For reasons that are unclear, the imperial government rebuffed his suggestions, perhaps because it too remained uncertain as to where to proceed.[20] The actual and profound reforms of criminal law can be credited to the chief justice of the King's Bench and eminent Tory John Beverley Robinson,[21] who described the impact of this legal reform at length in a charge to the grand jury of the Home district in April 1833. In tabulating the previous number of capital offences and those now remaining on the books, he found that with the passing of this legislation at least 121 and maybe as many as 150 capital offences had been abolished. Following these reforms, only some 15 offenses remained capital ones.[22]

The nature of this legal reform and the reduction in the number of capital offences remains somewhat misunderstood. It has sometimes been characterized as a retreat from cruelty and harshness.[23] While there is a small element of truth in this conclusion, the change represented more a recognition that, in practice, capital sentences were most often not carried out. This was the case both in England and Upper Canada, where the juries, magistrates, higher court judges, and ministers of the crown often extended 'mercy' in determining the final disposition of cases. Robinson lauded the historical 'lenity' of the law. In reflecting on the course of the previous forty years, he believed that no more than forty executions had ever been carried out. Eight of these had been for high treason during the War of 1812; most others were for murder.[24] The last execution for arson that he could remember had been twenty years before, and the last execution for stealing and forgery, thirty-five years.

Humanitarianism, idealism, and a retreat from the brutal application of the law were not then the only incentives for legal reform. There were in addition practical considerations, including the view that penal colonies were not of sufficient deterrent effect, that convict hulks were often unhealthy and inhumane, that banishment was too unreliable, and that the system of transportation was under criticism and review.[25] In short, as Blackwell and others have noted, the existing criminal law was losing its deterrent effect, for it imperilled the very survival of convicts for whom penal reformers increasingly advocated a correctional approach, or secondary punishment, over a system strictly based only on deterrence or vengeance.[26] Indeed, some reformers thought of prisons as 'hospitals for patients labouring under moral diseases,' though this was for most an extreme and probably not widely accepted metaphor.[27] Whether Robinson thought in such radically idealistic terms is unknown, but he was cognizant of these developments. In one grand jury address he remarked how the Kingston penitentiary now offered the courts a significant alternative to the implicit terror of former laws.[28]

In understanding the reduction in the numbers of capital offences and capital punishment during this era when relatively large-scale immigration, especially of assisted immigrants, exacerbated a whole host of social problems,[29] one must take into account cultural considerations. The volume of capital offences had increased dramatically under the reign of George III, but his death opened the door to change. English politicians active in legal reform, such as Lord Brougham, Lord John Russell, Wilberforce, Lord Shaftesbury, and others applauded the movement towards abolition of capital punishment first considered during the Enlightenment and subsequently placed under the veil of philanthropy and humanitarianism.

The final source of appeal for persons facing the ultimate penalty in the 1820s was Sir Robert Peel, the home secretary, who had been especially instrumental in initiating the reduction in capital offences. Though he was not a supporter of total abolition or noted for his leniency in supporting appeals for staying executions, Peel nevertheless lamented that the number of capital offences and punishments in England were 'more severe in this country, than in any other in the world.'[30] The ineffectiveness of capital punishment as a suitable deterrent, coupled with the comparative leniency towards criminals in countries such as Holland, Belgium (where capital punishment was abolished in 1829), Tuscany, and Russia, was a source of embarrassment to at least some British penal reformers and politicians,[31] especially when a new alternative in the form of the penitentiary came to the forefront. Moreover, by the late 1820s in the United States, a movement against capital punishment had gained international attention, in large measure because of the activities and influence of the Boston Prison Discipline Society. This broad-ranging groundswell for legal and penal reform coincided well with England's attempts to rationalize its legal system. Thus, in Robinson's words, Upper Canada too had decided to follow an openly 'humane course.'

Reform of the law in relation to capital crimes was paralleled by changes in penal ideology, the rise of so-called secondary punishment, and of course the penitentiary.[32] The penitentiary model had its antecedents in John Howard's proposed reforms in England and Belgium during the late eighteenth century and in the rebuilding of the Walnut Street jail in Philadelphia, but there was little widespread public interest.[33] Also, as more penitentiaries began to be built, there was no single model. Even Jeremy Bentham's panopticon, though an influential model, was only one among numerous alternatives.

The idea of introducing such a prison (and a lunatic asylum) in the Canadas was first raised in the early 1820s by Governor General George Ramsay Dalhousie, though nothing came of his proposal. He suggested a model like the English Millbank prison,[34] but this expensive institution, in existence since 1817, was already falling into disrepute. Then, late in the decade, some colonial penal reformers began to look at several American penitentiaries such as Auburn, the Eastern penitentiary at Philadelphia, and the Western penitentiary at Pittsburgh, all of which were completed during the 1820s and had proved far more successful.

In effect, some Americans had reinvented the penitentiary in the post-Napoleonic era and had brought about a renewed interest in the prospects of successful secondary punishment (especially of longer term imprisonment) in the segregation and classification of prison inmates, and in the use of hard labour, solitary confinement, and religious instruction, both to break the will of the convict and to reform him. Such detailed arrangements in the spatial ordering and in the regimen were embodied in the developing concepts of 'moral architecture' and 'prison discipline.' In the light of a rising crime rate and the Malthusian scenario of a rapidly growing population, especially among the poor during a time of industrial growth and prosperity, the international interest in penal reform was hardly surprising. In this 'age of improvement,' the penitentiary as a refined tool for social engineering joined the ranks of more glorified inventions such as the railroad and steamship.

The residue of the period of marked economic and social dislocation in Great Britain from 1826 to 1835 had made an impact on the Canadas, mostly through large-scale immigration, which more than doubled the population of what had been in many respects still a frontier society. This migration had also resulted in a perceived *relative* increase in crime and other social problems such as sickness and begging. The crime statistics, as previously noted, had not in themselves proved compelling. One must look elsewhere for an explanation of the combined appeal of legal reform and the introduction of the penitentiary. In part, the answer is to be found in the cultural transmission of ideas.[35]

The adoption of the idea of a penitentiary had much to do with deterrence and perhaps ultimate prevention. In a report by a select committee on the expediency of erecting a penitentiary, delivered in February 1831, the chairman, Hugh Thomson, carefully compared the advantages of the Glasgow bridewell with the Auburn penitentiary and recommended elements of both systems. The living conditions at these prisons were considered more humane, in the sense that convicts were guaranteed basic sustenance and more or less hygienic surroundings when compared to those of local jails. Yet the penitentiary was also feared owing to the enforced isolation of prisoners over long periods. Some believed that insanity could result from such harsh conditions and discipline. The treadmill, the tranquillizing chair, and hard labour at many early penitentiaries were by no means mild forms of punishment. Thomson claimed that 'people' in Glasgow and New York had little faith that these institutions actually reformed criminals at this stage in their development, but believed that they did offer deterrence. This satisfied Thomson, who observed that in his mind reform was to be 'only a secondary contention' in any event.[36]

A year later Thomson's tone and emphasis had notably changed. In a more detailed report on the penitentiary's efficacy, which laid the groundwork for its introduction into Upper Canada, Thomson and his fellow commissioner John Macaulay expanded upon those influences that now determined their recommendations. Uppermost was the rehabilitation of the criminal. Whereas Thomson had downplayed the importance of reform in the 1831 report, the apparent success of American institutions had resulted in a reappraisal and renewed confidence in the model penitentiary. The commissioners had also personally visited the Auburn penitentiary, the Mount Pleasant penitentiary (Sing-Sing), the Blackwell Island prison at New York City, and the Wethersfield penitentiary near Hartford, Connecticut. They would have visited others had not their visit been cut short by the outbreak of a cholera epidemic. Thomson and Macaulay responded favourably to reports from several notable British observers, namely, Captain Basil Hall, a popular author who had lauded prison developments in the United States and who supported corporal punishment, and Dr Whately, Bishop of Dublin, a commissioner of the British government's inquiries into the entire system of criminal punishment and an advocate of secondary punishment. In collecting additional supporting evidence, Macaulay and Thomson also corresponded with Colonel William Powers at Auburn and Warden Samuel R. Wood of the Eastern penitentiary at Philadelphia. They received reports from all of the abovementioned prisons and from the state of Louisiana, which contemplated penitentiary construction. Finally, Macaulay and Thomson made reference to 'Observations on the Penitentiary System of the United States,' a pamphlet written by James Buchanan, the British consul at New York City and a frequent correspondent with the lieutenant-governor, who wrote numerous tracts on public issues and brought matters and developments relevant to Upper Canada to the attention of its important public officials.

The influence of the Boston Prison Discipline Society on Upper Canadian developments has been only partially recognized,[37] yet it cannot be overemphasized. Through its vigorous and successful efforts, much international attention had been drawn to American model penitentiaries. Formed in 1825 specifically for 'the improvement of public prisons,' its role grew rapidly. In furthering the cause of penal reform, the society had by 1829 disseminated 16,000 copies of its reports throughout the United States and abroad. Among its practical accomplishments, the society had brought attention to the necessity of reforming the Auburn institution and thereby contributing to its acclaim as a model prison. Despite accolades, by the late 1820s management and conditions at Auburn had initially been less than exemplary; indeed, they had been described as inhumane. The society also furnished prison plans for Charlestown and influenced penitentiary construction at Wethersfield, Washington, and Baltimore. Little wonder that Upper Canadian penal reformers began to look to this world leader for advice.

It took only five years for the idea of a model colonial penitentiary to be introduced and put into planning. The first annual report of the Boston society was delivered to the House of Assembly of Upper Canada in 1827.[38] Discussions among reformers followed, and subsequently legislation was passed to obtain plans and estimates for a provincial penitentiary. Macaulay and Thomson forwarded their report to the legislature late in 1832, and asked that 'special attention' be given to the society's reports. In their view, its members had 'spared neither pains nor expense to accumulate information on the very important and interest[ing] subjects which form the objects of their Association, and who have thus collected and published a mass of most valuable intelligence respecting the penal laws, the prisons, and the prison discipline of the several States composing the Union, as well as foreign countries.'[39] To facilitate interest among legislators, the commissioners now placed all of the society's reports into a bound volume for legislators to peruse.

Not only did Upper Canadian penal reformers follow the society's activities, the society in turn paid considerable attention to Upper Canadian prison reform. The colony's efforts to reform its penal institutions found their place in the pages of the society's annual reports. In 1833, for example, the Kingston penitentiary (still awaiting completion) was included in a long list of prisons described as actively adopting the principle of solitary confinement, an element of penal discipline which the society strongly endorsed.[40] This same report included extracts from the Macaulay and Thomson Report. Mention of this report was significant, because the society had not as yet noted non-American publications relating to penal reform. Upper Canada's activities were joined by a commentary from the London Prison Discipline Society and excerpts from de Beaumont and Tocqueville's famous report which had only recently been translated into English. In creating an international focus and context for penal reform, it appears that the society was probably responsible for a newfound interest in the ideas of John Howard, whose past efforts were being resurrected, debated and lauded, thereby linking the forerunners of the penitentiary with its modern successors. At the annual meeting of 1833, for example, members passed a resolution commending penal reform efforts in France, Great Britain, Switzerland, and Russia, which they stated owed much to Howard's work sixty years earlier.[41]

Although Hugh C. Thomson, an active proponent of penal reform between 1827 and 1832, is generally given credit for the promotion of the Kingston penitentiary, it was really John Macaulay who stood at the very centre of Upper Canadian penal reform in this decade. Macaulay has been called by one biographer the quintessential Upper Canadian Tory, 'an embodiment of the consensus that underlay the political, social, religious, national, and geographical solitudes of Upper Canada.'[42] He was joined by two other eminent colonial reformers, Marshall Spring Bidwell and Charles Duncombe. As a commissioner of the House of Assembly, Macaulay more than Thomson (who had been in failing health, and died in 1834) carried on the investigation, construction, and finally the opening of the Kingston penitentiary.

Macaulay's contacts, especially with penitentiary officials and the society, were many and influential. In 1832, for instance, Macaulay was communicating with Levi Lewis, a chief keeper at the Auburn penitentiary, who on Macaulay's behalf requested plans and estimates for the project from William Powers. Macaulay was already well versed on specific penitentiary developments from the annual reports of the Auburn penitentiary forwarded to him, and from a study on 'Prison Architecture, Management and Discipline,' which summarized the most recent reforms of the era. Macaulay forwarded a copy of the report of the Legislative Committee on the building of a penitentiary to Powers who approved of its findings. The Auburn chaplain, B.C. Smith, a member of the Boston Prison Discipline Society, was also apparently Macaulay's friend. Smith received this same 'able' report (Smith's words) and replied that the proposed prison would be 'a great improvement upon the best system of prison discipline in existence.' Moreover, Smith then suggested to Macaulay that he hire Colonel Powers to superintend Kingston's construction. Smith's 'chief desire' was to forward Macaulay and Thomson's report immediately to the Reverend Louis Dwight, the prime mover of the society, because he wanted Macaulay's plans to benefit from Dwight's 'severest scrutiny and criticism.' While personally and entirely convinced that the Kingston model was a 'well-digested ... most perfect plan, carried out *in all its details*,'[43] no plan was truly perfect, and he promised to send Macaulay the annual reports of New York state prisons and the state's report of the Select Committee of the Legislature on Prisons to ensure perfection of Kingston's penitentiary.

Prior to March 1833 there was initial criticism of the penitentiary project within some circles in Upper Canada, based mostly on the question whether this institution warranted priority over other needed improvements, such as roads. There were also serious concerns as to the sources of the necessary funds. But enough support had been mustered to see the plan actualized. Smith's first plans for the Kingston penitentiary, a modified version of the Auburn plan, were forwarded to Macaulay in March 1833. During April, Powers also spent ten days in Kingston and found the site to be a good one. Dwight himself came to visit the site during the summer.[44] A penitentiary based on a reformed Auburn system was clearly in the offing.

Nevertheless, a new and more vehement opposition to the penitentiary among both Tories and reformers now surfaced. A chief critic was James Buchanan, the British consul at New York, who had several years earlier informed Thomson and Macaulay about developments in the American penitentiary system. He publicly outlined his objections in at least one Upper Canadian newspaper, specifically citing the penitentiary's substantial, growing, and ongoing operating costs, the lack of evidence that the system reformed criminals, the injustice of training convicts in skills that could be used to compete against honest tradesmen, and the stigma carried by ex-convicts, which would hamper their successful reintegration into society. Buchanan preferred to put tax money into other preventive methods, such as Sunday schools. He also worried that the failure to classify and separate prisoners made prisons a training-ground for crime.[45] Except for concerted opposition in Kingston, the site of the institution where local mechanics, backed by some Tories and reformers, engaged in protests to stop construction, Buchanan's criticisms were not sufficient to deter the penitentiary promoters. Whether or not to adopt a penitentiary in Upper Canada became a non-issue after the 1833 report of the penitentiary commissioners 'to organize a system of Prison discipline, and provide for the government and maintenance of the Penitentiary.'[46] The only outstanding issue for Upper Canadian penal reformers was 'prison discipline.' The House of Assembly had agreed to the construction of the penitentiary, although it would be over a year before the prison began receiving convicts. Two years later the provincial government also began inquiring into the state of the provincial jails, and the focus was 'On Prison Discipline.'

Throughout the early 1830s Upper Canadian interest in the Boston Prison Discipline Society's penal reform activities continued unabated. In 1834 lengthy excerpts from the society's yearly reports appeared in the Kingston *Chronicle*, and in the following year, when Dr Charles Duncombe was sent to investigate the American prison system, he also consulted with the society. He and his fellow commissioners were called upon to find answers to questions on the most effective regimen. There was little delay in completing this process. Legislation was passed in 1834, with the majority support of both Tories and reformers, 'to provide for the Maintenance and Government of the Provincial Penitentiary.'[47] Subsequently, on the basis of Duncombe's findings, the modified prison architecture and regimen of Auburn gained final approval over the so-called Pennsylvania system. If anything, Duncombe's findings reinforced the relative consensus that already existed among Upper Canadian penal reformers of all political leanings. Even the mere suggestion that treadmills attached to district jails be used found little support either in Upper Canada or Great Britain.[48]

Like the United States, the only organized opposition to the penitentiary – the most expensive public project of its day – came from Kingston-area craftworkers anxious about the impact of convict labour on their livelihoods and about the inhumanity of its regimen. Despite considerable opposition from these local craftworkers against convict labour, their protests were quieted when the Tory-headed provincial government deliberately and self-consciously appointed one of the workers' own supporters, James Nickalls, to the position of president of the Board of Penitentiary Commissioners.[49] Moreover, Macaulay, the government, and penitentiary officials made it a point to limit the type of work carried out by Kingston's convicts, despite their own misgivings about the exaggerated complaints of local craftworkers concerning the impact such labour would have on their future prospects for employment. Its handling of this conflict was a lesson on how the Upper Canadian state successfully diffused opposition to reform, and attempted to foster social and class harmony or at least diminish potential class conflict.

Parenthetically, there has always been some mystery as to why Duncombe was sent in 1835 to examine prisons, schools, and lunatic asylums. Susan Houston has suggested that 'ignorance, vice, crime, poverty, drunkenness, and lunacy comprised the staples of nineteenth-century social reform,'[50] and Duncombe's recommendations represented a 'package approach to social problems.' It is also widely, though incorrectly, assumed that in investigating institutions, Duncombe represented only the interests of reformers who, having gained a majority in the House of Assembly in 1834, were moving in a different direction from the previous government. But Macaulay, the quintessential Tory, also held to the 'profound conviction that proper institutions, whether they be constitutional, religious, or educational, could not only control conduct but transform men into persons as sober, sound, and respectable as himself.'[51]

Not surprisingly, both Duncombe and Macaulay shared the international belief in institutional methods of social reform which reflected the influence of the Boston Prison Discipline Society and its overall strategy. Such institutions were directly related to one another and to the wider problems they attempted to address. To effect change, an interrelated series of measures were required: changes in criminal law; improvements in public buildings through moral architecture, not only in prisons but in schools and almshouses; the promotion of labour 'not only as a means of support, but as an auxiliary of virtue'; 'unceasing vigilance' by government, and in families, schools, and factories; the protection of family government whereby obedience to parents was enforced; temperance and the better observance of the sabbath; solitude (including solitary confinement for criminals), prayer, and the reading of the bible; the promotion of Sunday schools; and justice, sympathy, and compassion towards fellow human beings, especially women, children, lunatics, debtors, and even criminals.[52] These elements are strongly evident and intertwined in both Duncombe's and Macaulay's reports and correspondence.

When the Kingston penitentiary finally opened in 1835 Macaulay visited the Auburn penitentiary, where he unexpectedly encountered William Crawford. Crawford had been sent by the British government to examine the Auburn system in its own efforts to apply American methods to prison problems. Voicing high praise for Crawford and the efforts of the London Prison Discipline Society, Macaulay boasted privately, in an apparent burst of colonial pride, that Great Britain appeared to be no further ahead, if not slightly behind, Upper Canada in revamping its national prison system.[53] The Kingston penitentiary had already anticipated in its design and regimen what was now being recommended for adoption in the mother country (later to be embodied at Pentonville).

Until 1835 American developments had been instrumental in guiding Upper Canadian prison reform. Thereafter, the influence of Great Britain and the Colonial Office became increasingly marked. By the mid-1830s all British colonies were being asked for information on district jails in their annual Blue Book. Anxious to get its own house in order – Crawford's visit to Auburn was but one example – the Colonial Office began forwarding various reports of a Select Committee of the House of Lords and related English statutes on prison discipline to the colonies.

Lieutenant-Governor John Colborne initially passed along Crawford's *Report on Prison Discipline* to Macaulay. In thanking Colborne, Macaulay informed his overseer that information on the progress of the English jail system had been until then beyond his reach. After these British initiatives, Macaulay began contact with his English counterpart, Samuel Hoare, secretary of the London Prison Discipline Society. In his first letter Macaulay used his loyalist leanings and tact to note that changes in penitentiary discipline had not originated in the United States. The Auburn system, as conceived by John Howard, had long ago become operative at Ghent, Belgium; and at Gloucester the English had practised the so-called Philadelphia system, which Macaulay remained unsure of but supported in principle.[54] The basis for supporting the Philadelphia over the Auburn system probably was that under its regimen and moral architecture prisoners were entirely isolated from one another.

British influence on Upper Canadian prison reform became steadily more marked towards the end of the decade, when all colonies were asked to submit information on their jail systems. The inspector of prisons for Great Britain had been given the responsibility of evaluating the existing state of jails within the empire, and sent his recommendations ('guidance') regarding prison discipline to steer colonial governments.[55] Moreover, Upper Canadian legislation governing the future erection of its jails was forwarded to the Colonial Office, where 'law officers' always reviewed legislation and made recommendations. Imperial law officers urged that the Society for the Improvement of Prison

Discipline in England be given the opportunity of offering suggestions for the Upper Canadian bill before the bill was ratified.[56] In retrospect, Upper Canadian prison reform thus was a product of both American and British influences.

Despite foreign influences on Upper Canadian penal reform, the extent to which Upper Canadian penal reformers initiated and participated independently in these international developments and discourse is unappreciated. Standing on the international periphery, Upper Canadian reformers such as Macaulay, Duncombe, and Bidwell, came to their own understanding of these issues and adapted them to colonial conditions. Macaulay, Bidwell and Dr Thomas Paddock, a lunacy reformer from New Brunswick, were directly associated with the Boston Prison Discipline Society as part of a select and influential group of twenty-one corresponding members, which included, among other affiliated non-Americans, the key penal reform figures of the day: Samuel Hoare, chair of the London Prison Discipline Society; Dr Julius, a penal reformer from Hamburg whom the society described as Germany's John Howard; and G. de Beaumont and Alexis de Tocqueville of Paris, authors of the famous 1830 study *The Penitentiary System in the United States.*

In seeking to ascertain who promoted penal reform in Upper Canada during the late 1820s and early 1830s, there is no evidence to indicate that political partisanship had any significant impact. Even as political tensions mounted in May 1837, the spirit of cooperation and common vision is undeniable. Members continued their affiliation with the society long after Bidwell had fled Upper Canada.[57] After Thomson's death in 1834 and the quick and unanticipated departure of Duncombe and Bidwell, owing to their association with rebels, in 1837, Macaulay continued to spearhead the penal reform movement in Upper Canada. He had been appointed president of the Board of Commissioners of the penitentiary in 1836 only to resign and take up a position on the Legislative Council, where his duties became increasingly onerous and diverse. Yet penal reform remained high on his list of priorities when he became inspector-general. He directed reform of the provincial jail system as part of a general effort to rationalize a number of important government departments in the wake of public criticism against colonial administration, including that in Lord Durham's report.

Macaulay's *Report of the Commissioners appointed under the Act regulating the future erection of Gaols in the Province,* issued in January 1840, reflected the latest developments in British and American penal reforms as evidenced in the use of reports respectively of the Boston and London prison discipline societies. The underlying continuity of prison reform over the previous fifteen years is evidenced in Macaulay's dissemination of the most recent *Report of the Boston Prison Discipline Society* and *the 1835 Report of the Committee on Gaols*, previously printed in the *Journals of the House of Assembly*.[58] The principles of classification, labour, religious instruction, and humane treatment were being earnestly implemented by the Upper Canadian government in the restructuring of its local jails.

This consensus among political opponents is, at first glance, somewhat surprising. To a degree, penal reform can be viewed as an extension of the political and ideological influence of the middle class. But such a reductionist analysis fails to do justice to the underlying ideological elements of the movement and diversity of its membership. Tocqueville believed that penal and other social reforms in the 1830s were initiated by a hybrid of highly motivated, largely upper middle-class, utilitarian, evangelically minded individuals. Upper Canadian reformers appear to have been no exception. They saw themselves as embarking on a mission to improve mankind, not merely on a quest to consolidate their class interests.[59]

The questions raised by prison and lunacy reform were not merely political and economic, but moral. I tend to agree with the notion that state penal policy indirectly supported the economic system by imparting a work discipline necessary in a market economy, and with the notion of the American penitentiary as pursuing profits by means of convict labour.[60] But I am not convinced by the argument that criminal law and its sanctions operated primarily as a class-control apparatus as opposed to an instrument of social order benefiting all classes in effecting rudimentary social order, though usually more to the benefit of the propertied.

A telling document helps to explain the self-perception of these social reformers. In a letter to Macaulay, a friend suggested a link between the late eighteenth-century reformers of the Enlightenment and the evangelical social reformers of the early nineteenth century. Both were 'among the best and wisest men of the age, though of adverse needs, and are the *only* men who have treated the subject philosophically, legally, morally, politically and analytically. What the modern (Heathen) philanthropists struck out in theory, the later equally benevolent and more christian worthies improved upon in their practical applications.' Their opponents, according to Macaulay's correspondent, were few. Despite opposition from some organized labour groups, not a single 'respectable' journal opposed these developments.[61]

What made the Kingston penitentiary qualitatively different from the one at Auburn was its 'moral' emphasis in the form of a permanent and full-time chaplain. This role was regarded as so vital to the success of the mission in 1837 that Macaulay requested the same rate of pay for the chaplain as that of the surgeon, because 'he must attend to the *moral cure* of *every* convict & for this purpose several hours each day is to be employed in separate intercourse with the prisoners. He can in fact attend to nothing else.'[62]

Lunacy Reform

Lunacy reform was in part closely related to the growing interest in penal reform in Upper Canada and elsewhere. Again, the Imperial government and the colonial state played an important role in raising and defining issues and then creating an institution to deal directly with the social problem. Towards the end of the 1830s, in his discussion of the general shortcomings of civil administration in the Canadas, Lord Durham wanted the imperial government to pay attention 'without delay ... to the existing want of any public establishment for the reception of insane persons either in Lower or Upper Canada.' This shortcoming headed his list of complaints about the 'bad' state of the jails, the Grosse Isle quarantine station, the ability of the medical profession in the countryside, and the existing system for dealing with the insane, the invalid poor, foundlings, and pauper immigrants.[63] But the problems and the assumed solution – a model asylum – were by then well known.

Colonial reformers had long anticipated this need, which had also become the subject of an international reform movement. For example, in its annual report of 1827 the Boston Prison Discipline Society had already concluded that 'a Jail is not the proper place for a human being suffering under one of the greatest of all calamities, the loss of reason.'[64] Likewise, the London Prison Discipline Society was directing attention to the evils of imprisoning lunatics in jails. The Boston society's depiction of the plight of the jailed lunatic, repeated in its endless variations, sums up well the content of such criticism.[65]

There is not upon earth a more affecting spectacle than an imprisoned lunatic. In viewing the ordinary inmates of a gaol, our sense of pity is in some degree counteracted by a feeling of justice; but in the criminal lunatic we behold an object of unmixed compassion – an irresponsible agent suffering under punishment – a sufferer from disease the most terrible, without the means which can alone contribute to his cure ... the lunatic is estranged from every comfort by which man is sustained in the hour of affliction; and if, as in the treatment of the criminal and pauper insane, the miseries of disease be aggravated by indigence and neglect, then is the measure of human calamity indeed.

In response to such inhumane conditions, which engendered feelings of pity and injustice, Massachusetts decided in 1830 to erect a hospital for poor and imprisoned lunatics. This project attracted the same degree of attention as the Auburn and Pennsylvania penitentiaries. Receiving its charges from jails, almshouses, and houses of correction, the Worcester asylum became the subsequent model for Upper Canada, and for eight other American states that soon followed suit.[66] But public support for the lunatic was a few years in coming. Even in the early 1830s the society had been preoccupied more with prison reform, prison architecture, and imprisonment for debt. Initially, only Massachusetts, New York, and New Jersey began to address and ameliorate the condition of destitute, insane prisoners.[67] By 1835 public lunatic asylums had been considered or built in Maine, New Hampshire, Vermont, and New York. The mid-1830s proved a turning-point. Nearly half the society's annual report for 1836 was devoted to the subject, and for the next ten years this topic received virtually as much attention as the prison.[68]

Lunacy reform was also beginning to make inroads in the United Kingdom. The days of the unregulated 'madhouse' were over. Conditions in existing lunatic asylums had been investigated by government committees, especially in 1815, and in the late 1820s the plight of pauper lunatics was being addressed. During the 1830s small public asylums, such as Lincolnshire under the direction of Robert Gardiner Hill and Hanwell under England's most famous lunacy reformer John Conolly, began to introduce moral architecture and moral treatment among psychiatric inmates.[69] The proliferation of state-funded county asylums was also in progress.

Newly developed scientific and medical approaches called for insanity to be treated like any other disease. Quaker laymen such as William Tuke of the York Retreat had practised 'moral treatment' for years with private patients. Kindness, adequate diet, hygiene, and less 'heroic' medical treatment (that is, bleeding and purging) underlay its growing acceptance and belief. In addition, the reconstructed lunatic asylums of the early nineteenth century incorporated moral architecture appropriate to their inmates in a style reminiscent of the penitentiary. Like the prison regimen, the regimen of the lunatic asylum was important. In short, psychiatric practices of the 1830s envisioned lunatics being removed from jails or other hostile environments and placed into a humane institution where they were subject to segregation, classification, labour, and religious instruction in an atmosphere vaguely but deliberately resembling a family's.

Calls for lunacy reform in the Canadas based on the model lunatic asylum and moral treatment followed very closely on the heels of a growing international debate. In 1829 Alexander Macdonnell, on behalf of the magistrates of the Home district, was the first to complain about having to support destitute lunatics in the jail and to request an 'insane asylum.'[70] This interest in lunacy reform reflected similar concerns in Lower Canada dating back to the turn of the century. In the early 1820s its Legislative Council struck a committee to inquire and report upon asylums, relief, and cure of the insane.[71] The acceptance of and move towards lunacy reform was surprisingly rapid. In 1830 a grand jury at York recommended the opening of a provincially funded 'general Asylum.'[72] A select committee of the House of Assembly was struck 'to report upon the best method of establishing a Lunatic Asylum.' The first recorded mention of the need for moral treatment of lunacy occurred in the same year in the petition of the Home district magistrates.[73]

Local magistrates had no legal authority to spend district funds. Yet it was not uncommon to find destitute lunatics, without family or friends to support them, and those who had become a public danger or social nuisance being put into jail. Non-violent lunatics without friends or family might also be boarded out by magistrates.[74] In order to meet these contingencies, the House of Assembly passed a statute in 1830 to provide the necessary funding for the Home district jail, and to make it 'a legal receptacle for insane persons,' since harmless lunatics could not be imprisoned without charge. Similar problems in other jails led in 1832 to the extension of such legislation to all districts.[75] Yet the persons supported in this manner were few. In 1835, for example, only eleven lunatics could be found in five district jails in the province.[76] Interest in the asylum cannot be attributed to a growing incidence of lunacy. Throughout this era no more than a few lunatics were incarcerated at any one time in the colony's district jails.[77] But where they were incarcerated they were often disruptive, noisy, violent, and needy, creating a nuisance and a burden for other prisoners and jailers.

The early ranks of Upper Canadian lunacy reformers include some now familiar names. The penal reformers Marshall S. Bidwell and Dr Charles Duncombe, supporters of the political reform faction, were joined by the Tory sheriff of the Home district, William Jarvis, and an unnamed political independent who sat together in 1832 on a government committee to inquire into the efficacy of asylum construction.[78] In response to their recommendations, Lieutenant-Governor Colborne authorized the newly constructed York hospital to add an adjoining building for an asylum, and a foundation was dug. Significantly, Dr Christopher Widmer, who headed the York hospital, denounced the practice in 1831 of leaving lunatics in jail, where 'neither medical or moral treatment can be successfully applied,' and suggested a 'suitable lunatic ward' at the hospital.[79] But the project came quickly to a halt when hospital trustees resisted the idea of admitting lunatics in 1833. In their minds, the presence of lunatics among other patients was disruptive. And in the light of severe underfunding, they worried that magistrates from elsewhere in the province would soon be sending lunatics to York, thereby overburdening the cash-strapped York hospital and the Home district.[80] The House of Assembly then considered establishing a committee to procure plans and estimates for 'an Asylum for Insane persons.' Hugh C. Thomson, a chief promoter who had also been a prominent figure in the adoption of a model penitentiary, was in ill health and soon died. Thus, Duncombe now looked to replace Thomson.

A grand jury lamented the condition of the Home district jail in 1834, and Dr Grant Powell, chairman of the Quarter Sessions, called on the government to remove 'maniacs to a proper Asylum.'[81] Powell was only one of a general chorus of complaining magistrates throughout the colony who urged immediate reform.[82] The cause was advanced once more in 1835. Dr Charles Duncombe headed a three-man commission, which included two fellow physicians, Morrison and Bruce, to obtain information on the subject. In a trip to the United States he questioned governors, officials, and heads of asylums – 'the best sources of information' – in the Upper Canadian government's quest for finding ways to improve colonial institutions. His report reaffirmed the ongoing international interest in the subject. He found various state governments in the process of sending commissioners abroad on similar missions both at home and in Europe, and he correctly observed that 'the promoters of [insane institutions, penitentiaries, and deaf and dumb schools] are now beginning to be alive to these subjects [cheapness, convenience, accommodation, or advantageous application] throughout this whole country [the United States].' Model asylums, such as Bloomingdale's in New York State and the Connecticut Retreat, were found unrivalled in their moral and medical treatment of the insane. But these institutions were well-funded private asylums and thus inappropriate models. Therefore, he came back utterly convinced of the merits of the Worcester asylum – modest in comparison with private asylums, state-funded, and applicable to Upper Canada's condition and resources.

Removing lunatics from jails, separating and classifying them in an asylum according to the nature of their afflictions, and providing an aesthetic, hygienic, and safe environment set the stage for possibly curing insanity, or at least eliminating the evils of a system of imprisoning lunatics that was now being widely and loudly condemned in reform-minded circles. In voicing his support for an asylum, Duncombe was convinced that this end would serve not only humanitarian goals but economic ones by reducing costs, either by restoring patients to society or by operating more cost-efficient institutions.[83] The medical board of Upper Canada, anxious to see a medical school attached to the proposed King's College with a chair in medical psychology and headed by Dr Widmer, also began lobbying the government.

Tabled in the House of Assembly late on 20 February 1836, Duncombe's report reaffirmed six years of thinking and agitation for a proper lunatic asylum. Four days later the speaker of the assembly wrote to the Boston Prison Discipline Society informing them that he found Duncombe's information 'very useful.' In the light of the continuing practice of jailing the insane, he confirmed that 'their comfort, their recovery, their safety, and that of others, all require some provision to be made for them.' Two thousand copies were ordered printed, and the House of Assembly soon resolved to set aside 10,000 pounds, Duncombe's estimate of the cost of such an asylum. The society was notified, presumably by Macaulay, of the 'striking' necessity of extending public relief to insane persons.[84] In turn, it immediately forwarded a copy of the *Report of the McLean Asylum* and a letter from Dr Lee. Thanking the society for its help, Macaulay noted that the province had begun a census that included a count of the number of insane persons in the province. Although the counting had not been done with care, and only 165 such persons were found, using comparable statistics in New England he estimated that 350 was a more realistic figure.

Lieutenant-Governor Francis Bond Head's opening address on 9 November 1836 specifically referred to long-existing problems facing the destitute insane, of 'cases of neglected misery and distress' and the need to provide them with a public refuge: 'I feel satisfied that the necessity of establishing a Provincial Asylum for Lunatics, need only be suggested to receive your benevolent consideration.' The Legislative Council concurred with Head's observation 'that humanity now calls loudly for the institution,' and acknowledged pleasure in working with other branches of government, 'so far as may be done by human means,' to put an end to this 'calamity so distressing.' According to Macaulay, the idea was 'cordially entertained by both houses.' The asylum bill was read for the third time and passed the House, but its timing proved unfortunate as the parliamentary session of 1836–7 'slipped away' without this goal being realized.[85] The most serious impediment was a constitutional crisis that had arisen between the lieutenant-governor, who decided to stop supplies, and the Legislative Assembly. There was no money forthcoming, and the Kingston penitentiary had problems paying its staff, even its warden. But the proposed project did not entirely stall. Despite the deadlock between the government and the House in 1836–7, the collapse of the colonial economy, and the outbreak of rebellion, a committee of the Legislative Council reported within the year on 'An Act to authorize the erection of a Lunatic Asylum in the Province.' The subject remained, in their words, an item of 'great importance and general interest.' The College of Physicians and Surgeons of Upper Canada also demanded an asylum 'for the cure of mental disorders' as an adjunct to the General Hospital, where medical students could be given instruction in 'the science of mental pathology.'[86] In 1838 the House again voted in favour of a lunatic asylum, but the question of how to raise funds delayed the project. A compromise led to legislation, passed by a vote of thirty-nine to one, in favour of extracting a regular small sum from property taxes to build a capital fund. Although reformers like Duncombe had by this time become *personae non gratae,* the committee's arguments were entirely consistent with his earlier proposals. The humanitarian nature and efficacy of a lunatic asylum remained unquestioned, and the committee's report was replete with similar references to the Worcester lunatic hospital, the McLean asylum, and other developments. What now concerned the committee was where to situate the institution and how to pay for its construction and operation. Although the House of Assembly had allotted five thousand pounds for asylum construction, half of what had been requested, the committee was absolutely convinced that this would be 'insufficient,' and it balked. In addition, because its members recognized the need to take 'great care ... to insure healthy air, abundance of pure water, and cheerful scenery,' no site had been approved. Meanwhile, they urged that the government provide temporary accommodation for lunatics, that a commission investigate possible sites, and that plans and estimates be given to the legislature in the next session for deliberate investigation and full funding.

On 11 May 1839, following years of unanticipated delays, 'An Act to authorize the erection of an Asylum within this province, for the reception of Insane and Lunatic persons' became law, and set forth not only the adoption of but a framework for the incarceration of lunatics and for the management of the institution.[87] The site and funding for a model asylum remained unresolved, and it would be another six years before the Provincial Lunatic Asylum opened. In the interim, the colony settled for a temporary asylum situated, somewhat ironically, in the recently abandoned Home district jail.[88]

In comparison with the penitentiary, there was little organized opposition to the creation of a lunatic asylum. But there were continuing concerns about funding. Like the penitentiary, this institution was enormously expensive, eventually costing £75,146, even though putting patients to work, as with convicts, was a consideration. But there were cheaper ways to deal with lunatics. The project was not promoted primarily for economic reasons, though a single, properly constructed institution was conceivably less expensive to operate in the long term than a host of ad hoc measures for lunatics in jails. Indeed, despite the hopes that inmate labour would reduce costs, neither the model penitentiary nor the lunatic asylum made much economic sense. They were and continued to be a capital drain on annual provincial budgets. At best, reformers hoped these more fiscally rational and accountable institutions would improve the province's finances incrementally.

Though the construction of such social control institutions might be interpreted as a ploy by the middle class to acquire or enhance their political hegemony, this group already exercised considerable power because no aristocracy of note nor sizeable upper middle class existed. The lunatic asylum was viewed with suspicion and avoided by some, but so were all hospitals. Otherwise, for the friendless, non-self-supporting, immoral, raving, dirty, wandering, violent, or maniacal lunatic, there was often no recourse but jail. Indeed, most citizens understood little of their condition and treated them with fear, ridicule, and even brutality. This abuse and unwillingness to care for lunatics contributed to the need for state intervention. No, the lunatic asylum was welcomed for other reasons than economic self-interest, emergent capitalism, or class hegemony. It was introduced as a possibly curative, preventative, and humane instrument that belonged in any civilized society and that promoted social harmony. Few promoters in this era could have anticipated its inherent, long-term dehumanizing qualities or its limited effectiveness.

Understandably, there is a tendency to view issues of poverty, crime, sickness, and insanity as qualitatively different in nature, or to group them together under the umbrella of social welfare concerns. In the minds of the 1830s social reformer, and even among politicians and others of influence who lamented the apparent tenuousness of the existing social order, these were concerns at the core of collective stability and security. In Tom Brown's words, 'lunacy reform reflected not only growing concern about the pauper insane and the cost of their maintenance but a deeper and more generalized anxiety and fear about the swelling ranks of the urban poor and ultimately about the state of the Upper Canadian social order itself.'[89] Such sometimes exaggerated anxieties stemmed from rapid social and economic change, the presence of growing numbers of strangers, the declining legitimacy of traditional moral and political order and its accompanying institutions, the apparent crumbling of the family, and other apprehensions. Yet these concerns were not exclusive to Upper Canada; they were also voiced during these years in the United States, Great Britain, and France.[90]

This argument, however, needs to be modified in at least two ways. First, officials were concerned not just about the urban poor, but about the rural poor. Second, it was not that 'Upper Canada appeared to be a society in dissolution in the 1830s,'[91] nor did contemporaries consider it to be. But by virtue of unprecedented levels of immigration, of which a sizeable number were paupers,[92] traditional institutions and practices were no longer effectively able to contain well-recognized existing problems. Apart from political and some class and ethnic tensions, these social concerns, it was feared, could seriously disrupt the harmony of the province if left unregulated. To ignore such problems when new institutional solutions presented themselves was unconscionable to those reformers imbued with an utilitarian or evangelical spirit. Suddenly there were clearly recognized opportunities for humanitarian expression, 'improvement' in social morality, and the overall administration of the state. The underlying issue was not possible dissolution, but how to prevent the erosion of the social order and how to control change.

In the months immediately preceding the outbreak of rebellion. Sir Francis Bond Head was clearly preoccupied with Upper Canadian social and economic problems. His prescription was the following. First, Upper Canada should not follow the lead of American republican democracy. 'We will not multilate the British constitution by concessions to democracy.' he wrote. Second, the Canadas would not be retained 'by force of arms.' Rather, Bond Head suggested, 'let us govern by moral power and not by military force; (i.e. let's clap the padlock on the mind).' This strategy would render 'a splendid moral triumph.'[93] Imperial and colonial authorities were unable to implement what *The Annual Register* described as Sir Francis' 'mystic maxims,' yet his pragmatic prescription was shared by other leading authorities.

Conclusion

The ideas of 'responsible government and legislative union' are widely viewed as the 'outstanding' recommendations of Lord Durham's report.[94] Other significant aspects of the full report should not be forgotten. Durham's 'task' in the aftermath of the Rebellions of Upper and Lower Canada of 1837–8 was to provide 'for the adjustment of questions affecting the very "form and administration of Civil Government." '[95] Consideration of topics such as poor relief, criminal administration and justice, and relief for lunatics did not escape his notice, and played a consequential role in his overall recommendations.

In acknowledging that a 'state of disorder' existed in the British North American colonies, Durham considered 'successful rebellion as the least danger in prospect.' Rebellion, he was convinced, could be crushed when necessary by 'enlisting one part of the population against the other, and of garrisoning the Canadas with regular troops sufficient to awe all internal enemies.' Equally important to Durham was the resolution of internal discontent and social disorder, and the establishment of 'a good and durable system of government' in which 'a good system of municipal institutions' was deemed essential.[96] The term 'municipal', as defined by Charles Buller, chief commissioner under Durham, meant 'in its largest sense ... every matter that may be properly submitted to local or municipal management.'

Chief among Durham's and Buller's concerns about municipal government were 'internal communication, the encouragement of industry, and the repression of crime.' This category encompassed police management, the nature of the magistracy, the lower levels of civil and criminal jurisdiction, and the 'general provision for the poor ... the system which has been established for the general relief of destitution and the suppression of mendicancy and vagrancy.'[97] What particularly vexed and disturbed them, for example, was the placement of destitute insane persons into local jails. Thus they recommended the construction of lunatic asylums, 'conducted on the humane and enlightened principles,' as in Europe.[98] To Durham, Buller, and their fellow investigator Edward Gibbon Wakefield, social disorder, poverty, crime, and lunacy were intimately related, and the British North American colonial governments needed to deal with all such matters in a more comprehensive fashion. In the case of Upper Canada and other colonies, the report was reaffirming, not initiating, what had been widely recognized and discussed as necessary social reforms.

In describing the state and the social process, Fernand Braudel states that in traditional European society, 'the mass of society ... was enclosed in the net of the established order. If the masses became too restive, the mesh was reinforced or tightened, or new ways of stretching it were devised.' The evolution of the Upper Canadian state during the 1830s can easily be seen in the manner envisioned by Braudel, as reinforcing and tightening the net and then developing alternative methods of maintaining a semblance of social harmony. In the casting of this net, crime and lunacy were handled neither in a crudely partisan nor in a formally political manner. Upper Canadian social reformers, a diverse group, appeared to have worked mostly in concert – paternalistically – hoping thereby to maintain a peaceful though inherently unequal social order. Further, one of the state's main tasks, Braudel writes, was 'to secure obedience, to gain for itself the monopoly of the use of force in a given society, neutralizing all the possible challenges inside it and replacing them with what Max Weber called "legitimate violence." '[99]

An imperial *and* a colonial preoccupation, social welfare in the broadest sense of the word necessarily employed this form of 'violence' against the criminal, lunatic, beggar, social nuisance, dissolute, and grievously malcontent. In this context the reformed role of the courts, magistrates, local officials, the Kingston penitentiary, district jails, the call for a lunatic asylum, legal and penal reforms, new laws governing social order, and the expansion of authority in the form of municipal police forces and a secret service can all be seen as products of a discourse in the 1830s that engaged the metropole and the hinterland. In the process some power shifted from individuals or groups – for example, from the lieutenant-governor or the Family Compact – to less personal forms. These forms reflected in different ways in the newly founded reform institutions, the rule of law, bourgeois egalitarianism, and, in general, the decentralization of power.

In the light of these changing mechanisms in the exercise of power, Upper Canadian reformers did not intentionally promote the hegemony of any single class (though the underlying ethos may have been middle-class) or privileged group.[100] They sought to create a mode of authority applicable to all classes by means of the depersonalization of power, as indicated in the legislation governing the management of both the penitentiary and the lunatic asylum. This structural shift in tradition and custom represents the birth of a technocratic state regulated by politicians and reformers. In their minds, they were protecting the public good, all private property, and individual rights, while fostering more humane attitudes towards criminals and lunatics. These beliefs and strategies appear not to have been a devious method for increasing authoritarian or class control; their intentions were stated explicitly.

In short, Braudel's depiction of the state as 'a looming presence, the coming together of many things,' rings true. On the basis of our colonial experience, the state became a more impersonal tool, a strategy by which to institutionalize the formative values of an emergent liberal capitalist society[101] and a changing moral and political economy. Institutional reformers aimed to create a new social and political consensus without endangering the relative and fragile stability in which they lived and which the past had provided for them. Criminals, paupers, and lunatics conceivably could arise from any class. If these classes of society were allowed to increase unchecked, they were potentially, and especially in their unpredictability and steadily increasing numbers, as dangerous to the wellbeing of local communities and society at large as any political radical or disaffected member of the labouring classes.

NOTES

1 Greg Marquis, 'Doing Justice to "British Justice": Law, Ideology and Canadian Historiography,' in *Canadian Perspectives on Law and Society; Issues in Legal History*, ed. W. Wesley Pue and Barry Wright (Ottawa: Carleton University Press 1988), 60.

2 Sean T. Cadigan, 'Paternalism and Politics: Sir Francis Bond Head, the Orange Order, and the Election of 1836' (1991), 72:3 *Canadian Historical Review*, 319–47, especially at 323.

3 R.C. Macleod, ed. *Lawful Authority: Readings on the History of Criminal Justice in Canada* (Toronto: Copp Clark Pittman 1988), 2.

4 See figures in J.E. Hodgetts, *Pioneer Public Service: An Administrative History of the United Canadas, 1841–1867* (Toronto: University of Toronto Press 1955), 36; Richard B. Splane, *Social Welfare in Ontario, 1791–1893; A Study of Public Welfare Administration* (Toronto: University of Toronto Press 1965), 282.

5 These terms are introduced in a discussion of education and the state in Bruce Curtis, *True Government by Choice Men? Inspection, Education, and*

State Formation in Canada West (Toronto: University of Toronto Press 1992), 175.

6 Paul Romney, 'From the Rule of Law to Responsible Government: Ontario Political Culture and the Origins of Canadian Statism' (1988), *Historical Papers*, 86–119, especially at 112–13.

7 Cited ibid., at 112–13. This era, apart from its reformist thrust, has also been described as 'the age of the mechanical engineer' and that of the rise of applied science. On the panopticon, see Michel Foucault, *Discipline and Punish: The Birth of the Prison* (New York: Pantheon Books 1978), 195–230.

8 For example, see Philip Corrigan and Derek Sayer, *The Great Arch: English State Formation as Cultural Revolution* (Oxford: Basil Blackwell 1985), 1–14; Philip Abrams, 'Notes on the Difficulty of Studying the State [1977]' (1988), 1:1 *Journal of Historical Sociology*, 58–89.

9 An early study of the relationship between crime, lunacy, poverty, and education is found in Susan Houston, 'Politics, Schools, and Social Change in Upper Canada' (1972), 53 *Canadian Historical Review*, 249–71.

10 Cadigan, supra note 2, at 323.

11 Russell Smandych, 'Beware of the "Evil American Monster": Upper Canadian Views on the Need for a Penitentiary, 1830–1834' (1991), *Canadian Journal of Criminology*, 125–47; Peter Oliver, 'From Jails to Penitentiary: The Demise of Community Corrections in Early Ontario' (1984), 4 *Correctional Options*, 4–10.

12 Bryan D. Palmer, *Working-Class Experience; The Rise and Reconstitution of Canadian Labour, 1800–1980* (Toronto and Vancouver: Butterworths 1983), 7–59.

13 Allan Greer and Ian Radforth, eds, *Colonial Leviathan; State Formation in Mid-Nineteenth-Century Canada* (Toronto: University of Toronto Press 1992), 11. In the same volume, see Ian Radforth, 'Sydenham and Utilitarian Reform,' 64–102; and Hodgetts, supra note 4, at 10–11.

14 Curtis, supra note 5; Susan E. Houston and Alison Prentice, *Schooling and Scholars in Nineteenth-Century Ontario* (Toronto: University of Toronto Press 1988), 97–123.

15 Hodgetts, supra note 4, at 33.

16 Philip A. Buckner, *The Transition to Responsible Government; British Policy in British North America, 1815–1850* (Westport, Conn., and London: Greenwood Press 1985), 250–90; Ged Martin, 'Attacking the Durham Myth: Seventeen Years On' (1990), 25:1 *Journal of Canadian Studies*, 39–59.

17 John D. Blackwell, 'Crime in the London District, 1828–1837: A Case Study of the Effect of the 1833 Reform in Upper Canadian Penal Law,' in *Historical Essays on Upper Canada: New Perspectives*, eds. J.K. Johnson and Bruce G. Wilson (Ottawa: Carleton University Press 1989), 555–91; John C. Weaver,

'Crime, Public Order, and Repression: The Gore District in Upheaval, 1832–1851,' in Macleod, supra note 3, at 22–48; Ann McEwen, 'Crime in the Niagara District, 1828–1851' MA thesis, University of Guelph (1987).

18 Annual Reports of the Inspectors of the Provincial Penitentiary, *Appendix to the Journals of the House of Assembly* (1835–40).

19 Blackwell, supra note 17, at 566.

20 Francis M. Quealey, 'The Administration of Sir Peregrine Maitland, Lieutenant–Governor of Upper Canada' Ph.D. thesis, University of Toronto (1968), 81.

21 Desmond H. Brown, *The Genesis of the Canadian Criminal Code of 1892* (Toronto: The Osgoode Society 1989), 18–19, 38–56. For background on Robinson, see Patrick Brode, *Sir John Beverley Robinson: Bone and Sinew of the Compact* (Toronto: The Osgoode Society 1984).

22 Statute 3d. Wm. IV, Chapt. 4. Relating To Capital Offence; with an exposition of its Provisions, in a charge of Chief Justice Robinson, to the Grand Jury of the Home District (York: April 1833), 28–34. For a comparison with other British North American colonies, see Jim Phillips. 'The Administration of the Royal Pardon in Nova Scotia, 1749–1815' (1992), 42 *University of Toronto Law Journal.* 1–49, and ' "Securing Obedience to Necessary Laws": The Criminal Law in Eighteenth-Century Nova Scotia,' (1993) *Nova Scotia Historical Review,* 87–124.

23 J.M. Beattie, *Attitudes Towards Crime and Punishment in Upper Canada, 1830–1850: A Documentary Study* (Toronto: Centre of Criminology, University of Toronto 1977), 8–13; Rainer Baehre, 'Origins of the Penitentiary System in Upper Canada' (1977), 69 *Ontario History,* 185–207.

24 Supra note 22, at 36.

25 A.G.L. Shaw, *Convicts and the Colonies: A Study of Penal Transportation from Great Britain and Ireland to Australia and other parts of the British Empire* (Melbourne: Melbourne University Press 1977), 127–45 and 249–65.

26 Leon Radzinowicz, *A History of English Criminal Law and Its Administration from 1750; I: The Movement for Reform, 1750–1833* (London 1948), 138; Douglas Hay, 'Property, Authority and the Criminal Law,' in *Albion's Fatal Tree; Crime and Society in Eighteenth Century England,* ed. Douglas Hay et al. (New York: Pantheon Books 1975), 48–49; Blackwell, supra note 17, at 558.

27 Francis Lieber, trans., 'Introduction,' Gustave de Beaumont and Alexis de Toqueville, *On The Penitentiary System in The United States and Its Application in France* (New York: Augustus M. Kelley 1970) vii; reprint of 1833 edition.

28 Supra note 22, at 37.

29 Rainer Baehre, 'Pauper Emigration to Upper Canada in the 1830s' (1981), 14:28 *Histoire sociale/ Social History,* 339–68.

30 Edward Gibbon Wakefield, *Facts Relating to the Punishment of Death in the Metropolis*, 2d ed. (London: Effingham Wilson 1832), 130.

31 'On The Decrease Of Capital Punishment,' 13 February 1839, National Archives of Canada (hereinafter cited as NAC) RG 5, A1, vol. 216, 11862–3.

32 This issue was the focus of attention in two separate investigations by committees of the British House of Commons in 1831 and 1832. On Hulks (158)–(547) vii. 559, 1830–1, and Gaols (128)–(276) vii. 519, 1831–2.

33 J.M. Beattie, *Crime and the Courts in England, 1660–1800* (Princeton: University Press 1986), 616–18; David J. Rothman, *The Discovery of the Asylum: Social Order and Disorder in the New Republic* (Glenview, Ill.: Scott, Foresman 1971).

34 Dalhousie Papers, 22 December 1822, NAC, MG24, A12, A-529.

35 With reference to the usefulness of this concept in the context of legal history, see the introductory remarks in Anthony Grafton and Ann Blair, eds, *The Transmission of Culture in Early Modern Europe* (Philadelphia: University of Pennsylvania Press 1990), 4. Particularly useful to our discussion are the following essays in that collection: Donald R. Kelley, ' "Second Nature": The Idea of Custom in European Law, Society, and Culture,' 131–72, and Lawrence Stone, 'Honor, Morals, Religion, and the Law: The Action for Criminal Conversation in England, 1670–1857,' 276–316.

36 Sundry Documents, report of Select Committee on expediency of erecting a penitentiary. *Appendix to the Journals of the House of Assembly*, 1831, p. 211–12.

37 C.J. Taylor, 'The Kingston, Ontario Penitentiary and Moral Architecture' (1979), 12: 24 *Histoire sociale/Social History*, 385–408.

38 Bidwell to House of Assembly, NAC, RG5, A1, 8 January 1827, 44142–3.

39 Report of the Commissioners on Penitentiaries, *Appendix of the Journals of the House of Assembly, 1831–32*, n.p.

40 *Prison Discipline Society, Eighth Annual Report, 1833* (hereinafter cited as BPDS) (Boston: 1833), 6.

41 *BPDS*, at 134–9, 4. The links between Howard and Dwight were indirect though plain. A member of Boston's Society for the Moral and Religious Instruction of the Poor, Rev. Bingham drew Dwight's attention to Howard on prisons. Dwight saw himself as fulfilling Howard's vocation. See William Jenkins, 'Memoir of Rev. Louis Dwight,' in Albert G. Hess, *Reports of the Prison Discipline Society of Boston* (Montclair, N.J.: Patterson Smith 1972), 32.

42 Robert L. Fraser, 'John Macaulay,' *Dictionary of Canadian Biography* (hereinafter cited as DCB) vol. 3 (Toronto: University Press 1985), 522; also see S.F. Wise, 'John Macaulay: Tory for All Seasons,' in *To Preserve and Defend; Essays on Kingston in the Nineteenth Century*, ed. Gerald Tulchinsky (Montreal and London: McGill-Queen's University Press, 1976), 185–202.

43 Macaulay Papers, B.C. Smith to Macaulay, 26 February 1833 and 12 March 1833, NAC, M-737.

44 Ibid., 31 July 1832; 26 February 1833, 12 March 1833, and 8 April, 1833.

45 Smandych, supra note 11, at 138–41.

46 'New Penitentiary at Kingston, Upper Canada' [25 November 1833], *BPDS, Ninth Report 1834*, 822.

47 Statutes of Upper Canada, (1834) 4 Wm. iv, c. 37.

48 David H. Shayt, 'Stairway to Redemption: America's Encounter with the British Prison Treadmill' (1989), 30:4 *Technology and Culture*, 908–39.

49 Bryan Palmer, 'Kingston Mechanics and the Rise of the Penitentiary, 1833–1836' (May 1980), 12:25 *Histoire sociale/ Social History*, 17–18.

50 Houston, supra note 9, at 166.

51 Wise, supra note 42, at 202 (cited in Smandych, supra note 11, at 143).

52 *BPDS, Fourth Annual Report, 1829*, 288–303.

53 *Report of William Crawford, Esquire, to the Secretary of State for the Home Department on the Penitentiaries of the United States, 1835*, Great Britain, House of Commons Reports (21) xix, 183.

54 Macaulay to Rowan, 16 October 1835. NAC, RG 5, A1, vol. 156, 86653.

55 Statutes of importance in regulating jails included 4 Geo. IV, c. 64; 5 Geo. IV, c. 35; 5 & 6 Wm. IV, c. 38; and 2 & 3 Vict., c. 56.

56 Law Officers Reports on Colonial Acts, Upper Canada, NAC, CO 323/53, 25.

57 *Twelfth Annual Report of the Board of Managers of the Prison Discipline Society, Boston, May, 1837* (Boston 1837), 3:163; reprinted in *Reports of the Prison Discipline Society of Boston*, vol. 3 (Montclair, NJ: Patterson Smith 1972).

58 J. Macaulay to S.B. Harrison, 18 January 1840. NAC, RG5, vol. 16, 130220.

59 A seminal discussion of the prevailing mentality among Upper Canadian authorities is G. Blaine Baker's ' "So Elegant a Web": Providential Order and the Rule of Secular Law in Early Nineteenth-Century Upper Canada' (1988), 38 *University of Toronto Law Journal*, 184–205.

60 Robert P. Weiss, 'Humanitarianism, Labour Exploitation, or Social Control? A Critical Survey of Theory and Research on the Origin and Development of Prisons' (1987) 12: 3 *Social History*, 337–42.

61 Macaulay Papers, supra note 43, Nelson to Macaulay, 22 February 1834.

62 Macaulay to Joseph, 10 April 1837, NAC, RG5, A1, 96493.

63 *Report on the Affairs of British North America from the Earl of Durham with Appendices* (Shannon: Irish University Press 1968), 49. This excerpt was deleted from G.M. Craig, ed., *Lord Durham's Report* (Toronto and Montreal: McClelland and Stewart 1963).

64 *BPDS, Second Report, 1827*, 95.

65 *BPDS, Third Report, 1828*, 207.

66 *BPDS, Twenty-Ninth Report, 1854*, 3–13. See also Rothman, supra note 33, at 130–54.

67 *BPDS, Eighth Report, 1833*, 23–4.

68 *BPDS, Tenth Report, 1835*, 1–9; *BPDS, Eleventh Report, 1836*, 5–29. Also see Daniel Francis, 'The Development of the Lunatic Asylum in the Maritime Provinces' (1977), 6:2 *Acadiensis*, 23–38.

69 Justin A. Frank Jr, 'Non–Restraint and Robert Gardiner Hill' (1967), 41:2 *Bul. His. Med.*, 140–60, especially at 155; Andrew T. Scull, *Museums of Madness: The Social Organization of Insanity in 19th Century England* (London: Croom Helm 1979), 34–40.

70 23 January 1830, NAC, RG5, A1, 55019–23.

71 André Cellard. *Histoire de la folie au Québec de 1600 à 1850: 'le désordre'* (Montreal: Boréal Express 1991): Peter Keating. *La science du mal: l'institution de la psychiatrie au Québec, 1800–1814* (Montreal: Boréal Express 1993): Jean-Marie Fecteau. *Un nouvel ordre des choses: la pauvrée, le crime, l'Etat au Québec, de la fin du VIIIe siècle à 1840* (Outrement, Qué.: VLB editeur 1989).

72 Representation of the Grand Jury of the Home District on the subject of an Asylum, *Journals of the House of Assembly*, Appendix (1831–2), 116; Report on petition of prisoners in gaol at York, ibid., 17 February 1830, 162.

73 Report of the York Dispensary, ibid., Appendix (1831), 4.

74 Meetings of the Home District General Quarter Sessions of the Peace, 24 February 1831, 6 May 1833, 12 May 1837, S105 Baldwin Room, Metropolitan Toronto Library.

75 An Act to Authorize the Quarter Sessions of the Home District To Provide for the Relief of Insane Destitute Persons in That District, (1830) 11 Geo. IV, c. 20, ss. 1–2; (1832), 3 Wm. IV, c. 45.

76 The Petition of the Justices of the Peace of the Midland District, *Journal of the House of Assembly*, Appendix No 6 (1835), n.p.

77 The same conditions were still evident in the subsequent decade. See Cathy E. Kindquist, 'Migration and Madness on the Upper Canadian Frontier. 1841–1850,' in Donald H. Akenson. ed. *Canadian Papers in Rural History*, vol. 7 (Gananoque, Ont.: Langdale Press 1992), 129–61.

78 G.M. Craig, 'Marshall Spring Bidwell,' *DCB*, vol. 10, 60–4; Michael Cross, 'Charles Duncombe,' ibid., 228–32; Robert J. Burns, 'William Botsford Jarvis,' ibid., vol. 9, 411–12. On Jarvis's role as a lunacy reformer, see Thomas E. Brown, ' "Living with God's Afflicted": The Origins of the Asylum in Upper Canada, 1830–1839: Towards an interpretation' (1984), 1 *Canadian Bulletin of Medical History*, 27–57, at 45.

79 Supra note 73, at 4.
80 J. Baby to Mudge, 14 May 1831, NAC, RG5, A1, 60760–71.
81 Supra note 74, 5 July 1834; 24 July 1834; 4 December 1834, n.p.
82 Supra note 76.
83 'Report on Lunatic Asylums,' *Appendix to the Journal of the House of Assembly of Upper Canada,* 1: 30 (1836), 2–6.
84 *BPDS, Eleventh Report, 1836,* 29.
85 *BPDS, Twelfth Report, 1837,* 117–18.
86 T.J.W. Burgess, 'A Historical Sketch of our Canadian Institutions for the Insane'(1898), 4 *Transactions of the Royal Society of Canada,* 17–18.
87 An Act to authorize the erection of an Asylum within this province, for the reception of Insane and Lunatic persons,' *Journal of the House of Assembly,* 15 March 1839; 3 April 1839; 16 April 1839; (1839) 2 Vict., c. 11.
88 The 1840s are discussed in Thomas Brown, 'Architecture as Therapy' (Summer 1980), 10 *Archivaria,* 99–123, at 117, and in R. Baehre, 'The Ill-Regulated Mind: A Study in the Making of Psychiatry in Ontario, 1830–1921,' Ph.D. thesis, York University (1985), chapter 3.
89 Brown, supra note 78, at 38.
90 Paul E. Johnson, *A Shopkeeper's Millennium; Society and Revivals in Rochester, New York, 1815–1837* (New York: Hill and Wang 1978), 5–9.
91 Brown, supra note 78, at 46–7.
92 Baehre, supra note 29, at 347.
93 *The Annual Register, or A View of the History and Politics of the Year 1838* (London: Thomas Curson Hansard, 1839), 235–42. This article summarized the background and events of the Rebellions and cited memoranda from Sir Francis Bond Head.
94 Craig, supra note 63, at viii-ix.
95 (John George Lambton) Earl of Durham, 'Report on the Affairs of British North America,' reprinted in *British Parliamentary Papers, Colonies, Canada, vol. 2, Session 1839* (Shannon: Irish University Press 1968), 5.
96 Ibid., at 138–9, 145. The implementation of more decentralized municipal control is discussed in C.F.J. Whebell, 'Robert Baldwin and Decentralization 1841–9,' in F.H. Armstrong et al., *Aspects of Nineteenth-Century Ontario* (Toronto: University of Toronto Press 1974), 48–64. Whebell suggests that Wakefield, Durham, and Buller saw municipal government as synonymous with colonial government, a means to decentralize the power vested in the Legislative Council and Legislative Assembly.
97 Copy of a Letter of Instructions addressed by the Honourable Charles Buller, MP, *Report on the Affairs of British North America,* Appendix C, 4–5.

98 Supra note 95, Appendix C, at 22.
99 Fernand Braudel, *Wheels of Commerce*, (New York: Harper and Row 1979), 493, 515.
100 Robert Gray, 'Medical Men, Industrial Labour and the State in Britain, 1830–50' (1991), 16:1 *Social History*, 19–43, at 42. The relationship between social, economic, scientific, and literary thought relevant to understanding reform ideology is discussed in Maxine Berg, 'Progress and Providence in Early Nineteenth-Century Political Economy' (1990), 15:1 *Social History*, 365–75.
101 This suggestion is indebted in part to Brown, supra note 78, at 45–6. A similar argument is made in Michael Ignatieff, *A Just Measure of Pain: The Penitentiary in the Industrial Revolution, 1750–1850* (New York: Pantheon Books 1978), 184.

8 The Blake Act of 1878: A Legislative Solution to Urban Violence in Post-Confederation Canada

SUSAN W.S. BINNIE

Introduction

Riot and collective violence have become closely identified in recent decades with the historical record of nineteenth-century Canada. This development may be partly or indirectly the result of a more highly developed appreciation of the phenomenon of riot as seen across time and cultures, as captured, for instance, for England in the work of E.P. Thompson, Eric Hobsbawm, and George Rudé[1]. But changing notions of the significance of riot derive too from recognition of the sheer prevalence of disturbances in nineteenth-century Canada. Recent studies have uncovered the history of riot as inscribed in reports of innumerable Orange-Green conflicts, in records of labour unrest, political meetings and elections, demonstrations by the unemployed, and ethnic hostility against minorities[2] This discovery of the incidence of riot has doubtless been more striking in the light of the emphasis in earlier Whiggish histories of Canada on the relatively peaceful progress of the country's development.[3]

If collective violence has become established as an integral part of the pre-Confederation record, the pattern of frequent and major riots persisting into the post-Confederation period has not been equally well recognized.[4] Parallels can be drawn, however, between the pre- and post-1867 experiences of riot. For, much as rioting climbed to new heights during the 1840s,[5] so collective violence appeared to reach alarming levels again during the 1870s, an especially turbulent decade marked by strikes, demonstrations, and sectarian violence across the country from Nova

Scotia to Manitoba. Again, the government reacted by passing new legislation specifically aimed at reducing the incidence of riot.

Violence and unrest, including deaths during some sectarian incidents, – were alarming to both central governments and local authorities. Collective violence during the decade of the 1870s was eventually seen as sufficiently serious for the federal Parliament to enact a draconian piece of criminal legislation, the Blake Act of 1878.[6] The act was purposely tailored to meet the situation in the province of Quebec, where large-scale and violent rioting had erupted in Montreal in the summer of 1877. The legislation was directed at controlling the carrying of guns and other weapons to prevent injuries and killings during urban violence. The Blake Act was enacted for one year and subsequently renewed annually until 1884, with both the Tory and Reform governments proclaiming it in force during their terms in office. Application of the statute was limited to restricted areas of the country, which were specified under each proclamation. The 'proclaimed districts' were in practice major cities: the Blake Act was applied to Montreal and the County of Hochelaga (for six years after 1878) and, later, to the city of Quebec in 1879 and to Winnipeg in 1882. After a rapid process of approval in 1878 for Edward Blake's bill, the subsequent history of the Blake Act demonstrated very occasional use of the legislation. Six years later, this restrictive new measure of Canadian criminal law was abandoned.

An explanation for the apparently novel legislative remedy of the Blake Act must answer the question of why riots in Montreal in 1877 were seen by political representatives as demanding a parliamentary response. A second and more specific issue is why a legislative approach through criminal law was considered particularly appropriate. No doubt the evidence of increasing public fear and concern that characterized political debate about sectarian unrest in the 1870s formed part of the government's picture of events. Furthermore, the practical difficulties of responding to violence were a repeated complaint by both local and provincial authorities. At the same time, the content of the Blake Act appeared inconsistent with broader popular perspectives: a basic contradiction existed in state legislation enforcing restrictions on possession of weapons in a largely agrarian society in which attitudes towards the ownership of firearms were generally positive. In addition, the decision to intervene was made by a federal Reform government that had previously strongly opposed central state interference in local disturbances.

Discussion of the origins and development of the Blake Act suggests a need to consider practical factors relevant to the phenomenon of riot at the political level of society as well as at other levels, such as the economic and ideological.[7] In analysing the Blake Act, the generation of new criminal statute law has been conceptualized and investigated primarily as a field of *political* activity within the state and its agencies and institutions.[8] In this perspective, problems developing in certain societal contexts arguably became identified as issues suitable for consideration in the political arena and deserving of parliamentary attention. In tracing such political processes in relation to the Blake Act, the focus moves from the question of how riot became a particular concern for the state to the issue of how the problem was deemed worthy of a legislative remedy.[9]

In addition, other more fundamental issues appear relevant first to the phenomenon of riot itself and second to the reactions of the central state. The pattern of increasingly frequent collective disturbances can be linked, for example, to changing socio-economic factors in the period. Considering the lives of the urban poor and working class in late nineteenth-century Canada, it is evident that conditions deteriorated for many during the 1870s. The prevailing hardships of urban working-class life were aggravated by a number of major economic developments and by geographic movements of population.

Moreover, official responses to riot, in the Canadian setting as elsewhere, were often highly contingent. In terms of policy, innovatory parliamentary law-making was only one possible new direction of several, including changes in policing practices and changes in reliance on military force. How different levels of the Canadian state responded to the violence and the ways in which these responses throw light on the nature of the state are two more focuses of this research.

From a more general theoretical perspective, it may be possible to use the Blake Act as one example of state processes of 'law making' (to use a Weberian term). The development and use of original legislation[10] offers an avenue to the general examination of broader state legislative processes. In this view, particular instances of law-making can throw light on the operation of state agencies, on the relations between them, and on the exercise of state discretion in the development and use of statute law. Innovative legislation may serve to illustrate how distinct state agencies and institutions interacted on particular issues and how they dealt with new problems and processes. In the case of the Blake Act, the federal Cabinet the federal political parties, and the Department of Justice, as well as their provincial counterparts in Quebec and local municipal authorities in Montreal, were some of the players concerned with finding solutions to urban sectarian violence. Studies of novel enactments may serve as potentially useful contributions to general theoretical work directed at analyzing legislative activity by the Canadian state in relation to the criminal law. As David Sugarman has suggested, legal historical analysis needs to be judged by 'its success in placing law and legal institutions within a satisfactory socio-economic and political context, and also the extent to which it sheds new light on the relationship between law, society, economy and politics.'[11]

The process this implies is wider than the usual scope of what is termed 'legislative history.' With a few exceptions, examination of the legislative history of criminal law statutes has developed as a relatively arcane field, characteristically as an exercise of greater interest to draughtsmen and lawyers than to historians. Some of the exceptions, however, hold considerable significance. One can point, for instance, to Bertha Putnam's groundbreaking work on the late medieval origins of the Statute of Labourers,[12] or to Styles and Innes's ongoing and illuminating research concerning eighteenth-century English criminal legislation.[13] The results in these two cases alone, widely divergent as they are in approach and period, suggest how much can be learned about the nature of more general state activities from studies of legislative processes and their outcomes.

Urban Riot in the 1870s

In relation to the claim of increasing riot,[14] existing work has helped to establish that riot was common in the new dominion. It has also clarified some of the distinct bases for riots, ranging from sectarian rioting to riot as a form of economic protest.[15] But little attention has been paid to the phenomenon of a sudden and rapid growth in the incidence of riot in the 1870s or to its underlying causes.

There is evidence that incidents regarded by the authorities as sufficiently serious to warrant military intervention escalated during these years. Involvement of the Canadian militia in incidents of unrest showed a marked peak by 1877.[16] Compared with an average of one military call-out per year in the late 1860s and two per year in the 1880s, call-outs averaged five a year across Canada in the 1870s and reached a new high of twelve in the most turbulent year of 1877. Over the decade of 1871 to 1880, militia call-outs built up slowly to the 1877 figure, showing a pattern of increasing demands for military assistance on the part of the civil authorities.[17] Furthermore, the incidence of riot in urban areas showed a marked increase, accounting for half the recorded call-outs in 1877 and 1878.[18]

The suggestion of a sudden and marked increase in major disturbances is borne out by the rhetoric of politicians in the city of Montreal. A series of violent incidents occurred between Protestants and Catholics in Montreal in 1877 and 1878. An examination of the discursive commentary and the perspectives adopted in local newspapers shows that the editors of both French- and English-language newspapers claimed that the violent episodes in Montreal were aberrations.[19] The accounts insisted on the peaceful nature of the city in the past. For instance, the Protestant *Daily Witness* reported a speech by an Irish-Catholic M.P., Bernard Devlin, in July 1877, and quoted him as saying that 'for half a century they had lived together in peace, and he would regret if that peace were now to be jeopardized.'[20] The Montreal *Gazette* similarly claimed: 'Fortunately for years all classes in Montreal have lived in harmony and peace, begotten of mutual respect for the feelings and convictions each of the others.'[21] And in reporting a joint meeting of the Protestant and Irish Catholic Societies in Montreal on 10 July 1877, the same paper referred to 'the peace, good order and social relations so long happily existing between the citizens of Montreal, of all classes and creeds.'

Evidently, the editors of the city's newspapers were convinced (or felt it important to persuade their readers) that violent incidents in 1877 were a new phenomenon, an anomaly in a usually peaceful city. But in effectively overlooking the well-known violence of previous decades relating to both political and religious issues, the press ignored the major riots at the time of the Rebellion Losses Bill in 1849, which led to the burning of the legislature in Montreal. They also failed to refer to the Orange-Catholic Gavazzi Riot of 1853, resulting from the visit of the Italian patriot and apostate Gavazzi, a riot that killed ten people and wounded fifty. The 1840s and 1850s had been marked by crowd violence in cities in all four of the North American colonies as well as by violence among labourers constructing canals. The 1860s, by contrast, had been a more peaceable decade, and this recent past may have allowed local leaders and press commentators, while recognizing the sudden upsurge in violence, to propagate a false estimation of the city's more distant history.

The Economic Factor in Riots

As suggested, the sudden sharp increase in the incidence of urban riot in Canada during the 1870s most likely found its sources in economic tensions associated with the Great Depression of 1874 to 1896. In order to explore the extent of the impact of the economic downturn on urban populations in the 1870s, the recession can be considered in relation to Canada's broader industrial development. Accounts by economic historians agree in pinpointing a degree of economic 'takeoff' of industrialization processes in Eastern Canada to the decades of the 1870s and 1880s.[22] This period was characterized by rapid industrial and commercial expansion, which coincided with the geographical enlargement of the country. In effect, Canada in the 1870s and 1880s left an initial era of early industrialization and entered into a more advanced stage distinguished by an increasing concentration and scale of industry and commerce. In relation to the analysis of public disorder and riot, this second stage of industrialization was accompanied by major and continuing upheavals affecting the labour force. Such changes were evidenced in increasingly overcrowded cities, continuing rural depopulation in eastern Canada, and large-scale movements of population westwards in the 1880s. In addition, these restructuring effects for labour occurred during years when economic conditions worsened owing to the downturns in the trade cycle typical of the Great Depression. Thus a broad picture of economic uncertainty and change emerges for the 1870s with serious repercussions or hardships for many members of the growing urban working class.

In terms of direct economic effects of the trade cycle, an initial downturn in the economic conditions of Canadian urban labour was evident by 1875:[23] urban unemployment had begun to grow with the migration of surplus rural labour to the cities – a development most marked in Quebec and Montreal,[24] but one that occurred in Ontario towns as well. One direct result was reduced wage rates for labourers. In Toronto and Montreal rates fell to fifteen cents an hour or one dollar a day – levels well below those required to sustain a family.[25] So severe were the hardships in Montreal and so high the level of unemployment that a local program of public works was hastily instituted to employ some of the surplus workforce.[26]

The economic problems facing the country no doubt added substantially to the picture of urban unrest presented to local, provincial, and federal levels of government. In one direct connection, Montreal workingmen regularly protested against cuts in wages, with crowds demonstrating to demand work from 1875 onwards.[27] Several militia call-outs in Eastern Canada in the 1870s also responded to economic disturbances including the Grand Trunk Railway strike of 1876–7[28] and the Lachine Canal strikes of 1875 and 1877.[29] But it would be incorrect to attribute the marked increase in the frequency of urban civil disorders directly or solely to economic hardship. Sectarian violence also increased. Sectarian disturbances were evidently exacerbated by the economic downturn, which caused Protestant-Catholic relations to deteriorate, especially in Montreal. This worsening of relations occurred partly through rivalry for scarce jobs, which was aggravated by increased population pressures in the over-crowded city. Not only were many labouring jobs seasonal, but certain occupations were reserved by custom for Catholic or Protestant labourers.[30] The worsening work situation pitted Catholic labourer against Protestant labourer in competition for fewer jobs. For skilled labourers, the situation made any changes in traditional exclusionary job practices appear to be attacks on sacred practice.[31]

As old cleavages of ethnicity and religion intensified in the mid-1870s, poor sectarian relations were aggravated as numbers affiliated with religious organizations reached new strengths. Membership in the Orange Order grew rapidly, and peaked in Ontario during the 1870s.[32] Membership in a Protestant fraternal order became more attractive, a phenomenon that probably was, as Greg Kealey has argued, associated with the strong benevolent function of the order in its role as a voluntary ethnic association. In Montreal, Catholic solidarity showed a parallel strengthening, with Irish and French Catholics coming together in uncharacteristic fashion to celebrate saints' days.[33] Such an intensifying of sectarian bonds during economic recession probably served as a practical response to the realities of financial hardship and unemployment. But the growth of religious societies also furnished stronger formal organizational bases, which in turn provided focuses for hostilities between rival sectarian groups, especially between extremist members of the anti-Catholic Orange Order and the French and Irish Catholic majority in Montreal.[34]

Violent incidents between Protestants and Catholics became common in Montreal by 1876. By 1877 small-scale sectarian clashes occurred regularly when members of rival groups crossed territorial divisions in the city. As research on sectarian violence in other cities in the period has shown,[35] riots frequently began from incursions into areas of the city identified with the other party. In addition, Protestant–Catholic violence occurred in Montreal, as elsewhere, in relation to parades and processions that marked anniversaries of significance to one of the parties. The resurgence grew from a new spirit of sectarian activity and Protestant hostility towards Catholicism, as reflected in the Orange Order's decision to restart the custom of parading in full regalia in 12 July.[36]

Major and serious incidents of urban sectarian strife in the period, which came to be of deep concern to the Reform government under Prime Minister Alexander Mackenzie in Ottawa, were not limited to

Montreal; they occurred in Toronto and other cities as well. While the present focus is on the Blake Act in relation to rioting in Montreal, there were commonalities in the sources of crowd violence and in the state's responses between riots in Montreal and those in other cities in these years. The latter included the Jubilee riots in Toronto in 1875, the Guibord riot in Montreal in 1875, the Montreal riots of 1877 and 1878, and the O'Donovan–Rossa riot in Toronto in 1878.[37]

State Reactions to Urban Riot

Central state responses to serious riot under Mackenzie's Reform government in the period from 1874 to 1878 illustrate the severe limitations in the means available to governments for suppressing riots. At the same time they reveal the timidity of the federal government's reaction to urban unrest and the state's fears of undertaking local interventions.

The principal method of state intervention remained that of ordering rioters to disperse by 'reading the Riot Act.' Under federal legislation enacted as a part of the process of unifying federal criminal law in 1868,[38] the crime of riot remained primarily, in one legal historian's words, 'a legal category, not a description of behaviour.'[39] Use of the act was highly discretionary. Admittedly much of this discretion was exercised at the local level, for the wording of the statute assumed action by a local justice of the peace, sheriff or mayor. Riot by more than a few people (twelve was the number specified in the statute) was an offence to be identified by authorized officials. No victims or complainants were necessary if an unlawful assembly threatened a disturbance (section 1), and prosecutions for riot were intended to be state-initiated (section 4). If rioters refused to disperse, the custom (again drawing on English practice under the Riot Act of 1715) was to summon armed troops or militia to suppress the disturbance. Troops who injured rioters by firing on a crowd were explicitly indemnified under the legislation.[40]

Despite previous use of a range of legislative responses for riot, the availability and appropriateness of different options in the Canadian setting were still far from clear. The Riot Act was too extreme an instrument to use without consideration for its consequences. The act remained uncertain in application; its use might end with armed militia firing on unarmed civilians,[41] or, as at Belleville in 1877 during the Grand Trunk strike, with strikers overpowering the militia.[42] In addition, the Riot Act was expensive to operate and led to disputes with local authorities about responsibility for the costs of calling out militia.[43]

Alternative legislative solutions had been adopted in Upper and Lower Canada in the pre-Confederation period in an effort to the reduce the level of sectarian violence in cities. Sectarian violence in Toronto[44] and Montreal,[45] had been of great concern to governments in the 1830s and 1840s. Precautionary and preventive measures such as bans on certain activities of religious secret societies, and even on the societies themselves, had been tried.[46] Despite the common sense inherent in the milder variant of banning public parades or processions, this answer was not considered workable in the 1870s. According to Sir Francis Hincks, it had not worked successfully in the 1840s, and in 1877, in his opinion, religious societies were likely to ignore any ban on parades. In addition, a ban would be particularly unwelcome to members of the Catholic church.[47] The more extreme variant of banning secret societies altogether could no longer be entertained by any government, given the growing membership of the Orange Order and its political significance. By the 1870s, as Waite has described, the order 'was an engine of intimidation before which governments, being representative, were bound to be circumspect.'[48]

The federal Reform cabinet's fear of direct state interventions in cases of riot, and its apprehension in particular over the prospect of religious riots in Montreal, were first demonstrated in October 1875 in relation to l'affaire Guibord. This lengthy dispute between 'liberal' and ultramontane Catholics in Quebec over the burial of the body of the excommunicated printer Guibord in consecrated Catholic ground had publicly split conservative and reform elements within the Catholic church in Quebec.[49] A riot in Montreal followed a first attempt to remove Guibord's body from a Protestant to a Catholic cemetery after a successful legal appeal by the reformers. The cabinet chose not to ignore the threat of further civil unrest, but to respond by passing an order in Council on 29 October 1875, offering written advice to the attorney general of Quebec on how to handle 'riot and disturbances of the peace.'[50] The cabinet did so in anticipation of opposition by conservative Catholics to a second attempt to rebury the printer's body late in 1875. The advice, perhaps a result of Edward Blake's new role as minister of justice, included a report on how the local authorities in Toronto had responded to the Jubilee (or Pilgrimage) riots of September 1875. Needless to say, this piece of wisdom did not receive an enthusiastic response from the Quebec attorney general.[51]

Despite cabinet concern over violence, Alexander Mackenzie declined all appeals to call out troops during the Grand Trunk strike of 1876–77 and the Lachine Canal strike of 1877. Mackenzie refused repeated requests for intervention in the first case from Hickson, the general manager of the Grand Trunk Railway,[52] and in the second from Beaudry, the Mayor of Montreal,[53] and from the canal contractor.[54] The difficulties of the federal government and the details of these two incidents serve to demonstrate the practical problems that faced the authorities in reacting to urban strikes: partisan local police forces, often drawn from sectarian or political groups that were the sources of their patronage positions;[55] the absence of any standing federal army;[56] and the uncertainty inherent in relying on a volunteer militia. In relation to riot, the governor general Lord Dufferin, had described the militia in Montreal in 1875 as 'a most unhandy instrument to employ in maintaining order,' adding 'the municipal police are of course useless.'[57]

The Orange Riot of 1877

A major riot broke out between Catholic 'toughs' and Protestant Orange Order members in Montreal in July 1877. The events helped to sharpen federal politicians'awareness of the difficulties of responding to sectarian violence and the limitations and inadequacy of available methods. The death of an Orange Order member, Thomas Hackett, in an Orange-Catholic riot on 12 July was undoubtedly the catalyst that inflamed Orange opinion across the country and raised serious fears in Ottawa of widespread sectarian unrest. A senior Orange leader and member of Parliament, John White, claimed that Hackett had been 'foully murdered.'[58] In fact, the victim had been holding a pistol in his hand when he was killed, but the potential parallels with another dead Orangeman, Thomas Scott,[59] must have raised alarming visions for the government. The events of July 1877 in Montreal threatened to reopen a Pandora's box of dissension from New Brunswick to Manitoba, wherever memories were retained of past sectarian discrimination and division.

The violent events in Montreal were clearly provoked by Orange Order intransigence. The Montreal leadership had insisted on the 'right' of members to parade through the streets on 'the Glorious Twelfth of July,' to commemorate the battle of the Boyne of 1690 and the Protestant English victory over Irish Catholics. In the months leading up to this anniversary in 1877, violent incidents had become more common in Montreal; fights and clashes between Protestants and Catholics had increased in frequency and seriousness, and were almost daily events. According to press reports, tensions over the approaching Orange celebration were already high by the beginning of July 1877. The existence of local organizations for each ethnic or religious group, referred to as 'national societies,'[60] provided vehicles for voicing concerns as well as for organizing members to respond to the threats of riot. But as a letter signed 'Freethinker' in a Protestant newspaper stated, efforts to prevent rioting on 12 July seemed likely to be ineffectual: 'The Orangemen of Montreal seem determined to parade the streets, and it is too evident that there is a counter determination on the part of the Irish Catholic Union. A collision seems inevitable. Confronted with a danger of such magnitude, ready to burst upon our comely city in countless horrors, it were criminal indifference to fold our arms and wait the issue.'[61]

As a result of intense local concern, volunteer militia units – mostly composed of Orangemen – were summoned to barracks by their officers in early July in readiness for anticipated problems. However, the mayor of Montreal, Jean-Louis Beaudry,[62] declined to take any special precautions in the face of threatened disorder. Tensions between opposing Orange and Catholic groups increased as newspaper reports emphasized potential disasters.[63] At the last moment the Orange leadership cancelled the march through the streets of Montreal, but went ahead with plans for a service in a downtown church.

On 11 July, the day before the Orange celebration, a sixteen-year-old member of the militia on guard duty became involved in an altercation with a passing Catholic labourer and killed him with a bayonet.[64] The labourer, John M'Keown, had stopped at the barrack-gates with a group of friends to hurl verbal abuse at the sentry. Harassing the guards was a common practice, according to evidence given later. However, the young militia member, Francis Fitzpatrick, was exonerated at a subsequent inquest.[65]

On 12 July, Catholics and Protestants stayed away from work in large numbers, despite threats of dismissal by employers[66] and pleas from their national societies. Perhaps provoked by the killing on 11 July, Catholic bystanders attacked Orangemen as they left their church service. Brawls broke out between rival elements, and fighting continued on the streets in several areas of the city. In one encounter the young Orangeman Thomas Hackett, 'a quiet respectable clerk from Ottawa,'[67] was shot and killed. After twelve hours Montreal police, eventually aided by the militia,[68] gained control and ended what the press referred to as 'mob rule' on the streets. Incidents of violence, including a number of shooting episodes and one serious but non-fatal injury, continued over several days.

Faced with these events, the Catholic church in Montreal responded by counselling patience and tolerance. Local priests advised Catholics to stay in their homes during the large and lavish funeral procession planned by the Orange Order for Thomas Hackett on 16 July. Despite such relatively pacifying statements, Orange Order members continued to rant against the Catholic church, portraying it as a threatening and monolithic institution bent on destroying other forms of Christianity. Orange assertions were vituperative and extreme: in his sermon on 12 July 1877 the Protestant order's chaplain had referred to the Catholic Church as 'drunken with the blood of the saints,' according to the Montreal *Daily Witness*. After Hackett's murder the same paper demanded that Catholic priests and laymen publicly disclaim 'sympathy with the outrages.' Even The *Times* of London was moved to comment on 'the fanatical Protestantism of the Orange Party' in Montreal.[69] The moderate French-Canadian press (*La Minerve, Le Franc-Parleur*) began to respond, attacking Orange denunciations of Catholicism, blaming Protestants for the violence, and calling for Catholics to respond verbally to Protestant attacks.

The State's Legislative Response

The claim that the Blake Act was the result of a decision to try new forms of state intervention in relation to public disturbances effectively subsumes at least two distinct changes in government policy. First, there was the new course of transferring consideration of the highly charged issue of sectarian violence to the political arena. This was already a risky approach, given the strong sectarian affiliations of many members of Parliament and Orange outrage over Hackett's murder. A second major change was the adoption and use of restrictive new weapons legislation by the central state.

Why did the entrenched, non-interventionist reaction to local riot favoured by the federal Reform government shift by 1878? Besides evidence of fairly widespread urban unrest, there was also support for the view of a general deterioration in Catholic–Protestant and French–English relations in several provinces. Anti-French moves in New Brunswick and Manitoba had deeply embittered the francophone minorities in those provinces as well as the francophone majority in Quebec. In addition, members of Parliament began to see that disturbances in Montreal were more serious than in the past and too serious to be ignored indefinitely. In other words, recourse to old methods of local control under the aegis of local magistrates was considered inadequate or inappropriate for the problems faced by the authorities in Montreal.

By the spring of 1878 Montreal representatives of both political parties, languages, and religions and all three ethnicities – French, Irish and English – concurred in demanding a federal solution to the continuing violence. Moreover, the parliamentary representatives' demands for action from Ottawa were coupled with a loud and strident public discourse in the city itself. This discourse spoke an economic language, emphasizing the effects of violence on trade and commerce in the city. Both the Montreal *Daily Witness* and the *Gazette* referred to the injury to Montreal's prosperity due to the rioting.[70] The central state's reluctance to respond was untenable after almost a year of federal government indecision and with the political leadership in the major city in the country demanding action. In effect, the Reform party government under Alexander Mackenzie was forced to be seen to act before the anniversary of Hackett's death. But Mackenzie's delay on the matter suggests that he and his cabinet remained at a loss as to what kinds of long-term moves would prove to be both relevant and politically acceptable.

If the government recognized the incidence of increased urban unrest by 1878 and its political implications, it was awkwardly placed to make political moves to deal with sectarian riots. A federal election was anticipated within a year or two. Mackenzie had relied for his majority in 1874 on an ill-assorted Reform constituency that included Orange Order Protestants and reform-minded French Catholics in Quebec, as well as Irish Catholics in Ontario and grit supporters and followers of George Brown. The Reform party's need to provide a political solution to unrest in Montreal had to be balanced against the views of factional and opposing sectarian elements in its own ranks.

The customary federal approach to riots earlier in the 1870s had been to refuse interventions, relying on the legal argument that repression of riot was strictly a local responsibility. Under the Reform party between 1874 and 1878, federally initiated interventions of any kind in local unrest were rare. The degree of government concern over events in Montreal was therefore evidenced by a federal decision to assemble a major contingent of militia – three thousand strong – in Montreal under the commander in chief, Sir Selby Smyth, on 12 July 1878, the anniversary of Hackett's death. The day passed peacefully. Later the same summer, however, Mackenzie again summoned troops to end riots in Quebec City. He suffered overwhelming anxiety over the outcome at the time.[71] The disastrous result, with troops firing on a crowd of unemployed workers and killing one demonstrator, caused Mackenzie and the Reform cabinet continuing concern and confirmed their view that direct interventions were highly undesirable. Effectively, if federal government involvement in unrest was considered necessary, the Reform cabinet under Mackenzie favoured indirect intervention over direct displays of force.

The Blake Act as a Legislative Solution to Urban Violence

Why did the Reformers come to the view not only that intervention through legislation was the most appropriate approach but that new legislation was necessary? By 1878 there was already a further legislative option available, a possible alternative to dependence on the Riot Act. Edward Blake, as minister of justice in 1877, had introduced an act to control the use of firearms.[72] The sectarian violence resulting in Hackett's murder in July 1877 and more violence leading to another murder in Montreal in April 1878[73] involved the use of handguns. As the 1877 firearms statute was mildly worded (creating the offences of carrying a gun without cause and pointing a gun at another person), an attempt to approach the problem of sectarian murders through stronger anti-firearm legislation seemed rational. By 1878, however, it was evident that Blake's new legislation had been ineffectual. Montrealers were still carrying weapons and using them in sectarian affrays. Canadians living outside areas of urban disturbances were unlikely to agree to a general prohibition on the carrying of guns. For many of Canada's citizens, whether urban or rural, the owning or carrying of firearms constituted an acceptable aspect of life,[74] and any attempts to limit or control the possession of firearms might be strongly resisted. Blake himself described the passage of the weak Firearms Act of 1877 as 'attended by many difficulties,' and stated that in his view additional measures against carrying firearms were likely to be rejected.[75] His new Firearms Act had come under attack in Montreal; in 1877, in the week before Hackett's death, it had already been termed a 'dead letter' in one newspaper editorial.[76]

After a lapse of almost a year, the matter of violence in Montreal was finally addressed in Parliament with the introduction of a new bill by Edward Blake in May 1878. Despite the enthusiasm with which Catholic members greeted the legislation when it was introduced in the House, the bill's apparent novelty was misleading. It was original neither in its conception nor in its contents, for Blake's draughtsmanship had been used to cobble together two existing pieces of legislation. The result was an amalgam of a Canadian statute based on pre-Confederation legislation controlling possession of liquor and arms among navvies (re-enacted after Confederation as the Peace Preservation Act of 1869) and an imperial statute, one of several enacted for use in Ireland in the 1870s, designed to prevent the possession of arms.[77] The bill prohibited the carrying of weapons and firearms in specified localities, and made licences necessary for carrying arms outside a residence in such districts (sections 1–3). Furthermore, the bill provided for the appointments of commissioners to issue the required licences (sections 6–7 and 9) and, by third reading, it provided for searches of persons and houses under suspicion of concealing weapons.

In this instance the Canadian statute provided the form – the notion of 'proclaimed districts' as defined by order in council – and the imperial statute provided the content. Edward Blake had clearly attempted to use criminal legislation to reach a constitutionally acceptable solution to the violence between the sectarian groups in Montreal. However, Blake weakened the Irish legislation considerably in drawing up his bill, omitting many of the more extreme provisions in the original. None the less, the bill appeared relatively strong when compared with the content of the Firearms Act of 1877, since it prohibited the carrying of weapons altogether. The significant difference was that the new bill had strictly *local* application – a point that was highly attractive to a government that had to be seen to act but was reluctant to impose arms control uniformly across the country.

Edward Blake no longer held ministerial responsibility for the department of justice, nor was he in the cabinet.[78] How then had Blake's bill come before the House? After a winter with more sectarian incidents in Montreal and no arrests of Hackett's murderers, Blake was reportedly approached by two moderate Reform party members of Parliament from Montreal, Louis-Amable Jetté, a French Catholic, and Bernard Devlin, an Irish Catholic, and asked to draft a legislative measure to contain further violence.[79] There were several likely reasons for Blake's agreement to introduce a private member's bill. Montreal's problems could have been seen as part of his unfinished business as minister of justice, and the new minister, Rodolphe Laflamme of Montreal, may have refused to become involved in the city's sectarian problems. Prime Minister Mackenzie may also have urged Blake to draft a bill. While the extent to which Blake's moves were made with Mackenzie's foreknowledge and agreement is unknown,[80] this silence does not preclude consultation. The political sensitivity of the topic of sectarian violence makes it likely that Blake's bill was cleared with the government in advance, and Mackenzie rose immediately to support the bill when it was introduced in the House.[81]

Debate in the Commons was prolonged and rancorous, despite general support for Blake's proposal. Protestant extremist opinion on the bill diverged from that of the majority and was strongly represented, with Orange Order representatives (such as John White, MP, grand master of the order in Eastern Ontario) remaining implacably hostile to the stat-ute.[82] Catholic Reformers from Quebec as well as moderate Quebec Tories demanded that the legislation be made stronger to include provisions for house-to-house searches of residences for weapons. As Hector Langevin argued in debate, the legislation should be 'harsh': 'The intention was to strike terror into the minds of those who were disposed to trouble society ... break the peace, and commit such violence as might lead to blood-shed.'[83] Even the intransigent Orange leadership found it difficult to press against urgent federal legislation introduced by a distinguished Protestant member of Irish descent ostensibly to protect Irish Protestants in Montreal. Blake's measure was grudgingly accepted by Orange supporters in the House and given rapid passage to third reading.[84]

What was lacking in the heated debates (and what may have subse-quently proved fatal to the functioning of the act) was any consideration of the practicality of the measures envisioned or their fit with current attitudes and practices relating to the ownership and possession of weapons. The emphasis in the House lay exclusively on obtaining a legislative measure agreeable to all parties, religions and races, leaving questions of subsequent operation and enforcement largely ignored. Discussion of the method of using appointed commissioners to licence guns, which relied on voluntary compliance by the citizenry, was missing from the recorded debates. Additional powers given to police to search suspected persons (in the bill as amended in committee) were questioned only as being inadequate. The overriding consideration in Parliament was to have emergency legislation in place before the approaching end of the session. The goal was to stem the increasing flow of violent incidents occurring in Montreal and to avoid the prospect of the city's dividing into two armed camps before 12 July 1878.

The Use and Impact of the Blake Act

Despite histrionics during the debate in the House, public concern, and newspaper attention, the Blake Act had little evident effect when pro-claimed for Montreal in May 1878, or later, in August 1879, for the city of Quebec. The statute was brought into force in Quebec two weeks after a riot between rival Irish and French port labourers had ended and after peace had been restored; in other words, after immediate threats of disorder had passed.[85] Its third and final proclamation, for Winnipeg in

1882, appeared to be an error, due to a misunderstanding between the local police and federal officials about the relevance of the Act to an outbreak of serious arson.[86]

In total, only five commissioners were appointed by the federal government to issue licences to carry arms in Montreal and Quebec under two proclamations of the statute.[87] Four commissioners were judicial officials, including two sheriffs and two judges; the fifth was a well-known local Montreal merchant. Each received a stipend of one hundred dollars a year and was issued fifty licences. The records of the Federal Department of Justic show that only two of the commissioners corresponded routinely with the department, usually about their annual stipends, and neither of them appears to have been very active in his post.[88]

The claim that the legislation was unfamiliar to most magistrates and to the judiciary is buttressed by the rarity with which it is mentioned in legal texts as well as the absence in law reports of references to its practical use. Apart from some highly favourable comments on 'la loi Blake' in liberal and Reform French publications in 1878 – especially in *L'Opinion Publique* edited by L.-O. David and the same L.-A. Jetté, MP – the legislation was rarely referred to in the press, even after proclamation in a city. Furthermore, it was not always listed in editions of magistrate's manuals or law digests published in the period.[89] As for the practical application of its powers, only one account of the use of measures under the act has been confirmed – when Mayor Beaudry acted in a precautionary fashion on 12 July 1878, and had train and boat passengers arriving in Montreal from eastern Ontario searched for weapons by his constables.[90] None was found.

After three more or less abortive proclamations of the statute, the Blake Act was allowed to lapse and was not renewed by Parliament in 1884. The Reform party appeared to lose faith in the legislation even before that date: when a member commented on the Blake Act during a debate in the House at the time of its annual renewal in 1881, he said, in Blake's presence: 'Many entertained the opinion that the Act had not worked as well as was expected by the hon. Minister of Justice.'[91]

Conclusion

Of the more than two hundred criminal law statutes[92] enacted in the period between Confederation and enactment of the Canadian Criminal Code in 1892, the Blake Act stands out for its sudden appearance and apparent novelty, its determined prohibition on carrying weapons, and its brief existence on the statute-books. Admittedly, the act did not become part of the state's standard repertoire of criminal statute law. However, if a preliminary examination suggests that the act was a case of legislative failure, that view is not necessarily accurate from the perspective of legislative historians. At the very least it underestimates the information that may be drawn from the experience of 'failed' legislation. To see the Blake Act only as a legislative embarrassment, as the poorly conceived and poorly designed brainchild of a distinguished politician, a piece of legislation to be expunged from the statute-books as soon as decently possible, is to dismiss what can be learned from statutory failures.

The act's significance lies in part in what it suggests about political and ideological aspects of Canadian society. First, that its provisions were seen as highly relevant to major problems of unrest in Canadian cities is a comment on the fears, concerns, and priorities of Canadian parliamentarians in 1878. Second, its adoption reflects the politicians' views of the public's concern for peaceful urban settings, settings wherein trade and commerce could proceed uninterrupted. Third the act offers insights into the Reform party's inability to respond to urban disorder in the 1870s. Indeed, it points up the limitations on the powers of any federal government to take action against riot. It also highlights some of the serious drawbacks to existing remedies for riot. Moreover, the fact that Edward Blake, who had withdrawn from the cabinet, was prevailed on to furnish a legislative solution for the problems in Montreal points both to the paucity of talent in the party and to Blake's continuing powerful, if unofficial, position. Last, that imperial legislation developed to keep the peace in Ireland should be modified for application to areas of riot in Canada is interesting, and probably attributable to Blake's familiarity with the dominion's constitutional law, his continuing interest in Irish affairs, and his concern with sectarian relations.

The Blake Act, relative to other minor criminal legislation, may stand as a limiting or marginal case in terms of its innovative design, successful passage, and subsequent ineffectiveness. None the less, some findings can be derived despite its brief existence. It is informative in several ways about state legislative activity and about processes of law creation and their effects. It shows that it was possible for a member of Blake's stature to bring forward a private criminal law bill and see it adopted.[93] In relation to process, the finding that a powerful alliance of Catholic, Protestant, French, and Irish members from Quebec effectively forced the state to be seen to act in relation to sectarian violence again reflects the government's assessment of the level of public concern. The government's choice of policy, however, remains interesting. In exercising its discretion the government first searched for a political solution to violence and then, reluctantly but necessarily in terms of its constitutional powers, accepted a form of weapons legislation as a relatively low-risk style of intervention. At the same time, the Blake Act did not reflect any popular or widely recognized demand for weapons control and, lacking any strong or discernible ideological basis, it is hardly surprising that firm patterns of implementation were not established after proclamation.

The act was arguably also significant in some of its effects. At a minimum, it provided a symbolic parliamentary solution to violence in Montreal. As a legislative measure restricted to disturbed areas, it furnished a politically acceptable solution in the interests of peace in Canada's leading city. The act translated parliamentary agreement on the necessity of acting into a form of law acceptable to a majority of political representatives. In terms of public discourse, Ottawa was seen to have produced a legislative answer, an offering to the cause of ending sectarian bloodshed. But in contrast to the government of the province of Quebec (which acted effectively, biting the political bullet by banning sectarian parades in Quebec)[94] the federal government's answer was formulaic, an unenforced and unenforceable gun-registration scheme that could hardly succeed in a divided city where guns were regularly owned, carried, and used. Its major significance probably lay in the fact that it constituted a warning by the state to Montrealers, a new and emphatic message delivered to sectarian leaders across the country to curb their members' activities or face threatened federal intervention.

Whether or not the Blake Act had a direct effect on the practice of carrying guns in urban areas, the outbreaks of violent incidents in urban areas had abated by the end of the decade. The 1877 wave of sectarian violence was not repeated, and urban riots had diminished in frequency across the country by 1880. A temporary upswing in the economy may have helped to diminish sectarian animosities; perhaps sectarian elements also tired of violent activities or found other outlets for traditional hostilities. Possibly they began to recognize that sectarianism was less appropriate in a New World setting. As Kealey and Morton have suggested, the emphasis of collective movements may already have begun to move away from sectarianism towards labour concerns. Whatever prompted the decline in violence, it was noted with relief by members of Parliament, and the act was subsequently dropped.

What can be said about these findings in relation to the broader project of studying minor criminal legislation? In what ways can the Blake

Act serve as a historical building-block for consideration of state legislative practices in relation to criminal law? Making assumptions about general processes of statutory development based on the Blake act would be highly premature, but the Act does serve to begin to point out the complex pattern of links that provided the impetus for development of new criminal legislation. Thus in Canada in the 1870s the economic recession and its effects for the growing urban labour force, the flare-ups of traditional patterns of sectarian violence, the alarm and concern expressed in public discourse, and the state's need to be seen to react were all part of the origins of new criminal law. Further, the development and use of the Blake Act suggest a marked lack of coherence in different levels of the institution of the state, a finding that implies that notions of the 'state' as a set of unified, purposeful, and functional agencies assumes too much in this period, at least in the legislative context of the Blake Act.

NOTES

I am grateful for editorial comments from Louis Knafla as well as for earlier helpful comments on a chapter of dissertation research (on which this paper is based) from Ian Taylor, Douglas Hay, and Barry Wright. The research was funded by a doctoral fellowship from the Social Science and Humanities Research Council of Canada from 1984 to 1988.
1 E.P. Thompson, 'The Moral Economy of the English Crowd in the Eighteenth Century' (1981), 50 *Past and Present*, and Eric Hobsbawm and George Rudé, *Captain Swing* (New York: Pantheon Books 1968).
2 A wide variety of riots is reported for the pre-Confederation period, including election riots, riots among canal and railway workers, and sectarian riots. The authors include Gordon Bale, *Chief Justice William Johnstone Ritchie* (Ottawa: Carleton University Press 1991), 24–6; Ruth Bleasdale, 'Class Conflict on the Canals in Upper Canada in the 1840s,' in *Pre-industrial Canada, 1760–1849*, ed. Michael Cross (Toronto: McClelland and Stewart 1982), and 'Unskilled Labourers on the Public Works of Canada, 1840–1880,' Ph.D. thesis, University of Western Ontario (1984); J.M.S. Careless, *The Union of the Canadas* (Toronto: McClelland and Stewart 1967); Michael Cross, 'Stony Monday, 1849: The Rebellion Losses Riot in Bytown' (1971), 63 *Ontario History*, 177–90, and ' "The Laws are like Cobwebs": Popular Resistance to Authority in Mid-Nineteenth Century British North America'(1984), 8 *Dalhousie Law Journal*, 103–23; H. Clare Pentland, 'The Lachine Strike of 1843'(1948), 29 *Canadian Historical Review*, 255–77, and *Labour and Capital in*

Canada (Toronto: Lorimer 1981); Paul Romney, *Mr Attorney: The Attorney General for Ontario in Court, Cabinet, and Legislature 1791–1899* (Toronto: The Osgoode Society 1986); and Scott W. See, *Riots in New Brunswick: Orange Nativism and Social Violence in the 1840s* (Toronto: University of Toronto Press 1993).

3 W.L. Morton's work, *The Kingdom of Canada* (Toronto: Bobbs Merrill 1963), provides one example of this genre.

4 Some exceptions include Greg Kealey's work on Orange-Green conflict in Toronto in 'The Orange Order in Toronto: Religious Riot and the Working Class,' in *Toronto Workers Respond to Industrial Capitalism, 1867–1892* (Toronto: University of Toronto Press 1980), 98–123, and Desmond Morton's account of the Grand Trunk Railway strike in 'Taking on the Grand Trunk: The Locomotive Engineers' Strike of 1876–7'(1977), 2 *Labour/Le Travail,* 5–34.

5 Cross has identified the 1840s as a period of 'modernization' in Upper and Lower Canada, during which societal 'tensions' became manifest in ways including riot; 'riot' is explained as the outcome of an economic shift from early to later industrialization and its ramifications at the political and social levels. See Cross, ' "The Laws are like Cobwebs," ' supra note 2.

6 The Blake Act was the common short title for 'An Act for the Better Prevention of Crimes of Violence in Certain Parts of Canada, until the end of the next Session of Parliament' (41 Vict., c. 17]). The act was named after Edward Blake, the eminent lawyer and federal minister of justice from 1875 to 1877.

7 These emphases lie in marked contrast to contemporary accounts, which treated Edward Blake's legislation as a rational, if ineffectual, solution to random urban sectarian violence. See the account given in *The Dominion Annual Register and Review* (Montreal: Dawson Brothers 1878). The present account is influenced by research on riot in other jurisdictions: for the United Kingdom, see supra note 1, and the summary by W.R. Cornish and G. de N. Clark in *Law and Society in England, 1750–1950* (London: Sweet and Maxwell 1989), 595–8. For Upper Canada, see J.M.S. Careless's discussion of the absence of violence during the elections of March-April 1844, attributed to the relative prosperity of the period: supra note 3, at 91.

8 *Political* in the sense used by French structuralist theorists, as demonstrated in the work of Louis Althusser and Nicos Poulantzas, in which the *political* level represents one level of the *social formation.*

9 This model suggests a temporal political link, moving chronologically from problem to political concern to legislative solution. Alternative patterns are recognized in which legislative solutions occur in conjunction with prob-

lems or are adopted before problems are identified. In the Canadian case, examples where pre-existing legislation was 'borrowed' from other jurisdictions (a relatively frequent experience), and questions of rationale and chronicity need careful investigation.

10 Or legislation new to the Canadian setting.

11 David Sugarman, 'Writing "Law and Society" Histories' (1992), 55 *Modern Law Review*, 292–308.

12 Bertha H. Putnam, *The Place in Legal History of Sir William Shareshall, Chief Justice of the King's Bench, 1350–1361: A Study of Judicial and Administrative Methods in the Reign of Edward III* (Holmes Beach, Fl: Wm. Grant 1968).

13 Discussed in Joanna Innes and John Styles, 'The Crime Wave: Recent Writing on Crime and Criminal Justice in Eighteenth Century England' (1986), 25 *Journal of British Studies*, 380–435, and in a second (unpublished) paper by the same authors.

14 While the history of riot in the decade of the 1870s in Canada has been investigated by several historians including Greg Kealey, supra note 4, and Desmond Morton, ibid., no comprehensive overview of collective disturbances is available.

15 Where 'sectarian' has been defined as 'of or belonging to a group of people with religious or other beliefs that differ from those more generally accepted' (*Oxford American Dictionary* 1980). In this study the term 'sectarian' is applied to conflicts between Protestant members of the Orange Order and French or Irish Catholics, as well as to conflicts in Quebec between right-wing ultramontane Catholics and liberals within the Catholic church, as, for instance, in *l'affaire* Guibord.

16 The figures used are derived from the work of the military historian J.J.B. Pariseau, *Disorders, Strikes and Disasters: Military Aid to the Civil Power in Canada, 1867–1933* (Ottawa: National Defence Headquarters, Directorate of History 1973).

17 The figures per annum for militia call-outs to disturbances were: 1871, 0; 1872, 2; 1873, 6; 1874, 3; 1875, 5; 1876, 5; 1877, 12; 1878, 7; 1879, 3; 1880, 4. Pariseau, supra note 16, at 23.

18 Where 'urban' is used to refer to larger towns such as Toronto and Montreal as well as to smaller centres, including St John, Belleville, Sarnia, and Charlottetown.

19 Newspapers examined included *La Minèrve*, *Le Franc Parleur*, The *Gazette*, and the *Daily Witness*.

20 *Daily Witness*, Montreal, 12 July 1877.

21 *Gazette*, 10 July 1877.

22 Sources relied on are W.A. Mackintosh, *The Economic Background of Domin-*

ion-Provincial Relations (Toronto: McClelland and Stewart 1939); *The Rowell-Sirois Report*, vol. 1 (Toronto: Macmillan 1978); Gordon W. Bertram, 'Economic Growth in Canadian History, 1870–1915: The Staple model and the take-off Hypothesis' (1963), 29 *Canadian Journal Economics and Political Science*, 159–84; Otto J. Firestone, 'Development of Canada's Economy, 1850–1900,' in National Bureau of Economic Research, *Trends in the American Economy in the Nineteenth Century* (Princeton: Princeton University Press 1963), 217–52; and Richard Pomfret, *The Economic Development of Canada* (Toronto: Methuen 1981).

23 According to economic historians such as Bertram, the Great Depression, experienced in the United States by 1874, had major effects in Canada by 1875; it was an international phenomenon to which Canada was especially vulnerable.

24 Brian Young's work describes the effects of rural migration to Montreal. According to Young's estimates, the population density in the city doubled between 1851 and 1871. See 'The Defeat of George-Etienne Cartier in Montréal-Est in 1872' (1970), 51 *Canadian Historical Review*, 386–406.

25 On 7 August 1877, the Montreal *Star* argued against lowering labourers' wages to eighty cents a day, stating that a labouring man and his family could scarcely survive on one dollar per day. Bleasdale, 'Unskilled Labourers,' supra note 2, at 161–2.

26 In one account the city is reported to have hired 'hundreds of destitute labourers to work on the roads at sixty cents a day.' Bryan Palmer, *Working-Class Experience: The Rise and Reconstitution of Canadian Labour, 1800–1980* (Toronto: Butterworths 1983), 95

27 Employment of labourers was highly seasonal; jobs were especially scarce in winter when living costs (including firewood) were markedly higher than in the summer: Bettina Bradbury, 'The Family Economy and Work in an Industrializing City: Montreal in the 1870s' (1979), *Canadian Historical Association Historical Papers*, 71–95. For the demonstrations of unemployed labourers in Montreal see Palmer, supra note 26, at 95; Bleasdale, 'Unskilled Labourers,' supra note 2, at 259–61; and Bettina Bradbury, *Working Families* (Toronto: McClelland and Stewart 1993), at 102.

28 Morton, supra note 4.

29 See Susan W.S. Binnie, "Explorations in the Use of Criminal Law in Canada, 1867–1892," Ph.D. thesis, Carleton University (1992), 184–7.

30 J.I. Cooper, 'The Quebec Ship Labourers Benevolent Society' (1949), 30 *Canadian Historical Review*, 337–43; and Bradbury, 'The Family Economy,' supra note 27, at 222.

31 Dorothy S. Cross, 'The Irish in Montreal, 1867–1896,' (M.A. thesis: McGill

University 1969), chapters 1 and 2; and Bradbury, *Working Families*, supra note 27, at 87.

32 Kealey, supra note 4, at 106. Scott See has suggested that membership strengthened in the 1840s in New Brunswick in direct response to levels of Catholic immigration: supra note 2, at 78–9.

33 Bleasdale, 'Unskilled Workers,' supra note 2, at 258.

34 For example, members of the cadet branch of the Orange Order, the so-called Young Britons, were known for their uncontrolled behaviour during Orange events. And Catholic organizations in Montreal were expressing concern over young Catholics who refused to join youth organizations and hung out on street corners with other Catholic youths – 'young toughs,' as the *Gazette* referred to them.

35 Cross, supra note 31, at 168–70.

36 Sybil Baker, 'Orange and Green: Belfast, 1832–1912,' in *The Victorian City: Images and Realities*, ed. Harold J. Dyos and Michael Wolff (London: Routledge and Kegan Paul 1973), 789–814; Nicholas Rogers, 'Serving Toronto the Good,' in *Forging a Consensus: Historical Essays on Toronto*, ed. Victor L. Russell (Toronto: University of Toronto Press 1984), 116–40; Kealey, supra note 4, at 115–16: See, supra note 2, chapter 4.

37 For details of several of these disturbances, see Desmond Morton 'Aid to the Civil Power: The Canadian Militia in Support of Social Order, 1867–1914' (1970), 51 *Canadian Historical Review*, 407–15.

38 31 Vict., c. 70. An Act respecting Riots and Riotous Assemblies

39 John Beattie, *Crime and the Courts in England, 1660–1800*, (Princeton: Princeton University Press 1986), 76.

40 The death of rioters could not therefore be charged as murder, as had been done in Lower Canada in 1832. See Elinor Kyte Senior, 'The Influence of the British Garrison on the Development of the Montreal Police, 1832–1853,' in *Lawful Authority*, ed. Rod Macleod (Toronto: Copp Clark Pitman 1988), 85–97, at 85.

41 As in Montreal in June 1878: Dale Thomson, *Alexander Mackenzie: Clear Grit* (Toronto: Macmillan 1960), 331.

42 Morton, supra note 4, at 21.

43 After the disastrous call-out at Belleville in December 1876, Edward Blake as minister of justice undertook an inquiry into the circumstances and introduced a new militia bill (Bill 102, 1877). It attempted to deal with the thorny question of responsibility for costs of call-outs, but was relatively ineffectual. See *Hansard*, 2 March and 4 April 1877.

44 Described in Rogers, supra note 36, at 118–20.

45 Dorothy Cross describes some of the violence in detail (supra note 31, at

168–72), as does Careless (supra note 2, at 125–6). On the question of local policing in Quebec and the control of riots, see Allen Greer, 'The Birth of the Police in Canada,' in *Colonial Leviathan: State Formation in Mid-Nineteenth-Century Canada*, ed. Allen Greer and Michael Radforth (Toronto: University of Toronto Press 1992), 17–49.

46 The Baldwins, father and son, tried at different times to introduce measures to control secret societies. William Warren advocated a bill banning religious processions in 1823 (Romney, supra note 2, at 156). After the election riots of 1841 in Upper Canada, Robert Baldwin succeeded in 1843 in banning all religious societies except the Freemasons, but the legislation was subsequently disallowed by the imperial government in 1851 (Careless, supra note 2, at 82; Rogers, supra note 36, at 118–19; Jean-Marie Fecteau, 'Les dangers du secret: note sur l'Etat Canadien et les sociétés secrètes au milieu du 19e siècle' (1991), 6 *Canadian Journal of Law and Society*), 91–111).

47 Francis Hincks published his views on the subject of controlling Orange Order parades in a letter to the Montreal *Gazette*, 30 July 1877.

48 Peter B. Waite, *Canada 1874–1896: Arduous Destiny* (Toronto: McClelland and Stewart 1971), 88.

49 An account of the Guibord affair from contemporary sources is given by Lovell C. Clark in *The Guibord Affair* (Toronto: Holt Rinehart and Winston 1971).

50 National Archives of Canada (hereafter cited as NAC). Order in council, RG2, p.c. 1074.

51 According to Richard Scott, dominion secretary of state, the lieutenant-governor of Quebec sent a hostile reply (Ontario Archives (hereinafter cited as OA), Blake Papers, Ms 20, Reel 6, Scott 13); however, the Quebec attorney general made moves that resulted in two local mayors of Montreal calling out the militia for the reburial (Pariseau, supra note 16, at 78).

52 According to Morton's account, Hickson made at least three requests to Mackenzie, but Mackenzie stood firm on the basis that 'the magistrates and local authorities alone can act': supra note 4, at 17.

53 The mayor, Jean-Louis Beaudry, telegraphed directly to Mackenzie on 18 December 1877, asking for action to preserve order along the Lachine Canal during the strike and Mackenzie again refused: NAC, RG11, B1(a), vol. 473.

54 The contractor, Davis, was accused of underpaying labourers, and 1,000 men were on strike in December 1877. Shots were fired at Davis through his office window, slightly injuring his son, and return fire seriously injured a worker. Davis applied to the federal minister of justice for 'protection on the works' and was turned down: supra note 53.

55 Concerning patronage in relation to urban police in the period, for Toronto practices see Helen Boritch, 'Conflict, Compromise and Administrative Convenience: The Police Organization in Nineteenth-Century Toronto' (1988), 3 *Canadian Journal of Law and Society*, 141–74; for Quebec see Elinor Kyte Senior, supra note 40, at 85–97; and Alan Greer, 'The Birth of the Police in Canada,' in Greer and Radforth, supra note 45.

56 The departure of British army units by the early 1870s (except from Halifax and Esquimault) left the country without an effective professional military presence, a matter of concern to John A. Macdonald and to Alexander Mackenzie. See Thomson, supra note 41, at 335, and Donald Creighton, *John A. Macdonald: The Old Chieftain* (Toronto: Macmillan 1955), 245, 411.

57 *Dufferin-Carnarvon Correspondence, 1874–1878*, ed. C.W. de Kewiet and Frank Underhill (Toronto: The Champlain Society 1955), 158.

58 *Hansard*, Commons, 6 May 1877. Speech by M.P. John White, Orange Order grand master for eastern Ontario.

59 Thomas Scott was executed at Red River Colony by Riel's followers during the first rebellion in 1870.

60 The Scots were represented in negotiations over the planned Orange parade by the St Andrew's Society, the French Catholics by the St Jean Baptiste organization, the Irish Catholics by the St Patrick's Society and their umbrella organization, the Irish Catholic Union. The Catholic church spoke indirectly through several newspapers funded by the church, including *Le Franc-Parleur* and the more extreme *Journal des Trois Rivières*. Even representatives of the German Society participated in public meetings.

61 Montreal, *Daily Witness*, 9 July 1877.

62 *Dictionary of Canadian Biography* (hereinafter cited as *DCB*), vol. 11 (Toronto: University of Toronto Press 1966–xx), 59–62.

63 The description of events is based on the accounts given in *Le Franc-Parleur*, *La Minerve*, the Montreal *Gazette*, the Montreal *Daily Witness*, and the *True Witness*.

64 See accounts in the Montreal *Gazette*, 12, 14, and 17 July 1877.

65 The verdict was reported in the *Gazette*, 18 July 1877.

66 Montreal *Daily Witness*, 13 and 14 July 1877.

67 As described at the inquest; see the Montreal *Gazette*, 16 and 17 July 1877.

68 Summoned and marched around the streets by their officers after the mayor, Jean-Louis Beaudry, refused to call them out – a refusal for which he was later strongly criticized by Orange Order members and other Protestants.

69 In an editorial on 19 July 1877.

70 Montreal *Daily Witness* 13 July 1877; The Montreal *Gazette*, 14 July 1877.

71 NAC, Dufferin Papers, 12–14 June 1878.

72 (1877) 40 Vict., c. 30. Certain weapons were already controlled under An Act respecting Offenses against the Person (32–33 Vict., c. 20, [1869]) which made it an offence to carry weapons including knives and daggers. Local forms of weapons control also existed under pre-Confederation bylaws and statutes, in New Brunswick and possibly elsewhere. (I am grateful to Greg Marquis for pointing this out.)

73 In this incident on 29 April 1878, about 100 men had gathered near the Wellington Bridge when shots were fired and one Irish Catholic, John Colligan, was killed, and others were injured (Montreal *Gazette*, 3 May 1878). Colligan's funeral on 6 May not only outdid Hackett's in terms of numbers, with an estimated 4,000 mourners, but took place on the same day that Blake's new bill received third reading in the House of Commons.

74 It is striking how frequently mention of handguns or other weapons is found in research on labour in this period: for instance, in relation to the building of the Pacific Railway, statements refer to foremen carrying guns as though it was a customary pattern; a similar situation prevailed during the 1877 riot on the Lachine Canal. See Binnie, supra note 29.

75 *Hansard*, Commons, 4 April 1878.

76 Montreal *Daily Witness*, 10 July 1877.

77 (1869) 31 Vict., c. 12 and (1876) 31 Vict. [Imp.], c. 14.

78 Having become president of the Privy Council in June 1877 and carried out his threat to resign from the Cabinet in January 1878.

79 The origin of the bill is clarified in the record of the parliamentary debates, in which both Devlin and Jetté spoke (*Hansard*, Commons, 2-6 May 1878). Jetté, a Reform Catholic lawyer and brother-in-law of the current minister of justice, Rodolphe Laflamme, had acted for the Catholic church in the Guibord affair in Montreal and had helped found the Parti National in Quebec. Devlin was a popular lawyer and well-known spokesman for Irish Catholics in Montreal (10 *DCB*, vol. 10, 229–30).

80 No correspondence appears to have survived on the subject between Blake and Mackenzie.

81 According to *The Dominion Annual Register and Review*, supra note 7, at 135, 'Mr Mackenzie, on behalf of the Government, entirely concurred with the principles and provisions of the bill.'

82 This is the same John White whom Donald Akenson portrayed as the transvestite prostitute Eliza McCormack in *The Life and Times of Eliza McCormack/ John White* (Montreal: McGill-Queen's University Press 1990).

83 *Hansard*, Commons, 4 May 1878.

84 The bill was rushed through the House of Commons between 2 and 6 May 1878.

85 Accounts of the riot between members of the Irish Ship Labourers Benevolent Society and L'Union Canadienne are provided in the *Dominion Annual
   Register and Review* for 1879; in Cooper, supra note 30; and in local newspapers, including the *Journal de Quebec.* The riot occurred on 15-16 August
   1879; the local magistrates requested a proclamation of the act on 19
   August, and the act was proclaimed on 2 September.
86 NAC, RG13, 86-7, 084, Box 8, 731 (43) 1882; RG13, A3, vol. 606 c. 14, 3331,
   10 May 1882. See also the Winnipeg *Daily Free Press* and the Winnipeg *Daily
   Times* for March 1882 for details of overcrowding in the city due to migration westwards, and ibid., 8-10 May, for details of a major case of arson.
87 Indexes to all federal orders in council were examined for the period
   1867–92 in the course of this research.
88 Files in federal Department of Justice records show little activity in relation
   to the act. The limited correspondence deals mostly with payment of
   annual stipends to the commissioners, who appear to have done little work,
   perhaps regarding the positions as sinecures. Thus, although the Blake Act
   was proclaimed for the city of Quebec in September 1879, as late as
   November 1879 one Quebec commissioner inquired whether there was to
   be a charge for firearms licences (NAC, RG13, A3, vol. 596, C14322, 12
   November 1879).
89 Such as Lewis's manual of 1884, admittedly published in Toronto. It was
   also omitted from Stephen's *Quebec Law Digest,* vol. 2 (Montreal: Périard
   1882) and mentioned briefly but without any reported cases in vol. 3
   (Montreal: Lovell 1886).
90 Morton, supra note 37, at 413.
91 *Hansard,* Commons, 4 February 1881.
92 See Binnie, supra note 29, at 572–603.
93 Although Blake failed in a similar endeavour in 1880 when he introduced a
   bill based on an English penal statute into the House (*Hansard,* 23 February 1880).
94 The province passed legislation to ban parades, although too late to be of
   use for 12 July 1878. Morton, supra note 37, at 413.

9 Civil Liberties and the Law: California during the First World War

DIANE M.T. NORTH

On 6 June 1788, in a speech defending the proposed new Constitution of the United States, James Madison argued: 'Since the general civilization of mankind, I believe there are more instances of the abridgment of the freedom of the people, by gradual and silent encroachments of those in power, than by violent and sudden usurpations.'[1] Madison's concern – encroachments of power – frames the thesis of this essay on civil liberties and the law in California during the First World War. I will describe briefly California on the eve of the United States' entry into the European conflict; I will address in detail the creation of federal, state, and local governmental units and private citizens' associations that cooperated to spy on, threaten, detain, arrest, and imprison dissidents, labourers, certain racial and ethnic minorities, and ordinary citizens; and I will examine and set forth ideas about civil liberties and the notion and role of the state in the creation of modern California, and indeed modern America.[2]

The Great War set in motion a variety of demographic, political, social, and economic changes in California. Although far removed physically from the battlefields of Western Europe and from the national capital in Washington, California's local, county, and state government functions expanded to meet new federal requirements as well as demands made by private citizens' associations. Governments and private organizations also devised new political surveillance techniques and restrictive legislation, and used the rhetoric of democracy to control behaviour and to suppress protest, certain racial and ethnic minorities – especially Asian-Americans and new Asian immigrants – and the radical labour organization, the

Industrial Workers of the World (IWW). Working within the Progressive party framework, which earlier had enacted notable social and political programs to correct many of the ills of industrialization and moderniz-ation, California citizens and their elected officials shaped a political culture that emphasized loyalty and conformity.

In addition to stimulating patriotic nationalism and uniting many Cali-fornians in a common humanitarian and political direction, an amalgam of characteristics peculiar to California, together with the extraordinary changes brought about by the First World War, combined to create a political culture in which distrust of dissent and state repression of rad-icalism would increasingly appear to be the rule rather than the exception.

In the years between 1910 and 1920 the state's population grew from 2.3 million to 3.4 million, of which approximately 200,000 persons were members of minority groups, the largest being the Japanese. California has a divisive and scandalous history of race relations and vigilante com-mittees, but in this pre-war period Asian immigrants seemed to threaten the equilibrium of ordinary citizens. Some Californians even worried about an invasion from Japan in the first decade of the new century. When the United States entered the war on 6 April 1917 the federal government launched a pervasive propaganda campaign to herald the nation's superiority and demand loyalty. Every corner of America was bombarded with sentiments about white, middle-class, Christian, capitalist virtues, and the resulting atmosphere of tension and distrust heightened the concern for social justice by the disenfranchised. At the same time the government used a strident rhetoric of democracy to create civic education programs that would 'Americanize' and assimilate new immi-grants and eliminate the threat posed by the anarchic 'foreign' doctrines of pacifism, socialism, and communism.

In California, which became a leader in positive efforts to improve the lot of workers and its ever-fluctuating itinerant seasonal labour force, countless men and women engaged in patriotic, humanitarian war work to raise money or provide material support for war victims, and took part in numerous food and energy conservation efforts. Yet some citizens, especially Valentine S. McClatchy, one of the owners of a Sacramento newspaper, and Anthony Caminetti, a congressional representative who would head the US Immigration Commission, used the war as an excuse to form a privately funded joint committee on immigration to try to get rid of the Japanese. The group eventually successfully lobbied for more stringent alien – that is, anti-Asian – land ownership laws and for national immigration restrictions, which were implemented in the 1920s.[3]

In economic terms, massive landholdings were concentrated in the hands of a few, and agriculture depended on an exploited cheap and ethnically diverse labour market. Extractive industries – oil, timber, fisheries – were expanding, as were food-processing industries, and transportation and water systems were being enlarged. The war provided a boost to California's economy and accelerated the process of corporate organization. The merchants and manufacturers' association in Los Angeles defied unionism and waged open-shop strikebreaking campaigns; San Francisco, by contrast, sustained a number of relatively successful trade unions in spite of the chamber of commerce's vigilant Law and Order Committee. The class-conscious, fiery, anti-capitalist rhetoric of the IWW, which advocated strikes, sabotage, higher wages, and shorter hours, was seen as a threat not only by leading capitalists but also by more moderate union leaders. Although the IWW scored some membership successes among migrant workers, its California membership was low and out of proportion to the harassment it encountered.[4]

In politics, Governor Hiram Johnson served as the catalytic force for the Progressive party, but his move into the US Senate when the country entered the war resulted in a leadership gap. Structural weaknesses developed in the party after the selection of William Stephens, a conservative southern Californian, as governor. Before Johnson left for Washington, he had overseen the enactment of pathbreaking reforms to the electoral system and for the establishment of pragmatic, centralized, humanitarian social programs.[5]

Californians were divided in their support of peace or preparedness for war. In July 1916 a bomb exploded in the midst of a San Francisco Preparedness Day parade, killing ten persons. The chief suspect, Tom Mooney, became a celebrated political prisoner, and studies have shown that his trial was an abrogation of justice.[6] Johnson fretted that the war was wrecking the Progressive agenda, and became a staunch opponent of President Woodrow Wilson. The new senator objected to the enactment of a Sedition Act because the bill's intent was 'to suppress the freedom of the press ... to prevent any man ... from indulging in fair and decent expression concerning the present Government.'[7] The president of the University of California, Benjamin Ide Wheeler, was opposed to war, as was David Starr Jordan, a former president of Stanford University and an internationally recognized leader of the peace movement. Wheeler's loyalty was questioned and his resignation called for because of his friendship with the Kaiser, while the new president of Stanford, Ray Lyman Wilbur, was adamant in his support of Wilson's war plans.[8] One of

California's most popular congressmen, Julius Kahn, was a strong advocate of preparedness, a founder of the National Defense League for improving the nation's military capabilities, and the initiator of the Selective Service Act. He strongly attacked those who opposed the United States' entry into the war and urged that 'fomenters of disloyalty be "taken before a court martial under military law and if convicted, punished in the way his crime implies." ' Without mincing words, Kahn declared, ' "Those who are not with us in this conflict are against us. They should be deterred from their treasonable course. This is no time to listen to the vaporings of pusillanimous pacifists or disloyal pro-Germans." '9

As the national government mobilized for war by creating various administrative units and enacting legislation to ferret out spies, saboteurs, enemy aliens, draft dodgers, and those suspected of disloyalty – including the press – state and municipal governments and private citizens' associations duplicated the federal model.10 Throughout US history, associations of private citizens have adopted extralegal and violent tactics to achieve their aims, as exemplified by a radical element in the anti-slavery movement, the Ku Klux Klan, anti-union activities on the part of capitalists, and certain political parties such as the Workingmen's Party in California.11 During the First World War, numerous patriotic organizations continued the tradition. For example, the American Protective League (APL), created in 1917 with the approval of the US attorney general and operating under the direction of the Federal Bureau of Investigation (FBI), was a privately funded, nationwide organization that recruited about 250,000 white, middle- and upper-class, morally sound male citizen volunteers. Because the Justice Department became responsible for enforcing major wartime legislation, including the Espionage, Sedition, Sabotage, and Selective Service acts and sections of the Food and Fuel Administration Act and regulations concerning enemy aliens, the APL volunteers would assist government agents in their work and report disloyal or enemy activities to the proper officials. The league regarded itself as a defender of the nation's security, and California became a key area of operation. According to various accounts, the work of the APL in California proved to be 'one of the most extreme examples of the surrender of the American people to irrationality.' Yet the attorney general described the assistance of the APL as 'invaluable' and as providing 'the greatest possible aid in thousands of cases.'12

The entire state of California was organized to allow the volunteer operatives to cover large cities, small towns, farming, ranching, and timber-production centres, packing companies, gas and electric utilities, railroads, oil fields, telephone and telegraph services, all manufacturing plants, and major bridges and water projects. League members busied themselves with their war against subversion by spending thousands of hours investigating and reporting on the character of citizens – enlisted men and officers, merchants, housewives, Red Cross workers, society women who entertained suspected German sympathizers, teachers, Boy Scout leaders, members of the Knights of Columbus and the YMCA, students, ministers, doctors, government officials, Germans, American citizens with German names, members of the IWW and suspected members, Mexicans, and radicals of any kind. The league secretly checked on people's citizenship, loyalty, and character, and on whether they had made seditious utterances orally or in print. When asked to report on prominent citizens recommended for important government posts, the APL tried to ascertain each individual's state of mind about the war before and after the United States' entry. Operatives also questioned those suspected of treason, sabotage, or interference with the manufacture of war material or obstruction of the draft. APL members relied on reckless undocumented accusations, on public opinion, and on hearsay. They illegally entered and searched people's homes and offices. On their recommendations, loyal citizens were denied jobs or detained by local, state, or federal authorities and punished.

These hyper-Christian moralists who excluded women and Jews from their ranks, tracked down alien enemies, slackers, and deserters and those who may have sold liquor illegally to soldiers or been engaged in 'vice and prostitution.' APL volunteers not only undertook investigations for the Department of Justice but worked for the War Department by collecting foreign maps and photographs, and for the Navy Department by searching for counterespionage activists who used wireless, lights, or signalling devices. The volunteers uncovered instances of hoarding, destruction, waste, and profiteering for food and fuel administrations, and checked on the legitimacy of passports for the Department of State. In addition, in order to make certain that service personnel or their families were not abusing the system, operatives followed through on assignments from the Treasury Department regarding war-risk insurance allowances and frauds. APLers also checked on citizens' character and loyalty for the US Shipping Board, and tried to guarantee the legitimacy of goods – or take care of alien enemy property transfers – for the alien property custodian.[13]

When the Orange County division submitted its final report to national

headquarters, the author boasted of the anti-German sentiment of the
devoted agents and described how the APL accomplished the elimination
of the teaching of the German language in public and parochial schools
and in the German Sunday schools. The division chief suggested that pro-
German organizations had been stamped out or muzzled and were no
longer a threat in Anaheim or Orange.[14]

Some league members sanctioned vigilantism. For example, the district
chief for Richmond, an East Bay town that housed several munitions
factories, noted that 'Local night riders tarred and feathered one alien
enemy for seditious utterances.' The APLer believed that this 'greatly
reduced the number of cases for investigation and stopped general
arguments on the war situation.' Someone, presumably at national headquarters, approved the action and wrote 'good' in the margin of the
report. The Richmond chief seemed to conclude that illegal aggression,
fear, and the ability of agitated citizens to take the law into one's own
hands were vital to democracy, for he believed that the work of the APL
'ha[d] been the means of making us all better Americans with a greater
love and regard for our Country than ever before.'[15]

Because many Californians lacked ties to family members and former
communities, associations were a way for people with shared ideas and
values to come together and unite around specific issues rather than
within traditional communities, and create a homogeneous society. Unfortunately, by the close of the war, certain branches of the APL, especially
in Los Angeles, used the framework of that association to create new
super-patriotic organizations, such as the Better American Federation,
which was concerned with maintaining law and order and the promotion
of an ultra-conservative and at times repressive political, economic, and
social agenda.[16]

The American Protective League was a voluntary association, in the
progressive tradition of volunteerism, with a special twist – a sanctioned
connection to the federal government and an ability to cooperate with
state and local governments. Organized by advertising executives and
patterned after the corporation and the military with strong leadership,
hierarchical command chains, numerous branches reaching into every
corner of the country, definite regulations, strict selection procedures, the
imperative to operate secretly, and a coordinated administrative network,
it also possessed an ethos. This ethos was the fervent belief that its activities protected rather than endangered democratic principles. Righteous
to a fault, the APL ignored the threat to society posed by their provoca-
tive and illegal surveillance. By acting within the federal and state bureau-

cratic apparatus, the APL contributed both to the expansion of governmental power and to the erosion of personal liberty.

In addition to the activities of private citizens' groups, various local, state, and federal entities cooperated to scrutinize the daily lives of citizens and to institutionalize mechanisms of political repression or forms of social control. One of the more unusual local developments occurred in the police department of Los Angeles city and county. On 1 April 1918 the police organized a separate bureau known as the 'War Squad,' 'for the purpose of aiding the various civil and military branches of the Federal Government' in the prosecution of the war. As there was no precedent for such work, the unit was experimental; by the close of the fiscal year, thirteen men worked for the squad, including ten who served as investigators. The office stayed open sixteen hours a day in order to register German aliens.[17]

The special unit worked indefatigably. In the three-month period the squad arrested 220 persons for seditious remarks, violations of the Espionage Act, failure to report for military duty or register as a German alien enemy, or desecrating the US flag. Police arrested individuals under suspicion as enemy aliens, spies, deserters, or slackers (the term reserved for those men who did not want to join the military); and presidential warrants were obtained for the internment of suspects. Within a year the unit had conducted approximately 9,000 investigations. No one seemed immune to suspicion. Even those citizens who neglected to contribute to liberty fund drives were identified and investigated by zealous agents. The police also responded to complaints made by conscientious Angelenos about the suspected unpatriotic conduct of others. In addition, the War Squad obtained information from and cooperated with numerous branches of the federal government, especially in cases involving press censorship of newspapers published by German-Americans and enemy aliens and by Mexican revolutionaries, including the legendary activist, Ricardo Flores Magón, who became a victim of anti-anarchist repression.[18]

The chief of police noted in his annual report for 1918 that at a recent convention of the International Association of Chiefs of Police at Kansas City, a high-ranking US intelligence officer 'generously approved the War Squad idea recommending it as a pattern for national activity.'[19] The mayor congratulated 'this pioneer organization among municipal corporations,' and indicated that Los Angeles law enforcement officials pursued a specific anti-labour and anti-radical political agenda. The mayor noted that by the end of 1918 the War Squad had trailed 'spies, terrorists, labour disturbers and hostile aliens – all new classes of malefactors so far as the Police Department was concerned.' He recalled how the 'police ha[d] watched the activities of labour agitators and held them powerless. The IWW and kindred groups have been restrained, with the result that Los Angeles, of all coast cities, has escaped serious labour trouble.'[20]

Other municipalities actively restrained the free speech and right of assembly of Californians. On 2 April 1918 the Berkeley city council unanimously passed an ordinance 'Prohibiting the Utterance or Use of Seditious Language, or of Words Tending to Disturb the Peace.' The ordinance forbade anyone in the city to use within the hearing of another person any seditious language, words, epithets, or expressions that had a tendency to 'create a breach of peace.' Violation and conviction of this vague but all-encompassing misdemeanour was punishable by a fine not to exceed five hundred dollars, six months in prison, or both. Oakland had a similar, though less punitive ordinance. There is a disturbing account in the APL papers about how volunteer operatives rounded up ten citizens with German names, who supposedly drank a toast to the Kaiser one evening at a local restaurant, and hauled these unsuspecting citizens off to jail for three months.[21]

A counterespionage agent for the Military Intelligence Division (MID) of the War Department reported a 'terrific increase in mob violence' throughout the western department in April 1918, when the 'public took the law into their own hands and punished enemies of [the] Government.' Angry residents tore down and burned the Berkeley Church of the Living God, headed by the Reverend Joshua Sykes, and tried to find Sykes in order to hang him. The pastor, under investigation by MID, previously had advised his congregation that he would protect them from the selective service draft. The War Department agent thought this action demonstrated 'the positive demand for more stringent laws to cover enemy activities.' A month later MID reported that citizens of the Santa Clara Valley were disgruntled with the cautious way in which local public officials treated suspected pro-German agitators, and formed vigilance committees under the name of the Knights of Liberty to administer a more personal form of justice.[22]

Other Californians, unable to join the soldiers in the trenches or work for the APL, expressed a willingness to contribute to the war effort by ensuring public security, and, with the coordinating skills of the state Council of Defense, organized loyalty committees in fifty-eight counties. Members 'actively and definitely engaged in the stamping out of disloyalists and seditionists,' aided in the detention of enemy aliens, and furnished valuable information to government authorities. The Council of Defense instructed each county council to appoint 'one cautious, level-headed, courageous man' to serve as chairman of the Loyalty Committee who would confidently report to the state the names and addresses of persons guilty of pro-German or anti-American talk, and also quietly urge the 'disloyal party' to refrain from making any remarks against the government or the prosecution of the war. In a bulletin issued by the council, committees were told: 'It is a grievous wrong, to the men who are offering their lives in support of the flag, that any of our people should make their undertaking more hazardous, by disloyal acts at home.' The council also set up an 'Intelligence Division' with volunteer agents in every county who worked closely with the federal Department of Justice, MID, and naval intelligence. The vice-chairman of the council, A.H. Naftzger, was convinced that California's security program kept it 'gratifyingly free' of 'overt demonstrations' and 'destructive enemy plots' that other states experienced.[23]

As mentioned earlier, the president of the University of California at Berkeley, Benjamin Wheeler, was criticized for his pre-war peace work and close ties to the Kaiser. The secretary of the board of regents wrote to citizens throughout the state assuring them of Wheeler's loyalty. But at the same time the regents set up a three-man, notably pro-British, advisory panel to help Wheeler with his administrative duties and to 'calm' the 'public restlessness over the current gossip.' However, several decisions by the university administration to eradicate dissident, or presumed dissident, behaviour and to enforce patriotism indicated how seriously it responded to accusations of disloyalty and how concerned it was to control the university community and create a homogeneous, stable setting. These decisions involved requiring faculty, employees, and students to sign loyalty pledges as a condition of employment and matriculation, cooperating with the American Protective League by asking it to investigate suspected personnel, and dismissing faculty members without due process because of their 'unsatisfactory attitude toward the present war,' including association with suspected pro-Germans. The evidence for the dismissal of several faculty members seems to have been based on rumour, the decisions based on the politics of fear. A dismissed professor of German language and literature appealed to have his case reviewed and be reinstated, but the procedures dragged on for six years, and he was unsuccessful.[24]

One aspect of the history of wartime hysteria is especially troubling because of the vigorous and concentrated manner in which local, state, regional, and federal authorities, industrialists, citizens' associations, and private individuals hounded the IWW. The exceptionally thorough nationwide effort was coordinated for California and the western region from the governor's office and overseen by the head of the Commission of Immigration and Housing, Simon Lubin, an otherwise enlightened and progressive department store executive who secretly paid an industrial spy to infiltrate the IWW. The district attorneys in San Francisco and Los Angeles cooperated with private detective agents hired by industrialists, with volunteers from the American Protective League and local councils of defense, and with agents from the departments of Justice, Labour, Treasury, and the Navy, and the War Department's MID.[25]

Even though the IWW membership was small, its presence was acutely felt, especially in the Central and San Joaquin agricultural valleys, in the oil fields, and in the forests because of its fiery, class-conscious rhetoric and its aggressive organizing tactics. Except in a few instances, it is difficult to ascertain accurately what criminal acts IWW members committed. When the Fresno membership initiated a free speech crusade in 1910, their meetings provoked mob violence, mass arrests, and extralegal repression. That is how the state and the people responded to the 'Wobblies' in the war years.[26]

Using presidential warrants and various wartime legislation, authorities spied on, harassed, and convicted countless members of the IWW throughout the country, and notably in Fresno and Sacramento. In addition to using the legal force of wartime controls, and the violence that accompanied that force, California's leaders helped shape the direction of the American labour movement by relying on its legislature and its courts to stifle the IWW, which was viewed as subversive before, during, and after the war. Throughout the war years the California legislature attempted to pass a Criminal Syndicalism Act aimed at silencing and punishing individuals or members of a group who expressed opinions deemed offensive to those holding power. The legislature finally succeeded in April 1919, and localities quickly duplicated the state's action. For example, Humboldt County, in the northwestern part of the state, passed a Criminal Syndicalism Ordinance that remained in force until May 1977. This legislation defined criminal syndicalism as: 'any doctrine or precept advocating, teaching or aiding and abetting the commission of crime, sabotage ... or unlawful acts of force and violence or unlawful methods of terrorism as a means of accomplishing a change in industrial ownership or control, or effecting any political change.'[27]

The state used this tool vigorously to prosecute the IWW and those so-called radicals who appeared to challenge the stability of Progressive plans and threatened to discredit what Progressive leaders saw as legitimate attempts to build a more just and orderly society. One scholar has argued that the IWW played the decisive role in the evolution of the federal government's anti-radical policy, for by 'eliminating the Wobblies, government officials passed legislation, evolved techniques and learned lessons that shaped their later course of conduct.'[28] Over five hundred indictments were handed down in California between 1919 and 1924, including several celebrated cases – specifically that of the active pacifist, IWW supporter, and member of a distinguished family, Charlotte Anita Whitney. The US Supreme Court upheld the constitutionality of California's Criminal Syndicalism law in *Whitney v. California*. Although the court overruled *Whitney* in *Brandenburg v. Ohio*, the law is still part of the California Penal Code[29] and is one of the few instances where a state legislature has repeatedly sought to ignore Supreme Court decisions by enacting minor changes in the law each time it is ruled unconstitutional.[30]

The First World War changed the dynamics of life in modern California. By permitting infringements on free speech and the press, by restricting and denying freedom of assembly and association, and by circumscribing due process, federal, state, and local governments, with the cooperation of the majority of citizens, undermined civil liberties and initiated coercive measures and intrusive, often inept habits of bureaucratic behaviour that persist today. The state sanctioned vigilantism and a reckless disregard for the truth, and turned citizens against each other by co-opting members of certain patriotic organizations as enforcers of wartime measures.

Civil liberties principles embodied in the Constitution and Bill of Rights have undergone a gradual evolution in the twentieth century, and were viewed differently before the First World War. The counsel to the Federal Commission on Industrial Relations pointed out in 1915 that the US Supreme Court, in its interpretation of the due process clause of the Fourteenth Amendment, 'does not apply the U.S. bill of rights to the states. Hence the protection of these personal rights and liberties are still left largely to the States, with certain definite limitations imposed by the due process clause.'[31] During the First World War the ideals of national security and loyalty were foremost concerns. The war tested and strengthened the resolve of the newly organized American Civil Liberties Union and other groups concerned with the defence of civil liberties and civil rights, and gradually brought the issue of civil liberties before the public.[32]

There is an awkward, fragile element to the preservation of civil liberties in a nation that believes itself to be democratic and uses the discourse of democracy to justify violations of civil liberties. The concept of civil liberties depends in part on how the state defines the democratic tradition and, in the case of wartime controls, on what constitutes a national emergency. The concept is continually being redefined by the prevailing power structure and by those groups not included in, but theoretically provided for by, the Bill of Rights. In American political culture both the sovereign state and the self-appointed voluntary guardians of the society have resorted to force in the name of security considerations. One of the persistent sources of tension between the state and the people has been the debate about how much state power is justified, particularly during periods of crisis. Wartime controls on dissent, bureaucratic surveillance agencies, and vigilantism all stimulate questions about whether the use of force is an expression of pre-war domination by certain groups, a desire to control internal dissent, or a response to a perceived alteration in the social status of challengers to the existing order.[33]

The First World War era witnessed the initiation of restrictive legislation, coupled with the rise of an entangled bureaucratic apparatus and administrative power with its own legal processes. This was a significant change for twentieth-century society. Security agencies competed with each other. The emphasis on administrative matters tended to overlook, ignore, or set aside concerns about integrity or justice. The key point in an administrative apparatus was (and is) to accomplish an assignment and sustain the power of the agency. In a commentary on the growth of early twentieth-century institutions, the political writer Walter Lippmann suggested that 'the effort itself has become the aim.'[34] The actual working out of administrative matters created a political climate that in each bureaucracy was insular, autonomous, inept, invasive, and that often permitted the institution to operate illegally.

Also, there seemed to be a special momentum to the process of gathering information on suspected persons. The process fed on itself. One memo or report led to another, and then to another. A file was created – often several files – because names were spelled erroneously. Other investigating agents in the same unit were asked to review a report. Copies were sent to the US attorneys' offices around the country and to other federal, state, and local departments. In addition, the new technology of the time made an enormous difference in how the work got done. Agencies and agents made creative use of the typewriter, carbon paper, the telephone and telegraph, efficient mail service, the new reliable automobiles, and crude wiretapping devices. This activity – the cooperation among investigating agencies and public officials and private citizens, the proliferation of investigations, the reliance on hearsay – set in motion an administrative process that enhanced state power at the expense of societal liberty. The process became established quickly, complete with formalized administrative practices. The state and those connected with it acted as if they were part of a vast new machine that took on a life of its own.

California's experience can be usefully compared and contrasted with that of other states. Within two weeks after the United States entered the war, the state legislature of Minnesota, anxious about the conduct of its large German-American population and eager to dampen the efforts of the agrarian activists – the Nonpartisan League – and traditional and radical labour unions, enacted a series of bills that placed the state 'under a virtual dictatorship for the duration of the war.' The legislature created an independent Commission of Public Safety with broad powers to defend the state and passed a criminal syndicalism measure and other bills prohibiting the possession of firearms or explosives by alien enemies and outlawing interference with the selective service process.[35] Not all Minnesotans wholeheartedly supported the war effort, for the quota of the first Liberty Loan campaign was not reached.[36] North Dakota and Iowa also vilified pacifists, German-Americans, and the IWW, and accused the Nonpartisan League of disloyalty, especially after the league members, concerned about low farm prices, high interest rates, and the dominance of corporate power over agriculture, opposed the Wilson administration's policy on the price of wheat. Although the league supported the war, its leaders raised issues of class when they 'blamed Eastern industrialists for America's drift toward war' and 'called for conscription of wealth as well as of men.'[37]

The demands of the war on California's people and resources dampened the formerly successful efforts of early twentieth-century progressive era reforms, and pointed out the limits of those reform activities because Progressives in California dramatized class and race divisions in American society. The Progressives' belief in the greatness of America – including a belief in the idea of progress and the notion of republican virtue – and desire to reshape and manage the society, the economy, and technology, resulted during the war years in an exaggeration of the opposition, a new definition of loyalty, and fear. The strident call for internal security played itself out in attacks on non-conforming radicals, on those who questioned or threatened the prevailing power structure, and on Asian-Americans and other racial and ethnic groups, rather than in concerns about the dangers of ultraconservative patriots or the loss of individual liberty. It also served as a catalyst for the growth of state power by being the stimulus whereby federal, state, county, and local units, private associations, and individuals scrutinized the daily lives of citizens and institutionalized a mechanism of political repression and forms of social control.

NOTES

1 *The Papers of James Madison*, ed. Robert A. Rutland et al. (Charlottesville: University Press of Virginia 1977), 11:79.
2 I have drawn on local, state, and national primary research materials either previously unavailable because of security classification concerns or unmined. I wish to thank the staffs of the National Archives and Record Service in Washington, the Bancroft Library at the University of California at Berkeley, the California State Library in Sacramento, numerous local historical societies throughout California, and the Office of the Attorney General for the State of California.
3 Richard B. Rice, William A. Bullough, and Richard J. Orsi, *The Elusive Eden: A New History of California* (New York: A.A. Knopf 1988); Roger Daniels, *The Politics of Prejudice: The Anti-Japanese Movement in California and the Struggle for Japanese Exclusion*, vol. 71 of the University of California *Publications in History* (Berkeley: University of California Press 1962; paperback 1977); Sucheng Chan, *Asian Californians*, in *Golden State Series*, ed. Norris Hundley Jr and John A. Schutz (San Francisco: MTL/Boyd and Fraser 1991); records of the California Joint Immigration Commission, Bancroft Library, University of California, Berkeley; State of California, Board of Control, *California and the Oriental* (Sacramento 1920); Joseph Giovinco, 'The California Career of Anthony Caminetti: Italian-American Politician,' Ph.D. thesis, University of California at Berkeley 1973); George Creel, *How We Advertised America* (New York: Harper and Bros. 1920); Thomas J. Archdeacon, *Becoming American: An Ethnic History* (New York: The Free Press 1983); State of California, Commission of Immigration and Housing, *Americanization: The California Program* (Sacramento: State Printing Office 1919); Edith Daley, *War History of Santa Clara County* (n.p.: Santa Clara Historical Society [1919]); State of California, Council of Defense, *California in the War* (Sacramento 1918).
4 William Issel and Robert W. Cherny, *San Francisco, 1865-1932: Politics, Power and Urban Development* (Berkeley: University of California Press 1986); Mike Davis, *City of Quartz: Excavating the Future in Los Angeles*, in *The Haymarket*

Series, ed. Mike Davis and Michael Sprinker (London: Verso 1990); State of California, Commission of Immigration and Housing, *A Report on Large Landholdings in Southern California with Recommendations* (Sacramento 1919); State of California, Bureau of Labour Statistics, *Eighteenth Biennial Report, 1917–1918* (Sacramento 1918), and *Nineteenth Biennial Report, 1919–1920* (Sacramento 1920); State of California, *Biennial Report of the Board of State Harbour Commissioners, July 1, 1916–June 30, 1918* (Sacramento 1919); Melvyn Dubofsky, *We Shall Be All: A History of the Industrial Workers of the World* (New York: Quadrangle/The New York Times Book Co. 1969); David F. Selvin, *Sky Full of Storm: A Brief History of California Labour*, rev. ed. (San Francisco: California Historical Society 1975); Michael Kazin, *Barons of Labour: The San Francisco Building Trades and Union Power in the Progressive Era* (Urbana: University of Illinois Press 1987).

5 George Mowry, *The California Progressives* (Berkeley: University of California Press 1951); Spencer C. Olin Jr, *California's Prodigal Sons: Hiram Johnson and the Progressives, 1911–1917* (Berkeley: University of California Press 1969); Mansel Blackford, 'Business and the Regulation of Railroads and Public Utilities in California During the Progressive Era' (1970), 44 *Business History Review*, 307–19; Mary Ann Mason Burki, 'The California Progressives: Labour's Point of View' (1976), 17 *Labour History*, 24–37; Jackson K. Putnam, 'The Persistence of Progressivism in the 1920s: The Case of California,' (1966), 35 *Pacific Historical Review*, 395–411; Jacqueline R. Braitman, 'A California Stateswoman: The Public Career of Katherine Philips Edson' (1986), 65 *California History*, 82–95, 151–2; H. Brett Melendy and Benjamin F. Gilbert, *The Governors of California* (Georgetown, Calif.: The Talisman Press 1965).

6 Richard H. Frost, *The Mooney Case* (Stanford: University Press 1968).

7 Hiram Johnson to C.K. McClatchy, 6 February 1918, in the Hiram Johnson Papers, Bancroft Library, University of California, Berkeley, as cited in Howard A. De Witt, 'Hiram Johnson and World War I: A Progressive in Transition' (1974), 56 *Southern California Quarterly*, 301–5.

8 Letter, Secretary of the Board of Regents V.H. Henderson to E.L. Finley, 7 December 1917, CU-1, Box 73, Regents' Files, file 1917, Archives, Bancroft Library, University of California, Berkeley; John Y. Cole, 'David Starr Jordan: Stanford's Tower of Strength' (1987), 13 *Imprint*, 5–9; *The Memoirs of Ray Lyman Wilbur*, 1875–1949, ed. E.E. Robinson and P.C. Edwards (Stanford: University Press 1960).

9 *New York Times*, 30 December 1917; and Kahn to General S.B.M. Young, 17 November 1917, Theodore Roosevelt Papers, Truman Library, as cited by Alan Boxerman, 'Kahn of California' (1976), 55 *California Historical Quarterly*, 348–51.

10 The historical scholarship is extensive. Consult David M. Kennedy, *Over Here: The First World War and American Society* (New York: Oxford University Press 1980); Ronald Schaffer, *America in the Great War: The Rise of the War Welfare State* (New York: Oxford University Press 1991); Robert H. Ferrell, *Woodrow Wilson and World War I, 1917–1921*, in *The New American Nation Series*, ed. H.S. Commager and R.B. Morris (New York: Harper and Row 1985); Neil A Wynn, *From Progressivism to Prosperity: World War I and American Society* (New York: Holmes and Meier 1986).

11 The Anti-Masonic party of the 1820s and 1830s, the antebellum Know-Nothings who became a successful force in the Republican Party, and the anti-Catholic American Protective Association were other extremist elements. For further information, see Seymour Martin Lipset and Earl Raab, *The Politics of Unreason: Right Wing Extremism in America, 1790–1970*, vol. 5 of *Patterns in American Prejudice Series* (New York: Harper and Row 1970); David H. Bennett, *The Party of Fear: From Nativist Movements to the New Right in American History* (Chapel Hill: University of North Carolina Press 1988); Neil Larry Shumsky, *The Evolution of Political Protest and the Workingmen's Party of California* (Columbus: Ohio State University Press 1992).

12 The major documentation for the following information on the American Protective League (APL) comes from the National Archives, RG 65, Federal Bureau of Investigation (FBI), American Protective League files; and from RG 165, War Department General Staff (WDGS), Military Intelligence Division (MID) correspondence, 1917–41; and U.S. Department of Justice, *Annual Report of the Attorney General, 1917* (Washington: GPO 1917). The attorney general's quote is from page 83. Both Joan Jensen and Harold Hyman have studied the (APL), but neither covered the group's operation in California extensively. See Joan Jensen, *The Price of Vigilance* (Chicago: Rand McNally 1968); 'extreme examples' is from page 28; and Harold Hyman, *To Try Men's Souls: Loyalty Tests in American History* (Berkeley: University of California Press 1959), 267–97.

13 The War Department general staff undertook surveillance of citizens at home. There are extensive files in the National Archives, RG 165, WDGS, MID, correspondence 1917–41. There is also material available on microfilm: *United States Military Intelligence Reports: Surveillance of Radicals in the United States, 1917–1941*, ed. Randolph Boehm, with a guide compiled by Randolph Boehm and Robert Lester, 34 reels (Frederick, Md: University Publications of America 1984). See Roy Talbert Jr, *Negative Intelligence: The Army and the American Left, 1917–1941*, in *The Twentieth Century America Series*, ed. D.W. Grantham (Jackson: University Press of Mississippi 1991); Joan Jensen, *Army Surveillance in America, 1775–1980* (New Haven: Yale University Press 1991).

14 RG65, FBI, APL, Box 1, Report, D. Jessurun to APL, 6 February 1919.

15 RG65, FBI, APL, Box 2, Report, Charles Renwick to APL, n.d.[after 20 November 1918]. In San Jose, George Koetzer, a brewery worker, was accused of making pro-German statements, tarred, feathered, and chained to a brass cannon in the city park. See Paul Murphy, *World War I and the Origin of Civil Liberties in the United States* (New York: W.W. Norton 1979), 129.

16 Edwin Layton, 'The Better America Federation: A Case Study of Superpatriotism,' (1961), 30 *Pacific Historical Review*, 137–47; and the Better America Federation Files, CB-1059, Carton 1, in the Simon J. Lubin Papers, Bancroft Library, University of California, Berkeley. A post-war indictment of the BAF is *Professional Patriots: An Exposure of the Personalities, Methods and Objectives Involved in the Organized Effort to Exploit Patriotic Impulses in these United States During and After the Late War*, ed. Norman Hapgood (New York: Albert and Charles Boni 1927).

17 Los Angeles, Police Department, *Annual Report of the Police Department, 1917–1918*, 2–10.

18 Colin M. MacLachlan, *Anarchism and the Mexican Revolution: The Political Trials of Ricardo Flores Magón in the United States* (Berkeley: University of California Press 1991). See also National Archives, RG28, Post Office Department, Recordings Relating to the Espionage Act, World War I, 1917–21, file 47595: *Los Angeles Germania*: file 47747, *San Diego Herald*; file 44548, 'Regeneracion.' There were other revolutionary groups active in California during the war, among them Asian-Indians seeking independence from British rule: see Joan Jensen, *Passage from India: Asian Indian Immigrants in North America* (New Haven: Yale University Press 1988).

19 Los Angeles, Police Department, *Annual Report of the Police Department, 1917–1918*, 6.

20 Los Angeles, *Annual Message, Frederic T. Woodman, Mayor, January 2, 1919*, 34–5.

21 The George W. Stewart Manuscript Collection, California State Library, Sacramento, Box 811, file 8. RG65, FBI, APL, Box 2, Letter, Joseph E. Caine to APL, 18 December 1918.

22 RG165, WDGS, MID, general correspondence 1917–41, Box 2239, file 10016-22, 5 January 1918; file 10016-38, Counter-Espionage Summary, San Francisco, 20 April 1918, 7; and file 10280-17, Box 2995, Counter-Espionage Situation Summary, week ending 18 May 1918, 3; RG65, FBI, APL, Box 1, R.W. Holabird to APL National Headquarters, 25 February 1918.

23 California, State Council of Defense, *Report of the Activities of the California State Council of Defense From April 6, 1917 to January 1, 1918* (Sacramento

1918), 43–4; California, State Council of Defense, 'Bulletin No 61,' 14 December 1917.

24 'Special Problem: Subversive Activities – Loyalty Oath, Tenure, No. 17-B, Supporting Cases, 1913–1952,' CU-5, Box 1208, Archives, Bancroft Library, University of California, Berkeley. This extensive file contains information on various individual faculty members and students. See also CU-1, Box 90, World War I; CU-5, Boxes 70, 77, and 80, president's files; and the university's archival pamphlet collection on the First World War. Information about the new committee comes from the above and from Verne A. Stadtman, *The University of California, 1868–1968* (New York: McGraw-Hill 1970), 196–242. In addition to the university's censoring its faculty and students, the state board of education launched an attack on German 'kultur' by banning the teaching of the German language and music and by banning certain history textbooks: State of California, Board of Education, *Third Biennial Report, 1916–1918* (Sacramento 1918).

25 The MID records, supra note 13; and the Simon J. Lubin Papers, Bancroft Library, University of California, Berkeley. The spy J. Vance Thompson wrote letters to Lubin and to George Bell, the director of the commission, describing labour conditions throughout the state. See, for example, J. Vance Thompson to George Bell, 24 May 1917, Lubin Papers, CB1059, Box 3, Thompson File; and 'Report on Special Investigation [of migratory work conditions in Stockton, Modesto, Turlock, Merced and Fresno] 30 May 1917, Lubin Papers, CB1059, Carton 1, file 13. Also housed in the Bancroft Library are the papers of the California Department of Industrial Relations, Division of Immigration and Housing, including numerous published reports. Extensive records are available from the National Archives, RG60, Department of Justice, Straight Numerical Files, correspondence, 186691–701, which deal with IWW cases.

26 National Archives, RG174, Commission on Industrial Relations, 'Fresno Free Speech Fight,' a report by H. Minderman, one of the IWW prisoners, 16 October 1910 to 3 March 1911, Serial No 819. See also *Report of Harris Weinstock, Commissioner to Investigate the Recent Disturbances in the City of San Diego and the County of San Diego, California to His Excellency Hiram W. Johnson, Governor of California* (Sacramento 1912); and Dubofsky, *We Shall Be All*, 173–97, 393–7, 438–41.

27 Cal. Stats., 199, c. 188, 281–2. Humboldt County's Ordinance No. 147 was passed by the Board of Supervisors on 18 November 1919. See also Woodrow C. Whitten, 'Criminal Syndicalism and the Law in California: 1919–1927' (1969), 59 *Transactions of the American Philosophical Society*, 1–73.

28 William Preston, *Aliens and Dissenters: Federal Suppression of Radicals, 1903–1933* (New York: Harper and Row, Harper Torchbooks 1966), 8.

29 *Whitney v. California*, (1927), 274 US 357; *Brandenburg v. Ohio* (1969), 395 US 444; and West, (1982), 11400.

30 Carol Jensen, *Network of Control: Supreme Court and State Security Statutes, 1920–1940, Contributions in Legal Studies* No 22, ed. by Paul L. Murphy (Westport: Greenwood Press 1982); William E. Forbath, *Law and the Shaping of the American Labour Movement* (Cambridge Harvard University Press 1991); National Archives, RG204, Pardon Attorney files, files 39–240 and 39–241, dealing with the aftermath of the IWW trials and the attempts in 1923 to secure pardons for the prisoners. For additional information on Whitney see Lisa Rubens, 'The Patrician Radical Charlotte Anita Whitney' (1986), 65 *California History*, 158–71, 226–7, and the Papers of John Francis Neylan, CB 811, Series 12, Box 100, folder 1, Bancroft Library, University of California, Berkeley.

31 National Archives, RG174, Commission on Industrial Relations, Memo by B.F. Moore, 'Constitutionally protected personal liberties,' February 1915, Serial No 1149.

32 The literature on civil liberties is extensive: National Popular Government League, *To the American People: Report upon the Illegal Practices of the U.S. Department of Justice* (Washington 1920); Zechariah Chafee Jr, *Free Speech in the United States* (Cambridge: Harvard University Press 1941); Mark E. Neely Jr, *The Fate of Liberty: Abraham Lincoln and Civil Liberties* (New York: Oxford University Press, 1991); Harry Kalven Jr, *A Worthy Tradition: Freedom of Speech in America*, ed. Jamie Kalven, Jr (New York: Harper and Row 1988); Samuel Walker, *In Defense of American Liberties: A History of the ACLU* (New York: Oxford University Press 1990); Christopher N. May, *In the Name of War: Judicial Review and the War Powers since 1918* (Cambridge: Harvard University Press 1989); Paul L. Murphy, *The Constitution in Crisis Times, 1918–1969*, in *The New American Nation Series*, ed. H.S. Commager and Richard Morris (New York: Harper and Row 1972); Donald O. Johnson, *The Challenge to American Freedoms: World War I and the Rise of the American Civil Liberties Union* (Lexington: University of Kentucky Press 1963); Harry N. Scheiber, *The Wilson Administration and Civil Liberties, 1917–1921*, vol. 6 of *Cornell Studies in American History, Literature and Folklore*, ed. R.H. Elias et al. (Ithaca: Cornell University Press 1960); and Robert K. Murray, *Red Scare* (Minneapolis: University of Minnesota Press 1955). See especially Mark A. Graber, *Transforming Free Speech: The Ambiguous Legacy of Civil Libertarianism* (Berkeley: University of California Press 1991).

33 For further discussion see James MacGregor Burns and Stewart Burns, *A

People's Charter: The Pursuit of Rights in America (New York: A.A. Knopf 1991);
Alan Dawley, *Struggles for Justice: Social Responsibility and the Liberal State*
(Cambridge: Belknap press of Harvard University Press 1991); Robert
Higgs, *Crisis and Leviathan: Critical Episodes in the Growth of American Govern-
ment* (New York: Oxford University Press 1987); Christopher L. Tomlins,
*The State and the Unions: Labour Relations, Law and the Organized Labour Move-
ment in America, 1880–1960* (Cambridge: University Press 1985); Stephen
Skowronek, *Building a New American State: The Expansion of National Adminis-
trative Capacities, 1877–1920* (Cambridge: University Press 1982); and
William E. Leuchtenburg, 'The Pertinence of Political History: Reflections
on the Significance of the State in America' (1986), 73 *Journal of American
History*, 585–600.

34 Walter Lippmann, *Liberty and the News* (New York: Harcourt, Brace and
Howe 1920), 57.

35 Carl H. Chrislock, *Watchdog of Loyalty: The Minnesota Commission of Public
Safety During World War I* (St Paul: Minnesota Historical Society Press 1991),
40–64, at 60. For an earlier, less critical study of the role of the commission,
see Franklin F. Holbrook and Livia Appel, *Minnesota in the War with Germany*, 2 vols, ed. Solon J. Buck (St Paul: Minnesota Historical Society 1928,
1932).

36 Holbrook and Appel, vol. 2, 200–2. The state of Missouri provides another
example of the lack of support for the war effort. According to a recent
study, 'the majority of Missourians continued to oppose American participation in the war all the way to the Armistice': Christopher C. Gibbs, *The
Great Silent Majority: Missouri's Resistance to World War I* (Columbia: University
of Missouri Press 1988), vii.

37 Robert P. Wilkins and Wynona Huchette Wilkins, *North Dakota: A Bicenten-
nial History* (New York: W.W. Norton; Nashville: American Association for
State and Local History 1977), 145. See also Nancy Derr, 'Lowden: A Study
of Intolerance in an Iowa Community During the Era of the First World
War' (1989), 50 *Annals of Iowa*, 5–22; Joel A. Watne, 'Public Opinion
Toward Nonconformists and Aliens During 1917, as shown by the Fargo
Forum' (1967), 34 *North Dakota History*, 5–29. Another state, Montana, provides an example of a unique wartime experience because of the domi-
nance of the Anaconda Copper Mining Company. See Arnon Gutfeld,
Montana's Agony: Years of War and Hysteria, 1917–1921 (Gainesville: University Presses of Florida 1979).

10 Wagging Tongues and Empty Heads: Seditious Utterances and the Patriotism of Wartime in Central Alberta, 1914–1918

JONATHAN SWAINGER

Participation in the First World War tested Canadian notions of citizenship, loyalty, and the responsibilities of empire. While for many a national identity was being forged in Europe's battlefields, anti-conscription riots in Quebec, internment camps for enemy aliens, and the suppression of free speech signalled that such an identity did not come cheaply. That freedom could be lost on the home front while Canadian soldiers were dying in Europe was indeed a dark irony of both world wars. Yet while we know of the resistance to conscription throughout much of Canada as well as the plight of those caught in the definition of enemy alien, the restraint of the so-called British heritage of free speech has largely escaped our historical attention.[1] Part of the omission is explained by an interpretation of the conscription crisis that reveals an inherent French-English tension in Canadian society. Further, the internment of enemy aliens draws notice not only because Canada had benefited from a considerable influx of immigrants in the fifteen years before the outbreak of hostilities but because the exercise foreshadowed the more infamous schemes aimed at Japanese Canadians during the Second World War.

In the end, however, the question of free speech in Canada during the First World War has not occupied a prominent place because the events do not correspond neatly with the dichotomies portrayed in the conscription crisis and the internment of enemy aliens. At the best of times defining the boundaries of free speech is a difficult undertaking involving issues of the common good, individual liberty, the role of criticism, and the responsibilities of the state towards its citizenry. Further, the inquiry cuts across many of the traditional questions focused on language, religion, ethnicity, and conceptions of loyalty. When added to the charged atmosphere of a community at war, charting the limits of free speech becomes an especially difficult nettle to grasp.[2] At its very heart, and perhaps most significantly, the issue of freedom of speech illuminates the complex interaction between ideas, laws, community, and the state.

The debate over the limits of free speech in Canada during the First World War involved a clash between jingoism and the desire to demonstrate the superiority of British law and government. In practice, this tension was revealed, on the one hand, in the urge to punish those who questioned the British cause and on the other, in the requirement that those who were charged with using seditious language receive a fair trial. These two ends were not mutually exclusive, of course. But as events developed, the judicial view of what constituted seditious language eventually espoused a far more restrictive perspective than the community may have wished. That such a view would in the end be swept away in the wake of the Winnipeg General Strike diminishes neither its existence nor the foresight of the judges who framed its tenets.

Raising Discontent or Disaffection

The war was not going well in the spring of 1915. On 22 April the Canadians fighting outside Ypres were some of the first to experience deadly chlorine gas. Two weeks later the Cunard ocean liner *Lusitania* was sunk by the German navy and eleven hundred were lost. Nerves were becoming frayed at home, and in central Alberta rumours of disloyalty among the immigrants west of Red Deer continued to circulate. Repeating the claims of the Calgary *News-Telegraph*, the Red Deer *News* warned those of pro-German sentiment that they should not expect much leniency in Canada at a time when their 'illustrious ancestors and cousins are doing their utmost to put Canadians to death by the rather barbaric chloride gas route.'[3] Within five weeks the first charge of using seditious language was laid in the Red Deer district and helped set in motion a chain of events that would eventually end before the Alberta Supreme Court. For the accused in that first case, Charles H. Von Holtum, a thirty-four-year-old clerk living near Evarts, west of Red Deer, the initial charge would soon be followed by another detailing his personal criticisms of the Allied war effort.[4]

There was little question that Von Holtum had offered some rather strong opinions. Although he admitted readily that he had come to Canada in order to evade German military law, he maintained a stout defence of his homeland. Suggesting that the sinking of the *Lusitania* had been no worse than 'the British efforts to starve the women and children of Germany,' Von Holtum added that the imposition of German government would greatly benefit Belgian society. Finally, he asserted that the good Germans of Calgary were being subjected to untold abuse, and that 'a German minister had his hair cut by force and had been hung up by the thumbs.'[5] It would later be questioned whether these opinions, while certainly inflammatory, were designed to 'raise discontent and disaffection among His Majesty's subjects.' Not surprisingly, such legalistic distinctions did not prevent the case from being placed on the docket to be heard at the Supreme Court in Red Deer, where, during a brief appearance before Judge Maitland McCarthy on 21 September, Von Holtum pleaded not guilty. It would be four months before Von Holtum would learn his fate at the next sitting of the Supreme Court in Red Deer.

The period between Von Holtum's plea and the resolution of his case provided the Supreme Court of Alberta with the opportunity to define the boundaries of free speech and sedition in a country at war. The task was not easy, and would challenge many other North American courts in the ensuing years. Yet in Alberta, where three of the eight Canadian precedent-setting decisions on seditious language were handed down, there emerged a jurisprudence embracing the notion that although the nation was at war, criticism of the war or the manner in which it was prosecuted was not inherently seditious. Further, while such criticism might offend the moral and patriotic sentiments of the community at large, it remained incumbent on the prosecution to demonstrate that the words spoken were done so in a manner to 'stir up discontent or disaffection.'[6] Criticism, no matter how ill-considered, was not inherently seditious. It is evident that a gap existed between those sentiments expressed in the local press and that handed down by the Supreme Court. However, the uncompromising stance was wholly consistent with a pattern of decisions in all aspects of the law, marking the early Alberta Supreme Court as a haven for innovative judicial interpretation.[7]

In these cases of seditious language, maintaining the court's innovative flair was largely the work of Judge Charles Allan Stuart and, to a lesser extent, Judge Nicholas Du Bois Dominic Beck. Unlike Chief Justice Horace Harvey, who would write the court's first precedent-setting decision on seditious language, Stuart and Beck were inclined to be more liberal and pragmatic in viewing the circumstances in which seditious words were allegedly uttered.[8] Both were apparently influenced strongly by the notion that the liberal state ought to tolerate all manner of dis-

senting opinion, and in the process 'encourage our differences, not for
the sake of difference but so that any man may be himself, sentient,
thinking, choosing, responsible.'[9] Putting words to action, Stuart, before
his rise to the bench, was active in Liberal politics, where his contribution
has been described by one biographer as being devoted 'to the public
good which places the welfare of the country before partisanship.'[10] For
his part, Beck not only was an active Liberal before his appointment to
the bench but also shouldered the additional responsibility of being a
converted Catholic fighting for separate school rights in western Canada.[11]
Stuart's and Beck's shared ideals prevented the law from becoming a
weapon of unbridled patriotic zeal.

When hostilities erupted in 1914, the Canadian criminal law pertaining
to seditious words was outlined in sections 132–4 of the Canadian Criminal Code.[12] These sections, in turn, appear to have been 'lifted verbatim'
from the 1879 English Draft Code, when Sir John Thompson set out the
Canadian code eventually passed in 1892.[13] While the latter does not
define the exact meaning of 'seditious words,' English law and textual
authorities such as Hawkins's *Pleas of the Crown* and Blackstone's *Commentaries* specified that language which has a direct tendency or intent to
incite or promote a breach of the peace or public disorder was seditious.[14] The code provided for two years' imprisonment for anyone found
guilty of speaking seditious words, publishing a seditious libel, or being
party to a seditious conspiracy. Noting that good faith criticism of the
monarchy or government did not entail a seditious utterance, section 133
provided practical guidance for prosecution of the offence. Essentially,
the offence of speaking seditious words was based on such words' being
expressive of 'seditious intention.'[15] 'The prime concern underlaying the
sedition provisions of the Code has been the tranquillity of the State'; but
what the question left unanswered was where the line between good faith
criticism ended and seditious intention began.[16] Specifically, the patriotic
fervour of the day raised the issue of whether that line was to be determined by non-legal forces such as the mood of a community at war.

The settlement history of central Alberta added yet another complication. Established initially in the early 1880s by a joint venture of Toronto
businessmen and the Methodist church, the community of Red Deer bore
the marks of Protestant Ontario loyalism. The surrounding district was a
broad mixture of American and European immigrants, whose connection
with all things British was fleeting at best. Given this environment, the
possibility certainly existed for a fundamental disagreement between the
'respectable' citizens of Red Deer and those of the outlaying district over

what 'seditious language' entailed. The *Red Deer News* of 30 June 1915 reported that the police had evidence to support charges of uttering sedition, but until that time had let the offenders off with only a warning.[17] This alleged leniency ended abruptly in the aftermath of Ypres and the sinking of the *Lusitania*. Thereafter, armed with a heightened sense of loyalty and the vaguely worded sections of the Criminal Code to guide their actions, justices of the peace throughout central Alberta turned to the task of sending those whose criticism crossed the undefined line to defend their words before the Supreme Court at Red Deer.

Seditious Utterances and Falsehoods

Charles Von Holtum was not alone on the docket when he recorded his plea of not guilty on 21 September before Judge McCarthy. In fact, three other charges of seditious language were scheduled for trial at the same session. The most notable defendant was John Reid, the Scottish-born socialist organizer and federal candidate, who faced three separate indictments of uttering sedition. Apparently the North West Mounted Police had known of Reid's political activities for some time, though there were no grounds for official action. However, in the wake of a speaking tour of west-central Alberta where Reid probably hoped to garner electoral support from immigrant voters, the police were finally provided with a reason to arrest the socialist candidate.

Reid's politics undoubtedly made him a subject of interest, but it was the content of his campaign speeches that brought him before the courts. Described by the *Guide* of Rocky Mountain House on 11 June 1915 as 'a forceful, level headed speaker and clear thinker,' the paper also offered the opinion that 'Comrade John Reid' and the socialists might give the 'other parties a hot run for their money' in the Red Deer constituency.[18] That evening Reid provided the assembled gathering in Rocky Mountain House with something more than expected. Rising to the occasion, Reid levelled an attack on the Allied war effort, stating that 'the capitalists would get all the glory, and that the soldiers would return to their country with wooden legs only to be disowned by the King.' Further, not only were Allied soldiers committing atrocities by order of Lord Kitchener, but 'British soldiers were cutting fingers from German soldiers and selling them.'[19]

Confronted with such statements, on 18 June the *Guide* retracted its earlier description of Reid and proceeded to attack his 'seditious utterances and falsehoods.' In a front page column, *Guide* editor J.D. Skinner reported that Reid's 'seditious remarks were very much resented, and it is a surprise to many that he was permitted to leave town without rough handling ... No loyal self-respecting man of whatever party would identify himself with such an individual. His chances of getting too [sic] Ottawa are mighty slim but he is making a good run for one or two other places.'[20] On 21 June, three days after Skinner offered this appraisal of Reid's future and ten days after he had delivered his address in Rocky Mountain House, Corporal W.J. Della Torre of the RNWMP laid the first of three charges for seditious utterances against Reid. A day later Reid once again addressed a gathering, on this occasion in the small community of Evarts between Rocky Mountain House and Red Deer, where he repeated his opinions on the war. As the meeting ended, Reid was reportedly saved from being 'thrown in the river' by the locals when the RNWMP arrived to arrest him on Della Torre's first charge.[21] At his preliminary hearing on 23 June before Justice of the Peace W.P. Lindsay, Reid pleaded not guilty to the charges arising out of his speech at Rocky Mountain House on 11 June. Two more charges were then filed in regard to Reid's speech at a socialist meeting in Evarts on 26 March, and again for a speech delivered in the same community on 22 June. Arraigned for a preliminary hearing on 25 June on the second and third charges, Reid once again pleaded not guilty and was committed to jail to await trial. Denied bail after the preliminary hearing, Reid remained in custody and off the campaign trail until bail was set at one thousand dollars by Judge James D. Hyndman on 3 August.

The other two defendants on the docket with Von Holtum and Reid were Theodore Clausen and F.L. Schacht. While having a drink in the Windsor Hotel bar in Red Deer on 23 June, Clausen, a well-known and respected seventy-year-old farmer living west of Red Deer, had suggested that the sinking of the *Lusitania* had not been without reason. A charge of making a seditious utterance followed four days later and after a preliminary hearing Clausen was bound over to appear before the next sitting of the Supreme Court.[22] Schacht was also before the courts to explain his defense of the sinking of the Lusitania, as well as his claims that he would rather eat with a cat than with King George, and his description of the RNWMP as 'the scum of England,' who would not arrest a man unless there 'was a crowd of them.' As well, Schacht had boasted that if the RNWMP came after him there would be a shootout.[23] In reporting Schacht's preliminary hearing, the Red Deer *News* concluded with a sneer that 'it is unnecessary to add that he was captured by one policeman and he came like a lamb.'[24]

In less than one month, between 18 June and 14 July 1915, a total of six charges of seditious utterances were filed in the Red Deer district. The three complaints against Reid attracted the lion's share of attention, but all the cases drew commentary from the local press. Most agreed with the sentiment expressed by J.D. Skinner of the *Guide*, who suggested that Reid's confinement to jail would provide him with the 'opportunity to reflect upon some of his foolish statements.'[25] Recognizing that there were wider issues at play, however, Skinner attempted to place Reid's comments, as well as those of the others accused of seditious language, into a broader context. 'Under normal conditions the utterances of Reid might be tolerated but the present is not time for loyal citizens to put up with such humbugging. The doctrine of free speech must not be abused. With men momentarily sacrificing their lives for the Empire, and some of whom are right from our own neighborhood, it is highly improbable that Britishers will stand silently by within the hearing of such objectionable statements as were made by Mr. Reid.'[26] Consistent with this line of argument, the Red Deer *News* assured Inspector W.P. Lindsay of the RNWMP that 'he will have all the loyal citizens of Alberta behind him' for taking 'the bull by the horns' in regard to these utterances.[27] Further, if there are those who question the war effort, 'the least these people can do is keep a civil tongue in their head and mind their own business.'[28]

Thus, as spring turned to summer and summer to autumn, a number of themes emerged in 1915 in the public discourse about seditious language. First, it appears that many people adhered to the notion that criticism of the war effort or the administration of affairs on the home front should expose the speaker to official censure. Essentially, criticism was viewed as inherently seditious. Second, it appears that for most people the concept of free speech necessarily involved certain responsibilities conditioned by the circumstances of the moment. Freedom of speech was not absolute and without limitation. Finally, most realized that in a community of immigrants there would be those who had no connections to the British empire and who therefore might not support the war effort. It was suggested that such opinions were unwelcome when spoken in public, and that it was best to keep them private for the duration of hostilities. Restraint was necessary for the protection of individuals holding contrary opinions; in the height of battle against foes at home and on the front, there were no assurances that loyal Britishers would be able to control their righteous indignation.

Words Expressive of Seditious Intention

For those burdened with the interpretation of the law, however, the questions arising from the charges of seditious language were more elusive than the public discourse suggested. The initial difficulty arose as soon as Reid's case was called before Judge Maitland McCarthy on 21 September in Red Deer. McCarthy refused to proceed with the matter unless the complaint against Reid contained the spoken words alleged to be seditious. The argument that the incriminating phrases were contained in a ninety-minute speech failed to move McCarthy; the Reid case, along with the other three, had to be adjourned until the next sitting so that the complaints could be redrawn.[29] Judge McCarthy's objection to the complaint indirectly attacked the vague definition of section 132 of the Criminal Code, which defined a seditious utterance as 'words expressive of seditious intention.'[30] The charge could not merely assert seditious language without specifying the words alleged to be seditious. In requiring the words to be quoted in the charge, McCarthy forced the crown to demonstrate that the specific words outlined in the indictment were indeed seditious.

Clarification of how the Albert Supreme Court would interpret charges of seditious utterance was provided in the case of *R. v. Felton*, delivered on 21 December 1915. Oscar Felton had been tried before Judge William Walsh at Okotoks on 27 August 1915 on two charges of uttering seditious words. The first complaint alleged that Felton had spoken such words as to raise disaffection and discontent and that the words were uttered 'with intent to promote public disorder.'[31] At trial, defence counsel had argued that the second count ought to be quashed in that it disclosed no criminal offence. Felton was found guilty on the first count, but the second was reserved for judgment by the Appellate Division of the Supreme Court sitting en banc. The central issue in the *Felton* case, as in all those concerned with allegations of seditious language, was the definition of 'sedition' and 'seditious intention.'

Drawing on a variety of sources, including Russell on *Crimes*, Stephens's *History of the Criminal Law*, Halsbury's *Laws of England*, the *Encyclopaedia of the Laws of England*, and English precedents, Chief Justice Horace Harvey outlined a number of conclusions in his judgment. First, 'on the principle that a man is presumed to intend the natural consequences of his act, it would always be open to a Judge or jury to infer the intent from the words and the circumstances in which they are spoken.' Second, Felton's opinion that he 'would like to see the Germans come across the Channel and wipe England off the map' and that 'England put Russia into the war and is letting them get licked,' was, in Harvey's eyes, intended both to bring hatred and contempt onto the government and also to promote ill will.[32] Finally, Harvey ruled that the offence of sedition 'covers a wide field ... and in this present day of the great war when all our people are in a state of nervous tension and excitement, and intense feelings against the enemy due to the struggle in which we are engaged, words which, in ordinary times, would have no effect in creating disorder cannot be used without much greater danger, and such words as those in question would not be likely to be used now unless with some intent to stir up trouble.'[33] Felton's conviction was affirmed. The decision implicity rejected the pre-war English precedent *R. v. Aldred*, which had specified that in locating the intent behind a seditious utterance, the court should look to the language *and* the circumstances of its use.[34]

Justice Charles Stuart agreed that the conviction was valid; however, he expressed some concern about Harvey's broad interpretation of 'seditious intention.' Stuart preferred the issue of intention, as defined by the circumstances in which the offending words were delivered, to be a factor in determining whether they were seditious. Inflammatory language uttered in a private conversation had a decidedly different character from the same language spoken in public. Second, and of considerable import-ance for all future prosecutions, Stuart refused to view 'very offensive expressions of dislike towards Englishmen' as seditious. To be considered seditious, the phrase under scrutiny had to be delivered in a context attacking 'Great Britain and the Dominions as a whole.' When this condi-tion was combined with Stuart's initial distinction between public and private speech, he appeared intent on drawing the court and its support-ing legal structure away from the role of monitoring society in search of every ill-conceived opinion. Increasingly the legal community embraced Stuart's rationale, and from this point forward he would write the court's precedent-setting decisions on seditious language.

When the four accused in the Red Deer district returned to court under redrawn complaints a month later, in January, 1916, the legal view of seditious utterances had been sharpened. For Charles Von Holtum, who had not only compared the *Lusitania* sinking with British attempts to starve German civilians but had claimed that German government would benefit Belgium and had spoken of ill-treatment of Germans in Calgary, this clarified perspective on the law produced an acquittal. In dismissing the charge against Von Holtum, Judge William Simmons 'commented favourably on the open manner in which Mr. Von Holtum had given his evidence. He had not concealed his sympathies for the German people in their war-sufferings. At the same time he must warn him to be careful of his utterances during the war.'[35] The other three defendants did not fare as well.

Despite defence counsel's argument that a conviction would 'strike a blow at the cherished British heritage of freedom and speech' and that 'the jury must take a broadminded view as to the rights of the advocate of an unpopular cause in citing his unpleasant facts,' John Reid received the harshest treatment. In charging the jury for Reid's case, Judge Simmons echoed the *Felton* decision by stating that 'every man must be assumed to intend the natural meaning and consequences of his words and actions. There must be some form of government and authority to maintain law and order, to protect the rights of all; and this authority must be supported in preventing what would tend to be animosity and tumult. Certainly words casting contempt, scorn and ridicule upon the authorized order should be carefully weighed before their utterance.'[36] If Reid's utterances brought unwarranted contempt on the cause or manner in which the war was being waged, discouraged enlistment, or subverted the duty that all citizens owed their country, they would be within the scope of the law. Provided with this view of the law, the jury returned a verdict of guilty and Reid was sentenced to fifteen months in the Lethbridge jail.[37]

The two other defendants, Theodore Clausen and F.L. Schacht, were found guilty and were fined fifty dollars each in lieu of incarceration. In charging the jurors in Clausen's case, Judge Simmons drew their attention to two basic principles. They first had to consider 'the freedom and liberty of speech allowed in this country: people had a right to criticize the administration of affairs without bringing themselves under the penalty for uttering seditious words with respect to this, the time and place under which the words were spoken were of prime importance.' Second, Simmons suggested that the government and laws of a nation must be respected and administered in such a fashion as to protect the public from riots, tumult, and a molestation of their rights.[38] In Schacht's case, the accused's praising of the sinking of the *Lusitania*, his threat that Englishmen who laid complaints against Germans in Canada would 'get a bullet some night after dark,' and his criticisms of the RNWMP as the 'scum of Great Britain' and of King George proved too much for the court. In giving Schacht the option of a fifty-dollar fine or three months in jail, Simmons reportedly suggested that 'if these people who took advantage of Canadian institutions were not sympathetic with Britain in this great war, the least they could do was to keep quiet and not advertise their views where it was sure to cause disturbances.'[39]

This first round of trials for seditious language in the Red Deer district provided an illuminating perspective on the development of the law to the end of January 1916. To be considered seditious, an utterance had to be public, derogating to the war effort or its administration, and delivered with an intent to promote ill will or hostility. By itself, criticism was not necessarily seditious. There is little question that these criteria added important substance to the elliptical sections of the Criminal Code that had initially guided the prosecution of seditious language.

However, clarification did not necessarily mean that free speech was better protected. Utterances promoting ill-will but not behaviour were apparently just as seditious as utterances that provoked actual tumult and riot. As the law stood in January 1916, seditious intention was equated with seditious action. The American legal historian Zechariah Chafee Jr has argued that in wartime only that speech which 'is clearly liable to cause direct and dangerous interference with the conduct of the war' should be subject to restriction; but the Alberta judiciary, in common with their American brethren, approached wartime cases with an eye to indirect and potentially dangerous interference in the war effort.[40] However, while Canadian and American jurisprudence began on parallel tracks, by the time the United States entered the war in 1917 the Alberta Supreme Court had taken Canadian law in a significantly different direction. As events unfolded after the initial round of seditious utterance cases, it slowly became apparent that a constituency existed for a peculiarly Albertan and, in a more general sense, a Canadian interpretation of seditious language.

'Play the Game Fair'

Two weeks after the first trials in Red Deer, riots erupted in Calgary over allegations that veterans were being fired from the White Lunch restaurant in favour of German-Canadians. The restaurant was razed by soldiers, and on the following day a similar fate befell the Riverside Hotel.[41] The allegations proved false and, while civic and military officials blamed each other for the outbreaks, Albertans were given pause to reflect on the patriotic fervour that had destroyed two businesses.

Many people undoubtedly shared the views of Florence Adderley of Red Deer, who chastised the soldiers for desecrating the king's uniform by participating in the riot, and suggested that if the government interned 'all Germans and Austrians' there would have been nothing to spark the soldier's ill-advised behaviour.[42] However, while Adderley may have reflected the views of a majority of Albertans, the Red Deer *Advocate* offered a surprising alternative. In a front-page column entitled 'Play the

Game Fair,' the *Advocate* suggested that while German-Canadians 'are bound to share a great deal of the opprobrium which attaches to Germany today ... Good German people who cannot possibly do this country any harm – are lumped together with the evildoers by hysterical, fanatical people, who want them driven out of the country.' And then, as if to press the point more forcefully, the writer declared that 'the duty rests upon all Britishers of sane, patriotic views, and especially upon all born Canadians to play the game fair, to uphold the cherished British heritages of asylum and just dealing for foreigners, and not to override indiscriminately all the rights of Canadian citizenship where the offender had a German name or had non-British sympathies.'[43] Revealing toleration that was rare in a society that often demonstrated a nativism bordering on xenophobia, the *Advocate's* defence of principle was extraordinary.

The Red Deer district experienced a brief lull in the prosecution of seditious utterances after the Calgary riot. The Alberta Supreme Court, however, in it judgment in *R. v. Cohen*, delivered in Calgary on 31 March 1916, continued to define the boundaries of free speech. In many ways the circumstances of the *Cohen* case were similar to *Felton* and Theodore Clausen's case in Red Deer. George Cohen, the operator of a secondhand furniture store in the Riverside community of Calgary, had claimed that Canadian troops were slaves to King George and that the remains of the Canadian dead would make good fertilizer. The words, heard only by one individual to whom he was speaking, were clearly in the form of a private conversation. Cohen appealed his initial conviction before Judge Simmons and jury on the question of whether sufficient evidence existed in law to fulfil the criterion of seditious intention. In confirming the conviction without defining the nature of public discourse, Judge Stuart admitted that the case rested 'on the extreme limit of the law.' He added, however, that the circumstances, 'not only of the particular occasion but also of times' had a real bearing on the case and were therefore a legitimate consideration for the jury. It remained for the jury to decide whether Cohen's utterance was likely to create feelings of ill will. Thus, despite the fact that the evidence of seditious intention was 'very weak,' it was strong enough to place the entire matter before a jury at the original trial. Cohen's appeal was denied.[44]

The *Cohen* decision potentially expanded the area that fell within the reach of prosecution for seditious utterances in a significant way. Consistent with the notions of bad tendency and possible danger, the utterance of a man in a private conversation was deemed suitable for prosecution. Stuart's admission that the case was at the extreme limit of the law and

Judge N.B. Beck's hesitant concurrence suggest, however, that this was a path not to be followed in the future.[45] For a court whose history marked it as one that preferred commonsense solutions to legal problems, assumptions about supposed intent seem to have been completely out of character. Thus, while the *Cohen* decision appeared to involve an expansion of the legal limits on free speech, the court's reticence suggested that the final word on the law of seditious utterances was yet to be heard.

A temporary respite from charges of seditious utterances in the Red Deer district ended four days after the *Cohen* decision was delivered. On 3 April 1916 Theodore Clausen was once again charged with using seditious language. On this occasion he was accompanied by his forty-one-year-old son Charles, who was also indicted. According to the depositions heard before Justice of the Peace W.P. Lindsay on 11 April, the elder Clausen had continued his criticism of the Allied war effort despite the earlier conviction and fine, claiming that King George had no business in the war and that Germans should rule the world.[46] For his part, Charles Clausen had claimed that 'he would shoot all the God damn green Englishmen' and that he hoped every ship carrying English or Canadian soldiers would sink. He also stated that if given the opportunity he would shoot King George.[47] Justice Lindsay found sufficient evidence for trial and bound Theodore Clausen on two sureties of $250 and Charles on two sureties of $2,500.

Availing himself of the opportunity to comment on the troubling state of affairs, Lindsay reportedly 'did not mince his words in describing the conduct of the accused [Charles Clausen] of using such language in a British country: had a Britisher spoken any one of such expressions in Germany, he would have been put up against a wall and shot, without benefit of a trial. He regretted that the law governing sedition was in such unsatisfactory shape and was not designed to meet the present emergencies.'[48] While it is doubtful that Lindsay actually advocated shooting individuals such as the Clausens, the tenor of his comments betrays a frustration with how the legal system in general, and probably the Supreme Court specifically, was dealing with the utterance cases. The turn of events in the ensuing sedition case involving William Flagg, however, doubtless provoked even greater alarm.

Of all the seditious utterance cases heard before the Supreme Court at Red Deer during the war, William Flagg's case may actually have met the standards of 'language damaging to the war effort.' According to Sergeant Robert H. Inglis of the 187th Battalion Canadian Expeditionary Force, who was supervising the recruiting office in Lacombe on 24 May

1916, Flagg called Private Harry Stokes out of the recruiting office and told him he was a fool to enlist.[49] Further, Flagg claimed he had as much right to discourage men from enlisting as Sergeant Inglis had to enlist them, and added that the army was 'in the habit' of getting possible recruits drunk and then signing them up for duty. Stokes testified that Flagg offered to whip some sense into him for leaving his wife and enlisting. In his own defence Flagg claimed the whipping comment had been made in jest, and admitted that he 'felt a little sore' because two soldiers had attempted to get his son Harry to enlist. Believing that the evidence was sufficient to place the matter before the Supreme Court sitting at Red Deer, Justice of the Peace Norman Carruthers committed Flagg to jail to await trial.

When court opened once again in Red Deer in late September 1916, three cases of seditious utterance were on the docket. Appearing before Chief Justice Harvey and a jury, both Clausens pleaded not guilty. Theodore Clausen was acquitted because the evidence against him was, according to the Red Deer *Advocate*, 'uncertain and prejudiced.'[50] Charles Clausen did not get off so easily; he was found guilty on three counts of uttering seditious language and given the choice of one year in jail or a fine of $500. Despite the continued plea that the charges were the result of personal malevolence against his family, Charles paid the fine and secured the necessary sureties guaranteeing his continued good behaviour. William Flagg pleaded guilty to the charge and begged for mercy because he had a wife and family and had already spent four months in jail awaiting trial. Hobbled by rheumatism and able to walk only with the aid of crutches, Flagg presented a pitiful sight before Chief Justice Harvey. Having displayed the appropriate remorse, Flagg received a suspended sentence and was released on his personal recognizance without surety.[51] His would be the last conviction for seditious utterances in the Red Deer district.

'A Wagging Tongue and an Empty Head'

The final act of the story was still to follow. On 3 November 1916 the last published decision on seditious utterances was handed down by the Supreme Court. In many ways Stuart's judgment in *R. v. Trainor*, heard by the Appellate Division of the Supreme Court in Calgary, demonstrated the lessons that had been learned in the previous year. The circumstances of the case were familiar. Suggesting that the sinking of the *Lusitania* was no worse than British attempts to starve German civilians, Arthur Trainor had called those who objected to his opinions 'hypocrites.' At the time Trainor made these statements, he was heard by three other individuals in the Strathmore drugstore where he was sitting at a desk writing a letter. Found guilty by Judge Simmons of uttering seditious words, Trainor appealed the judge's refusal to reserve a number of technical questions concerning the wording of the complaint. After dispensing with those issues, Stuart turned again to the issue of what constituted seditious language.

Beginning with the assertion that it was time to distinguish disloyal or unpatriotic sentiments from those of a seditious nature, Stuart declared that 'disloyalty of the heart' is not forbidden.[52] The courts can deal only with words expressive of an intention to create ill will against the monarchy, government, or war effort. Trainor had stated that the sinking of the *Lusitania* was good and that 'war was war.' Turning bravely to the heart of the issue, Stuart then wrote: 'Now I detest such an opinion as strongly as any one, but my present duty is to decide the law, not to express my moral or patriotic sentiment. For myself I am unable to see how the expression of such views, mistaken and detestable though they are, upon the proper limitations of the laws of war was calculated, or expressive of an intention, either to promote feelings of ill-will and hostility between different classes of His Majesty's subject or to incite disaffection against His Majesty's government.'[53]

Further, Stuart could not understand how the words, spoken in a country store, expressed an intention to stir up discontent. 'It is of course running counter to the opinion of everyone who has any moral instinct at all, but why should the expression of an erroneous or even detestable opinion on the proper limits of warfare be calculated, or expressive of an intention, to raise discontent and disaffection?'[54] Speaking for the majority, Stuart viewed Trainor's words as morally bankrupt, not seditious.

Finally, Judge Stuart devoted a few lines to what he saw as the alarming number of cases involving seditious utterances. 'There have been,' he wrote, 'more prosecutions for seditious words in Alberta in the past two years than in all the history of England for over a hundred years and England has had numerous and critical wars in that time.' While not wishing to 'repress the patriotic zeal of our public officials,' Stuart suggested that the dignity of the law was poorly served by bringing 'the foolish talk of men in bar rooms' before the courts, when it was clear that there was no real danger or deliberate purpose behind such words.[55] If Cohen's conviction had been on the extreme edge of the law, Trainor's had crossed the line, and therefore the appeal against conviction would be allowed.

Taking issue with a case based largely on a varied 'collection of technicalities' produced by a 'legal fine tooth comb,' Judge William Walsh dissented from the majority. Maintaining a faith in a doctrine of bad tendency and possible danger, Walsh asserted that since Trainor's utterances were heard by a number of people in the general store, they revealed a seditious intention because they amounted to an attack on the war effort. For Walsh, the language and the circumstances equated with seditious intention. He agreed with Stuart, however, that the incidence of these charges was a concern, for 'it is neither necessary nor wise to rush into Court every fool with a wagging tongue and an empty head, because of something which he has said about the war which savours of disloyalty.' Albertans must remain vigilant for, given the province's 'cosmopolitan' makeup, 'it certainly would be exceedingly dangerous to permit unbridled liberty of speech to every hot head in the community.'[56] Despite Walsh's concern, the ruling seemed to indicate the court's view that by the end of 1916 Alberta and the allied war effort were quite able to withstand the rigours of free speech.

The importance of 1916 for the prosecution of seditious language in Canada and Alberta is partially revealed in the available statistics for the war years.[57] The second full year of the war had more complaints and successful convictions both nationally and in Alberta than any other year. The 84 per cent conviction rate in Alberta is especially notable given the provincial attorney general's policy of allowing only those complaints likely to gain a conviction to reach the stage of a preliminary hearing.[58]

| | Canada | | Alberta | |
	Complaints	Convictions	Complaints	Convictions
1914	1	1 (100.0%)	1	1 (100.0%)
1915	14	7 (50.0%)	7	3 (42.8%)
1916	50	31 (62.0%)	25	21 (84.0%)
1917	29	15 (51.7%)	8	5 (62.5%)
1918	39	21 (53.8%)	7	2 (28.5%)
Total	133	75 (56.3%)	48	32 (66.6%)

Only in 1916 did more than eight cases meet the strict criterion specified by the attorney general's department; in that year the number skyrocketed to twenty-five. This was undoubtedly the figure that Judges Stuart and Walsh had in mind when they spoke of the high incidence of seditious utterance cases in the province. The message that in the future law enforcement officials should be more discerning, together with the legal boundaries established in the *Trainor* decision, produced immediate results. The number of cases fell by two-thirds in the following year.

These figures also testify to Alberta's central role in determining the nature of free speech in Canada. Over one-third of the complaints alleging seditious behaviour or language during the war were laid in Alberta. A further breakdown of national statistics reveals that 103 of the 133 complaints were from the provinces west of Ontario and, of those provinces, Alberta recorded twice as many as any other province. Finally, one out of every six complaints in Alberta was laid in the Red Deer district, a percentage that placed central Alberta behind only Edmonton and Calgary. Clearly the high profile of complaints in western Canada testifies to the region's settlement history and to the means whereby competing visions were played out in the context of free speech. Then as now, the question was of fundamental importance. Would the perimeters of speech or behaviour be framed within the context of the immediate community, or would the desire to import standards be maintained? In another context, Judge Stuart expressed his sentiment in compelling terms: 'In my opinion in a matter of this kind the Courts of this Province are not in every case to be held strictly bound by the decisions of English Courts as to the state of the common law of England in 1870. We are at liberty to take cognizance of the different conditions here, not merely physical conditions, but the general conditions of our public affairs and the general attitude of the community in regard to the particular matter in question.'[59] Clearly, in the cases of seditious language Stuart believed that 'the different conditions' in Alberta required a measure of flexibility. At the very least, the trials in central Alberta reinforced this commitment.

Allegations of seditious language continued in the Red Deer district throughout 1917 and 1918, but none produced convictions. A single complaint in 1917 charged Frank Vanstone with claiming that 'the Germans were coming over to Canada to kill all the Canadians, and he was going to help them.'[60] A subsequent complaint revealed that Vanstone and the chief witness to his utterance were involved in a dispute that ended in threats and broken windows. When the two cases were brought before Judge Walsh at Red Deer on 19 September 1917, the crown entered two motions of *nolle prosequi*.[61] A similar turn of events occurred in 1918 in the Dickson district, southeast of Red Deer. One month after

Alfred Schilling was charged with cattle theft, he was also charged with uttering seditious language.[62] At the preliminary hearing for the latter complaint, Schilling's defence counsel established the relationship between the initial charge of cattle theft and his client's subsequent voicing of ill-considered opinions. Despite being charged with having said that 'he would like to see Germany just whale the piss out of England,' a turn of phrase that almost certainly would have resulted in a conviction in the early days of the war, Schilling was acquitted before Judge McCarthy at Red Deer on 17 September 1918. He was also found not guilty on the charge of cattle theft.[63]

The final and perhaps most illuminating case was also scheduled for trial in September 1918. Ere Sturgeon of Red Deer had been charged on 21 May 1918 with having used seditious words against the king.[64] The depositions sworn on 22 May revealed that Sturgeon had been given a ride by the complainant, M.L. Roche. In the course of their conversation, the two argued about the war. Apparently Roche had called the accused a German and subsequently stated he would kill all Germans, to which Sturgeon replied that Germany would kill the Canadians and British as quickly as they could be sent over to the continent. Sturgeon denied having said anything about King George, but admitted that he claimed there would be 'a big stir when the soldiers come back.' The chief character witness for the accused was Sturgeon's employer, R.C.P. Gee, president of the War Veterans Association of Red Deer. Speaking for the accused, Gee stated that he 'certainly would not have employed him if he had any German tendencies.' Presiding Justice of the Peace Joseph Wallace determined that sufficient evidence for a trial existed and bound Sturgeon over on a surety of $1,000, provided by Gee.[65]

When the case was called on 17 September before Judge McCarthy at Red Deer, Sturgeon failed to appear; the Crown made application for estreatment of the bail provided by Gee. Two weeks later, John Quigg, the Red Deer agent for the attorney general, advised against estreating Gee's surety: 'If proceedings to estreat the bail are pressed, on account of Gee being a returned veteran (who I believe was never in the trenches but met with an accident at the base) a howl will go up from all the returned veterans from Newfoundland to Vancouver about the matter ... It amounts to this that when a returned veteran offers to go bail in any future case he must be refused.'[66] This was indeed an ironic twist. As the war came to an end, the attorney general's office received a concerned note about the feared outcry of estreating the bail of an individual charged with using seditious language.

Symk and Carruthers

The last month of the war provided a final indication of how far the Supreme Court had moved and the degree of continued resistance in some segments of the legal administration. Peter Symk, a naturalized Canadian citizen of German-American parents, stepped off the train in Lacombe, Alberta, a thriving community north of Red Deer, on 8 November 1918. Although he had attempted to enlist earlier in the war, Symk had been granted an exemption from military service because of his hunchback and his responsibilities as the sole supporter of his mother and family. Consistent with the conditions of his exemption, Symk had reported each change of address as he moved around the province looking for work. Shortly after leaving the train Symk was stopped by a Constable Goldring, who informed him that he was to report immediately to the registrar. Symk then wrote a brief note to the registrar in Calgary, notifying that office of his change of address; the letter was received on the following day. Later on 8 November, Goldring arrested Symk and brought him before Justice of the Peace Norman E. Carruthers. Before any charge was sworn out and without any oaths being taken, Carruthers began questioning Symk about his presence in Lacombe and why he had not reported. Symk explained that he had been granted an exemption, but Carruthers refused to accept the explanation and ordered him confined in the Red Deer jail for thirty days.

One day later, on 9 November, Arthur Russell, a Red Deer lawyer, filed a notice of motion for a writ of habeas corpus to obtain Symk's release from jail. Although Russell was unable to show that Carruthers had been served with a notice of motion, Judge Stuart, acting out of chambers in Calgary, was convinced that a grave injustice had occurred, and he ordered that Symk be released.[67] Russell then made application for twenty dollars in costs against Carruthers and filed the necessary motion with Stuart, who accepted it on the condition that Carruthers had ten days to appear and show reason why the costs should not be levied. Carruthers chose not to appear before Stuart; instead, he contacted the attorney general's office in order to secure its protection from Stuart's order. The attorney general preferred to let Stuart decide the matter, and the question of costs and liability was thrown open for yet another judicial decision. A somewhat annoyed Stuart determined that the costs against Carruthers would stand, and that if the attorney general's office was concerned about such a ruling, 'they are of course at liberty to pay it themselves.' Not bothering to hide his disgust, Stuart remarked that 'of course it is a

light thing for a man who is illegally and unjustly in jail to be forced to
make application to get out, but it seems to be an extraordinary thing in
the eyes of the Magistrate to be asked to make an application in person
to be relieved of costs which he would otherwise have been liable to pay
to the extent of $20.'[68]

Stuart's summary of the case left little question as to what had
occurred. Carruthers had never told Symk that he was being charged
under the Military Service Act for failure to report. He then questioned
Symk without any formal information or depositions being sworn, and did
all of this without suggesting that Symk might want to be represented by
legal counsel. Finally, Carruthers ignored the stipulations of the Military
Service Act requiring approval from the Department of Justice before any
prosecutions were initiated. Stuart's stinging conclusion cut to the heart
of Carruthers' actions, and revealed how far the court had travelled in
the prosecution of seditious utterances, Stuart closed his written decision
on the case:

> I have no doubt in the world that the real reason why this man was
> sent to jail was because he appeared to be German, although he was
> born an American citizen and was a British subject by naturalization
> and was complying with the law, and not at all because it was
> thought he had failed to comply with the law; and when such things
> as throwing this man in jail for a month in the manner I have
> described can happen in the name of loyalty and patriotism in this
> country, we ought to cease to wonder at what was being done in the
> name of the same things in Germany.[69]

Stuart's opinion was certainly influenced by the fact that the war had
already been won. But Stuart had also drawn the court in this direction
two years earlier when the judges wrestled with the limits of free speech
in a society at war.

That Judge Stuart and the Alberta Supreme Court expanded Canadian
jurisprudence on free speech to the extent that they did was a considerable accomplishment. The Red Deer district had proved to be an integral
element in demonstrating exactly how the emergent interpretation of the
law would work in practice. It remained clear, however, that while the
court developed its own perspective, patriotism and loyalty coupled with
opportunism compelled some lower-level officials to turn to the law as a
weapon in their personal battles against the foes and critics of Canadian
society. Thus it is certain that not everyone, and perhaps not even a

majority of Albertans, subscribed to what may have been viewed as rather lenient treatment of disloyal and dangerous utterances.

The Alberta court's unique perspective during the war years is especially striking when compared with the corresponding American jurisprudence.[70] The string of free speech cases decided after the war indicated that the United States Supreme Court did not embrace the reasoning that informed Alberta's judiciary.[71] Speaking for a unanimous court in *Schenck v. United States*, which concerned the distribution of anti-draft leaflets among members of the United States' armed forces, Judge Oliver Wendell Holmes unveiled the 'clear and present danger' doctrine. Holmes argued that 'when a nation is at war, many things that might be said in times of peace are such a hindrance to its efforts that their utterance will not be endured so long as men fight and no Court could regard them as protected by any constitutional right.'[72] This, of course, was substantively the same position that had been adopted by the Alberta Supreme Court three years earlier in January 1916.

However, while the two courts began with similar propositions limiting free speech, Holmes and the Alberta Supreme Court soon adopted a new perspective. After meeting with Zechariah Chafee Jr, Holmes reconsidered his earlier views; but he was unable to sway his brethren in the ensuing case of *Abrams v. United States*.[73] Abrams had been convicted of violating the 1918 Sedition Act when he published pamphlets criticizing the government's expeditionary force to Russia and calling for American workers to join with all those who opposed capitalism. Joined in his dissent by Justice Louis Brandeis, Holmes outlined the notion of a marketplace of ideas. Dismissing the allegedly seditious pamphlet published by Abrams as 'a silly leaflet by an unknown man,' Holmes asserted that 'the best test of truth is the power of the thought to get itself accepted in the competition of the market.'[74] The majority, however, chose to uphold the conviction and the view that Abrams's pamphlet was designed to excite disaffection and disloyalty in the United States at a time of war.[75] Unlike the Alberta Supreme Court, with its view that Canada at war could survive the burdens of free speech, the American court was apparently more sceptical.

For its part, the Alberta Supreme Court established its criteria for addressing seditious language issues, and then subsequently sharpened and defended those principles. Some contemporaries took issue with the perceived leniency of the court's interpretation, while those who would follow might question the fact that intentions were deemed just as seditious as actions. Yet at a time when criticism of any nature was viewed as inherently seditious, the Alberta Supreme Court stood for what it saw as the British heritage of free speech. It is clear that its members, like many Canadians, inclined to the sacrificing of individual rights for the protection of a wider and often ill-defined common good. But in the process they also protected the right of all fools with wagging tongues and empty heads, no matter on which side of the war they stood, to be given the opportunity to air their grievances.

NOTES

I would like to thank Professor Louis A. Knafla of the Department of History, University of Calgary, and Joanne Matthews of the University of Northern British Columbia Library, for their assistance in completing the final draft of this article.

1 For the conscription crisis, see J.L Granatstein and J.M. Hitsman, *Broken Promises: A History of Conscription in Canada* (Toronto: Oxford University Press 1977); Elizabeth Armstrong, *The Crisis of Quebec, 1914–1918* (New York: Columbia University Press 1937); and John H. Thompson, *The Harvests of War: The Prairie West* (Toronto: McClelland and Stewart 1978), 115–46. The internment of enemy aliens is discussed in Thompson, *Harvests of War,* 73–94; James B. Carruthers, 'The Great War and Canadian Enemy Alien Policy' (1978), 4 *Queen's Law Journal,* 43–110; *Loyalties in Conflict Ukrainians in Canada During the Great War,* ed. Francis Swyripa and John H. Thompson (Edmonton: Canadian Institute of Ukrainian Studies 1983); and Bohdan S. Kordan and Peter Melnycky, *In the Shadow of the Rockies: Diary of the Castle Mountain Internment Camp, 1915–1917* (Edmonton: Canadian Institute of Ukrainian Studies Press 1991). Discussions of both British and American internment operations can be found in William B. Glidden, 'Internment Camps in America, 1917–1920' (December 1973), *Military Affairs,* 137–41; Peter and Leni Gillman, *"Collar the Lot!" How Britain Interned and Expelled its Wartime Refugees* (London: Quartet Books 1980), 7–21; David Sanders, 'Aliens in Britain and the Empire During the First World War,' in Swyripa and Thompson, *Loyalties in Conflict,* 99–124; and Richard B. Speed III, *Prisoners, Diplomats and the Great War: A Study in the Diplomacy of Captivity* (Westport: Greenwood Press 1990), 141–66. An exception in regard to writing about sedition in Canada during the First World War is Joseph A. Boudreau, 'The Enemy Alien Problem in Canada, 1914–1921,' Ph.D. thesis, University of California (1965), 28–47; and Joseph A. Boudreau, 'Western Canada's "Enemy Aliens" in World War One' (Winter 1964), *12 Alberta*

Historical Review, 1–9. Gregory Kealey has offered a considerable reappraisal of Canadian domestic policy during the First World War in 'State Repression of Labour and the Left in Canada, 1914–20: The Impact of the First World War,' (September 1992), 73 *Canadian Historical Review*, 281–314.

2 For example, in writing about the crime of sedition in the epilogue to his study of the Canadian Criminal Code, Desmond Brown managed to avoid any substantive discussion of what the First World War cases of seditious utterance lent to the definition of sedition in Canada: Desmond H. Brown, *The Genesis of the Canadian Criminal Code of 1892* (Toronto: The Osgoode Society 1989), 151–2.

3 'Some Pro-German Publications,' *Red Deer News*, 5 May 1915.

4 The following is based on *R. v. Von Holtum* (1915, unreported), Alta. SC (Red Deer) Provincial Archives of Alberta (herein after cited as PAA), accession 79.220, file 1211.

5 'Charged with Sedition,' *Red Deer Advocate*, 25 June 1915. This report of the sedition charges west of Red Deer states that Von Holtum had been interned 'for a time early in the war' but had since been released and is undoubtedly a reference to the various federal provisions passed regarding the registration and internment of enemy aliens during the war. See, for example, 'Proclamation respecting German and Austro-Hungarian alien enemies,' *Extra Canada Gazette*, 15 August 1914, no 32, *Copies of Proclamation, Orders in Council and Documents Relating to the European War*, vol. 1 (Ottawa: The King's Printer 1915), 48–52. Amendments were passed throughout the war.

6 *R. v. Trainor* (1916), 10 Alta. LR 164, at 173.

7 Louis A. Knafla, 'From Oral to Written Memory: The Common Law Tradition in Western Canada,' in *Law and Justice in a New Land*, ed. Louis A. Knafla (Calgary: Carswell 1986), 62.

8 In his study of Harvey, Wilbur Bowker acknowledges that the chief justice probably did not agree with Stuart and Beck on how the seditious utterance cases should have been handled; Harvey's strict and literal application of statutes allowed little room for circumstances. See Wilbur F. Bowker, 'The Honourable Horace Harvey, Chief Justice of Alberta' (1954), 32 *Canadian Bar Review*, 933–81, at 948–9, and 1118–39.

9 Owen Chadwick, *The Secularization of the European Mind in the 19th Century* (Cambridge: Cambridge University Press 1975), 27 and 29.

10 Archibald Oswald MacRae, ed., 'Charles Allen Stuart,' in *History of the Province of Alberta* (Calgary: Western Canada History Company 1912), 1023.

11 John Blue, 'Nicholas Du Bois Dominic Beck' in *Alberta, Past and Present*, vol. 2 (Chicago: Pioneer Historical Publishing Co. 1924), 69–71.

12 Canada, Statutes of Canada (1906), c. 146, ss. 132–4.
13 William E. Conklin, 'The Origins of the Law of Sedition' (1972–3), 15 *Criminal Law Quarterly*, 277–300, at 284.
14 Ibid., at 279–83; and James E. Boasberg, 'Seditious Libel versus Incitement to Mutiny: Britain Teaches Hand and Holmes a Lesson' (1990), 10 *Oxford Journal of Legal Studies*, 106–21, at 113.
15 Supra note 12, s. 132.
16 Conklin, supra note 13, at 279.
17 'John Reid, The Socialist Candidate, and C.H. Von Holtum Committed for Trial for Seditious Utterances,' *Red Deer News*, 30 June 1915.
18 'Of Local Interest,' Rocky Mountain House, *The Guide*, 11 June 1915.
19 The following is based on *R. v. Reid* (1915, unreported), Alta. SC (Red Deer), PAA, acession 79.220, file 1205.
20 'The Socialist Candidate,' Rocky Mountain House, *The Guide*, 18 June 1915.
21 'Put a Stop to It,' *Red Deer News*, 30 June 1915.
22 *R. v. Clausen*, (1915, unreported), Alta SC (Red Deer), PAA, accession 79.220, file 1206.
23 *R. v. Schacht* (1915, unreported) Alta. SC (Red Deer), PAA, accesssion 79.220, file 1212.
24 'A Case of Sedition,' *Red Deer News*, 21 July 1915.
25 'John Reid Under Arrest,' *The Guide*, 25 June 1915.
26 'Heed the Warning,' ibid.
27 'John Reid, the Socialist Candidate, and C.H. Von Holtum Committed for Trial for Seditious Utterances,' *Red Deer News*, 30 June 1915.
28 'Put a Stop to It,' ibid.
29 'Supreme Court,' *Red Deer News*, 29 September 1915, and 'Supreme Court,' *Red Deer Advocate*, 1 October 1915.
30 Supra note 12, s. 132.
31 *R. v. Felton* (1915), 9 Alta. LR 238, at 239 (Alta. SC).
32 Ibid., at 242–3.
33 Ibid., at 244.
34 Conklin, supra note 13, at 280–2, and Boasberg, supra note 14, at 113.
35 'Supreme Court Sittings,' *Red Deer Advocate*, 4 February 1916.
36 'Supreme Court,' ibid., 28 January 1916.
37 The Reid case produced further charges in late April 1916 when I.J.W. Gold, who had testified against Reid, filed complaints against Alfred Isaacson, C.H. Macklin, and Sam H. Braton for publishing a defamatory libel. Isaacson had published affidavits sworn by Macklin and Braton in the *Western Clarion* of April 1916, to the effect that Gold had been either drunk or asleep during Reid's speech when the allegedly seditious phrases had been

uttered. Although the cases were sent for trial before the Supreme Court at Red Deer, all three prosecutions were ended through a crown motion of *nolle prosequi*. See *R. v. Isaacson, R. v. Macklin,* and *R. v. Braton* (1916, unreported), Alta. SC (Red Deer) PAA, accession 79.220, files 1307, 1308, and 1309.

38 'Supreme Court,' *Red Deer Advocate,* 28 January 1916.

39 'Supreme Court Sittings,' ibid., 4 February 1916. For a slightly different version of Simmons's comments, see 'Supreme Court,' *Red Deer News,* 2 February 1916.

40 Zechariah Chafee Jr, *Free Speech in the United States* (Cambridge: Harvard University Press 1948), 35. The persistence of the judicial doctrine of 'bad tendency' in the American sedition cases is discussed at 49–51.

41 See *The Albertan,* 11 and 12 February 1916, for details of the two riots. I would like to thank David Bright for bringing these references to my attention.

42 'The Pros and Cons of the Riots in Calgary,' *Red Deer News,* 16 February 1916.

43 'Play the Game Fair,' *Red Deer Advocate,* 18 February 1916.

44 *R. v. Cohen* (1916), 11 ALR 329, at 331–2 (Alta. SC).

45 Judge Beck wrote a *dubiante* concurrence questioning the soundness of the court's decision.

46 *R. v. T. Clausen,* (1916, unreported), Alta. SC (Red Deer) PAA, accession 79.220, file 1304.

47 *R. v. C. Clausen,* (1916, unreported), Alta. SC (Red Deer), PAA, accession 79.220, file 1303.

48 'Committed for Sedition – Clausens, Father and Son, Have Trial,' *Red Deer Advocate,* 14 April 1916. The *Red Deer News* of 19 April 1916 reprinted this column from the *Advocate.* Lindsay's allusion is probably to the case of Edith Cavell, who was captured by the Germans, tried before a court martial for assisting enemy aliens to escape from Belgium, found guilty, and subsequently shot. Local newspapers regularly compared Cavell's fate with the treatment of those accused of offences in Canada. See 'Justice,' *Red Deer Advocate,* 14 January 1916.

49 *R. v. Flagg* (1916, unreported) Alta. SC (Red Deer), PAA, accession 79.220, file 1310.

50 'Supreme Court Sittings,' *Red Deer Advocate,* 22 September 1916.

51 Ibid.; and 'Supreme Court,' *Red Deer News,* 27 September 1916.

52 *R. v. Trainor,* supra note 6, at 171.

53 Ibid., at 172.

54 Ibid., at 173.

55 Ibid., at 173–4

56 Ibid., at 174.

57 Figures are based on the yearly criminal statistics. See Canada, *Sessional Papers*, for the following years (publication dates in brackets): 1914, no. 17 (1915); 1915, no. 17 (1916); 1916, no. 17 (1917); 1917, no. 10c (1918); 1918, no. 10d (1919).

58 General circular, A.G. Browning, attorney general, 15 March 1916, PAA 69.210, G.R.D. Lyon, file 760.

59 *R. v. Cyr* (1917), 12 Alta. LR 320 (Alta. SC).

60 *R. v. Vanstone* (1917, unreported), Alta. SC (Red Deer), PAA, accession 79.220, file 1336.

61 Ibid., 1336–7.

62 *R. v. Schilling*, (1918, unreported) Alta. SC (Red Deer), PAA, accession 79.220, file 1354.

63 Ibid., 1350.

64 *R. v. Sturgeon* (1918, unreported) Alta. SC (Red Deer), PAA, accesion 79.220, file 1348.

65 John Quigg, agent for the attorney general in Red Deer, wrote to the deputy attorney general to advise against entering a stay of proceedings in the Sturgeon case. Citing the 'pretty strong language,' Quigg suggested that 'if stays are entered in these cases there is apt to be an outcry.' See Quigg to Deputy Attorney General, 5 June 1918, 'Re Ere Sturgeon,' PAA, accession 72.26, file 1514/C.

66 Ibid., Quigg to Deputy Attorney General, 4 October 1918.

67 Representing the Crown at Symk's hearing in Stuart's chambers, the Calgary law firm of Lent, McKay and Mann reported that 'this class of foreigner has proved that they were very apt to play foxy and resent inquiry into the requirements and facts of reporting, and would be sullen down to the point of a fine and imprisonment and then when they found that this did not work, they would be the first to squeal loud and long.' See Lent, McKay and Mann to Attorney General Browning, 29 November 1918, 'Re Peter Symk,' PAA, acession 72.26, file 1807/C.

68 'Magistrate at Fault,' *Red Deer Advocate*, 24 January 1919.

69 *Re Symk* (1919, unreported), Alta. SC (Red Deer), PAA, accession 79.220, file 1648; and in 'Magistrate at Fault,' *Red Deer Advocate*, 24 January 1919.

70 The argument has been made by James E. Boasberg, supra note 14, that, in practice, English decisions regarding seditious libel and incitement to mutiny were considerably more liberal than the views enunciated by Judges Learned Hand and Oliver Wendell Holmes in the United States. By extension, it might seem more useful to compare Canadian decisions with Eng-

lish cases rather than American. While Boasberg's views are compelling, they do not necessarily speak to Canadian conditions during the war. Neither of the British cases cited by Boasberg, and none of the American cases were heard during the war, whereas every Canadian case was tried and appealed during hostilities – an accomplishment that speaks to the credit of the Canadian courts. Second, although Canada and Britain obviously shared a great deal of history, Canada's current and future character would be determined by the fact that it was a North American nation and not merely an appendage, legal or otherwise, of Great Britain. Finally, Stuart and his western Canadian brethren were motivated by local conditions rather than bound by British decisions. It is of interest to note that the rationale behind *R. v. Aldred*, the case on which Boasberg builds his argument, was rejected by the Saskatchewan Supreme Court in *R. v Giesinger.* See (1915–16), 9 Sask. LR 423.

71 More pointedly, the absence of Supreme Court rulings regarding free speech during the war indicated to Chafee that 'we cannot rely on the Supreme Court as a safeguard against the excesses of war legislation': supra note 40, at 80.

72 *Schenck v. United States*, in *The Supreme Court and the Constitution: Readings in American Constitutional History*, 3d ed., ed. Stanley Kutler (New York: W.W. Norton 1984), 326.

73 Chafee argues that Holmes was biding his time after the Schenck case 'until the Court should have before it a conviction so clearly wrong as to let him speak out his deepest thoughts about the First Amendment': supra note 40, at 86, 110–11.

74 *Abrams v. U.S.*, in *The Supreme Court and the Constitution*, supra note 72, at 327–8.

75 Chafee, supra note 40, at 129.

11 Treaties, Trains, and Troubled National Dreams: Reflections on the Indian Summer in Northern Ontario, 1990

ANTHONY HALL

Land and Self-Determination

Rayno Fisher, Lenus 'Tubby' Door, and I sauntered along the main line of the Canadian National Railway. From heavy use the two steel ribbons usually glisten like the edge of a newly sharpened knife. But on this particular Sunday evening, 19 August 1990, the tracks were covered with a thin coating of rust. We walked to the outer border of Long Lake Reserve 58. Then we turned back towards our protest camp at the other end of the one-square-mile reserve about two hundred miles northeast of Thunder Bay. Only hours earlier we had removed the obstacles that had blocked east-west traffic on the line for seven days. About 80 miles to the south the people of Mobert Reserve held firm to their blockade of the main Canadian Pacific Railway line.

These actions were but part of an extraordinary Indian summer of activism initiated in June, when Elijah Harper successfully blocked the progress of the Meech Lake accord through the Manitoba legislature. Practically overnight Harper became a hero for millions of Canadians opposed to Meech Lake, but particularly for native people, who were suddenly given a champion in a system of Canadian government that until then had proved almost impervious to the direct exercise of aboriginal political will. No doubt some of the anger aroused by the aboriginal sabotage of Meech Lake found expression on 11 July in the armed assault of the Sûreté du Québec on the Mohawk defences against the expansion of a golf course in Oka, Quebec. Leading the successful repulse of the Quebec provincial police were members of the Mohawk Warriors Society.[1]

The striking television images of Elijah Harper and of the Mohawk warriors, the former working within the existing political order and the latter representing a radical alternative, struck a powerful chord in Indian country. Each alternative seemed to hold out a ray of hope. Implicit in the defensive tactics of both Harper and the warriors was a call to action. Aboriginal people throughout Canada answered.

The Mohawks of Kanewake on the south shore of the St Lawrence east of Montreal were the first to support their endangered relatives who were locked in siege with the Sûrèté du Québec. The Kanewake Mohawks placed blockades on the Mercier Bridge, infuriating commuters from nearby Chateauguay and Lasalle. Before the summer was over Canadians were to watch with astonishment as outraged mobs on the south shore burned Indians in effigy and stoned escaping vehicles full of Mohawk women, elders, and children, and as the nation's army was put under the direction of Quebec's Premier Robert Bourassa to deal with the mounting crisis.

Sympathy blockades and vigils sprung up across Canada in the days and weeks following the police attack on the Oka Mohawks. In some instances these protests involved non-natives who were drawn into aboriginal activism to an extent unprecedented in Canadian history. Many of the sympathy actions soon evolved into demonstrations of local frustration over the unwillingness of authorities to find just resolutions to aboriginal land issues. In British Columbia, for instance, where most native groups have never entered into treaty negotiations with the Crown,² the wave of protest blockades was particularly marked. In Southern Alberta a group of Peigan Indians known as the Lonefighters demonstrated their resistance to the building of the Oldman dam with particular bravado. They began digging a river diversion of their own to bypass an irrigation weir on the Peigan reserve.³

These expressions of resistance to the prevailing trend of Indian dispossession were truly spontaneous. No one coordinated the actions as part of a large masterplan. Rather, the example of Elijah Harper and the Mohawk warriors inspired relatively small groups of community people to begin taking their destinies more firmly into their own hands. In some instances these grass roots protests went beyond a show of resistance directed at federal and provincial authorities. The Aboriginal activism that showed such power during the summer of 1990 also involved an internal critique by native people of their own aboriginal leadership. The warriors and others were especially critical of the whole structure of elected chiefs, band councils, and Indian organizations such as the Assembly of First Nations. They charged that these structures of decision-making are rooted not in true aboriginal sources but rather in the federal parliament's Indian Act.[4]

The background of Long Lake 58's blockade is illustrative of the kind of hopes and frustrations that oozed from many native individuals and communities during the summer of 1990. Long Lake Reserve 58 is situated about one mile west of the predominantly French-speaking town of Longlac. Both the Indian and French communities lie at the northern end of Long Lake, a narrow body of water that cuts across one hundred miles of low-lying Canadian Shield country north of Lake Superior. The natural flow of Long Lake is northward towards James Bay. Thus the reserve lies in terrain that is part of the Arctic watershed. Nevertheless, the federal and Ontario governments' position was that Long Lake 58 is covered by the terms of the Robinson-Superior treaty, a land agreement covering territory drained by Lake Superior. This obvious incongruity is reflective of the inconsistency that has characterized the approach of successive governments towards the land regime in the area.

The difficulties surrounding the aboriginal land question largely lead back to the reality that many Indian groups north of Lake Superior were not represented in the negotiations leading to the treaties signed at Sault Ste-Marie in 1850. In fact, only three Indian communities participated in the original negotiations; as a result they were assigned reserves at Fort William, Michipicoten, and Gull Bay on Lake Nipegon. These reserves encompass respectively 14,274, 8,957, and 9,825 acres.[5] In comparison, the reserves assigned to the Indian groups that did not take part in the original treaty negotiations are much smaller. Those reserves were allocated in an ad hoc manner shortly before the turn of the century. They include Long Lake 58, a community of about eight hundred members who share a 537-acre reserve. They also include Pic Heron Bay (800 acres), Pic Mobert (33 acres), Pays Plat (580 acres), Rocky Bay (33 acres), and Red Rock (25 acres).[6]

The huge disparity in the size of reserves north of Lake Superior presents clear evidence that a number of native communities in the area have never been in a position to negotiate fair settlements of their aboriginal land title. The legal status of these communities is therefore similar to that of the Teme-Augama Anishnabai in Temagami, Ontario,[7] or of the Lubicon Crees in northern Alberta.[8] The traditional hunting territories of all these groups lie within land subject to the terms of Indian treaties, and yet the negotiation of the agreements left out the peoples in question. In each instance, however, the provincial governments have treated the land at issue as if they possess full and unfettered ownership of it. In the Long Lake 58 area the government of Ontario has asserted this claim of ownership by parcelling out logging permits to a number of operations, including the multinational Kimberly-Clark corporation.

The list of grievances that drove the band members of Long Lake 58 onto the railway track had been growing, especially during the last half of the century. In the late 1930s the Ontario government dammed up the northern end of Long Lake to reverse the flow of water so that logs could be floated down to pulp and paper operations at Terrace Bay on Lake Superior. After the Second World War, Kimberly-Clark took over this operation. The dam negatively affected the aquatic ecology of the Long Lake 58 area, a development compounded over the years by the wood bark and PCB contamination from Kimberly-Clark's activities. The cumulative result was that by the 1980s the Indians were told that it was dangerous to eat the fish from Long Lake. The rich trapping of earlier years has been drastically undermined by the damage from clearcut logging. More recently the Ontario Ministry of Natural Resources (MNR) and Kimberly-Clark have been spraying replanted parts of the region to kill off vegetation deemed unwanted. These poisonous chemicals, the hunters of Long Lake 58 charge, have been showing up in the game animals they catch. Tales are legion among these hunters of the heavy-handedness of MNR officials whose goal it seems to be to transform Indian hunting grounds into tree plantations.

During their lifetime, then, the elders of Long Lake 58 have witnessed a transformation from an era when they could harvest the rich wildlife of their homeland with few restrictions. From the liberty enjoyed during this era of relative abundance they have been pushed back and back into the narrow confines of their increasingly cramped reserve. Those individuals who have stuck tenaciously to their life on the land have been subjected to an increasingly bewildering array of regulations forced on them by the MNR.

With the example of Elijah Harper and the Mohawk defence of Mohawk lands to inspire them, the people of Long Lake 58, like native people throughout the country, reflected on their own experiences. They contemplated the future that seemed to lie in store for their children and their children's children if nothing changed. Out of this soul-searching came a flood of personal testimonials and collective declarations of shared purpose. The statement of grievances put together by the band council of Long Lake 58 is suggestive of the kind of commentary that came forward from many native communities in the charged atmosphere of those times. The following is an excerpt from that document:

In recent decades, far too many of our young people have chosen to take their own lives. Far too many have died violently and prematurely. Far too many have faced prison sentences and too many have suffered the nightmare of drug and alcohol abuse. While we must assume our share of the responsibility, can there be any doubt that the injustices and abuses we face have contributed to the loss of spirit among some of our people?

When governments continue to patronize us, or to push aside lightly our claims and grievances, we are implicitly being told again and again we don't count for much; that our Aboriginal nationalities are expendable; that we are awkward misfits who would make things easier for ourselves if we would just become brown little white men or white women. Is there any wonder that some of us internalize the signals we are being given at every turn? Is there any wonder that some of us lose a sense of who we are and how we can realize our full human potential in the midst of a province and a country that repeatedly shows itself so unaccepting of our Indigenous identity.

Why do we face such ruthlessness from officials who see our willingness to share the land as a signal it is OK to steal everything of value from us? The time has passed when we can any longer be patient with the continued theft of our resources. We must do what has to be done to secure for our future generations the political, economic and cultural tools we need to survive as a distinct Aboriginal society.[9]

As the discussion developed, there was growing agreement that many of the problems faced by Long Lake 58 and the surrounding bands could be traced back to the lack of clarity concerning underlying issues of land title. 'How come we have to do a land claim?' asked Frances Abraham, a seventy-one-year-old mother of fifteen who was to become one of the most steadfast bastions of resistance during the train blockade. 'Where did the MNR get the right to tell us what we can do and what we can't do on our own land? How come we have to do a land claim while the others who came and took our land never have to prove anything?'

Mrs Abraham's concerns were set against the background of an enormous backlog in the land claims process in Canada. Since 1973, when the federal government began accepting applications from Indian groups seeking to enter into land negotiations,[10] two different processes had been established. Comprehensive claims became an instrument of negotiation for native people not covered by the terms of any treaty.[11] In effect, therefore, the working through of such claims amounts to the negotiation of modern-day treaties. The specific claims process, by contrast, was to provide a means to address the grievances of those native groups who had already entered into a treaty relationship with the Crown.[12] Common problems addressed in specific claims involve charges that sections of Indian reserves have been improperly alienated or that the full extent of lands promised to Indian groups by the terms of treaties has never been properly allocated.

Although the federal government did expend some effort to advance native claims in the Yukon and the Northwest Territories during the 1980s, there was very little movement with respect to the great mass of aboriginal land disputes within provincial boundaries.[13] Most provincial governments had been unsympathetic to the prospect of sharing ownership and jurisdiction in land with aboriginal groups. Similarly, there was little political incentive for the federal government to fulfil its constitutional obligation to defend the aboriginal interest in Canadian lands against the encroachment of provincial interests. This trend became especially pronounced with the ascendancy in 1984 of Prime Minister Brian Mulroney and the federal Conservatives, a political regime that strongly favoured the facilitation of provincial agendas in the name of national reconciliation.[14]

By the summer of 1990 it was becoming clear to many observers that the land claims process in Canada was essentially broken for all but a few Indian groups. Long Lake 58 and several neighbouring Indian communities faced the added complication of being non-treaty peoples indigenous to a region claimed by the Crown as ceded territory. This assertion goes back to the negotiation of the Robinson-Superior treaty in 1850 and to the negotiation of Treaty 9 in 1905 covering Ontario lands drained by rivers flowing into James Bay and Hudson's Bay.[15] The other option available to the people of Long Lake 58 was to take their assertion of unceded aboriginal title to court. In making their case the Indians could point to the Royal Proclamation of 1763 and the constitutional tradition of treaty-making that flows from this foundational constitutional document.[16] The essence of their argument would be that the Crown has historically recognized the basic human right of aboriginal people not to be unilaterally dispossessed of their ancestral lands without fair compensation and provision for their future survival. Moreover, the band could look with some hope to an important string of Supreme Court of Canada judgments penned between 1984 and 1990 by Chief Justice Brian Dickson.[17] These findings were intended to begin the process of fleshing out the substance of what was intended by the positive affirmation of aboriginal and treaty rights in the Constitution Act, 1982.

However, the people of Long Lake 58 could look several hundred miles to the east to the experience of the Teme-Augama Anishnabai. This group asserts that it too was unrepresented in the treaty negotiations that took place in 1850, when William Benjamin Robinson also dealt with a number of bands living north of Lake Huron. It was not until 1971 that a reserve was finally allocated to the Teme-Augama Anishnabai on Bear Island in Lake Temagami. As Gary Potts, the chief of the band, claimed in 1973, the designation of Bear Island as a reserve still left unaddressed the deeper issues surrounding the band's unceded Aboriginal title. This assertion led to a bitter court battle that pitted the provincial and federal governments against the Temagami Indians.[18] For their efforts the Teme-Augama Anishnabai have been handed three very unfavourable court rulings.[19] Justice Donald Steele of the Ontario Supreme Court decided in 1984 that it was immaterial whether or not the Indians were represented at the treaty negotiations of 1850, because 'Aboriginal rights can be unilaterally extinguished by the sovereign power.' In his view the fact that land rights in Temagami had been distributed by the Ontario government to non-Indians was sufficient to obliterate whatever legal interest the Indians may have possessed in their ancestral domain.[20]

Judge Steele's finding on the Temagami land dispute, which was supported and even extended by the Ontario Court of Appeal in 1989, had a poisoning affect on aboriginal affairs in Ontario. Successive Conservative and Liberal provincial governments had marshalled all the legal arguments available to oppose the claim of the Teme-Augama Anishnabai. Officials acting on behalf of the provincial Crown resorted to a host of arguments originally developed in the nineteenth century to justify the dispossession of native people. In the final analysis, all these arguments are founded on the racist principle that Indians are inferior peoples who are doomed to disappear as distinct societies under the domineering weight of non-Indian progress. Provincial law officers' articulation of such abhorrent theories of racial hierarchy could not help but damage the reputation of the provincial government as an effective instrument for the protection and advancement of human rights. Judge Steele's lengthy finding helped draw the legal debates surrounding aboriginal and treaty rights more fully into the political forum. He stated that treaty negotiations essentially constituted little more than elaborate ceremonies to pacify Indians, because 'a treaty is not a conveyance of title ... title is already in the crown.' The major rule that determined whether a treaty was made with a particular Indian society involved the estimation of whether that group was contemplating 'insurrection.' Judge Steele wrote: 'Where there was no concern about an Indian insurrection, the Crown did not enter into treaties.'[21]

Frances Abraham and the other band members of Long Lake 58 were not contemplating insurrection when they decided to take their grievances to the court of public opinion during the summer of 1990. But, according to Judge Steele's logic, the threat of insurrection represented the only effective means to draw Crown officials into a modern-day treaty negotiation. And it was just such a negotiation that the people of Long Lake 58 sought, a negotiation that would confirm their capacity to bargain their way towards a decent collective future as a viable and stable aboriginal community. Of course, all the twists and nuances of the legal arguments concerning aboriginal title were not common currency in the community discussions that led to the railway blockade. The stories shared were naturally more personal. Community members remembered recurring instances when they had been pushed aside, ripped off, and cheated, often by individuals claiming to represent some distant authority with immense power to decide the fate of Indian lives. Band members told of how trapping-lodges full of equipment and supplies – the life-support system of whole families – had been burned by workers on the order of the MNR. They told of how hunters' gardens had been contaminated by chemicals sprayed over vast areas at the behest of the forestry industry; how rich trapping-grounds had been made barren and the surviving animals poisoned and sick; how students had been served so poorly in an alien system of non-Indian schools that received large portions of their funding from the Department of Indian Affairs (DIA); how so many mysterious deaths of band members seemed to go uninvestigated or inadequately explained by the police; how the apparatus of the law so often seemed to be enforced against Indians and how rarely the law seemed to work in Indians' favour; and how hard it was to maintain cohesive family lives when violent deaths, disease, alcoholism, incarceration, and poverty were regular fixtures of day-to-day life. As Diane Grant, one of Mrs Abraham's daughters, explained, many young people do try to escape the apparent dead-end of life on the reserve: 'Lots of our people have gone over to Winnipeg,' she said, 'but too many of them end up being shipped home in a box.'

In the charged atmosphere ignited throughout Indian country by Harper and the Mohawks, ideas and stories like these came rushing out in a flood. For the people of Long Lake 58, a major theme underlying all

these thoughts was the notion that they had never been formally acknowledged by the society of newcomers around them as the original inhabitants with prior rights to the land. Lacking this recognition, they had
never been able to bargain for a secure niche in the new economic
order. They had never been able to bargain for a reasonable degree of
access to the levers of political authority, levers that would enable them
to influence meaningfully the pace and form of change over the extent
of their ancestral lands. Nor had they ever been able to bargain for an
entrenched role in the management of schools, hospitals, and social
service agencies, institutions that would come to exercise enormous
control over their lives.

As the anecdotes and testimonials poured forth, they began to coalesce
into a larger picture which told of a major transformation that had
happened well within the lifetime of the elders of the community. People
had been deprived of a culture of relative independence, health, and
liberty; a culture of welfare, alcohol and jail had been put in its place,
bringing untold physical and emotional suffering to many of those
involved. I had a few ideas of my own to add to the growing body of
stories and theory that activated that month of protest in the ancient
heart of Ojibway country north of Lake Superior. We exchanged many
of our thoughts around the fires of the camps that encircled the old
Catholic church on the point jutting out from the northern shore of
Long Lake. Many of the old people still set up their tents on the point
as soon as it is warm enough to sleep comfortably outside. They return
to the grounds where their little townsite once stood in the days before
the DIA threw up the rows of box housing in the swampy terrain on the
other side of the highway. The intensity of activity on the point usually
builds as the summer progresses. By August the family camps have
become a main social centre of the reserve. The cool breezes from across
the lake thin out the legions of northern Ontario bugs.

Where most of the others talked largely from their own experiences,
much of what I said was drawn from reading. I had worked since 1982 as
a professor of native studies in Sudbury, Ontario, and never before had
I witnessed a moment so open to the seamless merging of theory and
analysis with the practical work of political activism. As we sipped our tea
I shared my conviction that the laws of Canada were being broken every
time non-Indian enterprises extracted wealth from the natural resources
in the Long Lake 58 area. I based this position on aspects of my reading
of Canadian constitutional history. Through this stream of history trickles
a developing, if sometimes submerged, recognition that aboriginal people

in the Crown's North American dominions have the basic human right not to be unilaterally dispossessed of their ancestral lands. Treaties are the essential instrument for Indian groups to signify their willingness to share their territories in return for various sorts of considerations guaranteed forever by the Crown.

I was able to quote a phrase from the *St Catherine's Milling* case, the grandpa of aboriginal land claims cases in Canada.[22] In 1888 the highest court in the British empire found that Canadian provinces can enjoy 'beneficial interest' in lands within their borders only after these lands have been 'disencumbered of the Indian title.'[23] All evidence pointed to the fact that this legal thing called 'Indian title' had never been the subject of any purchase or negotiations with the people of Long Lake band 58. This opinion, of course, was not a new one. A land claim based on this notion had been sporadically talked about and developed for almost two decades. But the electrified sensibilities in Indian country during the summer of 1990 created a new environment in which there was a far wider constituency of native people who were prepared to consider the connection between aspects of their day-to-day lives and the otherwise esoteric domain of constitutional argument. While most shared the feeling of having been cheated all their lives, a widening consensus began to emerge about what lay behind the swindle and about the kind of things that had to be done to address the injustice.

The visit, along with a series of band council meetings, led to a gathering of the whole community in the rec hall. It was clear that something significant was happening when the level of attendance challenged the turnout for bingo. Bernie Abraham, among the oldest of Frances's fifteen offspring, acted as master of ceremonies at one of the key gatherings. He is about fifty years old and one of the very few of his generation to leave the reserve for a lengthy period and survive. But much of his life has been tough, including the years spent in prison. Bernie's gruff playfulness lightened the atmosphere. With his encouragement many of the band members, young and old, gathered their courage to get up to the microphone and talk about their hurts and aspirations. Near the edge of the room sat my wife Lena and our two boys, Sam and Riley. They listened carefully as they snuggled up to their granny, Bertha Nabigon. Even the kids seemed to grasp a feeling of the importance of what was going on.

A brainstorming session produced a variety of suggestions about how to press the grievances of Long Lake 58 members and of native people throughout the country on the attention of the bureaucrats, the politicians, and the general public. The example of the Teme Augama Anishnabai, opposed relentlessly by the provincial government in the courts for almost two decades, effectively dampened hope of redress in the judicial corridors of power. And the broken mechanisms for the political negotiation of land issues, especially for groups disputing provincial claims to ownership and unfettered jurisdiction over aboriginal lands, offered no realistic opening to better changes. By a process of elimination, the people of Long Lake 58 decided to express their concerns for one hour across Highway 11 on 9 August 1990.

The police were duly informed of the band's intention to block the road on the reserve. At the appointed time the driver of the community school bus parked the vehicle across the highway. Several young men placed their drum on the road and began to sing. After about ten minutes the group was approached by an Ontario Provincial Police officer from Longlac detachment. He told us we were committing a crime and asked us if we would move off the road. I replied that we knew many laws had been broken over the years, with the people of Long Lake 58 suffering the negative consequences. And yet no one ever seemed to be held accountable, let alone go to jail for transgressing the constitutionally entrenched principles of aboriginal and treaty rights. On the other hand, the jails of Canada are filled with native people, many of them in prison for petty offences. Where was the equity? Where was the justice? The police officer looked somewhat deflated when no one flinched at the threat of being arrested. In the psychology of the encounter the weapon of fear was suddenly not his to wield. The exuberant Bernie Abraham seemed to be bouncing all over the highway. He jumped into the circle of discussion and announced that he had been arrested lots of times for 'garbage.' 'If you want to arrest me now, go ahead,' he said. 'This time it will be for something good.' Lena's mother Bertha mumbled an angry comment at the officer and tapped his elbow with her placard. The policeman meaningfully touched his arm and aimed back at Bertha the comment that she could be charged for assault. Then suddenly it was as if he stepped back from himself to notice how he must have appeared, flaunting his power as an officer of the law over this defiant grandmother. He smirked awkwardly and walked away.

When we lifted the blockade shortly afterward, we watched the passing of the cars and trucks that had been delayed. I was surprised how many of the motorists, mostly tourists, pointed thumbs up. A lot of truck drivers also honked their approval. During the summer of 1990 many Canadians had become exasperated with politics and elected officials of all stripes. I sensed in the reaction of some of the motorists the possibility of a more widely held sentiment. Perhaps there were many observers out there who in their heart of hearts would like to have demonstrated their displeasure with government as forthrightly as these native people. Perhaps there was a growing number of Canadians who were coming to get a small taste of what it felt like to be treated as Indians – that is, to be marginalized, to be deprived of access to the levers of real political power and to be lied to time and again. As we walked back to the rec hall I mulled over these thoughts and wondered how to present the best case possible to the court of public opinion.

There was a heightened mood of confidence as the group gathered to consider the next step. Early in the meeting Rayno Fisher stepped to the microphone. Rayno is a commanding figure, still strong in body. The father of many children, most of them with families of their own now, the clean lines on his weathered face speak of a vigorous life spent mostly outdoors. He seems to have only one good eye; the other is protected behind the fleshy configuration of a perpetual squint. 'A lot of the problems we face now go back to the way they put those rail lines through our reserve,' he said. 'The company never asked us if they could do it. They just pushed the lines through. And from that point on outsiders just seemed to think they could help themselves to what they wanted. The highway, they never asked us for permission to put it through. The same goes for the hydro line and the telephone line. To get back to the beginning of where the unfairness started, I think we should set up our blockade across the rail lines. We wouldn't be trespassing CNR. CNR has been trespassing us for the last seventy-five years.' The next day Bernie telephoned the train company to tell them of the community's decision. We typed out a notice of our intent and we faxed it to Toronto. The blockade was to begin on Monday morning.

First Nations, First Ministers

I have been visiting 58, Lena's home community, since around the time she became pregnant with our oldest son, Sampson Hall Nabigon. Sam was six in the summer of 1990. Sam came into the world during a decade when serious questions began to be asked in political circles about the place of aboriginal individuals and aboriginal societies in the Canadian federation. The patriation and attempted elaboration of the Canadian constitution proved to be the exercise that brought aboriginal issues into sharper political focus than at any other time during the twentieth century.

In 1980 Lena told me about the journey of her uncle George Finlayson to London, England. For many years Finlayson had been chief of Long Lake 58 band. He had last been in Great Britain as a soldier in the Canadian army during the Second World War. Now he was returning to Europe, together with almost half the Indian chiefs in Canada, to lobby the British government. A good-natured man who had cultivated his talent for conversation into a high art, he travelled to Britain with many other Indian leaders to oppose patriation of the Canadian constitution. In order to understand their opposition to the proposed shape of Canada's new constitutional order, it is necessary to appreciate the deep historic bonds that link many native people with the institutions of the British imperial monarchy.

In Canada the imperial monarch stands as the primary protector of aboriginal interests in lands and resources. For instance, the Royal Proclamation of 1763,[24] which some have called the Indian Bill of Rights or the Indian Magna Carta,[25] was issued directly by George III. In his personal capacity as sovereign of an expanded British empire, King George outlined the extent of the Indian territory in the North American interior. He then reserved for himself and his royal heirs the sole authority to negotiate the future disposition of land title with the aboriginal inhabitants of the Indian territory.[26] In this fashion, the proclamation established the Crown's constitutional framework for the subsequent negotiation of Indian treaties in Canada. The document stipulated that the native negotiators of treaties would deal with officials who represented the monarch as sovereign of the British empire; hence, the promises extended to aboriginal groups in Indian treaties are guaranteed personally by the monarch. There is no legislative dimension to the eighty or so treaties between Indian nations in Canada and the Crown of the British empire.

Finlayson and his fellow chiefs, therefore, had sound cause to fear that the constitutional status of their indigenous nations would be diminished by patriation. What was there to prevent Canadians from ignoring the treaty promises of the British sovereign once the locus of authority over the Canadian constitution passed from British to Canadian hands? What was to prevent politicians in the Canadian parliament and the provincial legislatures from changing the constitution to violate the Crown's historic promises that the land rights and the treaty rights of aboriginal peoples would be respected for as long as the sun shines, as long as the grass grows, and as long as the rivers flow? In my experience, this connection between some native traditionalists and the imperial monarch tends utterly to perplex those who are uninitiated into the ethos of Indian politics. Many younger native people are among those who have difficulty appreciating the sense of attachment to the queen felt by Finlayson's generation. A substantial portion of aboriginal youths, however, are still socialized into that aspect of their heritage that places land rights and treaties at the forefront of relations with non-aboriginal society.

An emphasis on treaties, both those that are made and those that have yet to be made, signifies a conception of aboriginal nations as allies of the Crown rather than as subjects of Canadian law.[27] The fact that most treaties were made directly with a king or queen is deeply suggestive of the nation-to-nation character of the agreements. One sovereign power recognizes the sovereignty of the other. Both parties to the treaty confirm their will to live harmoniously together in mutual enjoyment of shared territory and to hold in mutual respect each other's laws and customs. No doubt those native diplomats who negotiated treaties found great meaning in the fact that they were dealing with the highest authority in the imperial constellation. They were not dealing with politicians who come and go in the normal course of majoritarian democracy. They were not dealing with John A. Macdonald or career bureaucrats who were in no real position to assure the fulfilment of promises for as long as the sun shines. They were dealing instead with that part of the government of British North America that was meant to personify permanence and continuity, and to transcend the grimy tradeoffs of electoral politics. They were confirming a personal and perpetual relationship between their own extended families and the family designated to personify the best of the imperial heritage at the core of the empire.

The fears held by Finlayson and his generation of Indian leaders could not have been more thoroughly fulfilled than in the process that produced, in the spring of 1987, the Meech Lake accord. Eleven politicians known as first ministers met privately to change major components of the Canadian constitution. The assumption underlying the meeting was that these eleven men could legitimately represent all the inhabitants of a pluralistic Canada, including those who belonged to aboriginal societies. A further assumption was that many of the essential institutions of the Canadian state could be adjusted without reference to the impact of these changes on the crown's recognition of aboriginal and treaty rights.

The content of the accord reflected the bias of its authors, namely, Brian Mulroney and the provinces' premiers.[28] The new constitution would have contained a definition of the fundamental characteristic of Canada which included the famous phrase identifying Quebec as a distinct society. It spoke of Canada exclusively in terms of two major linguistic communities, English-speaking and French-speaking. The resulting impression of Canada was that of a kind of white man's country where the major measure of diversity would be embodied in the two 'official' languages imported from Europe. Nothing gave contemporary expression to the kind of principles articulated by King George in the royal proclamation, the document at the foundation of Canada's constitutional infrastructure. The Meech Lake accord therefore became a powerful symbol for many aboriginal people throughout Canada.[29] In order to appreciate the force of this symbolism – a symbolism that was eventually seized and channelled so effectively by Elijah Harper – one must look beyond the accord's 'legalese' and towards the politics that surrounded the document.

The factor that was probably most influential in mobilizing aboriginal opinion against the accord was the stark contrast between the first ministers' response to the constitutional claims of the Quebec government and their response to the constitutional claims of the aboriginal leadership. In four constitutional conferences on aboriginal matters between 1983 and 1987, the first ministers couldn't muster the political will to sanction a constitutional amendment that would have clarified the place of aboriginal governments in the Canadian federation. During the course of these nationally televised spectacles, aboriginal leaders were told that nothing must go into the constitution until a degree of certainty was achieved about how the courts would eventually interpret the new wording. Yet in March 1987 Brian Mulroney unilaterally terminated this series of conferences, which had included representatives of four national aboriginal organizations. The prime minister shut down the process without establishing any alternative processes to address those aboriginal issues that had been brought to national prominence over the previous four years. In April, the first ministers held the fifth of their post-patriation conferences on the constitution. This time they met in private at Meech Lake. Literally overnight, they came up with a sweeping agreement in principle that proposed a host of changes far beyond anything seriously contemplated at the conferences on aboriginal matters. And it all came down to crashing defeat at the bar of elected representation.

As we look back, the events at the Manitoba legislature seem to blend almost naturally with the events at Oka and Kanewake. It is almost as if the flare-up in Quebec was willed by some vast collective consciousness that requiring a theatre of action to work through the ideas and emotions stirred up by the death of Meech Lake. The ghost of Louis Riel haunted the convergence of Mohawk sovereignty with Québecois nationalism.[30] The breath of living history filled our lungs.

The Protest Camp

Lena came up with the slogan. We painted a banner saying: 'Let's Get Canada Back on the Right Track.' We put the sign along the edge of the tarp covering the eating area of the Nabigon family camp. The Fisher and Abraham clans organized their tents and gear in similar fashion, as the Long Lake 58 protest camp coalesced further with every passing day. The CNR had briefly tried running its trains along the more southerly CPR route. Within a couple of days, however, the chief of Mobert reserve moved his people onto the CPR track. The national rail service was effectively severed. The diversion of some Canadian trains began south of the Great Lakes via Chicago. Canadian trade unionists who were losing work began contemplating their own blockades to force the federal government to deal with the crisis. A few railway workers actually did block the trans-Canada highway north of Lake Superior for a few hours.

Was it realistic to imagine that the Indian protest of 1990 could help get the country back on track? Was it realistic to hope that the native blockades could contribute to a national reconsideration of the very purpose of maintaining a federation across the northern half of North America? The railways, after all, are one of the few reliable symbols of shared history and identity in a national mythology still awaiting extensive elaboration. These ribbons of steel were once at the very heart of the political and entrepreneurial visions that enabled a transatlantic dominion to emerge from the claim of an old fur trade company with a charter from the English king. But the old mythology needed reworking. The railway lines represented a conquest of geography to enforce an east-west flow of communications across a vast primal landscape. Brian Mulroney's obsession with the United States, however, rendered old ideals obsolete. The country was in need of new rationales to justify the elaboration of a Canadian nationality within the context of a continental trading-block.

Ironically, the stoppage of traffic created a moment of heightened contemplation all up and down the tracks. After a century of quiet accommodation, why had two obscure Indian communities in northern Ontario suddenly withdrawn their acquiescence to the flow of commerce across their lands? How strong was the frustration that had forced the people onto the tracks? What was the strength of their resolve? How contagious was it? How organized were they? How strongly were the actions in Northern Ontario connected to what was happening in Oka or in British Columbia? What might native people do next? Who would join in? Was the protest legitimate or was the action an insupportable assault on Canada's civil and economic order? One could almost feel the intensity of the questioning pass along the rails like an electric current.

When the railway lines were built, the Indians along the route were widely perceived, like the land, as wild forces of nature to be tamed. Engineers spanned the country with tracks at the same time as social engineers in church and state turned their energies to the transformation of aboriginal Canada. A principal instrument of the colonizing mission was the Indian residential school, where native youths were to have been re-created in Euro-Canadian images. But even as native people adapted with varying degrees of success to the tremendous changes imposed on their lands, most would not succumb to the drive to separate them from their indigenous identities. Indeed, as we entered the final decade of the twentieth century, the conquistadorial obsession to subdue the land and the peoples of the so-called New World no longer seemed credible. New national credos were demanded as we headed down the track towards the 500th anniversary of Christopher Columbus's arrival in continents that would henceforth be known as the Americas.[31]

Who was in a stronger position than native people to call into being a fresh vision of Canada's future? Who was in a stronger position to bring a knowing eye to outmoded conceptions of nation-building than those who have been pushed aside as primitive obstacles in the way of the arrogant newcomers' bulldozer progress? What national symbol is more evocative than the railway, that hefty engine of communications that opened Indian land to the large-scale penetration of peoples, cultures, and legal traditions exported largely from Europe? What would be the chemistry of mixing the politics of railways with the politics of Indianness? Might some kind of formula result from the blockade that would help get Canada back on the right track? Or was the imagery of masked Mohawk warriors so overpowering as to blank out receptiveness to the broader range of ideas coming forth from native people?

Ronnie Towegishig brought in the hindquarter of a moose when we were first setting up the protest camp. Later in the week someone contributed two large sturgeons to our communal food supply. Once the camp got going, an easy rhythm took over. During this part of the summer most of the people of Long Lake 58 live outside. Every day the elders walked the half mile or so between their camps at the point and the protest camp at the northern edge of the train yard on the reserve. At night some of the younger officers of the OPP would share tea, bannock, and moose meat with us. Uncle George Nabigon would usually stay up late cooking. Early on we had come to a good understanding with the

OPP that they would allow every opportunity for the peaceful resolution of the matter through rational negotiation. A provincial election was underway and there were sound motives for politicians in the provincial government to ensure that the whole affair didn't explode in their faces.

Largely because of the insistence of Lena's brother, Frankie Nabigon, a meeting took place between the Indian leadership in the area and the town council of Longlac. We wanted to do everything in our power to avoid the kind of ugly racial confrontations that had occurred in Oka and Chateauguay. Using a large map of the area, we tried to describe what was involved in the assertion of aboriginal title. We tried to provide reassurance that non-Indians had nothing to fear from a just resolution of the land dispute. In fact, it was our contention that everyone in the Longlac area stood to benefit from the economic rejuvenation that would probably develop in the aftermath of a modern-day treaty.

On 13 August we entered the CNR train yard on the reserve. Brad Lee, an executive of the federal Crown corporation, was there to meet us, accompanied by a CNR police officer. When we convinced Lee of our resolve, he announced his intention to advise head office to close the line. The gesture he made when he declared this decision reminded me of a baseball umpire signalling that the runner was safe at home plate. Later in the afternoon Lee met with the band council. He requested a letter outlining specific actions that might be taken by the CNR to bring the blockade to an early end. By the following morning we had a single page that asked the minister of transport to bring the grievances of Long Lake 58 to the prime minister's attention. In addition, we asked the company to describe its view of the nature of CNR's title to Long Lake 58 lands. Similarly, we asked the company to give us its legal opinion concerning the nature of the company's claim to land under the tracks in those parts of the country where aboriginal title remained unceded.

We marked our delivery of the letter to the CNR by raising a banner that read, 'Who's Trespassing?' In Rayno Fisher's mind there was no doubt. He kept repeating his reassurance: 'We're not trespassing CNR. They've been trespassing us for 75 years.' Our strategy was to reverse the logic of land claims. For once the onus would be on people other than aboriginal people to prove the legitimacy of *their* land claim. Let the Crown corporation prove the legitimacy of its claim to a federal Indian reserve. With the passing hours and days our web of communications from the band office widened dramatically. A stream of inquiries from the media turned to a flood. Then reporters began to show up in person. By the end of the week the national TV network sent crews out to the camp. We even fielded a telephone call from the *Wall Street Journal.* We also established contacts with the office of Ian Scott, attorney general of Ontario and minister of native affairs. It seems he left the campaign trail to deal with the blockades. In telephone discussions with his officials we soon arrived at an agreement that a major part of the problem was in the federal government. Although Indian land matters are the explicit constitutional responsibility of Ottawa, there was no political will there even to initiate a negotiating process. We agreed with officials in Scott's office that both Indians and the government of Ontario shared an interest in inducing the federal government to deal constructively with unresolved aboriginal land issues.

By 16 August we reached a bottleneck in the flow of the negotiations. Since we were ultimately appealing to the court of public opinion, we knew that it was important to show a good degree of consistency and moderation in our assertions. We tried to get the word out that we would allow Via passenger trains through the blockade but not cargo trains. This offer was never acknowledged. We also knew that it was unrealistic to expect immediate movement on the larger land issue. As we informed Lee, all that would be required for us to break the camp would be a letter from the minister of transport, Doug Lewis. That letter would merely have to acknowledge that there might be some legal uncertainties concerning the overlapping title of the CNR to Long Lake 58 reserve lands. Such an acknowledgment, we reasoned, would set in motion a chain of events that would eventually necessitate federal involvement in the larger land issue.

It seemed to us that we could force the federal government's hand by narrowing the issue to the nature of CNR's claim to Long Lake 58 lands. We would eliminate the argument of jurisdictional overlap, which is the federal government's usual justification for inaction on Indian land issues. CNR is a federal Crown corporation. Rail transport is a federal responsibility. Indians are federal creatures, according to the Victorian logic of the British North American Act. And Indian reserves have long been treated as federal domains. By boxing this Indian issue into an exclusively federal frame of reference, there should have been no way for federal officials to escape their responsibility by pointing to provincial claims of jurisdiction over lands and resources.

We decided to focus our attention on Doug Lewis rather than on Tom Siddon, minister of Indian affairs and northern development. What, we asked, is the role of DIAND? At the time of the building of Canada's second transnational railway, Indian agents tended to act both in the name of certain bands and on behalf of the minister of Indian affairs. Reserve lands were often simply signed over to railway companies and other interests, sometimes without the slightest effort to obtain the required sanction from the Indian community involved. We saw the old patterns repeated when officials from the DIAND in Thunder Bay moved forcefully to break a delicate emerging alliance between the railway unions and the native groups involved in the blockades. Was the department still tending to act on behalf of native people so as to keep them as isolated as possible in the larger political system? Does it persist in acting as if it represents aboriginal communities in their dealings with other state agencies?

It didn't take long for Doug Lewis to respond to our offer. Lena and I were driving over to the protest camp for a community meeting. Suddenly we heard a news bulletin on the car radio: 'A spokesperson for Transport Minister Doug Lewis announced that the OPP and CNR police have been asked to do whatever is necessary to remove the native blockade on the CNR line at Longlac Ontario.' We arrived at the camp and parked the car. A few minutes later an OPP helicopter hovered overhead. Perhaps the observers above were watching in the expectation that the group would break apart out of fear. What they witnessed instead was a movement of vehicles and people towards the camp. By this point many people at Long Lake 58 had decided that they wanted to be included if some were to be arrested.

We held the meeting as planned, fully expecting the police to arrive at any minute. The air was heavy with humidity. In this dense, tense atmosphere many of the most moving speeches were made. The train yard was wired with electricity so we could put the band's sound system to good use. Several young people who had not yet spoken in the community gatherings came forward. Diane Abraham talked with particular resolve about the importance of standing proudly together in the face of intimidation. So much had been stripped from the people; but here was a chance to regain a measure of dignity in the face of all the abuse. Diane's son, 'the professor,' also said a few words. Again and again the importance of holding together was stressed. It was natural to feel afraid, said Tubby Door, but it would be wrong now to be ruled by that fear.

The police did not come into the camp. Somewhere in the chain of command, probably at Scott's office, the federal order was flatly refused. We had passed through the bottleneck without losing ground. We could relax a little. Lee's role as go-between with the company and, indirectly, with the federal government came to an end that day. In a small ceremony we acknowledged the congenial diplomacy he brought to the affair. As Lee left the scene a new player entered. Mitch Phillips presented himself as the district manager of DIAND's Thunder Bay office. Essentially, he was the modern personification of Long Lake 58's Indian agent.

Mitch introduced himself at the microphone. He began by apologizing that in his years of service he had never actually visited the reserve. After these remarks he had to face questions from the audience of strangers before him. The harshest commentary came from Bernie Abraham. He took the microphone and made his gruff accusations only inches away from the Indian agent's nose. The photographer from the Toronto *Star* caught the encounter in a photograph that was widely distributed over the wire services. An image was captured of the moment when remote officialdom in the DIA was finally cornered into symbolic accountability to the people on the receiving end of the federal government's arbitrary rule.

The atmosphere at the camp on Saturday morning was especially calm. For some reason all the old people were there. Several of these elder statesmen of the Ojibway I had not seen before. They seemed to share a satisfied air of quiet understanding between themselves. There were several comments about how Mrs Abraham looked healthier than she had looked in years. In her bright patterned garments of plaid and paisley she cut a striking figure. A number of her fifteen children were among the mainstays of our action during a week that was for many of us one of the most intensely memorable experiences of our lives. It was a good moment for the elders to have been there in such numbers. The police officer of the CNR, with whom we had become reasonably friendly, walked into the camp with a thick file under his arm. In the file were Xerox copies of an injunction that had been granted earlier that morning to the CNR by Judge Joseph O'Driscoll of the Supreme Court of Ontario. The defendants were listed as Sidney Abraham, Bernard Abraham, Jocelyn Bouchard, Judy Desmoulin, Allan Towegishig, Veronica Waboose, Frank Nabigon, Rick Desmoulin, Ronald Towegishig, Tony Hall, and All Members of the Long Lake 58 Reserve Band and the Council Thereof. The document accused us of 'trespassing' upon 'property owned by or entrusted to the Plaintiff,' including the tracks, the right of way, and the 'Wye lands situate in and about Long Lake 58 Reserve.' The Wye lands cover the rail yard between the two major lines on the reserve, one running to Thunder Bay and the other to Winnipeg. Between these lines runs a circular connecting line where trains can turn around. Judge O'Driscoll demanded that the camp be entirely removed from the Wye lands.

A turning-point had been reached. The CNR man made a short announcement of his intention to serve individuals with a copy of the injunction. I moved quickly to the microphone to respond to his remarks. I suggested that only those individuals who felt entirely comfortable communicating in English should accept the injunction; those individuals who were more fluent in Ojibway should not accept the document. Rather, they should wait until translation services were provided to explain the court ruling in the Ojibway tongue. The suggestion, I thought, was a fair one. Throughout their lives the elders had been subjected to the imposition from afar of a bewildering array of rules and regulations they were expected to follow. Often these rules were enforced arbitrarily, even heavy-handedly, without sufficient explanation. What was the basis of the authority to which they were always expected to submit? Why was it that their own language, culture, and beliefs were never considered a legitimate factor to be taken into account in determining how their homeland would be used?

The chief and council, who along with myself had been named individually in the injunction, retired into the school bus parked at the camp. Already the bus had proved useful when groups of individuals at the camp wanted to meet privately. The band's lawyer, Marty Minuke, who had recently arrived from Winnipeg, gave us his view of the injunction's meaning. We asked one another about the ethics of what we should tell the elders. We reasoned that as long as the elders remained uncertain about the meaning of the injunction, it could not be legally enforced on them. It was only logical that the explanation of the injunction should be provided in Ojibway by those with the responsibility to enforce the court order. The decision was formalized with a show of hands. Although Marty Minuke was dubious, we decided to make a stand on the language issue. The group also passed a band council resolution asking Mitch Phillips to go to his superiors at the DIA to seek funding to meet the band's legal expenses. That seemed an appropriate role for the Indian agent; since the council was specifically mentioned in the injunction, and since band councils in Canadian law are technically administrative extensions of the federal government, the injunction was directed as much at the Crown as it was at us personally.

The court order changed the picture dramatically for the police. Their hand was being forced. Apparently the Longlac town council had agreed to make the Sportsplex, the biggest building in town, available to the OPP. It was possible that the hockey arena would have to be transformed into an incarceration centre. A major police operation was quietly set in motion. There were various estimates going of the number of officers involved. No doubt there were also a number of contingency plans involving different scenarios about what would happen if the police were forced to break up the camp physically. My impression is that about 230 police officers were involved, a major contingent in a sparsely settled section of northern Ontario. The emotional temperature started to rise quickly. I tried to keep calm by going on a solitary walk along the quiet, empty track. After having spent the winter on the bald prairie at Lethbridge, the site of my new teaching post, I still found rejuvenating solace amid the thick forest lands of the pre-Cambrian shield. That is the geography I most associate with home.

When I got back to the camp, a remarkable spectacle was underway. Two Indian OPP officers were sitting at a table engaged in intense discussion with a council of elders. The younger officer, Constable Larry Indian from Kenora, was endeavouring to explain the complex legal phraseology of the injunction in the Ojibway language. The experience was not easy for him. The elders seemed to be calling him to account for being on the opposite side of the table. Beside Constable Indian was a distinguished-looking older man with grey hair and green eyes. He later told me he was Saulteaux, from Fort Alexander reserve in Manitoba. Inspector D.W. Rupert did not speak the Ojibway language. In the hours ahead I came to see this officer as an effective interpreter of the band's position to the chain of command controlling the OPP. He was in a difficult position, and to my way of thinking Inspector Rupert rose to the challenge. By his actions he persuaded me that it is possible to work as an effective advocate of aboriginal interests from within the police.

Although I missed most of the specifics of this Ojibway discussion, I sensed a most serious gravity in what was being said. Obviously, the matters at issue went far beyond the specifics of the injunction. A group of native people were getting near the heart of the dilemma of how to cope with the massive intrusion of the white man's power in their midst. Constable Indian wore the uniform of the Crown, but in this context he became part of a deeper community of shared Indian interest that he was forced to address. Many onlookers listened intensely. Most of the younger people still understand Ojibway to some extent, even if they do not often speak the language. One could almost feel the ideas crackling in the air after the meeting. What should be done? When I spoke with Mrs Abraham she was clearly distraught. 'Where is the CNR's evidence?' she asked. 'How come they don't have to show any evidence? How come we always have to show evidence but they don't?' Of course the query got near the heart of the matter. I took her hand and we walked over to Constable Indian, to whom she restated her question. There wasn't much he could say.

I rose early on the following morning. Uncle George Nabigon was already outside brewing coffee over a small fire. Lena, Sam, Riley and Bertha continued to sleep deeply in our crowded little tent. This was the seventh day of the blockade and we were still holding our ground. With every passing hour the political profile of our issues rose higher as the effect of the rail blockades reached out more broadly into the economy. Where and how would the break occur before the weight of the mounting political pressure?

Marty Minuke went with Bernie to the Sportsplex on the morning of 19 August. The two understood each other well. The Winnipeg lawyer had represented Bernie in earlier times when Bernie was dealing with the criminal justice system on a regular basis. Their collaboration took another turn when Bernie included Marty in his efforts to found a national aboriginal hockey team to play exhibition games across the country. The effort to realize this vision was Bernie's greatest passion, together with his personal crusade to combat alcoholism on the reserve. He believed that a team made up of the country's best native hockey-players would give young Indians a positive role model. This need corresponded to one of Bernie's most persistent complaints, namely, the failure of the education system to meet the needs of his people. 'The education our kids are getting at the town school is unbelievably watered down,' he'd say again and again. Bernie kept telling us that his friend was 'the best lawyer in Canada.' Marty's Jewishness was significant to Bernie. 'Marty's people have burned in the ovens,' he'd say. 'Marty's people are in a good position to understand what's being done to us, even if the genocide we face is being done in more roundabout ways.' At a community gathering later that morning, Marty told us about the meeting with the OPP. He began by speaking of the 'sea of blue uniforms' in the hockey arena. The police officers he'd spoken to began by acknowledging the peacefulness of our action and the absolute absence of property damage. In retrospect, I believe the discipline we'd shown in this regard became one of our strongest bargaining-points. If even one of the young people had committed a small act of destruction, the police might have moved on all of us with the justification that their intervention was a protective measure.

Marty proceeded to outline the terms of the ultimatum given us by the police. If we did not move our protest camp within several hours we would be arrested for violating the injunction. Over the course of the day we faced a further succession of ultimatums. We balanced consideration of the ultimatums with our awareness that the OPP were really committed to search for a way out of the impasse without the use of force. There would certainly be unpredictable political consequences if the province's police force was to be photographed taking into custody a whole Indian band, including elders and children, for trespassing on their own reserve. The imagery would hardly enhance the public perceptions of the police or of the chain of command above them. The spectacle would have represented an embarrassment especially for Ian Scott, the minister of native affairs who was also the elected official ultimately in charge of the OPP.

An amazing chemistry took hold of the committed souls at the camp during the hours that followed. The genie was out of the bottle. The people divided and regrouped into a fascinating variety of entities and interests. At one point the elders wanted to meet in private, along with Bernie, in the school bus. At other points the chief and council met in the bus. Informal family gatherings also developed. Roy Michano, the thoughtful chief of Pic-Heron Bay, seemed to take it as his special responsibility to include the young people in the decision-making and to stimulate discussion of the larger context of the present controversy. Throughout the affair Chief Michano provided guidance and support in a quiet but effective way. The concept of self-determination began to take on deeper meaning for me. Some of the elders, including Frances Abraham, stuck to their hard and fast positions. So too did Frankie and Councillor Judy Desmoulin, an energetic young leader who provided much of the administrative know-how for the band. The possibility of arrest was in a sense our strongest weapon. There was a strongly held opinion that we should force the government into bringing down the full weight of the law upon us. Another community of interest saw wisdom in a less confrontational end to the affair. Those inclined to this approach argued that we had made our point and that it was time to pull back a little in the expectation that others would find their own ways to continue the pressure. As the issues were clarified through this intense exchange of ideas, there seemed to be a growing possibility of finding a middle ground.

In the late afternoon Marty returned from the Sportsplex with what he described as a final offer. He told us that if we did not move the obstacles from the tracks the OPP would certainly arrive to arrest us within twenty minutes. A small but significant modification had taken place, however, in what was demanded from us. We could retain our camp on the Wye lands as long as we agreed to stay eighty feet back from the tracks. That was it! Who's trespassing? We had our answer. No one gave the order. No one had to. Without even realizing it we had come to a consensus that was based on all the talk that had gone on beforehand. There was a simultaneous move towards the track. Young men and old men picked up the ties and rails that they had placed on the main CNR line. Others moved a picnic table back from the track. Some were visibly disappointed at the outcome. The women in the Abraham camp seemed particularly let down. Said Diane, 'All our lives we have been put down by officials in uniforms. They always get their way and we always have to bow down before their power. It's hard not to see what happened here today as a continuation of the old story.'

Most of the adults went home to rest and wash up. But as evening approached the camp began to come alive again. Sam and Riley and their cousins were in particularly high spirits. They waved at the freight trains as they rolled once again through the reserve. From the west came car after car of lumber, stripped from lands in British Columbia where the aboriginal title question also remains unresolved. I wondered how the Indians were doing in their actions out there. I met Rayno Fisher and Tubby Door shortly before nightfall, and we walked slowly westward from the camp along the main line.

The more I looked at the injunction, the more satisfied I became with the outcome. Technically speaking, we had not fully complied with the injunction. The retention of our camp on the Wye lands was a tacit admission that we were not trespassing. The CNR was in legal difficulty and a process would have to be set in motion to deal with the unresolved issues of land title. The federal government would have to be involved both on the side of the Indians and on the side of the Crown corporation. What we had obtained, then, was probably more significant than a letter from Doug Lewis. A start had been made. For Rayno, there was definitely a sense of getting even. As we returned to the camp he pointed to a rock outcrop. 'When I was a boy we lived up there in a log cabin,' he said. Apparently our protest camp was on the site of a small village where CNR workers had once lived. When Rayno would play in the community he was often treated as a trespasser. But he knew better. As his elders told him, the CNR workers were actually living on reserve land, even if they treated it as their own property. They made good wages during a time when it was very rare for an Indian to get a job with the company.

During the week, this short stretch of track came to hold all sorts of rich associations for me. The revelations about the ghosts on the site of our camp suddenly gave the whole landscape a deeper meaning. In earlier years, when I began visiting 58 with Lena, I would often encourage the people I met to tell me about the area's history. Only rarely did I receive more than puzzled looks. During recent days, however, stories about the old days began to pour forth from the people. It seemed almost as if the community was in the process of reclaiming its own history, as if it was staking a claim on the future by reorienting itself to a secure sense of where it had come from. Rayno chuckled to himself: 'It looks like we got the old CNR just in time.' He explained the comment by referring to what Lee told him earlier in the week. The wheels apparently were already in motion to sell the Crown corporation to the private sector, probably to the Japanese. Now here was a powerful symbol of Brian Mulroney's Canada: Privatize and sell out. Indian lands for sale at dirt cheap prices. Oka golfers and transnational corporations have the right of way.

In the following weeks I was able to reflect on what had happened with Lena's brother Frankie. He never did return to his job at the Weldwood plywood mill in Longlac. From his role in representing Long Lake 58's position to the outside world through the media, Frankie had gained a new sense of his own potential. 'I found out I can do that kind of work,' he said. Sometimes, however, Frankie experienced darker moments. He wondered if our action really had accomplished anything: 'What if you are wrong, Tony? What if in the long run there really isn't a place in this country for us Ojibways to be who we are?

In September the community chartered a bus to make the pilgrimage to Oka. Lena's sister Claire spoke of the trip as similar to earlier expeditions she had witnessed when groups went from 58 to visit Catholic shrines. Everyone who told me about the expedition mentioned the gregarious good humour of uncle George Nabigon. A victim of severe diabetes, he died shortly after returning to Leng Lake 58. Somehow the family drew consolation from the fact that George had made it to the Indian holy place before he was called to meet his creator.

NOTES

An edited earlier version of this paper has been published in A.-M. Mawhiney, ed., *Rebirth: Political, Economic and Social Development in first Nations* (Toronto: Dundurn Press 1993).

1 See Tony Hall, 'Indian Summer, Canadian Winter' (1991), 4 *Report on the Americas*, 34-8; Geoffrey York and Laureen Pindera, *People of the Pines: The Warriors and the Legacy of Oka* (Toronto: Little Brown 1991). On the background of the land dispute at Oka see, J.R. Miller, 'The Oka Controversy and the Federal Land-Claims Process' in *Aboriginal Land Claims in Canada: A Regional Perspective*, ed. Ken Coates (Toronto: Copp Clark 1992), 215–41.
2 Paul Tennant, *Aboriginal People and Politics: The Indian Land Question in British Columbia, 1849–1989* (Vancouver: University of British Columbia Press 1990).
3 Cy Gonick, 'Save the Oldman River' *Canadian Dimension* (December 1991).
4 See Tony Hall, 'The Politics of Aboriginality: Political Fault Lines in Indian Country' *Canadian Dimension* (January-February 1993).
5 Canada, *Atlas of Indian Reserves and Settlements, Canada, 1971* (Ottawa: Indian and Inuit Affairs Program, Reserves and Trust Group, reprinted 1978), reserve index to map sheet 3C.
6 Ibid.
7 Bruce Hodgins and Jamie Benidickson, *The Temagami Experience: Recreation, Resources, and Aboriginal Rights in the Northern Ontario Wilderness* (Toronto: University of Toronto Press 1989).
8 John Goddard, *Last Stand of the Lubicon Cree* (Vancouver: Douglas and McIntyre 1991).
9 The passage comes from a document entitled 'The Criminal Actions of the Governments of Ontario and Canada Against the First Nations Citizens of Long Lake Indian Settlement 58.' The document is part of the evidence presented by the CNR in its application for an injunction against Long Lake 58 Reserve Band on 17 August 1992: Supreme Court of Ontario, file no. 53538/90.
10 Thomas Berger, *Fragile Freedoms: Human Rights and Dissent in Canada* (Toronto: Clarke, Irwin 1982), 219-57.
11 Canada, *In All Fairness: A Native Claims Policy* (Ottawa: Minister of Supply and Services 1981).
12 Canada, *Outstanding Business: A Native Claims Policy* (Ottawa: Minister of Supply and Services 1982).
13 The reasons for the logjam in the settlement of land claims was the subject of a task force chaired by Murray Coolican: Canada, *Living Treaties: Lasting Agreements: Report of the Task Force to Review Comprehensive Claims Policy* (Ottawa: Department of Indian Affairs and Northern Development 1985).
14 Hall, 'Self-Government or Self-Delusion? Brian Mulroney and Aboriginal Rights' (1986), 6:1 *Canadian Journal of Native Studies*, 77-89.

15 John S. Long, 'No Basis for Argument: The Signing of Treaty Nine in
    Northern Ontario, 1905–1906' (1989), 5:2 *Native Studies Review*, 19–54.
16 See below at notes 26–7.
17 *Guerin v. The Queen*, [1985] 1 CNLR 120–62; *Simon v. R.*, [1986] 1 CNLR
    153–79; '*R. v. Sparrow*, [1990] 3 CNLR, 160–88.
18 Tony Hall, 'Where Justice Lies: Aboriginal Rights and Wrongs in
    Temagami,' in *Temagami: A Debate on Wilderness* ed. Matt Bray and Asheley
    Thompson (Toronto: Dundurn 1990), 223–53.
19 *Attorney-General of Ontario v. Bear Island Foundation*, [1985] 1 CNLR, 1–119;
    Bear Island Foundation v. Ontario, [1990] 4 CNLR, 3–7.
20 Hall, 'supra note 18, 237.
21 Ibid., 236.
22 Tony Hall, 'The St Catherine's Milling and Lumber Company Versus the
    Queen: Indian Land Rights as a Factor in Federal-Provincial Relations in
    Nineteenth-Century Canada,' in *Aboriginal Resource Use in Canada*, ed. Kerry
    Abel and Jean Friesen (Winnipeg: University of Manitoba Press 1991),
    267–86.
23 *St Catherine's Milling and Lumber Co. v. The Queen* (1888), 14 App. Cas. 46
    (PC).
24 The Royal Proclamation of 1763 is published in its entirety in *As Long as the
    Sun Shines and the Water Flows: A Reader in Canadian Native Studies*, ed. Ian
    A.L. Getty and Antoine Lussier (Vancouver: University of British Columbia
    Press 1983), 29–37.
25 The words were used by Lord Denning, master of the rolls, in *R. v. Secretary
    of State for Foreign and Commonwealth Affairs, ex parte: Indian Association of
    Alberta, and others*, [1982] QB 892.
26 On the significance of the royal proclamation as part of Canada's constitu-
    tion, see Bruce Clark, *Native Liberty, Crown Sovereignty: The Existing Aboriginal
    Right of Self-Government in Canada* (Montreal: McGill-Queen's University
    Press 1990); Brian Slattery, 'The Hidden Constitution: Aboriginal Rights in
    Canada,' in *The Quest for Justice: Aboriginal Peoples and Aboriginal Rights*, ed.
    Menno Boldt and J. Anthony Long ed. (Toronto: University of Toronto
    Press 1985), 114–38; Slattery, 'Land Rights of Indigenous People as Affected
    by the Crown's Acquisition of Their Rights,' Ph.D. thesis Oxford University
    1979). On the history surrounding the making of the Proclamation see
    C.W. Alvord, *The Mississippi Valley in British Politics*, vol. 1 (Cleveland: Clark
    1917).
27 On the forging of the alliance system, see Robert S. Allen, *His Majesty's
    Indian Allies: British Indian Policy and the Defence of Canada, 1774–1815*
    (Toronto: Dundurn 1992); Dorothy V. Jones, *License for Empire: Colonialism*

by Treaty in Early America (Chicago: University of Chicago Press 1982). On treaties generally, see Hall, 'Indian Treaties,' in *The Canadian Encyclopedia*, 2d ed. (Edmonton: Hurtig 1988). On prairie treaties, see Alexander Morris, *The Treaties of Canada with the Indians of Manitoba and the North-West Territories* Saskatoon: Fifth House 1991); *The Spirit of the Alberta Indian Treaties*, ed. Richard Price (Edmonton: Pica Pica 1987); Jean Friesen, 'Magnificent Gifts: The Treaties of Canada with the Indians of the Northwest, 1869–76' (1986), 5 *Transactions of the Royal Society of Canada*, 1:41-57. On treaties 8 and 1,1 see René Fumoleau, *As Long as This Land Shall Last* (Toronto: McClelland and Stewart 1975). On Ontario treaties before Confederation, see Robert J. Surtees, 'Indian Land Cessions in Ontario, 1763–1862: The Evolution of a System,' Ph.D. thesis, Carleton University (1982); Ian Johnson, 'The Early Mississauga Treaty Process, 1781–1819. An Historical Perspective,' Ph.D. thesis, University of Toronto (1986). For an aboriginal view of Treaty 7, see Chief John Snow, *These Mountains are our Sacred Places* (Toronto: Samuel Stevens 1977), 15–48. For a study of the relationship of Indian treaties to international law, see Miguel Alfonso Martinez, *First Progress Report of the Study on Treaties, Agreements and Other Constructive Arrangements between States and Indigenous Populations* (New York: United Nations Commission on Human Rights, 25 August 1992), G.E. 92-13653/48298 (E).

28 Peter Hogg, *Meech Lake Constitutional Accord Annotated* (Toronto: Carswell 1988). For various views on the accord, critical and supportive, see Thomas Courchene, *Meech Lake and Federalism: Accord or Discord?* (North York: York 1987); *Competing Constitutional Visions: The Meech Lake Accord*, ed. Katherine Swinton (Toronto: Carswell 1988); Bryan Schwartz, *Fathoming Meech Lake* (Winnipeg: Legal Research Institute of the University of Manitoba 1987); *The Meech Lake Primer: Conflicting Views of the 1987 Constitutional Accord*, ed. Michael D. Behiels (Ottawa: University Press 1989). For a narrative describing politicians' role in the Meech Lake fiasco, see Andrew Cohen, *A Deal Undone: The Making and Breaking of the Meech Lake Accord* (Vancouver: Douglas and McIntyre 1990).

29 Hall, 'What Are We? Chopped Liver? Aboriginal Affairs in the Constitutional Politics of Canada in the 1980s,' in *Meech Lake Primer*, supra note 28, 423-56. See also Alan C. Cairns, 'Citizens (Outsiders) and Governments (Insiders) in Constitution Making: The Case of Meech Lake,' *Canadian Public Policy*, special supplement (September, 1988), S121–S145.

30 Robin Philpot, *Oka: dernier alibi du Canada anglais* (Montreal: VLB 1991); Tony Hall, 'Aboriginal Issues and the New Political Map of Canada,' in *'English Canada' Speaks Out*, ed. J.L. Granatstein and Kenneth McNaught (Toronto: Doubleday Canada, 1991), 137–40.

31 On the new thinking associated with the quincentenary of Columbus's arrival in the Americas, see Ronald Wright, *Stolen Continents: The 'New World' through Indian Eyes since 1492* (New York: Viking 1992); and Thomas R. Berger, *A Long and Terrible Shadow: White Values, Native Rights in the Americas, 1492–1992* (Vancouver: Douglas and McIntyre 1991).

Part Three

GENDER

AND THE LAW

12 'If a Man's Wife Does Not Obey Him, What Can He Do?' Marital Breakdown and Wife Abuse in Late Nineteenth-Century and Early Twentieth-Century Ontario

ANNALEE E. GÖLZ

Many contemporary socialist feminists have located the family-household system as one of the primary sites of women's oppression under capitalism.[1] In the historical debates revolving around both the nature of the pre-industrial household and the impact of industrial capitalism on the working-class family, however, a more sympathetic and, at times, rather sentimentalized assessment has tended to predominate. In both cases Canadian historians have emphasized that the family-household system formed a crucial social and economic unit of subsistence, interdependence, and survival. Despite the persistent gendered division of labour in the household, these studies have largely focused on how each family member contributed vitally to the rural or urban family economy, whether through productive labour on the family farm, waged labour in the industrializing urban centres, or informal waged and unpaid reproductive labour in the household.[2]

The historical and theoretical insights of these recent Canadian studies cannot be discounted. They remain crucial to our fundamental understanding of the relationship between the family and the economy in nineteenth-century and early twentieth-century Ontario. At the same time, the family-household, notwithstanding its cultural, structural, and class differentiations over time and region, was not exclusively characterized by companionate marriage and the egalitarian economic cooperation that was necessary for rural or urban survival. In Ontario, familial and especially marital relations can also be examined both in terms of the shifting legal character of the husband and father's proprietary rights, and in terms of his increasingly regulated economic liabilities and responsibilities in relation to his wife and children.

324 Annalee E. Gölz

A general examination of these legally defined features of marital relations will provide the contextual framework for an exploration of marital violence. In my preliminary discussion of some of the more salient aspects of wife abuse, one of the harshest manifestations of a husband's real or perceived proprietary rights, I will attempt to specify the circumscribed legal options available to battered wives, and how married women struggled to articulate and assert their ambiguously defined right not to be abused or beaten by their husbands. At the same time I will endeavour to provide an alternative perspective into the qualitative nature of marital relations by focusing not only on the hierarchical relations of domination and subordination within the family unit, but also on some of the potential sources of tensions and antagonisms between husbands and wives. For, as Terry Chapman has pointed out, perhaps one of the most pressing tasks of Canadian historians should be to re-evaluate 'the myth of marital bliss which has dominated studies into the history of the family.'[3]

In the predominantly rural economy of Ontario, particularly in the first half of the nineteenth century, one of the major institutional sources for the protection of a husband's proprietary rights was rooted in English common law as well as subsequent legislation, in which these laws were adapted to local circumstances.[4] Both common and statute law, perceived as necessary to safeguard both social stability and public morality, vested in the state the power to define the framework of marital relations. While the important role of religious doctrine and social custom in upholding the sanctity of marriage and in regulating sexual behaviour cannot be underestimated,[5] common law did tend to define virtually every aspect of the matrimonial state. Thus, at least until the mid-nineteenth century, when the legal authority of the husband and father underwent a process of gradual, albeit limited, legislative modification, both legislators and the judiciary were concerned with the protection and reproduction of the traditional patriarchal family unit as one of the fundamental institutions of the social order. For instance, in 1844 one legal commentator, writing in the *Upper Canada Jurist*, stressed the potentially disastrous effects that would result from tampering with the inheritance and property laws that both structured and underpinned relations within the patriarchal family: 'Domestic duties are invaded, and parental authority disregarded. Children feel themselves no longer dependent, but are ready to indulge in any display of contempt of parental authority, and the fearful consequences that must ensue may ultimately destroy all rule and governance in the state.'[6]

Particularly within the earlier nineteenth-century family unit, the legally sanctioned property rights of the male head over his wife and children were exemplified in various ways. But the authority of the husband and father and the relations of domination and subordination within the family were rooted in the economic and social relations of the rural household economy. According to Marjorie Griffin Cohen, the power vested in the male head through his control over property and over the labour of his wife and children is 'crucial to understanding productive relations within the family economy' or what she terms 'patriarchal productive relations.' Thus, while the pre-industrial household economy relied on the pooling of unpaid family labour to enhance productivity, Cohen argues that 'the family in nineteenth-century Ontario was not an egalitarian unit and neither custom nor law considered that the family *per se* owned the means of production ... In the family economy, ownership of the means of production both in law and in practice was in the hands of the male head of the household.'[7]

Although the legal foundation and the social implications of a husband and father's control over property variously defined the status of female family members, a married woman clearly remained the most disadvantaged under the law. Her disabilities largely stemmed from the common law interpretation of marriage, which created a 'unity of legal personality.' In 1856 one legal commentator, writing in the *Upper Canada Law Journal*, explicitly described the absorption, or indeed the extinction, of a wife's legal identity as follows: 'The *natural* rights of man and woman are, it must be admitted, equal; entering the married state, the woman surrenders most of them; in the possession of civil rights before, they merge in her husband; in the eye of the law she may be said to cease to exist. Equal before marriage, she becomes legally an inferior. The man surrenders no legal rights – the woman loses nearly all.'[8]

While the subordinate status conferred on a woman through marriage carried with it various legal and socioeconomic consequences, in its simplest terms it entailed that her person, her children, her earnings, and most of the property she acquired both prior and after marriage were under the guardianship and control of her husband. The underlying assumption concerning the common law disabilities of a married woman largely rested on the notion that, like a child, she was both the responsibility of and under the protection of her husband. Moreover, her dependent status as a chattel of her husband was ultimately regarded as a privileged one and signified a societal concession both to her frailty and to her economic vulnerability.[9]

The sporadic legislative uncoupling of the 'unity of legal personality' and the modification of the absolute authority of a husband and father constituted a gradual process, which began in the mid-nineteenth century. In Ontario this process extended the rights of married women in particular areas such as child custody and guardianship, and accorded them some degree of control over their own property and earnings.[10] But as Constance Backhouse has argued, this was by no means an unambiguous process. For instance, as was the case with many nineteenth-century legal reforms pertaining to married women, the child custody legislation encoded a stipulation relating to adultery. In effect, an act of adultery, the gravest marital offence that could be committed by a married woman, would automatically render her morally 'unfit' and 'undeserving' of the legal custody and guardianship of her children.[11] Since, according to one late nineteenth-century Canadian legal scholar, the adultery of a wife carried more serious social consequences than that of a husband, it necessarily had to be 'punished' accordingly: 'Looking at it from a social, rather than from a moral standpoint, it is true that the wife's infidelity is followed by results of a graver character than those which follow the infidelity of the husband, and that it is therefore in the interest of society that the one should be punished more promptly and more severely than the other.'[12]

The legislative inclusion of the pervasive adultery clause carried with it even wider ramifications, which emerged from the extremely limited availability of divorce to Ontario women during this period.[13] While most Canadian legislators considered the costly and arduous parliamentary procedure as a necessary safeguard designed to uphold both the sanctity of marriage and the stability of the family, in cases of marital breakdown that involved desertion or cruelty there were at least two consequences for married women. First, as Jane Ursel has noted, it meant that 'a husband in effect maintained a lifetime ownership of his wife's sexuality.'[14] Second, the inclusion of the adultery clause in both common law and subsequent protective legislation relating to the maintenance of wives during marital separation meant that a 'guilty' wife, regardless of her circumstances, would forfeit any access to the economic resources of her negligent or abusive husband. One judge, for example, explicitly pointed out in 1869 that there were no legal grounds to justify a married woman's voluntary adultery: 'His compelling her to leave by his violence, or her leaving in consequence thereof, or his abandoning her without provision, alike fail to warrant or excuse her subsequent voluntary living in adultery.'[15]

While their sexual property interests continued to be protected by common law, husbands were not absolved of all obligations and liabilities. Perhaps their most entrenched legal responsibility was what one legal commentator described as their 'natural duty' to provide for the support and maintenance of their wives and children.[16] This liability sought to extend economic protection to wives in two fundamental ways.

First, one of the legally defined rights and benefits of marriage was a wife's entitlement to pledge her husband's credit for 'necessaries suitable to his station and circumstances.'[17] One commentator, writing in the *Upper Canada Law Journal* in 1856, specified the circumstances in which a wife could or could not claim credit:

> Where a husband wrongfully turns away his wife ... [or] personally ill-treat[s] his wife, and [is] guilty of cruelty towards her, so that from reasonable apprehension of further personal violence, she is obliged to quit his roof, he is responsible for necessaries ... Where a wife is guilty of adultery, and either elopes from her husband or is expelled from his roof on that account, or even when, being compelled by his cruelty to leave him, she is afterwards guilty of this offence ... he is not liable even for the bare necessaries of life supplied to her after her adultery and during their separation.[18]

This common law provision accounted for the advertisements concerning runaway wives frequently published in nineteenth-century Ontario newspapers in which a husband not only announced the fact of his wife's desertion, but explicitly sought to warn tradespeople or shopkeepers not to trust her or extend her any credit in his name. In this way he hoped to absolve himself of any economic liabilities for his wife's maintenance or for any debts she might contract during marital separation. Although the announcements provided few details regarding the circumstances surrounding a wife's desertion, a husband generally specified that it had been unprovoked by his behaviour[19] or that she had run off with another man.[20] In one 1870 case, however, a Mr Mills, on the day preceding his appearance before the Ottawa Police Court on charges of beating (or, as the Ottawa *Citizen* put it, 'reconstructing' his wife with 'a hard wood log') none the less published a warning: 'Caution. Martha Mills, my wife, having left my house without cause, the public are cautioned against giving her credit in my name.'[21]

Conversely, those wives whose husbands 'wilfully and without lawful excuse' refused to support them or were victims of spousal cruelty could technically seek redress in the civil courts and claim alimony for their maintenance during marital separation. But, as will be discussed in greater detail below, given the relatively high costs involved in civil litigation and the circumscribed judicial definitions of what constituted legal cruelty, this common law remedy remained limited, particularly for poor and working-class women. Moreover, in instances when a husband's non-support was a consequence both of his desertion and his disappearance, which seemingly was not uncommon in this highly transient era, these legal provisions were rendered largely ineffective.

Perhaps one of the most significant developments in the latter part of the nineteenth century was that, within the context of an industrializing economy, a husband's common law liabilities underwent a process of successive statutory reinforcement and became subject to more direct legal regulation. Under the provisions of Canada's 1869 criminal legislation, for example, a husband's wilful refusal to provide his wife and children with 'necessary food, clothing, and lodging' without 'lawful excuse' was explicitly defined as a criminal offence which, if it caused bodily harm or life endangerment, carried with it a maximum penalty of up to three years' imprisonment. (In 1892, the clause was slightly amended to include death, life endangerment, and permanent injury to health.)[22] Moreover, an 1869 act respecting vagrants included a stipulation that 'all persons who, being able to work and thereby or by other means to maintain themselves and families, wilfully refuse or neglect to do so' were subject to a fine of up to fifty dollars or to a prison term of up to two months. In 1874 the maximum term of imprisonment was extended to six months.[23]

While these legal provisions reflected an attempt to deter husbands from reneging on their marital and familial obligations, treating a husband's non-support as a criminal offence had various limitations, particularly for those working-class wives with children who did seek some form of redress in the courts in the 1870s and 1880s. For example, in one 1887 case Emiline L. charged her husband, a labourer from the village of Iroquois, with refusing and neglecting to support her. At the trial she not only intimated that her husband had squandered the family resources on gambling and alcohol, but she also testified that he had deserted her to live with another woman 'that he liked better than me,' leaving her and the children without household provisions. Despite her husband's adamant denials and his attempts to argue for 'just cause' by claiming that she had ordered him out of the house, he was found guilty. Under the provisions of the Criminal Code, however, his sentence of three months' hard labour in the common jail would have offered little hope of alleviating the evident economic distress of his abandoned wife and children.[24] Similarly, in 1877, when Andrew S. was convicted of both deserting and refusing to support his wife, the ten-dollar fine imposed by the Galt magistrate offered few guarantees that he would make any further economic contributions towards the survival of his wife and family.[25]

Given the economic dependence particularly of poor and working-class women on a male breadwinner and their often limited capacity to support themselves and their children, the withdrawal of economic support by husbands tended to show how economic vulnerability could quickly translate into material hardship or extreme deprivation. Consequently, those neglected and deserted wives who appeared in the courts often stressed how, in the absence of a male breadwinner's wage, they and their children had attempted to patch together a livelihood or had struggled to stave off destitution. While some married women sought out alternative sources of income, others were obliged to rely on the assistance of relatives, the community, or local relief for basic necessities. For instance, in 1875 Hannah R. of St Catharines testified that she and her infant had sought refuge at the house of a friend, Martin M., because her husband refused to support her despite her repeated applications to the court. Although her friend stated that he had agreed to shelter them during the winter, he had not expected to assume all the expenses for their upkeep. But he did emphasize that without his assistance 'she would have been exposed to extreme privation.'[26]

In some instances, however, a deserted married woman's perceived inability or refusal to live up to those characteristics associated with a 'dutiful wife' could elicit a more ambiguous response, particularly from neighbours and the community. For example, in 1888 Edward B., a sailor and labourer, made it clear to the Ontario County Court judge that his wife's persistent neglect of her domestic duties had compelled him to leave her after four years of marriage: 'About a year and six months ago I left my wife ... and said I would not live with her any longer. She was so dirty and neglectful ... The house was no cleaner than a pig pen & the children was very seldom washed and cleaned.'[27]

Neighbours were called as witnesses, and all corroborated Mr B.'s testimony: she and the children were living in a state of 'dirt and filth.' At the same time they stressed that the family was 'in a very destitute state,' without 'anything to eat and no wood to keep her & the children from freezing.' Although one neighbour stated that she felt that Mrs B. 'might do better with the means at her disposal,' and another had 'advised her to wash herself and [the] children and look a little decent,' the neighbours did not seem hesitant to assist her. While some offered food and fuel, a Mr H. managed to acquire two dollars in cash and a three-dollar food voucher from an extremely reluctant council of East Whitby. As Mrs B. herself pointed out, 'sometimes we could not [have] lived if it had not been for the neighbours.'

What is perhaps most striking about this particular case is that all the corroborating testimony focused almost exclusively on Mrs B's character rather than on her husband's neglect and desertion. She was described by the court recorder as a 'helpless, indolent creature,' and the underlying tension between her alleged laziness and her extreme destitution surfaced most explicitly when the question of the welfare of the children arose. Although Mr B. had on several occasions agreed to take custody of the children, his wife, regardless of how untenable her situation was, had refused to allow him access. The neighbours, however, unequivocally supported his parental claim by emphasizing that in their view she was not 'fit to care and bring up there [sic] children.' Unfortunately, the outcome is somewhat uncertain. While Mr B. claimed that his wife could support herself and insisted that she had received large sums of money from various sources, he did agree 'to provide for her to a certain degree.'

Often the harshest consequences of a husband's non-support or desertion were reserved for those wives whose spouses simply disappeared without a trace and who could no longer rely on the informal and usually temporary assistance of members of the community. In 1898, for example, twenty-two-year-old Mary Z. of the Township of Mornington explained to the Stratford police magistrate that her husband, a labourer, had deserted her, and that for six months his whereabouts had been unknown to her. She further testified that since she had no adequate means to maintain herself and her family, she had been obliged to take up temporary residence in the Stratford House of Refuge, had placed two of her young children in homes, and now felt that it was 'best and right' to surrender her two other infants to the Children's Aid Society.[28]

The enactment of the Ontario Deserted Wives' Maintenance Act in 1888[29] perhaps best represented an attempt to overcome some of the limitations associated with treating a husband's non-support as a criminal offence, particularly when it entailed a possible term of imprisonment or even a monetary fine. It also tended to reflect a more overt commitment on the part of the state to ensure that, whenever possible in instances of temporary or permanent marital separation, the costs of maintaining wives and children would remain the primary economic responsibility of the husband and would not become a social burden on the community. More specifically, as the political debates over the act suggest, the proposed legislation sought to grant poor and working-class wives the same opportunity to petition for maintenance costs in the lower courts that was enjoyed by middle-class wives seeking alimony payments in the civil courts. For instance, one legislator pointed out that the existing legal mechanisms were 'practically a denial of justice to the poor.'[30] Oliver Mowat explicitly outlined the purposes of the act: 'At present a husband who deserts his wife and family or neglects to support them is liable to fine and imprisonment, but this remedy is a very unsatisfactory one for the family. The bill proposes that the same tribunal, namely a magistrate or two justices of the peace, shall have power to order payment of an allowance in such a case. The Superior Courts now have this power, but the procedure is too expensive for many women.'[31]

Under this legislation a wife deserted by her husband could summon him before a police magistrate or two justices of the peace and obtain a court order for the payment of a weekly sum, not exceeding five dollars, towards her support and that of her children.[32] In 1897, the definition of a deserted wife was extended to include a wife voluntarily living apart from her husband because of his refusal or neglect to provide for her maintenance.[33] Not surprisingly, the main restrictive clause stipulated that if it was established that the female plaintiff had committed adultery (unless condoned) before or after the order for payments had been made, her right to maintenance would be disallowed or rescinded.[34]

The enactment of the legislation may have partially accounted for the growing number of neglected and deserted wives who sought redress in the courts between 1888 and 1920. This trend accelerated in 1913, when the definition of criminal non-support was substantially broadened through the exclusion of previous references to death, life endangerment, and permanent injury to health.[35] While non-support and desertion cases continued to be prosecuted under the Criminal Code and the Vagrancy Act in these decades, an average of 25 per cent of the neglected and deserted wives in my post-1888 survey were granted orders for weekly maintenance.[36] However, as a number of cases suggest, a court order for a weekly allowance was not always effective in forcing a recalcitrant husband to assume his financial responsibilities.

In 1897, for example, Florence P. of Toronto, formerly of the village of Merriton, laid a complaint against her husband, a carpenter, for non-support and desertion. Under the provisions of the act an 'amicable settlement' was reached whereby William P. agreed to take custody of two children and to pay his wife a weekly sum of three dollars cash to cover her maintenance and that of the other two children. Although the court recorder noted that the 'defendant positively refused to put his proposition in writing,' Mr P. 'solemnly promised' to carry out the settlement and 'husband and wife shook hands upon it.' Several weeks later Mrs P. returned to court and laid a second complaint for non-payment. In the absence of a source of income, she testified, she had had no choice but to move to Toronto, to rely on her mother's financial care, and to place her children in various Toronto shelters. After two days of testimony and extensive cross-examination, her husband was acquitted of the second charge. Although the court record remains unclear as to whether or not he remained liable for the original three-dollar weekly sum, this case points to some of the potential deficiencies of the act.[37]

The other significant aspect of this case was that much of the testimony hinted at some of the internal stresses experienced by at least some working-class families. The growing marital tensions between the increasingly estranged couple were largely precipitated by Mr P.'s successive periods of unemployment and compounded by the family's mounting debts. According to Mrs P., it was precisely during these periods of financial uncertainty that her husband's tyrannical behaviour intensified, making family life unbearable. He tightened his control over the family's sparse finances, and on one occasion, when she took ten dollars from his pocket in order to purchase supplies for her coming 'confinement,' he became angry and threatened her so severely that she felt compelled to flee to the neighbours.

The court testimony also disclosed that during these times of material uncertainty Mr. P. adamantly refused any form of assistance and prohibited any interference from the neighbours. For example, after discovering that one of the neighbours had brought some provisions to aid the family during a particularly difficult period, he apparently threw the foodstuffs out of the house and made it clear to her that 'I won't have people coming into my house bringing food for my children and that woman [his wife] disgracing my people like this.' Whether unable or unwilling to provide the 'necessaries' for his family, Mr P.'s behaviour implicitly hinted at the interrelation between his precarious status as the breadwinner and a crisis of masculine authority in the household. And both were seemingly linked to his inability to fulfil his expected role of maintaining the social respectability of the family.

In some cases, similar strains in the working-class family led to extreme acts of marital violence. Although by no means restricted to the working class nor confined to the late nineteenth or early twentieth century, wife abuse reflected one of the harshest manifestations of the unequal economic and power relations in the family. The economic vulnerability of married women, particularly those with children, coupled with the absence of effective mechanisms for legal redress, tended to restrict options when it came to obtaining some form of relief from marital cruelty. Within this unfavourable legal and socioeconomic context wives struggled to negotiate and defend their ambiguously defined right not to be beaten or abused by their husbands.

Although common law did offer married women (and children) some safeguards against the 'excessive cruelty' of their husbands, one of its underlying assumptions was that wives did not require the explicit protection of the law because they were under the guardianship of their husbands.[38] At the same time, the legally sanctioned rights of the male head of the household did extend to his use of some degree of physical force within the family. As legally responsible for the (mis)behaviour of his dependents, he was lawfully entitled to chastise his wife and children within certain limits. In 1883, for example, one Ontario judge stressed that some degree of violence was to be not only expected but tolerated within the private institution of marriage: 'At common law a man has the right to resort to the moderate correction of his wife for her misbehaviour, but not that I am aware to turn her out or lock her out of doors. She is entitled to the protection of his domicile, even if he takes her in and administers proper castigation for her faults. It is not, however, for magistrates or courts to step in and interfere with the rights of a husband in ruling his own household.'[39]

Despite the apparent reluctance of the legal system to intervene in private marital affairs or to interfere with the 'legitimate' rights of husbands,[40] married women were provided with some formal legal and economic protection, particularly in cases of marital breakdown involving 'unnatural' or 'intolerable' cruelty. As in cases of non-support, however, these legal remedies tended to underline how the intersection of class and gender shaped recourse to the law and the courts. Married women, particularly those with economic means, had the option of launching a relatively costly civil suit for alimony on the grounds of cruelty. If the higher courts ruled in a wife's favour, matrimonial relief from an abusive husband was coupled with at least the possibility of extracting some maintenance costs during marital separation.

This is not to imply, however, that the legal remedies accorded those married women who launched civil actions for alimony were without their limitations. As several scholars have pointed out, the judgments (at least in the reported alimony cases) suggest that the judiciary demonstrated a persistent reluctance to subvert the authority of the husband, to undermine the patriarchal institution of marriage, or to sanction the disintegration of the family unit. This reluctance was exemplified in the civil courts' circumscribed interpretation of what constituted legal cruelty and in their scrutiny of any evidence that suggested condonation or provocation on the part of the wife.[41]

In Ontario the judiciary's definition of legal cruelty tended to involve excessive and persistent acts that would 'cause danger to life, limb, or health, bodily or mental, or to give rise to a reasonable apprehension of such danger.'[42] Consequently, the civil courts tended to discount isolated acts of violence as sufficient cause for marital separation or alimony. As one Ontario judge pointed out in 1873, 'the law ... lays upon the wife the necessity of bearing some indignities, and even some personal violence, before it will sanction her leaving her husband's roof.'[43] The judiciary also tended to emphasize a wife's duty to placate and if possible to attempt to reform her husband's violent behaviour before seeking relief in the courts. For instance, in 1860 one judge expressed his unequivocal agreement with an 1844 English precedent in which this spousal responsibility was defined as follows: 'It is the duty of a wife to conform to the tastes and habits of her husband; to sacrifice much of her comfort and convenience to his whims and caprices; to submit to his commands, and to endeavour, if she can, by prudent resistance and remonstrance to induce a change and alteration.'[44] The female plaintiff, often caught in an untenable circle of proof, had to provide evidence that repeated and sufficiently brutal acts had occurred, and that she had not previously 'condoned' or 'forgiven' her husband's violent behaviour. In other instances the judiciary tended to consider a wife's defiance of her husband's authority or any indication of verbal or physical 'provocation' as sufficient justification to 'excuse considerable severity in the husband,' and as adequate grounds to undermine a married woman's entitlement to matrimonial relief.[45]

By the end of the nineteenth century, under the amended Ontario Deserted Wives' Maintenance Act of 1897, working-class wives were given the option of petitioning the lower criminal courts for maintenance on the grounds of marital cruelty. As noted earlier, this amendment extended the definition of a deserted wife to include a married woman who voluntarily separated from her husband because of non-support. This broadened definition also included a married woman who was living apart from her husband as a result of 'repeated assaults or other acts of cruelty.'[46] The major significance of this latter amendment was that, in contrast to the penalties imposed in the criminal prosecution of wife abuse, it provided the first statutory mechanism whereby abusive working-class husbands became economically liable for the maintenance of their battered wives. As noted earlier, however, one of the main challenges for those wives who used this legislation to achieve temporary or permanent separation from their violent husbands was attempting to ensure that the husbands fulfilled the financial conditions as specified in the mainten-ance orders granted by the lower courts.

In most instances, however, acts of physical aggression by husbands did not lead to marital separation. Throughout the late nineteenth and early twentieth centuries, the majority of married women, particularly those from the poor and working classes, sought legal redress in the criminal courts by charging their husbands with offences ranging from threats and intimidation to various degrees of assault. While it is arguable that most incidents involving wife abuse remained undetected because of the ideo-logical, socioeconomic and legal factors that tended to inhibit wives from launching criminal actions against their husbands, those cases that did manage to reach the courts were generally heard and adjudicated locally at the magistrate's or Police Court level. In some instances, more serious cases were referred to the County Court level or, less frequently, were tried before a jury at the Court of General Sessions or at the Criminal Assizes. When husbands were convicted, sentences varied according to the nature of the charge and the severity of the crime. On the basis of my sample of 332 cases involving wife abuse that surfaced at the Police Court and County Court levels from 1869 to 1920, the most common sentences included a monetary fine (19 per cent), a term of imprisonment (21 per cent), and, most often, a suspended sentence with or without a recogni-zance and sureties binding a husband to keep the peace, usually for a term of between six months and two years (59 per cent).[47]

These patterns suggest that in the majority of cases the criminal courts were less likely to punish violent husbands and more inclined to attempt to mediate marital relations, particularly by regulating the husbands' behaviour. One of the underlying premises of binding a husband to keep the peace was the extraction of a promise, often reinforced by a bond and sureties, of better conduct towards his wife. For example, the out-come of one 1897 case involving Cornelius B., who was convicted of assaulting his wife, was typical. The judge ruled that if the accused would take his wife back and treat her properly, he would suspend the sentence.

When the prisoner agreed to the conditions by entering into his own recognizance to keep the peace for one year and to appear for sentence when called upon, he was allowed to go free.[48]

Particularly for poor and working-class wives with young children, this form of mediation could potentially modify a husband's violent behaviour without risking the economic difficulties that a possible term of imprisonment would entail. Given the wives' dependency on a male wage and their economic vulnerability outside the confines of the family unit, even the temporary absence of the male breadwinner through imprisonment could seriously threaten the often precarious working-class family economy. At the same time, however, while many wives specifically requested that the courts bind their husbands over to keep the peace, this tactic was often ineffective in preventing further assaults. For example, in 1871, Catharine B. of Galt, having laid a complaint against her husband for brutally assaulting her, explicitly told the magistrate that 'when he was bound over last year to keep the peace towards me, he has been worse since, [I] do I not want him bound over to keep the peace again, it is no use.'[49]

Economic considerations, not to mention the element of fear, may have also partially accounted for the failure of some wives to appear in court, either for their withdrawal of complaints or for their seeming reluctance to testify against their husbands. In one 1881 case, for example, Charles C. of Whitby was brought before the Ontario County Court by Constable Bryan for 'striking, choking, and otherwise abusing his wife.'[50] According to the constable, this was not the first time he had been summoned to investigate 'similar rows' at the same household. At the trial several neighbours testified that they had heard Mrs C.'s screams and her repeated appeals to her husband 'not to choke her anymore,' as well as Mr C.'s threats that he would 'dash her brains out and break her neck.' Finding the door to the residence locked, at least two neighbours, apparently reluctant to enter the premises, watched the assault through an open window until the constable arrived on the scene to arrest the defendant. At the subsequent trial, however, Mrs C. displayed a decided reluctance to testify against her husband. As her brief statement at the trial suggests, she seemed inclined to justify her husband's behaviour: 'My husband did not hurt me last night. I was afraid he would. He never struck me in his life. My husband is kind to me except when he gets whisky. My husband locked the door, I don't know for what cause. He had his hands around my neck but he did not squeeze any. He was the worse of liquor last night or he would not have done it.'

This is not to suggest that married women passively accepted being beaten by their husbands. In most cases, the very presence of wives in the courts signified an attempt to defend their right to physical safety. At the same time, given the ambiguities associated with that right and the limited effectiveness of the legal system, married women used various strategies to articulate and assert their sense of entitlement to legal protection.

While the issue of a wife's provocation surfaced most explicitly in civil actions for alimony, it also emerged in the testimony of married women who appeared in the criminal courts. When presenting their case or when responding to the counter-accusations of their husbands, wives frequently assured the judge that they had not, for example, been drunk at the time of the beating or that they had not either verbally or physically provoked their husbands' violence. Moreover, as the cross-examination of Paraska T. by the Sault Ste-Marie police magistrate in 1920 indicates, a wife's conduct, regardless of the severity of the beating by her husband, was never completely ruled out as the possible cause of his violent behaviour:

Q. What was the fight about with your husband?
A. We had a little quarrel amongst ourselves.
Q. About what?
A. I asked him to help me do some little work around the house.
Q. And what did he do?
A. And he refused.
Q. So you went at him with the broom stick to make him work?
A. No, I just asked him if he would do any work and he refused, so I said two or three words again, and then he beat me.[51]

By contrast, the 1898 case involving Ellen W. of the Township of Pickering, who charged her husband with aggravated assault, was considerably strengthened by a series of character references submitted by neighbours and members of the community. Emphasizing that Mrs W. was not only an 'honest, hardworking, and respectable woman,' but also a 'good and faithful wife and mother ... worthy of the confidence of her husband,' the community tended to stress those traits that the County Court judge would conceivably interpret as those of a 'deserving wife.'[52]

The testimonies of other battered wives, however, showed that legal recourse to the criminal courts was a last resort or even an act of desperation, especially after an extended period of repeated or habitual abuse. In 1887 Ann B. of Port Perry laid a complaint against her husband for aggravated assault after ten years of persistent abuse. According to her testimony and that of her children, her husband, especially when 'worse of liquor,' had 'struck and kicked her a great many times before,' and had often threatened 'to take her heart out and kick it around on the floor.'[53] While the last brutal incident had occurred after she accidentally broke a dish in the pantry, Mrs B. stated that her reluctance to sleep with her husband because of his 'bad disorder,' and her attempts to curtail his drinking habits were among the many factors that had provoked previous and repeated beatings. Moreover, Eliza M. of the Township of Brock also testified in 1881 that her husband '[had] on several occasions abused [her] severely.'[54] The most recent beating had occurred after her husband had falsely accused her of stealing a quarter from his pocket. Even after finding the money intact, he proceeded to bite her and beat her with an umbrella. Although the magistrate suggested that because of Mr M.'s persistent and violent behaviour it was necessary 'to commit him for safekeeping' to prevent him from permanently injuring his wife, Mr McCarty was evidently bound in $100 and ordered to keep the peace.

For those married women who used the legal system to achieve some degree of protection from their violent husbands, the verdicts handed down by courts offered few guarantees that the incidents of abuse would abate or cease. Consequently, many abused wives tenaciously and often repeatedly returned to plead their cases before the magistrate. In 1885, for instance, Catherine D. of Peterborough testified that despite her repeated petitions to the court, her husband had 'twice taken the pledge and broken it.'[55] Although her husband's friends had 'always asked [her] to forgive him,' Mrs D. stated that because of her husband's habitual cruelty and, after the last nightmarish incident, her growing fear for her life, she had been compelled to take refuge at her brother-in-law's house and to lay another complaint against her husband.

One of the more blatant examples of the ineffectiveness of the criminal courts in stemming the incidences of habitual abuse was the case of Thomas Hinchey, identified in the Ottawa press as the 'notorious' wife beater.[56] In 1869 a battered and bruised Mrs Hinchey appeared at the Ottawa police station with her two young children to complain of 'the brutal treatment she had just received from her drunken husband.'[57] According to the newspaper account, it soon became evident that this was by no means an isolated incident. Rather, 'she [had] hitherto been afraid to bring him up for the ill-usage of her, but now she [could] bear it no longer and [would] appear against him.' At the subsequent police court proceedings, however, Mrs Hinchey, 'no doubt under the influence of fear,' reluctantly testified against her husband. The case was adjourned for one week to provide him with the opportunity to alter his conduct.[58] But Hinchey's subsequent and periodic appearances in the Ottawa police court on charges of wife-beating[59] may have at least contributed to a police court reporter's conclusion that 'every now and again, a whisky soaked of a male kind turns up charged with an aggravated assault on his wife and seldom, if ever do these demoralized creatures receive a punishment adequate to their misconduct.'[60]

The Ontario Woman's Christian Temperance Union expressed a similar sentiment several decades later. As strong supporters of a 1909 Criminal Code amendment that introduced whipping as a discretionary punishment for those husbands convicted and imprisoned for assault causing bodily harm,[61] members of the WCTU seemed confident that this would offer a more effective deterrent: 'The cycle of events was – "drunk, beat up wife (maybe the children too); hailed into court; fined." The only dint made was in the man's pocket book, and he soon forgot that and repeated the offence. So the exasperated women concluded that a dint in his anatomy might be more effectual.'[62] One legislator went even further: 'Instead of giving such a man six months in jail for beating his wife, I would give him thirty days and thirty lashes. If that is done, he will never beat his wife again.'[63]

Despite the confidence expressed by the WCTU and those legislators who supported the bill, my sample of cases suggests that this form of punishment was rarely ordered by the courts. In one instance, however, the Sault Ste-Marie police magistrate, after hearing the evidence in the brutal 1920 wife-beating case against Louis C., expressed great sorrow that 'such a thing as this can occur in any home in this country.' He further added that if the accused had not elected a trial by jury (where, five months later, he would be acquitted of the charge), 'I would have imposed the lash in addition to the sentence.'[64] It is also doubtful that the more liberal application of this punitive form of punishment would have acted as a decisive deterrent in stemming the incidents of wife abuse. Moreover, owing to its severity and the potential risks of retaliation, its more frequent use could have further inhibited wives from laying complaints against their husbands.

While the role of the legal system was generally limited in extending adequate protection to battered wives, the intervention of relatives, boarders, neighbours, and the community often served as an alternative. For instance, historical evidence indicates that extralegal community enforcement of appropriate domestic and marital conduct did provide one popular mechanism for third-party scrutiny and regulation of familial and marital behaviour. As Bryan Palmer has suggested, particularly in the first half of the nineteenth century, wife-beaters and disorderly households were frequent targets of the disciplinary practice of charivaris. While this popular custom could potentially relieve abused wives of the burden of complaint and the possible threat of retaliation associated with formal legal action, it could also be interpreted as one community response to the perceived 'deficiencies of legal authority' and to one aspect of marital relations 'where the rule of law could or would not intervene.'[65]

Although wives made up the majority of plaintiffs in criminal cases of abuse, the successful intervention of a third party would at least serve to halt the beating and would provide an abused wife with the opportunity to escape and to seek refuge at the house of a neighbour or relative. At the same time, a substantial number of wife-beating and other assault cases suggest that the interference of a third party with what some husbands considered their legitimate right could provoke violent and in some cases fatal responses. For example, in 1886, when several neighbours attempted to intercede on behalf of a Mrs S., who was being severely kicked and beaten by her husband on a village street in the Township of Kenyon, they testified that Mr S. pulled out a pistol and 'threatened to shoot any one who would interfere.'[66] In another case, Samuel McDowell of the Township of Nissouri, after seeing his brother strike his wife because she had let 'the cows into a field contrary to his directions,' threatened to strike him if he did it again. According to the testimony, the husband, John McDowell, responded to this threat by stating that 'it was none of [his brother's] business how often he struck his wife.' When his brother replied that it was his business and 'he would not let [him] strike her while he was there,' a violent and fatal brawl between the two brothers ensued. In this particular (and perhaps rare) instance, the husband was killed and the brother was convicted of murder.[67]

Underlying the ideological and formal restrictions imposed by both the law and the courts in protecting battered wives was the question of intemperance. As frequently discussed in the press, and as repeatedly alluded to in women's testimony, the brutish drunken husband signified the gravest threat to domestic harmony and one of the principal causes of the disintegration of the family unit.

In their testimony abused wives frequently mentioned whether their husbands were sober or 'worse of liquor' when the assaults or beatings occurred. While some married women presented the drinking habits of their husbands as an explanation for their violent misconduct, others denounced their spouses' habitual cruelty on precisely the same grounds.

In 1885 Catherine D. of Peterborough stated that because her husband became 'very violent when drunk' she was 'afraid to live with him,' and she described her seemingly futile efforts 'to humour him so as to ward off trouble.' But even though she linked her husband's persistent cruelty to his intemperate habits in much of her testimony, she did add that even when he was sober 'he would choke me if I interfered between him and my children.'[68] Conversely, drunkenness could potentially serve as one explanatory justification for some husbands' abusive behaviour. In 1882, for example, Patrick L. of Gananoque attempted to absolve himself of any responsibility for brutally assaulting and beating his wife by explaining to the judge that 'I don't remember striking my wife ... I think liquor was the cause of it.' In responding to her husband's claim, however, Sarah L. made it clear that even though her husband had been drunk when 'he hammered me from room to room,' he was 'not as drunk as he pretended to be.'[69] In 1905 Conrod S. of the Township of Ellice also blamed alcohol for what amounted to sixteen years of habitual violence when he stated, 'I did not intend to hurt, I did not intend to break her back ... I think I would get on all right if it were not for whisky. I was always sorry for what I did to my wife and I apologized to her. So far as drinking I intend to quit ... and become a sober man.' His wife, however, attributed his habitual abuse to another factor that had little to do with his intemperate habits: 'All his abuse is carried on in anger and wickedness, but with intent to boss me and control.'[70]

If intemperance became at least one pervasive social explanation for and recurring theme associated with spousal cruelty and domestic discord, it is arguable that it also tended to obscure and to displace attention from those sources of marital tensions linked with the unequal allocation of economic resources and the hierarchical relations of power that tended to structure relations between husbands and wives. Disputes over money and the possible conflicting interests associated with the survival of the family economy seemed to have enormous potential for creating marital tensions, particularly in poor and working-class families. In some instances it was precisely when wives reprimanded their husbands for squandering the family's economic resources on alcohol or for their failure to provide adequately for the family that their husbands became abusive. For example, in 1874 and again in 1884 Jane M. of St Catharines, the wife of a labourer, charged her husband with 'aggravated assault' and, on the second occasion, with the 'intent to cut and stab.'[71] In her 1884 statement Mrs M. complained to the magistrate that Mr M. 'only works occasionally and gets drunk with his evenings [and] I have three children living.' On the day in question, however, she had scolded him for not 'being at work that day' and for 'coming home drunk,' and had made it clear that he should 'stay away when he got his liquor.' 'When I said this to him,' she testified, 'he ran at me with the butcher knife, struck me in the back with the knife and struck me with his fist.' Fortunately for Mrs M. the knife apparently broke when it struck her corset and she was spared what could have been a fatal injury. And perhaps it was because of the sturdiness of her corset that Mr M. was acquitted of the charge of 'intent to cut and stab.'

In other instances, however, a wife's perceived disobedience and her real or alleged failure to fulfil an assigned duty or to provide expected services in the household precipitated acts of violence on the part of her husband. And the accused husband did not hesitate to present his wife's breach of her duties as a legitimate marital grievance. In 1892 Mary Ann D. of the Township of Uxbridge laid a complaint against her husband for kicking her and threatening to take her life and for ordering her and her children out of the house in the middle of winter while they were all still in their nightclothes. Although Mrs D. and her children testified that her husband had abused her and threatened to 'knock her brains out' often enough before, his most recent round of abuse was triggered by Mrs D.'s apparent failure to light the lantern in the house when he requested that she do so. Although Mr D. pleaded not guilty to the charges and denied having kicked his wife, he told the magistrate that his threatening language had been provoked by the actions of his spouse: 'She has not spoken a civil word to me for three months past. When I came home last night I called to have the lantern lit for me ... I went in the house to get the lantern. The lantern was not lit. They were all in bed but my wife. I swore and said 'you let a fellow break his neck.' I had worked all these years and had no body to light a lantern for me. I said people who would aggravate anyone like that should have their brains knocked out.'[72]

Similarly, in 1881 an Ontario County Court judge offered Matthew M. of Whitby the opportunity to respond to the assault charge laid by his wife. According to Mrs M., she frequently bought her husband some whisky in order to 'please him.' And, while she made it clear that he had struck her many times before, on this occasion, when her husband came home drunk and she had no whisky to give him, 'he commenced swearing and took me by the hair of my head and attempted to choke me. My sister came to my assistance and took him off. I then ran out with the children and have not been home since.'[73] In responding to his wife's statement, Mr M., unlike some husbands who found themselves in similar situations, did not deny abusing his wife, nor did he present a detailed explanation or justification. What his brief statement underscored, was one central component of nineteenth- and early twentieth-century marriage that tended to underlie the marital expectations of many abusive husbands and to shape the unequal relations of power within the marital unit. Whether interpreted as a rhetorical question or as a candid statement, the meaning inscribed in Mr M.'s words perhaps require little further comment: 'If a man's wife does not obey him what can he do?'

While abusive husbands like William D. and Matthew M. expressed their sense of entitlement in terms of wifely obedience and submission, others explicitly invoked the language of possession when referring to their wives. In 1900, for example, Mrs F of Galt took refuge in her parents' house after being assaulted by her husband. Thomas F. appeared at the house the next afternoon, determined to reclaim what he explicitly termed 'his property.' Although his father-in-law felt it necessary to inquire whether he 'would use his property right,' Mr F. remained adamant, replying that it was none of his father-in-law's business and that 'he would do as he liked.'[74]

Despite such overt proprietary claims, most abused wives who appealed for some form of protection from the legal system sought to modify, either through punishment or censure but more frequently through mediation, the most violent manifestations of this sense of male prerogative. The ambiguous definitions of the law and the practices of the courts left unquestioned the underlying unequal distribution of power and privilege that structured relations between husbands and wives. Thus, while marital breakdown took various forms in the late nineteenth and early twentieth centuries, criminal cases of non-support and desertion most clearly exposed the economic vulnerability of women, and particularly of poor and working-class wives with children. Instances of wife abuse revealed how economic vulnerability, together with the often ineffective yet seemingly prevalent mediatory efforts of the legal system left unchallenged the sexual hierarchy that continued to undergird and define the marital unit.

NOTES

This research was facilitated by the generous financial support of the Ontario Graduate Fellowship Committee, the Arthur and Evelyn Lower Fellowship Committee, and the Social Sciences and Humanities Research Council of Canada.

1 See, for example, Michèle Barrett, *Women's Oppression Today: Problems in Marxist Feminist Analysis* (London: Verso 1980); Roberta Hamilton and Michèle Barrett, *The Politics of Diversity: Feminism, Marxism and Nationalism* (Montreal: Book Centre Inc. 1986), 139–254.

2 Most recently, this general trend in Canadian family and working-class history has been shifting towards a more balanced approach to the study of the family. See *Canadian Family History: Selected Readings*, ed. Bettina Bradbury (Toronto: Copp Clark Pitman 1992) and Bettina Bradbury, *Working Families: Age, Gender and Daily Survival in Industrializing Montreal* (Toronto: McClelland and Stewart 1993). Also see Bryan D. Palmer, *Working Class Experience: Rethinking the History of Canadian Labour, 1880–1991* (Toronto: McClelland and Stewart 1992). For a discussion of the divergent theoretical and methodological approaches that have informed the studies written by family and feminist historians, see Louise A. Tilly, 'Women's History and Family History: Fruitful Collaboration or Missed Connection?' (1987), 12:1–3 *Journal of Family History*, 303–15.

3 Terry L. Chapman, ' "Til Death Do Us Part": Wife Beating in Alberta, 1905–1920' (1988), 36:4 *Alberta History*, 13–22. This kind of reevaluation is demonstrated in recent publications by Kathryn Harvey, ' "To Love, Honour and Obey": Wife-Battering in Working-Class Montréal, 1869–1879' (1990), 19:2 *Urban History Review*, 128–40; and 'Amazons and Victims: Resisting Wife-Abuse in Working-Class Montréal, 1869–1879' (1991), *Journal of the Canadian Historical Association*, 131–47; Judith Fingard, 'The Prevention of Cruelty, Marriage Breakdown and the Rights of Wives in Nova Scotia, 1880–1900' (1993), 22:2 *Acadiensis*, 84–101; Constance Backhouse, *Petticoats and Prejudice: Women and Law in Nineteenth-Century Canada* (Toronto: The Osgoode Society 1991); Karen Dubinsky and Franca Iacovetta, 'Murder, Womanly Virtue, and Motherhood: The Case of Angelina Napolitano, 1911–1922' (1991), 72 *Canadian Historical Review*, 505–31; and Karen Dubinsky, *Improper Advances: Rape and Heterosexual Conflict in Ontario, 1880–1929* (Chicago: University of Chicago Press 1993).

4 English civil law was introduced in Upper Canada in 1792 by An Act Introducing the English Civil Law into Upper Canada, (1792) 32 Geo. III, c. 1. In this act the legislators of Upper Canada stipulated that 'in all matters of controversy relative to property and civil rights, resort shall be had to the Laws of England as the rule for the decision of the same.' It should be noted that Upper Canada also received English criminal law.

5 Peter Ward, *Courtship, Love, and Marriage in Nineteenth-Century Canada* (Montreal and Kingston: McGill-Queen's University Press 1990), 15–49.

6 'The Law of Primogeniture' (1844–5), 1 *Upper Canada Jurist* 260.

7 Marjorie Griffin Cohen, *Women's Work, Markets, and Economic Development in Nineteenth-Century Ontario* (Toronto: University of Toronto Press 1988), 43–4.

8 (1856), 2 *Upper Canada Law Journal,* 217–18 (emphasis in original).

9 As the eighteenth-century English jurist William Blackstone pointed out, 'Even the disabilities, which the wife lies under, are for the most part intended for her protection and benefit – *so great a favorite is the female sex with the laws of England.*' Cited in Clara Brett Martin, 'Legal Status of Women in the Dominion of Canada,' *Women of Canada: Their Life and Work* (National Council of Women of Canada 1900), 37 (emphasis in original).

10 For a discussion of these various legislative developments and how they were administered in the courts, see Constance Backhouse, 'Shifting Patterns in Nineteenth-Century Canadian Custody Law,' in *Essays in the History of Canadian Law,* vol. 1, ed. David H. Flaherty (Toronto: University Press 1981), 212–48; Martin, supra note 9, at 34–40; Constance Backhouse, 'Married Women's Property Law in Nineteenth Century Canada' (1988), 6:2 *Law and History Review,* 211–57; Ward, supra note 5, at 38–49.

11 See Backhouse, 'Shifting Patterns,' supra note 10, at 219.

12 John A. Gemmill, *The Practice of the Parliament of Canada upon Bills of Divorce* (Toronto: Carswell & Co. 1889), 52.

13 For a discussion of Canada's changing divorce laws and procedures, see Gemmill, supra; C.S. McKee, 'Law of Divorce in Canada' (1922), 62 DLR 1–57; Constance Backhouse, ' "Pure Patriarchy": Nineteenth Century Canadian Marriage' (1986), 31 *McGill Law Journal,* 266–91; James G. Snell, *In the Shadow of the Law: Divorce in Canada, 1900–1939* (Toronto: University of Toronto Press 1991).

14 Jane Ursel, 'The State and the Maintenance of Patriarchy: A Case Study of Family, Labour and Welfare Legislation in Canada,' in *Family, Economy and State: The Social Reproduction Process Under Capitalism,* ed. James Dickinson and Bob Russell (Toronto: Garamond Press 1986), 176. The proprietary nature of a husband's control over his wife's sexuality was best exemplified in civil suits for criminal conversation, in which a husband sought material compensation for damages from his wife's adulterous lover. This occurred in Ontario as late as 1945. H.L. Cartwright, *The Law of Divorce in Canada and the Practice in Divorce Actions in Ontario* (Toronto: Canadian Law List 1945), 111. The most interesting case of criminal conversation I have uncovered thus far involved an 1852 civil suit against David Ryman, who was so incensed by the 'infamous' and 'unjust' nature of the civil action that he published a detailed statement in an attempt to restore his social reputation. Nonetheless, he was required to pay £800 in damages plus court

costs, which amounted to a stiff £1,000. See *Statement Made by David Rymal Relative to the Late Action Brought Against Him by David Gillett*, Archives of Ontario (AO), (1852) Pamphlet no 40.

15 *Woolsey v. Finch* (1869), 20 UCCP 135.

16 See *R. v. Bissell* (1882), 1 OR 515–16.

17 Supra note 8, at 181.

18 Ibid.

19 For example, Jacob Hillman published a notice in the *British Whig* twice weekly from 15 July to 4 November 1834, which characteristically read as follows: 'WHEREAS my wife, has left my bed and board without any just cause, I hereby forbid all persons harbouring or trusting her on my account as I will pay no debt of hers contracted after this date.'

20 For example, George Counter of Waterloo ran four ads during the month of May 1835 in the *British Whig* that provided more details: 'CAUTION. THIS is to give notice that in consequence of the absconding from my bed and board of my wife, Elizabeth Counter, late Elizabeth Whitcombe, widow. I will be no longer answerable for any debts she may contract. Elizabeth Counter left her home on the 16th of April in company with a young man named Frederick Thomas and a female child about ten years of age. The parties were last heard of in Watertown, N.Y. and are supposed to be now travelling towards the city of New York.' Mr Counter also requested that the New York *Commercial Advertiser* and the Albany *Argus* make the same insertion in their newspapers.

21 See Ottawa *Citizen*, 11 March 1870, 12 March 1870, and 14 March 1870.

22 (1869) 32 & 33 Vict., c. 20, s. 25; (1892) 55 & 56 Vict., c. 29, s. 210.

23 (1869) 32 & 33 Vict., c. 28, s. 1; (1874) 37 Vict., c. 43

24 (1887) The *Queen v. James L.*, AO, RG 22, United Counties of Stormont, Dundas, and Glengarry County Court Judges Criminal Court (CCJCC) Case Files, 1870–89. The following discussion is based on a sample of 257 non-support cases collected from a selection of Police Court Dockets and Minutebooks (Stratford, 1893–1906; Galt, 1857–82, 1884–1920; Sarnia, 1910–23; Belleville, 1874–7; Picton, 1851–82, 1887–1919; Sault Ste-Marie, 1907–1920), CCJCC Minutebooks and Case Files for ten counties (Perth, 1872–84, 1885–1901; Ontario, 1881–1920; Haldimand, 1869–91, 1911–20; Elgin, 1879–1908; Niagara North, 1869–1919; Carleton, 1908–20; Grey, 1869–1900, 1901–20; Stormont, Dundas, and Glengarry, 1872–1920; Leeds and Grenville, 1881–94; Peterborough, 1870–1907), Crown Attorney Case Files for Algoma, 1916–20, and Stratford Jail Register, 1876–1924.

25 (22 January 1877) *Agnes S. v. Andrew S.*, AO, RG 22, Waterloo County Police Court Minutebooks (Galt), vol. 5, 1875–7.

26 (1875) *The Queen v. Patrick R.*, AO, RG 22, Niagara North CCJCC Case Files, 1869–1919.

27 (1888) *The Queen v. Edward B.*, AO, RG 22, Ontario County Crown Attorney–Clerk of the Peace CCJCC Case Files, 1881–98.

28 (23 June 1898), *George D. v. Ludwig Z and Isidore Z.*, AO, RG 22, Perth County Police Court Dockets (Stratford), 1893–1906.

29 (1888) 51 Vict., c. 23 (Ont.).

30 *Ontario Legislative Assembly Debates*, 16 February 1888.

31 Ibid.

32 When the bill was first introduced, the maximum weekly allowance was fixed at $10, then reduced to $5. In 1911 the maximum weekly support was raised to $10 and in 1920 to $20. See *Ontario Legislative Assembly Debates*, 16 February 1888; 15 March 1888; (1911) 1 Geo. V, c. 34, s. 2 (Ont.); Allan M. Dymond, *The Laws of Ontario Relating to Women and Children* (Toronto: Clarkson W. James 1923), 36–41.

33 (1897) 60 Vict., c. 14, s. 34 (Ont.).

34 One legislator opposed the bill on the grounds that because 'the question of the wife's chastity' would inevitably be raised in these cases, the lower courts constituted an inappropriate forum. In his view, the issue of maintenance should remain the preserve of the higher courts, or at least be extended only to the County Court level. *Ontario Legislative Assembly Debates*, 15 March 1888.

35 (1913) 3 & 4 Geo. V, c. 14, s. 242a.

36 Because of the often ambiguous nature of the court records, in which the precise nature of the charge was not specified with any degree of consistency, it is difficult to ascertain if this represented a high or a low rate of success. But it is perhaps important to note that of the total number of cases in my post-1888 sample, 37 per cent resulted in a suspended sentence or an indefinite adjournment, 28 per cent were dismissed or settled out of court, 5 per cent resulted in a prison term, and 2 per cent resulted in the imposition of a fine.

37 (1897) *The Queen v. William P.*, AO, RG 22, Niagara North CCJCC Case Files, 1869–1919. Partially in response to these limitations, some police magistrates began to attach specific conditions to orders of maintenance, particularly with regard to the weekly payments. For example, in 1909 Robert B. of Galt was ordered to pay three dollars per week for the support of his wife and children. Nine months later he reappeared in the Galt Police Court on another charge of non-support. In the second case he was required to provide an order whereby the weekly sums would be paid through his employer. See (26 October 1901) *Julia O'D. v Peter O'D.*, AO,

348   Annalee E. Gölz

RG 22, Perth County Police Court Dockets (Stratford), 1893–1906; (22
October 1909) and (25 July 1910) *Mary B. v. Robert B.*, AO, RG 22, Waterloo
County Police Court Minutebooks (Galt), vol. 13, 1906–12.
38 See, for example, *Rodman v. Rodman* (1873), 20 Grant's Chancery Reports
443–4, where the duties of the husband in this regard are mentioned.
39 These are the words of a Judge Hughes and are cited in Erin Breault,
'Educating Women About the Law: Violence Against Wives in Ontario,
1850–1920,' MA thesis, University of Toronto (1986), 16.
40 In two excellent studies, Anna Clark and Pamela Haag use Carol Pateman's
distinction between the 'social contract' and the 'sexual contract' of marriage to account for the ambiguities of common law and the hesitancy of
the legal system to intervene in the relations between husbands and wives:
Anna Clark, 'Humanity or Justice? Wifebeating and the Law in the Eighteenth and Nineteenth Centuries,' in *Regulating Womanhood: Historical Essays
on Marriage, Motherhood and Sexuality*, ed. Carol Smart (London: Routledge
1992), 187–206, and Pamela Haag, 'The "Ill-Use of a Wife": Patterns of
Working-Class Violence in Domestic and Public New York City, 1860–1880'
(1992), 25:3 *Journal of Social History*, 447–77.
41 For a more detailed discussion of nineteenth- and early twentieth-century alimony cases in Ontario and other provinces, see Backhouse, supra note 13, at
295–312; Breault, supra note 39, at 31-46; Snell, supra note 13, at 97–102.
42 This definition stems from the late eighteenth-century case *Evans v. Evans*
(1790), which established the precedent in alimony litigation involving
cruelty. See R.R. Evans, *The Law and Practice Relating to Divorce and Other
Matrimonial Causes* (Calgary: Burroughs & Co. 1923), 43–52, 326–30. See
also Gemmill, supra note 12 at 222.
43 *Rodman v. Rodman*, supra note 38, at 430–1.
44 *Jackson v. Jackson* (1860), 8 Grant's Chancery Reports 506.
45 See *Bavin v. Bavin* (1896), 27 OR 571–82; *McKay v. McKay* (1858), 6 Grant's
Chancery Reports 380–3; *Severn v. Severn* (1852) 3 Grant's Chancery Reports
431–48.
46 (1897) 60 Vict., c. 14, s. 34 (Ont.).
47 This sample is based on the previously mentioned records: see note 24,
supra. In addition, some cases have been derived from preliminary research
into the Police Court reports for selected years published in the Ottawa
Citizen, the Ottawa *Times*, and the Toronto *Globe*.
48 (1897) *Eliza B. v. Cornelius B.*, AO, RG 22, Elgin County CCJCC Docket-
book, 1879–1908.
49 (14 February 1873) *Catharine B. v. Francis B.*, AO, RG 22, Waterloo County
Police Court Minutebooks (Galt), vol. 3, 1871–3.

50 (1881) *The Queen v. Charles C.*, AO, RG 22, Ontario County Crown Attorney–Clerk of the Peace CCJCC Case Files, 1881–98.
51 (1920) *Julia K. v. Andi T.*, AO, RG 22, Algoma Crown Attorney Case Files (Sault Ste-Marie), 1916–25.
52 (1898) *The Queen v. Frederick W.*, AO, RG 22, Ontario County Crown Attorney–Clerk of the Peace CCJCC Case Files, 1881–98.
53 (1887) *The Queen v. Albert B.*, AO, RG 22, Ontario County CCJCC Case Files, 1887–1901.
54 (1881) *The Queen v. Matthew M.*, AO, RG 22, Ontario County Crown Attorney–Clerk of the Peace CCJCC Case Files, 1881–98.
55 (1885) *The Queen v. William D.*, AO, RG 22, Peterborough CCJCC Case Files, 1881–1907.
56 Ottawa *Times*, 1 May 1869.
57 Ottawa *Times*, 4 February 1869.
58 Ottawa *Times*, 5 February 1869, 6 February 1869.
59 See, for example, Ottawa *Times*, 1 May 1869, 20 July 1870.
60 Ottawa *Citizen*, 24 November 1870.
61 (1909) 8 & 9 Edward VII, c. 9, s. 2(c).
62 S.G.E. McKee, *Jubilee History of the Ontario Woman's Christian Temperance Union, 1877–1927* (Whitby: C.A. Goodfellow & Son n.d.), 87.
63 See *House of Commons Debates*, 25 January 1909, 94. This amendment to the Criminal Code prompted considerable discussion in Parliament and in the Senate. It was first introduced into the House of Commons on 12 March 1883 but seems to have died in committee: *House of Commons Debates*, 12 March 1883, 287; 4 February 1909, 556–70; *Debates of the Senate*, 18 May 1909, 678–9.
64 (1920) *K. v. Louis C.*, AO, RG 22, Algoma Crown Attorney Case Files, 1916–25.
65 Bryan D. Palmer, 'Discordant Music: Charivaris and Whitecapping in Nineteenth-Century North America' (1978) 3 *Labour/Le Travail*, 5–62.
66 *The Queen v. Samuel S.*, AO, RG 22, United Counties of Stormont, Dundas, and Glengarry CCJCC Case Files, 1870–89.
67 *The Queen v. Samuel McDowell* (1865), 25 UCQB 108–15.
68 Supra note 55.
69 (1882) *The Queen v. Patrick L.* AO, RG 22, Leeds and Grenville CCJCC Case Files, 1882–94.
70 (14 December 1905) *C.P. v. Conrod S.*, AO, RG 22, Perth Police Court Dockets (Stratford), 1893–1906.
71 (1874) *The Queen v. Patrick M.*; (1884) *The Queen v. Patrick M.*, AO, RG 22, Niagara North CCJCC Case Files, 1869–1919.

350   Annalee E. Gölz

72 (1892) *The Queen v. William D.*, AO, RG 22, Ontario County CCJCC Case Files, 1887–1901.

73 (1881) *The Queen v. Matthew M.*, AO, RG 22, Ontario County Crown Attorney–Clerk of the Peace CCJCC Case Files, 1881–98.

74 (15 October 1900) *Joseph K. v. Thomas F.*, AO RG 22, Waterloo County Police Court Minutebooks (Galt), Vol. 12, 1898–1905.

13 Locking Them Up: Incarcerating Women in Ontario 1857–1931

WENDY RUEMPER

Introduction

In this paper I will explore the differential effect of the reform era on the criminalization and incarceration of women in the Andrew Mercer Reformatory of Ontario in Toronto and in two rural Ontario jails – Owen Sound and Kenora – from 1857 to 1931. Women received longer sentences and served longer terms in the Mercer Reformatory than in either of the rural jails. These differences were significant: on average, women sentenced to Mercer received 335 days, while women sentenced to the Owen Sound jail received 154 days and women sentenced to the Kenora Jail received 68 days. Women committed to Mercer for the first time received longer sentences than women who had been previously committed (an average of 356 days in comparison with 267 days) and served longer periods of time in the institution (276 days for first committals in comparison with 229 days for previous committals).

The Mercer Reformatory was the first prison for women in Ontario. The longer sentences were a result of the reform agenda at Mercer,[1] which took young first offenders, who were thought to require long periods of incarceration, and attempted to transform them into the institution's ideal of the proper woman. The jails had no such pretensions to reform, and the courts were more reluctant to incarcerate women in them. This was partly because the facilities were poor; the jails often lacked separate quarters for women and the staff to care for them. Paternalism was another significant factor. Particularly in the early years, many women were incarcerated on vagrancy and lunacy charges; the jails were used as hospitals and asylums when none existed within reasonable distance.

Government parsimony may have influenced sentencing decisions. The greater costs of running jails, as compared with penitentiaries, was a recurrent theme in the annual reports of the inspector of prisons and asylums. However, the tightness of government purse strings did not affect Mercer in the same way as other penal institutions. The superintendents of the reformatory called for longer sentences and a better class of inmate, but not for increased funding.[2]

The penal philosophy of the time also had a significant impact on the sentences the women received and the time they served, particularly at Mercer. With a move away from the classical belief in individual responsibility and moral weakness to a belief in scientific reform and a reliance on environmental explanations of crime, the progressive era brought demands for indeterminate sentences, probation and parole, and educational and vocational programs for inmates. At Mercer this meant that, over time, more women were given longer, indeterminate, or indefinite sentences, and that they served longer periods of time in spite of the increasing use of parole.

Methodology

The data collected here came from jail registers for Owen Sound in rural central Ontario, for Kenora in northern Ontario, and for the Ontario reformatory for women; from local histories and newspapers; and from the annual reports of the inspector of prisons and asylums for Ontario from 1857 to 1931. The Owen Sound jail was chosen because it was one of the early jails built in Upper Canada, its registers were available from 1857, and it served a large area of mid-southern Ontario. The choice of the Kenora Jail was predicated on its location in northern Ontario, its reputation as a frontier town, and its native population. In total, 3,106 cases of women incarcerated in the three institutions were included in the sample: 2,183 from Mercer,[3] 702 from Owen Sound,[4] and 221 from Kenora.[5] The experiences of the women in these three institutions, taken as a group, provide a reasonable picture of incarceration practices throughout the reform era in turn-of-the-century Ontario.

In this study, changing patterns in the social control and criminalization of women's behaviour are examined through incarceration practices over time. I have analysed the effect of a number of independent variables on the length of sentences and time served: the type of charge, the characteristics of the women, and a series of court variables. The characteristics of the women include age, birthplace, religion, race, moral habits, literacy, occupation, marital status, residence, recidivism, and (from the Mercer registers only) physical characteristics such as height, weight, skin complexion, eye and hair colour, and body marks or physical traits as described in the registers. The court variables include the option of paying a fine, the type of sentence,[6] and the reasons for release from the jail or reformatory.[7]

The Rise of the Liberal Welfare State in Ontario

Reform measures at Mercer reflected what Dorothy Chunn has described as the transformation of Ontario from a laissez-faire state to a liberal welfare state over the turn of the last century. This transformation

> entailed a philosophical and practical shift from legal formalism, premised on the ideology of individualism and the minimal state, to socialized justice, based on the ideology of individualization and the interventionist state. Thus, a mode of regulating the deviant and dependent grounded in legal concepts of liberty, equality, responsibility, and retribution was transformed into a hybrid one as non-legal categories of determinism, inequality, non-culpability and rehabilitation were incorporated within existing welfare structures.[8]

In the laissez-faire state, segregative institutions (such as jails, prisons, and asylums) followed the principles of individualism. The institutions attempted to 'remoralize' their deviant and dependent subjects and instil in them the virtues of discipline, hard work, rationality, and conformity. Remoralization was best achieved, according to this view, through segregation, hard labour, and moral and religious training, which, it was hoped, would train the deviant to exercise reason.[9] The deviant and the dependent were, in principle, to be strictly segregated. The state, through the criminal justice system, was to define and punish the deviant and the criminal. The private sector, including families, friends, and charities (and, if they failed, municipal authorities), was to support the dependent and the neglected.[10] As Chunn points out, and as is apparent from the jail data, it was difficult to maintain a rigid division between the private and the public. The poor, the old, and the sick were commonly incarcerated on vagrancy charges and indiscriminately housed with murderers, thieves, and other criminals in the Owen Sound and Kenora jails.

According to Chunn, the shift to individualization and the welfare state brought a multidisciplinary approach to dealing with the underclasses. The philosophical line between deviant and dependent blurred as the person was no longer seen as a free, rational subject but as a unique individual with particular characteristics who needed to be assessed and treated by 'professionals.'

> A mode of regulation that relied on "moralization" and legal pro-
> hibition / punishment was being transformed into one based on
> "normalization" and social control ... Whereas the former was
> aimed at forcing people to realize their weaknesses or potential
> weaknesses in order that they might begin to exercise their rational-
> ity and act conventionally, the latter attempted to bring the mar-
> ginal into line with normative requirements through positive tech-
> niques of intervention "for their own good" and that of society.[11]

With the development of the liberal welfare state, the civil–criminal distinction faded as functions performed by the private sphere (family, friends, churches) and by private agencies of normalization (such as Children's Aid Societies) merged with public mechanisms (courts), and the distinction between poverty and crime faded.[12] This change was evident at Mercer as representatives of religious, philanthropic, and voluntary associations came to the institution to minister to and care for the women incarcerated there. The federal and provincial governments assumed 'a direct, paternalistic role' in identifying certain categories of the poor as requiring state protection.[13] Deviant and dependent subjects were no longer responsible for their own reform. Under the liberal welfare state, professionals with specialized knowledge and curative techniques 'diagnosed and treated existing problems and proactively predicted and pre-empted their development.'[14]

At Mercer these specialists included the doctor who took charge of the women's sexual morality as well as their health; the ministers and their assistants who looked after the women's spiritual morality; the teachers who taught them obedience as well as reading and writing; the matrons who trained them in humility and the domestic arts; and other community agencies, such as the Prisoners' Aid Society, whose members helped the women re-enter society in their proper sphere.

Attempts were made to separate and classify different categories of deviant and dependent women. Segregative institutions introduced more complex classification systems, catering to various categories of deviants and dependents. In the Ontario penal system, asylums, reformatories, industrial schools, and prisons were established to permit classification and segregation of different kinds of offenders. At Mercer, segregation of the women was only partially achieved. The physical design of the institution made the total separation of different classes of women impossible. The jails were crowded, and although the administrators believed in the wisdom of classification and segregation, most failed to achieve either.

Women incarcerated in jails were much less likely to receive specialized attention, and the fading of the civil–criminal distinction took a different turn there. Provincial inspectors called upon local communities to provide shelter for their dependent citizens, to erect asylums and establish hospitals for those who were poor, ill, or destitute. Jails were only for criminals, they argued. But this civil–criminal distinction did not materialize in many communities. For example, in Owen Sound from 1857 onward, the jail served as a hospital, asylum, and poorhouse until other institutions were eventually built to house the poor, sick, insane, and indigent.

Determinism, inequality, non-culpability, the tenets of the liberal welfare state, and rehabilitation, resulted in women serving longer sentences at Mercer than in the jails. The effects of the philosophies and practices of the laissez-faire and the liberal welfare states can be found in the differential treatment of women incarcerated at Mercer Reformatory and the Kenora and Owen Sound jails from 1857 to 1931. In this analysis, four penal eras (1857–1882, 1883–1898, 1899–1917, and 1918–1931) have been delineated; the divisions are based on changing official views as reported in the annual reports of the inspector of prisons and asylums, other historical research on prisons in the United States and Canada,[15] and reports on the administration of penal policy in Ontario.[16] The differential effects of the reform era on women's incarceration experiences at Mercer and in the jails during each of the eras are analysed below.

The United States' Experience

Penal philosophies and practices similar to those in Ontario had already evolved in the United States. Prior to the 1840s, women had seldom been imprisoned. Men were active in the public sphere and had more opportunities to commit crimes, but women were still largely controlled by their families and churches: they were regulated by private rather than public institutions.[17]

After the 1860s there was an increase in the number of women committed to American prisons. This increase stemmed from the enforcement of new moral standards, which created a permanent category of female criminals. Women's criminal behaviour was predominantly sexually defined. Impure women were seen as a threat to social stability.[18] Previously, female immorality has been interpreted as a sin that required religious control; now it was also a sickness that required medical control.[19]

From 1870 to 1900 American (and Canadian) penologists advocated principles of rehabilitation rather than punishment for women. This was part of a broader current in prison reform based on the treatment approach. Leading penologists proposed new systems of discipline and rewards and emphasized the importance of classification of inmates to individualize treatment.[20]

Women increasingly moved into the public realm with the creation of new extradomestic institutions, including female reformatories. The American reformatories were based on the principle of separate spheres and innate sexual differences. Following the philosophy of Elizabeth Fry, penal reformers called for separate facilities for women. Their goal was to create 'true womanhood,' the ideal of 'purity, piety, domesticity and submissiveness.'[21]

Later, during the period from 1900 to 1935, crime became increasingly 'medicalized' in the United States: women's criminal behaviour was perceived as a disease that must be cured. Women were convicted of immorality and detained for treatment of venereal disease; prostitutes and brothel-keepers were incarcerated to prevent the spread of venereal disease.[22]

In the early twentieth century, American psychiatrists focused on the 'hypersexual female' – a woman who could not control her sexual desires. Women with this affliction were defined as 'psychopaths,' and psychopathy was said to be an inborn condition with no remedy. The term 'female psychopath' was used at first to refer to prostitutes and immoral young women. Later it was expanded to include other women who had violated middle-class views of proper feminine behaviour.[23]

Psychopathic hypersexual women were aggressive; men were their passive victims. This psychiatric view reversed the Victorian notion of women as victims in their sexual relations with men. In addition, the medical interpretation shifted away from moral explanations of women's deviant behaviour as 'bad.' However, middle-class social workers continued to view deviant and criminalized women as needing their protection, discipline and reform. A combination of the medical views of the psychiatrists and mental hygienists and the social reform views of middle-class workers shaped women's experiences in Mercer Reformatory (and to a lesser extent in the jails) over the turn of the century.

The Jails, Humanitarianism, and the
Laissez-faire State, 1857–82

The religious and philosophical concepts of the second half of the nineteenth century helped to determine the correctional policies and the extent and methods of social control that were used for women in jails and reformatories, as well as in asylums and other penal institutions.[24] All of these institutions tried 'to isolate their inhabitants from the outside world within an environment of order and regularity.' They shared the 'belief that the insane, the poor and the criminal led erratic, undisciplined lives which could be altered by the construction of an ideal social structure apart from society.'[25] The earliest jails were conceived as places of temporary constraint, but over time men and women were confined for longer periods of time 'in quarters completely unsuited to the housing of human beings and with no custodial philosophy or practices.'[26]

In 1859 a new Board of Inspectors of Prisons, Asylums and Public Charities first met in Upper Canada. The inspectors were required to visit the jails and reformatories twice annually and submit their reports to the Ontario government.[27] These annual reports described the humanitarian philosophy of the time and the jail practices that derived from it. Although the inspectors spoke of 'reform,' their statements primarily reflected a humanitarian concern grounded in the philosophy of John Howard. The humanitarians focused on issues of jail sanitation, 'supervision to prevent moral and physical corruption,' hard labour, and moral and religious instruction.[28] At this time criminality was seen as evidence of more serious evils that threatened the moral order of society. Widespread crime resulted from the failure of the poor and working populations to internalize the essential principles of social order. As a result, they succumbed to sin and immorality.[29]

Before the opening of Mercer in 1880, women were sentenced to local jails or, occasionally, to the penitentiary at Kingston. Women serving sentences in the Owen Sound Jail between 1857 and 1882 were charged with vagrancy (34 per cent), lunacy (17 per cent), theft (11 per cent), assault (8 per cent), and drunk and disorderly conduct (7 per cent). Most of the women charged with vagrancy had worked as labourers or servants. Many were single women with little education. They came from both rural and urban areas, some a considerable distance from Owen Sound.

It was not uncommon to find children in the jail registers who had been incarcerated on vagrancy charges, usually with their mothers, as well as elderly women. The women charged ranged from 1 year to 88 years of age. Many of the women were returned to jail repeatedly and the following case is illustrative of the vagrancy cases in Owen Sound jail in the period.

In 1878 Mary Jane Temple,[30] who came from a family whose female members were frequently charged with vagrancy offences, was convicted of vagrancy and sentenced to six months, hard labour. She was 24 years old and employed as a washerwoman. Mary Jane was incarcerated with her 4-year-old daughter Amelia, and during her stay delivered 'an illegitimate child,' Judith. The register showed that Mary Jane was incarcerated seven more times over the next six years with her two children.

Between 1857 and 1882, fifty women appear to have been incarcerated in the Owen Sound Jail on the ground of lunacy. No other reason was listed in the registers for holding any of these women.[31] The women's average age was 38, nine years older than the average age of the other women in the jail. They were more likely to be married and temperate, and they were better educated than the other inmates. Many had been born in Great Britain, and most came from surrounding rural areas rather than from the town of Owen Sound. Although they were not sentenced, they were held in the jail for longer periods than women convicted of offences.

The Owen Sound jail therefore served as a jail, a poorhouse, and an insane asylum. However, it was a holding tank, not a treatment centre. The principles of the laissez-faire state called for strict segregation and classification of the deviant and the criminal from the dependent and the neglected, but this was impossible in the jail, where lunatics, thieves, murderers, prostitutes, and drunks were incarcerated together with the aged and the poor. The neglected and the dependent were not necessarily cared for by the community – friends, family, and church – but more likely by the courts.

In contrast, Mercer, during its first years of operation (1880–2), was preparing to receive a restricted class of women – vagrants, prostitutes, unwed mothers, and other 'fallen women.'[32] Such women were deemed good candidates for reform. However, it took a few years before the judges appreciated this distinction and sent the 'right' kind of women to Mercer. The Toronto Police Court judges were regularly criticized in the inspector's annual reports for sending habitual drunks to Mercer on short sentences. The superintendents at Mercer were concerned that only women who showed good promise of reform should be sent there to benefit from their programs.

Andrew Mercer Reformatory, the Reform Agenda, and the Liberal Welfare State, 1880–98

The program at the Andrew Mercer Reformatory was built on two ideological precepts: the idea that reformation rather than punishment was the best antidote to crime, and the belief that women and men belonged in their proper and distinct spheres. The reformatory for women was based on the concept of a 'home,' with an all-female staff headed by a female superintendent who 'could "mother" her charges into respectable womanhood.' An 'ideology of maternalism' was borrowed from similar institutions in the United States, in which the superintendent and the matrons served as kindly but strict mothers who gently but firmly demanded obedience from their daughterly inmates.[33]

From the opening of Mercer until the turn of the century, the most common charges for incarceration were vagrancy, prostitution, drunk and disorderly conduct, and theft. Approximately half the women were Canadian-born, but the Irish were overrepresented in the reformatory population. More than half the women had worked in domestic or personal service, and about one-fifth were identified as prostitutes.

The Toronto and Hamilton courts sent most of the women to Mercer during this era, but those courts imposed shorter sentences than the courts in smaller centres. Over time the length of sentence and the length of time served by women at Mercer grew longer. For the first two years (1880 to 1882) the average sentence was 260 days; from 1883 to 1898 the average sentence was 283 days. The average time served was 236 days from 1880 to 1882 and 250 days from 1883 to 1898.

The administrators believed that moral reform could best be achieved through strict classification and segregation of criminal classes. They saw two types of inmates: the reformable and the non-reformable. The reformable were young women, preferably first offenders incarcerated on minor charges, whose backgrounds were conducive to programs aimed at improving their domestic skills, morality, and general demeanour. Young girls who were closer to the middle-class ideal (single, white, Canadian-born, Protestant, literate, temperate) and who already who had some experience in domestic or personal service were preferred. Unfortunately for the matrons at Mercer, this was not the class of women they always received.

The Mercer staff and the Ontario prison inspectors were particularly concerned about attracting 'reformable' women to Mercer. When they received 'non-reformable' women, the authorities advocated strict classification and segregation of the different classes of inmates. However, the physical structure of Mercer, with its separate cells and common corridors and work areas, was not consistent with the penal philosophy of classification and segregation.[34] An attempt was made to separate new entrants and disobedient women from the general ward. In the early years, new committals were placed in the refractory (punishment) ward for a month or so on probation, with the idea that, if they were obedient, they would be moved to the general ward and given employment. The officials thought that the privileges of the general ward would act as an incentive to obedience.[35]

A similar effort was later made to keep the novices away from the women who had been incarcerated for keeping houses of ill fame. The officials seemed concerned that the brothel-keepers would lure the young, apparently naïve women into a life of prostitution. The assumption was that if they kept the young first offenders separated from the older and more experienced criminals and bombarded them with moral training and proper examples of womanliness, the young women would adopt the morality and habits of ideal 'good' women – in other words the virtues exemplified by the staff and volunteers at Mercer. In 1884 an attendant was hired to take charge of inmates under 18 years of age and keep them away from the older women. She taught them reading and writing and various industries – shirt- and pant-making, hand sewing, and knitting.[36]

Work industries were established at Mercer for two reasons. Hard labour instilled discipline, and work programs were useful in training women for careers in domestic work, preferably in middle-class homes. (It is somewhat ironic that women sentenced to hard labour in the jails were less likely to be working than women at Mercer.) The women at Mercer were employed in a variety of industries, but most worked in the laundry. Besides doing the reformatory's laundry, the women also did the laundry for the Central Prison, the Canadian Pacific Railway, and some citizens of the City of Toronto. Other industrial work, principally knitting and sewing to order, responded to a less reliable demand. The women also performed domestic labour for the institution. They cleaned, cooked, baked, served in the dining-room, cared for the children in the nursery, nursed in the hospital, sewed, mended, and knitted.[37]

Community agencies, particularly those with educational and religious functions, were incorporated into the reform agenda at Mercer. Religion was an essential part of the philosophy and daily life of the Mercer Reformatory. God and discipline were joined together in all aspects of work. From 1880 until the turn of the century, women from the community came to the institution every Sunday morning to teach the Protestant inmates. A Protestant church service was held on Sunday afternoons and one or two evenings during the week. These services were led by clergy from the local ministerial associations.

Other religious organizations were involved in the reform programs at Mercer. The Upper Canada Bible Society sent bibles to all the inmates at Christmas. The Tract Society, the YMCA, and the Committee of the Hospital for Sick Children supplied religious literature. In 1893 the Salvation Army began conducting regular meetings on Monday evenings. References to Roman Catholic services and visits by priests were less common in the reports, although 32 per cent of the inmate population were Roman Catholic. Perhaps this was because the reports were written by the superintendent of the Protestant Sunday school. A Catholic mass was held each Sunday morning, and religious instruction given in the afternoon.

The Prisoners Aid Society was a community agency dedicated to helping the reformatory achieve its goals. It began to provide services that had previously been performed by the private sphere. It was, in effect, a 'public private agency' aimed at bringing the marginal into line through positive techniques of intervention 'for their own good.' In a characteristic blurring of the dependent–deviant distinction in the liberal welfare state, the Prisoners Aid Society workers acted as early practical, as well as moral, educational and religious counsellors.

The Prisoners Aid Society began to hold religious services and bible classes during the 1890s. A member of the association, referred to as a 'bible woman' in the annual reports, was assigned to visit with the women in the reformatory and to lead them in prayer, read from the Bible, and conduct religious classes. She would also visit the women individually in the corridors, cells, and hospital.

The Prisoners Aid Society worked with the teachers in the night school in a program aimed at teaching the illiterate women to read and write. At first, all of the women were required to attend the school a few evenings a week. But in 1884 Mrs O'Reilly, the superintendent at Mercer, decided to discontinue the practice of compulsory attendance, believing that it was useless to try to compel older women (the non-reformable ones) to learn when they had no interest. With the change in policy, daily classes were scheduled for the younger inmates (the reformable ones).

The Prisoners Aid Society also offered assistance and spiritual guidance to women after they were discharged. Members would meet the inmates on the morning of their discharge, provide them with clothing, and assist them in finding a place to work (generally as domestics in homes), lodgings (in a home, refuge, or Magdalen Asylum or in the Haven and Prison Gate Mission Home),[38] or in reaching friends and families. The teachers tried to offer support services to the women after discharge, but they appeared to have had mixed success in their efforts, with some former inmates falling into their 'old bad habits.'

The surgeon at Mercer was a key specialist in the realization of the philosophy of the early liberal welfare state. Like his medical colleagues in Europe[39] and in the United States,[40] he saw women's illnesses as peculiar to their sex. In his view, women's constitutions were weaker than men's, and women should be treated differently because of their propensity to develop 'women's illnesses.'[41] Women's sexuality was a major focus of his reports. He complained about pregnant women's lack of productivity and the problems of having to maintain a nursery at Mercer. He also wrote, in moralistical tones, about the sexual diseases the women had when they came to Mercer. Years of prostitution and a life of debauchery and drinking were hard on one's health, reported the surgeon. His description of the women's medical conditions illustrates his attempts to reduce their criminality (and morality) to their sexuality, with all of its 'problems.' This deterministic view blossomed after the turn of the century.

Although Mercer was an institution dedicated to reform, discipline and hard work were still considered important components for instilling the values of obedience and diligence in the servile domestic worker and the subservient wife. The staff complained about the 'incapables' who were committed to Mercer but were unable to work due to infirmity, insanity, idiocy, pregnancy, epilepsy, sickness, or a life of debauchery. In her report of 1888, Superintendent O'Reilly wrote about the condition of one 'incapable' on arrival at Mercer from Sudbury. Her feet had been frozen off and one finger was broken. She was unable to give a coherent account of herself and was certainly unfit for any work.[42] These administrators believed that women's sexuality, manifested in their unfortunate suscepti-bility to pregnancy and to diseases such as syphilis, and the requirements of caring for infants interfered with discipline and the proper moral work of the institution.

The Twentieth Century: A New Era of Reform, 1899–1917

The report of the 1890 Royal Commission on the Prison and Reformatory System of Ontario captured the concerns of penal administrators over the last two decades of the century. The commission recommended that people who were sick, elderly, poor, and insane be removed from the jails and placed in county houses of refuge and asylums, and that inebriates be sent to industrial reformatories. These moves, the commissioners estimated, would free up 50 per cent of the space in the jails so that individuals awaiting trial could be safely housed and minor offenders could be kept there for short-term punishment.[43] However, these changes had not been made in the Kenora and Owen Sound Jails by 1931, the end of the period under study.

The term 'reform' was popular before 1900, but its meaning changed in the twentieth century. In the earlier period, reform in the Ontario penal institutions had a religious and moral connotation and was applied to the individual. After 1900, the idea of reform took on a social meaning. The idea grew that reform should be scientific and based on rational thought. There was still an emphasis on morals, but morals could be formed (or reformed, in the case of inmates) through education and vocational training.

Religious and secular reformers shared the belief that social and moral reform were inseparable: 'The regeneration of the individual through social purity went hand in hand with science.'[44] Clergymen and charity workers joined forces. They believed that the church had a significant role to play in distributing material resources more equitably, and that this could be done through scientific philanthropy and sociology.[45]

Medicine was the link between personal regeneration and scientific urban reform. When doctors spoke of immorality, their professional status gave them scientific authority. By the turn of the century doctors claimed jurisdiction over morality issues, and particularly over sexuality. Venereal diseases, they claimed, were only a symptom of a graver social disorder.[46] Dr Margaret Patterson, the first magistrate of the Women's Court in Toronto, was the embodiment of the synthesis of social reform morality and science. Combining law and order with medicine and religion, she proposed the concept of the 'moral hospital'. The moral hospital was to be a combination of a rescue home and a modern lay hospital, but with the coercive force of a prison. Moral hospitals were required to deal with those criminals who were 'naturally vicious.'[47] Over the next thirty years, Mercer Reformatory, with its increasing medicalization of women's criminality, came closer to reflecting the ideal of the moral hospital.

The synthesis of science, morality, evangelism, and sociology was a powerful ideological system. The doctor, who already had the image of a learned scientist, a charity worker, and a reformer, played an important role both as a symbol and as a practitioner of reform.[48] The institutional-ization and medicalization of sexual and moral offenders were seen as cures for rampant immorality. Penal reformers supported a scientific approach to reformation and believed that institutionalization was the most efficient and effective means of achieving it. Applying the medical model, they argued that female offenders should be treated in reforma-tories in the same way that the sick were treated in hospitals and the insane in asylums.

Treatment was only for the reformable women, however. The large numbers of women incarcerated at Mercer in the years from 1899 to 1917 on drunk and disorderly charges were not considered to be reformable. About 23 per cent of the women at Mercer during this era had been charged with drunk and disorderly conduct; 26 per cent had been charged with vagrancy, 27 per cent with prostitution, and 14 per cent with theft.

The average sentence was shorter during this period (246 days), as was the actual time served (205 days) because of the large number of six-month sentences for drunk and disorderly conduct. The women were also slightly older (30 years of age) and were more likely to be married or widowed than in the previous era. The number of Roman Catholics incar-cerated at the reformatory increased to 36 per cent. Among those women labelled as habitual drunks, and who were dismissed by the Mercer staff as non-reformable, many were older, married, or widowed, Irish, and Roman Catholic.

Although the percentage of women charged with prostitution in this era was only slightly lower than the percentage in the previous period, very few (2 per cent) were listed as prostitutes (in comparison with 16 per cent in the previous era). Most of the women were labelled as servants, and many others were listed as 'non-productive.'[49] Since the introduction of the federal system of tickets of leave in 1899, 12 per cent of the women had been released on parole, a change from the previous era when most of the women served their full sentences at Mercer.

Multiple regression analyses for this era indicated that the women who received longer sentences were younger, lived in smaller centres (not in Toronto), and had been given a variable sentence (rather than a set sentence).[50] Women who served the longest time at Mercer were those who lived in smaller centres, had not been given the option of a fine, and had been given a variable, indefinite, or indeterminate sentence. The indefinite or indeterminate sentence allowed the Mercer staff to control the release time of the incarcerated women.

This period of progressivism (1899–1917) combined scientific rationality with moral reform and religious zeal. Religion, medicine, and secular organizations joined together in the cause of social purity. The Methodists and Presbyterians collaborated with the state to pass the Lord's Day legislation. They also lobbied the federal government to raise the age of consent, ban liquor, criminalize adultery, pass tougher obscenity legislation, and provide better care for criminals.[51]

Organizations such as the Women's Christian Temperance Union and the Salvation Army engaged in 'social purity' work in the community. The Women's Christian Temperance Union advocated moral education for children and upheld women's mission as 'mother of the race.'[52] The WCTU confined its work to other women of the same race and religion. This suggests that its members were interested in reforming women who were most like themselves, who may have fallen from their pedestal but were redeemable. These included white, Protestant, temperate women living in smaller communities, who needed some assistance and rehabilitation. These were the same candidates the staff at Mercer were hoping to attract for their good works programs. The WCTU was not directly involved in visitations or reform programs at Mercer, but the platform and its followers helped to set the stage for devising the model of the perfect woman – the one whom the reformable inmates at Mercer were expected to emulate.[53]

The Salvation Army rather than the WCTU developed contacts with criminals, prostitutes, and alcoholics. The Army's style, suggests Valverde, was attractive to members of the working class, and perhaps to the women incarcerated at Mercer. The Salvation Army confronted the real and pressing problems of the poor, such as domestic violence, drinking, unemployment, and crime. The Army was also authoritarian, a fact that undoubtedly appealed to the administrators at Mercer.

Evidence from the annual reports during the era from 1899 to 1917 indicates that the principles of scientific rationality were trickling into the penal philosophy of the time. Provincial Inspector W.R. Bruce Smith, in his annual report for 1905, discussed his version of the new penal philosophy. At this time there were 42 jails and 27 lock-ups in Ontario and an increase of about 800 committals over the previous year, mostly for drunkenness, disorderly conduct, and vagrancy.[54] Inspector Smith compared the correctional system to a corporation concerned with demonstrating financial success; he advocated a review and revision of the whole system to make it more effective and efficient. Smith argued that there was more to criminal behaviour than free will. 'The social environment was the culture medium of criminality. If there were no society, and no family, vice and crime could not exist.'[55] Societies, being responsible for their own criminals, must reform themselves rather than their victims; criminals were products of heredity and environment and were best helped by early intervention.

Applying this philosophy to the jailing of inebriates and the insane, Smith advocated a probationary system similar to the one used in Massachussetts. The 'rounders,' the chronic drunks 'with every organ of their bodies enfeebled and deranged from chronic alcoholic poisoning,' needed to be 'protected from themselves.' 'Their pitiable condition would be recognized and provided for, not by a prison cell, but by the establishment of an Industrial Home or farm.'[56]

Regarding the jailing of the insane, Smith called for a limitation on the length of time an insane person could be remanded to jail before being sent to an asylum, and for the abolition of the system of admission to asylums by warrant process.[56] In 1906 the law was changed: magistrates required evidence of insanity, and individuals had to be certified as dangerous before they could be sent to jail. The insane could be sent directly to the asylum without being first committed to jail.[58]

By 1906 Inspector Smith advocated the use of the indefinite and indeterminate sentence in Ontario in conjunction with probation and parole,[59] the cornerstones of reformist penal philosophy and manifestations of the liberal welfare system. Smith argued that those prisoners who showed a criminal tendency should be kept until they were reformed. The habitual offender who failed to heed warnings and take advice should be given an indeterminate or indefinite sentence. Smith believed that habitual offenders used short committals to recuperate and then returned, refreshed, to their former bad lives.[60]

Indeterminate sentences were based on the principle that the individual offender, not the crime, determined the length of detention. This suggested a need for careful analysis of the person's physical, mental, and moral status as well as a search for any 'natural depravity.' The purpose of the indeterminate sentence was to regenerate and resocialize the criminal to conventional society and prepare him or her for probation and parole. Treatment in prison should 'break down and eradicate the vicious and criminal traits of his character and build up and strengthen the best elements of his nature.'[61]

In 1917 prisoners at Mercer serving indeterminate sentences were granted the right to parole and the right to earn remission of a portion of their sentences – up to five days for every month during which they were 'exemplary in behaviour, industry and faithfulness' and did not violate prison rules. Further, a 'small gratuity' could be paid for worthy service and good conduct.[62]

Meanwhile, in the Owen Sound and Kenora Jails, rational scientific thought was slow to affect the incarceration experiences of the women. During this era (1899 to 1917) women were incarcerated for vagrancy (19 per cent), prostitution (24 per cent), lunacy (26 per cent), and theft (6 per cent). Women held as lunatics spent the longest periods in the jails. Most were eventually transferred to the insane asylums in Toronto and London. Multiple regression analyses showed that women committed for lunacy, or charged with prostitution, vagrancy, and other offences received significantly longer sentences than women charged with drunk and disorderly conduct. Vagrancy charges were also indicative of longer times served in the jails. The jails were still being used as poorhouses and hospitals at this time. Presumably there was no other place to send women charged with vagrancy.

Most (74 per cent) of the women incarcerated in the jails from 1898 to 1917 were born in Canada. In contrast to earlier periods, very few of the incarcerated women had been born in Ireland. About 13 per cent of the women were black and 7 per cent were native. Most of the women were employed in domestic and personal service occupations. Few were agricultural labourers.

Post-War: Heredity, Environment, Morality, and Disease, 1918–31

The post-war period brought a change in penal philosophy in Ontario. The application of rational thinking and scientific methods to the study of crime had a significant effect on the way in which administrators interpreted criminal behaviour. Influenced by such writers as Lombroso and Ferri, the scientific study of crime focused on the effect of heredity and certain physical characteristics on criminal behaviour. But philosophers and practitioners did not abandon the belief that moral deficiencies were related to criminal behaviour and that moral training and education were an integral part of punishment and reform.

By 1923 Inspector W.W. Dunlop advocated both punishment and reform, claiming that each was useful in dealing with different types of criminals. He believed that there were three causes of crime: 'Heredity, Environment, and a Fundamental Tendency to revert to a lower stage in moral development, in which man resolves to do evil in spite of the prohibitions of God, human government, and his own conscience.'[63] Inspector Dunlop thought that a bad inheritance (lack of moral sense) and a bad environment (bad homes, neighbourhood, friends) probably caused most crime. While a bad inheritance might explain drunkenness, vice, and sexual crimes, a bad environment could explain the higher incidence of crime in overcrowded areas – as, for instance, in Toronto, which had one-fifth of the population of Ontario but two-fifths of the crime. The fundamental tendency to crime or original sin might explain the incorrigible child, who was 'an unnatural creature' and 'absolutely useless', and whom 'nobody wants' (not even his parents).[64]

Dunlop thought that jails were meant to punish and deter criminals. He saw the common jails as valuable to society because they kept 2,500 criminals off the street, thus protecting people and property from harm. M.M. Robbins, a deputy provincial secretary in 1927, agreed with Dunlop's views, preferring the hard line of punishment to reform methods, particularly in dealing with confirmed criminals. He thought that most repeat offenders were confirmed criminals. The confirmed criminal was lawless and anti-social and 'resisted all appeals to live a better life.' He was a 'disturbing element in the community and a constant menace to public peace and safety.' He was dishonest. He begged, stole, lied, 'ravished women,' and killed others 'without the slightest feeling of remorse.' He was not deterred 'from committing a crime by fear of any penalty.'[65]

Confirmed criminals belonged in jail, argued Robbins, where punishment was paramount. He warned against stressing the humanitarian side of reformatories, because this would reduce 'the thought of punishment in the mind of the inmate.' The thought of punishment was supreme in the jail; the thought of reform was only a secondary consideration. Robbins did not believe it was possible to combine reform and punishment. He was concerned about the influence of confirmed criminals on first offenders and thought the two should be strictly segregated. In Robbins's view, only first offenders should be sent to provincial reformatories and industrial farms.

This theme of punishment was strong in official discussions of the county jails and less apparent in discussions of the Mercer Reformatory. The theme was also stronger in discussions of male criminality than in discussions of female criminality. Punishment was still an important part of penal philosophy in 1931, but the classical focus on individual responsibility had shifted. Now there was talk of the physical and social causes of criminal behaviour, over which the individual had limited control, and increased discussion of the role of heredity.

C.F. Neelands, the deputy provincial secretary in 1931, preferred treatment to punishment as a long-term solution to criminal behaviour, particularly for young men and women. He thought that younger people were being committed to penal institutions than in previous years, and that they were more likely to be first offenders. They were the reformable type of offender. Neelands believed that this group needed treatment, not punishment, and that treatment should start in the home, at school, and in church.[66]

Neelands's views, as opposed to Dunlop's and Robbins's, were those favoured by the staff at Andrew Mercer. The staff considered the type of offender who was sent to Mercer to be in need of treatment rather than punishment. Superintendent O'Sullivan, reporting in 1919, claimed that almost all of the admissions for that year were sex offenders. Further, the women were younger,[67] and 96 per cent of them were first offenders. The superintendent was confident that these younger women could be trained more successfully than the habitual drunks they had received in the previous era.[68]

In the final period of this research, 1918–1931, the treatment and medicalization of women's criminality blossomed as never before. Reformable women needed longer incarceration periods, according to the superintendents, staff, and inspectors. The courts obliged by sending women to Mercer for longer terms. In the era from 1918 to 1931 the average sentence was 492 days, twice as long as the average sentence in the previous era; the average time served was 348 days, almost 100 days longer. Only 53 per cent of the sentences given to the women were set sentences; 18 per cent of the women received indefinite or indeterminate sentences, and 29 per cent received variable sentences.

Police discretion affected the incarceration rates at Mercer and in the jails as broader societal and organizational factors influenced who was arrested and on what charges. In the nineteenth century, as upholders of public morality, urban police arrested drunks, prostitutes, and delinquent youth. These groups were targeted for two principal reasons. First, crimes of vice were believed to lead to more serious offences. Second, arrest was used as a form of class control. The police were, in a phrase, 'domestic missionaries' who supported moral reform agencies in cleaning up the city and spreading middle-class values of work, religion, and respectability. Police vigilance was aimed at the marginal urban poor (often Irish immigrants) and at supervising working-class recreations.[69]

By the twentieth century, the types of offences for which women were incarcerated had changed dramatically. Drunk and disorderly charges dropped from 23 per cent during the era from 1899 to 1917 to 2 per cent during the era from 1918 to 1931, and prostitution charges dropped from 27 per cent to 15 per cent. More women (41 per cent) were incarcerated on vagrancy charges than in the previous era (26 per cent). However, the use of two relatively new charges – liquor offences and breaches of the Venereal Diseases Act – reflected a changing focus in Mercer's program. From 1918 to 1931, 4 per cent of the women were incarcerated for liquor offenses and 5 per cent for venereal disease.

The women at Mercer during this final era were younger, averaging 25 years of age. More of the women were born in Canada (73 per cent) than in previous eras. Women born in Ireland now made up only 1 per cent of the reformatory population, about the same number as those born in Poland, Russia, and Italy. The women were less likely to have been labelled as intemperate than in previous eras, and were more literate. A larger proportion of women were listed as having no occupation or as housewives than in previous eras,[70] but women were still most likely to be engaged in domestic and personal work. Fifty per cent of the women were single, about 10 per cent more than in previous eras, and there was a decrease in the percentage of widowed women. There was also a significant decrease in the percentage of women from Toronto as more women from smaller cities and towns in Ontario were sent to Mercer. Eighty-eight per cent of the women were first offenders.

The multiple regression analyses for this era showed that the type of offence for which the women were incarcerated had little effect on the length of sentence they received.[71] Women who were younger, who were given indefinite sentences, or who worked as domestics received the longest sentences. Women who were older, married, born in non-English-speaking countries, and worked as prostitutes served the shortest time. Young women who worked as domestics were prime candidates for Mercer. They were considered the most malleable and closest to the ideal domestic workers which the staff at Mercer hoped to create. Longer indefinite sentences provided the staff with the best opportunities to reform the young women. The older married women, and those born in foreign countries, were less 'suitable' candidates for the institution's reform efforts. The administrators and staff at Mercer wanted women who were most like the middle-class ideal of femininity.

The medicalization of women's criminality reached its peak at Mercer with the incarceration of women for venereal disease. During this era, 51 per cent of the women (362 cases) were labelled as having some form of venereal disease. Mercer had been designated by the lieutenant-governor of Ontario as one of the public institutions to be used for the treatment of venereal disease. Under the Venereal Disease Act women could be held, examined, treated, and detained in the institution.[72]

The surgeon was a revered treatment specialist. Venereal disease was a physical sign of women's sexual immorality and a focal point for the surgeon's medical treatment. Women's sexual morality was thought to be tied to their physical sexuality, and both were used as indicators of their chances for reform. Mercer offered the opportunity for women to be purified medically and spiritually and then released as reformed women.

Surgeons at the Mercer were supported in their practice by the ideology of the Toronto Psychiatric Clinic and the Canadian National Committee for Mental Hygiene (CNCMH). Dr Charles K. Clarke, the director of the clinic and a prominent leader in the CNCMH, along with his colleague, Dr Clarence Hincks, established cooperative links with correctional and community agencies in Toronto.[73] These leading psychiatrists asserted that mental defects were the root cause of crime and delinquency; crime was the result of an inherited organic condition whose physical symptoms were visible to the trained psychiatric eye. The term 'feeble-minded,' used before the Great War with reference to prostitution, vagrancy, and poverty, was expanded. After 1918 'feeble-mindedness' was used to explain social disorder, moral contamination, unmarried motherhood, and the destruction of white, middle-class British lifestyles.

The intervention of the state apparatus in women's sexuality and the imposition of scientific rational methods in the reformatory was a manifestation of the ideals of the developing liberal welfare state in Ontario. The large number of cases of women incarcerated with venereal disease again illustrates the characteristics of this new welfare state: determinism, inequality, non-culpability, and rehabilitation.[74] These women, whose criminality was determined by their biology and sexuality and who operated in a separate and unequal sphere, were deemed not to be responsible for their behaviour. Rather, they were victims of miserable social conditions and their sexuality. Treatment in the reform program at Mercer could rehabilitate them if they were the right kind of women.

Such a liberal welfare agenda was not apparent in the jails. Women were given shorter sentences and served less time in the jails during the era from 1918 to 1931 than in any previous era. The average sentence was 153 days and the average time served was 21 days. More women (11 per cent) were released with fines than in earlier periods.[75] Significant numbers (39 per cent) of women were still being released by order of the judge,[76] 19 per cent were transferred to other penal institutions, and 8 per cent were transferred to an asylum.[77]

While it is difficult to exclude the possibility of changes in police charging practices, the jail appears to have served as a public order holding tank rather than a moral reformatory in this period. In Owen Sound and Kenora, from 1918 to 1931, two-thirds of the women were jailed on public order charges, while only 10 per cent were held for offences against public morals. Three per cent of the women were charged with prostitution, 28 per cent with vagrancy, 5 per cent with drunk and disorderly conduct, and 27 per cent with liquor offences. Most of the liquor offences were violations of the Temperance Act.

The women in the jails in this post-war era averaged 28 years of age. Sixty-three per cent of the women were born in Canada, while the others came from a wider range of countries than in previous eras. Few of the women were born in Ireland or Great Britain. There were few minority women in the jails – only 6 per cent were natives and 1 per cent were blacks. Surprisingly, considering the large number of liquor law offences, only 3 per cent of the women were described as intemperate. Perhaps because of the prohibition era in Ontario, few of the women admitted to drinking. The largest occupational category given was housewife (31 per cent) and the second largest was domestic and personal (20 per cent); 35 per cent of the cases had no occupation listed. The women were more likely to have lived in the main towns of Kenora and Owen Sound than in surrounding rural areas, a change from previous years.

Conclusion

The reform activity in women's prisons in Ontario varied over time and reflected the changing influence of contemporary philosophies and practices. As Ontario penal reform policies moved away from the regulation of women through moralization, legal prohibition and punishment and began to employ strategies of normalization and social control, marginal women were brought into line using positive techniques of intervention. These positive techniques were apparent in the Mercer Reformatory, but not in the two local jails. They resulted in the incarceration of women for longer periods of time and the use of indefinite, indeterminate, and variable sentences.

The inspectors and superintendents at Mercer treated the inmates paternalistically. They identified certain women as requiring intervention, and set up a reform program that combined basic education, religious, moral, and domestic training and taught obedience, servility, and the importance of knowing one's place in society. The plan was to bring potential candidates for reform into the institution and transform them into servile domestics and subservient wives. Preferred candidates were those women who met the ideals of middle-class reformers as typified by the members of the Women's Christian Temperance Union.

Specifically, the ideal inmates were young, single, white women who were Protestant, Canadian-born, literate, and temperate, and who had some experience in domestic and personal service. The inmates' reform was directed by specialists at Mercer, including the surgeon, ministers, teachers, matrons, and the early social workers from community agencies such as the Prisoners Aid Society and the Salvation Army. The specialists embraced the ideals of rational thought and the scientific method in developing a treatment program based on the medical model. As the focus shifted away from individual responsibility to an ideology that stressed the physical and social causes of criminal behaviour, criminal women were viewed as dependent, non-culpable, unequal, and deserving of a special rehabilitation program. This ideology culminated in the medicalization of women's criminality in the last era studied (1918–1931) and the incarceration of women, one-half of whom had venereal disease.

The philosophies and practices at Mercer were similar to those in American reformatories described by Estelle Freedman and Nicole Hahn Rafter. Criminal women were treated as fallen women who were victims of social problems, driven to crime.[78] However, women at Mercer experienced incarceration differently from those imprisoned in penitentiaries and reformatories in the United States. At Mercer the sentences and length of time served grew longer over time, partly as a consequence of the introduction of the indeterminate sentence. In contrast, Rafter reports that in the United States the switch to indeterminate sentencing did not increase the time served in penal institutions.[79] However, similar types of women were incarcerated in both countries. The tendency to incarcerate young, working-class, single women for public order offences in reformatories in Ontario and the United States has been reported by Estelle Freedman, Nicole Rafter, and Carolyn Strange. Further, all three scholars have pointed to the layers of social controls and domestication ingrained in reformatory programs. Social controls were both sexual and vocational, and the two were intertwined.[80]

The treatment of women at Mercer contrasted with women's experiences in the Ontario jails. The jails, still operating as laissez-faire institutions, embodied the principles of legal regulation, prohibition, and punishment. Jail policies and practices focused, in principle though not in practice, on classification, hard labour, strict discipline, and religious observance. But women incarcerated for vagrancy and lunacy were indiscriminately housed in the jails with women (and men) charged with theft, prostitution, drunk and disorderly conduct, assault, murder, and other offences. Reform ideals of the separation of dependents and deviants, with the care of dependents to be placed in the hands of family, friends, churches, and communities, had been lost.

NOTES

1 Carolyn Strange, 'The Velvet Glove: Maternalistic Reform at the Andrew Mercer Ontario Reformatory for Females 1874–1927,' MA thesis, University of Ottawa (1983).
2 I am grateful to Professor Peter Oliver for providing this information.
3 The data collected from Mercer begins with the opening of the reformatory in the summer of 1880. The sample is in excess of 20 per cent of all cases in the register. It is a systematic sample stratified by year.
4 Because the Owen Sound registers dated from the late 1850s, cases from these early years have been included in some of the analyses. All women in the registers were included in the sample.
5 The jail registers from Kenora dated from 1883. All women in the registers were included in the sample. Unfortunately, one of the Kenora Jail registers was found to be missing late in the data collection process, so the number of cases from this institution is disappointingly small.
6 The types of sentences included set sentences (for example, 18 months), variable sentences (for example, 18 months to 24 months), and indefinite and indeterminate sentences (which usually had no time given).
7 'Reasons for release' included time expired, transferred to an asylum or other non-penal institution, transferred to another penal institution, fine paid, released by the judge or court order, and died in custody.
8 Dorothy Chunn, *From Punishment to Doing Good: Family Courts and Socialized Justice in Ontario 1880–1940* (Toronto: The University of Toronto Press 1992), at 6–7.
9 Ibid., at 17.
10 Ibid., at 18.
11 Ibid., at 19.
12 Ibid., at 19–21.
13 Ibid., at 21.
14 Ibid., at 19.
15 Nicole Hahn Rafter, *Partial Justice: Women in State Prisons 1800–1935* (New

Brunswick: Transaction Publishers 1990); Estelle Freedman, *Their Sisters' Keepers* (Ann Arbor: University of Michigan Press 1981); Strange, supra note 1.

16 Richard Splane, *Social Welfare in Ontario 1791–1893* (Toronto: University of Toronto Press 1965).

17 Freedman, supra note 15.

18 Ibid.

19 Alexandra Dundas Todd, 'Women's Bodies as Diseased and Deviant: Historical and Contemporary Issues' (1983), 5 *Research in Law, Deviance and Social Control*, 83–95.

20 Rafter, supra note 15.

21 Freedman, ibid., at 54.

22 Rafter, supra note 15.

23 See Elizabeth Lunbeck, ' "A New Generation of Women'': Progressive Psychiatrists and the Hypersexual Female' (1987), 13 *Feminist Studies*, 513–43.

24 A.M. Kirkpatrick, 'Jails in Historical Perspective' (1964), 6 *Canadian Journal of Corrections*, 405–15.

25 W.A. Calder, 'Convict Life in Canadian Federal Penitentiaries 1867–1900,' in *Crime and Criminal Justice in Europe and Canada*, ed. L. Knafla (Waterloo: Wilfrid Laurier University 1981), 298.

26 Kirkpatrick, supra note 24, at 406.

27 Calder, supra note 25, at 298. After 1867 Ontario appointed a single inspector, John Langmuir, who served from 1867 to 1882: *Dictionary of Canadian Biography*, vol. 12, 1125–6.

28 Kirkpatrick, supra note 24, at 406.

29 John M. Beattie, *Attitudes Towards Crime and Punishment in Upper Canada, 1830–1850: A Documentary Study* (Toronto: University of Toronto Centre of Criminology 1977).

30 I have used pseudonyms to protect the privacy of the inmates' descendants.

31 Questions arise as to how so many women labelled as sane were incarcerated. Possibly they were found guilty of another charge but were insane, or perhaps they were convicted of lesser crimes and happened to be mentally ill, but I suspect that the women were committed for insanity. There is no evidence from the registers to support other explanations; there is no mention of other offences, and the 'comments' sections only contain notes on the women's mental health or behaviour. Further, the Owen Sound Jail was frequently chastised in the annual reports for its use of the jail as an asylum.

32 See Rafter, supra note 15, and Freedman, ibid.

33 Strange, supra note 1, 86.

34 Strange, supra note 1, at 84.

35 'Annual Report of the Inspector of Prisons and Asylums' of 1883, published in *Ontario Sessional Papers*, 1984 (hereinafter cited as 'Annual Report').
36 'Annual Report,' 1884.
37 'Annual Report,' 1883.
38 Some of the women discharged from Mercer stayed at the Haven and Prison Gate Mission Home. It was an asylum for fallen women and girls that incorporated religious instruction with domestic labour.
39 Ann Louise Shapiro, 'Disordered Bodies – Disorderly Acts: Medical Discourse and the Female Criminal in Nineteenth Century Paris' (1989), 4 *Genders*, 69–86.
40 Lunbeck, supra note 23.
41 'Annual Report,' 1888.
42 Ibid.
43 Splane, supra note 16.
44 Mariana Valverde, *The Age of Light, Soap, and Water: Moral Reform in English Canada 1885–1925* (Toronto: McClelland and Stewart 1991), 44–45.
45 Ibid., at 45.
46 Ibid., at 42.
47 Ibid., at 47–8.
48 Ibid., at 49.
49 'Non-productive' is the term used in the census data to describe women who had no occupation or who were housewives, spinsters, etc., or worked in their own homes.
50 Separate multiple regression analyses were run for time served and length of sentence for each of the eras. Groups of variables were entered in three blocks. The first block was the offences charged. Committals for lunacy and charges of prostitution, vagrancy, and other offenses resulted in significantly longer sentences than charges of drunk and disorderly conduct (adjusted $r^2.147$). The second block was the characteristics of the women. Women who were widowed received significantly shorter sentences than single women (adjusted $r^2.456$). The third block was the court variables. None of the court variables was significant (but the adjusted r^2 for the final model was .472). In the equations for time served, vagrancy was the only significant variable (adjusted $r^2.133$).
51 Valverde, supra note 44, at 52–8.
52 Ibid., at 60–1.
53 Ibid.
54 'Annual Report,' 1905, at 6.
55 Ibid., at 10.

56 Ibid.
57 Ibid., at 11.
58 'Annual Report,' 1906, at 14–15.
59 Referring to the enactment of a probation law in Great Britain, Smith quoted from the parliamentary address: 'Every human born is a fresh experiment from God, placed here on probation to work out his own destiny under the supervision of the Supreme Probation Officer of the universe.' This is an excellent example of a philosophy that blended science and religion in prison reform.
60 'Annual Report,' 1906, at 13.
61 'Annual Report,' 1907, at 13–14.
62 'Annual Report,' 1917, at 50.
63 'Annual Report,' 1923, at 19.
64 'Annual Report,' 1923, at 19–20.
65 'Annual Report,' 1927, at 3.
66 'Annual Report,' 1919, at 48.
67 Thirty-six per cent were under 20 and another 50 per cent were between 20 and 30.
68 'Annual Report,' 1919, at 48.
69 See Nicholas Rogers, 'Serving Toronto the Good: The Development of the City Police Force, 1834–1884,' in *Forging a Consensus: Historical Essays on Toronto*, ed. Victor Russell (Toronto: University of Toronto Press 1984); and Helen Boritch, 'Conflict, Compromise and Administrative Convenience: The Police Organization in Nineteenth-Century Toronto' (1988), 3 *Canadian Journal of Law and Society*, 141–73.
70 The word 'housework' appeared for the first time in this era.
71 Women charged with prostitution received significantly longer sentences than women charged with drunk and disorderly conduct (adjusted r^2 .102). Women listed as prostitutes also received longer sentences than women with no occupation (adjusted r^2 .134). None of the court variables was significant, but the final adjusted r^2 was .166. For time served, charges of prostitution and recidivism were related to a longer stay, but working as a prostitute was related to a shorter stay (adjusted r^2 .328). None of the court variables was significant, but the final adjusted r^2 was .347.
72 Strange, supra note 1.
73 See Jennifer Stephen, 'The "Incorrigible," the "Bad," and the "Immoral": Toronto "Factory Girls" and the Work of the Toronto Psychiatric Clinic,' elsewhere in this volume.
74 Chunn, supra note 8.

75 Most of the releases by fine were from the Kenora Jail.
76 This practice was most common in Owen Sound.
77 Fewer lunatics were incarcerated during this period.
78 Freedman, supra note 15.
79 Rafter, ibid.
80 Ibid.

14 'Just Plain Everyday Housekeeping on a Grand Scale': Feminists, Family Courts, and the Welfare State in British Columbia, 1928–1945

DOROTHY E. CHUNN

Gendering the Welfare State: An Overview

Since the 1970s the growing perception that welfare states are in moral, legal, fiscal, and social crisis has generated extensive research and writing on the origins of those states in liberal democracies, including Canada.[1] The literature reflects a general, though not total, agreement that the foundations of welfare states were laid during a period extending roughly from the 1880s to the 1940s, and that what took place was a fundamental reordering of western societies on two levels. First, in the sphere of production or the marketplace, the welfare state entailed the implementation of non-means-tested social security schemes, such as unemployment and health insurance, old age pensions, 'workmen's' compensation, which operated on the principle of universality for those who met eligibility criteria that were linked to participation in the paid workforce. Second, in the sphere of reproduction or the family, the welfare state was characterized by the development of legislation, policies, and programs governing child and family welfare, ostensibly universal in scope, which in practice were used primarily to regulate a select marginal segment of the working and dependent poor.[2] The emergent emphasis on social security at the level of production was matched by a growing focus on social work and eugenics in the realm of reproduction. At both levels of 'the social,'[3] state bureaucracies and regulatory structures were created to oversee and administer the new social welfare initiatives.

In short, the welfare state was a form of capitalist social organization and discipline that was qualitatively different from that of the nineteenth-century laissez-faire state.[4] The rigid ideological and practical distinctions between public and private and criminal and civil spheres that exemplified the classical liberal state were increasingly masked in the corporate liberal state as class control and repressive justice were transformed into social control and socialized justice.[5] Universal suffrage and citizenship rather than the discipline of the marketplace constituted the bases for social control.[6] Similarly, socialized justice emphasized rehabilitation and normalization rather than punishment and moralization in the quest to ensure that the deviant would be restored to good citizenship.[7]

Both social control and socialized justice represented governance through the nuclear family,[8] that reformers increasingly identified as the primary vehicle for inculcating and reinforcing dominant conceptions of masculinity and femininity across the entire population. Ultimately, the consensus that presumably characterized the relations among the members of individual families would exist on a societal level.[9] And, despite periods of intense class conflict, one of the most notable developments during the transformation of laissez-faire states into welfare states, particularly in Canada and the United States, was the construction of a liberal politics that rested on almost universal acceptance of bourgeois standards governing production and reproduction by the majority of the white middle- and working-class population. By the 1940s, then, most families were like autonomous, private 'havens,'[10] free from overt state regulation. Only those families that could not or would not comply with the norms governing social relations became the targets of official interventions by the agents of socialized justice.

The transformation of nineteenth-century welfare and legal structures into a system of socialized legal coercion organized around principles of social casework has been well documented in Canada and other jurisdictions.[11] At the same time, much of the existing literature is gender-blind: it does not examine the specific contribution of women, both feminist and non-feminist, to this development. Similarly, while there is a wealth of historical research on Canadian women reformers who individually or collectively pushed for the implementation of social legislation and socialized mechanisms for its enforcement,[12] theoretical work on the gendered nature of the welfare state is much less extensive. None the less, some of the existing literature clearly documents how the gender-based character of the welfare state emerged historically, with social security measures that were tied to paid employment and based on right being much more relevant to men and social welfare measures that were related to economic dependency and premised on paternalism being much more applicable to women.[13]

A few feminists and other researchers have also challenged the idea that the welfare state was created by men and foisted upon women by revealing how women were actively involved in constructing it as reformers, workers, and clients, particularly at the level of reproduction and socialized justice. Thus, women frequently initiated or joined campaigns for measures that ultimately transformed existing sociolegal structures that governed the deviant and dependent, or produced new ones; they peopled these welfare structures as volunteer personnel and, increasingly, as professionals; and they used them for their own purposes.[14]

In this paper I examine how feminists helped consolidate the sociolegal foundations of a gendered welfare state in British Columbia and Canada during the post-suffrage era from 1917 to 1945. There, as in other jurisdictions,[15] feminist women played a major role in promoting the development of social work and, to a lesser extent, eugenics among the poor. After all, the activities associated with sustaining and strengthening the reproductive or private sphere of the family were the ticket that allowed middle-class women – single or married, feminist or non-feminist – to participate in the public realm. Moreover, a core concern with the well-being of women and children and 'the family' generated a consensus among feminists and between feminists and non-feminists on welfare issues that frequently cut across political and religious lines.[16]

This gender collaboration was particularly visible in British Columbia during the post-suffrage era because the province boasted an unusual number of women in public life – politicians, judges, and other officials. Feminists were key players in campaigns to obtain both legislation that enshrined the hegemonic conception of femininity (and masculinity) associated with the nuclear family and heterosexual marriage (such as mothers' pensions, minimum wage and sterilization) and specialized mechanisms to administer these social laws (such as administrative boards and socialized courts).[17] In this paper I focus on the latter development, with specific reference to family courts. I present a preliminary analysis of why and how feminist women with loyalties and affiliations to three different political parties – Liberal, Conservative, and the social democratic Co-operative Commonwealth Federation (CCF) – supported and worked for the establishment of family courts in British Columbia, particularly during the period from 1928 to the opening of the Vancouver Family Court in 1945. The first section of the paper documents the shared assumptions and beliefs that were reflected in their collective view of the domestic relations court as a technocratic innovation for enforcing the 'white life for two' among marginal families.[18] The second part traces their formal

Dorothy E. Chunn

and informal political efforts to mobilize others, and especially other women, on this issue. The final part attempts to assess the relative importance of gender, race, and class in explaining the female consensus on the need for family courts that cut across political differences among women.

Social Work through Family Courts:
The Technocratic Fix

In most liberal democracies, the transformation of the sociolegal structures governing the underclasses during the transformation of laissez-faire states into welfare states was first evident with the establishment of separate, private justice systems for neglected, dependent, and delinquent children organized around juvenile courts and probation. Subsequently, similar socialized mechanisms for handling domestic problems between husbands and wives were created, which, in the United States and Canada, took the form of family courts. The latter signalled a shift in social work focus from children and the individual adults affecting them to the relationships among all the members of the nuclear family unit, and represented the increasing ascendancy of socialized justice, both ideologically and practically. Although the development of family courts in Canada mirrored the relatively slow and piecemeal construction of the Canadian welfare state, by the 1920s reformers in a number of cities were articulating demands for expanding the jurisdiction of juvenile courts to cover all domestic matters. Success came in 1929, when the first Canadian family court was proclaimed in Toronto.[19]

Fourteen years later British Columbia became the second province to adopt enabling legislation for the establishment of domestic relations courts, and the Vancouver Family Court finally began operations in February 1945 as the Second World War was drawing to a close.[20] However, as one editorial writer observed, there had been 'a persistent although not very vocal demand' for the creation of 'a proper family court' in the city for many years.[21] Moreover, in British Columbia, in contrast to Ontario, women were a primary source of this demand, including two feminists who were appointed to official positions by post-suffrage Liberal governments: Helen Gregory MacGill became British Columbia's first woman Juvenile Court judge and justice of the peace in 1917 at Vancouver; a decade later, Laura Jamieson succeeded her deceased husband on the Bench in Burnaby, thereby becoming the province's second female Juvenile Court judge. Even after men became the chief coordinators and decision-makers in the organized campaign for family courts during the early 1940s, women in public life continued to proselytize and mobilize support for this issue. Laura Jamieson, now a CCF member of the Legislative Assembly, and Tilly Rolston, the first woman Conservative MLA in British Columbia, spoke frequently on the topic of family courts, both inside and outside the House.[22]

As might be expected, given their divergent political affiliations, MacGill, Jamieson, and Rolston each had a somewhat different vision of family courts; yet they shared some basic assumptions and presented similar arguments about why such tribunals were necessary and what they could accomplish. First, the three women seemingly reached the same conclusion about the relationship between the family and social problems: 'normal' families, organized around a monogamous, heterosexual marriage relationship, the sexual division of labour, and the enforced dependency of children, generated conformist behaviour; pathological families – intact nuclear units whose members deviated from the norms governing their respective roles or nuclear units that were fractured by desertion, divorce, or death – bred pathological behaviour. As MacGill observed in 1939, 'the value of the good mother in the home' had become very apparent, since the children of widows and deserted women all too often followed a trajectory of neglect and then delinquency.[23]

Second, MacGill, Jamieson, and Rolston embraced similar explanations for the failure of family members to carry out their respective responsibilities and duties in the nuclear unit and for 'broken' families. They shared a core belief that individual deviance, exemplified by behaviours that flouted the norms governing femininity and masculinity, was usually the result of social pathology rather than personal defects. Thus, they illustrated the growing influence of sociological, and particularly ecological, explanations of crime and delinquency on Canadian reformers during the first half of the twentieth century.

Because she was a Fabian socialist as well as a feminist,[24] Jamieson went further than either MacGill or Rolston in drawing explicit links between 'bad' environments – specifically, poverty and inadequate housing – 'bad' families, and 'bad' behaviour. Speaking before the Legislative Assembly in November 1939, she stated flatly that 'poor homes and uncongenial conditions in the home' caused juvenile delinquency.[25] Two years later, in a provincial election campaign speech, she said that her eleven years of experience as a Juvenile Court judge had stimulated her interest in politics, because she came to realize that child delinquency 'sprang from poverty and lack of home training.'[26]

While they paid less attention to poverty per se, both Helen MacGill and

Tilly Rolston emphasized the importance of a 'good' physical environment in stimulating 'good' behaviour. For example, they were quite aware of the housing and delinquency issue during the early 1940s, when Vancouver was in the throes of an acute wartime housing crisis. As Rolston told delegates to the 1943 conference of the Vancouver Women's School for Citizenship: 'You can't have good families without good homes.'[27]

Not surprisingly, then, the shared assumptions of MacGill, Jamieson, and Rolston about 'the family' and what produced pathological families were reflected in similar ideas for preventing or rehabilitating deviant families. Again, Jamieson took the broadest view of what was required. Ultimately, she said, the problem of 'bad' families 'could only be remedied through political means.'[28] While preventive work was important and ought to be emphasized, 'little headway could be made until slums and poverty-stricken homes were eliminated.'[29] During the 1945 election campaign, Jamieson castigated the coalition government's refusal to do anything about the shortage of housing and nursery schools.[30] Forcing working mothers to leave their children, she said, 'condemns small children to bad housing and forces them to play in the streets,' which in turn means that the government must build new hospitals, mental hospitals, and reformatories 'to shut up those who have become diseased or criminal because of bad housing and lack of training.'[31] In short, there was a need for large-scale social as well as individual reform if structured inequalities that contributed to deviance were to be addressed.

However, the statements and actions of the three feminists also reveal a consensus that 'bad' families constituted a social work problem that was amenable to individualized, technocratic interventions by specially trained non-lawyers. Indeed, this consensus generated their collective support for the establishment of tribunals with more comprehensive jurisdiction over domestic issues than was entrusted to children's courts, both to prevent families from going 'bad' and to repair those that had. Helen MacGill was probably the first feminist activist to publicly promote the idea of family courts. By 1928 she was proposing that juvenile courts, including her own, should receive extended powers to handle matters pertaining to adoption, desertion, and non-support, and children of unmarried parents (but not divorce), as had already been done in some American states.[32] She presented the tried and true arguments of reformers: humaneness, economy, and, especially, effectiveness. As MacGill put it, juvenile courts with expanded powers to deal with all domestic problems would be a vast improvement on the status quo because they were already knowledgeable about delinquency and aware that it was a family rather than an individual problem; and they had the necessary machinery to supervise and carry on the necessary rehabilitative work (such as probation) without additional expense. During the 1930s, MacGill continued to focus on the need to develop domestic relations courts, adding to her arguments the success of the Toronto Family Court.[33]

Tilly Rolston embraced much the same concept of a family court although, in the midst of a world war, her major concern was a very specific one; namely, that such courts would not exercise jurisdiction over divorce, but would act to prevent it. Speaking in the Legislative Assembly, she cited divorce statistics for British Columbia that indicated a large increase from 1918 to 1942, and she lamented the fact that under wartime conditions 'not enough effort is taken to find the cause of domestic troubles which break up many homes each year.' After tracing the history and describing the success of family courts in other jurisdictions, Rolston said that she 'warmly supported' the government proposal to create a British Columbia domestic relations court 'where people can speak and understand one another,' differences can be straightened out, and possible reconciliations effected 'without the glare of publicity attending proceedings in ... [the ordinary police] courts.' The fiscal cost of such a tribunal 'would be light in proportion to the help it would give to a community' by counteracting 'the many family troubles that might be expected to develop through hasty wartime marriages' and 'averting broken homes.'[34]

The CCF was the only political party represented in the Legislative Assembly to draw an explicit link between family courts and the development of a welfare state structure, and to propose that such courts be accorded jurisdiction over divorce. In a 1937 speech to the House, Dorothy Steeves, MLA for North Vancouver, argued for the creation of 'special domestic relations and social welfare courts' that would use psychiatric and other expert advice to deal with divorce and with the victims in 'moral delinquency' cases.[35] Six years later, when the provincial government introduced enabling legislation for the establishment of family courts, Laura Jamieson urged the coalition to link the development of the new tribunals to a more comprehensive restructuring of the province's welfare structures. She argued that the processing of juvenile delinquency and domestic relations cases would be improved if as many as possible could be handled 'by social security department officials rather than ... by legal machinery.' What was required, then, was a ministry of social welfare with a mandate to engage in preventive social work, and with a bureaucracy selected on the basis of qualifications and merit rather than by patronage.[36]

None the less, the CCF recognized that the courts would continue to deal with domestic problems for the foreseeable future, and the party's conceptualization of socialized courts as technocratic mechanisms for 'normalizing' deviant families did not differ radically from that of the Liberals and Conservatives. After her election in 1939, Laura Jamieson frequently drew on her previous experience as a Juvenile Court judge in her speeches to the House about the need for the existing children's courts to adopt a social work rather than a legal approach to the resolution of social problems. It was crucial, she argued, that juvenile court judges and probation personnel have 'social service training instead of merely political influence,' and that juvenile courts focus on 'preventive' and corrective rather than 'punitive work.'[37] Similarly, in a speech supporting the proposed domestic relations court, Jamieson exhorted the government to appoint 'a quiet, sincere, sympathetic man or woman as judge with a full staff of psychiatrists, medical advisers, probation officers and social service workers'; experts who were nonexistent in the province's 'dummy [juvenile] courts.'[38]

To a greater or lesser degree, then, feminists affiliated with all three major political parties in British Columbia during the post-suffrage era used the same rhetoric to articulate the arguments advanced by the advocates of any reform – that it will be a more humane, effective, and economical alternative to the status quo. In this instance the family court was perceived to be a great improvement on the conventional police court as a means of enforcing 'the white life for two' in pathological, or potentially deviant, families among the working and dependent poor, a perception that was increasingly common among non- feminist women as well. The next section of the paper shows how women who espoused very different political philosophies worked collectively and individually to promote the establishment of domestic relations tribunals in the province.

Campaigning for Family Courts

Like their counterparts elsewhere, pre-suffrage women in British Columbia may have lacked voting rights but were none the less actively engaged in political life as members of numerous, autonomous women's organizations such as the Young Women's Christian Association (YWCA), the Federation of Business and Professional Women's Clubs, and, especially, the Councils of Women. The Councils of Women were made up of affiliated groups that represented diverse religious, political, and other interests and operated at the local, provincial, and national levels.

Clubwomen were usually middle-class feminists and non-feminists who opted for non-partisan cooperation to obtain legislation and policies that would benefit women and children, and thereby effectively wielded indirect power. Once female suffrage was attained, the situation did not change dramatically. Contrary to feminist expectations, women failed to enter electoral politics in large numbers, and their main political contribution continued to be channelled through the independent women's groups. During the Second World War, the Vancouver Women's School for Citizenship was added to this collection of organizations. Launched in 1941, the school's purpose was to inform women of all political affiliations about the important issues of the day.[39]

At the same time, opportunities for more direct political action opened up for some women during the post-suffrage era. Each of the three main parties in the province had a formal women's branch – Conservative and Liberal Women of British Columbia and the CCF Women's Council – that engaged in independent political projects and activities to a greater or lesser extent. And more women were elected or appointed to public office in British Columbia between 1917 and 1945 than anywhere else in Canada.[40]

In many cases, of course, the formal and informal political activities of individual women were intertwined. Thus, Helen Gregory MacGill, Tilly Rolston, and Laura Jamieson were not only influential clubwomen but also leading members of the women's branches of the Liberal, Conservative, and CCF parties respectively. In addition, MacGill was still on the bench and both Jamieson and Rolston were elected members of the Legislative Assembly during the Second World War. Although they entered the fray at different times, the three feminists worked in similar ways to generate political support for the establishment of family courts in British Columbia, particularly among women: through the traditional avenue of non-partisan organizations on the one hand, and through the women's branches of their respective political parties and female MLAs on the other.

Non-Partisan Women's Organizations and Political Action

Among the more important, informal sites of feminist agitation for the creation of family courts were the local and provincial Councils of Women, the Vancouver University Women's Club, women's church groups, and the Vancouver Women's School for Citizenship. Helen Gregory MacGill and Laura Jamieson were active members of the Vancouver and provincial Councils of Women from the pre-suffrage era onward, and Tilly Rolston was certainly a member of both organizations by the late 1930s. However, as the convenor of the Standing Committee on Laws for Women and Children from 1917 until her death in 1947, MacGill was probably the most directly influential of the three women with respect to the political activities of the Vancouver Council of Women. It was she who, as the resident expert on social welfare issues and eugenics, identified and analysed 'problems,' mobilized support for proposed legal reforms within the council itself, and organized submissions to the provincial and municipal governments for legislation and policies that would benefit women and children. And from the late 1920s, at least, one of the demands presented to the provincial government by the council's annual delegation to Victoria was the creation of family courts.[41]

After the Greater Vancouver Communities Council (GVCC) launched the organized campaign for family courts during the early 1940s, the non-partisan women's organizations took up the family court issue in earnest. Their resolutions reflected the increasingly dominant conceptualization of domestic relations tribunals as an end in themselves, emphasizing the technocratic functions of such tribunals in diagnosing and treating 'bad' families rather than the social pathologies such as poverty, which generated marital discord, delinquency, and other problems. MacGill continued to mobilize political support in the Vancouver Council of Women through her position as convenor. In November 1942 she persuaded the council to adopt a motion that commended Magistrate Herbert S. Wood, her associate in the Juvenile Court, for advocating what the council had 'long urged' – the implementation of an adult probation system. The motion also proposed that British Columbia should follow Ontario's example and create a domestic relations court with comprehensive jurisdiction over all matters concerning the family (except divorce) by extending the powers of the existing juvenile courts and implementing adult probation.[42]

When the coalition government passed enabling legislation in February 1943 but took no concrete steps to proclaim a family court, the Vancouver council adopted another resolution urging 'that a Family Court be established' in the city; the resolution was then forwarded to the Provincial Council of Women.[43] At its semi-annual meeting in November 1943, the latter group, in turn, declared that family courts were the best instrument for the prevention of juvenile delinquency, desertion, and divorce, and passed a resolution that was virtually identical to that of the Vancouver Council: 'Whereas we note that the Provincial Government has approved the Family Court and that the Attorney General is contemplating their [sic] setting up, we the Provincial Council of Women urge that the same be established and that they conform to the best known methods and approved lines as shown by successful Courts in North America.'[44]

Both Helen MacGill and Laura Jamieson were also lifelong feminist activists in another non-partisan women's group, the Vancouver University Women's Club. When the Legislative Assembly convened in February 1943, the VUWC sent a pro-family court resolution to the premier, the attorney general, and the five sitting women MLAs (including Jamieson), which pointed to 'maladjustment in family life' as 'one of the chief causes' of increasing juvenile delinquency, and specifically urged the women MLAs to promote legislation for the establishment of a provincial domestic relations court 'wherein adjustments of parental and marital differences may be made and harmony restored in the family.' The resolution reflects the influence of MacGill and Jamieson in its emphasis on the need for 'particular care ... in making the appointment of the presiding judge and the necessary personnel.'[45] Similarly, after the government enacted enabling legislation in the following month, the University Women's Club sent letters to the premier and the attorney general that commended them for their decision but also expressed regret that the government made no mention of appointing the 'trained personnel considered essential nor ... a judge specially qualified for that work,' an oversight they hoped would be rectified when the legislation was acted upon.[46]

Although little information has been located to date, church groups such as the Women's Missionary Societies were seemingly another site of non-partisan political action to promote the creation of domestic relations courts. As a member of the WMS of the Baptist church, Tilly Rolston may well have played a part in producing the statement, adopted at its annual convention in June 1944, which called for the 'immediate establishment' of family courts in British Columbia. A growing divorce rate, juvenile delinquency, and unsatisfactory homes were listed as reasons why the attorney general ought not to postpone implementing the plan.[47]

Meanwhile, Laura Jamieson was a driving force and an executive member of another influential women's group during the early 1940s – the fledgling Vancouver Women's School for Citizenship. As previously mentioned, the school was organized to inform women on important public issues so that they could be politically accurate and active. Undoubtedly through Jamieson's efforts, the VWSC decided to devote its annual conference in November 1944 to a discussion of marriage and divorce laws, delinquency, probation, and family courts. Milton Weber, chair of the Greater Vancouver Communities Council, which was spearheading the organized campaign for family courts, and Gordon Stevens, probation officer for the Vancouver Juvenile Court, were among the guest speakers.[48]

Jamieson herself spoke to the conference about family courts, placing particular emphasis on the need to appoint a judge with 'experience in the field of family relations' who could do more than 'patch up family squabbles.' Because parents were 'the largest group of unskilled workers in the world,' she said, a family court judge would have to carry out parent education, work for an end to poverty, and be concerned about housing.[49] The conference ultimately endorsed a statement which incorporated her views that a family court 'should not operate only within the narrow confines of law [but rather] should be the mediator right in the homes' (that is, preventive) and that the judge for the proposed Vancouver court should not necessarily be chosen 'from the rostrum of magistrates.'[50]

Women and Political Parties

For feminists like Helen MacGill and even more so for Laura Jamieson and Tilly Rolston, political activity in the non-partisan women's organizations was carried out simultaneously with and was not necessarily distinct from the work they did for their respective political parties. For example, the previously mentioned resolution supporting the establishment of a family court in Vancouver, adopted by the local council of Women in 1943, was actually a joint resolution from the Council's Moral Standards Committee and the CCF Women's Council. Laura Jamieson was a member of both groups, and the resolution, which also recommended that the judge 'be a woman with experience in marriage and motherhood,' clearly reflects the influence of both Jamieson and Helen Gregory MacGill.[51]

Similarly, Tilly Rolston was a member of both the Vancouver and the provincial Councils of Women when they adopted resolutions supporting the creation of family courts. At the same time she was an elected MLA in the coalition government, and was probably instrumental in selling the idea of family courts to her male colleagues. For example, when the Greater Vancouver Communities Council (GVCC) led a delegation to Victoria in January 1943 to meet with the government on the issue of family courts, it was Rolston who introduced them to the Cabinet even though she herself was not a minister.[52]

Another notable characteristic of British Columbian women engaged in partisan political activity during the post-suffrage era was their independence. They did not automatically accept or follow party policy. A year after she had introduced a GVCC delegation to cabinet, Tilly Rolston met with the premier, the attorney general and other cabinet members herself as the representative of the Conservative Women of British Columbia on a delegation to Victoria, which was again headed by Milton Weber from the Greater Vancouver Communities Council.[53] Nancy Hodges, another MLA in the coalition government, represented the Liberal Women of British Columbia. The delegation included the female heads of the Vancouver Parent-Teacher Association and the provincial Mothers' Allowances Board, as well as representatives from the Women's Christian Temperance Union (WCTU), and the Vancouver and Victoria Councils of Women. Emphasizing that the 1943 legislation pertaining to family courts 'did not go far enough to deal with the problems existing in BC today,'[54] the group urged the government to implement a province-wide system of family courts in British Columbia, adult probation, and an amendment to the Deserted Wives' Maintenance Act. Thus, both Rolston and Hodges were government MLAs acting on behalf of the women's branches of their respective political parties; they were also official participants in a group that was publicly critical of that government.

As a former Juvenile Court judge, Laura Jamieson became the CCF spokesperson in the Legislative Assembly on social welfare matters after her election in 1939. Until her defeat six years later, she fought hard for a comprehensive restructuring of the province's welfare structures, including the courts that handled social problems. Although the Liberals also supported the creation of a provincial social service department, Jamieson and the CCF had a much broader vision of what was required: a ministry of social welfare linked to a centralized system of socialized courts that would be staffed primarily by personnel who were graduates of a civil service examination, a social service course, and, preferably, a university social science course, with knowledge of law and civil administration, sociology, and child psychology.[55] When the coalition introduced enabling legislation for the establishment of family courts in February 1943, Jamieson exhorted the government to adopt her vision and to locate domestic relations tribunals within a revamped social welfare system. At the same time she clearly anticipated that the coalition had no intention of linking the creation of family courts to a wider reorganization of the province's welfare system when she admitted that if the attorney general went ahead with his plan to establish family courts on a piecemeal basis beginning in

Vancouver, the CCF would still 'welcome this as the proverbial half-loaf, which is better than no bread at all.'[56]

Nonetheless, Jamieson was determined to try to ensure that family courts would be staffed by personnel who had a social work rather than a legal perspective on family problems. Concerned that the government intended to use sitting police magistrates in the proposed domestic relations courts, she pointed out that the new courts would 'not function one whit better than the juvenile courts' because magistrates had a criminal law orientation and lacked training in non-legal sciences. Also unsuitable would be 'those pestiferous, sermonizing judges that sit on the benches of some of the higher courts in BC preaching platitudinous sermons on domestic relations to the couples to whom a divorce has just been granted.'[57] On second reading, Jamieson announced that the CCF would support the government bill to establish family courts if the attorney general would promise to appoint 'judges qualified in domestic relations and psychology, and trained for that particular procedure, and that the courts would be provided with thoroughly trained probationary officers and social service workers.'[58]

Attorney General Pat Maitland made no such commitment, but the CCF ultimately settled for the 'half-loaf' and voted in favour of the government bill. However, when the attorney general appointed the presiding police magistrate, Herbert S. Wood, to head the new Vancouver Family Court, Jamieson was quick to voice her disapproval and opposition: 'I do not see how a man who has spent the best years of his life as a police court magistrate considering cases of drunkenness and robbery and rape and murder, can be the best man available for the senior judge of a Family Court, where his task is to discover the qualities of tolerance and affection in the men and women with whom he has to deal.' Having observed the operations of the Vancouver Police Court under three different magistrates, she continued, 'it was quite evident legal technicalities took precedence above all else.'[59]

Jamieson (and the CCF) seemingly stood alone in criticizing Wood. In response, Tilly Rolston defended the appointment (and the coalition), stating that Jamieson's remarks were not justified. At the same time, Rolston censured the decision of the Vancouver City Council to locate the new family court in the old juvenile detention home, a criticism with which Jamieson concurred.[60] Moreover, women of diverse political affiliations could take satisfaction from the fact that, in some respects, the Vancouver Family Court did fit their collective expectations about the organization of socialized tribunals. For example, A.J. Cowan, appointed as the deputy Family Court judge, was a lawyer with an extensive social service background.[61] Similarly, Major the Reverend J.P. Gordon, hired as the 'contact officer who would deal with many of the cases alone,' had a long association with church-based social work agencies in the city.[62] Although he had no social service training, Gordon was the choice of the Vancouver Welfare Council for the position. Three women directors of social welfare agencies, who were professional social workers, sat on the council.[63]

Clearly, feminists were leading players in the events that produced the rudiments of a socialized justice system in British Columbia by 1945. Their growing unanimity during the post-suffrage era about the need for family courts was reflected in extensive political work, particularly among women, to mobilize public support for the establishment of these tribunals. In the final section of the paper, I examine some possible reasons for the consensus about domestic relations courts that cut across political party divisions and brought feminists and non-feminists together on that issue.

Gender, Race, Class, and the
Female Consensus on Family Courts

In analysing why pre- and post-suffrage women so frequently found themselves in agreement about legislative and policy reforms related to 'the family,' it is apparent that gender, race, and class were important and intertwined factors. More specifically, the majority of women who entered the political arena during this period, feminist and non-feminist alike, were white, middle-class, and upper-class women who had a common experience of gender oppression on the one hand and race and class privilege on the other. At the same time, they rarely challenged the conditions governing women's participation in the public realm: an acceptance of the sexual division of labour and a focus on 'feminine' spheres of endeavour (that is, issues related to women and children). Thus, the single, self-supporting woman was expected to carve out a niche in an acceptable 'feminine' career such as teaching, social work, or nursing. Moreover, the widespread assumption that married women were primarily responsible for the domestic sphere, especially child care, had immensely important implications for their activities outside the home. In particular, it meant that only those who were able to free themselves from domestic duties could actively participate in public life.

Therefore, married women who did venture into the public realm were frequently middle- and upper-class women in their late thirties or older, mothers with grown children who were finished with the most onerous years of child-rearing and who could hire domestic help to keep their homes running smoothly.[64] Furthermore, unlike many of their working-class counterparts who had to enter the paid workforce, these women were also free to engage in part-time volunteer work and activities connected with issues affecting the welfare of women and children. It is hardly a surprise, then, that the most common route to the outside world for affluent married women was through membership in the non-partisan women's organizations and associations.

The contradiction between privilege and oppression that characterized the public lives of both feminists and non-feminists during the pre- and post-suffrage years can easily be demonstrated with reference to the political 'careers' of Helen Gregory MacGill, Laura Jamieson, and Tilly Rolston. Although they were atypical in some ways, even among the relatively select group of white middle- and upper-class women actively engaged outside the home during the first half of this century, MacGill, Jamieson, and Rolston shared assumptions and experiences and faced constraints common to all women who ventured into public life. First, notwithstanding their political differences, they were clearly bound by race and class. They were all privileged white women – well educated and financially comfortable both in background and through marriage. Their class position made it possible for them to take up club work, and each of them, but especially MacGill and Jamieson, came to public prominence through a long history of volunteer work in women's groups and organizations. Their frequent interactions in the Vancouver and provincial Councils of Women and the University Women's Club very likely reinforced class (and race) affinities and softened political differences.[65]

Club work also brought them into contact with some white women from different class backgrounds and, sometimes, different political allegiances. This pattern was much more pronounced in Vancouver during the 1930s than elsewhere in the country: there were more working-class and socialist women involved in mainstream women's organizations of that city than elsewhere. Seemingly, the interclass experience had a radicalizing effect on many middle- and upper-class members of such groups inasmuch as women with political ties to the Liberals, Conservatives, and even the CCF were sometimes ahead of their own parties on issues.[66]

Indeed, socialist impact on the Vancouver Council of Women made it much more militant than any other in Canada during the Great Depression. Less is known about the provincial Council of Women, but a similar radicalizing tendency seems to have occurred. In 1938, for example, Tilly Rolston made her public debut when she presented the council's brief to the Rowell-Sirois Commission. The key problem, she told the commission, was the 'elimination of differences in standards of living, labour, and social legislation and cultural conditions in all parts of Canada ... and to elevate standards.' The council brief called for a program of social security measures that was probably more comprehensive than the Conservative party platform at that time: federal unemployment insurance, health insurance, federal responsibility for social services, a national housing scheme, and the elimination of government patronage appointments and the implementation of merit criteria.[67]

During the Second World War, this interaction among white women with differing political philosophies increased when the Vancouver Women's School for Citizenship and the British Columbia Housewives' League were organized. Although both groups were dominated by women from the CCF and Communist parties, other more conservative women were participants, if not actual members. For example, Tilly Rolston was a featured speaker at the 1941 convention of the Housewives' League.[68] Moreover, as elected MLAs, Rolston and Laura Jamieson worked together on some of the same government committees (such as welfare), and all the women sitting in the House during the early 1940s – one each from the Conservatives and Liberals and three from the CCF – were appointed to the post-war rehabilitation committee.

Similarly, it was female MLAs who acted as the primary spokespersons for their respective parties on family and 'women's' issues. Although political opportunism was a factor, both Tilly Rolston and Nancy Hodges, the Liberal MLA from Victoria, do seem to have been somewhat to the left of their respective parties on social welfare issues, judging by their speeches before the House. The newspapers declared them 'guilty of grand larceny of the CCF platform, to which they helped themselves without compunction' in their joint reply to the 1941 speech from the throne on behalf of the coalition government. In these, their maiden speeches before the House, they 'agreed in every particular' and 'advocated precisely the same reforms,' a coincidence that arguably reflected not only the leftward move of the coalition government to counter CCF growth but also the beliefs of the two women.[69] Among other things, Rolston proposed increased old-age pensions, a housing scheme, post-war planning and the compulsory saving and standardization of clothing to save money for the war. When the coalition government actually raised old age pensions, she was quick to point out that 'we have worked for it for 10 years at least – women's organizations, men's organizations, all over the province.'[70]

In addition to race and class affinities, Helen Gregory MacGill, Laura Jamieson, and Tilly Rolston also shared an adherence to maternal feminism. To a greater or lesser extent they all subscribed to the tenets of familial ideology: that the nuclear unit based on a biological division of labour and the public–private split was the most highly evolved and appropriate form of family. They may have chafed at but did not directly challenge the rules that governed women's participation in the public sphere: married women could legitimately engage in political activities aimed at enhancing the status of women (and children) in the home and protecting them from abuse, but they were still responsible for the domestic labour in their own homes, even if someone else did the actual work. These assumptions coloured their collective perceptions of what was necessary to protect and preserve 'the family' – mothers' allowances that would enable women to be at home with their children at least part-time; social legislation governing child and family welfare; and family courts.[71]

During the 1941 provincial election campaign in British Columbia, a newspaper story based on interviews with the eight 'feminine' candidates reported that they were all successful women in private life who were now willing to do a little 'mothering' for their less fortunate neighbours. Thus, the women viewed the prospect of electoral success not in terms of 'a career but a job that needs doing thoroughly and now.' They shared a 'belief in woman's part in the scheme of things' and were working for that goal regardless of their political party affiliation.[72]

As might be expected, Tilly Rolston was the most conservative defender of 'the family' among the women electoral candidates. Rolston had a literal belief in the sexual division of labour that would not have been out of place in the pre-suffrage era, and she was adamant that mothers ought to be at home with their children. In the 1940s she was articulating some of the same arguments for women's participation in public life as the suffragists had stressed during the late nineteenth and early twentieth centuries. None the less, although both Helen Gregory MacGill and Laura Jamieson recognized that some mothers with young children were forced to engage in paid labour, neither of them would have disagreed strongly in principle with the ideas about women's role that Rolston elaborated in a 1941 speech to the British Columbia Housewives' League:

'Women in wartime have an important role in the guarding of family standards ... A man may be head of the house, but it has been women's work always to make one dollar go as far as two in the feeding and clothing of her family ... It is the first job of women, particularly in wartime, to maintain the stability of her home, to keep it cozy and happy and see that her husband and children are properly fed. That is the only way they can have mental and spiritual health.'[73]

Similarly, neither MacGill nor Jamieson would have seriously disputed Rolston's views on the role of women politicians. Female MLAs had the primary responsibility to help and safeguard the interests of homemakers and their children by bringing their special talents and skills to bear – specifically, those related to housekeeping and caregiving. Women politicians would devote special attention to social issues that were of little concern to men. They would demand increases in mothers' pensions, for example, because 'we can't have our boys and girls growing up without sufficient bread and butter and milk.' And they would point out the inadequacies of social legislation and policy implemented by their male colleagues. Thus, when the coalition government allocated an additional five dollars to the aged but failed to raise pensions for widows, deserted mothers, and the blind, Rolston publicly expressed regret.[74]

For Rolston, then, Parliament was simply an enlarged domestic sphere: 'it's all there ... budgeting, bills, planning, keeping the family members happy ... in fact just plain everyday housekeeping on a grand scale.' 'After keeping house and raising a family' she felt she could 'face anything,' and, just as a husband and wife had to work together to have a 'balanced home,' so both men and women were needed in politics for the best results. Rolston also believed that, as mothers, women had a better understanding of youth and, since the war was demanding so much of youth, women politicians were especially needed to see that they received a 'square deal.'[75] As she stated in her maiden speech to the House, 'It all goes to show how women think alike and think in general along more advanced lines than men' and she went on to '[threaten] the gentlemen with a growing representation of women.'[76]

Gender-bonding among women of different political persuasions also developed through their direct experience of sexism in public life. As married women who accepted paid employment as state officials – Juvenile Court judges and MLAs – Helen Gregory MacGill, Laura Jamieson, and Tilly Rolston were perhaps even more vulnerable to overt gender bias than most women who ventured into the public realm during the post-suffrage era. Indeed, sexist treatment motivated each of them to leave one political party for another. In 1916 MacGill, who came from a bedrock Tory family in Ontario and was a lifelong Conservative, quit the party because of its intransigence on the suffrage issue. She joined the Liberal party, whose 1917 electoral success led to her appointment as a Juvenile Court judge. Thirteen years later she was unceremoniously fired by the Conservatives when they returned to political power. Thus, Pat Maitland, provincial leader of the Conservative party and attorney general in the coalition government during the 1940s, was an old enemy.[77]

Although she was reinstated as a judge when the Liberals regained office in 1934, MacGill also experienced shabby treatment at the hands of her adopted party. She was appointed to the 1936 ad hoc Advisory Committee on Juvenile Delinquency established by the Liberal government, and signed the committee's draft report on the understanding that certain offending items would be amended. However, some of these turned up in the final report that was issued in 1937. In addition, the original recommendation that there should be one senior juvenile court judge for the entire province with deputy judges to serve under *him* [my emphasis] had been changed to allow for women to be selected as well; but MacGill realized that she would not be the choice for senior judge and saw the recommendation as both a personal affront and a tactical move to relegate women to second place in Juvenile Court work.[78] Her subsequent announcement that she would never serve as a deputy may well have had something to do with the Liberal government's failure to act on the committee's report.

Similarly, Laura Jamieson was a committed member of the Liberal party until the late 1930s, when a male MLA in the Liberal government publicly chastised her for expressing outspoken views at public meetings where she was introduced as a Juvenile Court judge. This action prompted her to break with the Liberals, resign from the bench, and join the CCF.[79] In turn, Tilly Rolston was held back in the Conservative party and coalition government. Herbert Ascomb, who assumed the party leadership after Pat Maitland died unexpectedly in 1946, did not believe that women should be in public life and refused to give her a cabinet post. Ultimately Rolston left the Conservatives, sat as an independent, and joined the fledgling Social Credit party, later becoming the first woman cabinet minister with portfolio in Canada.[80]

Helen Gregory MacGill, Laura Jamieson, and Tilly Rolston also confronted sexism first hand through their membership in the women's branches of their respective parties. MacGill and Jamieson had actually organized the Liberal Women of British Columbia. Later, Jamieson became active in the CCF Women's Council and Rolston was involved in the Conservative Women of British Columbia. As previous discussion indicated, these groups did engage in some autonomous political activities; however, they were ultimately subordinate to the larger, male-dominated party structures. Thus, the CCF espoused a theoretical position of gender equality, yet it was typical of left-wing, socialist, and communist organizations at the time in that there was no real effort to rearrange the sexual division of labour to help women enter politics in the same way as men. The Liberals and Conservatives were more explicitly paternalistic, inasmuch as their women's groups were much like auxiliaries; the CCF Women's Council was at least an integral, albeit secondary, section of the party.[81]

Among the most telling extant records of the condescension and paternalism that so many men exhibited towards women who entered political life during the post-suffrage era are the diaries kept by Pat Maitland when the Legislative Assembly was in session. One 1943 entry describes the lone woman Liberal MLA in the coalition government as 'Nancy Pancy Hodges.' Another entry in 1946 refers to the fact that 'the three CCF bitches' were no longer in the House because of their electoral defeat the previous year. And even Tilly Rolston, a member of his own party, was the subject of patronizing references. Although Maitland had a sneaking admiration for her 'independence' and spirit, he viewed Rolston very much in sexist terms, commenting at one point that 'Tilly's stuff is as solid as she is built,' and that, she 'made a very fine speech. The best any female has made this year.'[82]

Overall, while race and class privilege bound women together, it appears that their shared assumptions about femininity and masculinity, encapsulated in the bourgeois family model, and their common experiences as women were most critical in forging consensus among and between feminists and non-feminists about social welfare issues, regardless of their political ties. Direct experience of sexism further cemented these bonds, especially among women who entered the male-dominated political arena. These conclusions are admittedly preliminary and are based primarily on a case study of three feminists in one province. None the less, the finding that British Columbian feminists assumed a leading role in promoting the development of family courts and, more generally, in constructing the sociolegal foundations of a gendered provincial welfare state is consistent with that of researchers elsewhere.[83] Clearly, more research that builds on these initial feminist analyses of women and state welfare remains to be done.

NOTES

The research for this paper was conducted during my tenure as the recipient of an SSHRC postdoctoral award in 1987–8 and 1989–90. I thank Shelley Gavigan and Carol Smart for their helpful comments on earlier drafts of the paper and Susan Binnie for her editorial skill.

1 Jim Dickinson and Bob Russell, eds, *Family, Economy, and State* (Toronto: Garamond Press 1986); Jacques Donzelot, 'The Poverty of Political Culture' (1979), 5 *Ideology and Consciousness*, 73–86; Alvin Finkel, 'Origins of the Welfare State in Canada,' in *The Canadian State*, ed. L. Panitch (Toronto: University of Toronto Press 1977); Dennis Guest, *The Emergence of Social Security in Canada* (Vancouver: University of British Columbia Press 1980); Allen Moscovitch and Jim Albert, eds, *The Benevolent State* (Toronto: Garamond Press 1987); James O'Connor, *The Fiscal Crisis of the State* (New York: St Martin's 1973); James Struthers, *No Fault of Their Own: Unemployment and the Canadian Welfare State 1914–41* (Toronto: University of Toronto Press 1983)

2 See Dorothy E. Chunn, *From Punishment to Doing Good* (Toronto: University of Toronto Press 1992); Patricia T. Rooke and Rudy L. Schnell, *No Bleeding Heart: Charlotte Whitton, a Feminist on the Right* (Vancouver: University of British Columbia Press 1987); Jane Ursel, 'The State and the Maintenance of Patriarchy: A Case Study of Family, Labour and Welfare Legislation in Canada,' in Dickinson and Russell, supra note 1.

3 Donzelot, supra note 1.

4 David Garland, *Punishment and Welfare* (Brookfield, Vt: Gower 1985), 6.

5 Chunn, supra note 2; Dorothy E. Chunn and Shelley A.M. Gavigan, 'Social Control: Analytical Tool or Analytical Quagmire?' (1988), 12 *Contemporary Crises*, 107–24; Roscoe Pound, 'The Rise of Socialized Justice,' in *National Probation Association Yearbook, 1942* (New York 1943); Edward A. Ross, *Social Control* (Cleveland: Case Western Reserve University Press 1969); Carol Smart, 'Regulating Families or Legitimating Patriarchy? Family Law in Britain' (1982) 10 *International Journal of the Sociology of Law*, 129–47.

6 Suffrage was 'universal' in Canada by 1918, but primarily for the white adult population. Aboriginal, Chinese, and Japanese persons did not gain the rights of citizenship until the 1940s and 1950s.

7 Jacques Donzelot, *The Policing of Families* (New York: Pantheon 1980); Michel Foucault, *The History of Sexuality*, vol. 1 (New York: Vintage Books 1980); Garland, supra note 4.

8 Donzelot, supra note 7.

9 See Varda Burstyn and Dorothy E. Smith, *Women, Class, Family and the State* (Toronto: Garamond Press 1985); Carol Smart, ed., *Regulating Womanhood:*

Historical Essays on Marriage, Motherhood and Sexuality (London: Routledge 1992); Eli Zaretsky, 'Rethinking the Welfare State: Dependence, Economic Individualism and the Family,' in Dickinson and Russell, supra note 1.

10 Christopher Lasch, *Haven in a Heartless World* (New York: Basic Books 1979).

11 Chunn, supra note 2; Garland, supra note 4; Rooke and Schnell, supra note 2; Russell Smandych, Gordon Dodds, and Alvin Esau, eds, *Dimensions of Childhood: Essays on the History of Children and Youth in Canada* (Winnipeg: Legal Research Institute of the University of Manitoba 1991)

12 Gillian Creese and Veronica Strong-Boag, eds, *British Columbia Reconsidered* (Vancouver: Press Gang 1992); Barbara K. Latham and Roberta J. Pazdro, eds, *Not Just Pin Money* (Victoria: Camosun College 1984); T.R. Morrison, ' "Their Proper Sphere": Feminism, the Family, and Child-Centred Social Reform in Ontario, 1875–1900' (1976), 68 *Ontario History*, 45–64, 65–74; Rooke and Schnell, supra note 2; Veronica Strong-Boag, *The Parliament of Women: The National Council of Women in Canada, 1893–1929* (Ottawa: Museum of Man 1976).

13 John Clarke, Allan Cochrane, and Carol Smart, *Ideologies of Welfare: From Dreams to Disillusion* (London: Hutchinson 1987); Jennifer Dale and Peggy Foster, *Feminists and State Welfare* (London: Routledge and Kegan Paul 1986); Linda Gordon, *Heroes of Their Own Lives* (New York: Penguin Books 1988); Thelma McCormack, *Politics and the Hidden Injuries of Gender: Feminism and the Making of the Welfare State* (Ottawa: CRIAW/ICREF 1991); Carol Pateman, 'The Patriarchal State,' in *The Disorder of Women*, ed. C. Pateman (Cambridge: Polity Press 1989); James Struthers, ' "Lord Give Us Men": Women and Social Work in English Canada, 1918–1939,' in Moscovitch and Albert, supra note 1; Zaretsky, 'Rethinking the Welfare State,' supra note 9.

14 Dorothy E. Chunn, 'Maternal Feminism, Legal Professionalism and Political Pragmatism: The Rise and Fall of Magistrate Margaret Patterson, 1922–1934,' in *Canadian Perspectives on Law and Society*, ed. W. Pue and B. Wright (Ottawa: Carleton University Press 1988); Chunn, supra note 2; Gordon, supra note 13; McCormack, ibid.; Rooke and Schnell, supra note 2.

15 Clarke, Cochrane, and Smart, supra note 13.

16 Ibid.; Veronica Strong-Boag, *The New Day Recalled: Lives of Girls and Women in English-Canada, 1919–1939* (Toronto: Copp Clark Pitman 1988); Susan Walsh, 'Equality, Emancipation and a More Just World,' MA thesis, Simon Fraser University (1983).

17 Allan Irving, 'The Development of a Provincial Welfare State: British Columbia 1900–1939,' in Moscovitch and Albert, supra note 1; Latham and Pazdro, supra note 12; Elsie Gregory MacGill, *My Mother the Judge* (Toronto:

Ryerson Press 1955); Helen Gregory MacGill, comp., *Laws for Women and Children in British Columbia*, 4th ed. (Vancouver 1928), *The Story of Vancouver Social Service* (Vancouver 1943); Elizabeth B. Norcross, '1918–1928: The Decade of Social Legislation' (1987), 17 *British Columbia Historical News*, 13–16; Strong-Boag, supra note 16.

18 ' "The White Life for two" has to be insisted upon': Rev. C.W. Watch, 'Social Purity Work in Canada,' in *The National Purity Congress: Its Papers, Addresses and Portraits*, ed. A.M. Powell (New York: American Purity Alliance 1896), 278; see also James Snell, 'The "White Life for Two": The Defence of Marriage and Sexual Morality in Canada, 1890–1914' (1983), 16 *Histoire sociale/Social History*, 111–28.

19 Chunn, supra note 2; James Snell, 'Courts of Domestic Relations: A Study of Early Twentieth Century Judicial Reform in Canada' (1986), 6 *Windsor Yearbook of Access to Justice*, 36–60.

20 The enabling legislation consisted of an amendment to the Juvenile Courts Act, SBC 1943, c. 13, and the Magistrates' Jurisdiction Act, SBC 1943, c. 36.

21 Vancouver News Herald (hereinafter cited as *News Herald*), 29 January 1944.

22 By focusing on three overtly political women in this paper, I am not suggesting that they were the most significant female proponents of family courts. Bureaucrats such as Laura Holland and directors of social agencies such as Mary McPhedran also played a significant role in promoting family courts and socialized justice.

23 Helen Gregory MacGill, *Laws for Women and Children in British Columbia*, 6th ed. (Vancouver 1939), at 22.

24 Strong-Boag, supra note 16; Walsh, ibid.

25 *News Herald*, 8 November 1939.

26 Ibid., 24 September 1941.

27 Vancouver *Province* (hereinafter cited as *Province*), 9 December 1943.

28 *News Herald*, 24 September 1941.

29 Ibid., 8 November 1939; see also Victoria *Daily Times* (hereinafter cited as *Daily Times*), 8 November 1939.

30 For an account of the coalition government, see the papers of the conservative leader, Attorney General 'Pat' Maitland: Public Archives of British Columbia (hereinafter cited as PABC), ADD MSS 781, Maitland Family 1911–72, Box 4, file 2, Pat Maitland to John Hart, 6 December 1941.

31 Vancouver *Sun*, 22 October 1945 (hereinafter cited as *Sun*).

32 H.G. MacGill, *Laws for Women and Children*, supra note 17, at 57–8; E.G. MacGill, *My Mother the Judge*, ibid., at 196.

33 H.G. MacGill, *Laws for Women and Children*, supra note 23, at 48; E.G. MacGill, *My Mother the Judge*, supra note 17, at 216, 233.

34 Victoria *Daily Colonist* (hereinafter cited as *Daily Colonist*), 5 February 1943; *Province*, 5 February 1943; *Daily Times* 5 February 1943.

35 *Daily Colonist* 3 November 1937; *News Herald*, 3 November 1937; *Daily Times*, 3 November 1937.

36 *Province*, 10 February 1943.

37 *Daily Colonist*, 8 November 1939; *Sun*, 20 November 1940.

38 *Sun*, 10 February 1943.

39 Latham and Pazdro, supra note 12; Strong-Boag, supra note 16; Walsh, ibid.

40 Latham and Pazdro, supra note 12; Strong-Boag, supra note 16; Walsh, ibid.

41 UBC Special Collections (hereinafter cited as UBC SC), Vancouver Council of Women, Minutes of Regular and Sub-Executive Meetings; E.G. MacGill, *My Mother the Judge*, supra note 17, at 173–6; H.G. MacGill, *Laws for Women and Children*, ibid.

42 UBC SC, Vancouver Council of Women, Box 8.6, Minutes of Monthly Meeting, 2 November 1942.

43 Ibid., Box 8.7, Minutes of Sub-Executive Meeting, 4 October 1943.

44 PABC, ADD MSS 1961, Provincial Council of Women, Box 3, Resolutions 1943, 15 November 1943; *Daily Colonist* 19 November 1943.

45 UBC SC, University Women's Club, Vancouver, MSS 872, file 22, Minutes of Meeting, 8 February 1943; PABC, Premier 1917–1954, Box 163, file 10, Theodosia Munro, Secretary, UWC, Vancouver to Premier John Hart 13 February 1943; Premier Hart, to Mrs Hugh Munro, 16 February 1943.

46 UBC SC, University Women's Club, Vancouver, MSS 872, file 22, Minutes of Meeting, 12 April 1943.

47 *News Herald*, 13 June 1944.

48 Vancouver City Archives, Vancouver Women's School for Citizenship, MSS 466, Minutes of Board Meeting, 10 July 1944.

49 *Province*, 29 November 1944.

50 *Sun*, 29 November 1944.

51 UBC SC, Vancouver Council of Women, supra note 42.

52 *Daily Times*, 15 January 1943.

53 *Province*, 15 February 1944, 2; *Daily Times*, 15 February 1944, 11; *Daily Colonist*, 16 February 1944.

54 *Daily Times*, 15 February 1944; *Daily Colonist*, 16 February 1944.

55 *Daily Colonist*, 8 November 1939; see also *Sun*, 20 November 1940.

56 *Province*, 10 February 1943; *Sun*, 10 February 1943.

57 *Province*, 10 Feburary 1943; *Sun*, 10 February 1943.

58 *Daily Colonist*, 12 March 1943; see also *Province*, 12 March 1943.

59 *Sun*, 16 February 1945; see also *Province*, 16 February 1945.

60 *Province*, 20 February 1945.

61 *Sun*, 16 February 1945; *Province*, 16 February 1945.

62 *Province*, 11 January 1945.

63 Ibid., 20 February 1945.

64 Strong-Boag, supra note 16; Walsh, ibid. Although widowed at the age of thirty-eight, Laura Jamieson was apparently able to maintain her middle-class lifestyle.

65 Connie Carter and Eileen Daoust, 'From Home to House: Women in the BC Legislature,' in Latham and Pazdro, supra note 12; MacGill, *My Mother the Judge*, supra note 17; Juliette Proom, 'Tilly Jean Rolston: She Knew How to Throw a Party,' in Latham and Pazdro, supra note 12; Walsh, supra note 16.

66 Strong-Boag, supra note 16; Gillian Weiss, 'The Brightest Women of Our Land: Vancouver Clubwomen 1910–1928,' in Latham and Pazdro, supra note 12.

67 *Province*, 24 March 1938.

68 Ibid., 13 November 1941.

69 *Sun*, 9 January 1942.

70 Ibid., 27 January 1942.

71 Speaking broadly, since it is clear that the three women often disagreed about the specifics of social legislation and policy directed at 'the family.' See Irene Howard, 'The Mothers' Council of Vancouver: Holding the Fort for the Unemployed, 1935–38' (1986), *BC Studies*, at 269–70; Proom, supra note 65; Strong Boag, supra note 16; Walsh, ibid.

72 *Sun*, 18 October 1941.

73 *Province*, 13 November 1941.

74 *Sun*, 27 January 1942.

75 Ibid., 18 October 1941.

76 Ibid., 9 January 1942.

77 MacGill, *My Mother the Judge*, supra note 17.

78 Ibid., at 217–18.

79 Walsh, supra note 16.

80 Proom, supra note 65.

81 Joan Sangster, *Dreams of Equality: Women on the Canadian Left, 1920–1950* (Toronto: McClelland and Stewart 1989); Walsh, supra note 16.

82 PABC, Maitland Family 1911–72, ADD MSS 781, Box 8, file 11, House Log, 8 February 1943; House Log, 5 March 1946; House Log, 30 March 1943

83 supra note 14

15 The 'Incorrigible,' the 'Bad,' and the 'Immoral': Toronto's 'Factory Girls' and the Work of the Toronto Psychiatric Clinic

JENNIFER STEPHEN

Introduction

In this paper I will explore the work of the Toronto Psychiatric Clinic (TPC) for the period 1918–1923, and examine how the category of feeble-mindedness was constructed and applied to young working-class women. As the flagship for the mental hygiene movement in Canada, the TPC was a social laboratory; it served as a centre for the production of knowledge about feeble-mindedness, its extent and mode of transmission through the general population, and the correct 'scientific' procedures required for accurate examination and diagnosis of its presence.[1] Its operation had significant effects on the lives of many young, single, and immigrant women.

The clinic did not operate in isolation. Instead, it was located within a widening network of state and extra-state agencies and institutions engaged in the criminal justice, immigration, and public health systems, and in education and social welfare work. As the research organ of the Canadian National Committee for Mental Hygiene (CNCMH), the TPC was charged with the task of producing 'evidence' to attest to the problem of feeble-mindedness during the post-war period of social reconstruction. Such 'evidence' was produced through examinations of working-class women referred to the clinic by a variety of state and extra-state agencies, and through 'mental hygiene surveys' conducted among incarcerated women.[2]

I will outline the social and political context in which the Toronto Psychiatric Clinic was located – specifically, its role in the production of knowledge which was then taken up by the leadership organ of the mental hygiene movement, the Canadian National Committee for Mental Hygiene, for its own ideological and propagandistic purposes. I will examine the technology of the clinical investigation itself to consider its deployment in relation to young working-class women who were its 'patients': by what social, moral, and economic criteria were they assessed and diagnosed? Finally, I will briefly survey the institutional apparatus that came into play at the level of 'treatment.' This apparatus involved a developing network of institutions used or at least recommended by the TPC practitioners to perform a continuum of functions that ranged from incarceration – temporary, indefinite, or permanent – to community surveillance and supervision with recommendations for vocational training and, finally, deportation.

Kathleen McConnachie has argued in her study of the CNCMH during the inter-war period that mental hygienists and eugenicists placed all social problems on the footing of biological and hereditary determinism.[3] However, what also emerges in this study is a textual, clinical approach that was rooted in the identification of individual pathology: in other words, an emphasis on the psychiatric case study. The new discipline of corrective and preventive psychiatry played a major role in defining the problems posed by feeble-mindedness and in refining the necessary diagnostic procedure. This work had important implications for social policy, particularly in its application to intelligence testing of school-children,[4] the psychiatric examination of offenders,[5] and the public health psychiatric exam of the immigrant population. C.F. Martin, a professor of psychiatry at McGill University and a Montreal representative of the CNCMH, divided the target population into three categories: (1) the paranoic; (2) the 'inadequate personality, which includes the mentally defective, the feeble-minded'; and (3) 'the emotional, unstable personality.'[6] Individuals of concern to mental hygienists, Martin argued in a 1920 article in the *Canadian Journal of Mental Hygiene,* could be classified into one of the three categories; indeed, such classification should comprise an important branch of the medical practitioner's work. Similar work conducted in the United States provided a substantial, even critical, boost. In an article in the July 1919 issue of the *Canadian Journal of Mental Hygiene,* Jessie Taft, the social service director for the New York State Charities Commission Committee on Mental Hygiene, summarized the links and the breadth of the work:

There is no question but that the swift rise of the mental test as a centre of interest and experiment in applied psychology has had much to do with the growth of popular recognition of feeble-mindedness as a social problem. Parallel to this development of psychology and aided by it has been the advance of criminology which by its disclosure of the intimate relationship between mental disability and antisocial conduct has perhaps done more than any one other thing to force the problem of feeble-mindedness upon the public.[7]

Dr Charles K. Clarke, after whom the Clarke Institute of Psychiatry in Toronto was named, was a major leader of the movement for mental hygiene in Canada. Clarke held degrees in medicine and law, and was a professor of psychiatry at the University of Toronto and the medical superintendent of the Toronto Hospital for the Insane before moving on to head the Toronto Psychiatric Clinic. Clarke was a significant contributor to the development and practice of forensic psychiatry in Canada. His sphere of influence extended well beyond the TPC into the criminal justice system; he was called upon frequently as an expert witness in notable trials during the period.

Dr Clarence Hincks was one of Clarke's closest collegues. Hincks along with Clarke and Dr Helen MacMurchy, formed the Canadian National Committee on Mental Hygiene in 1918. Dr MacMurchy, as inspector of the feeble-minded for Ontario, was also instrumental in helping to establish the clinic.

Although the historical development of the category of 'feeble-minded' has been buried or overlooked in most studies of English Canada during this period, ideas about population control and medical regulation exercised strong influences in social commentary and policy debates. For instance, Charlotte Whitton figured prominently among those who spoke against allowing so-called illegitimate mothers access to mothers' allowance. Similarly, Helen MacMurchy worked diligently to target 'immoral girls' during her tenure as inspector of the feeble-minded from 1910 to 1918. Like Clarke and Hincks, MacMurchy strongly supported legislative efforts to enable the identification and segregation of 'feeble-minded' persons from the larger population.[8]

Clarke considered that mental defect lay at the root of criminality and delinquency, that it was an inheritable organic condition which was manifested in physical symptoms, or 'stigmata,' such as a 'cleft palate.'[9] Thus the disease of feeble-mindedness could be mapped on the body and in the mind of the individual. Physical stigmata and certain moral and social behaviourial traits were read as typologies of the feeble-minded, although only a trained psychiatrist could accurately decipher their meaning. Most significantly, those connected with the TPC were certain that favourable environment could do little to mitigate the sentence of bad heredity or ameliorate the problem of mental degeneracy: feeble-mindedness was itself a disease transmitted through heredity.[10] As Frank Mort states in his study of British medico-moral politics: 'Human biology was now to be studied as a series of stages in the process of evolution. The life history of each and every individual needed to be grasped not merely in the context of his/her immediate environment, but as part of a broader racial history.'[11]

The work of the TPC is seen here as bound up in the emergence of what Nikolas Rose identifies as the scientific discourse of the 'psychology of the individual.' This discourse is located 'not within a history of reflections upon the nature of the soul, but within the changing conceptions of pathologies of thought, belief, intellect, emotion, and conduct.' In *The Psychological Complex* Rose states,

It is to these conceptions and practices of government regulation, surveillance, segregation, and therapy within which they were deployed, that we must begin to look if we are to begin to identify the conditions which made such a psychology [of the individual] possible. Not a history of ideas, then, but a history of practices, techniques, institutions and agencies, of forms of knowledge which made them thinkable and which they, in their turn, transformed. And a history of categories and problems around which such complex apparatuses formed, which provided the motivation for their emergence and the targets of their tactics.[12]

In looking at the *construction* of the *category* 'the feeble-minded woman,' I will explore the development of the range of practices, procedures, languages both verbal and statistical, institutional apparatuses, and agencies that were associated with the work of the clinic.[13] This discourse of feeble-mindedness was integral to shaping state regulatory powers over the 'delinquent girl,' in, as Kari Dehli has argued, its being 'constitutive of, although not determining, the social relations [it] describe[d] and in which [it] was produced and used.' Dehli identifies the power of state regulatory practices as central to making 'certain kinds of behaviour materially possible and socially acceptable, while at the same time containing and suppressing other ways of being.'[14] I would expand that practice to encompass extra-state agencies – those existing on the periphery of state regulatory process like the TPC, as well as agencies such as the Salvation Army's Haven and the Neighbourhood Workers Association, through which the network of state regulatory powers was operative. These agencies were integral to what Dehli terms the 'organized dominance' of the state while remaining just outside the ambit of the 'official' state.[15]

The mental hygienist's approach to social problems was directed first to the pathological psychiatric disorder of the individual concerned. Each case required examination, testing, and most important, expert diagnosis. On the rare occasions when the clinician could not find a diagnosis of feeble-mindedness, the clinic patients were pronounced 'apparently normal.' However, the search was not for the normal: the forms designed for use at the TPC could hardly remain blank. The point was to locate and identify the abnormal. Since there were not always overt physical signs, only the trained clinical expert could accurately diagnose the psychiatric disorder of feeble-mindedness. In fact, outward appearance, particularly of those women labelled 'high grade mental degenerates,' often conformed to physical cultural standards of female attractiveness. The body, as an instrument of moral misconduct, was deceptive. The point was made frequently that a young woman's 'good looks' were 'a menace to her' and society. Furthermore, such diagnoses had to proceed on a case-by-case basis, with careful, painstaking attention paid to intimate details of family history, heredity, the age at which the 'patient' commenced walking and talking, sexual habits, the age of onset of menstruation, and the employment history of 'patient' and parents. The centrepiece of the clinical investigation was the Binet-Simon test of intelligence. Such an intricate program of examination of each individual belied the underlying ideological approach that was operative throughout: social pathology was transmuted to individual pathology.[16]

The Mental Hygienist and Social Order

'Feeble-mindedness' as a category expanded after the Great War, and was fundamentally altered because of it. In an earlier pre-war period its explanatory power had been brought to bear on prostitution, vagrancy, poverty and destitution, and immigration, and what all of these meant to the survival of the purportedly 'superior race' of white middle class British empire-builders. By 1918 the practice of mass physical and psychiatric examinations of enlisted men, the expansion of public health and social welfare apparatus, the campaign against venereal disease, and the growing presence of psychiatry as a legitimate branch in 'state medicine' described a changed context in which the TPC was located. Industrial unrest, unemployment of men and particularly of women, military insubordination, the massacre of thousands of young men, and the return of survivors from overseas all converged in public discourse and were analysed by mental hygienists in a language emphasizing social unrest and its antidote – control of the social order. In one of his typically sweeping assertions, Hincks articulated the diagnosis of the current social malaise according to the mental hygienist: 'To feeble-mindedness or mental deficiency can be traced a considerable proportion of our crime, juvenile delinquency, educational inefficiency and moral contamination in primary schools; prostitution, illegitimacy, military insubordination, pauperism, unemployment and alcoholism.'[17]

The declining birth rate among women of the 'preferred stock,' together with the slaughter of so many young men, created fertile conditions for the production of propaganda to publicize and make tangible the threat allegedly posed by the feeble-minded. Statistics, which can be traced back to the crudest of estimates,[18] gained credibility and legitimacy as real, 'scientific' truth. 'Kit of the Kitchen,' a column in the popular journal *Social Welfare*, exhibited precisely this process of legitimation in the following 1918 excerpt:

> Canada has a population of some 7,500,000 of whom, at a conservative estimate, some 40,000 are feeble-minded. When one considers that the number of Canadians killed in this war amounts to 55,000 the problem comes home forcibly. It means there are 55,000 less of us to cope with this deficient 40,000. How is your community meeting the problem? Are 'Simple Jim' and 'Soft Maggie' and 'Daft Joe' wandering around at their 'own sweet will'? Do you know that from them and theirs, we recruit 60 per cent. of our prostitutes, 25 per cent. of our addicts and 40 per cent. of our juvenile delinquents?[19]

According to Hincks, Clarke, and their colleagues, feeble-mindedness was not a disease of external origin, a contagion originating outside, apart from the body, which could, like venereal disease, be treated, prevented, contained, and ultimately eradicated. Feeble-mindedness was within, hereditary, in the mind, defining the very identity of the individual from birth. The feeble-minded had no subjectivity apart from the identity conferred on her or him by the psychiatric disorder itself as diagnosed by the clinical expert. In fact, the problem lay not with 'Daft Joe' and 'Soft Maggie' at all; theirs was a 'mental defect' visible to all, an identity that had sufficient currency in popular culture that it could be recognized in the community as 'difference' and otherness. This was the point that the members of the Toronto-based Canadian National Committee for Mental Hygiene, led by Hincks and Clarke, felt compelled to make in order to identify the threat. In a deputation to the Toronto Board of Control in 1916, the argument was again rehearsed and the social and sexual danger alluded to: 'Mixing with the general population is that other large group whose mental condition is not so clearly apparent. Having the minds of children in adult bodies, they constitute, however, a very serious problem and grave danger to the moral and physical health of the community. Often attractive in appearance, but without the restraints and inhibitions that come with adult life, they constitute a serious social danger.'[20]

Regular reformatory methods were thought to be of little avail in dealing with the apparently growing problem of mental degeneracy. The question of whether the feeble-minded could be reformed or not was in fact rarely broached by TPC workers. Since the term was defined in such a way that all capacity for independent decision-making and subjectivity was suspended in these individuals, there was no individual consciousness to which the expert could address his or her reforming skills. In a 1916 article in the *Public Health Journal*, Clarke's daughter, Miss M.J. Clarke,[21] posed the problem that preoccupied those who worked in the area, in a manner which underscored the hereditarian definition of 'mental defect': 'We often find that those who used to be considered "incorrigible," "bad," and "immoral," are, as a matter of fact, feeble-minded, and not responsible for their actions. If this is proved to be the case we are of course, relieved of all necessity of trying to "reform" the individual or individuals, but we are still far from a satisfactory solution of our problem.'[22] In an article written for *Social Welfare* in 1918, Hincks elaborated on this view: 'Feeblemindedness is a condition of brain defect which renders the affected individual incompetent to earn a living, and incapable of conducting personal affairs with ordinary prudence. The defect is present in childhood and usually demonstrates itself by marked backwardness in learning to walk, to talk, and to obey simple commands, and by retardation in school. Heredity is the chief disposing factor.'[23]

The problem had broader implications for the population as a whole. At the level of the individual, feeble-mindedness indicated the degeneration of intelligence and thus the alleged incapacity to follow appropriate social, moral, and behavioral codes. But, on a larger scale the feeble-minded represented a growing population that was ultimately responsible for the deterioration and degeneration of the 'race.' As the work of the TPC proceeded the term was further refined, with the subsequent effect of establishing precisely what constituted infractions of moral, behaviourial, and therefore social 'norms.'

Fuelled by the success of their campaign against prostitution and venereal disease[24] and fear of the dysgenic impact of the First World War, the new professionals widened their scope to encompass all those whose social or moral misconduct was considered evidence of their 'mental deficiency' or 'feeble-mindedness.' What had begun as a loosely defined, overused term to explain deviancy in relation to prostitution or racist assessments of the immigrant population was soon deployed to address the chief concerns of the post-war period of reconstruction. The year 1918 marked both the formation of the CNCMH and the appointment of the Royal Commission on the Care and Control of the Feeble-Minded in Ontario and the Prevalence of Venereal Diseases. The Hodgins Commission, supported strongly by Provincial Secretary William MacPherson under the Hearst government, gave Clarke, Hincks, and their colleagues the platform they wanted. The commission's recommendations were an echo of the demands of the mental hygiene movement's leadership for a program of segregation following the 'farm colony' plan. The reasoning was internally consistent: far from dying out, as some had earlier believed, the 'feeble-minded' had the capacity to reproduce at a rate that vastly exceeded that of the 'superior stock' in the population.

As Kathleen McConnachie, Frank Mort, Jeffrey Weeks, and others have noted,[25] the science of eugenics and biological determinism gained ascendency during the first decades of the new century. Based on the genetic theory of unit transfer of characteristics, eugenics temporarily swept aside environmentalism. In Canada the fear of racial degeneration was allied with support for imperialist ideology. McConnachie notes a subtle shift after the First World War, in a continental partnership with the United States, from eugenic theory as a study of population to the direct application of hereditary determinism to social policy, a shift that, as Frank Mort notes, never occurred in Britain. Eugenic theory was almost as swiftly eroded after the war, its scientific basis ultimately debunked by research into theories of genetic crossover and multiple transfer. But although its theoretical base largely evaporated, its legacy remained in the practices, both clinical and ideological, developed under its influence.

The stated objectives of the CNCMH attest to a eugenic program that sought to intensify the moral regulation of women of childbearing age. Such regulation was integrally related to the class, race, and gendered interests of its membership and intended audience. A program of segregation was thought to be necessary, particularly since the only legislative provision that existed so far was a 1913 Ontario statute called the Female Refuges Act, which empowered physicians to certify 'feeble-minded' inmates and to keep them in houses of refuge after expiry of their sentences.[26] To the consternation of those concerned with the problem of feeble-mindedness, the legislation provided for short-term periods of incarceration. It was in this manner that the question focused from the outset on individual reproductive, and therefore sexual and moral behaviour. Constructing a broader reproductive strategy as a matter of social and government policy lay at the base of clinic practice. Further, the term 'feeble-mindedness' was itself transliterated from one that described inferior physical stock to one that connoted inferior intelligence.[27] The term 'mentally deficient' or 'mental and moral degenerate' gradually replaced 'feeble-mindedness' in the lexicon of the TPC's program of corrective psychiatry. In this case the target was the young 'mentally deficient' woman of childbearing age whose actions attested to her moral or social misconduct, and hence to her social inefficiency.

The 'Factory Girl' Meets the Psychiatrist

The problem of the 'girl delinquent' was thought to have been exacerbated by the disruption associated with the Great War. Drawn into the paid labour force by personal and familial economic needs and by the labour demands of an economy mobilized for wartime production, the 'factory girl' symbolized both economic and cultural transition. Economic independence and an increased sphere of personal autonomy, however, presented a series of problems which Clarke and his colleagues sought to address. Their concern was not that female exposure to the 'male' factory would prove debilitating for the nation's future mothers. Instead, Clarke chose to concentrate on what he termed 'occupational wanderers,' those young working-class women who moved from one job to another and whose apparent industrial inefficiency was subsidized by the newly legislated female minimum wage. Below is an assessment of a woman examined by Clarke, one that typifies his clinical analysis and prognosis:

This woman belongs to a very difficult type, and has very simply wandered from pillar to post for many years. She gave me a list of a dozen or more places she had been at ... [she] evidently is what we term an occupational wanderer, finding it impossible to get on anywhere on account of her violent and ungovernable temper ... She is suffering from a mental disease, and is, in my opinion, not fit to be left to her own resources. We have followed her record in Toronto, obtaining information from Mrs. Duff of the Employment Bureau, and it is quite evident that practically the same thing has happened wherever she has gone – she had outbursts of a wildly hysterical nature. I believe she should be placed in an institution, on account of her mental disability.[28]

Clarke operated on the view that a woman's efficiency in work was synonymous with her capacity for mothering, since both indicated adherence to the appropriate prevailing rules of individual moral self-government and discipline. The Ontario government's 1916 Commission on Unemployment shared a similar view, commenting disapprovingly on those young women who 'change from one factory to another and steadily lose the ability to become good workers ... Taking no interest in the work, they show a disrespect for property and material with which they bring disrespect on the factory girl as a class.'[29]

In an expanding culture of young women's work and leisure, it seemed that the moral welfare of the 'factory girl' was threatened on all sides: in the dance-halls, the factory cafeteria, the movie theatres and vaudeville, and on the ubiquitous joyride through dark country lanes on the city's outskirts. According to the dedicated child-saver J.J. Kelso, the problem, while not necessarily alarming, was none the less real and visible. 'There has been a larger number of delinquent girls from fifteen to eighteen in districts where the soldiers are assembled. Young girls are naturally attracted and a considerable number fall victim to their own weakness for men's society, and yet even here, the number is not sufficient to cause any general alarm.'[30]

As far as the editors of the popular journal *Social Welfare* were concerned, the problem was greater than that envisioned by Kelso. In an editorial in the November 1918 issue, the editor cautioned that the 'problem of girl delinquency [had] become very severe'; even though their numbers might be lower than young male delinquents, the offences were invariably more serious because related to sex and morality. According to the editors, poor social, moral, and environmental conditions at home and at work, including unsatisfactory parenting, could not entirely account for the problem:

The increase in the number of girl delinquents cannot be explained wholly by war conditions. The crowding of many girls into city districts where labour is wanted; the high nervous tension of overworked body and mind; the unwholesome influence of suddenly acquired superfluity of earnings and the too often frivolous reaction to the overcharged war-atmosphere (evinced in the boy by the spirit of adventure), – these contribute but do not suffice to explain conditions. Too many girls are 'let loose' to earn their living alone, and in a strange environment, under the sole protection of 'undefended innocence.' Many cases reported are of girls, almost too young to realize the social bearing of their crimes.[31]

The explanation, as was to be demonstrated over the ensuing period, lay in feeble-mindedness, alternatively termed mental degeneracy or mental deficiency. The editorial staff of *Social Welfare,* like the Toronto Local Council of Women, might advocate an 'equal moral standard between men and women,' one that would judge the male as harshly as the female offender for moral and sexual deviation. But it was not long before *Social Welfare*'s editors also hopped on the mental hygiene platform, calling for government action in the 'care and control of the feeble-minded.'

Clarke and his colleagues had found the solution in the science of psychiatry. Gordon Mundie, a psychiatrist practising in Montreal, claimed that the problem of 'girl delinquency' was particularly acute there. The majority of patients seen at the Montreal Psychiatric Clinic in 1919 were young women and girls. Mundie was particularly exercised by the refusal of young girls to follow the path of virtue. But by 1922 any attribution of delinquency to the war's disruptive force, hence the environmental influence, had to be abandoned. That year, Mundie vented his spleen against modern female youth:

The cause of the girl being brought before the Court is usually of a sex nature. With the spread of the dance hall, movies and automobiles, the average girl is not content to stay at home and do domestic work. She must take up a business career or work in a factory so that she can have her evenings free. Many of the girls are mentally deficient, but with a manner and a prettiness which, with their lack of mental control, leads to their delinquency. There is also the girl who thinks it is nobody's business but her own if she chooses to adopt an immoral career. One such girl when questioned about her life said it had been a delightful experience.[32]

Clarke prided himself on 'studying social failures from almost every angle imaginable,'[33] and felt that he could eschew with certainty any statements coming from the mouths of social reformers who, he felt, lacked the benefit of training in the methods and theory of psychiatry and scientific technique. In his view, careful empirical study and investigation far outweighed theory. 'It is all very well to talk of lectures on sex hygiene, and a dozen other plans, some excellent, but others almost as revolting as the conditions they strive to cure, but they are often as inadequate as would be the attempt to dam the St. Lawrence with a toothpick.'[34]

Flawed or nonexistent investigation, 'reforms verging on ill-digested radicalism,' tradition, even sentimentalism were useless as methods by which to deal with 'the poor girls who parade the blazing white ways at night, flit about the country roads and lanes joy riding in automobiles, or haunting the lower kinds of dance halls.'[35] These were the 'girls' with whom TPC practitioners were well acquainted: young women such as Beatrice B., who was examined while at the Industrial Refuge: 'This girl is a mental defective of the high grade type. She is slow-witted, affable and hypersuggestible. Her history indicates that supervision in an institution is advantageous for some time to come.'[36]

Affability and 'hypersuggestibility' were also the downfall of Dorothy F., another inmate of the Industrial Refuge. Not only was her moral and social misconduct an apparent threat to the social order, but she was infected with VD, which, on its own, constituted ample reason for her indefinite incarceration: 'This girl is a mental defective of the moron class. She is affable and hypersuggestible and too easy going to get along in the general community unless surrounded with the most careful and intelligent supervision. I would not recommend her discharge from the Industrial Refuge at present because I understand that she is suffering from gonorrhoea, and if she were paroled just now she might be a menace to society.'[37]

According to TPC practitioners, the greatest and most accurate test of social efficiency was employment, or, more specifically, occupation. Work habits, skills deployed, and longevity of employment, as well as loyalty, discipline, and obedience to one's employer, were all testimony to industrial and social efficiency. Clinic workers were convinced that the immorality of the girl delinquent could not be explained by low wages or poor working conditions. In fact, those who posited such an explanation were accused of looking at the horse from the wrong end. Clarke presented the argument in the form of a psychiatrist's law of supply and demand. The scarce commodity in this market was not skill, but intelligence and mental capacity: 'The explanation is not the one ordinarily offered, viz., that the low wages paid are the cause of immorality, the truth being that the mental capacity of the wage earners precludes them from receiving more than they are paid. It is one of the economic problems not clearly understood by those not in possession of the facts.'[38]

Undertaking the study of the young working-class woman from this angle opened up a new area, which, some considered, was a virtual fountain of social facts. Clarke could barely contain his excitement at the prospects. 'What our experience has taught us, is, that no more fertile field for investigation exists than that furnished by factory workers of certain types, where small wages and simple occupations go hand in hand.' A 'careful survey' of factories would reveal to the concerned public what was already common knowledge to clinic staff: that there were numerous factory girls who were defective, and therefore in need of identification and supervision. Surveillance was doubly necessary since VD was spread, in particular, by women factory workers who 'furnish[ed] a large proportion of the 'joy riders' and 'night hawks' who infest the country roads and streets after dark.'

The TPC did in fact conduct at least one special study of the 'factory girl,' since, following the view that proof had somehow to precede theory, only the direct hands-on mapping of the female factory worker could demonstrate that feeble-mindedness rather than working conditions was productive of immorality. The results of the 'survey' were published in the popular *Maclean's Magazine* in 1922 under Clarke's name. Protestations of scientific purity of purpose to the contrary, Clarke openly acknowledged that he intended to refute once and for all the misguided views prevalent among many social workers. Why did so many 'children,' as he put it, 'fall victim to the allurements of vice at an early age?' Clarke paraphrased the environmentalist's 'sentimental twaddle' with his usual acerbity:

'Oh, the low wages paid in factories are at the bottom of it all. Factory managers are indifferent, the girls do not receive remuneration at all adequate to enable them to live decently and they succumb very easily to the allurements of modern life with its dance halls, its joy rides, movies and cheap vaudeville.' The theory is plausible, but after all in social service, facts are essential.[39]

Clarke was more than willing to provide concrete facts that told a very different story from the villainous employer and victimized working girl of common, class-conscious lore. In a sample of 452 young women examined at the TPC, one-third were factory workers, 'nearly all of whom belonged to the low grade or high grade moron classes, most of them immoral, and often suffering from contagious disease.' Minimum wage legislation was just another example of misguided social policy that exacerbated the original problem by propping up the socially 'inefficient.' As far as Clarke and his colleagues were concerned, 'small wages have little to do with the matter, and the majority of misfits are earning far more than they are worth. Usually they only find employment when the demand for labour is great.'[40] The criminal justice system too perpetuated existing social problems, since the system dealt with the crime rather than with the individual. Criminal law was powerless to redress the harms done to the community by the feeble-minded woman: not only was she prone to recidivism and likely to transmit VD, but she also contributed her offspring to the growing ranks of the mentally defective.

> Mary Smith may receive ninety days in the Jail Farm for vagrancy, but who Mary Smith is, what her mentality is, what her history is, cannot be considered, – there is no time, and the wheels of justice must run with speed, otherwise the Court cannot get through. What of Mary Smith when she is finished her sentence? Of course, she is at liberty to go where she pleases unless it is necessary for her to receive further treatment in the hospital clinic and after that, – well she simply falls back into the old rut.[41]

Clinic Background

Those associated with the TPC and the CNCMH worked diligently to build a referral network linked to agencies and organizations throughout the Toronto region. The network would put the preventive and corrective program into practice, and therefore would protect society from women like 'Mary Smith.' Such a network was important for two reasons. First, a monitoring system could be developed among all agencies and institutional systems involved in the work of immigration, criminal justice, public relief and health, education, employment placement, and social welfare. Second, the apparatus provided for referral in the opposite direction – for the appropriate agencies to receive and care for those designated for 'treatment' and supervision. With that in mind, the clinic's work was to proceed as follows:

1 Free acceptance of all cases of suspected mental abnormality.
2 Evaluation of individual patients from the standpoint of social fitness, industrial efficiency, and capacity for education.
3 Advice to patients, guardians, employers, teachers, etc.
4 Industrial training of suitable types.
5 Employment Bureau for the partially handicapped.
6 Home supervision of cases.
7 Mental examination of patients attending S[pecial] T[reatment] Clinic (for venereal disease).
8 Co-operation with other social agencies.
9 Commitment to institutions of cases unsuitable for life in the general community.

In Clarke's view the clinic provided an organizational 'missing link' in the city's 'otherwise excellent chain of social agencies.' The Juvenile and Women's Court, Central Neighbourhood House, the Women's Jail Farm, the Toronto Board of Education and Department of Public Health, the Salvation Army's Haven and Prison Gate Mission for women, and the Belmont Industrial Refuge for women all opened their doors to facilitate the identification of 'mental defectives' in their midst. As Clarke himself noted, 'The chief value of the clinic has been its influence in educating the public in matters pertaining to mental deficiency and insanity – an influence that has extended to all parts of the Dominion.'[42]

In 1918 the CNCMH issued a 'plan of co-operation between the Toronto General Hospital Psychiatric Clinic and extra-hospital agencies.' This plan institutionalized the CNCMH's supervisory role in the 'care and control' of Toronto's 'mentally defective' population. The memorandum outlined the precise relationship that would exist between the TPC and the CNCMH on the one hand and the clinic and external agencies on the other. The CNCMH was to supplement the TPC's work 'for the purpose of giving advice for the education, training, vocational placement, and social adjustment' of 'cases' whom clinic medical staff thought might benefit. An official of the CNCMH was to be brought on staff at the committee's expense, and was authorized to have access to all 'patients.' The clinic's social service staff, charged with the task of social as opposed to psychiatric investigation, was instructed to cooperate fully with the CNCMH, and to provide the committee with 'a copy of all information appertaining to every case passing through the clinic.'[43] This arrangement gave Toronto's professional mental hygienists what they thought was the critically important set of data needed to prove their case. Local data drawn from the local population obviated the need to rely on easily refuted US statistics and case studies: it brought home the threat posed by the 'feeble-minded.'

By 1921 the CNCMH issued its first official study of the problem of mental deficiency for the Toronto region, noting the significance of the TPC as the prototype for the psychiatric research facility advocated by the mental hygiene movement: 'In the past we have had to draw on other countries for many of the figures on which to base theories, but since the advent of the Canadian National Committee for Mental Hygiene, advantage has been taken of the facilities offered by the Toronto General Hospital Psychiatric Clinic and its Social Service Department to collect accurate statistics.'[44]

Published under Clarke's name in the *Canadian Journal of Mental Hygiene,* the article's rather cumbersome title laid claim to the status of scientific fact: 'A Study of 5600 Cases Passing through the Psychiatric Clinic of the Toronto General Hospital. A Special Study of 188 Clinic Cases – Also a Survey of 767 Cases of Illegitimacy' appeared to compile and summarize all of the 'cases' examined at the clinic for the past seven years. But the study targeted only social matters pertaining to women and the 'girl delinquent' in a manner that revealed the priorities of the CNCMH, and hence the TPC, and that was intended to expose the allegedly hereditarian basis for prostitution, illegitimacy, and the 'occupational wanderer.' These were the specific categories into which the problem of 'feeble-mindedness' among women, like the study itself, was organized. Although more than half of the 5,600 cases examined were male, the 'problems' that were thought worthy of comment all related to and discussed women alone.

The clinic's purpose from the outset was to develop and implement a program of preventive and corrective psychiatry, to correct the 'failure of parents, employers, and others to recognize mental defectives and abnormals,' in a campaign of public education wherein all would share the work of controlling and caring for the 'feeble-minded.' An educated public was central to the success of such a preventive program. In this case, prevention did not mean that the 'disease' of mental degeneration could be prevented in the individual; rather, the afflicted individual could be, and in fact had to be, prevented from 'spreading the taint.' Commenting on the results of the TPC's 'Study of 5600,' Clarke alluded to the profligacy of the feeble-minded and the extent to which untrained non-initiates to the science of mental hygiene repeatedly missed the point, thereby adding to the problem. 'What does a careful study of these figures reveal?' Clarke asked rhetorically. 'Surely the first thought to strike the careful student is the fact that prevention has not received the consideration it deserved.'[45]

The first line of defence in the program of prevention was school inspection, which would identify and screen the feeble-minded at the earliest age possible. Not only would this census-taking permit accurate identification, but it would allow the mental hygienist to control the spread of other social problems. This emphasis on prevention in early childhood, while indicating the growth of childhood and behaviourial psychology as a separate discipline, also revealed the view shared by Clarke, Hincks and others that individual pathologies developed and could therefore be identified in early childhood. Consequently, immorality could also be detected from an early age; potential delinquency, later revealed in the prostitute and the occupational wanderer, could be exposed before it became manifest in concrete actions. Again, the idea was to *prevent* immorality before it was expressed in any of its forms. Clarke attempted to present the matter in a positive light, exhorting readers to share his confidence in both the diagnosis and the prognosis: 'A great majority of [prostitutes studied] were of school age when first becoming immoral, and were defective – some were insane. At all events, under a proper system of school inspection their defects could have been detected, and an intelligent line of care and treatment mapped out.'[46]

The clinical examination mirrored the agenda set by the CNCMH; weeding out the 'mental defectives' was translated into a search for social and industrial inefficiency, which in women was indicated by moral and social misconduct. The examination forms used by clinic workers reflected the underlying assumption that the social activities of the 'patient' held the key to the individual's position on the evolutionary ladder of mental development. Educational and occupational history were as significant as family history, moral and sexual activities as relevant as physical 'stigmata.' Every contour of the physical, social, and intellectual terrain was to be carefully scrutinized and documented.

The Clinical Examination

The entire clinical examination hinged on the Binet-Simon test, which was designed to measure an individual's degree of 'mental development' or 'mental age.' Canadian mental hygienists adopted the British classification system as set out in legislation enacted by the British parliament in

1913.[47] The three-tiered system ranged from the 'idiot' (low-grade defective), to the 'imbecile' (middle- range defective); but the greatest threat was alleged to spring from the 'feeble-minded' or 'moron' (high-grade borderline defective).[48] Since this latter group revealed no overt physical signs to indicate their internal malaise, the condition could be accurately diagnosed only by 'mental measurement.' This was Clarke's forte. According to Binet, a mental age of fifteen was considered an acceptable level of social maturity. Many of the women examined by Clarke measured below this mark. This, he explained, was proof of their mental defect, since 'ordinarily the term mental defective is applied to those who measure low in the scale of intelligence.' He was particularly concerned with those who 'do not reach a mental age of twelve, although their chronological age is much greater.'[49] Women 'with the minds of children in the bodies of adults' of course posed the greatest threat of all: sexually mature but lacking the 'mental stuff' that would compel them to social efficiency and moral conformity.

The eugenicist's view of the relationship between heredity and intelligence was reflected in the work of experts such as Peter Sandiford, an education professor at the University of Toronto and an educational adviser to the CNCMH. Sandiford was convinced that intelligence was genetically fixed according to the inherited quality of the individual's physiology and was therefore an absolute quantity, although it increased somewhat with chronological age. In Sandiford's usage, intelligence and mental age were one and the same.[50]

TPC practitioners took a similar approach and faithfully applied the Binet-Simon test. The women whose results gave the mental hygienists most trouble were those who reached a high score on the Binet-Simon scale. Such women were still considered mental defectives but were an anomalous group. Clarke described the group, which appeared to cause him the greatest degree of consternation, as 'factory girls' who were out for a good time, and who were guilty of moral infractions but had not turned their 'immoral careers' to commercial gain. 'Under this heading [of mental defectives] may be grouped the majority of the prostitutes examined, although others showed their defect more particularly in want of ability to realize their social obligations, and exhibited defects in character that were sufficiently clear to the investigators.'

Since it was difficult to classify such young women according to the legislatively defined gradations of mental deficiency outlined above, clinic workers found it necessary to develop a subcategory, the 'moral defective' whose inadequate social and moral intelligence made her a 'high grade moron,' whatever her score on the Binet-Simon scale. Clarke outlined the system thus: 'Take the girls, for example, who could do the Binet Simon tests up to twelve or thirteen, but whose failure even under advantageous circumstances, to recognize the most obvious moral obligations, clearly showed the defect of their organizations.'[51]

The purpose of the clinic investigation, and therefore the Binet-Simon test, was ultimately to determine the individual's social efficiency. Social efficiency was defined along the same lines as intelligence, as 'the capacity of an individual to live in accordance with the usages and dictates of society and to earn a livelihood.' The factors that determined social inefficiency included earning capacity or wage level, home life, and evidence of delinquency and immorality. 'Reasons for failure' were listed as unsuitable employment and lack of training; poor physical condition; 'unsuitable friends and associates'; 'personality peculiarities'; lack of affability; the absence of a 'sporting spirit,' that is, the inability to 'give and take with good grace'; and paranoia. Here, clinic investigators implemented their own classification system:

Class A – ability to conform to dictates and usages of society and to earn an independent livelihood without supervision.

Class B – fulfilling the requirements of Class A with the exception that occasional supervision is needed.

Class C – requiring more or less continuous supervision in the community

Class D – requiring institutional care.

A clinic questionnaire constituted another level of investigation, one that actively constructed the symptoms, knowledge and subjectivity of the 'patient' suspected of feeble-mindedness. The questionnaire was designed to probe more deeply into every aspect of the individual's social, moral, emotional and intellectual life and to locate pathological symptoms of degeneration. A series of notes written for clinic workers directed the route the 'interview' should follow. For example, the interviewer was instructed to determine in what way the subject was a 'social problem.' Appropriate pathologies to look for included 'delinquencies, immorality, venereal disease, dependency, marked retardation in school.'[52] It was especially important to decide whether the person was able to 'work satisfactorily' outside an institution; satisfactory work was defined as 'reliable employment with a living wage.' The investigator was aided in making this decision by noting the number of jobs held since school-leaving; clearly, a higher number of jobs indicated lower reliability. 'Salient causes' of unemployment were listed as low IQ, defects of character, and physical defects. There was no mention, and therefore no recognition, of how material conditions and personal or objective circumstances might contribute to job turnover or job loss. When asking about 'attitudes toward others and the world in general,' the examiner was to note that any complaints or avoidance showed the 'absence of [a] forward mind.'

Assignment of mental age, and especially its disparity with chronological age, stood either on its own to confirm the presence of mental degeneracy or in combination with moral and social misconduct. Anna McF., incarcerated at the Haven and Prison Gate Mission, was recommended for deportation because she was purported to be industrially 'inefficient.' Not only did she measure poorly on the Binet-Simon scale; she was also an 'occupational wanderer.'

> I have today examined this girl, and find she is of poor mental type, does not measure up to twelve years of age by the Binet Simon method, and is incompetent and unable apparently to work successfully. In Scotland she had only the most trivial kind of work to do and apparently changed about from one place to another pretty regularly. She says she has some money, and is anxious to be deported. Although the amount is probably insufficient to pay her fare, it would be well to assist her as she will simply become a burden on the community.[53]

The Program for Treatment

Practitioners at the TPC soon established a close working relationship with the social service agencies and correctional facilities in Toronto. The TPC served as a clearing-house: it received women referred to it as 'patients' and referred women, now processed through the examination and diagnostic apparatus, to appropriate facilities for supervision. The clinic developed important discretionary powers which permitted practitioners to intervene in and determine the future of many young women's lives. The histories of such women could be permanently altered, at the extreme by deportation or, perhaps more moderately, in the form of temporary 'supervision' within their communities, all at the recommendation of the clinic staff. The TPC also intervened in court proceedings to provide testimony, advice, and probationary services. Finally, in collaboration with the CNCMH, the TPC conducted a 'mental hygiene survey' among women held at the Toronto Women's Jail Farm (1922). This survey, like the clinic's other work, comprised extralegal recommendations pertaining to the advisability of parole, vocational training, or prolonged incarceration. Throughout, the information collected purported to strengthen the argument for the need for psychiatric intervention in cases pertaining to the alleged social and moral misconduct of young, working-class, immigrant women.

Community Supervision

The Big Sisters Association (BSA) provides one example of a volunteer agency that worked closely with the TPC to provide discipline and possibly some of the idealized guidance modelled on the relationship to which the organization's name alluded. The BSA also appeared to take on an extralegal probationary role, or to supplement the probationary period ordered by the Juvenile Court. In a letter to Dr G.W. Anderson of the Juvenile Court, Hincks recommended this practice for Helen D.L., a young woman whose actions did not provide legal grounds for incarceration but which were disturbing enough to require some level of community monitoring. Hincks thought that Helen was 'somewhat subnormal mentally but not definitely feeble-minded in the technical sense of the term.' Although in Hincks's estimation Helen was 'naturally industrious,' she was 'easily led' and would 'certainly fall along the lines of least resistance without strict and diplomatic supervision.' Helen already had a Big Sister, but Hincks diplomatically advised a switch to one who had 'a genius in dealing with girls' like her. Should she not reform through supervision, hard work and 'healthy recreation', the reformatory awaited. Hincks himself pronounced the sentence if probation failed: 'Helen should be warned that if she does not live within certain strictures she will be placed in custody.'[54]

Mary B., a seventeen-year-old recently arrived from Ireland, was brought to the clinic in 1921. Clarke was apparently reluctant to pronounce her entirely 'normal,' although any direct evidence of legal wrongdoing was not mentioned in her case. In Clarke's assessment, there was little need to wait for concrete evidence to emerge. The testimony of the subject was sufficient to indicate her need for supervision. 'While it is true that in intelligence she grades up to 14, at the same time her story in regard to her moral behaviour leads one to feel very sceptical of her truthfulness.

She tells of all sorts of requests to become immoral on the part of different individuals. The inference is that something must have happened in order to make men assume this attitude toward her, and I am by no means satisfied that her career has been free from indiscretions.'[55]

The most appropriate course of action for a young single immigrant woman like Mary B., according to Clarke, was to place her 'under very careful surveillance by the right kind of Big Sister.' In the event that such community surveillance or probation did not succeed in controlling Mary's sexual behaviour, Clarke advised deportation, adding that he was happy to offer his expertise in 'taking the necessary steps to have [deportation] effected.' Deportation proceedings were initiated the following year, since Mary B.'s inappropriate moral conduct appeared to continue. There was still no evidence of illegitimate birth or venereal disease. Had these been at issue, they would most certainly have been mentioned in Clarke's correspondence. The real issue was moral misconduct, of which illegitimacy and VD were only two of many symptoms. It is significant that Clarke drew a confession of immoral behaviour from his 'patient,' as though to legitimate his diagnosis: 'I have today examined Mary B., and still feel that she is not a safe girl to be at large. She has been immoral in the past, admits so today for the first time, and says she is very weak and easily led. I think she may be fairly classed as a high grade moron, and should, in my opinion, be returned to Ireland to her own people. The patient was in this condition before coming to Canada.'[56]

Deportation

To create a legal ground for deportation, clinic staff were required to establish that the women in question were feeble-minded when they arrived in Canada. The Canadian Immigration Act, which had earlier prohibited the entry of persons with infectious or contagious diseases, had been strengthened in 1906 to prevent other persons from emigrating to Canada, including any immigrant 'who is feeble-minded, an idiot, or an epileptic, or who is insane.'[57] Prostitutes and pimps were also prohibited, and those who were 'deaf, dumb, blind or infirm' were admitted only if their families guaranteed support. In this period the classes prohibited from entering Canada were grouped into four categories that reflected state priorities in the area of public health: mental defectives and the insane; those suffering from contagious diseases; those with physical disabilities; and those previously convicted of moral turpitude.[58] In addition, deportation was introduced for certain 'undesirables' under section 28 of the act: 'any person landed in Canada who, within two years thereafter, has become a charge upon the public funds, whether municipal, provincial, or federal, or an inmate of or a charge upon any charitable insitution, may be deported and returned to the port or place whence such immigrant came or sailed for Canada.'

In 1910 a new provision allowed for the subsequent removal of any immigrant belonging to the 'prohibited classes' as defined under the act. Other changes broadened the 1906 provisions against prostitution by specifically excluding pimps, a change that reflected the contemporary campaign against 'white slavery.'[59]

After 1913 the definitional model for the CNCMH was the British Mental Deficiency Act of that year, an inclusive piece of legislation that defined 'mentally defective' to include not only 'idiots' but also 'imbeciles,' 'feeble-minded persons' and 'moral imbeciles' under section 1 of the act: '... persons in whose case there exists from birth or an early age mental defectiveness not amounting to idiocy, yet so pronounced that they are incapable of managing themselves or their affairs ... children ... [who] by reason of such defectiveness appear to be permanently incapable of receiving proper benefit from the instruction in ordinary schools ... persons who from an early age display some permanent mental defect ...'[60]

The models for practical implementation were the intelligence test and the vast examination and detention facilities of Ellis Island in the United States. Statute law in, for example, New York and Missouri included the 'public charge' criterion, which was absent from the British statute, and the notion of community 'threat.' 'Mental deficiency in New York, therefore, referred to any person afflicted with mental defectiveness from birth or from any early age, so pronounced that he is incapable of managing himself and his affairs and of subsisting by his own efforts, or of being taught to do so, and who requires supervision, control and care for his own welfare, or for the welfare of others, or for the welfare of the community, and who cannot be classified as an insane person.'[61]

The communication addressed to Mr J.C. Mitchell of the Department of Immigration, Toronto, is typical of the clinics's recommendations concerning feeble-minded women, and of Clarke's diagnoses: 'She has already had two illegitimate children, and has absolutely no idea of responsibility. Is a mental defective measuring up to ten years of age. She should never have been admitted to the country, and if you cannot deport her she will become a burden on the community.'[62]

The notion that women might be deported simply because they had given birth to children outside marriage was controversial in law.[63] Conversely, the deportation of unmarried mothers pronounced mentally degenerate was much less so. From a sample of thirty-two people for whom deportation was advised, twenty were women. While 'chronic unemployment' was the single most important factor in deciding the fate of the men, 'illegitimacy' and 'immorality' provided the main justification for deporting the women. In this group two women were diagnosed as 'normal'; however, they both had 'illegitimate' children. The notations entered for individuals in entry after entry were intended to describe a grim allegory of 'social failures' and the inadequacies shown in medical and psychiatric immigration inspection.

- Mental age 11 yrs. Is a Barnardo girl. Has two illegitimate children. Suffering from venereal disease.
- Mental age 8 years. Has one illegitimate child. Is an occupational wanderer. Has been persistently immoral.
- Mental age between 7 and 8. Very irresponsible. Has one child 4 years of age. Says she was married twice and both men left her. This is doubtful.
- Married in 1917. Lived with husband 6 months, when he went overseas and was killed. Had one illegitimate child. Has venereal disease. Can neither read nor write.
- Generally poor knowledge. Is extremely careless about dress. One illegitimate child. Immoral before coming to Canada.
- [girl 15 years old] Immoral. Unsteady employment. Difficult case socially because of bad upbringing and undesirable habits.[64]

In the case of Grace A., Clarke's recommendation for deportation failed because she had already been in Canada fourteen years. She was originally brought to Clarke's attention by referral from the Toronto General Hospital Burnside 'lying-in' department (where Clarke was a regular visitor) and was found to have two 'illegitimate' children. Clarke's letter to immigration officials stated, 'If set at liberty she will no doubt continue to add to the defective population with a regularity that is very distressing.'[65] Two years later, Grace A. was again referred to the TPC. Since deportation was not legally possible, Clarke advised incarceration. Like the majority of cases examined, Grace A. had committed no discernible offence, nor was she in legal custody. Moral misconduct was itself tantamount to criminality.

I examined this girl first on September 13th, 1921 at the Toronto General Hospital. She has led an immoral career and has had two illegitimate children. At that time she had a mental age of ten years, and was diagnosed as a low grade moron. Today she appeared before me, and I found her to be if anything more childish than on the last occasion. In my opinion, she should be institutionalized, possibly in such a Home as the Haven, as she is not fit to be left to her own devices.[66]

Institutional Supervision

In 1922 the CNCMH, through the TPC, conducted a 'mental hygiene survey' of inmates at the Women's Jail Farm at Richmond Hill, north of the Toronto city limits. In a letter to the facility's superintendent, Dr Lillian Langstaff, Clarke commiserated over the legal hurdles that had to be overcome in such work; he felt 'greatly perturbed over many of these women ... they should not be at liberty, as they are not only a menace to themselves, but also to the public.'

> Let me congratulate you and your associates on the splendid institution you have developed. It is something to be proud of and although one feels much disturbed when it is realized that your hands are tied so thoroughly by red tape and legal practice. I am sure you agree with me that the majority of these unfortunates would be very much better institutionalized, much as one regrets to resort to institutions except when absolutely necessary. Take the case of Katie P. I pointed out years ago to the authorities that this woman should be locked up, and yet she has been allowed to go on adding from time to time to the defective population.[67]

Katie P. was initially brought to the TPC at the age of twenty-two, when she was pronounced 'hopelessly immoral, without any mental background to prevent her being so.' Her 'mental age' was rated at eight years. Four years later she was referred by Central Neighbourhood House. She had apparently 'added three more to the list of six defective children,' and, it was believed, would 'go on behaving immorally and adding to the defective population if not prevented.' At that time, Clarke advised that she be sent to the Haven and her children given into the custody of the Children's Aid Society. Clarke insisted on immediate action, since she had already cohabited with three men and was rumoured to have been seen frequenting a boarding-house 'for immoral purposes.' Six months later, they met again at the Jail Farm.

Since the Jail Farm was used as a facility to incarcerate women under the terms of the Venereal Diseases Control Act, it provided fertile ground to substantiate the argument for institutional custody of 'immoral' women. The presence of VD was thought to be intimately associated with moral misconduct, and therefore with mental deficiency. Similarly, although not recognized in legislation, the finding of 'occupational wanderer' attested to social misconduct. One working-class francophone woman, aged twenty-one, was found guilty in both respects.

> This girl has had very little education and can only read words of the simplest character. She married four years ago, and did not live with her husband any length of time. She came to Toronto and picked up another man, living in a restaurant ... She had worked in factories a good deal, Sunlight Soap factory, etc., waitress in a large number of restaurants – no less than four in Toronto. Has also done housework ... Her scale of intelligence is very low – for example, she states that Toronto is a city of 1000 inhabitants and Montreal is even smaller. Her general knowledge is practically nothing. Her manner is childish, silly, and she giggles a great deal while talking to examiner. Her emotional tone is very shallow. Has both G.C. and syphilis. Diagnosis; low grade moron.

Another young woman was first examined at the age of thirteen at the TPC. She had been referred by the Juvenile Court, where she had been charged with 'immorality.' Clarke pronounced her a mental defective. Three years later she was seen by clinic staff as part of the 'survey.' The language used to describe her 'history' typified the problem of young women's social and moral misconduct: 'L. is an occupational wanderer, having worked in candy factories, restaurants, etc. Has venereal disease. Has been immoral with two or three boys – would go to a park. Charged with not reporting for treatment. Is a mental defective.'[68] In all, the majority of women seen by clinic staff at the Jail Farm were pronounced mentally degenerate and, not surprisingly, best kept within the walls of the correctional institution. Segregation was considered the best possible course for young women of childbearing age, particularly once their 'immoral careers' had become entrenched in occupational wanderlust and moral misconduct.

Conclusion

The TPC's practitioners saw themselves as reformers of public health. Their work led them in and out of correctional institutions, factories, and even the dance-halls of Toronto. In following their efforts, I have begun to explore how such activity was part of a broader discourse that problematized young working-class and immigrant women through the categories of deviance, disease, and the practices of work and motherhood. The TPC's mental hygienists were committed to demonstrating that the 'state' had an interest in overseeing and intervening in the personal lives of young working-class and immigrant women, given its interest in regulating the conditions in which work, reproduction, education, and public health were carried out. The work of the TPC, through its documentary practices, clinical examination, and 'professionalization' of authorized practitioners, demonstrates the intended expansion of state social administration.

The notion of 'feeble-mindedness' cannot be approached as an ideational category, a new mental pathology, a method of separating out the normal from the allegedly abnormal. Serving rather as a mode of moral regulation, the view of 'feeble-mindedness' both created and responded to 'social problems' as problems of mental pathology. The administrative subjects such as 'factory girls,' VD transmission, illegitimacy, and the 'delinquent girl' intersected with established ideas of social 'problems' such as prostitution, unemployment, uncontrolled immigration, single women and their leisure patterns, marriage, and notions of 'race suicide.' These were all problem fields which TPC practitioners hoped to convince legislators were legitimate arenas for state intervention and regulation.

When the Royal Commission on the Care and Control of the Feeble-Minded was appointed in 1918, the mental hygiene community was confident that its concerns would be addressed. However, the moderately sympathetic Hearst government was defeated before any of the commission's recommendations were passed into law, even while pressure from the CNCMH continued unabated. None the less, with only slight legislative provision for the incarceration of so-called feeble-minded women in Houses of Refuge, a network of extralegal practices developed, at least around the Toronto Psychiatric Clinic. Large numbers of young women passed through this network after having been identified, diagnosed, and turned over into appropriate hands.

The Toronto Psychiatric Clinic served as a practical, influential instrument for the mental hygiene movement. The clinic marked an early high point in the significance of psychiatric practice in penological, immigration, and social welfare work. The psychiatric examination itself reflected a subtle shift in discourse that constructed 'feeble-mindedness' as it was applied to women. Although the 'fallen woman' lingered on, that identity was collapsed into the new diagnostic key: intelligence testing. The feeble-minded woman was mentally, and therefore morally degenerate.

Intelligence was itself construed as a broader social category, an index of the individual's social efficiency that was shaped by and in turn actively constructed notions of social and sexual deviance. In this practice, class, culture, gender, and race were identified as underlying vectors for social and moral misconduct as defined by the clinic practitioner. The mental test of knowledge, combined with assessments of employment history, sexual behaviour, and physical appearance, all became part of the terrain of the psychiatric examination, with the objective of assessing the moral and social conduct of young working-class and immigrant women. Similarly, clinic staff harboured a deep cynicism towards environmentally based, legislative, and structural social reform efforts. Biological, hereditary determinism motivated the work of the TPC. Even as the theoretical basis of eugenics was eroded, however, its practices were maintained. Social problems were not seen as structural or environmental in origin. Rather, periodic unemployment, poverty, and 'illegitimacy' were all seen as individual failings, indicative of individual pathological degeneracy. Past reform efforts, it was argued, had failed to grasp this point. They had, in fact, ignored the importance of placing all social 'work' on a firm scientific foundation. The answer, once the question was posed correctly, lay in the investigation of social 'failures' themselves. Thus Clarke and his colleagues could place responsibility for crime and delinquency, prostitution, poverty, and unemployment at the door of the 'mentally degenerate.' Not only did such individuals create the conditions that threatened the 'superior' stock; they reproduced the hereditary disease of mental 'degeneracy.' The so-called mentally degenerate woman, especially if 'diagnosed' as a 'high grade moral defective,' posed a formidable threat, given the greater freedoms and cultural laxity of the workplace, the dance-hall, and the movie theatre.

Only through scientific study and intervention by a trained psychiatrist could the 'socially inefficient,' mentally degenerate woman be identified. For the work to be effective, the professional program of preventive and corrective psychiatry initiated at the TPC had to be located at the nexus of an integrated network of agencies and institutions with which the women targeted by the clinic came into contact. In this way, too, TPC practitioners hoped to accomplish their goal of mapping the 'mentally degenerate' woman, by means of a census or register of the population. As an agency that existed on the periphery of the 'official' state, the TPC succeeded in adding another layer of professionalized intervention into the personal lives and identities of young working-class and immigrant women whom clinic practitioners sought to regulate, even in the absence of enabling legislation.

NOTES

I would like to thank Kari Dehli, Alison Prentice, Carolyn Strange, and Anne Healy for their assistance and encouragement.

1 The Toronto Psychiatric Clinic was initially established in 1909 as a small outpatient clinic for nervous and mental diseases at the Toronto General Hospital under the directorship of Dr Ernest Jones, 'with the idea,' wrote Dr Charles Clarke, 'of seeing what could be done in the way of getting in touch with mental cases in the early stages of the disease.' Two years later Clarke left his post as medical superintendent of the Toronto Hospital for the Insane to take up his new position as director of the formally established Psychiatric Clinic, now under the jurisdiction of the non-medical Social Service Department. That the clinic found its organizational support there reflected the reticence of the established medical profession to endorse the form and application of psychiatry practised by Clarke and Clarence Hincks. (Interview with Dr Jack Griffin.)

2 'Mental hygiene surveys' were also conducted among schoolchildren and the populations of Manitoba, Saskatchewan, and British Columbia. See, for example, E. Bott, 'Juvenile Employment in Relation to Public Schools and Industries in Toronto,' in *University of Toronto Studies: Psychological Series* (1920); and E.J. Pratt, 'The Application of the Binet-Simon Tests (Stanford Revision) to a Toronto Public School' (1921), 3 *Canadian Journal of Mental Hygiene*, 95–116 (hereinafter cited as *CJMH*). See also CNCMH, 'Mental Hygiene Survey of the Province of Saskatchewan' 3 *CJMH* (1922), 314–99. The Ontario government, unlike the governments of the western provinces, did not ask the CNCMH to conduct a 'mental hygiene survey.' There are several references to a 1906 survey's having been conducted, although no record of it has yet been located. Neither did the Quebec government appear to take up the call for a survey. According to Dr Cyril Greenland, this was due to the strength of opposition from the Catholic church.

3 Kathleen McConnachie, 'Science and Ideology: The Mental Hygiene Movement and Eugenics Movements in the Inter-War Years, 1919–1939,' Ph.D.
Thesis, OISE-University of Toronto 1987.

4 See Leonard P. Ayres, *Laggards in Our Schools* (New York: Russell Sage
Foundation 1913).

5 For a discussion of this work in relation to female criminology and penol-
ogy in the United States, see Estelle Freedman, *Their Sisters' Keepers: Women's
Prison Reform in America, 1830–1930* (Ann Arbor: University of Michigan
Press 1984). See also Helen Gregory MacGill, 'The Relation of the Juvenile
Court to the Community' (1920), 2 *CJMH* 232–36.

6 C.F. Martin, 'Psychiatry and Internal Medicine' (1920), 2 *CJMH* 137–43, at
141.

7 Jessie Taft, 'Supervision of the Feebleminded in the Community' (1919), 1
CJMH, 164–71, at 164.

8 Much of the secondary literature emphasizes the eugenicist focus, which
played a major part in the work of the CNCMH, particularly in connection
with compulsory sterilization. Provision for sterilization was legislated in
British Columbia but not in Ontario. For a discussion of compulsory sterilization and the role of popular social reform and women's organizations in
British Columbia, see Angus McLaren, 'The Creation of a Haven for
'Human Thoroughbreds': The Sterilization of the Feeble-Minded and the
Mentally Ill in British Columbia' (1986), 2 *Canadian Historical Review*
127–50. I differ from McLaren in so far as he, for the most part, adopts an
uncritical stance with respect to the diagnosis of 'feeble-mindedness' per
se. See also Angus McLaren, *Our Own Master Race* (Toronto: McClelland
and Stewart 1990). However, in the references I have consulted for this
paper, there is less discussion of compulsory sterilization and far more of
segregation, notably the plan for a farm colony for boys and girls in the
Toronto region – a plan that did not come to fruition during the period
discussed here.

9 In this Clarke demonstrated the continuing influence of the soon-to-be-
debunked criminological theories of Caesar Lombroso. See Caesar
Lombroso and William Ferrero, *The Female Offender* [1895] (New York: Wisdom Library 1958).

10 Not all agreed with this view, and the *CJMH* carried an article in its July
1920 volume which argued against the (later debunked) germ-plasm theory
of heredity. Its author, William White, saw the negative implications for
positive social reform of biological determinism. White was eager to establish psychiatry and psychology as a legitimate branch in the growing work
of preventive medicine, to elaborate what he called 'a comprehensive

approach to "preventive psychiatry,"' which concentrated first and foremost on early childhood. In what might be read as a critique of the TPC's
work, White disputed the relevance of the Binet-Simon test of mental age,
particularly where its results were interpreted as static and condemning.

11 Frank Mort, *Dangerous Sexualities: Medico-Moral Politics in England since 1830*
(New York: Routledge and Kegan Paul 1987), 172.

12 Nikolas Rose, *The Psychological Complex: Psychology, Politics and Society in England 1869–1939* (London: Routledge and Kegan Paul 1985), 6.

13 All of which together make up the discourse of 'feeble-mindedness' and
from which, I think, emerged the psychiatric / psychological / penological
category of the 'girl delinquent.'

14 Kari Dehli, 'Women and Class: The Social Organization of Mothers' Relations to Schools in Toronto, 1915–1940,' Ph.D. thesis, OISE-University of
Toronto (1988), 13–28.

15 Mariana Valverde and Lorna Weir, 'The Struggles of the Immoral: Preliminary Remarks on Moral Regulation' (1988), 17 *Resources for Feminist Research:
Feminist Perspectives on the Canadian State,* 31–4.

16 I would like to thank Deborah Brock for helping me clarify this idea.

17 C.M. Hincks, 'Feeblemindedness in Canada a Serious National Problem'
(reprinted from *Social Welfare*), Griffin-Greenland Archives, Queen Street
Mental Health Centre (hereinafter cited as QSMHC), Toronto(n.d.), 1.

18 Considerable hay was made of the early estimates produced at the TPC of
the percentage of 'feeble-minded' individuals in the population. For
example, Clarke gave what he considered a conservative estimate of 2,500
people, or 5 per cent of the Toronto population. Hincks took up the figure
for public propaganda and turned it into 40,000 for the country (out of a
total population of 8 million). The figure became the rallying cry, on
Hincks's lead. Hincks, supra note 17.

19 'Kit of the Kitchen,' (1918), 1 *Social Welfare,* 56.

20 Research Committee of the Toronto Mental Hygiene Society, 'The Problem
of Feeble-Mindedness in Toronto,' typescript, Clarke Papers, Clarke Institute of Psychiatry Archives (hereinafter cited as CIPA). Although the typescript is not dated, it is likely to have been presented to the Board of Control as part of the society's deputation.

21 Miss Clarke was an early graduate of the social work program at the University of Toronto. She worked at the clinic until the First World War, when
she used her skills overseas to assist in the war effort.

22 M.J. Clarke, 'The Attitude of the Neighbourhood Worker' (1916), 7 *Public
Health Journal,* 498.

23 Hincks, supra note 17.

24 The anti-VD campaign is discussed in my unpublished paper, 'For the Good of Coming Generations' (1989).

25 McConnachie, supra note 3; Mort, supra note 11. See also Jeffrey Weeks, *Sex, Politics and Society* (London: Longman Group 1981).

26 The statute, An Act Respecting Industrial Refuges for Females, (SO 1913, c. 79) included section 10, which read: 'Where a legally qualified medical practitioner, having the care of the health of the inmates of an Industrial Refuge, certifies that an inmate on account of natural imbecility is so feeble-minded as to render it probable that she would be unable to care for herself if discharged from the refuge, she shall not be discharged until such medical practitioner, with the approval of the Inspector, orders her discharge.'See also James McMeillie, 'Feeble-Minded Women in House of Refuge' (1914), 5 *Public Health Journal,* 225.

27 For a discussion of the shift from moral to intellectual categories in the causation of deficiency and defect based on the social control model, see Steven A. Gelb, 'Not Simply Bad & Incorrigible: Science, Morality and Intellectual Deficiency' (1989), 29 *History of Education Quarterly,* 359–79.

28 Letter from Clarke to Miss Allison, Welfare Branch, Department of Public Health, 21 January 1922. Re: Miss Catherine B., brought by Miss Jay, Council for Social Service, CIPA, Clarke Papers.

29 Ontario, *Report of the Commission on Unemployment,* 170–1, *Sessional Papers* no. 55, 1916.

30 Cited in editorial, 'Juvenile Delinquency and the War' (1918), 1 *Social Welfare,* 39.

31 Ibid.

32 Gordon Mundie, 'The Out-Patient Psychiatric Clinic' (1922), 3 *CJMH,* 311–12. Mundie was attached to the Psychiatric Outpatient Clinic, which opened in 1919 at the Royal Victoria Hospital. It is important to note that the term 'immoral career' was used frequently by TPC practitioners. Although the theme is not pursued here, the term often encompassed incestuous assault sustained by young women at the hands of their fathers or brothers. In several cases Clarke and his colleagues described these assaults as 'immoral activity' initiated by the young women, marking the beginning of their 'immoral careers.'

33 C.K. Clarke, 'Occupational Wanderers,' *Maclean's Magazine* 13 April 1922, 1. All references to this article are from typescript of same, CIPA.

34 Ibid., at 1–2.

35 Ibid., at 1.

36 Clarence Hincks, letter to Mrs Hind, Superintendent, Toronto Industrial Refuge, 12 September 1923, Griffin–Greenland Archives, QSMHC.

37 Clarence Hincks, letter to Mrs Hind, Superintendent, Toronto Industrial Refuge, 10 August 1923, ibid.

38 C.K. Clarke, 'A Study of 5600 Cases Passing through the Psychiatric Clinic of the Toronto General Hospital. A Special Study of 188 Clinic Cases – Also a Survey of 767 Cases of Illegitimacy' (1921–2), 3 *CJMH*, 18–19. The rationale for this study was to link the problems of criminality, prostitution, and illegitimacy to feeble-mindedness and uncontrolled immigration. The study's subjects included 3,274 males and 2,326 females. The report was organized into the following headings: 'Prostitution'; 'Nationality'; 'Illegitimacy'; 'Occupation'; 'Occupational Wanderers'; and 'What the Figures Teach'. Case histories were 'selected at random' to illustrate, with scientific and studied detachment, the broader categories described. The clinic population was composed entirely of referrals from the Juvenile Court, the Public Health Department, 'various societies' (such as the Big Sisters Association and child immigration organizations), and social agencies. Clarke's data, therefore, rely exclusively on case files derived through clinical exams conducted at the TPC. In turn, case referrals were determined primarily by informal access to agencies and institutional networks with which the TPC worked. While it is possible to conclude that the observations made in this study are an accurate assessment of those identities which clinic staff were at pains to construct, in no way can these data be systematically extrapolated to apply beyond the walls of the clinic itself, notwithstanding Clarke's claims.

39 Clarke, supra note 33, at 2.

40 Ibid., at 3–4.

41 Ibid., at 2.

42 C.K. Clarke, 'The Toronto Psychiatric Clinic: A Public Necessity' 1–2, (n.d., typescript) CIP Archives

43 'Plan of Co-operation Between the Toronto General Hospital Psychiatric Clinic and Extra-Hospital Agencies under the Supervision of the Chief of the Toronto General Hospital Psychiatric Clinic.' (1918) Griffin-Greenland Archives, QSMHC.

44 Clarke, supra note 38, at 11.

45 Ibid.

46 Ibid.

47 (1913) 3 & 4 Geo. V, c. 28, Part One, 'Power and Manner of Dealing with Defectives.' Especially pertinent are the provisions for institutionalization or guardianship of any 'person' 'who is in receipt of poor relief at the time of giving birth to an illegitimate child or when pregnant of such child.'

48 McConnachie, supra note 3, at 54.

49 Clarke, supra note 38, at 12.

50 Eugenecist views were questioned by some. For instance, E.J. Pratt, who was also a CNCMH member and on staff at the TPC, was part of a younger group of psychologists whose views tended towards the environmentalist perspective. Pratt, reporting on a survey of schoolchildren in Toronto commissioned by the CNCMH, stated that the survey results, 'as far as they go, indicate the effect of social status upon intelligence; whether the grounds are hereditary or environmental, or to some extent both, is another problem needing more data for discussion': supra note 2.

51 Clarke, supra note 38, at 12.

52 TGH Psychiatric Clinic, 'Sample Patient Questionnaire' (n.d.), and series of handwritten notes. TPC Papers, Box 15, file 3, Griffin-Greenland Archives, QSMHC.

53 Clarke letter to Wilcox, Department of Immigration, 28 February 1922, CIPA.

54 Letter from Dr C. Hincks to Dr G.W. Anderson, Juvenile Court, 24 January 1923, Hincks Papers, Griffin-Greenland Archives, QSMHC. The voluntary status of the BSA implied limitations in its dealings with young women under its unofficial jurisdiction who overstepped the bounds of social and moral misconduct; the services of the TPC could be useful in such cases. Olive G.S., referred to the TPC by the BSA, had attempted suicide by drinking a wine glass full of a toxic substance called Vapo Crysoline. (That action, however, does not appear to have directly prompted the organization to send Olive to the TPC, since it took place six months before her examination.) Hincks was unable to explain why Olive had tried to kill herself. He dismissed her action in two lines, concluding that 'perhaps the love of the dramatic entered into this incident.' He was more concerned over the young woman's desire for stimulation, and searched for the appropriate language to categorize such unusual behaviour. 'I had the opportunity of examining this girl a few days ago and learned something of her problem. She appears to be of a type desiring constant excitement and with very little ability for continuous effort in any form of productive work. I note that since her mother's death she has held, for short periods, four different positions and she tells me that she is not interested in anything she has taken up to date. She seems to be at a loss to know what she would like to do and will state frankly that all she wants is excitement.' Letter from Hincks to Big Sisters Association, Toronto, 3 April 1923, Griffin-Greenland Archives, QSMHC. In Olive's case the rules and regulations of an institutional existence were needed, since her father alone was unable to control her and supervision by a Big Sister would be inadequate.

55 Clarke, letter to Miss S. Gallagher, Rosary Hall, 8 June 1921, CIPA.

56 Clarke, letter to C.E. Wilcox, Department of Immigration, 30 January 1922, ibid.

57 Immigration Act (1906), 6 Ed. VII, c. 19, ss. 26–29. See also Barbara Roberts, *Whence They Came: Deportation from Canada 1900–1935* (Ottawa: University of Ottawa Press 1988), 12.

58 (1910) 9–10 Edw. VII, c. 27, s. 3. See Zlata Godler, 'Doctors and the New Immigrants' (1977), 9 *Canadian Ethnic Studies*, 6–17, at 8.

59 Supra note 58, ss. 3(a) to (i).

60 Supra note 47.

61 Ontario, 'Reports on the Care and Control of the Mentally Defective and Feeble-minded in Ontario,' 24 *Sessional Papers* (1920), 20.

62 Clarke letter to Mr J.C. Mitchell, Department of Immigration, 13 September 1921. CIPA.

63 Roberts, supra note 57, chapter. 6.

64 'Thirty two cases examined at the Toronto Psychiatric Clinic from April 22nd to September 22nd, recommended for deportation' (n.d.), Griffin-Greenland Archives, TPC Box 15, QSMHC.

65 Clarke, letter to J.C. Mitchell, Department of Immigration, 13 September 1921, CIPA.

66 Clarke, letter, 3 February 1923, ibid.

67 Clarke, letter to Dr Lillian Langstaff, Superintendent, Women's Jail Farm, 16 January 1922. The following table summarizes the clinical charges against the forty-three women included in the 'survey':

Age	No.	Immorality	Venereal disease	Illegitimacy	Occupational wanderer	Breach of Ont. Temperance Act
15–19	9	4	7	0	4	0
20–24	10	6	6	0	4	1
25–29	5	2	2	2	1	1
30–34	9	0	2	0	0	6
35–39	3	1	2	0	1	1
40–44	2	0	2	0	1	0
45+	1	1	3	0	1	0
NA	1	1	0	0	0	0

The survey results included the following summary of its findings: immoral 27; prostitute, 18; venereal disease, 27; mental deficiency, 21; dull normal, 11; apparently normal, 3; dementia praecox, 5; senile dementia, 1; married, 28.

68 CNCMH, 'Mental Hygiene Survey of Women's Jail Farm,' 1922 (typescript), Griffin-Greenland Archives, QSMHC.

Part Four

ARCHIVAL SOURCES
IN LEGAL HISTORY

16 'Law-ways,' 'Law-jobs,' and the Documentary Heritage of the State

LOUIS A. KNAFLA

Traditionally, 'archival sources in legal history' have been ascribed largely to the archives of the 'state,' whether the state has been the central, provincial, or local entity. Within that framework the archival documents at issue have been those under the custodianship of the ministers of justice, attorneys and solicitors general, parliaments, and legislatures. The documents in such custody, moreover, have been those produced by the activities of the courts, the judiciary, and related government departments whose functions are both administrative and facilitative. In this view the documentary heritage of the state relating to the law has often been coterminous with the research and writing of legal history.[1] The major body of historical literature that has come down to us comprises studies of those institutions and the civil, criminal, and regulatory problems and disputes that have been placed before them, tried and disposed of. 'Law' in this sense can be called state law because it has a common language, form, process, and substantive rules and doctrines that are both protected and facilitated by a professional body of people who derive their authority from the aegis of the state.[2]

The history of the law, however, has always emanated from more than the institutional and documentary heritage defined above. Law was derived originally from local customs, customs that embodied the folkways and normative values of the society. Most social and commercial relationships depend on these customs and norms for their conduct and success.[3] Thus it is the 'living law' (*lebendes recht*)[4] that represents the rules by which people conduct themselves, and 'law' or formal disputes are exceptions in the affairs of daily life. A dispute should be seen as a developmental stage in a

444 Louis A. Knafla

social or commercial relationship that has an element of conflict. Once it arrives on the table of the state it becomes a matter of state law. At this point the 'naming, blaming, and claiming' are refocused to fit the terms of the law by which they will be processed. The nature and language of the claim may change, and the dispute will be narrowed and crystallized to meet the demands of the gatekeepers and facilitators who will take the dispute down the road of litigation, guided by the procedural and substantive rules of the legal system.[5] In this sense there are two kinds of law: state law, and the normative rules of social and commercial ordering that form the larger social process of which law is simply one part.

The new field of 'law and society' encompasses those people who see law beyond the terms of state law and who study in the fields of social and commercial ordering as well as the interfaces with state law and comparative focuses. 'Legal pluralism' is a term that represents the wider field of law and society studies. In its narrow or more strict sense it refers specifically to the customs, norms, and rules of the community. In its broader sense it has been used to encompass not only social and commercial ordering but also the whole area of state law as part of social processes[6]. But legal pluralism also has a different intellectual focus. Associating 'ideology' with 'law,' it identifies law as 'legal centralism' or 'expository orthodoxy,' and legal pluralism as an ethnocentric view of multiple legal systems in a wide and diverse culture.[7]

Scholars of the law and society field who see themselves as 'legal pluralists' create a much wider horizon of documents for their research and writing. This broader horizon encompasses documents that are increasingly being referred to as 'quasi-' and 'non-statal' records. Quasi-statal legal records comprise those of organizations whose work includes state legal functions such as the police, but whose records have not been subjected to legislated controls, thus making authority and jurisdiction over them unclear. Non-statal legal records are of organizations whose work includes legal functions, but that are clearly private bodies outside the legislative framework of the state. The papers of law societies, bar associations, lawyers and judges, legal counsel of corporations and public and private groups, and jurists are among the more prominent in this category. Thus quasi- and non-statal legal records are less easily defined, less likely to be preserved, and more troublesome to locate and access; yet in the end they must rank at least equal with statal legal records in the research and writing of legal-historical topics.

'Law-ways' and 'law-jobs' are terms that have been employed primarily by legal anthropologists such as Karl Llewellyn and Adamson Hoebel to define the legal institutions and officials of native peoples whose institutional framework has rested chiefly on oral traditions. 'Law-ways' refers to all the processes by which disputes are resolved, and 'law-jobs' to the work of people who act as intermediaries in the resolution of such disputes. While more traditional legal-historical research discussed above uses courts as law-ways, and judges and judicial officials as law-jobs, the terms 'courts' and 'judges' do not fit well with many non-western post-medieval societies. Moreover, problems of distinguishing between customs and laws, the written and the unwritten, and local, regional, and national jurisdictions allow the terms 'law-ways' and 'law-jobs' to be used more effectively to examine the multifarious ways in which the living law is practised and experienced in both pre- and post-industrial societies.[8] The terms also encourage research into previously neglected legal systems, as well as engagement in comparative studies.[9] The standard bearers for 'colonial' countries have been the legal anthropologists, who look at 'law' as the artefacts of the speakers,[10] and who have revealed to us not only the substantive law of tribal legal systems but also a comparative understanding of the role of law in their societies.[11] Applied to the rich field of English legal history,[12] for example, this new wave of legal-historical research is full of insights. The insights offered by the approach have been exemplified in the writings of Brian Simpson.

Historiography

Simpson's earlier career produced numerous books and articles on more traditional legal history: law reports, contract, and land law.[13] But his current career is in the critical vein of sociolegal history, where he excels in taking unusual yet prominent cases and unwrapping them in relation to the entire contemporary world out of which they arose. This approach uses not only law reports and court records, but also records of government departments and private corporations, newspapers, lawyers' papers, and public and private correspondence. What emerges from such research is the suggestion that the law as legal custom, as the accrual of precedents, comprises a fiction from beginning to end.[14] This view draws support from the thinking of legal realists who distinguish between fact and law; for them, laws are artificial concepts created out of the transformation of facts.[15] The fiction of law can be deconstructed if examined as an interface of state, quasi-statal, and non-statal legal records together with their significance.[16] It is here too that the *paucity* of sources for traditional legal research can be transformed into *plenty*.[17]

The change of approach can be seen in Simpson's publication of *Cannibalism and the Common Law* in 1984, upon the hundredth anniversary of *R. v. Dudley and Stephens*.[18] Captain John Dudley and Mate Edward Stephens were convicted of murdering Ordinary Seaman Richard Parker, aged seventeen to eighteen, some 1600 miles off the Cape of Good Hope in 1884. These three men, with seaman Brooks, were aboard the yacht *Mignonette* when they had to abandon it in high seas for a rowboat. Drifting for nineteen days with two one-pound tins of turnips and drinking only the rainwater they could collect in their capes, they agreed (except for Brooks) to take the life of Parker. Thus on the twentieth day Stephens cut Parker's throat, with Dudley assisting, and they lived on his body and blood for a further four days until they were rescued by a passing ship.

Simpson researched the British press reports of the trial, citing twenty-seven newspapers from London and the regions, maritime correspondence and shipping records, and the ballads of seamen to demonstrate that there was a local custom of the sea for such occasions: faced with starvation, one ate one's colleagues, one by one, beginning with he who was the youngest or most junior, and who had the fewest dependents. Simpson demonstrated that the High Court decision accorded with the new code of middle-class Victorian morality, but went against maritime custom and did not represent the practised values of seafaring society. He was able to illuminate through this 'intertextual' study an important element of Victorian society: that the key to the *Dudley and Stephens* case did not lie in the traditional court record. It lay instead in a variety of texts: obscure newspapers, shipping records, oral history tapes, and seafaring ballads found in old phonograph-record collections. Furthermore, the full significance of the case was not to be found in the formal decision of the court, but in the sociocultural context disclosed in the evidence heard in the courtroom. The case is important not just for the point of law but for the window it provides into the operating cultural reality previously closed to us, and how that reality 'worked' in contemporary society.[19] Simpson showed that the case had two meanings: one in law and prevailing Victorian morality, and one in the cultural practices of seafaring.

The writing of how law works in society and its interrelations with political and socioeconomic structures is at the centre of the law and society field. They can be seen, for example, as subtle elements in John Beattie's acclaimed history of crime in eighteenth-century England. Beattie places criminal offences firmly in the streets and the workplace of the local community – contrasting urban and rural settings, and looks at the criminal law and punishments in fiscal and economic terms as well as legal and jurisprudential. These elements are also present in Alan Manchester's earlier modern English legal history, in which he introduced large sections on the law as it relates to labour, the family, and women.[20] How law works is even more prominent as the central focus of Gerry Rubin and David Sugarman's collected essays on the history of English law, economy, and society,[21] and of George Clark and William Cornish's major treatise in the field.[22] Clark and Cornish have broken new ground in English legal-historical studies. Their work is organized into sections on land, commerce, and industry, labour relations, poverty and education, accidents, and crime. Focusing on the interrelationship of legal, socioeconomic, and political change, the volume stands at the crossroads of what may well become the old and the new legal history. None the less, standing at the crossroads has its difficulties. In this pioneering effort there is too much context and insufficient law, too much statute law and insufficient attention to whether or how it worked, and too great an ideological focus on liberty and individualism at the expense of *mentalité*. But as learned commentators such as David Sugarman and William Twining have observed, the book is a milestone in legal historiography.

The underlying argument, then, is that the role of law-ways and law-jobs in the industrial or semi-industrial world of the nation-state should not be examined in isolation from the world that gave them birth. Once we recognize that statal, and quasi-statal legal records are only the visible edge of records that chronicle dispute-resolution in any society, we can begin to think as anthropologists as well as sociologists, lawyers, and historians. It is an often neglected and unspoken fact that few disputes in a common law country are resolved in a court of law. (It would be unbusinesslike to proclaim this!) Moreover, perhaps up to 90 per cent of disputes that reach lawyers' offices never make a court calendar. Therefore, the legal records of community associations, churches, charities, labour unions, corporations, lawyers, and judges underlie the framework of the formal courts in the modern nation-state. The terms 'law-ways' and 'law-jobs' can provide useful tools to examine dispute resolution both inside and outside formal court records.

Africa

British colonies in Africa serve as useful comparative laboratories for an examination of how common law as common custom, and common law as judicial precedent and legislative enactment, work in both pre- and post-industrial societies. English common law was carried to Britain's colonies on the back of imperial policy in its scramble for colonies in the eighteenth and nineteenth centuries. The Crown delegated its legal authority and powers to chartered companies; alternatively, it bestowed common law where favourable settlers would plant the seeds of queen, state, and established church. By the late nineteenth century, Britain had created constitutional mechanisms to protect the original inhabitants.[23] Rule was devolved to local rulers, where law was not imperial, magisterial, or hierarchical but the result of a supposed local consensus. The imperial government, desirous of creating stable regimes at a minimum cost, used indirect rule where possible, giving political power to local chiefs (in instances where some had held little power before). One result of this policy was to provide some protection to indigenous societies in areas where settlers permitted them to live. Into the twentieth century, for example, British Africa inherited a multitiered legal system of English and indigenous jurisdictions, which, like those of English medieval foundations, overlay one another and were never fully integrated.[24] What therefore marks 'colonial' societies is the separation and polarization of indigenous communities by the conqueror, followed by their gradual – but incomplete – absorption into artificial nationalities.

Legal historical writing on Africa until lately has rested chiefly in the hands of the constitutional historians in a way that bears a similarity to earlier English legal history. Using constitutions, orders in council, letters patent, royal instructions, and statutes of the imperial, colonial, and regional legislatures, the history could be and often was written as much from the perspective of London and the central archives as from the colonies themselves. The history that resulted is what a historiographer might term a school of 'metropolitan' history.[25] In other words, the law is seen primarily in imperial and 'British' terms. Seeing law as such a 'superstructural phenomenon,' as Martin Channock terms it, not only gives undue credence to state power in such societies, but also provides the state with a 'legalism' that gives it legitimacy and serves as an instrument for extending its powers further over the multifarious societies that reside within its borders.[26]

The colonial situation leads many historians of law and society to the necessity of seeing law as 'legal pluralism' in the broad sense of disparate legal regimes – the law-ways of a country. Thus, for South Africa, one must study not only the laws of the British but also Roman civil law, Anglo-Dutch law, and the laws of the local tribal communities. Since the indigenous peoples were ruled by European conquerors, the methodology of the 'critical studies' movement is important in identifying how 'law-govern-ment', 'law-ways,' and 'law-jobs' were created and how they were used in each society.[27] In this manner legal historical writing focuses not on the law of the state or on the hierarchical order of the 'Westminster model,' but on the law of quasi- and non-statal legal institutions, or law from the bottom up. The major problem here (as in England and Canada) is with the local, quasi-, and non-statal legal records. Channock likens their study to writing in the age of Sir Edward Coke: law as custom, custom that validates, contradicts, or creates law. As in medieval or early modern England, with its parallel legal systems, African countries become the modern equivalent of a 'comparative law laboratory.'[28]

Examples of what can be learned from the study of law and society have been identified in useful local studies of Senegal and Kenya. Francis Snyder uses a wide range of legal and non-legal records to explore the transition from communal land to capitalism in rural Senegal in the twentieth century. Relying on the French colonial archives, court cases, oral histories, linguistics, genealogies, aerial maps, and archaeological artifacts, his study of the Banjal village of Gasumay examines the history of its multiple legal systems, its land law, and the variable and independent factors that contributed to its development. Along the way he illuminates the patterns of land inheritance and transfers, kinship and marriage, and wealth and socioeconomic change.[29] As Simon Roberts has explained, the legal history of such societies cannot be written in the absence of a socioeconomic context: namely, how agricultural work was performed, how arrangements over land were handled, and how the family divided its responsibilities and planned the inheritance of land and other property.[30]

The need to move from the older positivist, hierarchical tradition in legal history to the more facilitative, living law approach was made brilliantly apparent in an earlier study by Professors Ghai and McAuslan on the history of public law in Kenya. Eschewing the methodology of lawyers and constitutional writers, they addressed a number of problems that modern legal historians of colonial societies are now taking into account. These include the legitimacy of colonial governments in the eyes of native communities, the relation of law to war, the use of law as coercion, assigning different rules to natives and settlers, keeping the law unknown to local communities (thereby precluding their members from using its possible advantages), and adhering to legal practice or its rhetoric in dispensing the powers of the state.[31]

In his study of local African tribes and communities, Richard Abel travelled over 2,500 miles in Kenya and found that 200 to 600 cases per year were heard in one hundred courts. Moreover, he found clear legal procedures, a substantive law that was well developed, and challenging legal rules and principles. For the law of tort alone he collected approximately

4,200 cases over a five-year period.[32] But the sources were also scattered and difficult to obtain. He noted with despair the terrible conditions in which surviving records were kept, and the necessity to do his own finding and listing. As Robin Luckham has found quasi- and non-statal legal records – particularly those of lawyers and businesses – were largely not extant or accessible.[33] But they are important. Again, in many colonies, as in England, the legal profession was instrumental not only in the growth of the state but also in major economic transformations.

The problems of legal records in one African society were clearly documented in a case study of Ghana undertaken by the Commonwealth Legal Records Project.[34] Based on the city of Accra, the project identified all records whose provenance was located in legal institutions. These included the papers of courts and government departments that reflected the views of state law, those of quasi- and non-statal institutions such as the university faculty of law and jurists who reflected the views of jurisprudential thought, and those of law firms that reflected the views of clients as understood by lawyers. An outsider could note that these different categories of legal sources represent the way in which people think in terms of relationships and the legally trained in terms of rules.[35] Recognizing the pluralistic legal system of common, customary, and religious law, the project sought to define the legal heritage of the region – albeit on the basis of an institutional framework. The researchers noted the great distance that existed, as in industrial countries, between national and other legal institutions, which would have been widened had they attempted to locate legal records in non-legal bodies. The project revealed not only the physical dimensions of the problems of records preservation, but also the relevance of the legal pluralism model to legal-historical writing.

The subjects such a model can examine are breathtakingly endless.[36] The insights into such subjects, however, break the sterility of much of the older legal-historical writing. Currently, scholars of African law and society are benefiting from the social history of the law being written by Europeans, while European and North American scholars explore how legal systems operate in Africa and how legal change is related to changes in socioeconomic relations, in the distribution of wealth, and in political power, legitimacy, and authority.[38]

Canada

In the Commonwealth, and particularly in Canada, the development of the areas of legal-historical scholarship which we can characterize as having traditional forms took shape in the 1960s, and grew slowly in the 1970s and 1980s as archivists turned their attention to the location, preservation, reconstruction, and listing of the court records being scheduled for disposition. Some of the original work in the reconstruction of court records was undertaken in Nova Scotia and Ontario.[39] Canadian provincial governments initially adopted some of the rather draconian destruction schedules of Britain's Public Records Office, which have made a quagmire for researchers of modern English court records.[40] But records scheduled for destruction for several provinces escaped the shredder or bonfire,[41] and disposition schedules for the Public Archives of Canada were not generally carried out, thanks to administrative bungling.[42] Fortunately too, some of the more ambitious and positive American attempts to schedule court records were emulated.[43] The debate between the records management and humanist traditions in collection and arrangement policies continues to this day, however, and involves scholars, bureaucrats, archivists, and librarians.[44]

Legal records, while they loomed large as physical holdings in the care of national and provincial archives, were not frequently consulted in Canada until the 1970s, when a number of scholars became engaged in writing on pivotal aspects the history of Canadian law. The early results included a number of major scholarly essays sponsored by the Osgoode Society. Edited by Professor David Flaherty, the first two volumes contained studies largely of institutional legal history, but within a political, British, and North American context.[45] This in itself marked a fundamental change in Canadian legal history. Essays that hinged on socioeconomic subjects such as master and servant legislation, workmen's compensation, nuisance, and rape were among the more innovative for the law and society and social control areas. Change has been even more dramatic in recent years, with the publication of Constance Backhouse's *Petticoats and Prejudice*, an examination of women and the law in the nineteenth century,[46] Carol Wilton's edited collection of essays on business and the law,[47] and a forthcoming multi-edited collection of essays on the history of crime and criminal justice, which includes work on race and gender.[48]

The problems of record linkage, however, which were discussed above for England, still exist for the history of Canadian law. Official legal histories may obscure as much as they reveal. A pertinent example is the myth of the 'Mounties,' and of the peaceful settlement of the Canadian west which can be attributed to dominion, federal, and territorial governments desirous of enticing European peoples to a harsh and uncharted landscape. For instance, British Columbia joined the new Canadian federation in 1871, and a rash of robberies in the Revelstoke (initially called Farwell) area led to a series of written complaints to the attorney general's office. A letter to Chief Justice Matthew Baillie Begbie, for example, told of 'cowboys' who terrorized the local population, and requested the chief justice to 'bring this drunken rabble under British justice.'[49] Another complained of a lack of constables in the area.[50] The local press of the Slocan region, which stretched out below Revelstoke, complained years later about the lack of constables and of police magistrates to try the accused, saying that the jails were too few and inadequate to hold offenders awaiting trial for the periodic assize sessions.[51]

As a result, the region had a history of vigilantism as a form of alternative justice from its earliest years of settlement. Thus when an American thief killed a local constable, a group of Kootenay men crossed the border, hunted him down, and shot him dead.[52] But a reading of the court records of the province for the second half of the nineteenth century reveals few serious criminal prosecutions, and in general a lack of 'traditional crime.'[53] It is only when one turns to the weekly local newspapers, correspondence, and business accounts that the 'vernacular' tradition becomes apparent. Such non-legal records moreover, can also highlight other legal problems. One prominent example that has emerged concerns a string of 'accidental' deaths in the lower Slocan region of British Columbia in the late nineteenth century.

The *Brooklyn News* reported a series of exposés from the mining industry in the autumn of 1898. A Swede working on a rockface near Brooklyn was killed when an improperly conducted explosion caused six hundred pounds of rock to fall on him. Three men were blown to 'smithereens' at Smith Falls, British Columbia, after twenty kegs of dynamite failed to explode; the men were asked to go in with an 'iron spoon' to loosen it, and did so all too successfully. John Oleson of Trail was asked to do a similar job with just a few kegs, and the resulting explosion sent the spoon through his heart and out his back. The district had no coroner, and often bodies had to wait several weeks before an investigation would be put in motion by a coroner from an adjoining region.[54] Suicides and accidental deaths were equally prevalent. Articles were written on bodies floating down the rivers of the Slocan.[55] None of these 'problems' appeared in the relevant court records of the province, all of which have survived for this district.

'Accidental deaths' are one of many black holes of legal-historical scholarship, and the recovery of coroners' inquests, together with company and hospital records, is essential for the history not only of crime, but also of medical practices, human psychology, negligence, and social and economic history. It is interesting to note that little has been done with accidental deaths in British history,[56] let alone Canadian or other common law countries.[57] Deaths ruled accidental did not go to trial, but coroners' juries heard and often recorded the evidence. Many kinds of deaths, ranging from homicide and infanticide to suicide and mercy-killings, were disposed of in this way. Here was a prominent instance where local communities, or their élites, could have a decisive impact upon how the criminal law worked by deciding which acts would be prosecuted and sent to a trial jury, and which would not. But this kind of research also requires other kinds of sources: the press, medical records, personal writings, and perhaps even ballads.

Black holes, however, are not limited to records concerning courts, violence, and death. They are also home to a wide range of quasi- and non-statal legal records that are essential for the study of sociolegal as well as traditional legal history. The problems identified above concerning the records of British police forces are also relevant to the records of Canadian forces. In a survey of these problems, Greg Marquis has noted that most Canadian police forces had little interest in their records, and many of their records have been disposed of. As in Britain, there is no legislation governing either their jurisdiction or their disposition. The result has been a history of the police written largely by amateurs in the form of hagiography, reproduced in popular literature and film, that has created among other things the 'myth' of the Mounties discussed above. As in Britain, the research potential is still largely undiscovered.[58]

Finally, non-statal legal records present an even greater quagmire. The combination of private ownership coupled with client-solicitor privilege bedevils the records of lawyers, as well as of law societies and bar associations, neither of which have developed standards of consistency for preservation of or access to their records.[59] Like the police, lawyers and judges form a profession that is important in its own right. With some exceptions, and as with the police, the inability of independent scholars to gain access to records has enabled the profession to write its own amateurish history, which often poses as hagiography and thus does little justice to standards of professional scholarship. In Australia, for example, neither lawyers nor law societies are 'records conscious,' and both actively practise the destruction of their records to save space and costs and to take advantage of the statute of limitations.[60] In Canada there are only four law societies currently involved in the maintenance of legal archives, and their practices vary considerably.[61]

The significance of private records is that their history reflects some of

the most prominent members of the communities, and the records of
lawyers contain perhaps more case materials than the records of the local
and central courts combined. Client files, depositions, and examinations for
discovery exist for many more disputes than those that go beyond the initial
statement of claim into a court of law. This has been recognized at least by
the Osgoode Society and the Legal Archives Society of Alberta.[62] However,
attempts to convince member law firms to deposit their records in archives,
whether public or private, have been less than successful. The example of
the Law Society of Alberta can be taken as reflecting the general reluctance
of the profession to move towards public openness.

A draft proposal for the papers held by lawyers and their firms, written
for the benchers of the Law Society of Alberta, suggests that their papers
should be closed forever to researchers, and that law firms should not be
encouraged to deposit such papers in any public or private archive.[63] In an
interesting but flawed and jaundiced review of the common law, the
recommendation states that all papers in the hands of lawyers belong to
their original owners, and that law firms themselves have no authority to
make them available. Citing a series of obscure cases from the eighteenth
to the twentieth centuries, the brief argues that only if a law firm obtains
the written permission of all the writers of the documents in a file or a
collection can it then make a disposition of that file or collection to another
body. Further, it is the responsibility of the researcher to obtain such
permissions.[64]

As we have seen, lawyers' papers are a crucial element of the legal
records of society. They lie at the heart of prominent studies, such as Brian
Simpson's exploration of the *Dudley and Stephens* case described above. Not
only can they illuminate a case that is important to the social, economic, or
financial history of a community or society, but in some instances they are
virtually the only extant and unimpeachable sources. The role of lawyers as
gatekeepers and facilitators of the law means that their private papers help
to close the circle of our snapshots of the dispute resolution system of the
state.[65] Their documents assist in excavating the links between statal, quasi-
statal, and non-statal legal records that must be established before further
research into law-ways and law-jobs can make another quantum leap,
perhaps equivalent to that of positivist thought of the nineteenth century.

Facilitative Law

The future of law and society studies depends on methodologies that are
not wedded to industrial societies or bureaucratic states, but are integrated

with the fabric of society. It is here that legal-historical writers and archivists must consider not only the anthropological models discussed above within the term 'law-ways,' but also the sociological: that which has been named facilitative law. Facilitative law is law wherever it is found, within or outside the public domain. Publicly, it is the law of the central state, provinces, counties or regions, and local communities. Privately, it includes both quasi-statal institutions that operate under legislation such as the police, social services, and utility boards, and non-statal institutions such as corporations, law firms, unions, and charities. It poses, however, that dangerous principle of all eclectic researchers and writers: we must keep everything.

More recently, there has been an openness on the part of many persons in the archival community to become more active in defining their mandate, and a realization among users that not everything can afford to be preserved. Giving the Society of Archivists' Maurice Bond Memorial lecture in 1992, R.C. Alston suggested that archives can no longer accept everything sent to them as 'dump heaping,' nor should they continue to collect 'historical debris which have been allowed to deteriorate into disorder.' He countered with the vision of an 'access library,' an archive that knows what it has and can produce it for anyone who walks through the door.[67] What is needed are comprehensive, interpretive descriptions of archival holdings,[68] lists of all the services to research them,[69] regional workshops to create a critical mass of donors and users,[70] and comparative studies for cross-disciplinary insights.[71]

What is also needed is a strategy for our documentary heritage in the common law world. In the past, archivists have been hesitant to define their functions. They must decide not only what should be collected, but how one can document society's past.[72] An interesting perspective on this approach was drawn by the German archivist Hans Booms in 1972 in an article that has recently been translated into English and is now influencing the archival debate in English-speaking countries. Booms sees the archivist as an appraiser whose mission is to create, out of the records of overly fragmented societies, a socially relevant documentary record that is storable and usable for future generations of researchers and writers. He sees the archivist as an empirical scientist whose job is to identify all the sources that illuminate the linear human existence, and that comprise 'completed reality.'[73] This involves an examination not only of archival methodology, but also of the methodologies of historians themselves. Booms's view – that the sum of government records does not equal the sum of life or of the state itself – is a clarion call to students of law and society.

The essential problem is to identify a documentation strategy for legal records that can generate the kinds of records necessary for the law and society or legal pluralist approaches, law-ways, or facilitative approach to legal history that have been identified in this essay, and that can also become part of any larger archival scheme for documenting society's past. The moment for this occurrence has already been identified, as various ideas and schemes coalesce in Canada, for example, on bringing non-statal legal records into the archival camp.[74] The ideas stem from an awareness within the archival community that current public records legislation is inadequate and that the reluctance of private holders to submit their documents to public scrutiny must be overcome.[75] The schemes stem from local archivists who have turned to regional structures, where jurisdictional conflicts are less awesome. Two such strategies which have been executed recently will be noted and explored in this conclusion. They pertain to documentation strategies for western New York State and for Quebec.

The New York Historical Records Program Development Project was formed in 1986 to question how well the state's western region was being documented. An advisory group of archivists, librarians, historians, and other researchers was asked to prepare a documentation strategy for the six counties of the region. The group sought to identify general topics that would span the entire breadth of human experience, past, present, and future. While the group found it impossible to complete its task, one of the fifteen topics into which the human experience was divided was politics, government, and the law. But the law was traditional law – the law of the central state. Other forms of law, such as quasi- and non-statal, were subsumed under other headings.[76] In the end, the use of 'traditional' forms was perhaps partly responsible for the group's failure to devise a documentary strategy that would stand the test of collection policy and user needs.

More successful was the limited documentation strategy for legal records created in Quebec through the Interministerial Committee on Court Records established by the Ministry of Justice.[77] Using the traditional concept of legal records, the committee of twelve was made up of representatives of the government, the judiciary, the legal profession, archives, universities, and the general public. Divided into 'producers,' 'custodians,' and 'users,' the committee members visited all the sites and documents of state legal records, established general principles concerning what legal records should be preserved, managed, and stored, and procedures for the retention schedules that would accompany the original production of the documents as future archival muniments. The result was a preservation policy that served the interests of the producers and the users, cut the storage costs by two-thirds, and used the funds saved for the production of the documents in a usable format with lists and, where relevant, indexes.

What is significant from the Quebec experience is that all parties interested in the legal records of the state were brought to the table to plan and implement a documentation strategy that covered fifty-nine court houses for thirty-six judicial districts. All too often decisions in these areas are made solely with reference to the single-minded interests of the holders of the records. In an age when we are being encouraged to solve problems collectively and within their larger contexts, the interests of the user should equally be reflected at the table. In this way the disposition schedule created by the province of Quebec in 1990 is a model for dealing with the problems associated with the generation of modern court records: a schedule that balances the problems of guardianship and institutional independence with those of administration, legal liability, and the needs of the various users who comprise the society that gave birth to the records.

What is needed is a similar approach to all classes of legal records, be they state, quasi-state, or private entities. One could suggest that given the difficulties of the latter two categories, and the fact that the traditional legal records of the state are a small part of society's law-ways, it would be useful for a model such as Quebec's to be devised to preserve the total legal records of a region under the legislative umbrella of the 'state.' The committee would be expanded to include members of the law society and of corporate, non-corporate, and municipal bodies. The goal would be to define the legal heritage of the region, identify the records that document it, determine which of those records are significant for retention (on both a cost- and user-benefit analysis), and propose how they can best be preserved and accessed, depending on the institutional structures that exist in the constituencies and communities of the region.[78] Only then can the interests of the holders be joined successfully with the needs of the users, and the folk-ways and law-ways of our societies be endowed with the rich and illuminating texture their people deserve.

NOTES

1 The theme is one that I have explored in several unpublished papers, and I wish to thank the conference organizers, panelists, commentators, and critics whose views have helped me to form those of my own: 'The Images of the Law and Legal Culture in British Columbia, 1866–1914: A Preliminary Discourse,' presented to 'Law for the Elephant, Law for the Beaver: A

Transboundary Conference on the Legal History of the West and North-west of North America,' University of Victoria, 23 February 1991; 'Legal-Historical Scholarship and Intertextuality,' presented to the Association of Canadian Archivists, Banff, Alberta, April 1991; 'Users of Legal Records: Case Studies from a Commonwealth Perspective,' presented to the Symposium on Legal Records in the Commonwealth, Institute of Commonwealth Studies, University of London, 4 July 1991; 'Statal, Quasi-Statal, and Non-Statal Legal Records,' presented to the Conference on Law, State, and Society in History, Osgoode Hall, Toronto, 16 May 1992; and 'Defining Legal Culture in Prairie Canada: A Prolegomenon,' presented to the Symposium on Contemporary and Historical Issues in Legal Pluralism,' University of Manitoba, 7 November 1992. I also wish to thank Susan Binnie, John McLaren, Robert Omura, Russell Smandych, David Sugarman, Jonathan Swainger, and William Twining for their useful comments and suggestions.

2 For an analysis of the terms see William Twining, *The Common Law Mind and the Making of the Textbook Tradition* (Oxford: Basil Blackwell 1986), 1–7; and the chapter by Brian Simpson, 'The Common Law as Legal Theory,' ibid., 8–25.

3 *People's Law and State Law: The Bellagio Papers*, ed. Antony Allott and Gordon R. Woodman (Dordrecht: Foris Publications 1985), is a collection of papers from an international conference on the history of folk law in western and non-western countries.

4 Eugene Ehrlich, *Fundamental Principles of the Sociology of Law* [1936], trans. W.L. Moll (New York: Arno Press 1975).

5 See the special issue of the *Law and Society Review*, vol. 15 (1980–1), devoted to disputes. The quotation is from William L.F. Felstiner, Richard L. Abel, and Austin Sarat, 'The Emergence and Transformation of Disputes: Naming, Blaming, Claiming,' 630–54.

6 For an overview of the literature see Brian Z. Tamanaha, 'The Folly of the "Social Scientific" Concept of Legal Pluralism' (1993), 20 *Journal of Law and Society*, 192–217; and the *Journal of Legal Pluralism and Unofficial Law*, which is becoming somewhat technical in focus.

7 Roger Cotterrell, *The Sociology of Law* (London: Butterworths 1984) and Leonard Pospisil, *The Ethnology of Law* (Menlo Park: Cummings Publishing Co. 1978) respectively.

8 For example, E.P. Thompson, *Customs in Common* (London: Routledge and Kegan Paul 1991), and Barbara Yngveson, 'Making Law at the Doorway: The Clerk, The Court, and the Construction of Community in A New England Town' (1988), 22 *Law and Society Review*, 409–48.

9 'Legal Pluralism in Industrialized Societies,' a special issue of the *Law and Society Review* (1993), edited by Carol J. Greenhouse and Fons Strijbosch.

10 There are an increasing number of important studies on the discordant voices of the law. See, in particular, John M. Conley and William M. O'Barr, *Rules Versus Relationships: The Ethnography of Legal Discourse* (Chicago: University of Chicago Press 1990).

11 Norman J. Singer, 'The Use of Writing as a Factor in the Integration of African Legal Systems: The Case of the Cambata (Ethiopia),' in *Law in Rural Africa* (1973), 22 *Rural Africana*, 57–68, discussing Ethiopia, Ghana, Nigeria, and Rhodesia. See the classic works of Bronislaw Malinowski, *Crime and Custom in Savage Society* (New York 1926, reprinted 1985), and of E. Adamson Hoebel, *The Cheyennes, Indians of the Great Plains*, 2d ed. (New York: Holt, Rinehart and Winston 1978) and *The Law of Primitive Man* (Cambridge: Harvard University Press 1954).

12 For a survey of the legal history field, its traditions, and developments, see my 'The Perspective of the Legal Historian: Legal- and Socio-Legal Historical Research,' in *Legal Records in the Commonwealth*, ed. William Twining and Emma Quick (London: Dartmouth Publications 1994). A fascinating exegesis of the theoretical development of the field is David Sugarman's 'Legal Theory, The Common Law Mind and the Making of the Textbook Tradition,' in *Legal Theory and Common Law*, ed. William Twining (Oxford: Basil Blackwell 1986), 26–61.

13 Most prominently, A.W. Brian Simpson, *A History of the Common Law of Contract: The Rise of Assumpsit* (Oxford: Clarendon Press, 1975).

14 See, for example, Professor Twining's critique of 'Cannibalism and Legal Literature' (1986), 6 *Oxford Journal of Legal Studies*, 423–30, where he notes the lawyer's position on 'what is law.'

15 See Karl N. Llewellyn, *Jurisprudence Realism in Theory and Practice* (Chicago: University of Chicago Press 1962).

16 See *Crime, Police and the Courts in British History*, ed. Louis A. Knafla (Westport: Meckler Corporation, 1990), vii–xxxviii, for the historiography. A fascinating analysis of the common law as fiction 'from beginning to end' is that of Brian Simpson, 'The Common Law as Legal Theory,' in Twining, *Legal Theory*, 8–25, supra note 12, at 8–25.

17 Clair Cowling, 'Legal Records and Archives Policy – A Case Study of England and Wales,' paper prepared for the English Records Project, appendix I. Cowling's survey of British archives reveals that few legal sources are actively researched in archives. Paradoxically, the state of many records and the lack and inaccessibility of lists and guides are important contributing factors. This paper is being published in *Legal Records*, supra note 12.

18 A.W. Brian Simpson, *Cannibalism and the Common Law: The Story of the Tragic Last Voyage of the 'Mignonette' and the Strange Legal Proceedings to Which It Gave Rise* (London and Chicago: University of Chicago Press, 1984).

19 A useful discussion of such reported cases as 'centripetal' and 'centrifugal' has been made by William Twining in 'Cannibalism and Legal Literature,' supra note 14.

20 A.H. Manchester, *A Modern Legal History of England and Wales, 1750–1950* (London: Butterworths 1980).

21 G.R. Rubin and David Sugarman, *Law, Economy and Society: Essays in the History of English Law 1750–1914* (Abingdon: Professional Books 1984). The essays here improve in many ways on the methodology used for some subjects in the Clark and Cornish volume, a book that was begun earlier but published later (infra note 22).

22 W.R. Cornish and G. de N. Clark, *Law and Society in England 1750–1950* (London: Sweet and Maxwell 1989).

23 Claire Palley, *The Constitutional History and Law of Southern Rhodesia 1885–1965 with Special Reference to Imperial Control* (Oxford: Clarendon Press, 1966). More generally, see R.T.E. Latham, 'The Law and the Commonwealth,' in *Survey of British Commonwealth Affairs*, vol. 1: *Problems of Nationality 1918–1936* (Oxford 1937).

24 For example, Ian Hamnett, 'Legal Change in Lesotho,' in *Labour, Law and Crime. An Historical Perspective*, ed. Francis Snyder and Douglas Hay (London and New York: Tavistock 1987), 83–91.

25 See, for example, B.O. Nwabueze, *A Constitutional History of Nigeria* (London: C. Hurst and Co., 1981).

26 Martin Channock, 'Writing South African Legal History' (1989), 30 *Journal of African History*, 265–88, at 266.

27 For example, the prominent and pioneering work of Charles van Onselen, *Studies in the Social and Economic History of the Witwatersrand 1886–1914*, vol. 1, *New Babylon*, and vol. 2, *New Nineveh* (Harlow 1982).

28 Channock, 'Writing South African Legal History,' quoting an unpublished paper by Anthony Allott, supra note 26, at 288. He notes that a problem of the English model lies in its concern with the politicization of the law rather than with any abuse of power.

29 Francis G. Snyder, *Capitalism and Legal Change: An African Transformation* (New York and London: Oxford University Press 1981).

30 Simon Roberts, 'Mmatlhong's Field,' in *Law in Rural Africa*, supra note 11, at 1–14.

31 Y.P. Ghai and J.P.W.B. McAuslan, *Public Law and Political Change in Kenya: A Study of the Legal Framework of Government from Colonial Times to the Present* (London and New York: Oxford University Press 1970).

32 Richard L. Abel, 'Law in Context: The Sociology of Legal Institutions, Litigation in Society,' in *Law and Social Enquiry: Case Studies of Research*, ed. Robin Luckham (Uppsala: Scandinavian Institute for African Studies 1981), 34–75.

33 Robin Luckham, *The Ghana Legal Profession: The Natural History of a Research Project*, in *Law and Social Enquiry*, supra note 32.

34 Pino Akotia, Harry Akussah, and Victor Dankwa, eds, *Legal Records in Accra: A Case Study*, (London: ACARM 1992). The comments below are taken from the report.

35 A view adopted by Conley and Barr in *Rules versus Relationships*, supra note 10, chapter 1, and at 6–7.

36 See, for example, the chapters of an early collection: G.W. Kanyeihamba and J.P.W.B., McAuslan, eds, *Urban Legal Problems in Eastern Africa* (Uppsala and New York: Scandinavian Institute of African Studies 1978); and the collection for Africa and Asia: *Law and Social Enquiry*, supra note 32.

37 The collected essays in D. Crummey, ed. *Banditry, Rebellion and Social Protest in Africa* (London: James Currey 1986).

38 For example, the prominent collected essays in Francis Snyder and Douglas Hay, eds, *Labour, Law and Crime: An Historical Perspective* (London and New York: Tavistock 1987).

39 For example, Barry Cahill, '"Bleak House" Revisited: The Records and Papers of the Court of Chancery of Nova Scotia, 1751–1855' (1989–90), 29 *Archivaria*, 149–67; and C.J. Shepard, 'Court Records as Archival Records' (1984), 18 *Archivaria*, 124–34, for both Chancery and Quarter Sessions.

40 Louis A. Knafla, 'Legal Archives: The National and Cultural Heritage,' in *1983 Meeting of Commonwealth Law Ministers – Memoranda* (London: Commonwealth Secretariat 1984), 545–52.

41 For Ontario the tragedies were outlined by C.J. Shepard, 'Court and Legal Records at the Archives of Ontario' (1987), 24 *Archivaria*, 117–20; for Alberta the tragedies were in part averted, and for other jurisdictions the results were mixed: Louis A. Knafla, '"Be It Remembered": Court Records and Research in the Canadian Provinces' (1984), 18 *Archivaria*, 105–23.

42 Now the National Archives of Canada. See Bryan Corbett and Eldon Frost, 'The Acquisition of Federal Government Records: A Report on Records Management and Archival Practices' (1983–4), 17 *Archivaria*, 201–32.

43 One of the classic disposition schemes was the Massachusetts Superior Court Records Project: Michael Stephen Hindus, Theodore H. Hammett, and Barbara M. Hobson, *The Files of the Massachusetts Superior Court, 1859–1959: An Analysis and a Plan for Action* (Boston 1979).

44 For example, the early 1980s debates in *Archivaria*: Terry Cook, 'Clio: The Archivist's Muse?' (1977–8), 5: 198–203; Tom Nesmith, 'Archives from the

Bottom Up: Social History and Archival Scholarship' (1982), 14: 5–26; George Bolotenko, 'Archivists and Historians: Keepers of the Well' (1983), 16: 5–25; 'The Debate over History and Archives' (1983–4), 17: 286–308; and Gordon Dodds, 'Provenance Must Remain the Archival "Bottom Line"' (1984), 18: 4–7.

45 David H. Flaherty, ed. *Essays in the History of Canadian Law*, 2 vols. (The Osgoode Society, 1981 and 1983).

46 Constance Backhouse, *Petticoats and Prejudice: Women and Law in Nineteenth-Century Canada* (Toronto: The Osgoode Society 1991).

47 Carol Wilton, ed., *Beyond the Law: Lawyers and Business in Canada 1830 to 1930*, (Toronto: The Osgoode Society 1990).

48 Jim Phillips, Tina Loo, et al., eds, *Crime and Criminal Justice in Canada*, (Toronto: The Osgoode Society 1994).

49 British Columbia Archives and Records Service (hereinafter cited as BCARS), RG 996, letter of John W. Wilson, 30 October 1885.

50 Ibid., letter of G.B. Wright to the attorney-general, 4 February 1885.

51 *The Ledge*, 14 January 1897.

52 Cariboo *Sentinel*, 25 July 1867.

53 For example, my research in BCARS, the assize calendars in GR 996 for 1883–1914, and the county court books in GR 5812 for 1867–1914.

54 *Brooklyn News*, 20 August, 3 September, 10 September, 29 October, and 5 November 1898 respectively.

55 Ibid., 8 October 1898, where the phenomenon is reported and the problem is discussed.

56 For examples, see the various calendars of coroners' records that have been published over the years by Dr R.H. Hunnisett, who is currently writing a history of the English coroner; also the article by P.E.H. Hair, 'Deaths by Violence in Britain: A Tentative Secular Survey' (1971), 25 *Population Studies*, 5–24.

57 Few coroners' inquests survive, for example, in the province of Ontario: Guy St-Denis, 'The London District and Middlesex County, Ontario, Coroner's Inquests, 1831–1900' (1990–1), 31 *Archivaria*, 142–53. For an interesting case study, see Roger Lane, *Violent Death in the City: Suicide, Accident and Murder in Nineteenth-Century Philadelphia* (Cambridge: Harvard University Press 1979).

58 See Greg Marquis, 'Towards a Canadian Police Historiography,' elsewhere in this volume.

59 James W. Whalen, 'The Application of Solicitor-Client Privilege to Government records' (1984), 18 *Archivaria*, 135–41; and Doug Whyte, 'The Acquisition of Lawyers' Private Papers,' ibid., 142–53.

60 Peter Moore, 'Waiving History Goodbye?' elsewhere in this volume.

61 The law societies of Alberta, British Columbia, Quebec, and Upper Canada, with a program under development in Manitoba. For a survey, see Rick Klumpenhouwer, 'Private Sector Legal Archives in Canada,' elsewhere in this volume.

62 As set out in a recent newsletter of the Legal Archives Society of Alberta; see Rick Klumpenhouwer, 'An Archival Perspective on Lawyers' Records II' (1993), 3 *Arch-i-types*, 6. See also Roy Schaeffer, 'The Osgoode Society Survey of Private Legal Records in Ontario' (1987), 24 *Archivaria*, 181–5.

63 A copy of the proposal is in the possession of the author.

64 The brief was later revised and the intent overturned by the benchers, but only after considerable pressure from archivists and potential users. To this date, however, records of the law society that were used by previous researchers are still technically unavailable.

65 Aviam Soffer, 'Beyond Mirrors: Lawrence Friedman's Moving Pictures' (1988), 22 *Law and Society Review*, 995–1016.

66 For example, the discussion in Tullio Caputo, Mark Kennedy, and Charles E. Reasons, eds, *Law and Society: A Critical Perspective* (Toronto and London: Harcourt Brace Jovanovich 1989).

67 R.C. Alston, 'Preserving the Record' (1992), 20:88 *Archives*, 181–9, quotation at 183, 186.

68 Such as R.E. Ingram, ed. *Sources of Jamaican History, 1655–1838*, 2 vols (Zug: Inter Documentation Company, 1976).

69 As, for example, *Basic International Bibliography of Archive Administration*, ed. Michel Duchein (New York: UNESCO 1978).

70 An example was the proposed regional Institute of Archives Sciences for Southeast Asia that was planned for the National Archives of Malaysia in 1973 but not fulfilled.

71 For law, for example, a guide similar to Charles A. Jones, *Britain and the Dominions: A Guide to Business and Related Records in the United Kingdom concerning Australia, Canada, New Zealand and South Africa* (Boston: G.K. Hall and Company 1978).

72 Helen Samuels, 'Who Controls the Past' (1986), 49 *American Archivist*, 109–24.

73 Hans Booms, 'Society and the Formation of a Documentary Heritage' (1989), 24 *Archivaria*, 69–105, the quotation at 80. His empirically constructed 'grids' representing that reality are perhaps more problematic.

74 Rick Klumpenhouwer, 'Private Sector Legal Archives in Canada,' elsewhere in this volume.

75 See, for example, the trenchant work of Lisa B. Weber, ed., *Documentary*

America: Assessing the Condition of Historical Records in the States (New York: National Historical Publications and Records Commission 1984).

76 Richard J. Cox, 'A Documentation Strategy Case Study: Western New York' (Spring 1989), 52 *American Archivist*, 192–200, where the project is outlined.

77 *Report of the Interministerial Committee on Court Records*, the English summary of the three-volume French-language report by Jessica Pottier, revised by Evelyn Kolish (Montreal: Ministry of Cultural Affairs 1991). The working committee created by the Archives nationales du Québec was established under the auspices of both the National Archives and the Ministry of Justice. The report discusses previous experiences in Britain, France, and the United States.

78 For a thoughtful survey of the issues, Douglas Hay, 'Archival Research in the History of the Law: A User's Perspective' (1987), 24 *Archivaria*, 36–46.

17 The Archives of the English and Welsh Police Forces: A Survey

CLIVE EMSLEY

For generations the history of the English and Welsh police forces was incestuous, Whiggish, and oriented towards metropolitan London. It was incestuous in that most of those who wrote it were either former police officers or civilians, sometimes civil servants, who enjoyed close connections with the police. It was whiggish because it tended to see 'great, far-sighted reformers' of the late eighteenth and early nineteenth centuries as creating a liberal, progressive system in response to potentially serious threats from criminals and rioters. Given the good sense of the majority of the British public and its political leaders, this system was soon to develop into a lynchpin of the British constitution and, in consequence, a model for other, less fortunate nations. It was oriented towards metropolitan London because it stressed that the first English force was the Metropolitan Police created by Sir Robert Peel for London in 1829, and it rather assumed that this provided the model for the rest of the country.[1] Overall, the English police were portrayed in this model as more responsive to the general public and less military than the police of continental Europe, and as more restrained and less party-political than the police of the United States. There is an element of truth in this assessment. However, during the last two decades this Whiggish picture has been considerably revised, particularly by a generation of academic social historians who have moved out from the study of crime and crowds to focus on the machinery deployed to enforce the law on the streets. Much of this recent work has concentrated on the origins and early development of the police, and has stressed the role of the new police in enforcing a new threshold of order demanded by persons of property.[2]

Where the new work has extended into the twentieth century, again it is
the high-profile public order role of the police that has received most
attention.[3]

The older histories, which surveyed the police in England and Wales
as a whole, tended to depend on printed sources and central archives.
The fact that the Metropolitan Police were the only force answerable
directly to the home secretary and not to any local police committee
meant that many of its archives were deposited in the Public Record
Office at Kew. The ready availability of these archives, once weeded, to
researchers probably accentuated the metropolitan orientation of the
histories. But there was also a tendency to rely uncritically on the assessments of nineteenth-century police reformers. One of the most celebrated
printed sources on early nineteenth-century policing is the Report of the
Royal Commission on the Rural Constabulary, which deliberated between
1838 and 1839. The Home Office files in the Public Record Office contain the detailed responses of county magistrates to the questionnaires of
the royal commission, but it was much easier to read the printed version
of the commission's report and to assume that Edwin Chadwick, himself
a 'great reformer' and the report's principal author, had dealt fairly and
honestly with the information submitted. Contemporaries, not unsympathetic to police reform, voiced suspicions of some of Chadwick's conclusions;[4] and recent research suggests that he drew heavily on the
material that supported his arguments for a new national police and
discarded much of the rest.[5] The authors of the traditional histories of
individual police forces – and a considerable number of such histories
were written at the time of the major force amalgamations of the 1960s[6]
– used such material as they could find still scattered around the force in
question or deposited in a local record office. But they also used the
Whiggish framework of Charles Reith and T.A. Critchley, and often found
that the most manageable way to tell their story was by beginning each
new chapter with the appointment of a new chief constable and chronicling the major events and reforms of his tenure of office. Some of the new
revisionist police history has used local material, but usually that to be
found in county archives. The police created in the nineteenth century
were nothing if not bureaucratic. Bureaucratic organizations by definition
generate vast amounts of paper, but seem not always certain about what
to do with it, and this has been the case with police paperwork.[7]

In the second half of the nineteenth century there were upwards of
two hundred police forces in England and Wales, and even before the
Second World War there remained well over one hundred. A succession

of amalgamations during the 1960s and 1970s meant that at the beginning of the 1990s there remained just forty-three; and in the spring of 1993 there were rumours of Home Office proposals in circulation to reduce this number by some two-thirds. Where particular police forces had occasion to correspond with the Home Office, and vice-versa, there are sometimes surviving papers in the Public Record Office in Kew. There are also police papers in county, and sometimes borough, record offices. But there are also papers that remain in police hands.

The surviving archives of the English and Welsh police forces, which remain in police hands, are an invaluable means of illuminating not only the police themselves but also the realities of law enforcement on the streets, perceptions of the law, and a variety of much broader aspects of social history. My aim here is to provide a brief introduction to these sources, the problems in their use, and an outline of the kinds of things they contain. The archives were explored and listed by myself and Ian Bridgeman as the result of grants from the Economic and Social Research Council and the Open University between 1986 and 1989.[8]

One of the problems with police archives is knowing exactly to whom they belong: are they the property of the chief constable or of his police committee? It has long been the duty of local government to 'make proper arrangements,' in the words of the 1972 Local Government Act, for any documents that it has originated or that are in its custody. However, the curious constitutional position of chief constables appears to put them and their forces outside the provisions of this legislation.[9] The problem is knowing who should take responsibility for the preservation of surviving archives and for a policy of preserving documentation for future historians. The Police History Society, an organization that includes in its membership a large number of serving police officers and ex-police officers, has made the preservation of archives a principal reason for its existence and has published a pamphlet on the necessity for a coherent policy, which has been sent to chief constables.[10] But given the day-to-day tasks and pressures of policing, senior officers have tended to give the matter a low priority.

The amalgamations that have taken place, particularly since the 1960s, and that have often united police forces across county boundaries have confused the situation still further. The current Cambridgeshire constabulary has material from a variety of older forces whose jurisdictions now lie within its borders, namely, the old county forces of Cambridgeshire and Huntingdonshire, the boroughs of Cambridge and Peterborough (once in Northamptonshire), and the Isle of Ely. From 1963 to 1975 the Cambridgeshire constabulary itself was part of an even bigger Mid-Anglia Police; it also holds the surviving records of this force. Fortunately, the Cambridge-shire force has established a museum and archive at its principal police station in Peterborough, but this has come about as result of a deter-mined effort by a group of interested policemen rather than because of an initial policy decision from the top. The West Mercia constabulary, covering an even wider area of the old counties of Worcestershire, Here-fordshire, and Shropshire, established its museum and archive under rather similar circumstances; while the Greater Manchester and the South Wales police have established museums and archives following directives from the top, and have recruited professional archivists to organize and staff them. Sadly, though perhaps not surprisingly, other forces lack both direction from the top and enthusiasm from the bottom to preserve their archives and artifacts. Most surprising, however, even though the Metro-politan Police boasts of being the premier force in Britain, the plans to establish a museum and archive initially put forward in 1948 still have not come to fruition. The invaluable collection of artefacts and documents that constitute the basis for this museum were stored, until very recently, on the top floor of a warehouse-cum-factory in Brixton, just a few hun-dred yards from the scene of the major disorders of the summer of 1981.

In the late 1980s the lack of direction in many forces over what to do with historical documents led to some confusion during the investigations into how much and what kind of archival material had survived. On one or two occasions the work had to rely on the good offices of an assistant chief constable, a senior figure in the Police History Society, to jog forces into responding to inquiries or arrange visits. There were attempts to charge the researchers admission to one or two of the 'archives'; at least one of the archive collectors, a former detective, made no secret of his suspicions about the intentions of investigating academics, and some of those responsible for the documents sought to impose fifty- or even hundred-year embargoes on the material in their possession. Possibly encouraged by the efforts of the researchers and the recognition that they possessed material of interest and value, some forces decided to deposit their surviving archives in county record offices. But it is also apparent that there were more prosaic reasons for this; the Sussex consta-bulary deposited its archives in the local county record office because it needed the office space taken up in the force headquarters. Some new documentation has come to light since the cataloguing was completed in 1989; but sadly, a few of the documents that were catalogued have subsequently disappeared.

It is difficult to describe succinctly the kind of documentation that survives in these archives. It takes a variety of forms – written, printed, photographic, cinematic. It begins in the middle of the nineteenth century after police forces became obligatory for local government by the County and Borough Police Act of 1856, but it remains patchy, since documentation has survived largely by accident rather than design. It covers law enforcement by the police from top to bottom, ranging from chief constables' letterbooks and force orders to the chargebooks of police stations and the journals of individual constables. For most of the major forces there survive recruitment registers and personnel books giving physical details of individual policemen and chronicling their police careers – promotions, rewards, disciplinary offences, postings, retirements, and pension. Generally, and unfortunately, these are the only documents for which there are long runs. For relatively short periods there are regulatory registers listing licensed cabs, public houses, street sellers, and so on. Some forces have kept rare runs of Petty Sessions books; the Avon and Somerset force, for example, has five volumes of the Pensfold, Gloucestershire, Petty Sessions, 1850–84, and Staffordshire has eleven volumes of the Petty Sessions Books for Cheadle, 1906–62. While county record offices generally have in their care the surviving records of the magistrates' police committees, which supervised country forces until 1888, and the joint standing committees of magistrates and county councillors, which supervised these forces until the 1960s and 1970s, the police archives also have some of this material and thus, potentially, fill gaps. Borough forces were supervised by watch committees from the Municipal Corporations Act of 1835 to the 1960s and 1970s. Sometimes borough watch committee archives have found their way into county record offices; but the police archives also have watch committee documentation: the Greater Manchester police, for example, have 365 volumes of the City of Manchester watch committee minutes running from 1895 to 1972, an invaluable source for anyone interested in the administration of, as well as the policing of, the city in the twentieth century.

In general these archives take us away from the great men and famous crimes to deal with the day-to-day issues of regulation and petty offences. Many of the documents in the Metropolitan Police repository are the kinds of things which the Public Record Office would not be interested in holding and preserving, since its primary focus is central government and administration. But the notebook of PC Alexander Hennessy for the period 1867–88, or the typewritten reminiscences of PC Arthur Battle, beautifully illustrated with a colleague's cartoons, need a home that is readily accessible to researchers.[11] It is precisely this kind of document which provides a nugget for the social historian seeking to reconstruct street life and police regulation during the mid-Victorian or inter-war periods. One of the social historian's problems at the moment is convincing those who make decisions about which documents should be preserved for future reference that the 'common or garden' is as important, and some might argue even more important, than the papers relating to great or notorious events; it is, perhaps, also a problem for legal historians.

The uses of such a motley of documents are, of course, potentially vast. They can help to fill some of the gaps left by the weeders and by accidents. While researching *The Origins of the Vigilant State*, Bernard Porter was informed that Scotland Yard had pulped all its Special Branch files 'to furnish recycled paper' during the Second World War.[12] Some correspondence with Special Branch and MI5 can, however, be found in surving letterbooks of provincial chief constables during the First World War and immediately afterwards. The archives of the Humberside police, for example, contain the memoranda of the chief constable of Hull for the First World War and inter-war years. These include, among a variety of other things, a confidential letter from Sir Leonard Dunning, HM Inspector of Constabulary, expressing concern about strikes in munitions factories: 'There is without doubt an organized attempt to create trouble in munition works which has more than local importance.' Any information gleaned by the local police was to be sent to Basil Thomson, the head of the Metropolitan Police Special Branch. The letter also enclosed a 'list of persons who have come under notice, but it does not pretend to be complete, and [Thomson] will be glad to hear of the movements not only of those whose names may appear upon it, but also of others whom your local knowledge may bring under suspicion.' The list contains forty-one names, including Labour and ILP parliamentary candidates, local councillors, and union officals.[13]

The police personnel registers provide probably the best record of the physical characteristics of working-class males for the late nineteenth and early twentieth centuries. These men were exceptional in that they met the physical requirements of the police, and that they volunteered for the police. But then any single occupational group is likely to be exceptional, and it is rare that historians can work from perfect sources covering every potential angle. Using Metropolitan Police recruitment data in the Public Record Office, Haia Shpayer-Makov has produced a series of illuminating articles on the recuits for the London force from 1870–1914. While her work concentrates essentially on the police institution, it shows also the potential value for studies of migration and of the anthropometry and medical condition of the working class.[14]

There is similar evidence in the provincial recruitment registers, and preliminary work on these already shows the dangers of relying on the Metropolitan experience as the model for elsewhere in the country. Some forces, especially, it would seem, the county constabularies, drew heavily on locally–born men for their constables; Kent and East Suffolk, for example, found about three-quarters of their recruits from men born in their jurisdictions. Others, generally the urban forces, relied far less on local men; only a fifth of the men who joined the Birmingham police in the late nineteenth century had been born in the city. Some forces were keen to recruit former soldiers; others were less so. Just over one-half of the men recruited into the Bedfordshire constabulary from the mid-1920s to the Second World War were former soldiers; but in neighbouring Cambridgeshire under a third of the recruits had served in the army. The extent to which agricultural labourers were favoured as police recruits, as the traditional histories assert, remains a complex issue. Up to the beginning of the First World War most entries under the heading 'Previous Trade' describe the recruit as a 'labourer,' but labourer was a catch-all term in the nineteenth century. As the century drew towards its close the number of agricultural workers was declining in the country. But at the same time the recruitment registers offer far more detailed descriptions even under the heading of labourer – such as 'builder's labourer,' 'labourer and fisherman,' and 'agricultural labourer.' Probably a majority of nineteenth-century police recruits came from rural districts, but it would be erroneous to consider every 'labourer' as a former agricultural worker.

Two further points of interest emerging on a preliminary reading of the records – the nineteenth-century recruits have, first, the largest number of recruits who had served as soldiers, and, second, the largest number of Irishmen. The number of men who gave their trade as 'soldier' constituted under 1 per cent of the recruits to the Metropolitan Police between 1850 and 1909, but the number of men with military service never fell below 12 per cent from the 1860s. The Irish recruits came particularly from the poor, backward counties of the west, and in much higher numbers than their proportion of the overall population. The Irish were notorious for their turbulent behaviour in Victorian cities, yet the evidence of the recruitment books suggests that they were significant on both sides of the law-and-order divide. Overall, recruits appear to have been younger as the nineteenth century wore on, possibly reflecting a growing awareness of the police as a lifetime career, with prospects, for a young working-class male, and especially after the guarantee of a pension with the legislation of 1890.[15]

In addition to giving information on what men did before they joined the police, these registers give details of each man's career in the police and, in some instances, what they did afterwards and their pensions. Some resigned because they could not stomach the work, particularly night patrols. John Partridge, for example, resigned from the Worcestershire constabulary in July 1882 after four and a half months; he returned to his former trade of blacksmith because the 'night air did not agree with him.' Many were dismissed or were asked to resign because of disciplinary offences, not the least of these being drunkenness. There are scores of examples of the latter. In February 1879, after just six weeks in the force, Edward Henry Hudspith, a wheelwright and former artilleryman, 'resigned' from the Worcestershire force, having been 'absent from his beat 4 hours and helplessly drunk' and 'asking people in the streets to give him drink and insulting them upon their refusal to do so.' Nine years later another ex-soldier, George Biggs, was dismissed after a police career of six years, during which time he had been severely disciplined twelve times. On half of these occasions drinking was involved; the last straw was 'omitting his conference point at 2 a.m. on 22nd. Septr. and at 12 midnight 24th. Septr. Also drinking at the Manchester Inn, Romsley on Sunday night the 23rd. Septr. 1888, while on duty and inducing or ordering the manageress Miss Johnson to supply ale after 10 p.m. when the house should have been closed.'[16] Discipline was enforced harshly with fines and removals to other posts, generally at a man's own expense; it seems only gradually to have been softened from the inter-war period.

Comment in these registers also enables, in part, enables the reconstruction of the origins of modern cop-canteen culture. Certainly from the late nineteenth century, some men believed that their uniform and their authority as constables gave them power over the public, women, and their neighbours. By the same token, comment in these registers and in some of the manuscript memoirs and autobiographies held in these archives shows that the avuncular tradition of the English 'bobby' was an important role model for some English policemen.[17]

In the same way that the recruitment registers might be used for a morphological study of working-class males, it seems probable that the discipline books and other material in police archives, might be used for a glimpse of the working-class family, as well as of attitudes to the law and to the police. Again the sources might not always be ideal, but they are some of the best that we have. Policemen's wives were subjected to investigation by senior officers, and the men were held responsible for their wives' behaviour. In July 1917, for example, Robert Chadwick, a constable in the Lancashire Constabulary, was disciplined for permitting his wife to run up debts over the previous two years. Chadwick was ordered to pay his wife's debts, and was transferred 'for the good of the service' to another station. The slightest whiff of scandal between a constable and his wife could lead to a disciplinary hearing. In June 1925 PC Alfred Redford was ordered to resign from the Lancashire Constabulary for 'discreditable conduct.' His fault was 'fighting with his wife ... thereby causing annoyance to the neighbours.'[18]

Joanne Marie Klein's doctoral dissertation, a pioneering study in this area, draws upon the police achives of Birmingham, Liverpool, and Manchester from the turn of the century until the Second World War. Her work offers valuable perspectives on working-class marriage and family life as well as on policing.[19] Chief constables organized welfare and charity agencies; the Devon and Cornwall Constabulary Archive held rare advertising films from the 1920s urging cinema audiences in Plymouth to donate to the widows and orphans fund created by the city's chief constable for the local poor.[20] Chief constables responded to enquiries about missing persons and relatives with whom families had lost touch, while from the early years of the twentieth century they dealt with a new and socially superior class of offender – the motorist.

The welfare and assistance roles of the English police have not been much explored by historians, but they may well have contributed to a grudging acceptance and even appreciation by sections of the working class.[21] The traditional view is that it was the Motor Traffic Act of 1930 which began to poison relations between the police and the middle class, but the evidence from the police archives suggests that the friction was developing well before. In September 1906, for example, the chief constable of Huntingdonshire sought to appease an angry friend who had been stopped for speeding:

My dear Balfour,
I have received your letter and also a police report. I am quite satisfied that the duty was correctly done, as I never allow any Motor duty to be taken on until I have selected the place and satisfied myself that all is fair. I quite believe that you, like every Motorist who has fallen into any 'trap' (Motorists' term), has no idea of the

great pace at which you were going, and for old acquaintance sake the matter shall drop, but please keep it to yourself as I have a very difficult and unpleasant duty with these motor cases, and have often had occasion to proceed against my friends and even relations.[22]

While one of the founders of the current interest in the history of crime has castigated recent research for its conceptual timidity and its increasing transformation into the 'history of administration or "the machinery of justice,"'[23] the letterbooks of chief constables, police orders, chargebooks, refused chargebooks, and a variety of other documents held in the police archives will be the best way in to exploring the imperatives of policing. In the same way that some of these records suggest there were different attitudes about who made the best recruits, policing ideas and imperatives varied between borough and borough, between borough and county, and between county and county. Serious academic local studies are just getting under way into different police forces, and they are drawing heavily on the local police archives. This does not have to result in historians' learning more and more about less and less, cowering in conceptual timidity and losing their historical imagination. When these studies are complete, a much better picture should emerge of the role of the police in English society, of the contrasts between the Metropolitan Police and its provincial cousins, and of the steady encroachment of the Home Office on the powers of local police committees. Indeed, from a solid historical base it may even be possible to challenge some of the hallowed constitutional twaddle that still surrounds the English police and to make a serious assessment of their uniqueness.

NOTES

1 The key Whiggish texts are those of Charles Reith, notably *The Police Idea* (Oxford: Oxford University Press 1938), and *British Police and the Democratic Ideal* (Oxford: University Press 1943). Among others in the Whiggish mold is T.A. Critchley, *A History of Police in England and Wales*, 2d ed. (London: Constable 1978), who was secretary to the royal commission on police, 1960–2, and a senior member of the police department in the Home Office.

2 The essays of Robert D. Storch mark the beginning of this shift. See, in particular, 'The Plague of Blue Locusts: Police Reform and Popular Resistance in Northern England 1840–1857' (1975), 20 *International Review of*

Social History, 61–90, and 'The Policeman as Domestic Missionary: Urban Discipline and Popular culture in Northern England, 1850–1880' (1976), 9 *Journal of Social History*, 481–509. See also Carolyn Steedman, *Policing the Victorian Community: The Formation of the English Provincial Police Forces 1856–1880* (London: Routledge and Kegan Paul 1984).

3 Jane Morgan, *Conflict and Order: The Police and Labour Disputes in England and Wales 1900–1939* (Oxford: Clarendon Press 1987); Barbara Weinberger, *Keeping the Peace? Policing Strikes in Britain, 1906–1926* (Oxford: Berg 1991).

4 See, for example, *Justice of the Peace*, 13 April 1839, 206–7, and 20 April 1839, 221.

5 My thanks to David Philips and Robert Storch for information on this point, and for a preview of their current joint study of policing before the police.

6 Dennis T. Brett, *The Police of England and Wales: A Bibliography 1829–1979*, 3d ed. (Bramshill: Police Staff College 1979), is a useful guide.

7 Joseph Fouché's police in Napoleonic France were regarded as particularly efficient and certainly appear to have been on top of potential conspiracies against the regime. However, Jean Tulard has noted of this police, 'Son goût des fichiers, des registres, des rapports, bref du papier, a été poussé jusqu'à la manie.' He goes on to describe 'Le culte du reseignement pour le reseignement.' Jean Tulard, 'Le mythe de Fouché,' in *L'etat et sa police en France (1789–1914)*, Jacques Aubert et al. (Geneva: Droz 1979), 31.

8 Ian Bridgeman and Clive Emsley, *A Guide to the Archives of the Police Forces of England and Wales* (Cambridge: Police History Society 1989).

9 The celebrated ruling in the case of *Fisher v. Oldham Corporation*, [1930] 2 KB 364, and subsequent judicial rulings, while still the subject of debate, denied that a police constable was in any respect a 'servant' of a municipality; see, inter alia, Laurence Lustgarten, *The Governance of Police* (London: Sweet and Maxwell 1986) 56–61.

10 L.A. Waters, *Towards a Record Management Policy for Provincial Police Forces in England and Wales* (Cambridge: Police History Society 1992).

11 Metropolitan Police Archive MS 1116, Note Book of PC Alexander Hennessy; MS 175.88 PC Arthur Battle, 'This job's not what it used to be'

12 Bernard Porter, *The Origins of the Vigilant State: The London Metropolitan Police Special Branch before the First World War* (London: Weidenfeld and Nicolson 1987), xi.

13 Humberside Police Archives, Hull City Police, Chief Constable's Memorandums, 1916–26, fol. 77. For other examples of the links between MI5, Special Branch, and provincial forces, see Clive Emsley, *The English Police: A*

Political and Social History (Hemel Hempstead: Harvester Weatsheaf 1991), 101–2 and 121.

14 Haia Shpayer Makov, 'The Making of a Police Labour Force' (1990), 24 *Journal of Social History*, 109–34; 'Notes on the Medical Examination of Provincial Applicants to the London Metropolitan Police on the eve of the First World War' (1991), 47 *Histoire Sociale/Social History*, 169–79, and 'The Appeal of Country Workers: the Case of the Metropolitan Police' (1991), 64 *Historical Research*, 186–203.

15 Emsley, supra note 13, at 178–85. Together with Mark Clapson I am currently using these records for a study of recruits to the English Police forces circa 1840–1940; see Clive Emsley and Mark Clapson, 'Recruiting the English Policeman c. 1840–1940' (1994), 3 *Policing and Society* 269–86.

16 West Mercia Police Museum, Worcestershire Constabulary Descriptive Register and Record of Service, 1877–1883, fols 26, 147, and 155.

17 See, in general, Emsley, supra note 13, at 201–6.

18 Greater Manchester Police Museum, Lancashire Constabulary, Manchester Division Misconduct Book 1912–35, fols 34 and 89.

19 Joanne Marie Klein, 'Invisible Working-Class Men: Police Constables in Manchester, Birmingham and Liverpool, 1900–39,' Ph.D., thesis, Rice University (1992).

20 The films were in a poor state when discovered in the late 1980s. Video copies now exist in the Devon and Cornwall Constabulary Archive at Exeter and in the European Centre for the Study of Police at the Open University. The original films have been deposited for safekeeping and restoration with the British Film Archive.

21 In contrast, the welfare role of the police in American cities is central to Eric H. Monkkonen's *Police in Urban America 1860–1920* (Cambridge: University Press 1981). For a brief comparison of a British city (Manchester) and a German city (Wuppertal) exploring Monkkonen's ideas and using police archival holdings, see Barbara Weinberger and Herbert Reinke, 'A Diminishing Function? A Comparative Historical Account of Policing in the City' (1991), 1 *Policing and Society*, 213–23.

22 Cambridgeshire Constabulary Archives, Huntingdonshire Constabulary, Chief Constable's Letter Book, 1906–1915, fol. 14; and see in general, Clive Emsley, ' "Mother, What Did Policemen Do When There Weren't Any Motors?" The Law, the Police and the Regulation of Motor Traffic in England, 1900–1939' (1993), 36 *Historical Journal*, 357–81.

23 Peter Linebaugh, *The London Hanged: Crime and Civil Society in the Eighteenth Century* (London: Allen Lane 1991), xviii.

18 Towards a Canadian Police Historiography

GREG MARQUIS

A decade ago Eric Monkkonen, in his essay 'From Cop to Social History,' reported on an encouraging trend: the recognition that the police were a worthy subject of social history inquiry.[1] Over the last two decades American and British historians, influenced by contemporary controversies surrounding policing, have produced an extensive historical literature, and there are signs that more is on the way. In Canada the Royal Canadian Mounted Police are a national or, more properly, an international symbol. Yet our police history lags far behind other jurisdictions. With the exception of R.C. Macleod's monograph on the North West Mounted Police for the period 1873–1905,[2] we have nothing approaching the work of Monkkonen, Fogelson, Walker, Johnson, and Harring on the United States, nor of Emsley, Steedman, Palmer, and Reiner on England and Ireland (and Miller on both England and the United States).[3] Despite the flowering of social history, Canadian academics have all but ignored one of the most important institutions of the state.[4] In this paper I look at the emergence of historical writing on the Canadian police, the current status of the literature, and its likely directions. In the last section I examine four important research questions using examples from Vancouver police records.

The Red Shadow: The RCMP

Non-Canadians are often surprised and even disappointed to learn that Canada has been home to law enforcement organizations other than the Mounted Police. The Mounties and their partisans (prior to the 1970s virtually every journalist, historian, and novelist who wrote on the subject) have not gone out of their way to disabuse the world of this notion. History has been very important for the RCMP's public relations. Since 1919 RCMP veterans have published a journal, *Scarlet and Gold*, which contains historical pieces. The *RCMP Quarterly*, which first appeared in 1934, has also featured countless historical items. The RCMP maintains a museum at Regina, its original western headquarters, as well as staff historians and a photo archives at its Ottawa headquarters. Historians of municipal, provincial, and private police must work under the 'red shadow.' For decades the Mounted Police were the subject of the only histories of policing in Canada, and most of this literature was Whiggish, anecdotal, and ethnocentric. As Macleod has pointed out, it never questioned 'why Canada should have departed so abruptly from the British tradition in law enforcement' by appointing a national constabulary to secure the west.[5] Although the early twentieth century was a golden age of English Canadian historiography, scholars avoided the topic of the Mounted Police. Journalists and amateurs did not. The first full history of the force, by Ernest J. Chambers, a participant in the 1885 Northwest Rebellion, appeared in 1906. J.W. Turner, a journalist, worked for decades on his two-volume history, which was published in 1950. Although Turner interviewed members of the force and relied on few official documents, he produced a bland chronicle.[6]

Until Akin's balanced treatment in 1973, historical accounts of the Mounted Police were unambiguously pro-police. Popular historical treatments, like fiction, tended to repeat core characteristics: the ability of the Mounties always to 'get their man'; their élite nature; their respect for natives; their aversion to violence; and their honesty and sense of uncompromising duty to queen and country.[7] The works of Harwood Steele, the son of Mountie Sam Steele, bordered on hagiography. The further the frontier receded, the more gilded the image of the police.[8] With the waning of imperialism, other priorities arose. After the Second World War the Mounties were portrayed as Canadian G-men; good 'cold warriors' and up-to-date crime fighters. This was an image the RCMP consciously cultivated at the time.[9] In 1973, the RCMP's centennial year, William and Nora Kelly produced a competent if somewhat biased semi-official history. William Kelly had headed the RCMP's controversial security and intelligence branch. After retirement Kelly, a law enforcement 'hawk,' became involved in journalism and co-wrote a massive police textbook that reflected the anxieties of a Cold War crime fighter.[10] On the left, Lorne and Caroline Brown's polemical *An Unauthorized History of the RCMP* assailed cherished myths associated with the force by examining its treatment of natives, labour, the peace movement, and radicals. That volume's revisionism signalled a period of 'Mountie-bashing' unleashed by the social changes of the 1960s, Québécois nationalism, and revelations that the RCMP had been engaged in 'dirty tricks' and surveillance against legitimate political parties and organizations. The RCMP's role in security and intelligence, much of it aimed at domestic subversion, became the object of two royal commissions, countless press articles, and a number of critical books.[11] Yet, as Walden noted in 1982, the Mounted Police, despite contemporary allegations of wrongdoing, remained popular with the public.[12]

The key to the popularity of the early twentieth-century Mounted Police is invented tradition, fuelled by the popular culture of imperialism and the American entertainment media.[13] As Walden notes in his study of the Mounties and popular culture, 'The image of the police was a popular fabrication.' From the 1890s onwards, in novels, magazine articles, children's stories and popular history, the Mounted Police were 'a shining symbol of Anglo-Saxon superiority.'[14] They embodied manliness, order, and British fair play. Their habitat, the western frontier and later the Arctic, was romantic, unspoiled, and dangerous. The partly mythical image of the Mounted Police became a source of pride for English Canadians. The fictional Mountie was a composite character, a Canadian version of James Fenimore Cooper's Deerslayer who preferred duty – and the frontier – to settled life. Dime novels and motion pictures developed what mid-twentieth-century Mounties would later deride as a 'Rose Marie' image of the force, but the RCMP welcomed and cultivated its heroic image in popular culture.

In terms of territory the North-West Mounted Police (1873–1905) and the Royal North-West Mounted Police (1905–19) was a powerful federal agency, and the organization's records are, by the standards of the municipal police, impressive.[15] Yet it was not a 'national' police force. Even with acquisition of security and intelligence duties in 1920, expansion into provincial policing and anti-smuggling patrols in the early 1930s and moves into Newfoundland and British Columbia in 1950, the RCMP (as it now was) did not become a truly national constabulary. Despite its official pretensions, and its control of the national criminal records collection, the force encountered a mixed reception in the Maritime provinces[16] and hostility in Quebec. Ontario, the heartland of English-Canadian nationalism, whose interests were safeguarded by the original NWMP, has not encouraged RCMP intrusions into provincial and municipal law enforcement. The western and eastern provinces contracted with the Mounties for rural policing between 1928 and 1950, but did so more for financial reasons than for purposes of standardization. RCMP contract detachments, as many provincial and municipal officials readily understand, are not only subsidized by the federal treasury; their personnel are forbidden to join unions. Since the 1930s the RCMP, despite their international reputation, have for the most part served as federally subsidized traffic cops.

Internal Affairs: Official Histories

Two forms of police literature with a long tradition are the memoir and the official history. A number of ex-NWMP officers wrote memoirs, some of them reminiscent of the writings of Royal Irish Constabulary officers who served on another imperial frontier, late nineteenth-century Ireland.[17] Most 'participant-observers' flattered the force, although the occasional indiscretion, such as a report of heavy drinking, slipped out. One of the best contemporary accounts is *Mounted Police Life in Canada* by R.B. Deane. Deane, a former superintendent, wrote in 1916 that the force had outlived its usefulness in the west and should be disbanded. After the Second World War no fewer than three senior RCMP officers produced autobiographies.[18] Although Mounted Police memoirs are the most visible, a few municipal and provincial officers took up the pen.[19] *The Memoirs of a Great Detective* (1904), the autobiography of Ontario detective John Wilson Murray, followed in the tradition of nineteenth-century French, British, and American detective autobiographies and biographies. A rare urban work is George T. Denison's *Recollections of a Police Magistrate* (1920), the musings of the noted imperialist, police magistrate, and architect of the late Victorian Toronto police department.[20]

Urban police departments invariably produced at least one amateur historian, usually a constable, NCO, or detective, who functioned as unofficial archivist and chronicler. From these efforts emerged local police 'museums,' small-scale operations with an emphasis on lurid crimes and acts of bravery. Despite the efforts of individual departments, much valuable material has been lost. In recent years a number of municipal departments have produced commemorative histories that vary in terms of quality of research. Most official histories are organized according to the regimes of various police chiefs, make liberal use of anecdotes, and are aimed at members of the department and public-spirited citizens.[21] Two exceptions are Turmel's overview of the Montreal police and

Swan's centennial history of the Vancouver department. In both cities police administration has been heavily politicized and scandal ridden; the result, particularly in the case of Swan (a former police detective) is both instructive and entertaining. Given that 'in-house' historians have both insiders' knowledge and access to sources, collaborative efforts seem a fruitful avenue. One such project is *The Saint John Police Story*, jointly attributed to sociologist Peter McGahan, detective William Higgins, and the late police chief Gerald Wallace.[22]

Police Patchwork: Case Studies

Canada's academic police historiography began with R.C. Macleod's 1976 study of the North-West Mounted Police. Morton and Horrall had previously discussed the role of the NWMP as an agent of the central government.[23] Macleod concluded that the NWMP prior to 1905 was successful in mediating between white settlers and western natives, and rarely abused its powers. Unlike earlier chroniclers, Macleod examined the role of patronage, an inescapable fact of Canadian public administration. He concluded that the Mounted Police survived the turn of the century not because of heroic exploits or British fair play, but because of circumstance: it had become useful to settlers and to local and federal politicians. He also noted the force's distaste for enforcing liquor laws once white settlement was well established. This functional hypothesis, based on the realization that police did more than fight crime, was developed further by Betke, who examined the NWMP's service role in relation to settlers. Like the Royal Irish Constabulary, the NWMP fulfilled a number of administrative tasks that benefited both state and populace. Morrison's study of the mounted police in the Yukon and the Arctic in the period from 1894 to 1925 also examines the police as an administrative entity. Morrison argues that the police 'changed the north from a largely unregulated society to one which operated, in theory and increasingly in fact, under much the same rules and terms [as] the rest of the country.'[24] Recently Macleod has written on the twentieth-century Mounted Police, but we still know little about the force's post-1919 operational history, its impact on Canadian policing, and its relations with American agencies such as the Federal Bureau of Investigation.[25]

Nineteenth-century advocates of provincial police took as their model the Royal Irish Constabulary. Lower Canada (1837–40) and the United Canadas (1842–67) experimented with government-controlled rural police to meet the threat of French-Canadian unrest and labour strife on public works. These constabularies were never intended to be permanent, but neither was the North West Mounted Police. In the 1850s New Brunswick passed, but did not proclaim, legislation authorizing a colonial police. Prince Edward Island contemplated a similar policy when it was threatened with the removal of its British garrison. In 1856 the Canadian government, in the face of bitter municipal opposition, withdrew its bill proposing a provincial police. And the new colony of British Columbia in the late 1850s engaged an RIC officer to act as police superintendent. The best nineteenth-century example of a provincial police, however rudimentary, was the Newfoundland Constabulary, formally constituted in 1871, a consolidation of earlier policing efforts in St John's and various outport communities. Ontario and Quebec organized small detective forces which developed into provincial constabularies in the age of the automobile, an example followed by both western and eastern provinces, including tiny Prince Edward Island.

Provincial policing was rooted in rural society, an area of growing interest to Canadian historians. Greer's article on the 1839–42 Rural Police of Lower Canada is a rare academic treatment of rural policing. Greer, a leading social historian of New France and Quebec, argues that the rural police and its urban counterparts extended 'the reach of the state over civil society.'[26] In Lower Canada, as Lord Durham noted, the state barely existed outside the environs of Quebec and Montreal, which is precisely why a temporary gendarmerie was organized following the insurrections of 1837–8. As Greer points out, the NWMP was not the first police force controlled by the Canadian government. Other than Greer's piece and Phyne's article on provincial policing in Nova Scotia, academics have ignored rural policing. Once again, amateurs and journalists have filled the gap.[27] Fox's history of the Newfoundland Constabulary, although rich in documentary evidence, is a scissors-and-paste rendering that leaves room for a more systematic study of an important facet of Newfoundland society. Stewart and Hudson's account of the Saskatchewan Provincial Police, geared for the popular market, concentrates on the politics of rural policing from 1917 to 1928. Higley's detailed chronicle of the Ontario Provincial Police benefits from access to primary records and an insider's knowledge of the OPP. Although an encyclopaedic official history, Higley departs from tradition by introducing more of a 'warts and all' approach, however muted: he admits, for example, that the OPP assisted in breaking strikes. A more readable work is Stonier-Newman's account of the British Columbia Provincial Police, absorbed by the RCMP in 1950. Stonier-Newman, the daughter of a BCPP highway patrolman, makes use of both archival sources and interviews with veteran officers.[28]

Research on the urban police, who were organized as early as the 1830s and 1840s, has appeared in dribs and drabs in article form or as part of urban history. One valiant attempt at synthesis, based largely on official histories and a limited secondary literature, is the work of three Ottawa sociologists.[29] The historical background provided by commentators on contemporary policing usually is far from satisfactory. A recent history of Canadian crime and criminals, oddly enough, totally ignores the police, whose appearance in the nineteenth century constituted an important shift in state power and in the construction of criminality.[30] The case study method, favoured by social and urban historians, makes sense for municipal departments, whose development reflected local economic, social, and political factors. Academic journal articles on the Canadian municipal police first appeared in the 1980s. Similarly, a number of historians discussed the police in urban history.[31]

In *The Politics of the Police*, the British sociologist Robert Reiner contrasted the 'cop-sided' view of police history with that of 1970s and 1980s revisionists. The Canadian literature on nineteenth-century police reform is insufficiently developed to allow a historiographic analysis as sweeping as Reiner's, yet some observations can be made.[32] Historians who approach the police within a Marxist framework are more conscious of police reform's relation to state development under capitalism. Kealey, a working-class historian, has discussed police reform in early Victorian Toronto in terms of 'a new bourgeois consensus,' 'bourgeois order,' and a 'new bourgeois hegemony.' Translation: capitalism produced the police in Toronto and elsewhere. Rogers, whose speciality is eighteenth-century British social history, adopts a similar stance in his discussion of nineteenth-century Toronto police reform. In his view the police originated, in Reiner's words, as 'the advance scouts of the state' – an interpretation adopted in the United States by Harring.[33] Greer's study of policing in Lower Canada adopts a similar perspective, although the situation in that colony in the 1830s was more analagous to Ireland than to industrializing Britain.

Researchers who have approached the subject from the point of view of police history have been less certain of the institution's class instrumentality. Senior and McCulloch acknowledge the political nature of police reform in Montreal and Quebec from the 1830s to the 1850s, but the initial impetus for police innovation was fear not of the working class but of the anglophone élite's desire to contain French-Canadian nationalism.[34] Boritch, a sociologist, hovers between a class control and a pluralist model of police history, with a slight tendency towards the former. In a detailed examination of nineteenth-century Toronto she recognizes class control, but also a service role and 'self-determination and self-maintenance' – the police department's bureaucratic imperative. Boritch, with Hagan, has also produced a quantitative study for a sociology audience on Toronto policing.[35] Weaver's article on the Hamilton police does not reject class analysis. Yet it questions suggestions that the police existed primarily to break strikes, to enforce morality, or even to fight crime. 'Community entanglement' led the Hamilton police down these paths, but its fundamental role was that of an urban service bureaucracy.[36] The police service role, which for decades was open-ended, helped legitimize the institution in the eyes of the working class.

Studies of nineteenth-century Saint John, Charlottetown, and Quebec City and twentieth-century Toronto reach similar conclusions.[37] The example of Charlottetown, a minor town in a minor British colony, supports Monkkonen's assertion that exactly when a nineteenth-century community decided to create a police force depended neither on public disorder nor on rising crime, although these factors could give a boost to institutional development. In the case of Charlottetown, crime 'rose' precisely because of the organization of a police establishment in 1855. Those sociologists and critical criminologists who rarely have anything positive to say about the contemporary police, and historians influenced by British working-class and European social historiography, will by nature stress class instrumentality. Most police historians will be less sweeping in their claims. The difference between the overt class-control interpretation and a more nuanced case-by-case approach may be the difference between objective and subjective considerations of class.

Directions

Because of its decentralized police system, Canada's police history must be prosecuted on a city-by-city, province-by-province basis. In the final part of this paper I examine four organizing principles for further research, using examples taken from police and civic records deposited at the City of Vancouver Archives. Although the following themes are urban, they can be adapted to rural jurisdictions. Vancouver, Canada's Pacific metropolis, was incorporated in 1886 with the arrival of the Canadian Pacific Railway. Its police force, now one of the largest in Canada, was for much of the twentieth century the subject of innumerable controversies, most of them centring on morality enforcement.

Police and the Law

The exact relationship between law and its enforcement is not always discernible, even where records have survived. And the questions asked by historians who focus on the police often differ from those who examine legal thought, the bench, the bar, important trials, and law reform. For many decades the municipal police were closely associated with the magistrates' courts. Even where courts were provided with city or crown attorneys to supervise important prosecutions, it seems that the police were key players. Vancouver's Crown attorney explained in 1928, 'We must take what the officers say.'[38] Much like magistrates who tailored their sentences to fit the circumstances of the crime, the police appear to have used discretion in reducing charges in drug and bootlegging cases. Police actions were controlled by law, as certain judgments and citizens' litigation indicate, but official records do not easily reveal the degree to which informal procedure governed the day-to-day operations of police departments. Neither do court records easily reveal the quasi-judicial role of the police. Historians of the police should be prepared to uncover the informal justice system, a process that was often far removed from official versions of reality.

The cash bail controversy of the 1920s is a good example. The official reality was that the police routinely arrested and charged prostitutes by the score. The informal reality was that most offenders were not expected to show up in court. Either through custom or deliberate strategy, the police, the Crown attorney, and the magistrates perpetuated a routine processing of 'found-ins,' women arrested in disorderly houses. In most cases these women, their names neatly typed in monthly morality reports, posted cash bail, failed to appear in court, and thus forfeited the bail. Although technically there had been no conviction, the authorities regarded the forfeited bail as a fine and were satisfied. This situation outraged women's and social service groups, which demanded that prostitutes be jailed for their own good. Cash bail was also routinely granted to alleged liquor law violators.[39] According to arrest statistics and 'fines,' the Vancouver police in the 1920s were cracking down on vice; but reform groups understood the reality.

Police and Crime

Records send mixed messages concerning the relationship of the police to crime. It is evident that the police developed a narrow view of criminal behaviour; this selective attitude extended even to Criminal Code offences. Occurrence books – records of incidents, persons, and lost property encountered on patrol – are the basic police record. Little serious criminal activity is recorded in these registers, as suggested by the occurrence record for pioneer Vancouver (1889–94). (The notebooks of individual officers, mandatory in many departments, are other useful sources for routine experience, yet they are rare in archival collections.) The policing of suburban districts, such as South Vancouver, which came under Vancouver's police system in 1929, was even less dramatic, at least according to the occurrence books. South Vancouver's major public order problems in the late 1920s, it seems, were boys, dogs, and quarrelsome neighbours.[40] This does not mean that all police work was trivial or that serious crimes were not committed. South Vancouver, admittedly, was not Gastown. But occurrence reports caution us against automatically linking the police to crime. Other administrative records important for departmental housekeeping are the minutes of boards of police commissioners and city council police committees.[41]

Although patrol officers were more important numerically, whether on the beat prior to the 1930s or in subsequent more motorized decades, records relating to detective work tell us more about police-defined crime. The records of small and medium-sized police departments are not as specialized. Even in a major city such as Vancouver, with its reputation for drug abuse, transiency, and prostitution, the war on crime was waged by a mere handful of officers. Correspondence from the chief constable to the city licence inspector for the period 1920–36 suggests that detectives, in addition to combatting drug peddlers, sporting women, gamblers, and thieves, made regular reports on rooming-houses, hotels, cafes, apartment buildings, and taxi drivers. If morality and other offences were committed on the premises, or if the police took a disliking to the character of proprietors, employees, customers, or tenants, the chief would suggest that licences be cancelled.[42] This bureaucratic relationship gave the police great discretionary power in the urban economy, and indicates a concern with 'respectability.' By contrast, the 'crimes' that outraged moral reformers, women's groups, social service workers, and journalists in 1900–45 were viewed as inevitable by the enforcers. The head of the Vancouver 'dry squad' reported that bootlegging was not regarded as a dishonourable occupation by most residents, and other detectives testified in 1928 that gambling, both in Chinatown and outside, was not strictly criminal, the Criminal Code notwithstanding. And a morality squad member revealed that the department's policy on disorderly houses was 'keep them where there is no outcry against them ... where there is no disease in the house or no thieving.'[43]

Police and Community

Police records, as Monkkonen and others have pointed out, can be rich social indicators. Monkkonen's study of American municipal police in the period from 1860 to 1920 emphasized not crime-fighting but the need for a centralized municipal bureaucracy as the motive behind police reform. If one agrees that the police institution, until the rise of the regulatory welfare state, was the city's paramount bureaucracy, then its documents, if extant, are potentially the most important municipal record group.[44] Yet a rich collection of documents does not alleviate problems of interpretation. Municipal police records prepared for political masters tend to reflect a middle-class view of the institution. Records also reflect the internal needs and priorities of the police bureaucracy.[45] Furthermore, oral communications and 'understood' procedures and practices are absent from the official record, as are documents that have been culled, accidently destroyed, squirrelled away, or simply forgotten. Finally, police records can distort our perception of police work. Vancouver's records, for example, reflect morality and detective work more than patrol and traffic duties, despite the fact that the latter consumed the greater share of resources.

Vancouver records provide insights into a host of themes not directly related to police history: working-class culture; race relations, particularly Anglo-Canadian views of the city's large Chinese minority; control of wayward girls; labour relations; and domestic violence. A large number of organizations, ranging from the Ku Klux Klan and the Moral Reform Association to the Canadian Labour Defence League, made demands on the police authorities. Records such as the transcripts of the 1928 Lennie Inquiry, although difficult to sift through as evidence, provide glimpses of Vancouver's lower-class 'night life': drinking dens, gambling joints, and prostitutes operating in small brothels and rooming-houses. Although there are no separate records in the City of Vancouver Archives on the Women's Division, its activities surface in other record groups. The Women's Division, which in the 1920s consisted of several policewomen working under a female head, did preventive and social service work with juveniles, especially girls, who became involved in domestic disputes and attended court. Like its contemporary, the Toronto Police Morality Department, the Women's Division was involved in the enforcement of court-ordered maintenance payments.[46] Juvenile and social service work, which in large urban departments involved matrons and policewomen, should be studied closely; otherwise police history is in danger of remaining unbearably masculine.

The image of the Chinese community found in Vancouver police records is predictably stereotypical; Chinatown was, in the eyes of the police, a distinct society wherein a certain amount of gambling and opium-smoking was both expected and tolerated. This is evident in the testimony of detectives and senior officers before the 1928 Lennie Inquiry into morality enforcement.[47] Most of Vancouver's narcotics arrests and a great deal of its gambling prosecutions centred on Chinese males. Otherwise, the Chinese, according to the official record, were extremely law-abiding. The drug issue, the cause of periodic moral panics in Vancouver from the 1910s to recent years, is treated in routine fashion in police testimony and records in comparison with the press and pulpit. Indeed, one could go so far as to suggest that Vancouver detectives, in their own crude way, were culturally sensitive to the Asian minority. They noted, for example, that Chinese clubs, the object of the periodic wrath of Oriental exclusionists as nests of dope fiends and white slavers, performed a vital social welfare function. One detective testified that while Chinese élites preferred to maintain amicable relations with the civic authorities, 'if a Chinaman talks to a detective in the streets, he will be seen as a stool pigeon.'[48] The Vancouver Police Department published statistics on race and crime as late as the 1960s. Such material should be exploited by historians of ethnicity and race relations.

Working-class historians have identified the police as an important institution in the state's arsenal.[49] In Canadian working-class history, Vancouver is associated with the pre-First World War Industrial Workers of the World, the activities of relief camp strikers, which culminated in the On-to-Ottawa Trek of 1935, and violent labour confrontations such as the 1935 waterfront strike. Specific record groups do suggest that the Vancouver police gathered intelligence on Communist organizers, unemployed leaders, and certain trade union officials, particularly during the Great Depression. And the general files and minutebooks of the board of police commissioners, two of the most useful record groups in the City of Vancouver Archives, indicate protests on the part of conservative trade unions and Communist organizations against police handling of unemployed parades and meetings. To argue that the Vancouver police evolved largely in response to working-class protest or to the threat of class conflict, as Harring has argued of American cities, may be ideologically appealing. The events along the Vancouver waterfront in 1935 lend credence to Harring's thesis. Yet the 'radical threat' pales in comparison to other concerns such as drugs, prostitution, gambling, and major crimes.[50] As Baker has recently discovered, Canadian labour historians have tended to assume rather than prove the class instrumentality of the police in industrial relations. Baker's assessment of the NWMP's response to the 1906 Lethbridge coal strike is ambivalent – a conclusion that will satisfy neither pluralists nor class-conflict theorists, but an important one none the less.[51] We know that the RCMP monitored radical and ethnic organizations and that the police as a whole, like most Canadians, did not like Communists. But we are still awaiting an in-depth treatment of the history of policing of strikes in Canada.

Police and Professionalism

Professionalism for the early twentieth-century police encapsulated a cluster of goals: freedom from political interference; adequate personnel, wages, and equipment; insulation from 'malicious prosecutions' in the civil courts; and the reform of 'soft' laws. Crime-fighting came to dominate the public image, if not the actual duties, of North American policing by the early twentieth century. Handling criminals was the core of police professionalism. Big-city police tracked known criminals on the basis of their habits, clothing, lifestyle, and acquaintances. The ability to 'read' people on the street has remained fundamental in detective work.[52] (Joseph Ricci, Vancouver's first 'ethnic' detective, testified in 1928 that he could tell at a glance whether an individual was a Scotsman or a Jew).[53] An institutional record reflecting this interest in the criminal class was the rogues' gallery, a collection of identification photographs dating from the late nineteenth century. The Vancouver police department's early photographic records concentrate on thieves, vagrants, confidence men, and the odd prostitute (including one who claimed to be from Paris, France). They reveal, among other things, that turn-of-the-century Vancouver criminals were natty dressers. They also suggest the racial aspects of crime and policing. A large proportion of those arrested were black. Vancouver later added fingerprint cards, building up one the largest criminal records collections in Canada by the Second World War.[54]

Primary records for large police institutions also suggest differences of opinion on the meaning of professionalism. Chief constables, the object of ongoing study as a professional group, did not speak for the entire police service.[55] Vancouver's many police chiefs appear, in the records, as victims – of political intrigue, rank-and-file resistance, and their own ambition. Unlike chief constables in Toronto, Vancouver chiefs do not appear to have developed an arm's-length relationship with their political masters, at least before the Second World War. Detectives, the élite of the Vancouver department, and patrol officers do not seem to have enjoyed mutual respect. Police unionism, or rank-and-file militancy, is an appropriate subject, given the current strength of municipal police associations. The early emergence of the Vancouver Police Federal Union No 12 as a thorn in the side of senior officers and municipal politicians is evident in the minutes and correspondence of the board of police commissioners. Post-Second World War records suggest the importance of labour relations in the institution.[56] A full treatment of the police union would constitute a key chapter in Vancouver's municipal political history. Vancouver archival holdings are not conducive, however, to investigating the social profile of police personnel, as Marquis, Weaver, and McCulloch have done for Toronto, Hamilton, and Quebec City.[57]

Conclusion

The 1970s and 1980s were lean years for the history of policing in Canada. In the same period British historians and sociologists produced sophisticated studies that discussed the police in relation to state theory and class relations. American scholars began to shed their fascination with the political history of policing and examine its social context. In Canada much of the police history beat remains to be covered. Over the next decade, it is hoped, a fuller historiography will emerge, the product of historians as well as of sociologists, policemen, and journalists. Canadian police history has unique characteristics – notably the existence of a national territorial constabulary that in this century began to contract out to provincial and municipal governments. It is likely that no one ideological or theoretical interpretation will enjoy hegemony.

As the discussion of Vancouver sources suggests, police records can benefit scholars of many persuasions. Specialists in urban, working-class, ethnic, and women's history are especially advised to consider these sources. In the narrower field of police history, potential topics include municipal and provincial case studies; the operational history of the RCMP; the relationship of the police to reform groups and other criminal justice institutions and actors; police use of deadly force; the policing of strikes; police involvement in domestic disputes; policewomen; the treatment of ethnic and racial minorities; the social history of the rank and file, police unionism, and professional networks; the history of private policing; the role of technology; metropolitization and regionalization; and the gradual extension of provincial supervision over the municipal police.[58] Canadians are debating questions such as police recruitment and training, the use of deadly force, and the general problem of accountability. Such issues are rooted in the past, and historians have a role to play in the debate. The time seems opportune for a new police historiography.

NOTES

I would like to thank the staff of the City of Vancouver Archives for their assistance.

1 Eric Monkkonen, 'From Cop to Social History: The Significance of the Police in American History' (1982), 14 *Journal of Social History*, 575–91. See also Monkkonen, *Police in Urban America, 1860–1920* (Cambridge: University Press 1981).

2 R.C. Macleod, *The North-West Mounted Police and Law Enforcement, 1873–1905* (Toronto: University of Toronto Press 1976).

3 Robert Fogelson, *Big City Police* (Cambridge: Harvard University Press 1977); Samuel Walker, *A Critical History of Police Reform: The Emergence of Professionalism* (Toronto: Lexington Books 1977); David R. Johnson, *Policing the Urban Underworld: The Impact of Crime on the Development of American Policing, 1800–1887* (Philadelphia: Temple University Press 1979); Sidney Harring, *Policing a Class Society: The Experience of American Cities, 1865–1915* (New Brunswick: Rutgers University Press 1983); Clive Emsley, *Policing and Its Context, 1750–1850* (Hong Kong: Macmillan 1983); Caroline Steedman, *Policing the Victorian Community: The Formation of the English Provincial Police Forces, 1856–80* (London: Routledge and Keagan Paul 1984); Stanley Palmer, *Police and Protest in England and Ireland, 1780–1850* (Cambridge: University Press 1988); Robert Reiner, *The Politics of the Police* (New York: St Martin's Press 1985); Wilbur Miller, *Cops and Bobbies* (Chicago: University of Chicago Press 1977).

4 William Baker, 'The Mounties and the Miners: The Royal North-West Mounted Police and the 1906 Lethbridge Strike' (Spring 1991), 27 *Labour/Le Travail*, 55–96.

5 Macleod, supra note 2, at 4.

6 E.J. Chambers, *The Royal North-West Mounted Police* (Montreal: Mortimer Press 1906); John Peter Turner, *The North West Mounted Police, 1873–1893*, 2 vols (Ottawa: King's Printer 1950).

7 A.L. Haydon, *The Riders of the Plains: A Record of the Royal North West Mounted Police of Canada, 1873–1910* (Toronto: Copp Clark 1910); L. Charles Douthwaite, *The Royal Canadian Mounted Police* (London: Blackie and Son 1939); R.G. MacBeth, *Policing the Plains* (London: Hodder and Stoughton 1922); T. Morris Longstreth, *The Silent Force* (New York: The Century Co. 1927); Richard Neuberger, *Royal Canadian Mounted Police* (New York: Random House 1953); Paul F. Sharp, *Whoop-Up Country: The Canadian-American West, 1865–1885* (Minneapolis: University of Minnesota Press 1955); Ronald Akin, *Maintain the Right: The Early History of the North West Mounted Police, 1873–1900* (New York: John Day Co. 1973).

8 Harwood Steele, *Policing the Arctic* (Toronto: Ryerson Press 1936); *To Effect an Arrest: Adventures of the Royal Canadian Mounted Police* (Toronto: Ryerson Press 1947).

9 Alan Phillips, *The Living Legend: The Story of the Royal Canadian Mounted Police* (Boston: Little, Brown 1954); Delbert Young, *The Mounties* (Toronto: Hodder and Stoughton 1968).

10 Kelly and Kelly, *The Royal Canadian Mounted Police: A Century of History, 1873–1973* (Edmonton: Hurtig 1973); *Policing in Canada* (Toronto: Macmillan 1976).

11 Lorne and Caroline Brown, *An Unauthorized History of the RCMP* (Toronto: James Lorimer 1973); Jeff Sallot, *Nobody Said No* (Toronto: James Lorimer 1979); Robert Dion, *Les crimes de la police montée* (Montréal: Editions cooperatives Albert Saint Martin 1979); Richard Fidler, *RCMP: The Real Subversives* (Toronto: Vanguard 1978); En collaboration, *La police secrete au Québec: La Tyrannie occulte de la police* (Montreal: Editions Québec 1978); Edward Mann and John Allan Lee, *RCMP vs. the People: Inside Canada's Security Service* (Don Mills: General Publishing 1979); John Sawatsky, *Men in the Shadows: The RCMP Security Service* (Toronto: Doubleday 1980), and *For Services Rendered: Leslie James Bennett and the RCMP Security Service* (Toronto: Doubleday 1982); S. Horrall, 'The Royal North West Mounted Police and Labour Unrest, 1919,' in *Lawful Authority: Readings in the History of Canadian Criminal Justice*, ed. R.C. Macleod (Toronto: Copp, Clark and Pittman 1988), 133–50.

12 Keith Walden, *Visions of Order* (Toronto: Butterworths 1982).

13 Robert Thacker, 'Canada's Mounted: The Evolution of a Legend' (Fall 1980), 14 *Journal of Popular Culture*, 298–312.

14 Walden, supra note 12, at 3, 5.

15 Macleod, writing in 1976, noted that Mounted Police records for the period 1885–1920 amounted to over three thouasand volumes. Most of the 1873–85 records were destroyed by fire.

16 R.A. Maclean, *Bill Fraser, Mountie* (Hantsport: Lancelot Press 1991).

17 John G. Donkin, *Trooper and Redskin in the Far North West* (London: Sampson, Low, Marston, Searle and Rivington 1889); Charles P. Dwight, *Life in the North West Mounted Police and Other Sketches* (Toronto: National Publishing 1892); Murray Hayne, *The Pioneers of the Klondyke* (London: S. Low, Marston and Co. 1898), Samuel B. Steele, *Forty Years in Canada* (Toronto: McClelland, Goodchild and Stewart 1915); Cecil Denny, *The Law Marches West* (Toronto: Dent 1939).

18 R. Burton Deane, *Mounted Police Life in Canada* (Toronto: Cassell 1916); Vernon Kempt, *Without Fear, Favour or Affection* (Toronto: Longmans, Green 1958); Charles Rivett-Carnac, *Pursuit in the Wilderness* (Toronto: Little, Brown 1965); C.W. Harvison, *The Horsemen* (Toronto: McClelland and Stewart 1967).

19 E.M. Slader, *From the Victorian Age to the Space Age* (Saint John: New Brunswick Historical Society 1973); Hugh Corkum, *On Both Sides of the Law* (Hantsport: Lancelot Press 1989); Margaret Gilkes, *Ladies of the Night: Recollections of a Pioneer Policewoman* (Hanna, Alta: Gorman and Gorman 1989).

20 John W. Murray, *Memoirs of a Great Detective*, ed. V. Speer (London: William Heinemann 1904); George T. Denison, *Recollections of a Police Magistrate* (Toronto: Musson Books 1920).

21 See, for example, Robert Hutchinson, *A Century of Service: A History of the Winnipeg Police Department* (Winnipeg: Police Department 1974); Leonard Harkness, *History of the Amherst Police* (Sackville: Tribune Press 1989); Dave Brundage, *Pride in the Past: City of Edmonton Police Department, 1894–1982* (Edmonton: Police Department 1982); George Megeney, *History of the Stellarton Police* (Stellarton: Centennial Committee 1991); Peter Worrell, *Policing the Lakehead, 1874–1988* (Thunder Bay: Guide Printing and Publishing 1989).

22 Joe Swan, *A Century of Service: The Vancouver Police, 1886–1986* (Vancouver: Police Centennial Museum 1986); J. Turmel, *Police de Montréal: Historique de service: Premières structures et évolution de la police de Montréal, 1796–1971*, 2 vols (Montréal: Service de la police de la CUM 1971); Peter McGahan, William Higgins, and Gerald Wallace, *The Saint John Police Story: The Clark Years, 1890–1915* (Fredericton: New Ireland Press 1991); Jean-Paul Brodeur, *La délinque de l'ordre: Recherches sur les commissions d'enquête I* (Québec: Editions Hurtibise 1984).

23 Desmond Morton, 'Cavalry or Police: Keeping the Peace on Two Adjacent Frontiers' (Spring 1977), 12 *Journal of Canadian Studies*, 27–37; S.W. Horrall, 'Sir John A. Macdonald and the Mounted Police for the Northwest Territories' (1972), 53 *Canadian Historical Review*, 179–200.

24 Carl Betke, 'Police and Pioneers on the Canadian Prairies, 1885–1914,' in

494   Greg Marquis

Macleod, *Lawful Authority*, supra note 11, 98–119; W.R. Morrison, *Showing the Flag: The Mounted Police and Canadian Sovereignty in the North, 1894–1925* (Vancouver: University of British Columbia Press 1985), xiv.

25 R.C. Macleod, 'An Uneasy Relationship: The RCMP and Provincial Policing,' in *Police Powers in Canada: The Evolution of Practice and Authority*, ed. R.C. Macleod and David Schneiderman (Toronto: University of Toronto Press 1994).

26 Greer, 'The Birth of the Police in Canada,' in *Colonial Leviathan: State Formation in Mid–Nineteenth-Century Canada*, ed. A. Greer and Ian Radforth (Toronto: University of Toronto Press 1992), 43.

27 John Phyne, 'Prohibition's Legacy: The Emergence of Provincial Policing in Nova Scotia, 1921–32,' (1992) 7 *Canadian Journal of Law and Society*, 157–84; Cecil Clark, *Tales of the British Columbia Provincial Police* (Sydney: Gray's Publishing Co. 1971); *British Columbia Provincial Police Stories* (Surrey: Heritage House Publishing Co. 1986); Jose Villa Arce, 'Alberta Provincial Police' (Autumn 1973), 21 *Alberta Historical Review*, 16–19. See also Greg Marquis, 'The History of Policing in the Maritimes: Themes and Prospects' (October 1990), 19 *Urban History Review*, 84–99.

28 Arthur Fox, *The Newfoundland Constabulary* (St John's: Robinson Blackmore Publishing Co. 1971); Chris Stewart and Lynn Hudson, *Mahony's Minute Men: The Saga of the Saskatchewan Provincial Police, 1917–1928* (Riverhurst: Modern Press 1978); Dahn D. Higley, *OPP: The History of the Ontario Provincial Police Force* (Toronto: Queen's Printer 1984); Lyne Stonier-Newman, *Policing a Pioneer Province: The British Columbia Provincial Police, 1858–1950* (Madeira Park: Harbour Publishing 1991). See also Sean Moir, 'The Alberta Provincial Police,' MA thesis, University of Alberta (1991).

29 C.K. Talbot, C.H.S. Jayewardene, and T.J. Juliani, *Canada's Constables: The Historical Development of Policing in Canada* (Ottawa: Crimecare Inc. 1985).

30 D. Owen Carrigan, *Crime and Punishment in Canada: A History* (Toronto: McClelland and Stewart 1991). Neither the Kellys in *Policing in Canada* nor John Sewell in *Police: Urban Policing in Canada* (Toronto: Lorimer 1985) provides firm historical analysis.

31 Desmond Morton, *Mayor Howland: The Citizens' Candidate* (Toronto: Hakkert 1973); T.W. Acheson, *Saint John: The Making of a Colonial Urban Community* (Toronto: University of Toronto Press 1984); Nicholas Rogers, 'Serving Toronto the Good: The City Police Force,' in *Forging a Consensus: Historical Essays on Toronto*, ed. Victor Russell (Toronto: University of Toronto Press 1984), 116–40; Greg Marquis, ' "A Machine of Oppression Under the Guise of the Law": The Saint John Police Establishment' (Autumn 1986), 16 *Acadiensis*, 58–77; 'Working Men in Uniform: The Early Twentieth Century

Toronto Police' (November 1988), 20 *Histoire sociale*, 259–77; 'Enforcing the Law: The Charlottetown Police Force,' in *Gaslights, Epidemics and Vagabond Cows: Charlottetown in the Victorian Era*, ed. Douglas Baldwin and Thomas Spira (Charlottetown: Ragweed Press 1988), 86–102; Bill Rawling, 'Technology and Innovation in the Toronto Police Force, 1875–1925' (March 1988), 80 *Ontario History*, 53–71.

32 Reiner, supra note 3. See also John Weaver, 'Introduction: Trends and Questions in New Historical Accounts of Policing' (October 1990), 19 *Urban History Review*, 79–83.

33 Gregory S. Kealey, 'Orangemen and the Corporation: The Politics of Class during the Union of the Canadas,' in Russell, *Forging a Consensus*, supra note 31, 67–77; Rogers, ibid. Reiner, supra note 3, at 28; Harring, ibid.

34 Elinor Senior, 'The Influence of the British Garrison on the Development of the Montreal Police, 1832–53,' in Macleod, *Lawful Authority*, supra note 11, 85–97; Michael McCulloch, 'Most Assuredly Perpetual Motion: Police and Policing in Quebec City, 1838–58' (October 1990), 19 *Urban History Review*, 100–12.

35 Helen Boritch, 'Conflict, Compromise and Administrative Convenience: The Police Organization in Nineteenth Century Toronto' (1988), 3 *Canadian Journal of Law and Society*, 141–74; Helen Boritch and John Hagan, 'Crime and Changing Forms of Class Control: Policing Public Order in "Toronto the Good," 1859–1955' (1987), 66 *Social Forces*, 307–35.

36 John Weaver, 'Social Control, Martial Conformity and Community Entanglement: The Varied Beats of the Hamilton Police, 1895–1920' (October 1990), 19 *Urban History Review*, 113–27.

37 Marquis, 'A Machine of Oppression', supra note 31; 'Enforcing the Law,' ibid.; 'The Police as a Social Service in Early Twentieth Century Toronto' (November 1992), 25 *Histoire sociale*; McCulloch, supra note 34.

38 City of Vancouver Archives (hereinafter cited as CVA), RG 37 D(6), 4, Vancouver Police Inquiry Testimony (1928), 1755. See also G. Marquis, 'The Contours of Canadian Urban Justice, 1830–1875' (February 1987), 15 *Urban History Review*, 269–73.

39 CVA, RG 75 (B), Vancouver Police Commission General Files, vol. 5, G.M. Macleod to W.H. McKay, 23 October 1922; RG 75 (B), 6, Blanche Denman to Chairman of Board of Police Commissioners, 14 November 1923.

40 CVA, RG 37 (C), 2, Police Department Occurrence Book, 1889–94; RG 37(C) 12, Occurrence Book, 1929.

41 CVA RG 75 (A) 1; Minutes of the Board of Police Commissioners, (1904–8); RG 26 (B) 2C, Vancouver City Council, Minutes of the Standing Committee on Fire and Police, 1894–1948.

42 CVA RG 43 (C) 1–2, Chief Constable's Office Correspondence, 1920–36.

43 CVA, Vancouver Police Inquiry Testimony, 2617.

44 Monkkonen, supra note 1; Peter McGahan, *Crime and Policing in Maritime Canada: Chapters from the Urban Records* (Fredericton: Goose Lane Editons 1989).

45 Rogers, supra note 31, at 133; Boritch, 'Conflict, Compromise and Administrative Convenience,' supra note 35.

46 For policewomen, see Gilkes, supra note 19; Marquis, 'Police as a Social Service,' supra note 37.

47 Vancouver Police Inquiry Testimony, vols 6–7. The 1928 Lennie Inquiry testimony fills eleven boxes.

48 CVA RG 42 (B), 32, Vancouver Police Court, Drug Offences Register, 1921–2.

49 Bryan Palmer, *Working Class Experience: The Rise and Reconstitution of Canadian Labour, 1800–1980* (Toronto: Butterworths 1983); Gregory S. Kealey, 'State Oppression of Labour and the Left in Canada, 1914–20: The Impact of the First World War' (1992), 72 *Canadian Historical Review*, 281–314.

50 CVA RG 75 (E)5, (E)7, Chief Constable's Reports, vols 1–3, 1935; RG 75 (F) 1–7, Chief Constable's Reports, 1929–35.

51 Baker, supra note 4.

52 Greg Marquis, 'Canadian Police Chiefs and Law Reform: The Historical Perspective' (October 1991), 33 *Canadian Journal of Criminology*, 385–406; Johnson, supra note 3; Weaver, 'Introduction: Trends and Questions,' supra note 32.

53 CVA, Vancouver Police Inquiry Testimony, 2006.

54 CVA RG 37 (C) 8, Prisoners' Record Book, 1898–99.

55 Marquis, supra note 52; Guy Tardif, *Police et politique au Québec* (Montreal: L'Aurore 1974).

56 CVA RG 75 (A) 4, Minutes of Board of Police Commissioners, 1920–7. For unionism, see Greg Marquis, 'Police Unionism in Early Twentieth Century Toronto' (June 1988), 81 *Ontario History*, 109–28.

57 Marquis, 'Working Men in Uniform,' supra note 31; Weaver, supra note 36; McCulloch, supra note 34.

58 Some of these issues are treated in Greg Marquis, *Policing Canada's Century: A History of the Canadian Association of Chiefs of Police* (Toronto: The Osgoode Society 1993).

19 Private Sector Legal Archives in Canada: A Source of Concern

RICHARD KLUMPENHOUWER

The professions of history, law, and archives share a common conceptual and methodological ancestry in western society. Modern historiography began in the disparate schools and academies of early modern Europe essentially as a study of community laws and customs as preserved in the archives of the state. Constitutional law was regarded as the main engine of historical progress. European law, especially common law, developed as the accumulation of historical custom and precedence, of which state and judicial archives served as the only true evidence. The ancient role of church and state archives as 'the people's' evidences' was expanded and transformed in the nineteenth century to include the role as the 'arsenals of history.' Historicist concepts of organicism and historical context formed the basis of, and still dominate, modern archival methodology, reinforcing at the same time the value and integrity of archives as authoritative legal evidence. Historians, lawyers, and archivists studied similar problems and topics, held common intellectual objectives, and moved in the same social and political circles.[1]

In the late nineteenth and early twentieth centuries, history, law, and archives began to diverge. The centrifugal forces that encouraged this divergence have not been adequately explored, but a few of the more obvious are professional specialization, intellectual and social pluralism, and the increased complexity of information. In Canada, as in many of the former European colonies, the traditional links between the disciplines were even less certain, and needed to be forged in a new way. In recent years, however, the emergence of Canadian legal history and the advent of Canadian 'legal archives' has renewed the discourse among historians, the legal community, and archivists. At the same time the relationships among them are much different from what they were before. Archives are no longer conceived and administered primarily as a body of legal evidence, nor are legal historians confined to the traditional internalist study of statutes, courts, and government bodies. The commons in this new research village, while not yet fully surveyed and staked out, encompasses the broad area of interaction between law and society. The legal profession, however, a principal subject and documentary source for historical research in law and society, remains only an occasional and bemused visitor to the commons.

The role and contributions of non-governmental, private sector legal archives in Canada is significant, but is perhaps the least understood of any of the elements in this new equation. Defined in the negative, 'non-governmental' sense, they comprise the records of participants in the legal system who do not fall under the direct jurisdiction of the state and hence are not subject to public records legislation, as is the case for justice ministries, the police, and the administration of the courts. In the positive, 'private sector' sense, they are the records of the independent players in the legal system – lawyers, judges, and professional and service organizations. Given the high status of an independent judiciary and bar in a liberal society such as Canada, private sector legal archives constitute a considerable segment of the total documentary record of Canadian law within Canadian society.

In this paper I will deal with the concepts, issues, and practical realities relating to private sector legal archives. This paper begins with an overview of recent efforts of historians and archivists in Canada to promote, preserve, and use the archival records of the private sector legal community. This discussion will serve as an introduction to the archival problems addressed in the second part of the paper. Key to the solution of those problems is the active support of a naturally reluctant legal profession and its independent associations in these efforts, a support that is crucial yet problematic. Matters are complicated by the often conflicting professional attitudes of the legal community and historical researchers towards the value of private sector legal archives. The archivist is faced with the challenge of reconciling these interests within a viable administrative structure. Archival principles of appraisal and program administration may present some practical directions for building on the precarious foundation achieved so far.

Programs and Projects to Date

In all, as of this writing, four major programs for preserving private legal archives in English Canada have been established: the Osgoode Society for Canadian Legal History, the Law Society of Upper Canada Archives, the Legal Archives of British Columbia, and the Legal Archives Society of Alberta. It is fair to say that the first project was dominated by the requirements and initiatives of legal historians. While archivists and lawyers were certainly involved, it was the urgency of legal historians to establish a viable research base for a fledgling Canadian legal history that powered the enterprise. The other three projects combined the work and input of legal practitioners and archivists with the administrative priorities of the provincial law societies.

The high-profile establishment of the Osgoode Society in 1979 as an institution dedicated to the promotion of research in the history of Canadian law provided a major impetus for a new burst of activity in Canadian legal history. The directors of the Osgoode Society immediately identified the development of legal archives as a priority and launched an ambitious campaign to collect, preserve, and allow research use of private sector legal records in Ontario. The society hoped to build upon the work achieved by the Archives of Ontario in the 1970s, which, along with many other provincial archives, had successfully located and acquired many of the extant records of the various courts in the province. By 1979, however, it seemed evident that similar success would not be so easily achieved for non-government materials. The Archives of Ontario in particular appeared unable and unwilling to begin acquiring the high volume of private lawyers' records while the inevitable legal issues surrounding solicitor-client privilege and research access remained unresolved.[2]

This failure prompted the Osgoode Society's editor in chief and legal historian Peter Oliver and Catherine Shepard of the Archives of Ontario to declare in 1980 that 'almost nothing has been done to collect private legal records' and that 'on the face of it, it seems safe to assert that this circumstance at least in some measure is responsible for the appallingly weak state of legal history in Ontario.' Their description of Canadian legal historical scholarship without private legal archives expressed the magnitude of the problem:

> The result has been that while we know that lawyers and legal matters have had a substantial impact on the Canadian political, economic, and social systems, and that the nature of the legal influence changed considerably as Canada underwent its transition from rural-commercial society to an urban-industrial one, we remain entirely unable to analyze with any precision the nature and extent of the

legal influence. We are even unable to say with any assurance
whether the role of the law in several areas has been primarily active
or reactive. The result of the failure of legal history to develop as a
significant discipline is that some of the most important and substantial areas of the Canadian experience remain unilluminated by
historical scholarship.[3]

The Osgoode Society attacked this neglect on two fronts. It initiated
legislative reform to allow archival deposit and research access to privileged lawyers' records, and it began a province-wide survey to determine
the nature and extent of law firms' archival material and the profession's
attitude to the prospect of transferring such records to the Archives of
Ontario. In 1987, when the chair of the society's legal records committee,
Christine Kates, reported on the progress of these two projects, the
Ontario legal historians seemed on the verge of a significant breakthrough; appended to the report were a model deposit agreement for
lawyers' and law firms' records and appraisal guidelines.[4] Yet the society's
legal recordkeeping role had become minor by 1990. Overcoming the
professional culture surrounding the absolute confidentiality of law firm
and judicial records evidently required a groundswell of awareness and
support in the legal community on a scale not even the Osgoode Society
could muster. Instead, the society has focused on its publications and an
oral history program.

An alternative program for acquiring and maintaining private legal
archives was already operating by the time the Osgoode Society's project
to preserve lawyers' records in the Archives of Ontario had run its course.
In 1983 the Law Society of Upper Canada established, with a grant from
the Law Foundation of Ontario, an archival program for its own prodi-
gious record holdings dating back to 1797, the first law society archives
program in Canada. As the self-governing regulatory body of Ontario's
legal profession, the Law Society of Upper Canada initially conceived of
its archival program as one that would cast its net well beyond the administrative records of the society itself. In 1980 an official of the society
expressed a desire to 'encourage the deposit of important material available in the profession and elsewhere that might otherwise be lost. As a
research tool the collection would form a valuable resource for both the
social and professional history of the bar in Ontario.'[5] But this element
of a proposed mandate was never brought to fruition beyond maintaining
the eclectic collection of manuscript materials retrieved from the laby-
rinth of Osgoode Hall and received from donors. The Law Society of

Upper Canada Archives remains by and large a records management and archives service for the Society itself, which now provides its entire core funding. Outside researchers must obtain the approval of the secretary for access – another indication of the program's strong internal administrative focus.

Another model for preserving private sector legal records was attempted in British Columbia in the mid-1980s. A historian in the law faculty at the University of British Columbia, Dr DeLloyd Guth, along with some high-profile members of the provincial bench and bar, established the Legal Archives of British Columbia with a broad-based mandate within the British Columbia Courthouse Library in Vancouver, again with substantial Law Foundation support.[6] This program was immediately successful in securing the archives of legal professional organizations, notably the Law Society of British Columbia and the British Columbia branch of the Canadian Bar Association. However, the immediate custodians of the program, the British Columbia Courthouse Library Society, were reluctant to pursue deposits of law firm records without resolving the problems of client privilege, confidentiality, and public access. Eventually, responsibility and funding for the program was transferred to the Law Society of British Columbia, and a new facility was opened in 1992. The functions of the Legal Archives of British Columbia are now more or less confined to administering the current and inactive records of the Law Society of British Columbia. As in Ontario, no formal research access policy to the records has been established.[7]

Alberta provides yet another program model. The Legal Archives Society of Alberta was established in 1990 as an independent institution with the mandate to acquire and make available archival records of lawyers, judges, and private legal organizations in Alberta. The organization grew out of a series of projects sponsored by the Heritage Committee of the Law Society of Alberta, which, with the input of a professional archivist, were gradually directed towards a coherent archival program. The Legal Archives Society owes its autonomous status mainly to the Alberta Law Foundation's condition that the program maintain a corporate identity separate from the Law Society. [8]

The Legal Archives Society of Alberta has enjoyed the benefits and suffered the consequences of its independent status. On the one hand, not all of its resources are channelled into administering the records of the host institution. The types of organizational and personal records, or fonds, acquired to date represent all areas of its mandate, including the records of the Law Society of Alberta, the Edmonton and Calgary bar associations, various justices of the Supreme Court of Alberta, and the records of a significant number of law firms. Because the program is not operated as an office of the Law Society, a formal research access policy to Law Society records was concluded before these records were deposited with the Legal Archives Society.[9] On the other hand, though the Law Society has a permanent representative on its board of directors, the Legal Archives Society cannot count on the almost instant attention which Law Society letterhead garners among members of the legal profession. In addition, the Law Society maintains a critical distance from the operations and policies of the Legal Archives Society. Perhaps the most serious problem for the Legal Archives Society, and for any independent legal archives program, is stable and ongoing funding. Without a secure, direct institutional sponsor such as the Law Society, the Legal Archives Society is vulnerable to imminent funding cuts from its major source of support, the Alberta Law Foundation.[10]

It is stating the obvious, then, to say that beyond the administrative frameworks of law societies and their records, historians, archivists, and interested members of the legal community in Canada have gained only the narrowest of toeholds on the major task of preserving and maintaining an adequate archival record of the private sector legal community. The only common denominator in all of the Canadian projects has been the funding source: the provincial law foundations which since the early 1970s have collected and dispensed funds received from the interest accrued on lawyers' trust accounts. No clearly superior program model has emerged. Yet it must be remembered that all practical efforts in this field have been pioneering, and much has been learned about the nature of the private legal community's documentation and the unique approach required to gain what is perhaps the key to future development: the widespread and direct support of the legal profession itself for preserving its own archives as a long-term information resource.

An Archival Perspective on Future Developments

As the projects described above illustrate, legal archivists are placed in the unenviable position of reconciling the research interests of historical researchers with those of the original creators and custodians of the archival records – the legal profession. Such a position may appear uncomfortable, but it is in many ways a natural one for an archivist to assume. Perhaps the single most important principle of archival theory and methodology is that in order to maintain its documentary value for historical or any other kind of research, as much evidence as possible of the administrative and cultural context of the original use of the records must be preserved along with the records themselves. As a consequence, archivists pay a great deal of attention to establishing and maintaining the presence and participation of the creators of the archives by various means, including records management operations, arrangement and retrieval systems, and administrative histories. Furthermore, it has been a longstanding principle of Canadian archival development that the institutions creating the records should preserve and support their own archival programs.[11] A balance must be struck between the interests and requirements of the archives program to maintain the support and context of archival material, and the interests of society as a whole, represented in part by public researchers.

The role of the private sector legal archivist is particularly demanding. To define as an 'institution' a collection of individual law practices, legal service and professional organizations, and judges in federal and provincial courts seems to stretch the meaning of the word to its limits. Nevertheless, some commonalities exist: all of these community members operate under self-governing regulations, they are conscious of and fiercely protect their independence from the state, the professional education of their personnel is remarkably homogeneous, and there is a strong 'institutional culture' that defines community attitudes and mores. Hence the major challenge facing any legal archivist (and, by extension, any legal historian) is this: How does one enlist the support and participation of an atomized community of independent professionals with a collective ethic about its records seemingly at odds with historical inquiry?

The specific problems associated with depositing and accessing lawyer's records and, to a lesser degree, the records of judges and private legal organizations, are familiar enough. Client files, some law firm administrative records, and many disciplinary documents produced by law societies fall either under solicitor–client privilege or under a general ethical principle of confidentiality, both of which are considered absolute and maintained on behalf of the client. Judges, wishing to preserve the finality of their judgments and to avoid undermining the authority of the court, regard their benchbooks and working papers as immediately obsolete or at least as completely confidential once the judgment is delivered. Archivists, lawyers, and historians point to these problems of access as the most serious obstacles to an effective legal archives program for the private sector legal community.[12]

As has already been shown, a narrow focus on changing these legal principles of access to allow the preservation and use of private legal records has generally been unsuccessful. These fiercely defended principles are at heart expressions of a more basic objective - to protect the independence and integrity of the legal community as a system and a self-regulated profession. It may be useful to identify and address some of the relevant foundational elements of the legal profession's institutional culture and the role of information in the institution as part of an attempt to foster its archival awareness.

From the historian's perspective, the cultural attitudes of the legal profession towards information does not look promising. The Canadian legal historian Douglas Hay has identified 'deeper habitual modes of thought' among members of the legal profession and the judiciary about the value and use of information. Hay argues that lawyers, working within narrowly defined rules of evidence and competing interests in creating and disclosing information, are 'committed not only to developing some evidence and inferences, but equally committed to suppressing others ... In short, while the ethical lawyer is not supposed to suppress legally relevant evidence, her or his whole training suggests a very narrow definition of relevance.'[13] Hay cites the American legal historian Robert Gordon's attempt to explain how and why the lawyer's perception of evidence and documentation is at odds with the historian's. Lawyers 'think of the law above all as a logical structure, from which sure conclusions can be drawn provided the right technique is used.' For them, the law is not subject to the historical contingencies, shifting allegiances, and intellectual contexts with which the historian is concerned. To legal practitioners, Gordon concludes, the law is 'largely ahistorical.'[14]

Hay's portrayal of the legal community as historically unreflective and simplistic in its use of documentary evidence, though tempting, is in the end unfair. The Canadian medical profession, for example, has been even less willing to preserve its archives, indicating that something more than the bad habits and attitudes of lawyers and judges is to blame. Virtually any government, business, university, or community archivist would say that the same mindset dominates the institutions from which his or her program acquires its records. From an archival perspective, it is not difficult to understand why.

Every practitioner, official, public servant, and private individual creates and uses records to accomplish an appointed task at a certain time – *to do* something specific, not particularly to document *how* it was done. One of the most important documentary qualities of archives – their authority as impartial evidence – derives from the assumption that the documentation was produced and used not as historical evidence for historical research, but as a tool for completing an action. In the interests of legal historical research, then, the reasons any lawyer might have to create, use, and, in the proper circumstances, destroy records cannot be questioned.[15]

In terms of archival theory, Hay has confused 'primary' and 'secondary' value: he does not distinguish between the ways in which members of the legal profession record their actions, produce required legal documentation, and use other sources of collected information to fulfil their current functions with the ways in which the legal profession may regard those records as historical evidence.[16] Perhaps the real questions are whether members of the legal community are capable of perceiving the secondary value of the records they produce beyond their original context in the legal system, whether they are willing to preserve their inactive records to accommodate this value, and whether they feel they possess the proper analytical and administrative tools to forge the natural continuum between the primary and secondary values of their records. The answers to these questions will emerge only when the legal profession is presented with three sets of facts: first, a coherent explanation of what secondary value is and which records possess this value (an archival appraisal issue); second, the connection to their primary activities as lawyers, judges, and legal organizations (a records management and access issue); and, third, an opportunity to take responsibility for preserving their own archives in an organized, systematic method (an administrative and funding issue). The objective of such a program is to incorporate the concepts and values of archives in the institutional culture of the private sector legal community, in the process ensuring enduring support for programs to preserve the archival record of the history of Canadian law and society.

One of the key elements of the effort to make archives an integral part of the legal community's identity is the acquisition and appraisal program. This entails the development of criteria and methodology for selecting which documents, out of the whole body of documentation produced by the institutions within its mandate, can and should be preserved. There is an immediate, obvious reason for doing this: the collective volume of all the records produced by lawyers, judges, and legal organizations is too great to be stored in its physical form or retrieved and comprehended for research purposes. Information must be reduced to a manageable physical and intellectual scale. This appraisal is also crucial to the preservation of the records: without such criteria and methodology, inactive private sector legal records will continue to be destroyed indiscriminately. When a policy for determining what is valuable and what is valueless is formulated, legal practitioners will have a much clearer picture of their place in the larger context of historical documentation. Essentially, then, the entire process of dealing with what a legal archives program will select and preserve, and why, is an exercise in defining the value and role of the program in the legal community.

For private sector legal archives in particular, there are other, possibly even more urgent and practical, reasons for developing and implementing a clear acquisition and appraisal program. By virtue of their intermediary functions as advocates, counsellors, and judges, members of the legal profession naturally collect and produce a great deal of information that is duplicated in the archives of other prominent bodies, notably governments. Identifying and reducing duplication results in substantial savings of resources for the lawyer, judge, and organization, as well as for the archives program. In addition, implementing acquisition and appraisal criteria for private legal records achieves a crucial practical advantage in dealing with the ethical issues of solicitor-client privilege and client confidentiality. As its stands, client waiver is a prerequisite for disclosure of the bulk of material produced and kept by lawyers and of some records kept by law societies. To obtain individual waivers for all the client records of a firm is unfeasible. Once the records have been appraised, however, the prospects for obtaining such waivers for the small core of remaining records improve considerably.

It is not enough to say that acquisition and appraisal criteria for private legal archives is essential to maintain a manageable body of records, to explain the secondary value of the records, and to help deal with the problem of archival access. A more formidable problem immediately arises: what are these criteria, and how are they developed? This, of course, is a central problem in archival science: to build a body of documentation that is authoritative, objective, and useful for current researchers as well as for generations of researchers in the future. Needless to say, there is no universally valid and absolute solution to this problem, but archivists have developed useful categories and concepts for making the function of archival acquisition and appraisal more effective.

It is generally accepted that archives, by their nature, hold two kinds of secondary value. First, the records document the actual functions and people who created them – in this case the law firm, judge, or legal organization – and therefore are of 'evidential value.' Second, the records may document any number of people, organizations, communities, events, ideas, and places which the lawyer, judge, or legal organization served or dealt with, and therefore are of 'informational value.'[17] These two kinds of documentary value are dependent upon each other. Documentation of informational value can be understood only within the context of evidential records, and the same record often holds both kinds of value. Identifying evidential and informational value separately is useful, however, for consistency and efficiency in the appraisal analysis. There is a tendency for archival programs to focus their appraisal priorities on adequately documenting the functions and history of the people or institutions from which they receive the records, and to pay little or haphazard attention to the informational value of the records. The prime mandate of most private legal archives programs, in fact, is to support the history of the legal community. However, if the full value of private legal archives as records of the interaction between law and society is to be realized, both values must be recognized in the acquisition and appraisal process.

The ultimate question remains: Is the game worth the candle? Lawyers, judges, and legal organizations are prominent players in Canadian society, and they generate a large number of records for their own purposes. But will any significant amount of that material actually prove to be of secondary value for future research? Archivists have had very little professional experience with appraisal and user patterns for private legal records. Most of their expressed opinions about the value of such records have been conjectural. Some have argued that lawyers' records provide crucial additional information not found in court records and paint a fuller picture of the law's impact on society,[18] that judges' records and working papers show the influences and personalities behind judgments and the development of case law,[19] and that the records of professional organizations chronicle how the legal community defines and controls its role in the legal system.[20] Others are sceptical of the historical significance of lawyers's records in particular. Brian Bucknall seriously doubts that much or any client material found in lawyers' records documents anything significant and, when it does, the information is often already in the public domain.[21] Many judges would claim that their benchbooks reveal very little beyond the facts of the case and that most of their thoughts and opinions contributing to a case were never recorded. It may well be that only a small fraction of the total records produced by the private sector legal community is of either evidential or informational value in documenting the law and society. However, in view of the scarcity of documentation on the legal profession, even this small remnant is worth pursuing. Only a concerted attempt to analyse and appraise a significant body of private sector legal records will provide the knowledge and experience on which to base a conclusion.

The information produced by the legal profession is complex and voluminous, and the process of identifying and selecting records of archival value must be comprehensive and systematic. Case files, in the form of a law firm's client files or a law society's member files, are perhaps the most obvious appraisal challenge. For a time archivists were dazzled by the ultimate selection system – social science sampling – and various forms of sampling have been applied to court records in the United States and Canada.[22] In order to gain a reliable record, however, the form and information structure of the individual units of the sample must be homogeneous, a criterion law firm case files do not meet, and the sample is useful only for specific research projects. By and large, random sampling is not an option for archival case files and, for lawyers' records in particular, the application of purposive sampling methodologies, while providing important structure to the appraisal procedure, raises more questions than it answers.[23] In the end, building a selective body of archival documentation of the private sector legal community requires defining what is being documented as much as analysing the documentation generated by the community. This kind of thinking is at the basis of a new acquisition and appraisal technique developed by American archivists called 'documentation strategies' and the earlier European 'documentation plans.'[24] The methodology of this macro approach involves defining a specific jurisdictional scope, usually geographical and topical, formulating subject and functional categories or classifications, and identifying people, institutions, events, and phenomena to be documented in each category. Once the documentation plan is complete, the archivist is better able to target the institutions and functions that are most likely to provide source material, instead of appraising a mass of documents as they present themselves. Only thereafter does the actual appraisal of records begin, on the basis of how well certain elements of the grid have been covered or over-documented, whether the sources provide substantive documentation of evidential or informational value, and the legal and physical implications of preserving the records and making them available.[25]

In the context of the private legal archives program, the jurisdictional scope could be defined as the interaction of the functions of law in and affecting society. Topical categories might include such broad areas as land, family, commerce, environment, and legal structures.[26] The final form of the documentation plan would resemble a historical outline identifying not only significant and representative lawyers, firms, judges, courts, legal organizations, trials, judgments, legislation, and professional programs, but also governments, policies, businesses, labour groups, social groups, communities, political events, and economic conditions that were directly affected by the actions and functions of the legal community.

While daunting in its scale and problematic in its definition, the documentation plan has some attractive features for the private sector legal archives program. The final plan is not merely a reference tool for archival acquisition and appraisal; it points out, directly and concretely, for the benefit of a naturally sceptical private legal community, the value of their records in documenting the history of law and society. In addition, the process of constructing and implementing the documentation plan provides a forum for the legal community to participate, along with archivists and legal historians, in building their own archival heritage.

The criteria and methods used in acquiring and selecting private legal archives are crucial in allowing the legal profession to understand and work towards preserving its records. Where the actual program is located, how it is sponsored, and the form of the services it offers will encourage and reflect the acquisition approach. It is best to establish and administer private sector legal archives programs not as 'thematic archives,' which collect all material relating to a research or social theme, but as genuine 'institutional archives,' providing archival services to a clearly identified, coherent institution – the legal profession. In other words, while the acquisition and appraisal program based on a documentation plan may be subject-based, the administrative context and collecting activity are focused on a defined institution. The legal profession is more likely to view and support such an archives program as its own, the program will be better able to maintain closer ties with the current activities and practices of the profession, and it will serve the research community by preserving the records within their functional context.

The 'institution' of the legal profession is not a unified bureaucracy but a regulated association of autonomous members, and therefore the authority and lines of communication in the community are more difficult to establish. There is no doubt that the provincial law society, as the one organization to which all members of the profession belong, must have a strong hand in endorsing and administering the private sector legal archives program as a service to all members. Also, as the largest single recipient of the legal profession's 'taxes,' it is an obvious source of ongoing funding for a program to preserve the legal profession's documentary heritage. However, while the law society's support is crucial, administrators of private legal archives programs must actively resist the natural conservative tendency to focus exclusively on law society records and avoid dealing with ethical concerns relating to lawyers' records.

Altogether, the problems involved in developing private legal archives in Canada must be seen as more than just historical research or legal problems. They are archival problems. Methods and theories of archival practice in the areas of records acquisition and selection are not only tools for managing the volume and complexity of private legal records; they define the role of archives in the institution law as a vital component of its professional identity and practice. An effective acquisition and appraisal program should present a feasible explanation of the long-term documentary value of the records and a clear demonstration of how they can be identified, preserved, and used in the future. Only then will the private legal community be in the position to accept or reject the concept of legal archives, deal seriously with the issues of research access, and commit the resources necessary to sustain a viable program.

Conclusion

By any standard, the existing programs and systems for preserving and using private legal archives in Canada are in their infancy. More pessimistic observers might claim that the cradle is really a deathbed, and that client confidentiality, professional indifference, and informational complexity are insuperable obstacles. From the archivist's perspective, the task of developing and implementing a coherent, viable archival program for the private sector legal community, like any other groundbreaking archival enterprise, is challenging but not overwhelming. The essential theory, methodology, and administrative requirements are recognizable: archivists have had to face these challenges in every institution where they have managed to gain a foothold. Progress will be achieved not by berating the legal profession for its lack of historical awareness or its bad documentary habits, but by understanding the role of documentation in legal practice, building a concept of the continuum between the primary and secondary value of this documentation in the institutional culture, and providing useful, practical means and methods for the profession to participate in and build its own archives. The problem of what kind of information to keep, for how long, for what reasons, and in what form is as much a concern for the legal profession as it is for a government or a business. An archival program can provide services and expertise to help the legal community deal with such problems: techniques and theories of archival appraisal and acquisition can be applied to private sector legal records just as effectively as they can to any other institutional records, provided that they are systematic and connected to a larger documentation scheme. Private sector legal archives programs will always have difficulty maintaining an adequate administrative profile and authority in such an atomized institution. But the support of the provincial law societies can go a long way towards achieving an effective position within the legal profession.

NOTES

1 Ernst Breisach, *Historiography: Ancient, Medieval, and Modern* (Chicago: University of Chicago Press 1983), 161–220; Ernst Posner, 'Some Aspects of Archival Development since the French Revolution,' in *Archives and the Public Interest:Selected Essays by Ernst Posner*, ed. Ken Munden (Washington: Public Affairs Press 1967), 25–7.

2 Catherine Shepard and Peter Oliver, 'The Osgoode Society, the Archivist and the Writing of Legal History in Ontario' (1980) 14 *Law Society of Upper Canada Gazette*, 193–4.

3 Ibid.

4 Christine J.N. Kates, 'The Osgoode Society: Preservation of Legal Records' (1987), 21 *Law Society of Upper Canada Gazette*, 58–70.

5 Roy Schaeffer, 'The Law Society of Upper Canada Archives' (1987), 21 *Law Society of Upper Canada Gazette*, 48–57, at 51.

6 DeLloyd Guth, 'Stow and Tell, Part Two' (November 1986), 44 *The Advocate*, 863.

7 Bernice Chong, 'BC Legal Archives Finds a New Home' (Spring 1993), 3:2 *AABC Newsletter*, 7.

8 Minutes of Benchers' Convocation, Law Society of Alberta, September 1989; letter from the Alberta Law Foundation to the Heritage Committee, 20 October 1989.

9 Minutes of Benchers' Convocation, Law Society of Alberta, February 1992.

10 In fact, the Alberta Law Foundation informed the Legal Archives Society of Alberta that, as of 31 October 1994, the foundation would not provide any operational grant funding to the society. The annual grant of $106,000 represents over 75 per cent of the society's entire budget. Annual and capital fund-raising campaigns are currently underway.

11 Consultative Group on Canadian Archives, *Canadian Archives: Report to the Social Sciences and Humanities Research Council of Canada* (Ottawa: SSHRC 1980), 61–6.

12 Thorough overviews of issues surrounding archival access to lawyers' records are found in Brian Bucknall, 'The Archivist, the Lawyer, the Clients and their Files' (Winter 1991–2), 33 *Archivaria*, 181–7, and Doug Whyte, 'The Acquisition of Lawyers' Private Papers' (Summer 1984), 18 *Archivaria*, 142–53. Insight into judges' attitudes to public access to their working records is provided by the statements of DeLloyd Guth in 'BC Professor Preserves Forgotten Legal Archives,' *Lawyers' Weekly*, 28 June 1991, 2, 8.

13 Douglas Hay, 'Archival Research in the History of the Law: A User's Perspective' (Summer 1987), 24 *Archivaria*, 36–46.

14 Ibid., 45

15 Hilary Jenkinson, *Manual of Archive Administration*, 3d ed. (London: P. Lund, Humphries & Co. 1965), 12–13.

16 The American archival theorist T.R. Schellenberg developed the concepts of the primary and secondary value of records: records hold primary value for the agency that produced them and used them for its own administrative, operational, and legal purposes; records hold secondary value for all other users of the information, for whatever purpose, after the records have served their primary value. Theodore R. Schellenberg, 'The Appraisal of Modern Public Records' (October 1956), 8 *Bulletins of the National Archives* , 6–7.

17 T.R. Schellenberg labelled these appraisal values 'evidential value' for the purposes of documenting the records creator, and 'informational value' for the purposes of documenting people, places, and phenomena with which the record creator dealt. Schellenberg, supra note 16, at 3.

18 Whyte, supra note 12, at 152; Shepard and Oliver, supra note 2, at 194–5; Kates, supra note 4, at 59.

19 Guth, supra note 12, at 8.

20 W. Wesley Pue, 'The Legal Profession in Prairie Culture' (April 1992), 1:4 *Architypes*, 5–6.

21 Bucknall, supra note 12, at 185–6.

22 Terry Cook provides a thorough overview of sampling techniques and their application to archives in ' "Many Are Called but Few Are Chosen": Appraisal Guidelines for Sampling and Selecting Case Files' (Summer 1991), 32 *Archivaria*, 25–50.

23 The Legal Archives Society of Alberta suggests using a combination of exemplary and exceptional sampling for law firm client material in its brochure *Selecting Law Firm Records of Archival Value: Guidelines for Lawyers* (Calgary 1992).

24 A rationale for descriptions of this acquisition and appraisal approach can be found in Helen Samuels, 'Improving our Disposition: Documentation

Strategy' (Winter 1991–2), 33 *Archivaria*, 125-40, and Hans Booms, 'Society and the Formation of a Documentary Heritage,' ed. and trans. Hermina Joldersma and Richard Klumpenhouwer (Summer 1987), 24 *Archivaria*, 69–107.

25 Case studies of how documentation strategies and documentation plans were implemented can be found in Richard J. Cox, 'A Documentation Strategy Case Study: Western New York' (Spring 1989), 52 *American Archivist*, 192–200, and Hans Booms, 'Uberlieferungsbildung: Keeping Archives as a Society and Political Activity' (Winter 1991–2), 33 *Archivaria* 25–33.

26 The Legal Archives Society of Alberta has begun construction of a documentary plan for the law and society in Alberta. These examples are taken from the preliminary proposals developed at the first meeting of the society's Documentation Plan Working Group.

20 Waiving History Goodbye? Lawyers' Records and the Scholar

PETER MOORE

The law, society, and the state conspire to leave the legal side of the history of Australian society under-written. Courts and lawyers, and the subjects that attract their attention, escape the kind of scholarly review that the executive, the legislature, and business regularly receive. This is because the non-current records of law firms are not treated as business archives. Many Australian lawyers believe that legal records, like much else about lawyers, are 'special.' Archivists and users alike find this an impenetrable barrier; in fact, if lawyers and scholars work together, they will find that it is no more than a soluble impasse.

Neither Australian lawyers nor their professional societies are exemplars of the proactive principles and practices of records management that are so well known in government and business. Legal practices treat client-matter file management as little more than file titling and numbering, usually in conjunction with an accounting system's need for a billing name and address and an alphanumeric code for recording professional time, disbursements, and trust account movements. Yet law firms (like government and commercial organizations) need their files to report on the state of a matter, to initiate or respond to developments in a matter, to facilitate the delegation of tasks to junior personnel, and to use as a precedent for 'how we did it before.'

If file creation has little long-term strategic significance, retention is worse. Australian lawyers either retain their firm's and their clients' files for inordinate lengths of time or destroy them with ruthless monotony: not to escape long-term accountability, but because few lawyers recognize a research interest in their records. File destruction responds to legal and commercial interests that are set up by the statutes of limitations, the law of evidence, the vague spread across the statute-books of document creation and retention provisions, professional misconduct rulings from professional bodies, the perversities of file ownership, and the high cost of commercial storage. Indeed, the risk of records seizure by corporate and taxation 'watchdog' authorities seems positively to recommend destruction as early as legally permissible or financially feasible.

Lacking a proactive 'records consciousness,' law firms fail to recognize the long-term informational value to themselves in their own internal records. Partnership archives cover the firm's constitution, partnership accounts (proprietors' and non-equity partners), mergers, entry and withdrawal from partnerships, minutes of meetings, firm investments, personnel, premises, practice management and development, financial planning, library, computers, and continuing education programs. Current records document the firm as a business in accordance with commercial laws and accounting practices. Non-current, permanently valuable records fall squarely within well-settled criteria for 'business archives.'

'Legal business archives,' a refined core of records retained permanently, would serve the firm's ongoing administration, its need to refer to past practice for guidance on present circumstances, as a historical account of the law firm as an entity, and its long-term financial status, at least at the annual level of profit-and-loss accounting. The 'archival values' of law firm records certainly qualify them as vital records.

Actually, Australian law firms probably do not realize the extent to which so-called practice management system software achieves a high level of records management capacity. This software goes further than accounting systems, deeds registers, and safe custody facilities ever did. It integrates file creation, conflict of interest checking, and closure processes with overall costing, billing, and sophisticated analysis and reporting. Some systems include pure information management functions, such as research and precedent databases. Never before have lawyers captured so many details about files and how they are handled. Lawyers can set retention schedules more accurately according to statutes of limitations, statutory retention periods, and best evidence rules, as well as for internal reference and research needs, either for subsequent matters or for practice analysis and development. Of course, the dissection of data retained about a file answers many of the needs that lengthy file retention once purported to supply. It can also serve to facilitate archival preservation and scholarly research. Alteratively, advanced practice management systems may be used to liberate the bulk of client-matter files for even earlier destruction than at present.

Why has no records culture developed in such an intensely documentative profession? First, business law is complex, obscure, and inward-looking. Second, the principle of judicial independence has led to a national archival regime that largely denies scholarly access to judicial records. Third, the conservatism of legal professional bodies lends a defensive spirit to broad-based 'accountability' arguments that has meant slow progress in a variety of extralegal areas. Fourth, lack of vigour in the national legislative archival regime lets the judicial system escape the statutory net of archives and freedom of information laws. Finally, the scholarly community fails to demand legal sources for their work in order to scrutinize lawyers, the legal system, particular laws and practices, and the infinitely broader areas in which lawyers' clients operate.

As a result, only a few law firms have deposited their records with cultural institutions that collect archives. Admittedly, lawyers' records that are returned to clients also turn up in the archives of businesses, trade unions, and private individuals. Yet the research value of a legal firm's records applies the law's own 'best evidence' rule to history, politics, economics and society. Lawyers often have the best possible record of the transactions that they document, because the clients did not create similar records, have since destroyed them, have died or dissolved, moved away, or gone out of business.

A lawyer's client-matter records often contain the richest veins of research material for topics spanning the spectrum of scholarly interest. They document the behaviour of the lawyers themselves, their levels of skill and enterprise, their writing and negotiating skills, the constitutions of their partnerships, their finances, and their personnel. Client files are records of crisis and resolution, of dispute and settlement, of new initiatives, and of changing policies about former initiatives. They cover relations between the state and the individual, between individuals, between individuals and corporations, and between corporations. They mirror the world around them: the drama of interpersonal relations, the stark reality of capitalism at work, the relevance of law and of laws in the life of the citizen and the state.

Social, legal, and economic historians, economists, political scientists, sociologists, and analysts of public administration, banking, and manufacture would find evidence, proof, or indicia of various lines of inquiry in the 'big cases' – the very stuff of 'history from above.' But law firm records also contain the mundane, the humdrum, the routine – the very stuff of 'history from below' – reflecting the style of the practice and the way the legal system affects most people. Local, business, and family history would be well served by these sources. But historians and cognate scholars do not clamour for legal professional sources; even legal historians appear to be able to bypass them in their researches into the study of the law in history. Legal records are little used, partly because their presence in archives is not well known and partly because scholars do not seek them out. Neither archivists nor scholars are guilty of self-help here.

Are law firm records 'special' business archives? No; they are different. Client-matter files must cover them against professional negligence actions. This function is perhaps more pointed for lawyers, but protection against attack – whether at a public relations level or one of strict legal liability – is also true of businesses and governments. A happy byproduct of the legal profession's (near) paranoia in this respect is that lawyers' records are often more comprehensive and accurate than commercial or government files: another argument for their retention for scholarly use.

All records are property. But client-matter files have a money value amounting almost to cash in a lawyer's hands, a quality less common in government and commercial files and forming no part of archival convention. Files also represent marketable property: work-in-progress or money's worth, the basis for costing and billing, and a component of a law firm's valuation. The lawyer's lien for payment of fees arises only because files are physical property. Whose property? Items created by lawyers for clients generally belong to clients; items created by lawyers for their own use usually remain theirs; items sent by third parties may remain theirs or someone else's (but exactly whose is often unclear). Those principles relate to the file's physical contents. By contrast, intellectual property in the text contained in items on file does not always belong to the owner of the paper or other medium on which it appears.

It is commonly felt that clients own their files but let the lawyers hold them until it is lawful to destroy them, on the tacit assumption that once the bill is paid the files have no further financial or other value. Some lawyers charge clients for storage and even for microreprography in an entrepreneurial attempt to reduce file storage overheads, though this does not settle the matter of co-ownership. Others return items from the files the clients supplied or originals that they signed,[1] though this certainly confounds the archival principle of record integrity.

The real problem with legal records is confidentiality. The lawyer-client relationship is dominated by the lawyer's fiduciary duty to serve the client in trust and confidence.[2] Significant corollaries include the duty to maintain the client's confidences, breach of which constitutes professional misconduct even if it does not amount to a breach of the law itself. Confidentiality affects business and government records too, though the relationship between business and consumer, and between government and citizen, is not as onerous or so well worked over.

The main outcome of the confidentiality principle – that oral and written communications received by a lawyer from a client with a view to receiving legal advice get special protection – is often called 'legal professional privilege,' though it is actually the client's privilege. A lawyer's client cannot be compelled to disclose these communications in the course of legal proceedings, nor can the lawyer do so without the client's consent. A client may restrain a lawyer from disclosing communications or may waive the privilege. Until the client waives the privilege it is the lawyer's duty to claim it on the client's behalf if requested to disclose during legal proceedings. Client privilege is justified as a matter of public interest; citizens should be able to confide in their legal advisers to obtain all the help they need to protect their rights. Recently, however, the High Court of Australia held that in some circumstances[3] client privilege may be subordinate to the public interest.

Beyond the realms of client privilege, the general law of confidentiality still applies. Information provided by a client which is divulged to a third party gives rise to an action for breach of confidentiality, not because of the special status of lawyer and client but because that relationship is of the kind that gives rise to an obligation to keep confidences. The consequences for lawyers may, of course, be more onerous because professional misconduct may occur as well as tort.

Sheer market forces also force law firms to maintain client confidences. Lawyers are loath to ask their clients, either at file opening or at closure, for permission to transfer their files to an archival institution. That would admit that confidential conversations and documents would one day be open to public scrutiny. No law firm would want to tarnish its public relations and marketing efforts by appearing to be a firm that 'talks.' Law firms have to provide an efficient, prompt, and cost-effective service, or risk losing a client's business. They have to market their practices and work long hours to meet client deadlines. Occasionally they even have to forfeit fees - or pride - to keep their clients happy. In this way they are in the same position as other businesses that provide services and deposit their non-current records with research institutions, although perhaps law firm commercialism is necessarily more sensitive to the confidentiality question.

In addition to statutes and common law, lawyers are bound by ethical and practical rulings made by their professional bodies.[4] Professional bodies also act as detective, prosecutor, judge, and jury in cases of alleged professional misconduct. Some law society journals print accounts of misconduct inquiries and findings as a warning to would-be defaulters. Law society rulings balance the lawyer's ethical responsibilities with his or her ability to earn a living, reinforce the economic basis of legal practice, and protect lawyers in the earning and collecting of fees. (As constructs of an influential and well-rewarded vocational group, they raise the interesting question of society's or the state's price for their perpetuation.)

Concerning records, law societies provide members with little more than regulations about the lawyer's lien over his or her clients' files.[5] Only the Law Society of Western Australia supplies guidelines to members on general file retention and destruction. Their tenor is the relatively short-term ambit of the statutes of limitations and other statutory rules supplemented with prudential considerations for some grey areas.

No Australian law society has an archival program in place. Three of the ten societies have considered establishing an archives program relating to the profession and itself. Two have appointed committees – one 'to improve on our historical record keeping,' the other a 'low-key Archives Committee which is specifically charged with locating, identifying, labelling and displaying appropriate materials of historical interest within the Law Society building.' One law society suggested that it might make its own records available for public research use, subject to the terms of its constituting statute. Another deposited its non-current records with a university that collects business and labour records, but has discontinued this in favour of an internal committee. No society has a settled policy or view on scholarly access to legal practice records, and none has ever discussed developing one. No society provides members with guidelines on the deposit of legal practice records with public bodies. Consequently, no society has recommended controls on deposits to cultural institutions. One even suspects that law firm 'partnership, personnel and financial records' would 'be of little interest to others.'

Clearly, law society officials have not realized the purpose of archival administration for their own organizations, let alone for their law firm members. The societies are concentrating on the curiosity side of archives work: salvaging oddities rather than totalities, preoccupied with interior decoration rather than internal efficiency. This is the stuff of antiquarianism, not the service of posterity.

The Australian Capital Territory's Law Society is bound by federal freedom of information legislation because its statutory public purpose character has been held to be a 'prescribed authority' under the federal Freedom of Information Act.[6] A corollary is that the society's 'public purpose' records (including any that are indistinguishable as to private and public functions) might be national archives under the federal Archives Act. The other statute-based societies may find themselves caught similarly by state FOI and archives legislation. It remains open for a law society to rule, as one has virtually done, against the deposit of their members' client-matter files in archival institutions. Their reasons would probably include:

- breach of faith and trust (the fundamental fiduciary duty);
- breach of confidence (disclosing information provided in confidence);
- breach of client privilege (lack of consent to its waiver);
- conflict of interest with past and present clients;
- risk of invasion of privacy;
- public relations (commercial objections).

Lawyers generally take the view that client-matter files are beyond the reach of scholarly inspection. Comparable arguments have been raised about cabinet records, church archives, and private papers of influential people. The fear of hurting individuals, corporations, and governments is often cited. The 'frankness' argument asks how can anyone divulge secrets knowing that one day they will become public property. But does not scholarship depend on access to records of this kind?

The legal profession's fiduciary duty means that lawyers must not benefit from actions that are in any way inconsistent with their clients' interests. Benefits could include file storage and retrieval at the archival institution's expense and income tax relief by depositing records in recognized public cultural institutions. However, these are not the sorts of benefits that the law has proscribed.

The law seems to say that sending files to research institutions discloses information to strangers that was provided in confidence, and that client privilege cannot expire even though consent to disclosure may become impossible – for example, with the death of an individual or the dissolution of a corporation. Lawyers ask how law firms can disclose to scholars what could not be brought as evidence before a court of law. Perhaps the deposit of records with a cultural institution is professional misconduct. While it may be possible to sustain that argument, the real question is, Should it succeed? For most practical purposes, privilege from production in evidence in court proceedings ceases to matter once the proceedings are over – or if they cannot be initiated. After the statute of limitations prevents proceedings on the subject of documents that would have been privileged, there is no one for privilege to protect. Time kills the privilege.

The same is true, in reality if not in law, of confidentiality in general.

The circumstances that give rise to confidentiality are *present* events and relationships. The law of confidentiality does not recognize that the passage of time reduces the information's sensitivity and its potential for trouble-making because time cannot extinguish the fact that it was given in confidence. Yet the 'heat' of confidences does diminish once personal or commercial circumstances change. When the client's matter is over, the bill paid, and the file put away, most records in most law firms begin to lose their controversy and impact. This is not to say that access should be universally available. Particularly in cases involving interpersonal matters, the secrets of the client-matter file could contain details about persons living or dead that might distress, offend, or injure persons still living. Archivists have proved competent to manage these issues, to which they are particularly sensitive.

The problem, then, is a practical one, and one with broad cultural implications. The usual lawyers' arguments against placing law firm records in public cultural institutions are not persuasive. Established controls on archival access to confidential records will answer their worst fears. Settled policies and procedures will assure lawyers that their professionalism is protected and posterity benefited. Scholarly, archival, and legal professions must strike a pragmatic balance between the competing interests. This is certainly possible, as every polity that has passed archival legislation knows. There is also a role for the state in constructing a legislative framework within which the parties can coexist.

Abstract and objective questions of archival accountability alone are insufficient to delay the development by lawyers and archivists of mutually satisfactory arrangements for depositing legal client records in archival custody. However, a parallel case for a real need for this kind of material must also be made. This crusade is for the scholars to mount, and, like so much else in Australian archival administration, the campaign for access to lawyers' records will probably be led by amateurs rather than academics.

Debate and discussion can proceed only when lawyers have a proper understanding of the benefits of archival administration, what it offers, how it is conducted, and how lawyers' records fit into its principles and practices. Archivists have to 'sell' their profession's objectives, in particular the control of access to records. The archival community works on the premise that when records are accepted, they can be used for research. Access is therefore crucial. Conditions may vary a little. Most custodians of law firm archives permit bona fide researchers to use those parts of collections that are already in the public domain, such as transcripts of evidence and exhibits. Other documents are subject to a thirty-year rule: the permission of both the law firm and the client is required, though if the client cannot be reached, client permission is waived by the custodial institution. Material written from the records must also be cleared before presenting theses or delivering papers at conferences. Of course, many non-legal records held in public institutions are restricted in various ways. Specific access is negotiated with particular donors, depending on the contents of the archival accumulation.

Proper records management in law firms would ensure efficient file description and overall practice management, and support the effective delivery of client service during the matter's life. Lawyers could assess the importance of closed files to decide on an appropriate retention period and to regulate retirement to cheaper storage sites. Ultimately, records management would also take care of the scholarly archival issue. Law societies and law firms should develop records disposal schedules,[7] such as those used in federal and state government departments and large corporations. Special funding recently generated a disposal schedule for local government records in New South Wales. The management value to societies and firms will be matched by the control the schedule affords of subsequent deposit and access in archival institutions.

Once the Law Council, law societies, and privacy authorities accept that legal practice records have a research value, they should work with public cultural institutions to create a set of guidelines, consistent with ethical and practical rulings, for deposits of records in cultural institutions and scholarly access to legal client-matter files. If deposit with public cultural institutions is problematic, Australia's law societies should consider establishing records management and archives services for their law firm members. The state's role consists of changing the law. Legislation to apply a thirty-year rule to access to client-matter files would also provide for the automatic waiver of client privilege and amnesty from breach of fiduciary or confidentiality duties.[8]

A new balance *can* be achieved between conflicting interests: the archivist's indignation that things are not more purely archival; the historian's frustration that material exists and is likely to yield rich returns but is unavailable or, if available, is inaccessible; and the lawyer's lament that overheads are so high, client files are such a dead weight, and surveillance authorities are poised to pounce.

NOTES

1 The Western Australian Law Society's guidelines on records retention recommends this action.

2 For example, *Tyrell v. Bank of London* (1862), 10 HLC 26, at 44, by Westbury LC, endorsed at *Law Society of N.S.W. v. Harvey*, [1976] 2 NSWLR at 154, by Street CJ, at 170.

3 *Corporate Affairs Commission of NSW v. Yuill and Others* (1991), 4 ASCR 624; and see Climpson and Proctor, 'Eroding Legal Confidentiality Down Under' (1992), *International Financial Law Review*, 9–10, and *Butterworths Corporation Law Bulletin* (Sydney 1992), no. 3 para. 58.

4 Law societies exist in every Australian state; all but one are incorporated by act of Parliament. The Australian Law Council, a non-statutory federation of law societies, operates as a national legal lobby, but does not make ethical or practice rulings.

5 For example, *Solicitor's Handbook* (Brisbane: Queensland Law Society 1988), parts 6 and 11.

6 *Re Brennan and The Law Society of the Australian Capital Territory* (1984), 6 ALD 428–41 (Hall, Deputy President).

7 They could do no better than to follow the example of some of their Canadian colleagues. For instance, the Law Society of Upper Canada is currently developing retention schedules for its records.

8 The longest limitation period in Australia, thirty years, is also the common statutory archival period for the release of government archives.

Contributors

EDITORS

Louis A. Knafla
Dr Knafla is professor of history at the University of Calgary and holds his
Ph.D. from the University of California, Los Angeles. He serves as editor in
chief of *Criminal Justice History* (Greenwood Press). He has published extensively on English and Canadian legal history, and has edited a number of books
including *Law and Justice in a New Land* (1986), and *Kent at Law 1602: Assizes
and Sessions of the Peace* (1994).

Susan W.S. Binnie
Dr Binnie is research coordinator at The Law Society of Upper Canada
Archives, and has taught part-time at York University and the University of
Toronto. She holds degrees from Cambridge, Toronto, and Carleton. Her
Ph.D. work analysed developments in criminal legislation in nineteenth-century
Canada, and she has published in the fields of criminology and legal history.

FOREWORD

David Sugarman
Professor Sugarman is professor of law and director of the Law and History
Program at Lancaster University. He has published widely in the fields of legal
history, company law, the sociology of law, and the legal profession, including
Legality, Ideology and the State (editor, 1983) *Law, Economy and Society, 1750–1914*
(co-editor, 1984), *Law and Social Change in England, 1780–1950* (1993), *Pro-*

fessional Competition and Professional Power: Lawyers, Accountants, and the Social Construction of Markets (co-editor, 1995), *The Law Society, 1825–1995* (1995), and *Law in History* (editor, 1995).

AUTHORS

Rainer Baehre

Dr Baehre is associate professor of history at Sir Wilfred Grenfell College, Memorial University of Newfoundland. He has written articles on nineteenth-century Canadian social history and on mechanisms of legal, social, and moral regulation.

Dorothy E. Chunn

Dr Chunn is associate professor of criminology and former co-director of the Feminist Institute for Studies in Law and Society at Simon Fraser University. She holds a Ph.D. in sociology (criminology) from the University of Toronto. Her publications deal with issues surrounding feminism, criminology, and family law, and her research emphasizes Canadian history.

Anton Cooray

Dr Cooray is the associate head of the Department of Law at City University of Hong Kong. He was formerly Dean of the Faculty of Law, University of Colombo. He holds Ph.D.s in law from London and Colombo. Dr Cooray specializes in constitutional and administrative law, and has written extensively on the function of law in Sri Lanka.

Clive Emsley

Professor Emsley holds a personal chair in history at the Open University in Milton Keynes, England. His area of specialization is mid-eighteenth-century to late nineteenth-century English legal history, and he has published a number of books, including *Crime and Society in England, 1750–1900* (1987) and *The English Police: A Political and Social History* (1991).

Christopher English

Christopher English has taught French history at Memorial University of Newfoundland since 1967. A graduate of Dalhousie Law School in 1990 and a member of the Law Society of Newfoundland, he has published several articles on the emergent legal regime of Newfoundland.

Paul Finkelman

Professor Finkelman holds a Ph.D. from the University of Chicago. He is Visiting Professor of Law at Chicago-Kent College of Law. He has taught at

Virginia Tech Institute and State University and recently spent two years as Visiting Associate Professor in the Brooklyn Law School. His numerous publications include *Slavery in the Courtroom* (1985) and *American Legal History: Cases and Materials* (with Kermit L. Hall and William M. Wiecek, 1991).

Annalee E. Gölz

Annalee Gölz is a doctoral candidate at Queen's University. She is currently working on her dissertation, entitled, 'Dis/membering the Family: Marital Breakdown and Family Violence in Ontario, 1820–1920.' Her thesis explores various aspects of marital breakdown, including bigamy, non-support, and the physical abuse of wives and children.

Anthony Hall

Dr Hall holds a Ph.D. in history from the University of Toronto, and has specialized in Canadian history, with particular focus on aboriginal affairs. He is an associate professor in the Department of Native Studies at the University of Lethbridge. He has published academic and journalistic articles on aboriginal rights and legal claims, and has done related broadcast and media work.

Kusha Haraksingh

Dr Haraksingh graduated from the School of Oriental and African Studies, University of London, and now teaches at the University of the West Indies, Trinidad, where he has served as head of the History Department and chair of the Institute for African and Asian Studies. He writes on labour and plantation studies, and on aspects of the Indian diaspora. He has served as a senator in Parliament and is a barrister of Lincoln's Inn.

Richard Klumpenhouwer

Richard Klumpenhouwer has been archivist of the Legal Archives Society of Alberta since its inception in 1990. He holds master's degrees in history and in archival studies from the University of Western Ontario and the University of British Columbia and has published in the areas of archival history and appraisal theory.

Greg Marquis

Dr Marquis obtained his Ph.D. from Queen's University. He has published articles on the history of Canadian urban justice and is the author of *Policing Canada's Century: A History of the Canadian Association of Chiefs of Police* (1993). He has a particular interest in the history of policing in the Atlantic provinces and elsewhere in Canada.

Peter Moore
Mr Moore holds his LLB from the University of Adelaide and his Dip. Archiv. Admin. from the University of New South Wales, Australia. He was admitted to practice in the Supreme Court of South Australia, and is a consultant with Information Management for Lawyers. He has published and given seminars on records management and legal archives in relation to legal practice.

Diane M.T. North
Diane North is a Ph.D. candidate in US history at the University of California, Davis, and has lectured in US and California history at San Francisco and San Jose State Universities. She holds an MA in museum studies from the State University of New York and has worked for museums and historic preservation agencies in the Unites States. She has published one book and several scholarly articles on the American west.

Wendy Ruemper
Dr Ruemper received her MA in sociology from the University of Windsor and her Ph.D. from the University of Toronto. She is a member of the social science faculty at Georgian College in Barrie. Her research interest is in the field of women and criminal justice in nineteenth-century Ontario.

Russell C. Smandych
Dr Smandych is an associate professor of sociology at the University of Manitoba. He has published numerous articles in the field of Canadian criminology and legal history, and has co-edited a bibliography of Canadian criminal justice history. He is currently working on a study of the administration of criminal justice under the Hudson's Bay Company in the Canadian west prior to 1860.

Jennifer Stephen
Jennifer Stephen has worked as a researcher with the Metro Labour Education Centre, Labour Council of Metropolitan Toronto and York Region. She has completed a master's degree with the Department of History and Philosophy at the Ontario Institute of Studies in Education, University of Toronto.

Jonathan Swainger
Dr Swainger is lecturer in history, the University of Northern British Columbia. His Ph.D. is from the University of Western Ontario. His current research projects include a major paper, " 'Governing the Law': The Canadian Department of Justice, 1867–1878" and a study of Canada-US extradition in the post-Confederation period.

Table of Cases

Abrahms v. United States (US, 1919) 283

Brandenburg v. Ohio (US, 1969) 253

Campbell v. Hall (UK, 1796) 146, 149–50, 160

Firearms Act (Canada, 1877) 228–9

Ho Tsz Tsun v. Ho An Shin (Hong Kong, 1915) 164

In Re Anderson (Upper Canada and UK, 1861) 37–63

In Re the Estate of Ng Shum (Hong Kong, 1990) 161–2

In Re Tse Lai-Chin (Hong Kong, 1969) 161, 168

In Re Wong Chio-ho and Another (Hong Kong, 1969) 161

Lebbe Marikkar's Application for a Writ of Habeas Corpus (Sri Lanka, 1890) 154

Lui Yuk Ping v. Chow To (Hong Kong, 1962) 164

Non Sooja's Case (Sri Lanka, 1930) 154

Paththuma v. Seni Mohammadu (Sri Lanka, 1921) 155

R v. Butler (Newfoundland, 1819) 16, 90

R v. Cohen (Alberta, 1916) 274–5

R v. Dudley and Stephens (UK, 1884) 446

R v. Felton (Alberta, 1915) 270, 274

R v. James Lundrigan (Newfoundland, 1820) 16, 90–1, 93

R v. Trainor (Alberta, 1916) 276, 279

Ratwatte v. Habana (Sri Lanka, 1898) 153

St Catherine's Milling (UK, 1888) 299

Schenck v. United States (US, 1913) 19, 283

Siripina v. Korale (Sri Lanka, 1898) 153

Tikiri Kumarihamy v. de Silva (Sri Lanka, 1906) 154

Ummah v. Pathumma (Sri Lanka, 1913) 154
Whitney v. California (US, 1927) 253
William Dawe v. John Broom et al. (Newfoundland, 1822) 73, 93

Table of Statutes, Charters, and Proclamations

Administration of Estates Act (UK, 1925) 166
Adoption of Children Act (UK, 1926) 165
Adoption of Children Ordinance (Hong Kong, 1956) 165–6
Adoption Ordinance (Sri Lanka, 1944) 155
An Act to authorize the erection of a Lunatic Asylum in the Province (Upper Canada, 1839) 202–3
An Act to reduce the number of cases in which Capital Punishment may be inflicted (Upper Canada, 1833) 184
Bill of Rights (US, 1787) 253–4
Blake Act (Canada, 1878) 215–34
British North America Act (UK, 1867) 308
Charter of Justice (Sri Lanka, 1801) 150
Chinese Wills Validation Ordinance (Hong Kong, 1856) 169
Consolidated Statutes (Newfoundland, 1877, 1916) 80
Constitution of the United States (US, 1787) 44, 243, 253
Constitutional Act (Canada, 1791) 47
Constitutional Act (Canada, 1982) 296
Country and Borough Police Act (UK, 1856) 469
Criminal Code (Canada, 1892) 231, 266–7, 270, 273, 328, 331, 339, 486
Criminal Syndicalism Act (California, 1919) 252–53
Criminal Syndicalism Ordinance (California, 1919) 252
Deserted Wives' Maintenance Act (British Columbia, 1944) 391
Deserted Wives' Maintenance Act (Ontario, 1888) 330–1
Deserted Wives' Maintenance Act (Ontario, 1897) 331, 334
Espionage Act (US, 1917) 246, 249

Female Refugees Act (Ontario, 1913) 413
Food and Fuel Administration Act (US, 1917) 246
Fourteenth Amendment to the Constitution (US, 1868) 253
Freedom of Information Act (Australia, 1984) 519
Habitual Idlers Ordinance (Trinidad, 1920) 134
Immigration Act (Canada, 1906) 426–7
Independence Act (Ceylon, 1947) 153
Indian Act (Canada, 1872) 292
Intestates' Estate Ordinance (Hong Kong, 1971) 166–7, 169
Judicature Act (UK, 1791) 81, 83, 105–6, 112
Judicature Act (UK, 1809) 81, 83
Judicature Act (UK, 1824) 77–8, 80, 83, 91
King William's Act (UK, 1699) 83
Labour Ordinance (Trinidad, 1935) 136
Local Government Act (UK, 1972) 467
Marriage and Divorce Ordinance (Sri Lanka, 1859) 154–6
Marriage Law of the People's Republic (China, 1950) 163–4
Marriage Reform Ordinance (Hong Kong, 1970) 161–2, 164–6
Married Women's Property Ordinance (Sri Lanka, 1923) 158–9
Masters and Servants Ordinance (Trinidad, 1846), 133
Matrimonial Causes Ordinance (Hong Kong, 1967) 165
Mental Deficiency Act (UK, 1913)
Military Service Act (Canada, 1917) 282
Motor Traffic Act (UK, 1930) 473
Municipal Corporations Act (UK, 1835) 469
New Territories Land (Exemption) Ordinance (Hong Kong, 1994) 168
New Territories Ordinance (Hong Kong, 1910) 167
Palliser's Act (UK, 1775) 82
Paris, Treaty of (UK, 1814, 1815) 76
Peace Preservation Act (Canada, 1869) 228–9
Probates Ordinance (Hong Kong, 1897) 166
Proclamation of 1763 (UK, 1763) 184
Quebec Act (Lower Canada, 1774) 104–5, 113, 184
Real Chattels Act (UK, 1834) 91
Rebellion Losses Bill (Canada East, 1849) 219
Riot Act (UK, 1715) 222
Robinson-Superior Treaty (UK and US, 1850) 292, 295
Royal Charter (Hong Kong, 1843) 160
Royal Charter (UK, 1825) 78–80, 85, 87
Royal Proclamation (UK, 1763) 295, 302

Sabotage Act (US, 1917) 246
Sedition Act (US, 1916) 245–6
Selective Service Act (US, 1917) 246–50, 255
Statute of Labourers (UK, 1351) 218
Succession Ordinance (Sri Lanka, 1917) 155–6
Supreme Court Ordinance (Hong Kong, 1844) 160
Treaty of Nanking (UK, 1842) 159
Truck Ordinance (Trinidad, 1920) 135
Venereal Diseases Control Act (Canada, 1918) 370–1, 430
Webster-Ashburton Treaty (US, 1842) 37, 39–43, 45, 48–9, 51–2, 56, 58, 63
Wills Ordinance (Sri Lanka, 1844) 155
Workmen's Compensation Ordinance (Trinidad, 1920) 135–6

Index

This index has been prepared by the editors. Major entries are identified by bold-face headings, as follows: **Canada, Common Law, Communities and the State, Corrections, Courts, Crimes and Offences, Criminal Law, Economics, Government and Politics, Great Britain, Health and Welfare, Human Condition, Law, Police, Professions, Religion, Social Relations, Society, United States, Violence,** and **War.**

Subject entries can be found by checking under the relevant major heading or main entry; for example, listings of 'jails' appear under the major heading '**Corrections,**' while 'Law Society of Western Australia' is found under the main entry 'Australia.'

Published works are listed by author. Cases, as well as statutes, charters, and proclamations, are listed in two separate tables.

Abel, Richard 449–50
Aberdeen, Lord 40
Abraham, Bernie 299–300, 310, 313
Abraham, Diane 309, 315
Abraham, Frances 294, 297, 299, 314
Abraham, Sidney 310
Adderley, Florence 273
Africa 26; colonial 26; East 130; law and society in 447–50; slave trade 39–40; South 448–49; state formation 4
Akenson, Donald 107–8

Akins, Ronald 478
Albany (New York) state prison 20–1
Alberta 291; dissent in 18–19, 22; Law Foundation of 501–2; Law Society of 454, 501–2; Legal Archives Society 454, 499, 501–2; Supreme Court 19, 21, 264–6, 270–84
Alston, R.C. 455
Anderson, Dr G.W. 425
Anderson, John 15, 17–18, 37–63
archives: *see* professions
Ascomb, Herbert 398

Ashburton, Baron, Alexander Baring, 40–1
Asia 30, 145–72 passim; immigrants 14; law and society 5; Southeast 26
asylums: *see* **Corrections**
Auburn (New York) penitentiary 188–92, 194, 197–8
Australia: Capital Territory's Law Society 519; *Freedom of Information Act* (1984) 519; historiography 3; Law Council of 522; Law Society of Western Australia 519; lawyers in 28, 453; lawyers' records 514–22; New South Wales 522; settlement of 15
Avon and Somerset (England): police force 469

Baby, Jacques 109
Backhouse, Constance 326, 451; *Petticoats and Prejudice* (1991) 451
Baehre, Rainer 19–21, 102–3
Bagot, Sir Charles 41
Bahamas: governor of 42
Baker, William 489
Barres, Augustus Wallet des 87, 93
Bathurst, Lord 77, 91
Battle, Arthur 469
Beattie, John 446
Beaudry, Jean-Louis 224–5, 231
Beaumont, G. de 190, 195; and Alexis de Tocqueville, *The Penitentiary System in the United States* (1830) 195
Begbie, Matthew Baillie CJ 452
Belgium 186–7, 265, 271
Bell, David 92
Bell, George, 260n25
Bentham, Jeremy 187
Benton, Thomas Hart 42

Berkeley California 245, 250–1; Church of the Living God 250
Betke, Carl 481
Bidwell, Marshall Spring 190, 195, 199
Biggs, George 472
Binet-Simon intelligence test 409, 421–4
Binnie, Susan 3–33, 20–2
Birmingham (England): police 471, 473
Black, Sir Jeremiah S. 61–2
Blackstone, Sir William 16, 93, 182; *Commentaries* 266
Blackwell, John 184
Blackwell Island Penitentiary (New York) 188
Blake, Edward 223, 228–32
Blake, Governor 167
Bloomington's Asylum (New York) 200
Boasberg, James E. 288–9
Bond, Maurice 455
Booms, Hans 455
Boritch, Helen 483–4
Boston Prison Discipline Society 20–1, 186, 189–91, 193, 195–7, 201; *Report of the McLean Asylum* (1836) 201
Bouchard, Jocelyn 310
Boulton, Henry John CJ 89
Bourassa, Robert 291
Brandeis, Louis J 283
Brantford (Ontario) 38, 43–4, 49, 53–4
Braton, Sam H. 286–7
Braudel, Fernand 206–7
Brenton, Edward J 87
Bridgeman, Ian 467
British and Foreign Anti-Slavery Society 47, 50

British Columbia 291, 305, 315, 379, 381–2, 385–89, 392, 396, 451–2, 479, 482; Advisory Committee on Juvenile Delinquency (1936) 398; Communist party 395, 399; Conservative party of 381, 383, 386–7, 391, 394, 398–9 Co-operative Commonwealth Federation 381, 383, 385–6, 387, 390, 391–2, 394–5, 398–9; family courts 23–5, 379–99; Federation of Business and Professional Women's Clubs 386; feminists and the welfare state 379–99; Housewives' League 395–6; immigrants 14; Legal Archives 499, 501; Liberal party of 381, 386–7, 390–1, 394, 398–9; Mothers' Allowance Board 391; Provincial Council of Women 388–90, 394–5; Provincial Police 482–3; Social Credit party 398

Brode, Patrick 52, 54

Brooklyn News (British Columbia) 452

Brougham, Lord 186

Brown, Desmond 285

Brown, George 54, 227

Brown, Lorne and Caroline: An Unauthorized History of the RCMP (1973) 478–9

Brown, Tom 204

Brownrigg, Robert 155

Bruce, Dr 200

Bruce Smith, W.R. 365–6

Bryan, Constable 336

Buchan, David 990

Buchanan, James 189, 191

Buchanan, James (US president) 60, 62–3

Bucknall, Brian 507

Buller, Charles 184, 205

Burke, Edmund, 103: Reflections on the French Revolution (1791) 104

Burnaby (British Columbia) Juvenile Court 382–3, 386

Burton, Jack 38–9

Burton, Moses 38

Cadigan, Sean 78, 183

Calgary 264, 273–4, 276, 279, 501

Calgary News Telegraph 264

Calhoun, John C. 42

California: civil liberties 21–2, 243–62; Council of Defence 250–1; Criminal Syndicalism Act (1919) 252–3; dissent in 18–19; economics 245–7, 249–50; labour 243–6, 249–52, 255; law in First World War 243–56; pacifists 245–6, 255; politics 244–5, 255–6; Progressive party 21, 23, 244–5, 252–3, 255; security agencies 243, 246–50; University of, at Berkeley 245, 251

Cambridge (England): constabulary 467

Cambridgeshire (England): constabulary 467–8, 471

Caminetti, Anthony 244

Canada 3, 5, 9, 15–19, 23, 27, 37–63, 215–34, 263–4, 266, 272–3, 278–9, 284, 290–1, 295, 302–6, 355–6, 370, 379–82, 387, 407, 410, 419, 426–8, 449–54, 456, 477–91, 497–511

Anti-Slavery Society of Canada 38, 46, 54

civil liberties 19, 21–2

Confederation 19, 22

Conservative party 216, 230, 296

Department of Indian Affairs 297–8, 308–10

Department of Justice 217, 229, 231
federal legislation 215–34
federal-provincial relations 215–34,
    290–316
government of 46–7
Grand Trunk Railway strike
    (1876–7) 220, 222–4
historiography 3–6
intergovernmental relations 40–63
Lachine Canal strikes (1875, 1877)
    220, 222–3
law and society 5–6
lawyers in 28
Liberal party 266, 296
maritime colonies 17
militia 218
National Committee for Mental
    Hygiene 371, 406–7, 411–12,
    418–22, 425, 427–31
North-West Mounted Police 267–8,
    272, 477, 479, 481–2, 489
Orange Order 215, 219, 220, 221,
    223–7
Parliament 216–17, 226–33
police 27–8
private sector legal archives
    497–511
Public Archives of 451
Rowell-Sirois Commission 395
Royal Canadian Mounted Police
    477–80, 489–90
Supreme Court of Canada 295–6
War Veteran's Association 280
Whigs 216
Women's Christian Temperance
    Union 391
Women's Missionary Society, Bap-
    tist Church 389
Young Women's Christian Associ-
    ation 386

Canada East: see Quebec
Canada West: see Ontario
Canadian Journal of Mental Hygiene
    406, 420
Canadian National Railway 20, 290,
    293–4, 297, 301, 305, 307–16
Canadian Pacific Railway 290, 297,
    305, 316, 360, 484
Caribbean: law and society of 5
Carleton, Guy (Lord Dorchester)
    110, 113–14
Carrington, Rev. Frederick Hamilton
    90
Carruthers, Norman JP 276, 281–2
Carson, Dr William 82, 90
Cartier, P.M. 60
Cartwright, Richard 109, 120
Cass, Lewis 61
Ceylon 130; laws and customs 149,
    152–5
Chadwick, Edwin 466
Chadwick, Robert 473
Chaffe, Zachariah Jr 273, 283
Chambers, Ernest J. 478
Channock, Martin 448–9
Chapman, Terry 324
Chichester-Fortescue, Lord 49
China 14, 146, 160, 170–1, 487–8;
    laws and customs of 14, 17, 145–6,
    159–72; marriage customs 16;
    southern 170
Chunn, Dorothy 23–5, 353–4
Citizen (Ottawa) 327
Civil law: see law; Roman law
Clark, George N. 3, 447
Clarke, Dr Charles K. 24, 371, 407,
    411–14, 416–17, 419–23, 426–30
Clarkson, Thomas 41
Clausen, Charles 275–6
Clausen, Theodore 268, 272, 274–6

Cochrane, Sir Thomas 88–9
Cockburn, Sir Alexander CJ 47
Cohen, George 274, 277
Cohen, Marjorie Griffin 325
Coke, Sir Edward 449
Colborne, John 194, 200
Colclough, Caesar 79, 81
colonies 3–5, 10–11, 13–18, 21, 26–8,
    35–177 *passim*, 219, 445, 447–50;
    law and customs of 5, 14–18, 26,
    145–72; Upper Canada 181–207

Common Law
    adoption 155, 163, 165–6, 384
    alimony 25, 327–8, 331–5, 337, 488
    bankruptcy 99–100, 102, 112–15, 118
    contracts 16, 113, 134–6, 445
    debt 16, 84, 86–7, 89–90, 92, 102,
        113, 133, 182, 327, 473, 517
    divorce and matrimonial 24, 84,
        89, 141, 155–6, 158–9, 163, 165,
        328, 335, 383, 388–90
    equity 77, 103, 161
    evidence 28, 84–5, 137–9, 454
    inheritance and succession 15, 17,
        91, 154–7, 161–3, 449
    injunctions 311–12, 314
    intestate 84, 139, 155–6, 163–4,
        166–70
    land law 22, 449
    nuisance 451
    probate 166
    procedure and process 28, 84–86
    tort 449
    trusts 167
    wills 86, 155, 168–9

Commonwealth Legal Records Pro-
    ject (Ghana) 450

Communities and the State 18–22,
    27–8, 74–5, 86–92, 137–8, 205, 207,
    263–84, 330, 339–40, 360–1, 365,
    371, 374, 385, 409, 416, 418–19,
    425–6, 443–9, 453–7, 484–90, 497–8,
    503–4, 506
    disorder and dissent in 18–22
    imperial authority in Upper
        Canada 181–207
    law of 9–13, 17, 21, 29, 79–80,
        169–71
    legal records of: *see* professions,
        archivists
    municipalities 9–10, 20, 36, 88–90,
        119, 205–6, 246, 250, 465–74,
        484–5, 487–91
    and natives 290–316
    policing of 465–6, 469–74, 482
    urban communities 215–34
    welfare state, 6, 24, 354–5, 359–62,
        371, 379–99 *passim*

Connecticut Retreat Asylum 200
Conolly, John 198
Conrad, Charles M. 42
Cook, Terry 28
Cooper, James Fenimore 479
Cooray, Anton 14, 16–17, 145–77
Cornish, William R. 3, 447

Corrections
    almshouses 198, 358
    asylums 7–8, 19–20, 22; female 353,
        355, 357, 362–3, 366–7
    banishment 185
    corporal punishment 16, 91
    deportation 23, 406, 424–9
    executions 18, 156, 185–6
    fines 89, 137, 250, 272, 276–7,
        328–31, 335, 485
    forfeitures 89
    galleys 7
    hard labour 187–8, 357, 360, 373

houses of industry 198, 355, 363, 366, 368
houses of refuge, 413, 416, 419
hulks 7, 185
jails 8, 38, 43–5, 49–51, 61, 116–17, 136, 184, 188, 203, 205–6, 250, 272, 276, 281, 298, 300, 328, 339, 425, 429–30, 452; female inmates 351, 355–9, 363–9, 371–4
parole 352, 364, 366, 425
penal reform 181–3, 181–98, 206–7
prison reform 357, 359–67, 372, 384
prisons 6–8, 19–23, 25, 39, 57, 250, 297, 328, 330–1, 335; female inmates of 351–2, 355, 357, 360, 362–3, 372
probation 352, 360, 366, 382, 386, 388, 390, 392, 425–6
reformatories 23, 351, 354–66, 368–73, 411
tickets of leave 364
transportation 185
treadmill 188
whipping 90, 276, 339

Courts 3, 6–8
admiralty 74, 77, 84
appeal 85, 90, 148, 270, 296
central court records 8, 25–9
chancery and equity 77, 83–4, 89, 103, 161, 300
circuit courts 74, 84–6, 335, 452
clerks of 9, 92
common pleas 16, 50–4, 57–60, 75, 83
coroners' 452–3
ecclesiastical 26
family 23–4, 379, 381–99
feudal 26

franchisal 26
juvenile 382–6, 390, 402, 419, 425, 430
King's Bench at Westminster 18
local (undesignated) 8, 16, 25–9, 148, 153, 167, 170–1, 205, 334–7, 342, 363, 449–50, 504
magistrates' 335, 402, 480, 485
manorial 26
police 25, 335, 338–9, 392
superior (undesignated) 11, 21, 24, 83, 331, 446, 503
supreme 11, 19, 21, 37, 43–6, 49–63, 77–80, 83–90, 148–9, 152–4, 158, 160–2, 168, 264–6, 270–84, 295–6, 310
surrogate 86, 90
women's 363, 419

Cowan, A.J. 392
Crawford, William 193–4
crime: and deviance 182, 353–5, 358, 361, 366, 374, 381, 384, 386, 431–2, 448; and juvenile delinquency 369, 383, 385, 388–90, 392, 398, 414–16, 420–1, 423, 430–2, 488; and recidivism 353, 418; and social control 6, 8, 20, 23–4, 106, 181–207 *passim*, 226, 233–4, 256, 369, 372–3, 380, 410, 451, 483–4

Crimes and Offences
abduction 54
abuse and neglect 24, 323–43
adultery 156, 326–7, 331, 365
arson 39–40, 231, 250–1
assault 38–40, 90, 92, 225, 290, 300, 335–6, 338–42, 357, 368, 374
bawdy house 356, 360, 485, 487
begging 187, 206, 368

bigamy 151
conspiracy 266
defamation 138
desertion 25, 247, 249, 327, 329,
  331, 334, 343, 383–4, 388
disorderly 7, 266, 270, 340, 357,
  359, 364–5, 369–70, 481, 484–5
drugs 294, 410, 485–6, 488–9
drunkenness 193, 294, 297–8, 313,
  328, 336–8, 340–2, 357–9, 362–6,
  368–70, 372, 374, 392, 410, 480,
  487
forgery 39, 185
fraud 247
gambling 328, 486, 487–9
homicide 40, 453
indecent assault 368
infanticide 453
libel 48
manslaughter 56
murder 38–40, 42, 45–6, 51, 54–7,
  61, 89, 184–5, 219, 225–6, 228–9,
  245, 279, 340, 353, 358, 368, 374,
  392, 446, 452
negligence 452, 515
obscenity 365
piracy 39
prostitution 25, 356, 358–60, 364,
  367, 369–72, 374, 409–10, 412,
  420–1, 426–7, 431, 486–7, 489
rape 392, 451
riot 17, 20, 54, 83, 132, 215–34
  passim, 272–6
robbery 39–40, 42, 392, 452
sedition 5, 18, 22, 263–84
sexual (general) 156, 363–4, 368,
  371
smuggling 74, 479
suicide 431, 452–3
theft 12, 40–1, 76, 185, 280,

358–9, 364, 367–8, 374, 452, 486,
  489
treason 18, 48, 85, 89
trespass 20, 90, 301, 307, 310, 315
vagrancy 25, 134, 187, 205, 351,
  353, 357–9, 364–5, 367, 371–82,
  374, 409, 489
vice 193, 368–9, 417, 485
See also crime

Criminal Law
  arrests 19, 38, 55, 85, 134, 252, 268,
    300, 309
  bail and recognizances 268, 276,
    280, 335–6, 338, 485
  contempt 90
  evidence 55–8, 270–84, 330, 332,
    334, 337, 452–4, 487
  indictments 56–7, 253, 268–70
  juries 41, 75, 85, 89–90, 116, 185–6,
    199–200, 225, 271–2, 452–3, 518
  pardons 89
  remands 89
  searches 229
  witnesses 38–9, 329–30, 407, 454
  writs 43, 47–52, 60, 63, 281
  See also crime; crimes and offences;
    criminals

criminals: and accomplices 20;
  convicts 192–3, 203, 207; gangs of
  76
Critchley, T.A. 466
Crompton, Lord Justice 48
culture: and leisure 4, 108, 130, 141,
  145–8, 181–2, 187, 306, 311, 323,
  395, 411, 414–17, 425, 430, 432,
  446, 453, 469, 473, 479; and education 23, 82, 92, 116, 183, 244, 251,
  313, 352, 354, 357–61, 363, 372–3,
  390–1, 405, 410, 418–20, 431, 447;

and schools 9, 12, 28, 75, 193, 248,
297–8, 306, 311, 369, 384, 410–11,
423–4; and universities 12, 387,
389, 394; Enlightenment 186, 196;
legal 8–9, 11–17, 20, 27, 91, 303–4;
mentalities 11–12; newspapers 75,
119, 191, 219, 249, 327, 338, 340,
352, 395, 445–6, 452–3, 478, 490;
and value systems 8

Dalhousie, George Ramsay 187
Dallas, George M. 61–2
David, L.-O. 231
Deane, R.B., *Mounted Police Life in
Canada* (1916) 480
Dehli, Kari 408–9
Denison, George T., *Recollections of a
Police Magistrate* (1920) 480
Devlin, Bernard 219, 229
Devon and Cornwall (England)
police achive 473
Dickson, Brian CJ 295–6
Digges, Seneca P. 38–9, 45, 50, 58
Door, Lenus 'Tubby' 290, 309, 315
Draper, William H. CJ 52, 57, 60
Duckworth, Sir John 77
Dudley, Captain John 446
Dufferin, Lord 224
Duncombe, Dr Charles 190, 192–3,
195, 199–202
Dundas, Henry 109–10, 116–18
Dunlop, W.W. 367, 369
Dunning, Sir Leonard 470
Durham, Lord John 184, 186, 197,
205, 482
Durham Report (1839) 183–84, 205
Durkheim 12
Dwight, Louis, Rev. 191

East India Company 149

Eastern Penitentiary (Philadelphia)
187–8

Economics
agriculture 82–3, 134–5, 156, 158,
168, 183, 189, 216, 246, 252, 255,
291, 323, 366–7, 449, 471
business and commerce 12, 16, 20,
74, 90, 112–13, 134–5, 139–40,
146–7, 159, 183, 187, 231–2, 245,
444, 447, 469, 508, 514–15, 517,
520
capital and wealth 7, 24, 87, 140,
146, 159, 172, 192, 203, 207,
244–5, 255, 323, 379–80, 444–5,
447–51, 455, 457, 483, 515
communications 254–5, 301, 307–8,
310–11
corporations 9, 19–20, 28
entrepreneurs 7, 78
fishing 13–14, 16, 73–93, 245, 293,
471
forestry 245, 247, 293, 297
gleaning 12
Great Depression (1874–96)
219–20, 488
hunting 292, 297
industry and manufacture 7, 80–1,
131, 135, 146, 181, 187, 193, 205,
220, 244–5, 252, 255–6, 328, 360,
365, 413–18, 421, 431, 447, 450,
454, 483, 489, 509, 516
inflation 135
interest rates 255, 515
laissez-faire 353, 357–9, 380, 382
land 20, 80, 82, 85–6, 88, 113, 116,
118, 138–9, 159, 167–8, 245,
290–316, 447, 449, 508
leases 75, 82–3, 91, 153–4, 160
markets 76, 80, 140, 196

merchants 76–8, 83, 112, 114–15

mining 255, 452, 489

plantations 131–41

profits 14, 134–5, 515

property 15–16, 75, 77, 80, 82–3, 86, 89–91, 104, 112, 117, 138–40, 152, 156–9, 165–9, 171, 207, 247, 324–6, 343, 414, 449, 465, 517

public utilities 9, 28, 247, 301, 455

rent 87, 117

settlement 13–14, 16–17, 74, 78, 80, 82–3, 91, 107–8, 117, 147

strikes 132

sugar industry 14

taxation 17, 100, 116–18, 189, 191, 520

technology 255, 491

transport 190, 231, 245, 247, 290, 297, 300–1, 305–6, 308–10, 315–16, 446, 473–4

unemployment 215, 220, 330, 332, 365, 379, 395, 410, 424, 428, 431–2

unions 9, 12, 28, 132–3, 243–5, 249–53, 305, 447, 455, 470, 490, 479–80, 487–90, 509, 516

work and wages 4, 7, 15, 23, 76, 80, 89, 102–3, 117, 131–6, 140, 191–3, 196, 199, 217, 221, 234, 243–6, 249–52, 255, 315, 323, 325–6, 329, 353, 360, 362, 365, 367, 369, 379, 383, 393–4, 396, 399, 409, 413–17, 423, 428, 447, 469

Elliot, Charles 159–60

Ely, Isle of (England) constabulary 467

Emsley, Clive 27–8, 465–77

England: see Great Britain

English, Christopher 13–14, 16, 73–98

English Ladies Association in Aid of Coloured Refugees 46

Errington, Jane 107, 118

Europe 4–6, 8, 79–80, 205–6, 243, 263, 266, 304, 450–1, 465, 484, 497, 508; state formation 4, 6–8

Felton, Oscar 270

Finkelman, Paul 15, 17–18

Finlayson, George 302–3

First Nations, Assembly of 291

Fisher, Rayno 290, 301, 307, 315–16

Fitzpatrick, Francis 225

Flagg, William 275

Flaherty, David 451

Fogelson, Robert 477

Forbes, Francis 79, 81, 90, 92

Forsyth, John 40

Fort William (Ontario) Reserve 292

Fox, Arthur 482

Fox, Henry Stephen 40

Franc-Parleur, Le (Quebec) 226

France 4, 6, 11, 14, 20, 74, 76, 80, 190, 204, 449; Annales School 4, 11–12; colonies 449; creoles 131; French Revolution 7; monarchy 6

France, Anatole 10

Freedman, Estelle 373

Freeman, Samuel B. 38, 51, 57

Friedman, Lawrence M. 3

Fry, Elizabeth 356

Gambier, Governor 82

Garvin AJ 158

Gazette (Montreal) 219

George III 186, 302, 304

George V 267–8, 272, 274–5, 280

Germany 19, 21, 195, 264;

historiography 4; people of 246–51, 267, 270, 272–82, 455
Ghai, Yash P. 171, 449
Glasgow Bridewell 188
Goderich, Lord 87–8
Goldring, Constable 281
Gölz, Annalee 24–5
Gordon, Rev. Major J.P. 392
Gordon, Robert 504
Gore district, Upper Canada 184

Government and Politics
attorneys general 8, 43, 53, 58, 88, 164, 223, 246, 254, 278–86, 388–9, 391–2, 398, 443, 452, 485
bureaucracy 6, 21, 182, 243–4, 246–56, 297, 303, 379, 385, 451, 454, 466, 484, 486–7, 509
censorship 245–62
central state 18–23
civil service 391, 465
Colonial Office 51, 78, 46, 109–11, 110, 114, 134, 183, 194–5
Communists 395, 399, 488–9
conscription 263
Conservatives 295–6, 381, 383, 386–7, 391, 394–9
Co-operative Commonwealth Federation: see British Columbia
corruption in 78, 118, 479
dissent 5, 7, 18–22, 254
elections 105, 117, 304, 396
Fabians 383
free speech 245–6, 248–50, 252–3
Home Office 73, 186, 466–74
intergovernmental 20–2, 25, 28–9, 145–8, 215–34, 243–4, 253–6, 293–6, 301–6, 445–55
justice department 8, 217, 229–31, 246–52, 254, 282, 443

Labour 470
legislatures 7–8, 16–18, 24–8, 80–2, 87–9, 99–100, 105–6, 109–20, 146–7, 151–65, 169, 184–5, 189–91, 194, 199–203, 215–34, 244, 246, 250–4, 290, 304, 324–6, 331, 339, 379–80, 385–9, 392–4, 397, 407, 413, 427, 430–1, 443, 447, 455, 467, 472, 498, 508, 516, 519
Liberals 266, 296, 381, 386–7, 390–1, 394, 398–9
local 19, 388
Marxists 4, 7, 12, 483
monarchy and the prerogative 6–7, 74, 86, 90–1, 147, 302–4, 448, 478
municipal 20–1, 469, 479–80, 484–91, 503, 509
Parliament 37, 41–2, 44–9, 58, 73, 75, 83, 88, 91, 105, 111, 114, 170, 216–17, 228–33, 326–33, 397, 421–2, 443, 470
patronage 385, 395, 399, 481
Privy Council 49, 90, 134–5, 149
Progressives 21, 23, 244–5, 212–13, 255
secretary of state 40, 61, 63, 73, 114, 247, 254
Social Credit 398
socialists 268, 323, 383, 394–5, 399
solicitors general 8, 163, 677, 443
sovereignty 7, 21, 49, 91, 160, 171, 296, 302–3
surveillance 243–4, 246–56
Tories 21
Treasury Department 247, 252
treaties 39–43, 45, 48–9, 51–2, 56–8, 63, 290–316 passim
Whigs 21, 88, 216, 465–6, 478
Workingmen's party 246

See also **Communities and the State**

Graham, Aaron 75
Gramsci, Antonio 12
Grand Banks, Newfoundland 73, 77,
    84, 91
Grant, Diane 297

Great Britain 3, 6–7, 10–11, 13–14,
    19, 22, 25–7, 37–63, 73–93, 100–1,
    104–7, 111–14, 118–20, 131, 135,
    146, 251, 263, 269–72, 277, 280,
    284, 299, 302, 324, 358, 372, 412,
    422, 427, 446–9, 451–3, 465–74,
    477–8, 481–4, 490
    Admiralty Court 74, 77
    Colonial Office 109–11, 114, 134
    colonies 13–18, 21, 26, 73–93,
        99–120, 130–41, 269, 302, 409,
        447–50, 478–9, 484
    Commission of Oyer et Terminer
        74, 84, 89
    conquests 16–17, 78, 112, 146, 149,
        448
    Convention of Chuenpi 159
    Convention of Peking (1860) 160
    Corn Laws 81
    Court of Exchequer 83
    Court of Queen's Bench 37, 49–50,
        60, 83
    draft criminal code 266
    Economic and Social Research
        Council 467
    English police forces archives
        465–74
    historiography 3–4
    Home Office 466–7, 474
    intergovernmental relations 40–63
    Labour party 470
    marriage law 16
    MI5 470

    monarchy 6–7, 478
    Parliament 7, 73–5, 78, 83, 88, 91,
        105, 111, 114, 421–2
    Police History Society 467
    police in 27–8, 477
    poor laws 99–103, 112–20
    Privy Council 85, 90, 134–5
    Public Records Office 451, 466–7,
        469
    Quarter Sessions 74
    Reform Acts 81
    Royal Commission on the Rural
        Constabulary (1839) 466
    royal navy 80–1
    royal prerogative 74, 86, 90–1
    Society of Archivists 455
    Society for the Improvement of
        Prison Discipline 194–5
    Special Branch 470
    Strickland Committee (1948) 161,
        163, 165, 168
    Treaty of Nanking (1842) 159
    Whig party 465–6

Green, James S. 63
Greenhous, Brereton 101
Greer, Allan 477
Grenville, Lord 15, 105–6, 109–10
Grosse Isle quarantine station
    (Upper Canada) 197
Gull Bay reserve (Ontario) 292
Gunning, James H. 38, 55
Guth, DeLloyd 501
Guyana 141

Hackett, Nelson 40–1
Hackett, Thomas 224–9
Hagan, John 483
Hagarty, John H., J 58
Hall, Basil 188

Hall, Lena 299, 301, 307, 313, 316
Hall, Riley 299, 313, 315
Hall, Sam 299, 313, 315
Hall, Tony 17, 20-1
Hamilton, Robert 109, 120
Hamilton, Sir Charles 76, 81, 91, 93
Haraksingh, Kusha 15-16
Harper, Elijah 290-1, 293, 304
Harring, Sidney 477, 483, 488-9
Harris, William H. 46
Harvey, Horace CJ 265, 270-1, 276
Hawkins, William: *Pleas of the Crown*
266
Hay, Douglas 504
Hayward, William 93
Head, Sir Edmund 61
Head, Sir Francis Bond 201-2, 204-5

Health and Welfare 86, 113, 146, 165,
183, 188, 198, 206, 353-5, 366, 371,
379-82
charities 9, 78-80, 101, 154, 186,
196, 353-4, 357, 363, 447, 455, 473
children's aid societies 23
hospitals 9, 23, 24-5, 28, 75, 186,
198, 200, 298, 352, 361, 363, 384,
419-20, 428-9, 452
mental hygiene 405-7, 409-13,
418-22, 425, 427-31
pensions 379, 469
poor laws 14
psychiatric clinics 405-33 *passim*
public health 298, 331, 334,
409-10, 418-19
social welfare 22-4, 76, 204,
329-31, 334, 379-80, 385, 388,
391, 395-6, 399, 405, 410-11,
418, 432, 455, 473, 486
workmen's compensation 135-6,
379, 451

Hennessy, Alexander 469
Henning, Thomas 54
Higgins, William 481
Hill, Robert Gardiner 198
Hillsborough, Earl of 114
Hincks, Dr Clarence 24, 371, 407,
411-12, 421, 425
Hincks, Sir Francis 223
Hindus: laws and customs of 14, 16,
139-40, 147
Hoare, Samuel 194-5
Hodges, Nancy 391, 395, 399
Hoebel, Adamson 444-5
Hogan, CJ 161
Holland, Laura 402
Holmes, Oliver Wendell J 283
Holtum, Charles von 264, 267, 271,
285
Home District (Upper Canada) 185,
199-200, 203
Hong Kong 14 Council of Women
163-4; family inheritance 16-17;
laws and customs 145-72; New
Territories 159-60, 168-70
Horowitz, Morton 7
Horrall, S. 481
Houston, Susan 193
Howard, John 187, 194-5
Hudson, Lynn 482
Hudspith, Edward Henry 472

Human Condition
caste 156
death 38, 42, 138, 186, 224, 226-8,
245, 279-80, 294, 331, 336, 342,
446, 452-3
disease 187-8, 198, 204, 297, 316,
353, 355-6, 362-3, 371, 373,
410, 412, 418, 420, 423, 426,
430-1

eugenics 23–4, 379, 381, 388,
  412–13, 422
gender 15, 451
heredity 163, 366–72, 406, 409–11,
  421, 432
illegitimacy, 358, 384, 407, 410,
  420, 426, 428–9, 432
insanity 20, 84, 181–4, 193,
  197–207, 351, 357–8, 363, 366–7,
  374–5, 384, 413–14, 419, 421,
  426–7
morality 145, 155, 181, 183–7, 193,
  196–9, 207, 246–7, 277, 324,
  353–5, 357, 359, 363–5, 369,
  371–2, 385, 406–16, 418, 421–4,
  426, 428, 430, 446, 484–9
poverty 20, 76, 83, 99–120, 136,
  182, 187, 193, 197, 203–7, 297,
  329, 331, 341, 353, 355, 357–8,
  371, 381, 383–4, 386, 388, 390,
  409–10, 432, 447, 473
pregnancy 362
race and racism 4–5, 14–15, 19, 37,
  52–6, 131, 151, 230, 243–5, 255,
  296, 365, 382, 393–4, 396, 399,
  408–9, 412, 431, 451, 486–8, 490
sexuality 6, 22–3, 25, 324, 326, 343,
  354, 356, 362–3, 371, 373–4, 383,
  393, 396–7, 399, 409, 411,
  413–14, 416, 421–2, 426, 430,
  432
temperance 23, 365, 372, 391

Humberside (England) police force
  470
Humboldt County (California)
  Criminal Syndicalism Ordinance
  252
Huntingdonshire (England) constabulary 467, 473

Hutchings, Richard 74
Hyndman, James D. J 268

India 134, 147; migrants to Trinidad
  131–40; state formation 4–5. *See
  also* East India Company
Indian, Larry 312–13
Industrial Workers of the World
  244–5, 247, 250–3, 255, 488
Inglis, Robert H. 275–6
Innes, Joanna 218
Ireland 47, 93, 107, 228, 367, 370,
  372, 425–6, 480; battle of the
  Boyne (1690) 224; creoles 131;
  Royal Irish Constabulary 477,
  480–2
Irish 219, 221, 224–5, 227, 229–30,
  359, 364, 369, 471, 476
Irvine, R. Douglas 61
Isaacson, Alfred 286–7

James, Edwin John 47
James Bay (Ontario) 292, 295
Jamieson, Laura 382–7, 389–92,
  394–8, 404
Japan 244, 263, 316
Jarvis, William 199
Jetté, Louis-Amable 229, 231
Johnson, A.K.: *Becoming Prominent*
  (1989) 117–18
Johnson, Hiram 245
Johnson, J.K. 117
Johnson, Sir John 104–5
Johnston, Sir Alexander 148–9, 152,
  155
Johnston, David 477
Jordan, David Starr 245
Julius, Dr 195

Kahn, Julius 246

Kaiser, the 245, 250–1
Kandyan: laws and customs 146–51,
    154–7, 171
Kanewake Nation 291, 304
Kates, Christine 500
Kealey, Greg 221, 233, 463
Keats, Sir Richard 83
Kelso, J.J. 414
Kenora (Ontario) 312; jail 351–2,
    355, 363, 367, 372
Kent (England) constabulary 471
Kimberley-Clark Corp. 293
King's College (Upper Canada)
    201
Kingston (Ontario) 59, 116–19; peni-
    tentiary 184, 186, 190–7, 202, 357,
    367
Kitchener, Lord 267
Klein, Joanne Marie 473
Klumpenhouwer, Richard 27–8
Knox, William 73

Laflamme, Rodolphe 229
Lancashire (England) constabulary
    473
Langevin, Hector 230
Langstaff, Lillian 429

Law
    aboriginal, 17, 148–59, 167, 169–71,
        290–316 passim
    arbitration 9–10, 17, 74, 91
    bar associations 9, 28
    civil rights and liberties 18–19, 99,
        104, 112, 243–56, 447
    common law 8, 21–2, 25–6
    courthouses 116–17
    customary 5, 9–17, 26, 29, 148–72,
        443–9, 497
    extradiction 39–43, 45, 50–1, 56, 59

law reform 16, 20–1, 77, 85, 183–4,
    187, 206, 383–4, 466, 483
law societies 9, 28
legal fictions 445, 459
legal pluralism 3–5, 8–13, 17, 25,
    27, 444, 448–50, 454–7, 489
mercy 453
positive 10, 12, 15
precedents, 11, 26, 115, 149–50,
    168–9, 271, 445, 447, 515
proclamations 8, 22, 136, 149, 156,
    160, 167, 184, 230–1, 295
Roman (civil) 14, 151–2, 438, 497
See also Common Law; Criminal
    Law; Corrections

Law Magazine and Law Review 45
Lee, Brad 307
Lee, Dr. 201
Leigh, Rev. John 90
Levy, J.C. 101–2
Lewis, Doug 308–9, 315
Lewis, Levi 190
Liberator, The 62–3
Lincoln, Abraham 62–3
Lindsay, W.P. 268–9, 275
Lippman, Walter 254
Llewellyn, Karl 444–5
local communities: see Communities
    and the State
London (England) 37, 46, 62, 74–6,
    80–1, 105–6, 114, 134, 197, 301,
    446, 448, 465; London Prison Disci-
    pline Society 190, 194–7; Metro-
    politan Police 465
Long Lake Reserve (Ontario) 20–1,
    290–316
L'Opinion Publique (Montreal) 231
Los Angeles 245, 248–50, 252; Ameri-
    can Protective League 248; Mer-

chants and Manufacturers' Association 245; War Squad 249–50
Low Countries: sovereignty 6
Lower Canada 197, 199, 205, 481–2; Court of Common Pleas 16; courts of 16; Rebellions (1837–8) 205, 482. *See also* Quebec
Lubicon Cree (Alberta) 292
Lubin, Simon J. 252
Luckman, Robin 450
Lundrigan, James 16, 90–1, 93
Lushington, Dr Stephen 41
Lusitania 264–5, 267–8, 271–2, 277
Lyons, Lord 61

Macaulay, John 188–97, 201–2; *Report of the Boston Prison Discipline Society* (1840) 196; *Report of the Commissioners* (1840) 195–6; *1835 Report of the Committee on Gaols* (1836) 196
Macauley, George Trevelyan 12
McAuslan, W.B. JP 449
McCarthy, Maitland J 265, 267, 270, 280
McClatchy, Valentine S. 244
McConnacie, Kathleen 406, 412
McCulloch, Michael 483, 490
Macdonald, John A. 43, 53, 58–60, 303
Macdonnell, Alexander 199
McDowell, Samuel 340
Macfee, J 164
McGahan, Peter, et al.: *The Saint John Police Story* (1991) 481
MacGill, Helen Gregory 382–5, 387–90, 394, 396–8
Mackenzie, Alexander 221–4, 227–9
Macklin, C.H. 286–7
McLaren, John 11

McLean, Archibald 38, 43–45, 53, 55–6
McLean Asylum (Upper Canada) 202
Maclean's Magazine 417
Macleod, R.C. 477–9, 481
McLintock, A.H.: *A Study in Retarded Colonization* (1941) 78
MacMurchy, Dr Helen 407
McPhedran, Mary 402
MacPherson, William 412
Madison, James 243
Magna Carta 59, 302
Mahavamsa 147
Maitland, 'Pat' 392, 398–9
Maitland, Sir Peregrine 185
Maitland, Thomas 155
Malthus, Thomas 187
Manchester (England): police of 469, 473; police of Greater Manchester 468–9
Manchester, Alan 447
Manitoba 216, 224, 226; legislature of 304
Markland, Thomas 119
Marquis, Greg 27–8, 453
Martin, C.F. 406
Marx, Karl: and Marxism 4, 7, 12
Massachusetts: prisons 19, 198
Mathews, William 38–9, 43, 51, 54–5, 58–60, 62
Matthews, Keith 78
Mealing, S.R. 116
Meech Lake 290, 303–4
Michano, Roy 314
Michipicoten Reserve (Ontario) 292
Mid-Anglia Police (England) 468
Milbanke, Mark 75
Millbank Prison (England) 187
Miller, Wilbur 477

Mills, Martha 327
Mills, Mr 327
Minèrve, Le (Quebec) 226
Minuke, Marty 311, 313–15
Missouri: and slavery 37–9, 43–6,
    55–6, 58, 60, 63
Mitchell, J.C. 427
M'Keown, Francis 225
Mobert Reserve (Ontario) 305
Mohawk Nation 290, 293, 304, 306
Mohawk Warriors Society 290–1
Molloy, John William J 87
Monkkonen, Eric 477, 484, 487
Montreal 20, 216, 220–1, 229, 231,
    291, 406, 415, 430, 480–3; McGill
    University 406; police of 480; Prot-
    estant-Catholic riots (1877–8) 222,
    224–5; Psychiatric Clinic 415; riots
    in 216, 219–21, 223–8, 230, 233
Mooney, Tom 245
Moore, Peter 27–8
Morris, Patrick 90
Morrison, Dr 200
Morrison, W.R. 481
Mort, Frank 408, 412
Morton, Desmond 233, 481
Mount Pleasant Penitentiary (Sing-
    Sing) 188
Mowat, Oliver 331
Mulroney, Brian 295, 303–5, 316
Mundie, Gordon 415
Murray, David 103, 113
Murray, John Wilson 480; Memoirs of
    a Great Detective (1904) 480
Murray, General James 113
Muslims: laws and customs of, 16,
    139, 146–8, 150–5

Nabigon, Bertha 299–300, 313
Nabigon, Francis 307, 310, 316

Nabigon, George 306, 313, 316
Nabigon, Sampson Hall 301
Nafzger, A.H. 251
Neelands, C.F. 369
Netherlands 186; colonies 14, 145–51,
    155; conquests 146
New Brunswick 224, 226, 482; law
    profession 92; Loyalists 105; penal
    reform 195; poor relief 101
New England: immigration 84, 93
New York: Charities Commission
    Committee on Mental Hygiene
    406–7; Historical Records Program
    Development Project 456; prisons
    19, 198
New York: City of 188–9
New Zealand: historiography 3
Newcastle, Duke of 46
Newfoundland 280, 479, 482; ad-
    miralty courts 84; circuit courts
    84–6; constabulary of 482; law and
    legal development of 13–14, 17,
    73–98; marriage laws 16; Supreme
    Court 79, 83–7
Nickalls, James 192
North, Diane 19, 21
North, Frederick 149, 155
Northamptonshire (England): con-
    stabulary 467
Nova Scotia 113, 215–16, 451; Bishop
    of 89; Loyalists 105

O'Donel, James 75
O'Driscoll, Joseph J 310
O'Flaherty, Patrick 7
Ojibway Nation 298, 310–12, 316
Oka (Quebec) 290, 304–5, 307, 316
Oldman Dam (Alberta) 291
Oleson, John 452
Oliver, Peter 499

Ontario 357, 372–3, 382, 388, 451,
    479; Archives of 499–500; Chil-
    dren's Aid Society 330, 354, 429;
    Commission on Unemployment
    (1916) 414; Court of Appeal 296;
    Court of Common Pleas 50–2, 54,
    57–8, 60; Court of Queen's Bench
    37, 43, 45–6, 49–51, 53–9, 62–3,
    296, 310; dissent in 18; incarcer-
    ation of women 351–74; Law Foun-
    dation of 500; Law Society of
    Upper Canada 500; Law Society of
    Upper Canada Archives 499–501;
    Ministry of Natural Resources 293,
    297; northern 290–316; Prisoners'
    Aid Society 354, 361–62, 373; Prov-
    incial Police 300, 306–7, 309,
    311–15, 482; reform party 21; Royal
    Commission on the Care and Con-
    trol of the Feeble-Minded 431;
    Royal Commission on the Prison
    and Reformatory System (1890)
    362–3; Supreme Court 296; Tract
    Society 361; wife abuse in 323–43;
    Women's Christian Temperance
    Union 339; YMCA 361. See also
    Upper Canada
Open University (Milton Keynes,
    England) 467
Orange Order 59
Osgoode, William CJ 99, 104–6,
    108–12, 115, 118–19
Osgoode Society (Toronto) 451, 454,
    499–500
O'Sullivan, Supt 369
Ottawa 224–5, 227, 233, 268, 308,
    338, 478, 488; Police Court 327,
    338–9
Owen Sound (Ontario): jail 351–2,
    355, 357–8, 363, 367, 372

Paddock, Dr Thomas 195
Palmer, Bryan 340
Palmer, Stanley 477
Palmerston, Lord 39, 45–7, 49–51, 60
Paris 10, 195, 489; Treaty of 76
Parker, Richard 446
Partridge, John 472
Pashukanis, Evgeny 4
Pays Plat Reserve (Ontario) 292
Peel, Sir Robert 186, 465
Peigan Indians 291
Pentonville Prison (England) 194
Peterborough (England) constabu-
    lary 467
Phillips, Mitch 310–11
Phyne, John 482
Pic Heron Bay Reserve (Ontario)
    292, 314
Pic Mobert Reserve (Ontario) 292
Pitt, William 105–6, 109

Police 27–8, 45, 57, 76, 86, 90, 205,
    231, 249–50, 297, 307, 335, 339,
    369, 371–2, 453, 455, 465–74,
    477–91
    Canadian National Railway 307–10
    Continental Europe 465
    English 465–74
    historiography of, in Canada
        477–91
    International Association of Chiefs
        of 249
    London Metropolitan 81, 465–6,
        468–71, 474
    North-West Mounted 267–8, 272,
        451–3
    Ontario Provincial Police 300,
        306–7, 309, 311–15
    Ottawa Police Court 327
    and policing 7–8, 25

records of 27–8, 486–7,
Wales 46–67

Port, Samuel 38, 55
Porter, Bernard: *The Origins of the Vigilant State* (1987) 470
Portugal: colonies of 145, 147–8
Pottinger, Henry 159
Potts, Gary 296
Poulantzas, Nicos 1
Powers, Colonel William 188, 190–1
Prest, William 92
Prince Rupert's Land: marriage customs 16

Professions
anthropologist 9–10, 22, 445, 447, 455
archivist and archives 6, 443–5, 450–1, 453–7, 465–74, 497–511, 514–22
historian 8–10, 12–13, 22, 323, 445–8, 450–7, 466, 470, 473–4, 477–91, 497–500, 502–3, 505, 509, 516–17
judge 9–10, 16, 20–2, 24, 28, 53–60, 79, 84–6, 92–3, 131, 150–5, 159, 162, 170, 185, 265, 270–84, 324, 326, 334, 381–2, 389–90, 393, 398, 444–5, 447, 453, 456, 485, 498–503, 505–8
lawyer 8–9, 12–13, 16, 22, 27–8, 46, 52, 57–8, 79, 86–7, 92–3, 311, 313, 393, 407, 429, 444, 447, 449–50, 453–7, 485, 497–511, 514–22
magistrate 10, 46, 74, 77, 79, 84–6, 89–90, 103, 119, 185, 199–200, 205–6, 231, 281–2, 329–31, 336–9, 341–2, 366, 382, 390, 392, 444, 452, 469, 485

medicine 92, 197, 200–2, 362–3, 365, 369–71, 407, 429, 452, 470, 504
psychologist and psychiatrist 23, 198, 201, 356–7, 371, 386, 405–35 *passim*, 452
sociologist 8–9, 363, 383, 391, 447, 455, 481, 483, 490, 516

Prowse, D.W. 78
Public Health Journal 411
Putnam, Bertha 218

Quebec 99–100, 104–5, 112, 114–15, 216, 223, 226–7, 263, 303–4, 479; civil law of 14, 16; Interministerial Committee on Court Records 456; legal records of 456–7; provincial police 290; reform party 21. *See also* Lower Canada
Quigg, John, 280

Rafter, Nicole Hahn 373
Rawlyk, George 107, 118
RCMP Quarterly 478
Red Deer (Alberta): patriotism and sedition 263–83
Red Deer Advocate 273–4, 276
Red Deer News 264, 267–69
Red Rock Reserve (Ontario) 292
Redford, Alfred 473
Reeves, John, 75, 78, 81
Reid, John, 267–70, 272
Reiner, Robert: *The Politics of the Police* (1985) 483
Reith, Charles 466

Religion 5–6, 8–9, 15–16, 22, 89, 137, 187, 196–9, 223, 230, 263–4, 306, 324, 339, 353–4, 357, 360–1, 363,

365, 368–9, 372–3, 381, 386, 393, 448, 450
Anglicans 82, 92
Baptists 389
Buddhists 147, 157
Catholics 20, 81–2, 84, 90, 147–8, 219, 221, 223–30, 266, 298, 316, 361, 364
churches (unspecified) 9, 12, 354–5, 358, 363, 369, 447
evangelicals 204, 363
Islam 147
Jews 82, 247, 313, 489
Methodists 266, 365
Presbyterians 365
Protestants (undenominated) 20, 219, 221, 223–7, 359, 361, 365, 373
Quakers 82, 198
Scriptures 137, 193, 361
Sunday schools 191

Ricci, Joseph 489
Richards, William B. 58
Riddell, William R.: *The Life of John Graves Simcoe* (1926) 115–16
Riel, Louis 304
Robbins, M.M. 368–9
Roberts, Simon 449
Robinson, John Beverley 43–5, 57–8, 185–6
Robinson, William Benjamin 296
Roche, M.L. 280
Rocky Bay Reserve (Ontario) 292
Rocky Mountain House Guide 267, 269
Rogers, Nicholas 483
Rolston, Tilly 382–5, 387–92, 394–9
Romney, Paul 107–8, 118, 182
Rose, Nikolas: *The Psychological Complex* (1985) 408

Rothman, David 23
Royal Gazette (St John's) 75
Rubin, Gerry R. 3, 447
Rudé, George 215
Ruemper, Wendy 23, 25
Rupert, D.W. 312
Russell, Arthur 281
Russell, Lord John 49–50, 58, 61, 186
Russell, Peter 109, 120

St John's (Newfoundland) 74–6, 81, 83, 85, 89–92, 482
St Madeleine Sugar Co. Ltd 134
Salvation Army: Haven and Neighbourhood Workers Association 409
San Francisco 252; Law and Order Committee 245; Preparedness parade 245
Sandiford, Peter 422
Saskatchewan Provincial Police 482
Saulte Ste-Marie (Ontario) 292, 337, 339
Scallan, Bishop 76
Scarlet and Gold (RCMP) 478
Schacht, F.L. 268, 272
Scott, Ian 308–9, 314
Scott, Thomas 224
Senior, Elinor 483
Seward, William F. 63
Shaftesbury, Lord 186
Shepard, Catherine 499
Shillings, Alfred 280
Shpayer-Makov, Haia 470–1
Siddon, Tom 308
Silverman, Jason 53
Simcoe, Lady Elizabeth 111
Simcoe, John Graves 17, 99–120
Simon, W.R. Bruce
Simpson, Brian 445–6; *Cannibalism*

and the Common Law (1984) 446,
454
Sinhalese laws and customs 147–51,
155–7
Sissons, William 271–2, 274
Skinner, J.D. 267–9
Smandych, Russell 14, 17, 21
Smyk, Peter 281–2, 288
Smyth, Sir Selby 227
Snyder Francis 449

Social Relations
abolitionists 37, 40–3, 46, 50, 63
anti-slavery 39, 49, 54, 57–60,
62–3
bootlegging 485–6
custody and guardianship 325–6,
419
domestic relations 382, 384–6, 389,
392
employer-employee 15, 132–4, 225,
417, 419–20, 486
family 6, 9, 11–13, 18, 24, 138–40,
151–71, 193, 199, 276, 299–301,
303, 305, 323–43, 353–5, 358,
370, 374, 379–99 *passim*, 421, 447,
449, 472–3, 508
gender 4–6, 15, 18, 22–5, 321–439
passim, 374–82, 393–9, 451
indentured workers 130–41
landlord-tenant 153–4, 486
marriage 15–16, 24–5, 75, 81–2, 88,
139–41, 151–2, 154–66, 171,
323–43 *passim*, 370, 381, 389–90,
393–4, 396, 428, 430–1, 449, 473
master-servant 15, 38–9, 53, 63, 86,
116, 451
paternalist 118, 353–54, 372, 380,
399
patriarchy 23–4, 29, 165, 170

polygamy and polyandry 157,
163–4, 171
slavery 15, 18, 37–63, 131, 155, 246,
427
voluntary associations 243–4,
246–50, 253–6

Social Welfare 410–11, 414–15

Society
aboriginals 7, 12, 14, 20–2, 26,
136–7, 140, 182, 290–316, 445,
447–50, 479, 481
Afro-Americans 51–5, 58, 131, 367,
372, 489
aliens 89, 246–51, 255, 263
bourgeoisie 183, 206, 399, 483
children 139–40, 154, 164–6, 193,
265, 291, 293–4, 310, 323–30,
332–8, 343, 358, 379, 383–4, 387,
393–4, 396–7, 406, 413, 417, 422,
427–9
class 4, 7–8, 15, 19, 23, 138, 183,
193, 196, 203–4, 219, 244, 246,
255, 323, 369, 380, 382, 393–4,
399, 483–4, 488
creoles 131, 136–40
debtors 193
élites 7, 14, 17, 21, 107–9, 113, 118,
132, 136, 183, 241, 393–4, 478
immigrants 5, 12, 14–19, 25, 75–76,
84, 93, 107, 117, 131, 133, 135–6,
147, 186–7, 197, 204, 244, 263,
266–7, 369, 405, 409, 412, 418,
425–8, 431–3, 470, 481
merchants 78, 109, 112–13, 115
middle class 22–4, 107, 109, 135,
139–40, 183, 196, 203, 206, 331,
356–7, 359–60, 369–71, 373,
380–1, 387, 393–4, 409, 446, 473,
487

Mohawk Nation 290–316
nobility 6
patriarchy 324, 332, 341, 343
servants 357, 359, 362, 364, 367,
    370, 394
strangers 204
study of 9–13
women 6, 12, 18, 22–5, 29, 152,
    156–9, 163–4, 168, 171, 193, 244,
    247, 253, 265, 291, 323–43,
    351–74, 405–35, 447, 451, 472–3,
    486–8, 490
  feminists 22–3, 25, 29, 323,
    379–99
  widows 138–39, 364, 370, 383,
    397, 473
  working class 23–4, 156, 207,
    220–1, 234, 243–7, 249–53, 255,
    323, 328–43, 357, 360, 367, 369,
    373, 380–1, 394, 396, 405–35
    passim, 447, 470–3, 483–4, 487–8,
    490
  youth 351, 369, 383, 385, 388–90,
    392, 398, 410, 414–16, 420–1,
    423, 425–7, 430–2, 488

South Carolina: secession 63
Spain 74, 131; creoles 131; monarchy
    6
Speenhamland system 103
Splane, Richard: Social Welfare in
    Ontario (1965) 100–1
Sri Lanka 14; laws and customs
    145–72
Stanford University (California)
    245–6
Star (Toronto) 310
Steedman, Caroline 477
Steele, Donald 296–7
Steele, Harwood 478

Steele, Sam 478
Steeves, Dorothy 385
Stephen, Jennifer 23–5
Stephens, Edward 446
Stephens, William 245
Stevens, Gordon 390
Stewart, Chris 482
Stokes, Harry 276
Stonier-Newman, Lynne 482–4
Stowe, Harriet Beecher 49
Strange, Carolyn 373
Stratford (Ontario) House of Refuge
    330
Strickland, George 163
Stuart, Charles 41, 52
Stuart, Charles Allan 265–6, 271, 274,
    277–9, 281–2
Sturgeon, Ere 280
Styles, John 218
Suffolk East (England) constabulary
    471
Sugarman, David 3, 29, 218, 447
Superior, Lake 292, 298, 305
Sussex (England) constabulary 468
Swainger, Jonathan 19–21
Swan, Joe 481
Sydenham, Lord 183–4
Sykes, Rev. Joshua 250

Taft, Jessie 406
Tamils: laws and customs 146–8,
    151–2, 158–9
Tappan, Lewis 41
Teme-Augama Anishnabai reserve
    (Ontario) 292, 296, 299–300
Thatcher, Margaret 146
Thompson, E.P. 4, 12
Thompson, Sir John 266
Thomson, Basil 470
Thomson, Hugh H. 188–91, 195, 200

Tocqueville, Alexis de 190, 195–6
Toronto 42, 48, 62, 181, 220, 301,
    331–2, 360, 364, 367–8, 370–1, 413,
    418, 424, 430–1, 483–4, 486, 490;
    Andrew Mercer Reformatory
    351–2, 354–5, 357–66, 368–73; Bel-
    mont Industrial Refuge 419; Big
    Sisters Association 425–6; Central
    Neighbourhood House 429; Clarke
    Institute of Psychiatry 407; family
    court 382, 385; General Hospital
    419–20, 428–9; Haven and Prison
    Gate Mission Home 362, 419, 424,
    429; Hospital for Sick Children
    361; Jubilee riots (1877–8) 222–3;
    Juvenile Court 419, 425, 430;
    Magdalen Asylum 362; O'Donovan-
    Rossa riot (1878) 222; Osgoode
    Hall 4; police court 358; Psychia-
    tric Clinic 23–4, 371, 405–35; riots
    in 219, 222–3; Salvation Army 361,
    365, 373; University of 407, 422;
    Women's Christian Temperance
    Union 365, 373; Women's Court
    363, 419; Women's Jail Farm 425,
    429–30; working-class women of
    405–35
Torre, W.J. Della 268
Towegishig, Allan 310
Towegishig, Ronald 306, 310
Trainor, Arthur 276–7
Trinidad: law of 14–16, 130–41; legis-
    lature and legislation 131, 133–4;
    marriage customs 16
Tucker, Richard 79, 87, 93
Tuke, William 198
Turmel, J. 478–81
Turner, J.W. 478
Tuscany 186
Twining, William 447

Tyler, John, President 42

United States 3, 5, 7, 15, 17–18, 20–1,
    37–43, 45, 49–53, 60–3, 76, 84,
    106–7, 119–20, 184, 188, 190–2,
    194–5, 200, 204, 243–4, 247, 253,
    255, 273, 282, 255–7, 312, 373, 380,
    382, 384, 451–2, 465, 477, 479–80,
    487–8, 490, 504, 508
    American Civil Liberties Union 253
    American and Foreign Anti-Slavery
        Society 41
    American Protective League
        246–52
    anti-German sentiment in 247–51,
        255
    anti-labour movements in 243–5,
        249–52, 255
    Asian-Americans 243–4, 255
    Better American Federation 248
    Bill of Rights 253–4
    Congress 42, 63
    Constitution 44, 243, 253
    Declaration of Independence 44
    Department of Justice 246–7,
        251–2, 254
    Department of State 247
    Department of the Treasury 247, 252
    Federal Bureau of Investigation
        246, 481
    Federal Commission on Industrial
        Relations 253
    government of 37, 63
    historiography 3–5
    intergovernmental relations 40–63
    Knights of Columbus 247
    Knights of Liberty 250
    Ku Klux Klan 246, 487
    labour movements 243–5, 249–53
    law and society in 5, 17

Liberty Fund 249, 255
National Defense League 246
Nonpartisan League 255
police in 465, 477
prisons 355–6
Progressive party 21, 23, 244–5,
    252–53, 255
Red Cross 247
Supreme Court 19, 253, 283
War Department (Military Intelli-
    gence) 250–2
Wobblies 252–3
Workingmen's party 246
YMCA 247
See also named states and cities

Upper Canada 357; asylums 181–4,
    187–93, 197–205; Bible Society 361;
    Chancery 103; College of Phys-
    icians and Surgeons 202; crime
    and social order in 181–207; dis-
    sent in 19; Family Compact 206;
    justices of the peace 103, 119;
    judiciary 18; law of 15, 17, 21–2;
    legislature 99–100, 105–6, 109–20;
    Loyalists 104–9, 117–20; prisons
    182–207; provincial lunatic asylum
    203; Rebellions (1837–8) 183–4,
    202, 205; settlement of 14; state
    and social order 181–207; Tories in
    106–8, 111, 118, 183, 190–3, 199,
    21; Whigs in 183. See also Ontario
Upper Canada Jurist 324
Upper Canada Law Journal 48–9, 325,
    327
Ursel, Jane 326

Valverde, Mariana 365
Van Leeuwen, Simon: Commentaries
    on the Roman-Dutch Law 152

Vancouver 280; City Council 388,
    392; Council of Women 388,
    390–1, 394; Court House Library
    501; Family Court 381–2, 390, 392;
    Greater Vancouver Communities
    Council 388, 390–1; Juvenile Court
    382, 390; Parent-Teacher Associ-
    ation 391; Police Court 392; Police
    Department 477, 481, 484–90; Uni-
    versity Women's Club 387, 389,
    394; Welfare Council 392;
    Women's School for Citizenship
    384, 387, 389, 395
Vanstone, Frank 279

Violence 20, 78, 91–2, 183, 203, 206,
    246, 252, 452, 478, 490
    arms and weapons 228–9, 231–3
    guns 216, 228–9, 255, 268, 340
    knives 38–9, 51, 55–6, 290, 341–2
    in Canada 215–34
    domestic 23–5, 327, 333–42, 365,
        382, 396, 473, 487
    Montreal riots (1877–8) 219
    Orange-Catholic Gavazzi Riot
        (1853) 219
    public disorder 18
    rebellions, revolutions and revolts
        7, 18, 48, 249, 482
    riots 17, 20, 54, 83, 132, 215–34,
        263, 291, 46
    strikes 220, 264, 481–2, 484, 488–9
    vigilantism 248, 250, 253–4

Virginia: loyalists 58

Waboose, Veronica 310
Waite, Peter B. 223
Wakefield, Edward Gibbon 205
Waldegrave, William 76
Walden, Keith 479

Wales: police forces archives 465–6
South, police in 468
Walker, Samuel 477
Wall Street Journal 308
Wallace, Gerald 481
Wallace, Joseph 280
Walnut Street Jail (New York City)
187
Walsh, William 271–2, 279

War 6, 18, 88–9, 246–54
American Revolutionary 99, 104, 106
Civil War 17, 53, 63
conscription 263
First World War 19, 243–62, 371,
409–10, 412–13, 415, 470–1, 488
military and soldiers 6, 117, 205,
217, 222, 224, 247–52, 263, 267,
273–6, 280, 283, 409–10, 414,
471–2
militia 20, 218, 220, 222, 224–5
Napoleonic 75–6
navy and sailors 247, 252, 329
of 1812 76–77
Second World War 263, 293, 302,
382, 384–5, 387, 395–7, 466, 471,
473, 478, 480, 489–90

Ward, Henry, Gov. 157
Warwick, University of 4
Washington, DC 37, 61, 189, 243
Weaver, John 103, 484, 490
Weber, Max 12, 206
Weber, Milton 390–1
Webster, Daniel 40, 42

Webster-Ashburton treaty 37, 39–43,
45, 48–9, 51–2, 56, 58, 63
Weeks, Jeffrey 412
West Mercia constabulary (England)
468
Western Penitentiary (Pittsburgh)
187
Wethersfield Penitentiary (Hartford)
188–9
Whately, Dr. 188
Wheeler, Benjamin Ide 245, 251
Whitehall (Westminster) 18, 41, 59,
82, 87, 91
Whitney, Charlote Anita 253
Widmer, Dr Christopher 200–1
Wilberforce, William 186
Wilbur, Ray Lyman 245
William Bibb Institute 38
Williams, Sir William Fenwick 46,
61
Wilson, Woodrow 245–6, 255
Winks, Robin 52–3
Winnipeg 216, 230, 310–11, 313;
general strike 264
Wise, S.F. 106–7
Wood, Herbert S. 388, 392
Wood, Samuel R. 188
Worcester Asylum (Pennsylvania)
198, 201–2
Worcestershire (England) 468; con-
stabulary 472

York Hospital (Upper Canada) 200
York Retreat (Upper Canada) 198